SHOREBIRDS

An identification guide to the waders of the world

SHOREBIRDS

An identification guide to the waders of the world

Peter Hayman, John Marchant and Tony Prater

Sponsored by the American Birding Association

Houghton Mifflin Company
Boston

© 1986 John Marchant, Tony Prater and Peter Hayman
First Published in the USA in 1986 by
Houghton Mifflin Company, Two Park Street, Boston,
Massachusetts 02108.

Library of Congress Cataloging in Publication Data

Marchant, John 1951-
    Shorebirds: an identification guide.

    Bibliography: p.
    Includes index.
    1. Shore birds—Identification. 2. Birds—Identifi-
cation. I. Prater, Tony, 1943-   . II. Title.
    QL696.C4M37 1986   598'.33   85-8230

ISBN 0-395-37903-2
ISBN 0-395-60237-8 (pbk.)

Colour separation by Alpha Reprographics, Middlesex

Printed and bound in the Netherlands
by Royal Smeets Offset b.v. Weert

CONTENTS

THINOCORIDAE

FOREWORD
By Roger Tory Peterson

The field identification of birds has become an immensely popular sport or recreation during the last two or three decades. It has also become much more sophisticated, pushing ahead on several fronts. One of the most popular of these frontiers is the identification of waders, or shorebirds, the hordes of soberly-coloured sandpipers and plovers that swarm along the beaches, marshes and tidal flats during migration.

'Fieldmarks' as portrayed in the standard field guides are the 'Trademarks of Nature' by means of which one species can be readily separated from another with some certainty. In recent years, a polarisation has developed in field techniques beyond the scope of the field guides. On the one hand, some practitioners in the sport seem able to identify a bird at a distance by shape alone, or by a combination of impressions such as form, wing-action, and other intangibles — for example, the thin-necked, pigeon-headed look of an Upland Sandpiper and, in flight, its shallow wing-action. The sophisticated wader-watcher sometimes speaks of a bird's 'jizz', a term derived from the fighter pilots' acronym, 'GIS' — General Impression and Shape. I prefer to call it the 'Holistic Method' of recognition. This approach is almost more of an art than a science.

This is in direct contrast to the 'Micro-Method' of some elite birders, who no longer rely solely on binoculars and who are fortunate enough to own a Questar, Celestron, or one of the other telescopic devices designed for amateur astronomers. With these instruments mounted on sturdy tripods, they can see even the parasites on a Dunlin or the nasal grooves on a tattler. They may speak of 'worn tertials' or 'barred secondary coverts' and other fine points. Field birding of this sort, in a sense, has come almost full cycle back to the specimen tray.

This monographic work embraces both extremes, the art and the science, a service that no general field guide designed to fit the jacket-pocket can fully accomplish. This is not to denigrate the standard field guides; they do the job admirably more than 95% of the time. But if you would extend your horizons — if you wish to be sure of that stray Least or Western Sandpiper in Britain, or that improbable Temminck's or Long-toed Stint on the west coast of North America — you will find confirming evidence in these pages, both in the text and in the illustrations. This book will also make you more aware of ages, seasonal moults, and migration patterns, as well as the variety of vocalisations.

In as much as birds have wings — and they use them — it is not surprising that some sandpipers and plovers occasionally switch sides from the Old World to the New and vice-versa. Dowitchers, yellowlegs and Pectoral Sandpipers turn up regularly in Britain; Ruffs, Curlew Sandpipers and others find their way each year to North American beaches. In Alaska, especially in the outer Aleutians (which are technically part of the United States), nearly 20 Asian sandpipers and plovers have been recorded, some of them with regularity. Those modest little sparrow-sized brown-and-grey sandpipers known in Britain and Ireland as 'stints' are an especial challenge to the stintomaniac who is looking for rarities.

Two hundred and fourteen species of waders or shorebirds swarm over the beaches, marshes, mudflats, plains and tundras of the world. This impressive guide by a team of skilled field experts is the first attempt to describe and illustrate them all within the covers of a single book.

Many birders no longer confine themselves to their own continent, they travel. Even for those who don't, it is illuminating to learn that there is not just one kind of oystercatcher, but ten others elsewhere in the world; and that their woodcock is not the only one, but that there are five others. Whereas there is but a single lapwing in Britain and none in North America (except as a storm-blown accidental), there are 23 other lapwings or lapwing-type plovers of the genus *Vanellus* elsewhere in the world, mostly south of the equator.

Many waders that breed on the arctic tundra tend to be circumpolar, occurring in both the New World and the Old. Those which breed farther south, where continents are farther apart, show more speciation. Although sandpipers predominate in the northern hemisphere, plovers and snipes show greater diversity below the equator.

We owe a debt to Peter Hayman, John Marchant and Tony Prater, who have so painstakingly and skilfully portrayed and described the many plumages of the world's waders, some of which had never been illustrated before. If you are not already addicted to the shorebirds, you will be after studying this landmark volume.

INTRODUCTION

Waders (shorebirds) are among the most attractive and popular groups of birds in the world. Special interest has focused on them for three main reasons.

Firstly, they are among the world's greatest migrants; many species travel from the high Arctic to the southern limits of Australasia, Africa and South America. In regions such as Australasia where there are few passerine migrants, waders may constitute most of the long-distance migrants. Because of the huge distances travelled, virtually any of the migrant species is capable of turning up unexpectedly, even in the 'wrong' continent. Any birdwatcher who watches a wader haunt regularly might be lucky enough to come across such a bird.

Secondly, the individual features which enable positive identification to be made, even of common species, are relatively poorly known and have been the subject of much debate. A number of important features are described for the first time in this book. The treatment of waders in most general field guides is often too sketchy to allow species to be identified with certainty, especially bearing in mind the possibility of vagrancy from other continents.

Thirdly, wetlands throughout the world are under threat and waders are a good indicator of their state of health. Man so often misuses these areas by altering the volume of or polluting the water flowing in, by drainage for agriculture or forestry, by reclamation for industrial or urban growth, or by otherwise over-exploiting the natural resources.

This handbook is the first comprehensive review designed to enable birdwatchers anywhere in the world to identify any species of wader in the field. It provides information to help the advanced observer or the careful beginner to identify not only the species but also, where possible from field characters, the age, sex or geographic origin of the bird. However, it also draws out the essential details, both in the illustrations and in the text, to enable any observer to make a positive identification of any species.

All species of waders in the world are described and illustrated. They belong to the order Charadriiformes and are subdivided into the families Jacanidae, Rostratulidae, Dromadidae, Haematopodidae, Ibidorhynchidae, Recurvirostridae, Burhinidae, Glareolidae, Charadriidae, Pluvianellidae, Scolopacidae and Thinocoridae. Recently-extinct species and species presumed extinct are included.

Other long-legged birds (such as herons, cranes and ibises) which have been termed 'waders' by some authors do not fall within the scope of this book. The two species of the Chionididae (sheathbills) of the Antarctic are also excluded as they are so different from the true waders and are well covered by the field guides to the seabirds, particularly Harrison (1983). Harrison's *Seabirds* and the present volume together cover all the charadriiform species.

HOW TO USE THIS BOOK

Especially for those not familiar with waders it is important, as a first step, to try and decide to which family or group an individual bird belongs. Once recognised as a godwit, for example, the species can be quickly confirmed by turning to the appropriate plates and text. To assist the basic separation of wader families, we have described each group in a separate section on pages 23-28. Birdwatchers who are diffident with wader identification are recommended to read that section before turning to the plates or consulting the detailed species texts.

The Species Texts

Heading

Each species is given a reference number, which serves as its identification label both on the plates and in the texts. These numbers are used purely for convenience within the context of this book.

To some extent the names chosen represent a compromise with the current moves, particularly from the USA, to give every bird species an English name which, like the scientific name, cannot possibly be confused with any other. Thus we have used Northern Lapwing, originally an American name for the Palaearctic *Vanellus vanellus*, and added adjectives to the names of the birds most frequently known in Britain as Snipe, Curlew, Dotterel, Avocet, Golden Plover, and so on. We have, however, stopped short of inventing names with qualifying adjectives where no satisfactory ones yet exist. The widespread *Burhinus* of the Palaearctic and Oriental regions remains just 'Stone-curlew' ('European' has been added by some authors, but this is not satisfactory for a species which breeds from the Canaries east to Burma!). Other 'problem' species names are Painted Snipe, Ringed Plover, Redshank and Greenshank.

The number and order of species vary with each treatment by different taxonomists. Indeed, it surely cannot be possible to represent the evolutionary tree of waders, branching so profusely in time and space, in the form of a universally-agreed one-dimensional species list. Our species list has been drawn up for convenience of use, and we make no claims as to its evolutionary exactness. It is based on Clements (1982), with a few changes in the treatment of closely-related taxa and in the scientific names where further work has indicated the need.

After the species heading, a few introductory sentences highlight features of special interest or any peculiarities of the bird.

Identification

This section incorporates the essential features which enable a rapid identification of the species regardless of age, sex, race or state of plumage. Similar species or those most likely to be confused

are described and cross-referenced. Bare-part colours, although arguably most logically part of the description, are given here because of their great importance in the identification of waders.

Voice

Many species will first be detected by their calls. Familiarity with the calls of a variety of species is a valuable aid to rapid identification, and often enables a positive identification even of an unseen bird. The song and the contact and alarm calls are described, concentrating on those which are of particular value in identification. (Note that many species have a wide vocal repertoire which cannot be fully documented in a work of this kind.)

Habits

This section summarises the main elements of the behaviour of the species, such as feeding, breeding and display, and describes the habitats used. These characters combine with others to give each species a special 'feel' or 'jizz', which may be almost as useful in identification as plumage characters or voice.

Movements

The sedentary or migratory nature of the species is indicated here. For migratory species the main migration routes are given (if known), along with a summary of records of vagrancy. Long-distance migrants are the most likely species to be encountered outside their normal range.

Description

This section describes the different plumages of breeding and non-breeding adults and of juveniles. For most species, this should enable the reader to discover the colours and patterns present throughout each plumage, whether or not all parts of the bird appear on the plates. Elements of the plumage important in identification or in determination of age, sex or race are also referred to under those headings.

Age and sex

Any features which may enable an observer to identify the age and sex of the bird are summarised here, with emphasis on those which can be seen in the field. Further characters distinguishable on birds in the hand are described by Prater, Marchant and Vuorinen (1977) for the 117 species which occur in the Holarctic region.

Races

A brief summary is given of the races (subspecies) described for each species, and of the characters by which they can be distinguished. Where alternative treatments are available, we have usually opted for the most recent or the simplest (that with the fewest subspecies). Any known geographical variation within described subspecies is also discussed.

Measurements

Measurements are given as a guide to the size of species and subspecies in comparison with their relatives. In many cases, measurements are critical for the identification of species. Metric units are used throughout; average total length is also given in inches.

'Length' is the total body length from bill-tip to tail-tip, measured with the bird laid flat on its back but without undue force being applied. This measurement is given here because it is traditionally used in bird books to indicate size. However, since the lengths of bill, neck and tail vary so much in waders, and size is often so difficult to judge, the figures should be interpreted carefully. No new data on body lengths are presented in this book; the collection of accurate data really requires a supply of freshly-killed birds — not available to us, nor indeed readily obtainable in these more enlightened times. Jones (1983) has drawn attention to the fact that the lengths given for several species of wader vary (sometimes markedly) between different books. We have tried to use only the most authoritative sources.

'Wing' is measured from the carpal joint (the bend in the wing) to the tip of the longest primary, using the flattened-chord technique. Since for most species suitable series of live measurements are not yet available, museum measurements are used throughout. These are roughly 2% shorter than the 'real' values for birds caught for ringing or found freshly dead (Prater et al. 1977). Even on museum skins, wing measurements depend on the measurer! For all but a few species, the measurements given are ones we have taken ourselves from the specimens at the British Museum (Natural History) in Tring, which houses the largest collection of skins anywhere in the world.

'Bill' is the measurement from the bill-tip to the farthest point of exposed, non-feathered culmen ridge. Difficulties arise where the base of the culmen is concealed by forward-growing feathers or covered by a wattle or a shield. In some of these cases, non-standard techniques have been used and these are described in the text. Particularly in such birds, some measure which does not involve the feathering on the culmen would be a desirable alternative. Such a measure now coming more into favour for live birds is total head length ('THL') from the bill-tip to the back of the skull, measured using vernier calipers. Preliminary studies show that THL can give better separation of, for example, sexes and races of migratory calidrids than does the shorter and more variable measure of bill length, but few data are available on this as yet.

'Bill depth' is measured at the deepest part of the bill, usually either at the gonys or near the base.

'Tarsus' is measured from the centre of the 'knee' joint on the back of the leg to the middle of the joint between tarsus and middle toe on the front, sometimes characterised as the last scale before the toes divide. The word 'tarsus' is conventionally used to describe the tarsometatarsus.

'Tail' is measured from the tip of the longest feather to the skin at the base of the central feathers.

In a few cases, other, more specialised measurements useful only for small groups of species are described.

References

A few of the most useful sources in the literature for each species are given in abbreviated form. In general, these are biased towards identification and behaviour, and towards recently-published works which can act as a key to earlier studies. All references given in the species texts appear in the specific bibliography on page 401.

Standard reference texts, recommended reading for a larger number of species, are not referred to individually; the principal ones are listed in a separate general bibliography on page 401. The reader is also referred to the many regional field guides, which do not appear in the bibliography.

The Plates

All major plumages of most species are illustrated on the plates, with important features highlighted in a brief text on the facing page. Juveniles constitute the majority of vagrant and thus unfamiliar waders, yet all too often in previous works the juvenile plumage has been omitted or mislabelled. We hope that we have avoided all such basic errors. The species are depicted in approximate taxonomic order, with adjustments to ensure that similar species or those from the same geographical area are shown together as much as possible. See also pages 35-36.

The Maps

The maps are designed to show breeding and non-breeding distributions of all species in as much detail as space allows. They are placed opposite the plates in order to provide maximum information in accessible form. More detail on distribution and migrations is usually to be found in the species texts.

Conventions used in the maps are explained below.

Conventions used on the distribution maps:

Yellow — regular breeding areas; sporadic nesting areas are mentioned in the text where appropriate.

Green — areas where regular breeding occurs and birds are found regularly in non-breeding season.

Blue — areas where birds are regularly present during the non-breeding period. Birds may be seen on migration between areas coloured blue and yellow. Migration routes, where known, are discussed in the species text.

Shaded pale blue — areas where birds are widely dispersed outside the breeding season either on the sea (phalaropes) or on island groups.

Heavy black border to map indicates species which are probably extinct or very close to extinction.

HOW TO IDENTIFY WADERS

There are two basic points which all birdwatchers should bear in mind when identifying waders. Firstly, there is no substitute for getting to know thoroughly the common species. Usually there are only a dozen or so species in this category in any one locality and, once their behaviour, habits, calls and variations of plumage have been learnt, then it becomes much easier to locate and identify the scarce waders. Secondly, by definition, rare waders are very few in number! The great majority seen will be of the commoner species, so when identifying an odd-looking wader it is prudent to consider seriously an unusual individual of a common species before the possibility of a rare one.

Careful unbiased observation is the key to successful identification.

Shorebird topography

Throughout this handbook we use various technical terms referring to the *topography* of the bird. In order to identify some waders — and especially to determine the age, sex or race — it is important that particular feather tracts or parts of the bird are accurately located and carefully observed. We have followed the standard names now recommended by the authoritative *British Birds* magazine. The drawings overleaf show these on a typical wader.

Frequent reference is given in the species texts to patterns of markings on feathers. Terms such as 'fringed', 'edged' or 'tipped' are not used as alternative descriptions, but have separate meanings. Some typical patterns are illustrated below.

Plumage sequence

Wader identification can be much easier if the observer is aware of the age of the individual. Thus, if a bird of unknown species can be aged as a juvenile, then all adult plumages can be disregarded and only juveniles considered in further attempts to identify the species. Many misidentifications happen needlessly because of the failure to appreciate the age of the bird.

Migratory northern species are normally well synchronised in their breeding seasons, plumages and moults, so that for example it is possible to find a calidrid in full juvenile plumage only during July to November, no matter where in the world you happen to be.

The typical plumage sequence for such a bird is described below. Several systems are in use for naming plumages; we have chosen one which can cope with a worldwide approach. Our 'breeding' and 'non-breeding' correspond respectively to the widely-used American terms 'alternate' and 'basic'. Terms such as 'summer plumage' and 'winter plumage' may obviously lead to confusion when describing species which cross the equator. Where

Types of patterns found on feathers

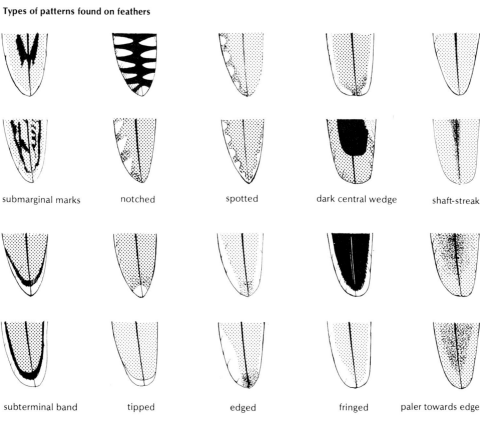

| submarginal marks | notched | spotted | dark central wedge | shaft-streak |

| subterminal band | tipped | edged | fringed | paler towards edge |

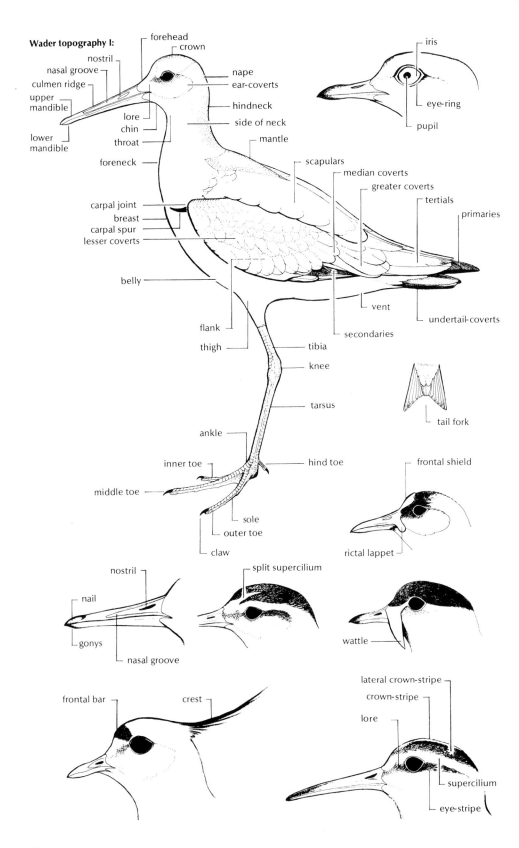

Wader topography I:

forehead
crown
nostril
nasal groove
culmen ridge
upper mandible
lower mandible
lore
chin
throat
foreneck
nape
ear-coverts
hindneck
side of neck
mantle
scapulars
median coverts
greater coverts
tertials
primaries

carpal joint
breast
carpal spur
lesser coverts
belly
flank
thigh
vent
secondaries
undertail-coverts
tibia
knee
tarsus
ankle
inner toe
middle toe
hind toe
sole
outer toe
claw

iris
eye-ring
pupil

tail fork

frontal shield
rictal lappet

nostril
nail
gonys
nasal groove

split supercilium

wattle

frontal bar
crest

lateral crown-stripe
crown-stripe
lore
supercilium
eye-stripe

Wader topography II:

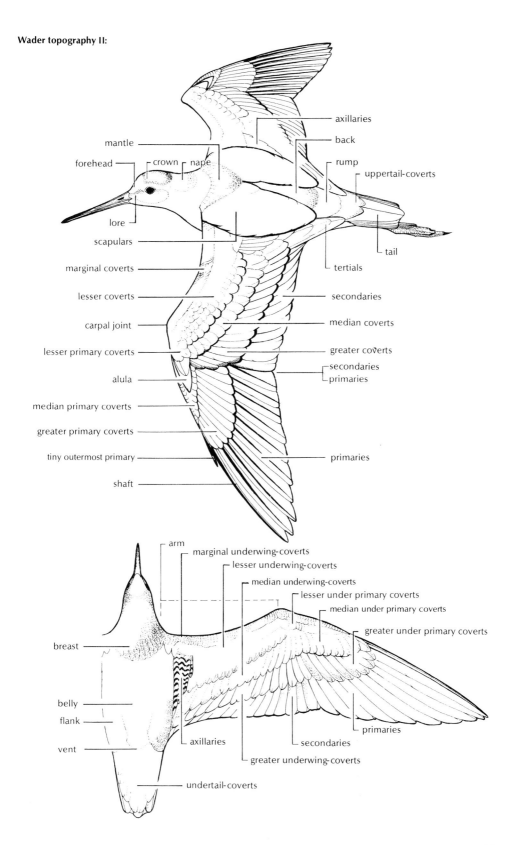

axillaries

back

mantle

forehead — crown — nape

rump

uppertail-coverts

lore

scapulars

tail

marginal coverts

tertials

lesser coverts

secondaries

carpal joint

median coverts

lesser primary coverts

greater coverts

secondaries
primaries

alula

median primary coverts

greater primary coverts

tiny outermost primary

primaries

shaft

arm

marginal underwing-coverts

lesser underwing-coverts

median underwing-coverts

lesser under primary coverts

median under primary coverts

greater under primary coverts

breast

belly

flank

primaries

vent

axillaries

secondaries

greater underwing-coverts

undertail-coverts

we write of 'winter quarters' or 'spring migration', we are however referring to the season prevailing in the breeding area.

The newly-fledged young bird is the *juvenile*. During its first few weeks after flying some loosely-structured downy feathers may remain, especially on the nape and rear flanks and sometimes as down-streamers on the tip of the tail. Once these disappear, the full juvenile plumage is characterised by rather small, neat and usually strikingly-patterned feathers. These feathers were grown almost together, and tend to show a fairly uniform degree of wear and fading (although those most exposed to abrasion and sunlight wear faster). Probably as a result of the physiological strain of growing so many feathers at once, these juvenile feathers all tend to be smaller than those of the adult and not so strongly structured. In most, if not all, species, juvenile primaries are shorter and narrower than those of the adult and wear more rapidly to a pointed shape. In many species, rows of juvenile coverts are exposed below relatively small and neat scapulars; this is in contrast to adults, where the large, rather loose scapulars droop over most lesser, median and greater coverts:

Adult and juvenile: length of scapulars

juvenile

adult

Typically, the wing-coverts and back feathers in juvenile *Calidris* species are fringed with whitish-buff or chestnut; in *Tringa* species they are spotted buff or whitish; while in *Charadrius* species they are finely fringed pale buff with a fine subterminal band of darker colour. The plates show these and other patterns. During the period when juveniles are fresh, the adults are at the end of the breeding season and in worn plumage, and so there is great contrast between the ages.

The juvenile plumage is retained for a few weeks, exceptionally up to three months. It is then usually partially replaced by a *first non-breeding plumage* which at least superficially resembles that of the adult; in the hand it can be seen that most individuals usually retain a number of the characteristic juvenile inner wing-coverts. The juvenile flight feathers are also normally retained and are paler brown, more pointed and more worn than those of adults, owing to a faster rate of abrasion. This age can be distinguished with certainty by field observation only in a few species, although in the hand it is relatively easy. Juveniles of some small and highly migratory species may moult some or all of the primaries as part of the post-juvenile moult, and thus become very difficult or impossible to separate from adults after only about six months.

As the breeding season approaches, birds hatched ten months previously may attain a full *breeding plumage* indistinguishable from that of the adult. Most larger waders, however, do not breed in their first year, and either retain very worn first non-breeding feathers or moult partially into a very poor version of the breeding plumage. During the latter part of the breeding season, first-year birds undergo a complete moult and enter adult non-breeding plumage. Any retained feathers from the juvenile plumage, including the primaries, are replaced during this moult, having lasted for up to 12 months.

Eventually the adult breeding plumage is attained. In many species (calidrids, godwits and golden plovers, for example), the breeding plumage is dramatically different from the non-breeding plumage: pale underparts may become red, black or strongly barred. Few non-migratory species exhibit great changes in pattern between breeding and non-breeding plumages.

After the breeding season the plumage of adults becomes very worn and is replaced in a complete moult (of both body and flight feathers), which usually takes place later than that of first-year birds.

In some species the two groups of feathers are moulted simultaneously, in others body moult precedes wing moult, while yet others show the opposite pattern. The bird thus returns to its *adult non-breeding plumage*; this is retained throughout the non-breeding season, which may be as long as nine months. The strong, dark, fresh-looking primary feathers prove to be a good indicator of adults when birds are examined in the hand.

Other factors affecting colours and patterns

The changes in appearance of shorebirds are due primarily to the moult sequence as described above, but there are a number of other variables which may cause the birds to look different.

Strong sun, particularly in tropical areas, results in the bleaching of colours, so that buff goes rapidly to whitish and brown becomes pale brown. At its most extreme, one-year-old birds which have not replaced all body feathers can become very pale and 'washed-out'. In addition, bright sun may make a bird appear pale: for example, Western Sandpipers in South America or Little Stints in Africa may look as pale as Sanderlings. As the feathers fade, they become weaker and *abrade* faster. This contributes to changes in the overall neatness as well as in the colour of the individual. Abrasion is ultimately the reason why feathers are replaced by moult: they steadily lose their functions of flight, insulation and display. Tertials and scapulars overlie and protect most of the feathers of the wing; being much more exposed to light, they abrade faster than other feather tracts. On all feathers the pale areas (usually fringes or tips) are lost first, and it is only later that the dark central areas start to break down.

Particularly on the upperparts, wear is very important in determining the appearance of birds in breeding plumage. Often, the fresh feathers are tipped grey, and have bright edges and a dark centre: thus the upperparts first appear greyish, then brightly patterned, then blackish towards the end of the season.

Some typical patterns of feather-wear are illustrated:

with examples ranging from the very rare pure albino (white with pinkish bare parts) to the much more frequent partially albinistic (showing abnormal white patches). Leucistic (colours paler, tending towards dull yellowish-white) and melanistic (colour tending towards black) individuals are generally less frequent than partial albinos, although they occur more commonly among some species (for example, Common Snipe and Eurasian Woodcock) than among others.

During detailed ringing (banding) studies on shorebirds in many countries throughout the world, a number of species are being *colour-dyed*. This technique enables the birds to be followed without having to be recaptured. Picric acid (orange-yellow) is the commonest dye, but other colours such as pink, blue, violet and green may be used. It should always be obvious when a bird has been dyed, but

Patterns of wear on feathers

    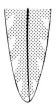  

fresh　　slightly worn　　　heavily worn　　　　pale-notched tertials

Moult does not occur randomly, but in a well-defined sequence within each feather tract. Typically, moult starts with the innermost (first) primary and progresses outwards. When primary moult is about half completed, the outermost (first) secondary is dropped and secondary moult progresses towards the body. At this stage, waders in flight show a large gap half-way along the trailing edge of each wing. The loss of flight feathers impairs flying ability, so birds may flap faster in order to keep up speed; this can alter the characteristic 'jizz' of the species. The tertials are replaced soon after secondary moult starts; in most waders, the innermost secondary is then lost and secondary moult proceeds in two directions towards the inner central secondaries. Tail feathers are replaced during the period of secondary moult, mostly from the middle (first) feathers outwards towards the edge of the tail. Typically, primary moult spans the entire period of wing and tail moult. The tertials are frequently replaced again during the partial body moult into breeding plumage.

There are many slight variations in the replacement patterns of flight feathers, but these are detectable only on birds in the hand. The timing of moult depends on many complicated and interrelated factors, such as the age of the individual bird, latitude of its breeding grounds, wintering grounds, timing of breeding season, length of migration, feeding conditions in different parts of its range, etc. Comments made here are, of necessity, generalised summaries and exceptions do occur.

Albinism, leucism and *melanism* all occur in shorebirds. There are many degrees of albinism,

there is a potential hazard to identification which should be recognised. Colour-marked birds should always be reported (see page 31). In some areas natural staining may occur.

Dirty legs, caused by dirt such as soft black mud or orange dirt from sand- or gravel-workings, may obscure the true colour of the legs and toes, and this possibility should be borne in mind. Leg colour is in general a very useful identification feature, but has a slight inherent variability; apparent leg colour can also depend to an extent on the quality of the light.

Size and shape

When attempting to identify a wader, it is important to gain an impression of its size and shape, but it must be realised that neither is absolute, even for a single individual bird.

Size may not always be easy to judge, particularly if there are no other birds for comparison (see Grant 1980). Grant (1983b) has drawn attention to the fact that, when using powerful optical aids such as a telescope or a telephoto lens, optical illusion ('size-illusion') can play tricks on the unwary: birds behind the plane of focus tend to appear larger, and those in front smaller, than they really are. Thus a Dunlin photographed against a background of Little Stints or Least Sandpipers may turn out looking the same size, although it is actually a larger bird!

Waders wintering in the tropics tend to weigh less than those in colder zones and may actually appear smaller. This impression is heightened by the feathers being flattened against the body, rather than fluffed up to retain heat.

Most waders have a characteristic **shape**, but many factors can influence this in the field. The stance may vary depending on whether the bird is alert or relaxed, feeding or resting, or in a strong or light wind. A bird feeding in a hunched attitude in the chill of the early morning may appear erect and slim when disturbed by a raptor in the afternoon. The diagram below illustrates the variety of attitudes and poses which may be adopted by a single individual bird.

the legs tucked into the body feathering rather than trailing behind. Grant (1983a) has drawn attention to the potential this habit gives for misidentification, for example between a Spotted Redshank flying with legs retracted and a dowitcher.

Behaviour

The way a bird is behaving is often a vital clue to its identity. Important elements of the behaviour of individual species are mentioned in the 'Habits'

Range of postures possible for a single individual bird

The relative length of the folded wing against the tail is an important identification pointer in several species. The exact distance from wing-tip to tail-tip in an individual bird, however, varies to some extent depending on how neatly it has folded its wings. Where possible, this feature should be observed over a long time-period, so that the typical value can be assessed.

Similarly, on a flying wader, the projection of legs or toes beyond the tip of the tail should be looked for. A number of long-legged waders, however, particularly in cold weather, may fly with

section of the text.

It should, however, be recognised that the value of behaviour in identification is limited. Most species have a repertoire of feeding methods, and the mode of feeding at any one time may depend on many factors, including the food items being taken, their spacing and density, the presence or absence of other feeding birds, and so on.

Where vagrants are concerned, habitat choice and feeding habits are often not representative of the behaviour of the species within its normal range.

Behaviour

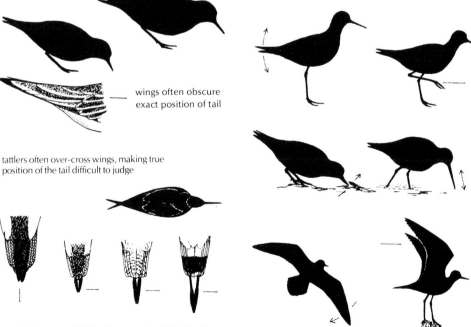

wings often obscure exact position of tail

tattlers often over-cross wings, making true position of the tail difficult to judge

projecting central tail feathers may look like feet

GENERAL NOTES ON FAMILIES AND GROUPS OF WADERS

JACANAS (Jacanidae) 8 species
Pages 215-221
Plates 1-3
The jacanas (normally pronounced with a hard 'c') are an extraordinary group of birds with representatives throughout the tropical continents. They all have greatly elongated toes and claws and are thus able to walk across floating vegetation. The female is generally the larger of the sexes; in most species she is polyandrous, and leaves incubation and care of the brood to the male. Several species have an unusual bone structure of the wing which enables the eggs to be brooded, and young to be carried, between the adult's wings and body. Most species are relatively sedentary, but one, the extraordinary Pheasant-tailed, is a strong migrant. Jacanas are rather diverse in plumage and in presence or absence of wing-spurs and wattles (as are the lapwings *Vanellus*), but there are arguments for putting all but Lesser and Pheasant-tailed into a single genus.

PAINTED SNIPES (Rostratulidae) 2 species
Pages 221-222
Plate 4
These species resemble snipes in shape but are shorter-billed, more brightly coloured and have woodcock-like rounded wings. They live in chiefly tropical and subtropical marshlands. The plumage patterning, particularly in the widespread Painted Snipe, is highly intricate; the female is the larger and brighter, and leaves incubation and care of the brood to the male. The South American Painted Snipe is smaller, duller, and shows less marked sexual dimorphism. Activity is greatest at dawn and dusk and at night.

CRAB PLOVER (Dromadidae) 1 species
Pages 222-223
Plate 9
This bird is highly distinctive in its pied plumage and huge black bill, and also in its habits. It is unique among waders in nesting underground in a burrow, laying a white egg, and rearing the chick at the nest. Parental care continues for several months, even after migration. The species is restricted to northern and western parts of the Indian Ocean. Crabs form a large part of the diet.

OYSTERCATCHERS (Haematopodidae) 11 species
Pages 223-231
Plates 5-8
Oystercatchers are almost cosmopolitan, occurring in perhaps as many as 20 separate forms. All are remarkably similar, but there are limited variations in size, shape of bill and legs, iris and eye-ring colour, and distribution of black, white and brown in the plumage. The taxonomy of this group is still not satisfactorily resolved.

All oystercatchers are bulky waders with black/brown or black/brown-and-white plumage, a long stout orangey bill and fairly short pinkish legs. They are chiefly coastal, but inland nesting occurs in three of the pied species. Rocky-shore oystercatchers tend to be blacker in plumage, thicker-billed and stouter-legged. Bivalve molluscs form a high proportion of the diet, but oystercatchers, particularly pied species, also probe for worms and other prey on mudflats or inland.

IBISBILL (Ibidorhynchidae) 1 species
Page 231
Plate 9
The Ibisbill is a most unusual-looking wader, combining superficially curlew-like and stone-curlew-like features with a unique plumage pattern. It is perhaps most closely related to the oystercatchers. It is restricted to glacial riverbeds in the Himalayan region and Tibetan plateau, descending to lower altitudes in winter. In flight, the downcurved bill and rather rounded wings may suggest a similarity to ibises.

STILTS AND AVOCETS (Recurvirostridae) 7 species
Pages 232-237
Plates 10-12
These species live around wetlands, chiefly brackish and saline, in warm or hot climates, and are colonial or semi-colonial nesters.
  Stilts (3 species): Stilts are so named because of their very long legs. All three species also have a long, thin, almost straight bill. The Banded Stilt (*Cladorhynchus*) is an Australian species with a brown breast-band and extraordinary nesting habits. Other stilts (*Himantopus*) comprise up to eight separate forms, varying chiefly in the patterning of black and white in the plumage, from which we have recognised two species.
  Avocets (4 species): Avocets have strongly-upcurved bills, and often feed by making vigorous sideways sweeps through water or soft mud. Their plumage is mostly pied, but two species also have reddish on the head and neck. The feet are webbed; avocets often swim and up-end to feed.

STONE-CURLEWS (Burhinidae) 9 species
Pages 238-244
Plates 13-16
These are chiefly birds of the southern continents, although one migratory species reaches middle latitudes of Eurasia. All have black or black-and-yellow bills, a large yellow eye, brownish, cryptically-patterned plumage, and longish yellow or greenish legs with a characteristically large 'knee' joint. Most are essentially birds of arid or semi-arid open country, but some live near fresh water or on the coast. Activity is chiefly nocturnal. Voice includes very loud wailing songs, often reminiscent of curlews. Feeding actions are lethargic and plover-like. Larger species are powerful predators and take lizards or even small mammals.

COURSERS AND PRATINCOLES (Glareolidae) 17 species
Pages 244-259
Plates 14, 17-21
This family is widespread in warm or hot climates, but does not occur in the Americas.

Coursers (8 species) and Egyptian Plover: True coursers are long-legged, fast-running, cryptically-plumaged birds of dry habitats. Several species are crepuscular or nocturnal.

Egyptian Plover is a brightly-plumaged, rather stocky bird of African rivers which nests in sandbanks and often buries both eggs and young in the sand to cool them or to hide them from predators.

Pratincoles (8 species): These are very long-winged waders which feed extensively by aerial hawking for flying insects. Their flight is fast and graceful, with an easy swallow-like or tern-like wing-action, full of fast jinking turns after prey. Most feeding is done at dawn and dusk, the birds resting inconspicuously for much of the day. The forked tails and short legs of most species are also reminiscent of terns. Pratincoles are highly gregarious and nest in colonies. Some species are strongly migratory. The Australian Pratincole is more terrestrial than the others and may be intermediate between coursers and pratincoles.

LAPWINGS AND PLOVERS (Charadriidae) 65 species
Pages 259-310
Plates 22-47
This is a cosmopolitan group of birds which are relatively short-billed and are chiefly visual feeders. Feeding action is typified by the succession of run-pause-run-dip or run-pause sequences. During pauses the bird is actively searching for signs of possible prey.

Lapwings (24 species): These are large, round-winged, rather showy species which often have wing-spurs or wattles. They are found almost worldwide, but are absent from the Arctic and from North America (except as vagrants). Most species are sedentary and tropical, but several are strongly migratory. Their flight is rather slow and heavy, but can be highly aerobatic at times. Three species have wispy upstanding crests.

Golden and Grey Plovers (4 species): The genus *Pluvialis* contains four rather large and dumpy species, all strong migrants which breed mostly in arctic regions. The upperparts are spotted or spangled in all plumages, while in breeding plumage the underparts become extensively black. The colour of the axillaries is important for identification.

Small plovers (37 species): This is a varied group comprising the genus *Charadrius* and a number of single-species genera which show similarities to it and are probably closely related. Almost all patterns of migration and distribution shown by waders as a whole are represented within this group: some are high-arctic breeders and long-distance migrants; some are non-migratory and restricted in their distribution (in several cases to remote islands or island groups); and others nest in the far south and migrate north before the southern winter. The genus *Charadrius* is cosmopolitan, and includes species nesting in a wide variety of habitats: from the edges of snow-fields at high altitude or in the Arctic, to areas of baking tropical sand where eggs often have to be cooled rather than warmed by the incubating adult. Within the single-species genera are several rather distinguished birds including Wrybill, one of very few bird species with a lateral asymmetry to the bill.

MAGELLANIC PLOVER (Pluvianellidae) 1 species
Page 311
Plate 87
It is not clear whether 'plover' is a suitable name taxonomically for this bird, which does not appear to show close affinities with any other wader family. In the field it shows several similarities to turnstones, including the habit of turning seaweed and stones to look for hidden prey; uniquely for a plover-like bird, it will also dig some distance into the sand for food. Another of its peculiarities is a large crop which is distended in display and is used to carry food to the young.

SANDPIPERS, SNIPES AND ALLIES (Scolopacidae) 88 species
Pages 311-387
Plates 48-86
This is a large and varied family of waders, comprising ten well-defined groups of species. Of these groups, all but three (the Polynesian sandpipers, the woodcocks and the snipes) are confined to northern latitudes as breeding birds. Most, however, are strongly migratory and many reach the tips of the southern continents as non-breeding visitors. In contrast to the plovers, most waders in this group rely chiefly on tactile rather than visual cues when feeding.

Godwits (4 species): Godwits are large, tall and elegant waders with long, fractionally-upcurved bills. Non-breeding plumages are rather curlew-like, but in three of the species the underparts become to some extent chestnut-red in breeding plumage. Two species show boldly black-and-white wings and tail in flight. All four species typically feed and roost in large flocks. Females are appreciably larger than males and often feed in deeper water.

Curlews (8 species) and Upland Sandpiper: Curlews are easily recognised by their brown plumage, with little if any seasonal change, and long, downcurved bills. The bill shape distinguishes them from the closely-related godwits. There are two small species, about the size of a large *Tringa* sandpiper, three intermediate, and three large; these last birds are among the largest waders in the world, and are certainly the longest-billed. The curved bills are well adapted to removing worms from deep burrows in intertidal mud, but curlews also eat such items as crabs and small molluscs, and even the eggs and young of other birds.

Upland Sandpiper is a rather singular species with a short, straight bill, but appears to be most closely allied to the curlews.

Shanks, tattlers and allies (16 species): These are small to medium-sized birds, often with longish, brightly-coloured legs and a bill rather longer than the head. Most feed actively by pecking or chasing

visible prey, and probe less often than most other sandpipers. All nest in temperate or subarctic zones rather than in the high Arctic: the Redshank nests regularly in North Africa, and the Willet just reaches Venezuela as a breeding bird. More than most sandpipers, the *Tringa* species (shanks) are birds of freshwater margins. Some nest in trees, using the old nests of passerine birds.

Polynesian sandpipers (2 species, one now extinct): The Tuamotu Sandpiper is a rare wader restricted to a few remote Pacific atolls. It is small, short-billed and short-legged, with rather short and rounded wings and rather plain, dull brown plumage. Its relative the White-winged Sandpiper, once found on Tahiti and Moorea, is now extinct. Their closest relatives may be the tattlers, or perhaps the Upland Sandpiper and the curlews.

Turnstones (2 species): This distinct tribe contains only two species, both breeding in the Arctic. The Black Turnstone is restricted to the northeast Pacific, but the Ruddy Turnstone can be encountered almost anywhere in the world. These are fairly small, stout, squat waders with short, strong legs and a short, deeply-based bill which, although strongly pointed, has a distinct upward slant to the lower mandible. The powerful neck muscles, strong legs and unusual bill are used for turning over (hence the common name) stones or seaweed to find hidden food items. Turnstones are primarily birds of rocky or stony coastlines, and are strictly coastal when not breeding or on migration. They fly strongly on pointed wings, when the flashing white patches on the wings, tail and back provide a striking contrast to the otherwise inconspicuous plumage.

Phalaropes (3 species): These are the most aquatic of the waders, and the only ones which are at home swimming on the open ocean. They swim buoyantly, often spinning around and picking items off the surface. To aid swimming, all have enlarged flaps of skin on their toes, although in the most terrestrial species, Wilson's Phalarope, these are less well developed. In non-breeding plumage they are mainly sparkling white and greyish with a dark smudge running backwards from the eye (the 'phalarope-mark'). When breeding, however, they are transformed, with blacks and chestnuts; in all three species the female is brighter than the male in breeding plumage and, apart from egg-laying, takes little part in the breeding cycle.

Woodcocks (6 species): Two species of woodcocks are widespread; the others are restricted to islands, mainly in the East Indies. They are essentially crepuscular and nocturnal woodland birds, cryptically coloured with deep red-browns and blacks and with diagnostic blackish bars across the rear crown and nape. The underside of the tail is tipped silvery-white. In flight, the stocky shape, broad rounded wings and long straight bill are noticeable. Woodcocks are very difficult to see on the ground, and are most likely to be observed during display. They feed in soft ground by probing deeply with the long bill. The eyes are set in large sockets right on the side of the head, and thus give good all-round vision without the need to turn the head.

Snipes (18 species): The snipes are typical

inhabitants of grassy marshland, especially where there are muddy edges to pools; some prefer more wooded country. Typical snipes have parallel pale buffish lines down their backs and are superbly camouflaged by a mixture of buff, browns and black. They often crouch motionless when initially disturbed and then explode away, sometimes from underfoot. The bill is long and straight, with many sensory cells in the distal half. The feeding technique is to probe rapidly, with a 'sewing-machine' action, almost vertically into soft ground. Aerial displays are well developed in most species, usually taking place at dusk and dawn; in several, a drumming noise is made by tail-feather vibrations during steep downward dives. Snipes vary in the number and shape of their tail feathers. The two subantarctic snipes are very different from the other species and may be primitive forms. They live in woodland and dense grassland on a few isolated islands to the south of New Zealand, and are in danger of extinction.

Dowitchers (3 species): Dowitchers are snipe-like in bill shape and feeding behaviour, but more like godwits in plumage. They are, however, rather smaller and shorter-legged than godwits, with thicker and straighter bills. There are two American species, very similar to each other, and a third species in eastern Asia; all are migratory.

Calidrids and allies (25 species): These species all breed between 42°N and 83°N, and many only in the high Arctic. All are migratory and two species, despite their breeding range and relatively small body size, are among the waders which occur regularly almost everywhere. The members of the genus *Calidris* are abundant nesters on the arctic tundra, and are paramount among those many birds which are adapted to exploit the short-lived but prolific flush of life in the arctic summer. After breeding, several of the species gather on estuaries in huge flocks which are spectacular in flight. The bill-tips of calidrids have many sensory cells to detect vibrations from hidden prey; the birds feed busily, pecking or probing almost continuously to obtain a constant supply of small prey items. In flight, the wings are relatively long and slim, and many species show clear white central wingbars and dark-centred rumps and tails. Among the allied species, the Surfbird and the Spoon-billed Sandpiper are divergent from the rest in bill shape, and the Ruff has a highly-developed lekking display and spectacular male breeding plumages.

SEEDSNIPES (Thinocoridae) 4 species
Pages 387–390
Plates 87–88
The seedsnipes are inland waders of South America which are similar in some respects to grouse or partridges in their biology. They are generally found in cold climates in the far south of the continent or at high altitude. The diet is chiefly vegetarian. They have short legs, a stocky body, a short neck and a short, broad, decurved bill. Two large species in the genus *Attagis* resemble partridges, while the two *Thinocorus* species are much smaller and may look almost lark-like on the ground. In all four species the plumage is superbly camouflaged.

CONSERVATION OF WADER HABITATS AND SPECIES

In these pages we have already alluded to the problems that face waders and their habitats. Unless rational and practical conservation measures can be introduced, then the future of many species will be bleak indeed! As a corollary, birdwatchers too will find fewer species and smaller numbers. Much more work is urgently needed to document wader numbers, distribution and population ecology in order to understand fully the implications of all the pressures we are placing upon them.

For centuries, before technology changed the balance, man's main impact on waders was through killing them, normally for food. This was, and still is, widespread in many parts of the world. Once the gun was refined, man's influence became enormous. We can look back with sadness and amazement to the documented slaughter of birds such as the Eskimo Curlew (once known as the Dough-bird) in the second half of the nineteenth century on the plains of North America. Here was a bird once exceedingly abundant, but which was killed in many cases just for sport, with piles being left to rot. From being abundant, it was reduced almost to extinction soon after the turn of the century. Similar pressures were applied to the American Golden Plover (Audubon describes a spring shoot near New Orleans in which 48,000 were killed in one day) and to the other curlews, Upland Sandpiper, Red Knot and many other species. It was blithely assumed that migratory waders were an inexhaustible resource.

While better sense now reigns in North America, there remain several blackspots where hunting is popular but poorly controlled. These include the Mediterranean, where the rare Slender-billed Curlew is greatly at risk to indiscriminate shooting, and Java, where tired migrants are netted in huge numbers for the pot and where one endemic wader has been extinguished in recent years.

During voyages of exploration, the accidental introduction of rats has put many indigenous island species under great pressure. This is perhaps best exemplified by such waders as the New Zealand and Chatham Islands Snipes, the Tuamotu Sandpiper and the New Zealand Shore Plover. Similarly, deliberate introductions of sheep, goats, pigs, cats and other animals have had enormous repercussions on such species, either through predation or through destruction of habitat.

Even today, lack of appreciation of the impact of developments can introduce similar problems. In South Africa the linking of Marcus Island, site of a colony of the scarce African Black Oystercatcher, to the mainland has given a bridgehead to predators such as Cape foxes (Hockey 1983b).

Modern man is assaulting his surroundings in ways undreamt of a few hundred years ago. It is difficult to summarise the impact of this, but with particular reference to waders there are five main, often interrelated categories. These are reclamation of coastal wetlands, agricultural intensification, drainage, pollution and disturbance.

'Reclamation' is a word often used to describe the claiming (for the first time) of a natural wetland for man's purposes. Major schemes for claiming some of the largest wetlands in the world are continually being put forward: in Europe, for example, there have been recent plans for the Wash, Morecambe Bay, the Rhine delta and the Waddensea, to name but a few. The impact of such losses on the populations of migratory waders would be enormous, but fortunately the immense financial costs have prevented many such catastrophic plans from reaching fruition. Much more insidious, however, is the continual attrition, or nibbling away, of sites. Surely everyone who knows a large estuarine or coastal area of significance for waders can think of his or her own examples of loss. This could be for a variety of different purposes, among them petrochemical-works, power-stations, roads, airports, ports, housing, rubbish dumps, coastal-protection schemes, a place to dump dredged material, marinas and agricultural land. Added together on a regional or world scale, small habitat losses add up to a staggering assault on these vital areas for waders. The importance of recognising this problem and trying to minimise or preferably stop the loss cannot be emphasised too strongly.

There have been trends in most human societies towards population growth and the acquisition of wealth. The associated needs of feeding the population better or maximising the income from a given area have both contributed to agricultural intensification. In many parts of the world, there is no longer a need for land to lie fallow to recover from previous crops, and conditions cannot justify a low-input/low-output system. Through the application of fertilisers, herbicides and pesticides, land can be made to crop almost continuously. Very few waders are capable of breeding in fast-growing crops. In western Europe, the trends towards using fast-growing rye-grass for silage, rather than the slower-growing hay meadows, and towards autumn-sown cereals, have virtually forced breeding waders such as the Northern Lapwing and the Stone-curlew on to the ever-decreasing areas of wet meadowland and spring-sown cereals, or into fringe habitats. Numbers of these breeding birds are, not surprisingly, declining in many areas.

Often associated with agricultural intensification is land-drainage. Wet meadows, especially those regularly flooded by fresh water, maintain a good natural fertility, but drainage may enable different, temporarily more valuable crops to be grown on them. As the nature of a site changes, so the waders adapted to that habitat disappear. Land-drainage may also be carried out to prevent occasional flooding, for mosquito-control, or for housing developments. In Britain, over 90% of old meadowland has been destroyed during the present century. Water-extraction for industrial, urban or agricultural use is reducing the size of some lakes and giving rise for concern; an example is Mono Lake in California, a reservoir for Los Angeles, where tens of thousands of Wilson's Phalaropes have traditionally moulted and fattened for onward migration.

Pollution of wetlands through oil, chemical, pesticide or nutrient input can have major repercussions. Undoubtedly, the massive doses of organochlorine pesticides used to combat the malarial mosquito must have had an impact on waders of tropical wetlands, as they did on many other birds when used less liberally in North America and Europe in the late 1950s. Oil and chemical pollution are relatively small problems at present, but are potentially serious. A high input of nutrients such as phosphates and nitrates to inland or sheltered coastal wetlands is more significant. Eutrophication is a reality in many areas, with dense algal growth smothering and killing the vital invertebrates on which the larger animals depend. Acidification of wetlands through acid rain is likely to affect waders similarly by destroying lower elements of the food-chain.

Disturbance is a broad heading; it ranges from people simply walking through breeding or feeding grounds or roosts, to more aggressive and noisy human occupations. A major problem is the physical destruction of beach and dune habitats and their associated nesting waders through the ever-increasing use of 'off-the-road' vehicles, especially in North America. The more often a breeding bird is forced off the nest, the more likely are the eggs or newly-hatched young to succumb to predators or to the elements. In cold weather, or while birds are on migration, energy is especially at a premium; disturbance increases stress and the need for additional food, while at the same time reducing the time available for foraging. Wider discussions on conservation problems can be found in Prater (1981) and Evans and Dugan (1984).

Waders show a high degree of site-fidelity, returning to their breeding or wintering sites year after year. More surprisingly, they often show a remarkable return-rate to the vital 'stepping-stone' wetlands on the migration route: many birds will return to the same area of the same beach or estuary each year on migration. The patterns of breeding, migration and wintering distributions of waders have been built up over many thousands of years and it is all too easy for man to change or destroy them, often with no real benefit to himself. The aim of all birdwatchers who care about the birds they watch must be to do everything possible to ensure survival of the habitats and with them the birds that depend on them.

HOW TO STUDY WADERS

Identification of waders is a skill which demands detailed study, careful observation, often under difficult conditions, and preferably a background of accumulated experience. A visit to the local estuary or sewage-farm (a favourite haunt of waders!) at a passage time of year is a highlight for many a birdwatcher; at a good site, it would be surprising if there was not a wader in unusual plumage, or in some other way presenting an interesting exercise in the skills of identification.

Knowing the identity of a bird gives added pleasure to watching its habits and behaviour, but should not, we believe, be regarded as a satisfactory end in itself. Observers should always consider the question 'How can my observations aid the study or conservation of the species?' Our state of knowledge of most species is so basic that every observation properly recorded is a valuable particle of information which can eventually help to build up a picture of the habits, movements or population size of the species concerned.

'What should I do if I find a rare wader?'

If you suspect that you have found a rarity, even a local rarity, the first thing is to be sure to take as many notes or sketches as possible (no matter how rough!) of the bird in the field. Plumage, bare-part and structural features are important, but so too are call, behaviour and the impression of the whole bird. These can be written up into a neater version (but not a doctored one!) when you get back to the car or home. For most countries with well-organised ornithological societies, there are *records committees* to whom records of rare waders should be sent and who will keep the description on file for the benefit of future reviewers. It is clearly imperative that only *bona fide* occurrences are incorporated into the permanent records of the country or region.

Owing to the difficulties of wader identification, it is advisable to try to obtain some corroboration from experienced observers. This is not always easy, but birds seen by more than one observer are far more likely to be accepted as genuine! Whether the location of the bird should be revealed widely, thus possibly attracting a large number of observers, is a difficult question which must be left to the judgement of the finder. In many cases no harm will come to the bird or the environment, nor will local residents or landowners be inconvenienced, but in others real problems may be foreseen. In general, locations of rare breeding birds should not be divulged except to the relevant conservation bodies.

'What do I do if I find a colour-marked wader?'

Many population and migration studies use plumage-dyeing, colour-rings (bands) or, more rarely, coloured or numbered wing-tags to allow recognition of individuals or classes in the population. If a colour-marked bird is seen, it is important to record in detail the exact colour of any dye and where it is on the bird, as well as the exact positions, colours, shapes, patterns or numbers of colour-rings or flags placed on the legs, or tags fixed to the wings. This information should then be reported, along with date, place and species.

Unfortunately, the migration of waders across national boundaries means that co-ordination of record-keeping is difficult; this task has recently been taken on by the Wader Study Group (c/o Dr DJ Townshend, Department of Zoology, University of Durham, South Road, Durham, UK), who will pass on sightings to the relevant organisation or research worker. Information (if available) on the origin of the bird will be returned to the observer. In a few cases (for example, where some marks have been lost), it is not possible to identify the individual bird, but observers should not be deterred from reporting any subsequent sightings of colour-marked waders.

'How can my ordinary observations help?'

In many countries, wader studies are organised and co-ordinated by local or national ornithological societies. The contact names and addresses of such societies are often obtainable from information libraries or natural history museums. Regular counts of migratory waders, such as for the Birds of Estuaries Enquiry in Britain, can provide much useful information.

Among the main organisations concentrating on wader work are:

WADER STUDY GROUP. The WSG is an international association of amateur and professional workers on waders, formed in 1970 and now with a membership of about 500. It aims to co-ordinate wader studies on an international scale, and publishes a regular bulletin for news and notices, including preliminary publication of results. The general secretary (also for the New World section) is Dr Stephen Baillie, 8 Little London, Whitchurch, Aylesbury, Buckinghamshire HP22 4LE, UK. The WSG can act as a clearing-house for information on waders from all parts of the world, including sightings of colour-marked birds.

INTERNATIONAL WATERFOWL RESEARCH BUREAU. The Wader Research Group of IWRB co-ordinates counts of wetland sites. Help is required from resident or visiting birdwatchers in all parts of the world, especially in areas poorly covered by national organisations. The contact address is Drs Cor Smit, Rijksinstituut voor Natuurbeheer, Postbus 59, 1790 AB Den Burg, Texel, The Netherlands.

In addition, membership and support of national bird conservation bodies is a tangible way of helping to protect the waders and their habitats from man's many excesses.

ACKNOWLEDGEMENTS

Although we have all been watching waders for many years, this project did not really begin until after the publication of the 'wader guide' to the Holarctic species (Prater et al. 1977). During this long period of preparation, we have received a tremendous amount of help from wader-watchers all over the world.

Special thanks are due to the staff of the British Museum (Natural History) at Tring, particularly Michael Walters, Dr Philip Burton, Peter Colston and Derek Read, for allowing our frequent reference to their skin and spirit collections over a protracted period and for constant help and advice; to the other museums worldwide which loaned skins and birds in spirit; to Dr Stephen Baillie for loan of his microcomputer and software; to the British Trust for Ornithology (particularly for word-processing facilities, use of the library, and for granting a short period of scientific leave); and to typists Gill Marriott, Christine Albone, Margaret Millner, and Jane Marchant. We are especially indebted to Jane, who devoted many long evenings to typing the whole book onto the word-processor, also adding the typesetting commands, and collected many of the references.

At Christopher Helm Ltd, we should like particularly to thank David Christie and Jo Hemmings (editing), Ann Doolan (design), and also Christopher Helm and Mark Beaman.

The library staff of the Royal Society for the Protection of Birds have been of great help in finding obscure references and in the loan to the artist of a considerable number of books and publications. Especial thanks are due to Ian Dawson, Chris Harbard and Rob Hume.

The artist owes particular thanks to his wife and family for putting up with all the skins etc lying around the house and for providing innumerable cups of coffee during the work.

The authors, and particularly the artist, owe a great debt of gratitude to Martin Bragg and Barry Highland of Alpha Reprographics for their enormous help throughout this project and for their expertise in producing the most excellent colour reproductions.

In addition, the following people assisted the project by providing stimulating discussion, unpublished field-notes or photographic material, accommodation or information on foreign trips, or by commenting on early drafts:

Worldwide
Dr Allan J Baker, Dr Nigel J Collar, Simon Cook, Richard Fairbank, Peter J Grant, James Hancock, Lars Jonsson, Richard Loyn, Nigel Redman, Monica Vizoso.

Eurasia
Per Alström, Francis Argyle, Tim Cleeves, Nick Dymond, Dr Vladimir Flint, Rodney Martins, Andrew Moon, Urban Olsson, Richard Porter, Tony Pym, Craig Robson, Mike Rogers, Edward van Ijzendoorn, Keith Vinicombe, Alan Vittery, Pierre Yésou.

North America
Elizabeth Copper, Tom H Davis, Jon Dunn, Kevin Griffith, Paul Lehman, Guy McCaskie, Don Roberson.

South America
David Bishop, Theodore A Parker III, Dr J van Remsen, Martin Sutherland.

Africa
Chris Balchin, Tim Dee, Dr Peter Lack, Dr David Pearson, Barry Taylor.

India and Southeast Asia
Paul Andrew, David Bishop, Dr Simon Cox, Tim and Carol Inskipp, Colin Mackenzie-Grieve, David Melville, Duncan Parish, Phil Round.

Australia
Chris Corben, Dr Stephen Davies, David Eades, Phil Gregory, Roger Jaensch, Brett Lane, Dr Clive Minton, Shane A Parker, Adrian Riegan, Fred TH Smith, Bob Swindley.

New Zealand
Brian Bell, John Fennell, Barrie Heather, Ann Lindsey, Colin M Miskelly, Dr Ray J Pierce, Paul M Sagar.

Antarctica
Peter Prince.

NOTES ON THE PLATES

by Peter Hayman

The aims in producing the colour plates are twofold: firstly, to provide the most comprehensive illustrations available, with equal treatment for rare or little-known species; and, secondly, to produce accurate scale drawings of every species. The emphasis, and time spent, on measurement to gain accuracy is not so much to show the relative sizes of birds, although this is useful, but to gain an insight into the physical differences or similarities, however subtle these may be. From a taxonomic viewpoint, we can show the differences between two closely-related species and, in terms of identification, we may be able to separate them on silhouette alone. For instance, the Stone-curlew (31) and the Senegal Thick-knee (32) show differences in the length of the body (a), in relative tail projections (b), in the proportion of the arm (c) to the outer wing or hand (d) and in the wing-tip configuration (e).

The skin collection is used to supplement details taken from the dead bird and as a further plumage reference. Measurements may have to be taken from skins alone, a laborious process and open to error.

The National Museum of New Zealand has started the excellent practice of preserving new skins with one wing, complete with scapulars, detached and set in a fully open position, thus providing a perfect pattern and feather reference. This might be followed by all with advantage.

Scales used on plates

All of the illustrations on the plates are drawn to scale, but, because of the size-range from curlews to stints, we have had to use two scales for flying and two for standing birds.

Each species on a plate has a principal flight illustration, all to the same scale, with smaller inset drawings as space permits. Likewise, standing birds have all principal illustrations to the same scale, with

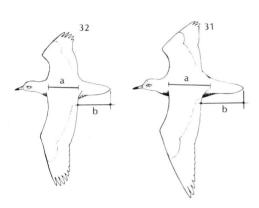

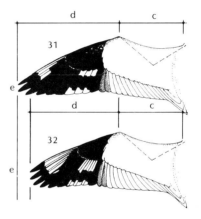

These features combined produce a rather bustard-like profile for the Senegal Thick-knee and are points which, however subtle, can be discerned in the field. It might have taken much comparative work with the two species together to 'work out' these differences in the field, but, once the *mind* is aware of such features, the *eye* is able to pick up the difference; it is much more time-consuming and difficult to work the other way around.

To produce the scale drawings, the following reference material was used:

Dead birds kept in deep-freeze (European material only)
Spirit collections
Skin collections
All available photographs, field sketches and notes (photographs are invaluable for the correct facial expression, checking feather patterns etc)

It is necessary to have a dead bird in order to produce a completely accurate flight drawing (see technique on page 36). Deep-frozen birds are the most convenient to use, but the majority of material available is kept in spirit. When taken out and partly dried, the specimen is usually perfectly flexible.

smaller supplementary drawings fitting the space available. Some of the smallest drawings are designed specifically to show the distant views that one often gets in the field. Some smaller species, stints especially, have additional larger drawings.

The principal scale for *flying* birds, scale A, is used on 60 of the 88 plates. The principal scale for *standing* birds, scale B, is used on 78 of the plates. The exceptions are as follows:

Large flying birds, scale C
Plates 5-16 (note that Egyptian Plover on Plate 14 is in the majority scale, i.e. flight A, standing B)
Plates 22-30
Plates 48-53
Plate 65 (note that Eurasian and American Woodcocks are shown at the majority scale on Plate 64 for size-comparison with the snipes, and Eurasian again at the smaller scale on Plate 65 for comparison with the remainder of the woodcocks)
Large standing birds, scale D
Plates 5-8
Plates 13-16
Plates 52-53

Technique used to measure a dead bird for scale drawings

The proportional dividers (1) are set to scale required, and measured off the dead bird (2) to produce the scale drawing (3) of a Willet (146, Plate 59). Only the main dimensions are shown on 2. These include the wing bones, ulna (C) and humerus (D), which form the inner wing. The tail (J) and its position in relation to the rear edge of the wing are vital. One of the most important dimensions is E (front of open wing to tip of tail). The length F has to be gauged from field experience, photographs if available, or intuition. All of the primary feathers, wing-coverts and feather tracts have to be measured.

Drawings are done on tracing paper, making overlay corrections easier. An average of five drawings may be produced before a final tracing-paper negative is made; this is reversed onto the colour-washed plate and rubbed down to produce a pencil image.

Willet, 146 Plate 59

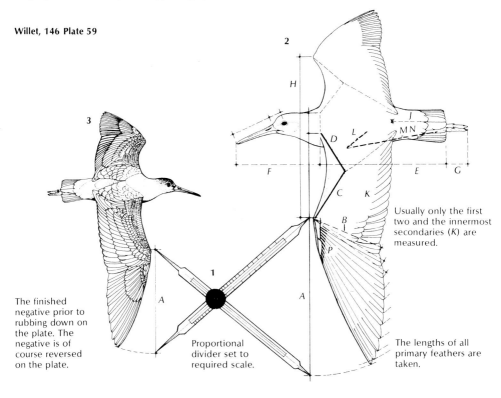

Usually only the first two and the innermost secondaries (K) are measured.

The finished negative prior to rubbing down on the plate. The negative is of course reversed on the plate.

Proportional divider set to required scale.

The lengths of all primary feathers are taken.

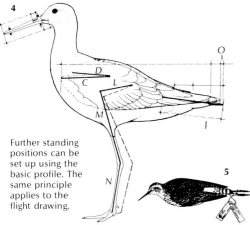

Further standing positions can be set up using the basic profile. The same principle applies to the flight drawing.

The procedure for the standing bird is the same as for the flying bird (3). The femur (L), tibia (M) and tarsus (N), when set out, confirm the foot projection in flight (G). Some of the dimension lines are indicated but not labelled. Approximately 50 measurements are taken for the flying bird and 30 for the standing bird, depending on the complexity of the species. Much the same procedure is used for skins, but the wing is set up in the closed position, with the skeleton and quills at P (see drawing 2) set up, then transferred to the radiating profile of the open wing.

Illustration 5 shows the appearance of a museum skin, in this case of a Wood Sandpiper (145).

PLATES 1-88

2 African Jacana *Actophilornis africana*

Text page 215

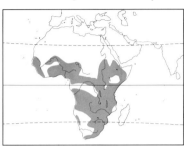

The widespread jacana of Africa; typical of large wetlands with floating vegetation, but often seen on small or temporary pools.

a ADULT: Deep chestnut body contrasts with black head and hindneck and with white cheeks, side of neck and throat. Golden-yellow upper breast. Bill and large frontal shield are blue.

b ADULT: White anterior supercilium is partly obscured by the frontal shield.

c ADULT: When flying, shows enormous trailing feet, short tail, and rounded wings. Apart from blackish head, neck and flight feathers, upperparts are all-chestnut. White foreneck is conspicuous.

d ADULT: Underwing-coverts are deep chestnut.

e JUVENILE: Dark brown cap, hindneck and eye-stripe contrast with long white supercilium from bill to behind eye. Upperparts glossed green, but rump, secondaries and outer greater coverts are chestnut. Underparts white with golden-yellow breast-band and chestnut thigh-patches. Frontal shield small. Obviously larger than 1.

f PART-GROWN CHICK: Like 1, but lacks rufous cap and paler patch on wing-coverts.

3 Madagascar Jacana *Actophilornis albinucha*

Text page 216

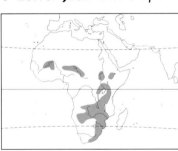

Replaces its close relative, 2, in Madagascar.

a ADULT: Strikingly different from 2; head and neck pattern is reversed. Crown, hindneck and sides of neck white, bordered below by golden-yellow. Crown flecked dark. Face and foreneck mostly glossy black. Body and wings chestnut, except for a band of white from thighs over uppertail-coverts. Bill and frontal shield are blue.

b ADULT: In flight, the white hindneck and band over uppertail-coverts contrast strongly with the chestnut back and wing-coverts. Primaries blackish.

c ADULT: Chestnut wing-linings are continuous with chestnut belly. Band of white at the rear is conspicuous.

d JUVENILE: Virtually identical to 2e, but crown, hindneck and eye-stripe tend to be blacker, and eye-stripe broader near the bill. Underparts white, with some golden on breast and dull chestnut o flanks and belly. Bill-shield small.

1 Lesser Jacana *Microparra capensis*

Text page 215

A tiny, crake-like jacana, often inconspicuous. May occur alongside 2.

a ADULT: Very like juvenile of 2, but much smaller, more like a small crake. Note pale brown panel on the closed wing, and chestnut-red crown, nape and eye-stripe. Long supercilium is orangey from bill to eye, but becomes white at the eye. Sides of neck yellow, upper flanks chestnut. No bill-shield.

b ADULT: In flight mainly dark, with clear, pale brown panel over the larger coverts and a striking white trailing edge to the secondaries and inner primaries. Long legs, trailing feet and rounded wings are crake-like.

c ADULT: Underwing-coverts and flight feathers blackish, showing little contrast with chestnut axillaries. Strong contrast with white belly. White trailing edge is also visible from below.

d JUVENILE: Virtually identical to adult, but faint buff fringes to scapulars may aid identification.

5 Pheasant-tailed Jacana *Hydrophasianus chirurgus*   **Text page 217**

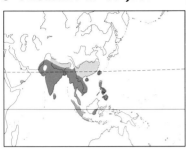

This is a highly distinctive bird, found typically on large freshwater lakes. Its seasonal plumage changes and migratory habits are unique among jacanas.

a ADULT BREEDING: Quite unmistakable. Long, drooping, dark brown tail. Dark brown body contrasts with brilliant white panel on wing and with face and throat. Hindneck golden-yellow. Small black nape-patch. Peculiar elongated outer primaries.

b ADULT NON-BREEDING: Tail is much shorter. Underparts white, except for blackish-brown breast-band which runs up the neck and joins the eye-stripe. Crown and hindneck blackish, sides of neck golden.

c ADULT: Breeding bird in flight shows mainly-white wings, above and below, contrasting with dark body and wing-tips.

d JUVENILE: Rufous-brown cap and fringes to wing-coverts. Dull buff sides to neck. Fresh juvenile lacks anterior supercilium. Breast-band rather indistinct.

e ADULT NON-BREEDING: Wing-coverts (except leading lessers) mostly brownish.

6 Bronze-winged Jacana *Metopidius indicus*   **Text page 218**

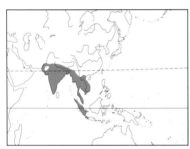

A heavy-looking, short-tailed jacana, often found on small waters.

a ADULT: A very dark glossy jacana with a long, brilliant white rear supercilium. All glossy black, apart from greenish mantle, scapulars tertials and wing-coverts and deep rufous tail and undertail. Heavy bill is yellow or yellow-green, and bill-shield red.

b ADULT: In flight looks very dark; blackish with bronzey-greenish wing-coverts and dark rufous tail and rump. The white supercilium is prominent. Legs trail far behind the short tail.

c ADULT: Underwing and underparts are all blackish, apart from the rufous undertail.

d JUVENILE: The dark upperparts contrast with the deep buff neck and whitish lower breast and belly. The tiny white supercilium and absence of a darkish breast-band separate it from 5, while 4 is white underneath and has no dark rear eye-stripe.

4 Comb-crested Jacana *Irediparra gallinacea*   **Text page 217**

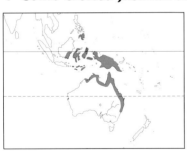

The only jacana of the Australasian region.

a ADULT: At distance, brown wings show clearly against black hindneck, upper mantle, breast and flight feathers, which in turn contrast strongly with white rear belly, face and upper neck. Sides of neck bright golden-yellow. The unique bright reddish-pink comb is prominent. Female is often noticeably larger than male.

b ADULT: In flight, the brown wing-coverts are obvious against the rest of the blackish upperparts. White undertail-coverts sometimes show beyond the short black tail.

c ADULT: Underwing-coverts and axillaries are solidly blackish.

d JUVENILE: Browner than adult, with chestnut cap. Black breast of adult is absent. Comb and wattle very small.

7 Northern Jacana *Jacana spinosa* Text page 219

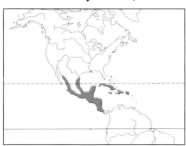

The northern relative of 8, this species is found on marshes and wetlands as far north as Texas.

a ADULT: Very dark, with black head and neck, dark maroon-chestnut belly and brighter chestnut coverts and mantle; all colours have strong glossy sheens. Sometimes, when primaries droop, a green-yellow streak is visible on the wing.

b ADULT: Three-lobed yellow wattle contrasts with the black head. No rictal lappet.

c ADULT: In flight, the bright greenish-yellow primaries and secondaries form a flashing contrast with remaining dark plumage. Very long legs trail far behind the short tail.

d ADULT: Wings are often held aloft, showing bright greenish-yellow, dark-tipped flight feathers contrasting with dark maroon-chestnut underwing and belly. Long, pointed, yellow carpal spurs.

e JUVENILE: Dark brownish cap, hindneck and upperparts contrast with long white supercilium and mainly-white underparts. Breast is buff and flanks maroon-chestnut. The frontal wattle is small, but still three-lobed. Coverts and scapulars show inconspicuous buff fringes. Rump is chestnut. Flight pattern like adult.

8 Wattled Jacana *Jacana jacana* Text page 220

This jacana, the only one in South America, has six races; the widespread ones are very like 7, but differ in shape and colour of the wattles.

a ADULT: All races show a dull red, two-lobed frontal wattle and a lateral (rictal) lappet which overhangs the side of the bill.

b ADULT race *jacana* (most of South America): Always shows dark chestnut mantle, scapulars and coverts and black head and neck. Central belly always black, unlike 7, but flanks may be tinged dark maroon on some.

c ADULT: All races show greenish-yellow, dark-tipped flight feathers, contrasting with otherwise dark plumage. In all except *hypomelaena*, there is a contrast between dark chestnut mantle and black hindneck. Male is often appreciably smaller than female.

d JUVENILE: Virtually identical, except race *hypomelaena* (h, i), to 7e, with dark brown upperparts and white or buffish underparts and supercilium. Rictal lappets absent, but very small frontal wattle is two-lobed, providing the only certain separation from 7.

e JUVENILE: Same plumage as d, in flight; greenish-yellow flight feathers.

f ADULT race *scapularis* (W Ecuador): Adult shows some black feathers among the upper scapulars and, in flight, almost whitish outer primaries.

g ADULT race *hypomelaena* (W Panama to N Colombia): All maroon-chestnut is replaced by black.

h JUVENILE race *hypomelaena*: Flanks, axillaries and underwing-coverts are black (dark maroon in other races and in 7e).

i JUVENILE race *hypomelaena*: Blacker back, wings and tail than in other races and in 7e.

9 Painted Snipe *Rostratula benghalensis*   Text page 221

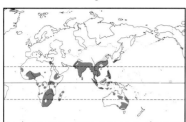

A skulking, snipe-like wader of inland marshes. Pale 'harness' and eye-patch are distinctive. Sexes are very different in adult plumage, the female being much brighter.

a ADULT FEMALE: Brightly and clearly patterned. Eye-patch and 'harness' are clean white, and neck dark reddish-brown. Green wing-coverts, finely barred black, are diagnostic of females. Flight feathers are like those of male. Australian race *australis* is depicted. Nominate race (above right), covering rest of range, is noticeably smaller.

b ADULT MALE: Smaller than female, with plumage duller and more cryptic. Wing-coverts show large paired golden-buff spots.

c ADULT MALE: In flight, coverts appear mainly golden-buff. Wings and tail are broad and rounded; legs often dangle. There is a narrow black wingbar.

d JUVENILE: Juveniles of both sexes superficially resemble adult male, but wing-coverts are greyer with smaller, paler buff spots. Initially, darker band on lower breast is virtually absent and down-streamers are present on the tail-tip.

e IMMATURE FEMALE: Duller than adult. Spread wing may show retained juvenile (buff-spotted) coverts.

10 South American Painted Snipe *Nycticryphes semicollaris* Text page 222

A small, dark, snipe-like wader of inland marshes. Apart from being smaller and darker, it differs from 9 in its graduated tail of narrow, pointed, brown feathers and in its virtual absence of sexual dimorphism.

a ADULT: Head, neck and breast are sooty-brown. Blacker cap contrasts with thin pale crown-stripe. Larger coverts and scapulars show some clear white spots. Lacks eye-patch of 9, and has a more sharply-decurved bill-tip. Male is depicted; brighter individuals (as to the right) are perhaps more likely to be females.

b JUVENILE: Throat and breast are buffish, with darker streaking and spotting. Small buffish-white patches on sides of breast. Coverts are brown, fringed and barred buff but not spotted. Scapulars show some creamy-buff spots.

c JUVENILE: In flight, wings appear short and rounded and legs often dangle. Flight feathers in all plumages are darker than in 9, with smaller spots and less prominent barring.

12 Eurasian Oystercatcher *Haematopus ostralegus*   Text page 223

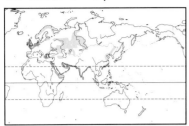

The most widespread and migratory of the world's 11 species of oystercatcher. Breeds widely inland as well as on the coast. The white throat-band of non-breeding and immature plumages is found only in this species.

a ADULT BREEDING race *ostralegus* (Europe, W USSR): Strongly contrasting pied plumage. No white neck collar. Eye-ring scarlet; iris deep red.

b ADULT BREEDING race *osculans* (Kamchatka to N China): As 12a, but bill slightly longer. Shows slightly more white on closed wing.

c ADULT BREEDING race *longipes* (central USSR): As 12a, but bill averages longer and upperparts slightly browner.

d JUVENILE: Browner back, no neck collar. Dark bill is usually pointed. Eye-ring dull orange and iris muddy-brown. Legs greyer.

e IMMATURE: Large white neck collar is gained during first winter.

f ADULT NON-BREEDING race *ostralegus*: As breeding, but gains white neck collar; bill-tip duller. Long white wingbar, and white area extending up back.

g ADULT BREEDING race *osculans*: White lacking on outer primaries, but extending more onto median coverts.

h ADULT BREEDING: Very white underwing.

i In breeding season, adult (above) has brighter bare parts than immature (below). Immature has white neck collar, and tends to have more pointed bill.

15 African Black Oystercatcher *Haematopus moquini*   Text page 226

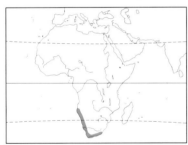

The only southern African oystercatcher except for 12, which occurs as a vagrant. Nests in dense colonies on some offshore islands. Compare with other black oystercatchers on Plates 7 and 8.

a ADULT: All-black oystercatcher, identified by scarlet eye-ring, red eye, and range. Legs deeper coral-pink than on other oystercatchers. Heavy legs and bill related to rocky habitat and shellfish diet.

b ADULT: In flight, plumage unmistakably all-dark. Wings show fairly long arm (body to carpal joint), and quite broad primaries.

c ADULT: Whitish shaft of outer primary is only contrast with uniformly dark plumage.

d JUVENILE: Bare parts are duller and browner than in adult. Upperparts show some brown fringes.

16 Canarian Black Oystercatcher *Haematopus meadewaldoi* Text page 227

Not recorded with certainty since 1913, and probably now extinct; known only from Lanzarote, Fuerteventura and adjacent islands in the E Canary Islands. Almost identical to 15.

a ADULT: All-dark and virtually identical to 15, but with slightly shorter tail and shorter arm.

b ADULT: Underwing on some birds provides the only clear separation from 15; note indistinct pale silvery flash at the base of the outer primaries.

13 American Oystercatcher *Haematopus palliatus*   **Text page 225**

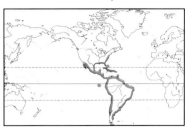

A more sedentary and less gregarious species than 12. It nests entirely on or near the coast: only vagrants are seen inland. Its yellow iris and brown (not white) back are simple identification features.

a ADULT: On all birds, the brown back and coverts contrast with the black head and neck. Never has white neck collar. Nominate race (Caribbean, Atlantic south to Uruguay) is depicted.

b ADULT: Iris yellow, with red-orange eye-ring. Bill orange, slightly yellower at tip.

c JUVENILE: As adult, but feathers of mantle, scapulars and wing-coverts spotted or finely edged buff. Bill pinkish-brown, tipped darker. Iris brownish, and legs dull grey.

d ADULT race *palliatus*: Has white flash on inner primaries in addition to band on greater coverts. Contrast between brown back and black neck is clear. All races have much less white in wing, especially on primaries, than 12. Back and rump always dark, with white restricted to a band on uppertail-coverts.

e All races show darker undersides to primaries and secondaries than 12. Race *palliatus* shows some pale on bases of inner primaries.

f ADULT race *frazari* (W Mexico): The lower breast line is usually very irregular. Intermediates with 14 sometimes occur.

g ADULT race *frazari*: Shows rather broad wings, and slight dark flecking on uppertail-coverts.

h ADULT race *pitanay* (W South America): Has intermediate-width wings and even-width white bar on greater coverts. No white on primaries.

i ADULT race *durnfordi* (Argentina): Has narrow wings, with less white on outer greater coverts.

j ADULT race *galapagensis* (Galapagos Is.): Bill heavy, legs rather short and stout. Breast often shows irregular lower border.

k Race *galapagensis*: Uppertail-coverts usually flecked darker.

l Pacific populations generally lack white in the primaries.

14 American Black Oystercatcher *Haematopus bachmani*   **Text page 226**

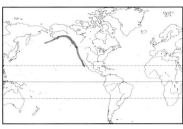

This coastal oystercatcher is virtually identical to 21, but is found only on the North American Pacific coast.

a ADULT: The yellow iris is typical of all American oystercatchers. This species has an orange-red eye-ring, black head, neck and underparts, and slightly contrasting brown mantle, scapulars and coverts. Legs pale pink. Tail fractionally longer than in 21.

b JUVENILE: Initially the iris is orange-brown, but it soon becomes yellowish. Bill dull orange with dark tip. Feathers of mantle, coverts and scapulars obscurely fringed with brown or buff.

c In flight looks all-dark, but the slight contrast between hindneck and mantle may be visible.

21 Blackish Oystercatcher *Haematopus ater*   **Text page 230**

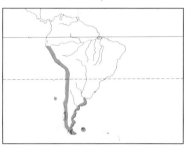

A rather heavy-billed black oystercatcher, found only on South American coasts. Very similar to 14.

a ADULT: Virtually identical in plumage and bare-part colours to 14, with brownish back and black neck and underparts. Slight differences are the fractionally shorter tail, hardly projecting beyond the wing-point, and the heavier bill, usually with a clear step on lower mandible.

b JUVENILE: Differences from adult are as for 14. Bill-tip may be yellowish. Many feathers, especially on mantle, scapulars and coverts, have narrow brown or buff fringes.

c Virtually impossible to tell from 14 in flight, except by range.

19 Magellanic Oystercatcher *Haematopus leucopodus*   **Text page 228**

This pied oystercatcher is yellow-eyed like its American relatives, but also has a yellow eye-ring. Its wing pattern and its cocked tail in display are highly distinctive.

a ADULT: Uniquely among oystercatchers, shows a yellow eye-ring in addition to yellow iris. Mantle, scapulars and coverts are as black as the neck, separating it from 13 in the area of overlap in Argentina.

b In flight, has a unique pattern for an oystercatcher, with entirely-white secondary panels and small areas of white on inner primaries and greater coverts. These contrast sharply with the black plumage.

c The underwing shows a sharp division between all-black under primaries and under primary coverts and all-white under secondaries and under secondary coverts. The leading edge of the underwing is black.

17 Variable Oystercatcher *Haematopus unicolor*   **Text page 227**

This sedentary and coastal oystercatcher has pied, black and intermediate phases. Its habits are more similar to those of black oystercatchers than to those of pied species.
a ADULT DARK PHASE: Sooty or glossy black. Red eye-ring and iris
b DARK PHASE: Virtually identical with 22, except for shorter tail which does not project beyond folded wings. Posture typically angular.
c ADULT PIED PHASE: Breast has broad and variable smudgy band at lower border. White shoulder of 20 is absent. In flight, shows wingbar like 20 but white only on uppertail-coverts.
d INTERMEDIATE PHASE: In flight, some individuals show obscured white band on uppertail-coverts and well-separated small white patches on greater coverts.

18 Chatham Islands Oystercatcher *Haematopus chathamensis*
     Text page 228

Restricted to Chatham Is. Appears to be very closely related to 17. It has a shorter bill, but heavier legs and feet. Plumage is like pied phase of 17, but the pectoral division is usually more smudgy. In flight, very like 17d.

20 Pied Oystercatcher *Haematopus longirostris*   **Text page 229**

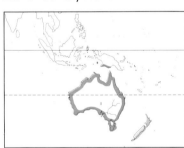

There are two, well-differentiated races.
a ADULT Australian *longirostris*: Has red eye-ring and iris, and black-and-white plumage with white shoulder-patch.
b ADULT South Island Pied Oystercatcher (SIPO) of New Zealand, race *finschi*: Superficially like Australian form, but rather smaller.
c Race *longirostris*: Short wingbar, not meeting trailing edge. White rump extends onto the lower back.
d Race *longirostris*: Flight feathers and median under primary covert dark. Wing fairly broad.
e Race *finschi*: All-white greater coverts form a longer bar than in *longirostris*. Some show white also on inner primaries. White rump extends well up the back to end in a point.
f Race *finschi*: Underwing is similar to *longirostris*, but slightly more white shows on bases of flight feathers.

22 Sooty Oystercatcher *Haematopus fuliginosus*   **Text page 230**

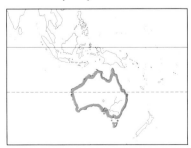

Only black oystercatcher in Australia. Entirely sooty-black, with red iris. Longer-tailed than other oystercatchers. Occurs on rocky coasts and nearby beaches and sandflats, typically singly or in small groups.
a ADULT: Faintly bulkier than Australian race of 20. No white in plumage.
b ADULT: Posture typically horizontal. Wing-tips fall short of tail-tip.

11 Crab Plover *Dromas ardeola*   Text page 222

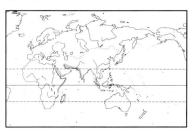

An extraordinary wader, found only on Indian Ocean coasts. Crabs form a major part of the diet.

a ADULT: One of the most distinctive waders, with startling black-and-white plumage and a disproportionately heavy black bill. Head is typically white with a dusky smudge around the eye, but, as 11b, may have variable dark streaking on the rear crown and nape. Legs long and pale greyish-blue.

b ADULT: In flight, the primaries, secondaries and their greater coverts are black, forming a dark triangle which contrasts with the white forewing. Whitish bars cross the primary bases and primary coverts. Mantle and inner scapulars black, the latter emphasising the long white 'V' of the lower back. Massive bill obvious. Feet trail behind the white tail.

c JUVENILE: Very like adult, with dark streaking on the rear crown, but the black of the mantle and inner scapulars is replaced by dark silvery-grey. White of wings, rump and tail is slightly sullied with grey.

d JUVENILE: Upperparts show much less contrast than in adult.

e All individuals show a very white underwing with dark at tips of primaries. An adult is depicted.

23 Ibisbill *Ibidorhyncha struthersii*   Text page 231

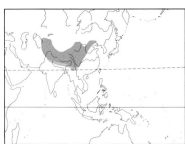

Virtually confined to stony river valleys in the mountains of southern Asia.

a ADULT BREEDING: Once seen, unmistakable. Remarkable combination of strongly-decurved bill, black face outlined by white and all blue-grey upperparts. Black-and-white breast-bands. Bill and legs bright red.

b ADULT BREEDING: Upperparts all blue-grey, but outer wing darker with clear white patch at base of inner primaries and white spots towards the tips of the outer primaries. Head pattern clear.

c ADULT NON-BREEDING: Area around base of the bill becomes whitish. Bill red-brown, legs pink-grey.

d JUVENILE: Brown face heavily mottled with white gives quite a pale appearance. Upperparts darker and browner, with slight scalloping owing to buff-orange fringes. Has brown breast-band, but the white band is lacking. Bill dark pink-grey, legs pink- or green-grey.

e ADULT NON-BREEDING: Amount of white in primaries is variable (compare 23c).

f ADULT BREEDING: Underwing mostly white, with dark tips to most flight feathers.

24 Black-winged Stilt *Himantopus himantopus*

Text page 232

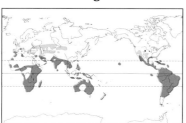

An unmistakable species with pied plumage, thin pointed bill and extremely long pinkish-red legs. Immatures are browner, but readily recognised by shape. The races fall into three groups: 'Black-necked' and nominate Black-winged Stilts are illustrated here, and 'Pied Stilts' are shown on Plate 11.

a ADULT MALE race *mexicanus*, 'Black-necked Stilt' (North America and N South America): In all races, adult male has black mantle and scapulars, uniform with wing-coverts. In this race, crown, nape an hindneck are always black. Some individuals show pink-flushed underparts.

b ADULT FEMALE race *mexicanus*: Mantle and scapulars are brownish, contrasting with black hindneck. Head pattern is similar to male's.

c ADULT: In flight, upper wing surfaces are entirely blackish, contrasting with white back and rump. Female of race *mexicanus* depicted. Long legs trail far behind tail, giving a very distinctive silhouette.

d ADULT: From below, underwings are entirely blackish except for small triangle of white on the inner coverts.

e JUVENILE race *mexicanus*: Pattern of head and hindneck is like adult's, but black is tinged brown. Both sexes show brownish mantl and scapulars. Secondaries and inner primaries are tipped white.

f ADULT FEMALE race *knudseni*, 'Hawaiian Stilt' (Hawaii only): Head pattern as in *mexicanus*, but with more black on cheeks and forehead and smaller white spot above the eye. Sexual dimorphism is less than in *mexicanus*.

g ADULT MALE race *knudseni*: Some show extensive black on sides of neck, extending slightly onto upper breast.

h ADULT MALE race *melanurus* (Peru and Brazil southwards): Like *mexicanus*, but averages larger and shows variable white crown and white or greyish collar around base of hindneck. This race intergrade with *mexicanus* in Peru.

i ADULT FEMALE race *melanurus*: Mantle and scapulars are browner than in male, but sexual dimorphism is less than in *mexicanus*.

j ADULT FEMALE race *melanurus*: Head pattern is like male's, but mantle and scapulars are browner.

k ADULT MALE of nominate race (Eurasia, India, Africa): Crown and hindneck patterns vary from pure white to dusky-grey, but black patterning of other races is absent.

l ADULT FEMALE of nominate race: Across the whole range, crown and hindneck patterns show same extent of variation as in male. Mantle and scapulars are brownish.

m JUVENILE of nominate race: In fresh plumage, dull buffish feather edgings may give a scaly appearance to the upperparts. Crown and hindneck are always dusky.

n IMMATURE of nominate race: First-year non-breeding individuals are typically muddy-brown above, with greyish crown and hindneck Some show a small patch of pale red at base of bill.

o In flight, nominate race shows relatively narrower wings than othe races. Adult male is depicted.

p Underwing pattern is similar in all races.

24 Black-winged Stilt *Himantopus himantopus*　　　See Plate 10

q ADULT MALE race *leucocephalus*, 'Pied Stilt' (Australia, New Guinea, New Zealand): White upper mantle. Black of nape and hindneck often stands out as a raised ridge of feathers. Black collar may be almost complete. An example from Australia is depicted.

r ADULT MALE race *leucocephalus*: Like nominate race in flight, but neck pattern differs and wings are a little broader.

s JUVENILE race *leucocephalus*: Upperparts are brownish, initially with paler fringes, and wings show a narrow whitish trailing edge. Very similar to juvenile of nominate race.

t ADULT MALE race *leucocephalus* (an example from W Australia): There is some (as yet undefined) regional variation within Australia.

u ADULT FEMALE race *leucocephalus*: A little browner than male, but sexes are very similar.

v ADULT: In flight, some W Australian individuals are shorter-winged.

w ADULT MALE race *leucocephalus* (an example from New Zealand): The New Zealand population averages shorter in the leg, and longer in the wing and bill measurements. Black on neck is usually more extensive. Interbreeds commonly with 25.

25 Black Stilt *Himantopus novaezelandiae*　　　Text page 234

Extremely long pink legs and straight thin bill are like 24, legs are slightly shorter and bill slightly longer. All but young juveniles show black on the underparts. See text for drawings of hybrids with 24.

a ADULT: Most are entirely blackish, apart from bright pink legs. Upperparts are mostly glossy black, head and underparts sooty-black. Some show white flecking on underparts.

b ADULT: Shape in flight is clearly stilt-like, but legs trail less than in 24.

c JUVENILE: Apart from shape, very like juvenile of Pied Stilt (24), but upperparts lack pale fringes. White underparts and forehead. Hindneck greyish. Bill dull grey-pink. Usually accompanied by parents at this age.

d IMMATURE: Typically shows whitish breast and large black smudges on belly and flanks. Hindneck greyish.

26 Banded Stilt *Cladorhynchus leucocephalus*　　　Text page 235

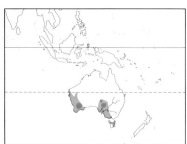

Long orange-pink legs and a straight or slightly-upcurved bill. Head and neck are always entirely white.

a ADULT BREEDING: Mostly white, with black wings and chestnut breast-band which extends backwards and becomes blackish-brown on belly. Looks pied at a distance.

b ADULT NON-BREEDING: Breast-band and belly-patch are partially obscured by white- and brown-tipped feathers.

c JUVENILE: Underparts are entirely white. White mantle is simple distinction from Pied Stilt (24).

d ADULT: In flight, white mantle and completely-white secondaries, forming a white trailing edge to the inner wing, contrast strongly with black wing-coverts and primaries. Wingbeats are flickering.

e JUVENILE: As adult in flight, but breast-band is lacking and plumage is generally duller. White trailing edge extends farther onto inner primaries.

28 **American Avocet** *Recurvirostra americana* **Text page 236**

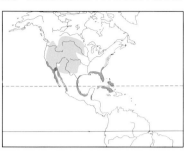

The only avocet with seasonal plumage changes. Very long legs.
a ADULT MALE BREEDING: Orange-brown neck, shading into white on back and breast, with paler face. Narrow white bar on outer scapulars and inner coverts. Male typically has longer, straighter bill.
b JUVENILE FEMALE: In females, bill tends to be shorter and more upcurved. In juvenile, crown is pale brown, washed pinkish-buff, and hindneck orange-brown.
c ADULT NON-BREEDING: Head and neck very pale grey, almost white at distance. Some individuals are difficult to sex.
d ADULT BREEDING: In flight, upperwing appears dark: all have dark primary coverts, unlike 27 and 29, and broad dark wing-tips and covert bar.
e ADULT NON-BREEDING: Underwing much whiter than upperwing, with dark primaries.
f JUVENILE: Wing pattern differs from adult in white tips to inner 5 primaries.

27 **Pied Avocet** *Recurvirostra avosetta* **Text page 235**

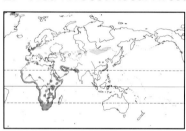

All avocets have a clearly-upcurved bill, but this is the only blackish-capped species. Particularly in tropical regions, crown may fade to whitish, leaving a dark mask and hindneck.
a ADULT: Black cap and hindneck; very extensive white patches on the coverts and secondaries of the closed wing. Long blue-grey legs.
b JUVENILE: All black is tinged brown, and white of mantle and on wings is mottled with pale brown and buff. Crown is particularly liable to fade.
c ADULT: Tip of wing black, but inner primaries and primary coverts white. Fairly small but well-defined black bars on coverts and scapulars. Stiff-winged flight gives flickering appearance.
d Underwing is very white, except for black outer primaries.

29 **Red-necked Avocet** *Recurvirostra novaehollandiae* **Text page 237**

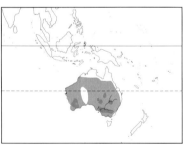

Unlike 28, coloured head and neck of adult is present at all seasons.
a ADULT: Dark chestnut head and neck, much darker than breeding 28 and sharply divided from the white lower neck and breast. Some pale colour around base of bill. Broad white scapular patch and blackish-brown coverts. Juvenile has paler, browner head and neck, and brownish fringes on upperparts and coverts.
b ADULT: Strongly dark-and-white plumage. Alula and inner primaries white, unlike 28. More blackish on coverts and tertials than 27 or 28. Blue-grey legs are very long, and toes trail well behind tail.
c Underwing white, with strongly contrasting head and outer primaries.

30 **Andean Avocet** *Recurvirostra andina* **Text page 237**

Found at high altitudes in the Andes, and exceptionally on the Peruvian coast.
a ADULT: A bulky avocet with relatively short legs and strongly-upcurved bill. The completely-white head and neck contrast very strongly with the dark brown upperparts. Unusual orange iris.
b ADULT: In flight, the dark brown, very broad wings and dark brown mantle and tail contrast with the white neck, head, back and rump. Feet project a little behind tail.
c Underwing shows silvery-black flight feathers, contrasting with the rest of the underparts which are white.

28d

28c

27c

27b

28b

28e

28a

28f

27a

27d

30c

30b

29a

29b

30a

29c

31 Stone-curlew *Burhinus oedicnemus*   **Text page 238**

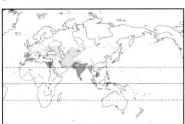

The big, staring yellow eye, the long, thick, yellow legs, and the fairly hunched posture are features in common with all *Burhinus*. Black lower border to white lesser-covert bar is diagnostic of this species. The relatively small bill typically has an all-yellow base and black tip.

a ADULT: Neat white lesser-covert bar, prominently bordered above by dark brown and below by black. Tips of greater coverts pale grey Race *oedicnemus* (Europe and east to the Caspian) is rather dark brownish, streaked darker; southern birds *saharae* (Mediterranean and N Africa) are more sandy, and *harterti* (south and east of the Caspian) greyer. Male is depicted (see Appendix).

b ADULT race *indicus* (Pakistan to Sri Lanka and Burma): Smallest race showing slightly more dark on the base of the culmen ridge.

c JUVENILE: Distinguished from adult with difficulty by rufous-buff fringes to tertials, rear scapulars and inner coverts. The white lesser-covert bar is slightly obscured, and bordered only obscurely below by blackish-brown. Tips to the greater coverts are slightly whiter. Tail-down, when present, is diagnostic.

d ADULT: White flashes on outer primaries and on base and tips of inner primaries are usually prominent. Toes do not project beyond long tail. Race *oedicnemus* has relatively dark covert panel.

e ADULT race *indicus*: Paler covert panel. Dark culmen ridge.

f Some individuals, mainly juveniles, lack white on bases of inner primaries.

g Underwing mostly white; breast streaked dark.

h In flight, larger than 32 and with relatively longer primaries.

32 Senegal Thick-knee *Burhinus senegalensis*   **Text page 239**

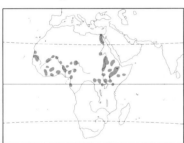

Diagnostically, large pale grey wing-panel lacks a white band above. Compared with 31, has a larger bill with a smaller amount of yellow on the base; the black of the tip extends along the culmen ridge to the bill-base. Found mainly in riverine habitat.

a The pale grey covert bar is distinct, sometimes appearing paler towards the top edge. Legs long, yellow but slightly tinged brown. Adults and juveniles are virtually identical, except for retained tail-down on some juveniles.

b In flight, has a similar white pattern in the primaries to 31, but the white may be more prominent. Pale grey covert panel is prominent. Has a relatively short tail, long arm and more rounded wing-tip.

c Underwing looks very similar to 31, although the white outer primary flash may be more prominent.

d In flight, looks smaller and more compact than 31.

31c

31e

31f

31b

31a

31g

31d

32b

32a

32c

31h

32d

33 Water Dikkop *Burhinus vermiculatus*   Text page 239

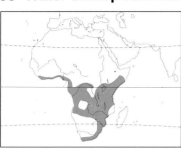

A typical *Burhinus*, but rather dark. Has a broad greyish covert pane as 32, but with a white line above; this line lacks the black lower border of 31. Uniquely, the upperparts have fine vermiculations, visible at close range. The heavy bill has only small green-yellow patches on the base. Found in close association with water.

a ADULT: Race *vermiculatus* (E and S Africa) is depicted.
b Race *büttikoferi* (W Africa): Darker brown above and less grey.
c JUVENILE: Unless tail-down is present, appears indistinguishable from adult.
d In flight, feet project beyond the tail. Clear white patches on primaries, and a fairly pale covert panel. Wings are rather broad and rounded.
e Underwing-coverts mostly white, with a dark bar at covert tips.

34 Spotted Dikkop *Burhinus capensis*   Text page 240

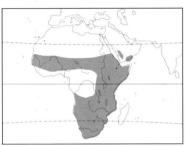

Uniquely, is boldly spotted, barred and streaked, and lacks any sign of a pale covert panel. Very long yellowish legs.

a ADULT: Scapulars and coverts are clearly and boldly marked with big dark subterminal spots, contrasting with pale fringes. The ground colour varies locally from pale sandy to rich brown. Tail and tertials are barred. Note lack of contrast between scapulars and coverts.
b JUVENILE: Larger lesser, median and greater coverts show a mixture of feathers with dark central bars, pale edges and indistinct submarginal washes. This gives a more streaked appearance, contrasting more with barred tertials and tail.
c In flight, looks long-winged and long-tailed with plain coverts and small white primary flashes. Inner white spot is variable, sometime virtually absent.
d Underwing variable, but usually shows a strong dark bar at the cover tips.

40 Egyptian Plover *Pluvianus aegyptius*   Text page 244

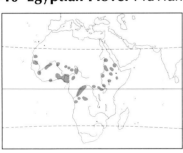

Colours and patterns of this chunky, riverine wader are quite unlik those of any other species.

a ADULT: Deep blue-grey coverts, scapulars and tertials contrast with the black crown, mask, hindneck, mantle, back and breast-band. Supercilium, chin and throat are brilliantly white, while the belly is deep peachy-buff. Short legs are blue-grey. Feeds with plover-like pecks, scratches sand, and chases insects.
b JUVENILE: Rather duller than adult, with rusty feathers mixed in brown-black of head. Leading lesser and median coverts rusty.
c In flight, an amazing expanse of flashing white on the coverts and flight feathers contrasts with a black diagonal bar and grey lesser an median coverts. Tail is white-tipped. Wings rather broad-based.
d Underwing brilliantly white, with long black bar crossing flight feathers. Belly contrastingly orangey.

35 Double-striped Thick-knee *Burhinus bistriatus*   Text page 241

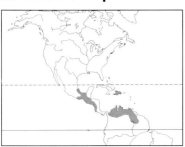

Long, broad, white supercilium, bordered above by a sharp black line, gives this stone-curlew a striking appearance. It is very like 36, but has darker upperparts, neck and upper breast, with sharper division between dark breast and white belly. Ranges are widely separated.

a ADULT nominate race (Central America): In adults of all races, upperparts have broad, darkish brown feather centres and fairly narrow tawny-buff fringes. Note strongly-streaked appearance. This race is relatively large, and dark above, with breast tinged greyish. Race *pediacus* (N Colombia) is paler above, with cinnamon-buff feather edges.

b ADULT race *vocifer* (Venezuela to Brazil): As dark as nominate, but breast is browner.

c JUVENILE: Very like adult, but paler. Upperpart feathers have narrower dark centres and broader, brighter buff edges. Head, neck and breast are strongly tinged buff.

d In flight, note long legs and relatively long wings and tail. Large white flash at base of inner primaries and a smaller (but variable) one subterminally on outer primaries.

e White of belly continues onto underwing-coverts and axillaries, contrasting with darker breast and neck.

36 Peruvian Thick-knee *Burhinus superciliaris*   Text page 241

Shares striking superciliary pattern and greenish-yellow legs with 35, but is clearly smaller and paler. Upperparts are finely streaked, looking uniform at a distance. Pale brown of neck and breast merges into white of belly.

a ADULT: Upperparts pale grey-brown, with slightly darker lower scapulars and lesser coverts. Larger wing-coverts pale grey, sometimes slightly mottled.

b JUVENILE: Very like adult. Upperpart feathers are slightly darker brown, with warmer buff fringes. Grey coverts have irregular dark submarginal lines and buff fringes. Typically, nape is pale and white supercilia appear to meet.

c In flight, relatively pale coverts and upperparts contrast with dark lesser coverts and blackish flight feathers.

d Pale underwing contrasts less with the breast than in 35.

36c

35d

35e

36d

36b

35c

35b

35a

36a

37 **Bush Thick-knee** *Burhinus magnirostris* Text page 242

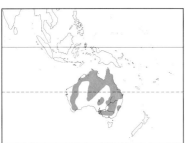

A large stone-curlew, similar in structure to 35 and 36, but longer-legged than other species. Unlike 39, strongly streaked, and not restricted to coastal regions.

a ADULT: Forehead off-white. Crown and nape grey, finely streaked dark. Upperparts mostly grey-brown, but pale grey coverts form a striking panel on closed wing. Fairly prominent supercilium, bordered below by sooty-brown. Breast and upper belly tinged buff and strongly streaked brown. Posture may be upright, or furtive and horizontal. Juvenile is very similar, but is paler than adult owing to broader, relatively distinct buff fringes.

b In flight, wing-action is noticeably stiff. Feet trail behind tail. Pale covert panel contrasts with darker upperparts and blackish primaries. Distinct white flashes in primaries. Ash-grey is continuous from crown to tail-tip. Underwing is largely white.

38 **Great Thick-knee** *Esacus recurvirostris* Text page 243

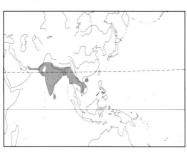

A very large, unstreaked, greyish stone-curlew with a massive uptilted bill. Found near water, both coastally and inland on rivers and lakes.

a ADULT: Striking black-and-white head pattern is like 39, but lores and forehead are mostly white. Plain brownish-grey above. Contrasting blackish lesser-covert bar is bordered narrowly by white below. Rest of coverts are pale grey. Juvenile is very like adult, except that upperpart feathers have buff fringes. Looks slightly paler than adult at a distance.

b In flight, the rounded wings and flashing white, pale grey and black are almost bustard-like. Note broad black subterminal band on inner primaries.

c Underwing is white, apart from dark bands near tips of primary coverts, primaries and secondaries.

39 **Beach Thick-knee** *Esacus magnirostris* Text page 243

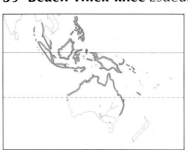

A massive stone-curlew with a heavy, straight bill and stout, relatively short, pale greenish or brownish legs. Very striking white supercilium is surrounded by black. Lores are mainly black, and forehead shows black band. Strictly coastal.

a ADULT: Most of upperparts are an unstreaked brownish-grey. Dark lesser-covert bar, bordered below by a sharp but narrow white line. Rest of coverts evenly pale grey. Distinct yellow patches on base of the black bill. Iris clear yellow. Bill shape and head pattern are ready distinctions from 38. Juvenile is very like adult, but paler owing to buff-fringed upperparts and coverts. Covert pattern less distinct. Iris and base of bill dull yellow.

b In flight, rounded wings show extensive white and very pale grey; this contrasts with blackish outer primaries and dusky bar at tips of secondaries. Toes project only slightly beyond tail.

c Underwing-coverts mostly white. Inner primaries form a bright, translucent triangle. Underwing contrasts slightly with breast and upper belly.

d JUVENILE: Very similar to adult, but coverts are initially darker.

37a

37b

39b

38b

38c

d

39c

39a

38a

PLATE 17: African coursers

48 Temminck's Courser *Cursorius temminckii*   Text page 252

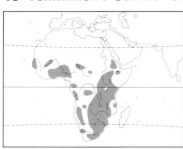

Marginally the smallest of the coursers. Often seen on grassland. Compare with Burchell's (46) and with Indian (47).
- a ADULT: Plain upperparts. Rufous belly. Nape and crown both rufous. Pale lores distinguish it from 47.
- b ADULT: In flight, note strong contrast between brown coverts and black flight feathers. Black or mainly-black secondaries distinguish from all races of 46. Lacks 47's white band on uppertail.
- c Underwing shows dark coverts and black undersides to primaries and secondaries. White rear belly and undertail contrast strongly.
- d Some show narrow white trailing edge to secondaries. Tail shows white fringe and dark subterminal bar.

41 Two-banded Courser *Rhinoptilus africanus*   Text page 245

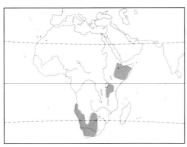

A small, short-billed courser of arid, mainly open plains. Colouring varies widely between regions according to soil colour. Always has strongly scaly upperparts and two black breast-bands.
- a ADULT: Foreneck finely streaked. Upperparts show broad pale fringes and dark subterminal lines.
- b In flight, shows very striking chestnut trailing edge to the wing, blackish wing-tips and tail, and narrow white patch on uppertail.
- c Pale example of nominate race (SW Africa).
- d Dark example of *granti* (E Cape Province, Transvaal), to show full range of variation.

42 Heuglin's Courser *Rhinoptilus cinctus*   Text page 246

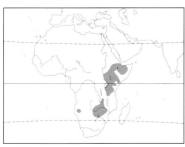

A large courser of grassy scrub and light woodland. Owing to nocturnal habits, rarely seen. Compare with Jerdon's (44).
- a ADULT: Three breast-bands: middle one broad and streaky brown, others narrow and chestnut. Upperparts scaly.
- b ADULT: Note minor variations in head pattern.
- c In flight, upperwing shows little contrast. White band across uppertail. White-fringed tail.
- d Underwing is mostly pale, except for blackish wing-tip and dark markings on primary coverts.

43 Violet-tipped Courser *Rhinoptilus chalcopterus*   Text page 247

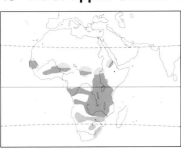

Largest courser. Often occurs in thick bush and light woodland. Mainly nocturnal. Migrations not yet understood.
- a ADULT: Plain above. Head shows dark mask, mainly-dusky throat and pale patch behind the eye. Bare parts reddish.
- b In flight, brown coverts contrast strongly with black flight feathers. Unique iridescent primary tips are not a field character. White band across uppertail. Tail white-fringed.
- c JUVENILE: May show broader pale tips to greater coverts, suggesting a lapwing (see Plates 26 and 27). Pale tail-tip is lacking.
- d JUVENILE: Very like adult. Pale tips to greater coverts.
- e Underwing shows broad black tip and trailing edge, contrasting with white bases of flight feathers.

PLATE 18: Cream-coloured/Burchell's complex, and Indian coursers

45 Cream-coloured Courser *Cursorius cursor*

Text page 248

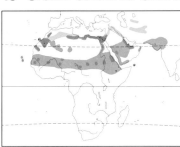

A pale courser of sub-desert habitats, sandy-cream in all plumages. Grey rear crown is shared with 46.
a ADULT: Very clearly-marked head pattern, with supercilia meeting on the nape. Underpart colour slowly pales from cream to whitish on vent. Upperparts an even sandy-cream.
b JUVENILE: Head pattern less distinct, especially supercilia. Upperparts finely scalloped with narrow, dark subterminal lines.
c Upperwing shows a strong contrast between sandy coverts and secondaries and black primaries. Narrow white trailing edge to secondaries. Feet extend a little past tail.
d Underwing-coverts and axillaries entirely jet-black, contrasting abruptly with secondary tips and pale sandy body.

46 Burchell's Courser *Cursorius rufus*

Text page 249

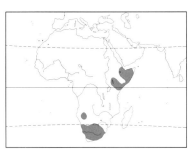

Found mainly in semi-arid or dry grassland habitats. A close relative of 45: E African races have previously been treated as part of that species.
a ADULT race *rufus* (S Africa): Like 45, has long white supercilia and grey rear crown. Upperparts darker and browner. Breast grey-brown. Mid-belly shows black line, sharply contrasting with white rear belly and vent.
b Race *rufus*: Upperwing much darker than on 45, with broader white tips to the secondaries.
c Race *rufus*: Underwing-coverts grey-brown, contrasting with all-white secondaries and rear belly.
d ADULT race *littoralis* (Kenya): Paler brown than 45, with clearer division of fore-belly from white rear belly. Much smaller than 45.
e Race *littoralis*: Upperwing like 45, but less contrasting.
f Race *littoralis*: Underwing-coverts pale brown-grey; broad but slightly-obscured white trailing edge to secondaries.

47 Indian Courser *Cursorius coromandelicus*

Text page 251

The only courser over most of its range, and the only *Cursorius* species with a white uppertail. Diagnostic black lores, white supercilium starting at eye, and all-chestnut crown.
a ADULT: Supercilium all-white, eye-stripe from bill to hindneck all-black. Upperparts an even darkish grey-brown. Breast rich cinnamon-brown, darkening towards mid-belly to a black central patch; rear belly and vent white.
b ADULT: White uppertail-coverts contrast with upperparts; narrow white trailing edge to secondaries. Primaries all-black.
c Underwing-coverts dark grey-brown. Black flight feathers and dark coverts contrast with white secondary tips and white rear belly.

44 Jerdon's Courser *Rhinoptilus bitorquatus*

Text page 248

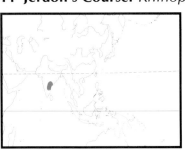

Probably now extinct. This very distinctive, large courser was found in rocky, hilly country with light scrub and tree cover.
a ADULT (juvenile not known): Has a head and breast pattern markedly different from 45 and 47, the only other coursers of India. Short, broad supercilium, broad darkish mask. Chestnut throat-patch surrounded by white. Breast has two darkish brown lines separated by a prominent white band. Compare with 42.
b In flight, the prominent white flashes on the tips of the outer primaries are diagnostic. Also has white uppertail-coverts and a whitish bar on outer greater coverts.
c Creamy-white underwing, with black flight feathers and white terminal flash, is reminiscent of Stone-curlew (31).

50 Common Pratincole *Glareola pratincola*

Text page 254

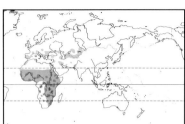

Like all *Glareola*, a graceful, tern-like, mainly aerial feeder. White rump and long forked tail. Very like 51 and 52, but has white edge to secondaries.

a ADULT BREEDING: As 52, but black on lores less extensive and red area on bill large, reaching to nostril. Sharp black outline to creamy throat.

b ADULT BREEDING: Distinguished from 51 and 52 by mid-brown wing-coverts and mantle, showing contrast with blackish primaries and by clear but narrow white trailing edge to secondaries. Tail fork deeper, and black terminal bar more extensive.

c ADULT BREEDING: Underwing-coverts and axillaries deep chestnut-red, but may appear darker; white edge of wing clear. As in 51 and 52, whitish belly is conspicuous overhead.

d ADULT NON-BREEDING: Creamy throat is edged by a band of fine streaks. Breast becomes a more mottled grey-brown. Wing and tail roughly equal in length on adults. Upperparts paler brown than 52.

e JUVENILE: Coverts and scapulars clearly fringed pale buff and with dark subterminal bands. Paler than 52. Throat pale, lacking a dark border. Wings longer than tail.

f JUVENILE: Shows pale-looking coverts, white trailing edge and shallower tail fork than adult. White-tipped secondaries and relatively long tail distinguish from 51 and 52.

g ADULT BREEDING (Africa): As nominate race, although underwing is generally duller and browner. White edge of wing may abrade rapidly and become difficult to see.

52 Black-winged Pratincole *Glareola nordmanni*

Text page 255

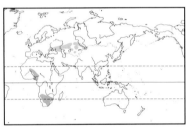

Very like 50, with which it overlaps in range, but more like 51 in many plumage features.

a ADULT BREEDING: Head dark, with broad black on lores; red patch on base of bill small, not reaching the nostril.

b ADULT BREEDING: Slightly broader-winged than 50. Coverts are evenly dark brown, showing little contrast with flight feathers. Secondaries blackish with no sign of white tips. Tail fork is shallower than 50, with a narrower black terminal band.

c ADULT BREEDING: Underwing-coverts and axillaries entirely black so no contrast on underwing.

d ADULT NON-BREEDING: Creamy throat is edged by a band of fine streaks. Breast becomes a more mottled grey-brown. On all adults, as on juveniles, the wings extend well past the tip of the tail. Upperparts slightly darker than in 50.

e JUVENILE: Feather patterns are very similar to juvenile 50, but mostly fractionally darker. Wings extend well past tail-tip, only slightly more than in 50.

f JUVENILE: In flight, looks dark with shallow tail fork. Inconspicuous buffish tips to the secondaries are rarely visible in the field. Black underwing distinguishes from 50 and 51.

g JUVENILE: Underwing is mostly black, but some larger underwing-coverts are often narrowly and indistinctly tipped chestnut.

53 Madagascar Pratincole *Glareola ocularis*   Text page 256

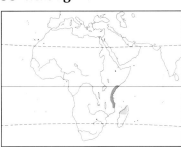

This fairly large, dark pratincole breeds only on Madagascar, but from Apr to Sept it occurs in flocks on the E African coast.

a ADULT: A dark brown pratincole, with folded wings always extending far beyond the tail. The lower breast and fore-belly are chestnut, the rear belly white. Dark cap and white patches around eye are conspicuous. Typically looks bulky and short-legged. Bill rather heavy and mostly dark.

b ADULT: Dark wings look very long, and contrast with white uppertail. Shallowly-forked dark tail. White around eye obvious.

c Spread tail shows square end, broad black tip and white on outer feathers.

d ADULT: Underwing-coverts and axillaries chestnut, often quite pale, colour merges into chestnut on belly. White rear belly and undertail are continuous with white patch on uppertail-coverts.

e From below, chestnut on underwing and belly may not be distinct, but note short tail and white confined to rear of belly.

54 Rock Pratincole *Glareola nuchalis*   Text page 257

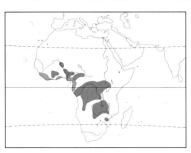

A small, dark pratincole, typical of rocky riverine habitat.

a ADULT race *nuchalis* (Gabon eastwards): Mainly dark grey, with small clear white line behind the eye merging into a white hindneck collar. Bright red legs are clear distinction from 53.

b ADULT race *nuchalis*: Small and dark, with contrasting white uppertail and hindneck collar. Closed tail has shallow fork.

c Underside shows white tail-base, under-greater-covert patch and rear belly.

d ADULT race *liberiae* (W Africa): As *nuchalis*, but hindneck collar and rear of eye-stripe chestnut, with white in eye-stripe restricted to area behind the eye.

e Race *liberiae*: As *nuchalis*, but head looks mostly dark at a distance.

f JUVENILE: Both races are dark grey-brown, with many small buff spots; no eye-stripe or hindneck collar. Legs orange-red.

55 Grey Pratincole *Glareola cinerea*   Text page 257

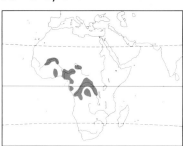

A small, distinctively pale, W African pratincole, found mainly along rivers with large sandbanks.

a ADULT: Small size, pale dove-grey upperparts and all-pale underparts prevent confusion with other pratincoles in Africa. Also note neat, curving black eye-stripe and white supercilium, broad pale chestnut collar, and pale chestnut breast. Legs bright orange-red. Juvenile is similar to adult, but lacks black eye-stripe and white supercilium. Upperparts are slightly more sandy-grey, the coverts have wide buff fringes, and the breast is washed pale cinnamon.

b ADULT: In flight, the small size combined with brilliant white wing-panels on secondaries and primaries, and white on the uppertail and base of tail, give a highly distinctive appearance.

c Underwing is white, the inner wing particularly brilliant; clear white patch under outer primaries.

49 Australian Pratincole *Stiltia isabella*   Text page 253

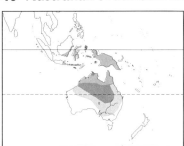

Distinctive, with very long wings, short tail, and long, dark legs. Sandy-rufous head and upperparts of adult become browner when worn.

a ADULT BREEDING: Head and upperparts bright sandy-rufous, lores blackish and chin white. Dark chestnut patches on lower breast and belly appear almost black at a distance. Bill is sharply defined black and red. Outer primaries very long.

b ADULT NON-BREEDING: Slightly duller, and lacks dark lores. Dark chestnut patches reduced in size and almost separated.

c ADULT BREEDING: Exceptionally long-winged in flight. Legs project well beyond squarish tail, and sometimes dangle. Black outer primaries contrast strongly.

d Underwings show black coverts and axillaries, contrasting with silvery secondaries and inner primaries and with white rear belly.

e JUVENILE: Upperparts browner, with sandy fringes. Inner primaries finely tipped buff, and outer primary shorter than on adult.

51 Oriental Pratincole *Glareola maldivarum*   Text page 255

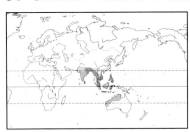

The eastern relative of 50 and 52 (Plate 19). Always has shorter tail than those species. Upperwing is like 52, but chestnut wing-linings are like 50.

a ADULT: Upperparts and upper breast an even darkish brown. Creamy throat outlined neatly in black. Bill mostly black, with a very little red on lower mandible. Tail always falls roughly half-way between tertial tips and primary tips. Tends to show more orange-buff on the lower breast than 50.

b ADULT: Dark brown wing-coverts show little contrast with flight feathers. Shallowly-forked tail (see also Plate 19). No trace of white on trailing edge of wing. Outer primary shaft dusky from above.

c ADULT NON-BREEDING: Throat well streaked. Rest of underparts duller.

d ADULT NON-BREEDING: Chestnut underwing-coverts and axillaries, as 50, but secondaries all-dark.

e JUVENILE: Upperparts have buff fringes and dark subterminal lines. All flight feathers are narrowly tipped buff.

f JUVENILE: Obscure pale tips to secondaries, some of which may be retained for up to a year.

56 Little Pratincole *Glareola lactea*   Text page 258

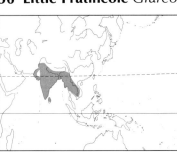

A tiny, pale, swallow-like pratincole, which shows a white wing-panel. Often found on rivers.

a ADULT BREEDING: Dark brown crown becomes pale grey-brown on hindneck. Lores black; throat pale pink-buff, breast buffish-grey and belly white. Tail falls well short of wing-tips. Very short, dark legs. Non-breeding adult lacks black lores and has streaking on throat. In juvenile, chin is whiter compared with non-breeding adults, with sharper division from throat. Close views show that primaries have buff fringes and upperparts buff fringes and spots.

b ADULT BREEDING: Black outer wing contrasts with large white wing-panel on bases of secondaries and on larger coverts. White uppertail-coverts and sides of tail. Some show a bold white flash in middle primaries. Shallow-forked tail looks square when spread.

c Underwing at all stages shows black underwing-coverts, axillaries, tips of secondaries and outer primaries, and a brilliant white wing-panel.

57 Northern Lapwing *Vanellus vanellus*

Text page 259

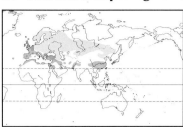

A highly distinctive, crested wader, found mainly on grasslands and farmland, often in huge flocks. The most migratory lapwing.

a ADULT MALE BREEDING: Upperparts very dark green with metall gloss. Head pattern clearly black-and-white, typically with all-blac chin and throat merging into breast-band. Long crest.

b ADULT FEMALE BREEDING: Head less clearly marked than male's always with white flecking on throat. Crest averages shorter.

c ADULT NON-BREEDING: Head blackish and buff, with clear whit chin and throat. Buff fringes to scapulars and coverts are often extensive, but lesser coverts are dark.

d JUVENILE: Dull head as c, but with short crest. Neat buff fringes t upperpart feathers.

e ADULT MALE: In flight, deep jerky wingbeats are characteristic. Distinct dark upperwing with whitish at wing-tips. Adult male show very broad bulging primaries.

f ADULT FEMALE: Outer wing rather slimmer than e, and wing-tip more pointed. Flight feathers and under primary coverts are black

g JUVENILE: Outer wing much slimmer than on adult.

71 Sociable Plover *Vanellus gregarius*

Text page 269

A migratory lapwing which nests semi-colonially. Seen mostly on grasslands or farmland.

a ADULT BREEDING: The brilliant white supercilia which run from th forehead to meet on the nape are striking and, like the chestnut-and-black belly, are reminiscent of the much smaller Eurasian Dotterel (120). The black of crown and belly is most intense in males. Legs and bill black.

b ADULT NON-BREEDING: Clear supercilium, but crown and lore are paler. Black and chestnut are entirely lost from belly.

c JUVENILE: Supercilia as a, but infused buff. The grey-brown upperparts are neatly scaled with dark subterminal lines and buff fringes. Underparts whitish, but breast has dull wash and is heavil streaked brown.

d In flight, in all plumages, shows completely-white secondaries, contrasting with black wing-tips and brown coverts. Tail is mainly white, with black subterminal bar. Juvenile is depicted.

e ADULT NON-BREEDING: Belly is white, breast a mottled greyish-brown. At all stages shows brilliant white underwing with black wing-tips.

f ADULT BREEDING: The underwing is even more striking against dark belly.

72 White-tailed Plover *Vanellus leucurus*

Text page 270

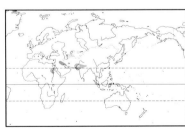

A long-legged, slender-billed lapwing, often seen wading in edges inland wetlands.

a ADULT: Fairly pale brownish-grey, with pale face, large eye, and relatively small body on very long yellow legs. Lilac sheen on upperparts and rosy-buff infusion on lower breast. A white panel shows to variable degree on the closed wing.

b ADULT: Often adopts slim, erect posture.

c JUVENILE: Upperparts have dark-centred feathers with bright buff fringes, giving a blotched appearance. Neck and breast paler than adult, a mottled brown-grey. Tail-tip faintly brownish.

d In flight, the prominent all-white tail is diagnostic. White wing-pan extends to the forewing. Very long legs trail well past tail.

e ADULT: Underside like 71, but outer secondaries are black-tippe and breast is always noticeably darker than belly. Feet project muc farther beyond tail.

57e

57a

57b

57c

57d

57f

57g

71a

71d

71c

71e

71f

72e

71b

72a

72b

72c

72d

76 Grey-headed Lapwing *Vanellus cinereus*   Text page 273

A fairly dark, heavy lapwing, typical of freshwater wetlands. Bill yellow, with sharply-defined black tip. Iris red. Tiny yellow wattles at base of bill. Long yellow legs.

a ADULT BREEDING: Whole of head and neck grey, sometimes quite pale on the face. Grey on lower breast darkens to a neat black breast-band.

b ADULT NON-BREEDING: Head and neck mostly brown, tinged grey; chin and throat white. Black breast-band partly obscured. Wing-coverts show more extensive pale tips.

c JUVENILE: Head and breast entirely brownish. Breast-band absent or smudged brown. Brown of upperparts is neatly fringed buff.

d In flight, jet-black wing-tips contrast with bright white secondaries and outer coverts. Uppertail white; tail white with subterminal black band. Toes project partly beyond tail-tip.

e Underwing totally white, except for black primaries. Strong contrast with sharply-bordered dark breast.

60 Spur-winged Plover *Vanellus spinosus*   Text page 261

Very distinctive pied head and underparts and brown upperparts. Dark red eye. Blackish legs and bill. Found mostly near inland wetlands.

a ADULT: Black pattern is well defined and lacks any pale markings. Upperparts uniform brown. Black spur on carpal joint, slightly longer in the male.

b In flight, strongly black, white and brown. Tail mostly black. Uppertail and lower rump white. Black primaries and tips of secondaries contrast with long, but relatively narrow, diagonal white wing-panel. Toes project beyond tail-tip.

c White underwing-coverts, axillaries, rear belly, vent and undertail contrast very strongly with black flight feathers, breast, upper belly and tail.

d JUVENILE: Black is tinged brown and, especially on the chin and forehead, speckled with white. Coverts and scapulars show broad (but not conspicuous) buff fringes. Spur is relatively short and blunt.

61 River Lapwing *Vanellus duvaucelii*   Text page 262

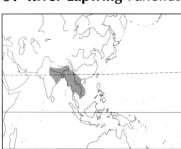

Distinctive patterning separates easily from 60, its close relative. Note grey on cheeks, mid-grey breast-band, and black central patch on white belly. Rarely seen away from rivers.

a ADULT: Black crown and nape can be raised as a helmet-like crest during display. A narrow white line surrounds the black on the head and neck. Upperparts relatively pale sandy-brown. Black-and-white wing pattern often shows on the closed wing. Long, curved, black carpal spurs. In juvenile, black is partly obscured by white tips, sandy-brown upperpart feathers have slightly darker subterminal marks and buff fringes, and spur is relatively short and blunt.

b In flight, shows broad diagonal white wing-panel which separates black of primaries and tips of secondaries from sandy-brown of upperparts. Isolated black crescent near carpal joint is main distinction from 60; note also more extensive white on inner secondaries. Broad black terminal tail-band. White uppertail and lower rump. Head appears black and grey, with white hardly detectable.

c Underwing-coverts and axillaries white, meeting white of belly, but contrasting with black belly-patch and flight feathers.

76e

76d

76a

76b

76c

60a

60d

61a

60b

60c

61c

61b

58 Long-toed Lapwing *Vanellus crassirostris*

Text page 260

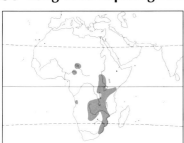

An unusual lapwing associated with freshwater marshes. Its relativel long toes help it to walk on floating vegetation. White face and foreneck contrast with black nape, hindneck, sides of neck, and breast. Bill longish and fairly heavy. Legs reddish.

a ADULT: Mantle and scapulars are an even light grey-brown. Wing-coverts white, showing clearly on closed wing. Black areas glossed with bluish.

b Nominate race *crassirostris* (northern): In flight, shows contrast of mostly-white wing-coverts and glossy black flight feathers. Uppertail-coverts mostly black, but with a narrow white band bordering black tail. Legs often dangle.

c Race *leucoptera* (S Tanzania and Malawi southwards): Wings are entirely white, except for black outer primaries. Intermediates occu in which flight feathers are silvery-grey or dappled black and white.

d JUVENILE: Differs as follows: grey-brown of upperparts slightly mottled buff; white wing-coverts mottled brown and buff; black feathers tinged brown and tipped buff with no bluish gloss.

59 Blacksmith Plover *Vanellus armatus*

Text page 260

Usually found near water. Remarkable and distinctive plumage pattern. Long blackish legs. Black bill. Iris deep red.

a ADULT: No brown in plumage. Black, grey and white patches are all sharply defined. Long black carpal spur, longer in the male.

b JUVENILE: Pattern is like adult, but white crown is tipped brown, chi and throat are whitish, and upper scapulars show some blackish feathers. All black feathers are tipped buff-brown. Wing-coverts ar fringed buff. Tertials are boldly barred. Relatively short and blunt carpal spur.

c In flight, shows black back and upper rump, white lower rump and uppertail, and a broad black tail-band. Upperwing is entirely blacl and grey, except for a small white wedge on the bases of the inner secondaries. Toes project well beyond the tail.

d From below, white underwing-coverts, axillaries and belly contras with black flight feathers, tail-band and breast.

62 Black-headed Plover *Vanellus tectus*

Text page 263

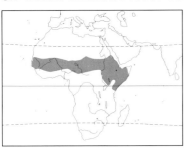

Distinctive wispy black crest like Northern Lapwing (57). Neat whit wedge from eye to nape. White patches on forehead and chin. Long black feathers in central breast. Bill red, tipped black; small red wattles on forehead; iris golden-yellow; longish, slender red legs. bird of dry, often bare, plains.

a ADULT nominate race (most of range): Black and white on head, neck and breast are sharply defined. White on forehead largely obscured by wattles. Upperparts evenly brown. Bare parts bright. Crest long.

b JUVENILE: Pattern recalls adult, but black of head and neck and brown of upperparts are strongly fringed buff. Centre of breast and crest are brownish; crest is relatively short. Tertials and scapulars strongly barred dark brown and buff. Legs and base of bill dull brown-pink. Wattles small.

c In flight, distinctive white primary coverts and white bases of fligh feathers form a strong contrast with broad black wing-tip and trailin edge. Uppertail-coverts white. Tail mostly black, with white at bas and tip.

d White of underwing-coverts extends well onto bases of flight feathers

e ADULT race *latifrons* (E Kenya, S Somalia): White forehead is broade than distance from bill-base to eye. Not known to intergrade with nominate race.

64 White-headed Lapwing *Vanellus albiceps*　　　　Text page 264

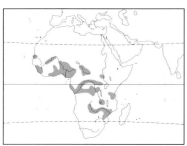

A highly distinctive lapwing found mainly by larger rivers.
a ADULT: Crown-stripe and chin clean white. Black and white conspicuous on coverts of folded wing. Long black, curving carpal spurs. Wattles very long and prominent. In juvenile, white on head is less extensive and partly obscured, wing-coverts are fringed buff, and brown of mantle and scapulars is mottled with pale buff. Spurs and wattles are initially relatively small, but grow quickly.
b ADULT: In flight, whole bird is strikingly pied. White areas on wing contrast with black outer primaries and squarish black patch on outer coverts. Broad black tail-band. Silvery-white patch on lower back is obscured by scapulars. Compare Long-toed Lapwing (Plate 24).
c Underwing-coverts and axillaries very white. From below, appears totally white except for black outer primaries and tail-band and grey sides of neck.

67 Crowned Lapwing *Vanellus coronatus*　　　　Text page 267

Found on dry inland plains. Except in juvenile, almost horizontal white and black bands surrounding black crown form a highly distinctive head pattern. White sides of breast form a 'peak' between brown breast-band and folded wing.
a ADULT: Black-and-white on head sharply defined. Brown of upperparts and breast evenly coloured, except that darker lower breast ends in a sharp blackish line.
b JUVENILE: Forward part of white head-band is suffused buff-brown leaving a brighter, whitish 'U' on rear crown. Black on head is tipped brown. Brown upperparts and breast are marked with strong dark subterminal lines and buff fringes and notches. All primaries except outermost are typically fringed buff.
c In flight, shows a prominent white bar which extends across secondaries and greater coverts and onto primary coverts. Lower rump and uppertail are white. Broad black subterminal tail-band. Wingbeats are rather slow.
d Underwing-coverts and axillaries are white; belly is also white. Breast is contrastingly brown.

68 Senegal Wattled Plover *Vanellus senegallus*　　　　Text page 267

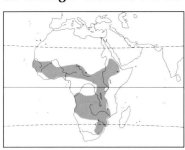

A large, tall lapwing typical of damp grassland. Plumage is mainly brown, but with white forecrown and black chin and throat. Bill yellow and black. Large bicoloured wattles. Long legs are usually bright yellow, sometimes greenish-yellow.
a ADULT race *lateralis* (E Zaïre and S Uganda southwards): Chin black. Brown median coverts uniform in colour. Sharp black carpal spur. In *lateralis*, grey-brown fore-belly darkens and forms a blackish line just in front of the legs, and bill-tip is solidly dark. Uniform grey-brown breast and mid-belly and reduced black on bill are characteristic of northern races, nominate and *major* (south to N Uganda).
b JUVENILE: Wattles very small. Chin and throat whitish. White head-patch is slightly obscured. Some show a few narrow buff fringes on median coverts, but upperparts generally as adult.
c In flight, mainly-black flight feathers contrast with a large square-ended white panel across the outer coverts and bases of secondaries. Lower rump and uppertail white. Black-and-brown tail-band. Toes project well beyond tail-tip. Nominate race is depicted.
d Race *lateralis* is very similar from above.
e Underwing-coverts are white, contrasting with dark flanks (*lateralis* only) and black-tipped flight feathers.

65 Senegal Plover *Vanellus lugubris*

Text page 265

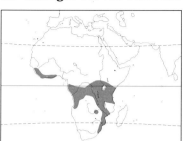

A small lapwing typical of open, dry plains. Darkish brown above, with grey-brown head, neck and breast. Distinct white 'peak' between the dark wing and breast. Bill is black, iris orange-yellow and longish legs dull red-brown. Closely resembles the larger 66, but is slimmer, taller and stouter-billed. Forehead shows a relatively small white patch. Flight pattern obviously different.

a ADULT: White forehead-patch sharply defined, contrasting with darkish brown crown and lores. Green-glossed coverts are uniform in colour. Lower breast shows a relatively narrow, well-defined black band.

b JUVENILE: White forehead-patch and black breast line partly obscured by buff tips. Brown coverts and scapulars fringed and spotted buff. Tertial edges are notched with buff.

c ADULT: In flight, note characteristic all-white secondaries and all-brown coverts. Trailing edge of wing is white in this species, black in 66. In adult, inner 4 primaries are narrowly tipped white. Tail shows broad black terminal band, but outer feathers are all-white. Toes project farther beyond tail-tip than in 66.

d JUVENILE: In flight, shows dull head and breast and buff fringing and spotting on coverts. Inner 8 primaries are tipped buff.

e Underwing is mainly white, contrasting with brownish under primary coverts and black primaries.

66 Black-winged Plover *Vanellus melanopterus*

Text page 266

Very like 65, but larger, stouter, shorter-legged and thinner-billed. Occurs mainly at higher altitudes. Brownish upperparts lack a green sheen. White forehead-patch is typically larger and less well defined. Wing pattern very different: white on outer coverts shows on the closed wing, as well as in flight. Black on lower breast is usually broader.

a ADULT: Head, neck and upper breast are mostly a clean, fairly pale ash-grey, sometimes tinged pale brown. Broad black breast-band. Upperparts are uniformly darkish brown.

b ADULT: Face and breast patterns are rather variable.

c JUVENILE: Head, neck and breast are pale brown, mottled buff. Dark breast-band is initially absent. Feathers of upperparts have broad buff fringes, giving a scaly appearance.

d ADULT: In flight, shows broad black tips to secondaries. White wing-panel extends across outer coverts to the base of the primary coverts. Broad black subterminal tail-band extends to outer feathers.

e JUVENILE: Like adult in flight but with buffish scaling to brown upperparts.

f Underwing-coverts, axillaries and bases of flight feathers are white, contrasting strongly with black bar on secondary tips and mostly-black primaries.

69 **Spot-breasted Plover** *Vanellus melanocephalus*   Text page 268

A very striking lapwing, restricted to moorland and grassland in the Ethiopian Highlands. The boldly spotted and streaked breast-band is unique among lapwings. Juvenile plumage is not yet described.

a ADULT: Neat black face, crown and hindneck. Prominent white supercilium. Long feathers of nape can be raised to form a crest. Sides of head and neck pale grey-brown. Breast spotted and streaked. Brown upperparts are slightly glossed with green. Some white is usually visible on the closed wing. Bill black, with yellow patch at base of upper mandible. Small yellow wattle in front of eye. Iris pale yellow or yellowish-grey. Relatively short, pale yellow legs.

b In flight, shows diagonal white wingbar which extends from inner secondaries across greater coverts and onto outer median and lesser coverts. Tail shows fairly narrow black subterminal band.

c Underwing-coverts, axillaries and belly are white. Flight feathers, except inner secondaries, show black tips.

70 **Brown-chested Plover** *Vanellus superciliosus*   Text page 269

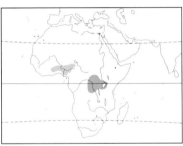

A small lapwing found mainly on dry, short grassland. Bill black, with yellow patch at base of lower mandible. Legs dark grey or reddish-brown.

a ADULT: Unique combination of dark chestnut breast-band, pale chestnut forehead, and yellow wattle above and in front of eye. Cap black. Chin whitish. Foreneck and upper breast ash-grey. Upperparts greeny-brown, with narrow rufous edges when fresh. Iris yellow.

b JUVENILE: Face, neck and breast dull grey-brown. Crown slightly darker brown. Forehead and supercilium pale rufous. Upperparts brown, with broad rufous fringes. Iris dull brown. Wattles relatively small.

c ADULT: In flight, shows a short, diagonal white wingbar. Tips of all flight feathers are black. Lower rump and uppertail white. Tail show black band, narrowing towards outer feathers. Feet project less beyond tail than in Black-winged Plover (Plate 26).

d JUVENILE: Like adult in flight, but head and breast are duller.

e Underwing-coverts, axillaries and belly clear white, contrasting with dark-tipped flight feathers and with dark breast.

69b

69a

69c

70e

70a

70c

70d

70a

70b

63 Yellow-wattled Lapwing *Vanellus malabaricus*   **Text page 263**

A sandy-brown lapwing often found in dryish lowland habitats. Dark crown bordered by white supercilia which almost meet on the nape Bill slender, yellowish at base and black at tip. Large yellow wattle hanging down in front of eye. Iris pale yellow. Long yellow legs.

a ADULT BREEDING: Crown, chin and throat black. Brown breast, bordered below by narrow black breast-band.

b ADULT NON-BREEDING: Black crown has brown feathers admixed Chin and throat also more brownish.

c JUVENILE: Crown all-brown; chin and throat white. The sandy-brown upperparts have dark subterminal bars and buff fringes especially on median coverts and tertials. Breast-band obscure. Wattles relatively small and dull.

d In flight, narrow white wingbar on inner wing only. Lower rump and uppertail white. Central, subterminal, black bar on tail.

e Underwing-coverts and axillaries white. Black tips to primaries and secondaries.

77 Red-wattled Lapwing *Vanellus indicus*   **Text page 274**

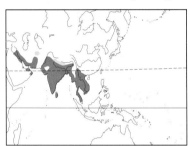

A large, striking lapwing, typically found near water. Centre of breast throat, crown to hindneck black (but see c), ear-coverts and sides of breast white. Legs long and yellow; bill-base, eye-ring and wattle red bill tipped black.

a ADULT BREEDING: Black on head, neck and chest. Upperparts pale brown, glossed green and purple. Bare-part colours bright. Non-breeding individuals may show some brown tips in black on crown, and white speckling on throat. Largest and palest race *aigneri* (Iraq to W Pakistan) is depicted. Races *aigneri*, *lankae* (Sri Lanka) and *indicus* (E Pakistan, India, Nepal and Bangladesh) have white line down side of neck joining ear-coverts with lower breast. Black of hindneck meets brown mantle.

b ADULT BREEDING race *atronuchalis* (Assam and Burma eastwards) Black line across base of side of neck isolates a white ear-covert spot. Narrow white base of hindneck.

c JUVENILE: Much duller than non-breeding adult. Chin and throat almost white; white speckling on crown. Rest of black areas are dar grey-brown. Wing-coverts less glossy, obscurely fringed buff. Wattl tiny, legs tinged dull greenish.

d ADULT: In flight, shows a diagonal white wing-panel and whitish lower rump to base of tail; narrow black subterminal tail-band. Rac *indicus* is depicted.

e ADULT race *atronuchalis*: Relatively small and dark, like *lankae* an southernmost *indicus*, but shows white collar and isolated ear-cover spot.

f Underwing-coverts and axillaries white.

78 Javanese Wattled Lapwing *Vanellus macropterus*   **Text page 275**

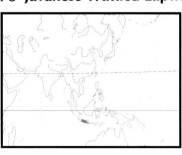

Once found around inland wetlands, this very dark lapwing is almos certainly extinct. The juvenile has never been described.

a ADULT: Head sooty-black, with glossy black crown and nape. Breas grey-brown, but large glossy black belly-patch contrasting with shar white rear belly. Upperparts an even dark brown. Bill black with pale yellowish base, large hanging creamy-white wattles. Long, curving black spur and long yellowish legs.

b In flight, like Masked Lapwing (Plate 29) in lacking white in the upperwing, but wings are much narrower. There is a small white patch on base of uppertail-coverts and tail and a broad black tail-band.

c Underwing-coverts white, axillaries grey-brown, underside of bod brown, black and white.

79 Banded Lapwing *Vanellus tricolor* Text page 275

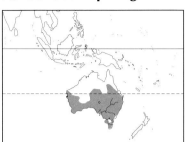

A medium-sized lapwing of short, dry grasslands. Identified by complete blackish U-shaped breast-band and broad, clear white rear eye-stripe. Unlike 80, shows white on upperwing in flight. Iris and eye-ring yellow, with small red wattle in front of eye. Bill yellow, with dusky nail. Relatively short legs are dark purplish, redder above the joint.

a ADULT: Glossy black on head, neck and breast. The brown upperparts have a slight purple sheen and appear uniform in colour. Colours of bare parts clear and bright. Wattle distinct.

b JUVENILE: Crown is brown, fringed buff. Band down neck and across breast is blackish-brown, with broad, irregular buff bars. Brown mantle, scapulars and coverts show broad pale buff fringes. Tertials irregularly barred buff. Bare parts all duller, wattles tiny.

c ADULT: In flight, shows a narrow but clear diagonal line of white from inner secondaries to carpal joint. Rump, uppertail-coverts and tail are mostly white, with a narrow black subterminal band. Feet do not project beyond tip of tail.

d JUVENILE: Patterns of wing and tail are as on adult.

e Underwing-coverts and axillaries white, like belly, contrasting with black primaries, tips of secondaries and breast-band. Some show white at base of primaries.

80 Masked Lapwing *Vanellus miles* Text page 276

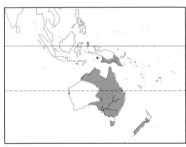

A large and distinctive lapwing with enormous yellow wattles around the eyes. Always has a dark crown and entirely-white underparts. The bill has a bright yellow base and paler tip. Legs are long and red. Long yellow spur on carpal joint.

a ADULT race *miles* (New Guinea, NE Australia): Black is restricted to crown and nape. Wattle is enormous and extends well behind eye.

b ADULT race *novaehollandiae* (SE Australia, New Zealand): Black runs down hindneck and spreads slightly onto sides of breast. The wattle, though very large, does not extend much behind the eye.

c ADULT: Individuals showing intermediate characters are frequent, especially in overlap zone around 25°S.

d JUVENILE race *novaehollandiae*: Pattern as adult, race for race, but black is tinged brown and obscured by many buff tips. The olive-brown upperpart feathers are irregularly mottled and barred dark brown, and fringed buff. Wattles are initially small, but grow rapidly.

e ADULT: In flight, lacks white in the large rounded wings but has a clear white rump to base of tail. Tail mostly black, with narrow white fringe. Nominate race (depicted) shows white hindneck.

f ADULT race *novaehollandiae*: Hindneck and breast-sides are black. This race averages longer-winged.

g Underwing-coverts and axillaries white, like underparts, contrasting with black flight feathers.

79c

79d

79a

79b

79e

80e

80a

80c

80b

80f

80d

80g

73 Pied Plover *Vanellus cayanus*

Text page 271

A small lapwing-like plover, strikingly pied on head, scapulars and breast, and with long orange or red legs.

a ADULT: Face mask from forehead to nape mostly glossy black, duller sooty-black on ear-coverts. Forehead sometimes shows a little white. Neat glossy black breast-band. The even greyish upperparts show two V-shaped lines: inner white line on mantle and inner scapulars, and black line on outer scapulars. Sharp black carpal spur.

b JUVENILE: Face mask strongly tinged brown, often with whitish forehead; black scapular lines absent, and breast-band dusky-grey. Brown scapulars and coverts fringed pale cinnamon-buff.

c ADULT: In flight, primaries and primary coverts black, but large white central patch in wing extends from bases of inner primaries to inner secondaries. Large white area from lower back to base of tail contrasts with broad black tail-band. Feet project beyond tip of tail.

d Underwing-coverts, axillaries and bases of flight feathers are white, like belly.

74 Southern Lapwing *Vanellus chilensis*

Text page 272

A large crested lapwing of lowland grassland. Bare parts including carpal spur are dark reddish, with bill tipped black.

a ADULT race *chilensis* (central Chile and Argentina): Black face joins breast-band; white on face narrow but clear; head blue-grey; large bronze patch on mantle; shortish crest. Race *fretensis* (southernmost South America) is similar.

b ADULT race *cayennensis* (north of Amazon): Little black on lower throat, much white on face, cinnamon-brown head and neck.

c ADULT race *lampronotus* (Amazon south to N Chile and N Argentina): Black face joins breast-band; little white on forehead; head and neck brown-grey; mantle with bronze patch.

d JUVENILE: Racial variation is slight. As adult but with brownish feathers tipped buff on head, throat line virtually absent, and white on face infused buff. Crest and spur shorter. Breast-band dull sooty-brown. Glossed greenish-brown upperparts are browner, with buff fringes and indistinct buff barring.

e ADULT: In flight, broad white and silvery patch across centre of wing contrasts with black primaries and mid- to outer secondaries. Narrow white band on rump and uppertail, broad black band on tail. Nominate race is depicted.

f Underwing-coverts and axillaries white, as belly, but contrasting with black breast-band and flight feathers.

75 Andean Lapwing *Vanellus resplendens*

Text page 273

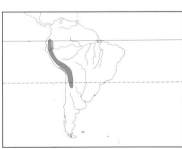

A large lapwing of high-altitude grasslands in the Andes. Distinctive pale creamy-brown head, with diffuse dusky eye mask. Slender bill is red at base, brown at tip. Iris and legs pink.

a ADULT: Head and neck have slight grey infusion. Breast darker grey, ending in a sharp, dark grey line. Most of upperparts brown, strongly glossed green, but the lesser coverts have purple sheen showing on the closed wing. Small carpal spur. Juvenile is like adult, but head and neck creamier; grey breast is mottled buff; upperpart feathers, including lesser coverts, dull brown-green, with dark green submarginal band and pale buff fringes; pale buff spot internally on tip of tertials.

b In flight, has a broad white diagonal band from inner primaries and inner greater coverts right to carpal joint. Outer wing and tips of secondaries are black; also contrasting are purple lesser coverts anterior to the white band. Square white patch over rump and uppertail; tail has broad blackish subterminal band. Feet do not protrude beyond tail-tip.

c Underwing-coverts, inner secondaries and axillaries white, as belly.

81 **Eurasian Golden Plover** *Pluvialis apricaria*   **Text page 277**

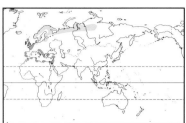

A bulky, golden-spangled, mainly inland plover. Compare with other golden plovers on Plate 32. Poorly-marked supercilium. Relatively small bill, short legs and short wings. Distinctive white underwing.

a ADULT BREEDING: Black underparts are bordered by white; partly obscured whitish flank line. Undertail mostly white. Upperparts show bright gold spots. Bright male of northern form is depicted. Extent of black is variable; on females, black underparts are tinged brownish.

b ADULT BREEDING male of southern form: Face obscurely blackish, with white-tipped feathers. Amount of black is very variable.

c ADULT BREEDING female of southern form: Black may be absent on face and throat.

d ADULT NON-BREEDING: Black underparts are lost. Breast is mottled golden-brown, lower flanks and belly whitish. Occasional individuals are much greyer than shown.

e JUVENILE: As non-breeding adult, but at close range shows fine dark bars on flanks and sparsely on belly.

f In flight, looks uniform except for narrow white wingbar, most obvious across primaries.

g Axillaries and most underwing-coverts obviously white, unlike American (83) and Pacific (82) Golden Plovers. Toes fall roughly level with tail-tip.

84 **Grey Plover** *Pluvialis squatarola*   **Text page 280**

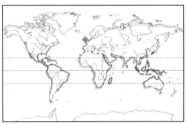

Larger and greyer than 81, and rarely seen inland. The bill is heavy and the actions rather languid. In flight, the diagnostic black axillaries, white rump and strong white wingbar are revealed. Legs dark grey.

a ADULT MALE BREEDING: Underparts from face to belly uniformly black; vent and undertail always white. Brilliantly-spangled silver-grey upperparts. Extensive white on crown and sides of neck and upper breast, but none on flanks.

b ADULT FEMALE BREEDING: Underparts have browner tinge and many white flecks. Upperparts sometimes browner.

c ADULT NON-BREEDING: Becomes much plainer grey or brownish-grey with upperparts spotted whitish. Distinct dark ear-covert patch, but no obvious supercilium.

d JUVENILE: Like non-breeding adult, but upperparts are darker and browner and spotted pale yellowish, and flanks and lower breast show some fine dusky bars. Compare with American Golden Plover (Plate 32).

e In flight, looks pale but shows long white wingbar and squarish white patch on rump and uppertail, often obscurely barred.

f Underwing-coverts white, but axillaries are always black, forming an extremely obvious isolated patch in non-breeding or juvenile plumage.

81a

81b

81f

81d

81e

81g

81c

84f

84d

84e

84b

84c

84a

82 Pacific Golden Plover *Pluvialis fulva*   Text page 278

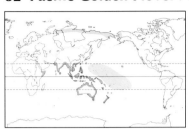

A small, slender, long-legged golden plover, but proportions not always obvious in isolation. Tends to be more coastal than Eurasian (81) or American (83). Bright golden-spangled plumage, with distinct supercilium. Brownish-grey underwing is shared with American.

a ADULT MALE BREEDING: Underparts black, typically with white splashes on undertail and continuous white flank line. Male averages slightly blacker than female, with less white flecking.

b ADULT NON-BREEDING: Loses all clear black and white on underparts. Gold spotting on upperparts is less prominent but still yellow. Breast is sometimes greyish, but less so than on 83.

c ADULT NON-BREEDING: Typical adult, compared with juveniles of all three species to the left.

d JUVENILE: Very like non-breeding adult, but breast clearly mottled brownish-yellow and grey-brown; flanks and fore-belly finely barred dark brown. Supercilium clear pale yellowish-buff.

e In flight, shows slighter wingbar than Eurasian. Toes typically project beyond tail-tip. Wings are relatively shorter and blunter than on 83. Juvenile is depicted.

f Underwing-coverts and axillaries are always brownish-grey, as on 83.

83 American Golden Plover *Pluvialis dominica*   Text page 279

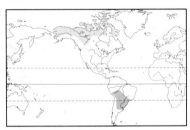

The middle-sized, but proportionately the longest-winged and largest-billed golden plover. For much of the year, greyer than other golden plovers. Typically, an inland species. Underwing pattern like Pacific (82). Distinct whitish supercilium. Compare carefully with 82 and with Grey and Eurasian Golden Plovers (Plate 31).

a ADULT MALE BREEDING: Gold-spangled upperparts and black underparts from face to undertail are like 82. Flank line usually absent; typically, shows large white patches on breast-sides. Male has underparts usually solidly black, including undertail-coverts, while female shows more white feathers on underparts. Moulting birds especially may closely resemble 82.

b ADULT NON-BREEDING: Upperparts dull brown-grey, whitish supercilium. Breast greyish. Belly pale whitish.

c ADULT NON-BREEDING: Some, especially worn individuals, may lack gold altogether.

d JUVENILE: Crown, mantle and scapulars dark brown with pale yellowish spots. Prominent whitish supercilium and dark ear-covert spot. Breast, flanks and upper breast strongly mottled greyish. Primaries project farther beyond tertials and tail than on 81 or 82.

e In flight, wings proportionately longer than those of other golden plovers. Whitish supercilium may be evident. Toes do not project beyond tail-tip.

f Underwing-coverts and axillaries are brownish-grey as on 82, distinctly darker than on 81.

86 Ringed Plover *Charadrius hiaticula*

Text page 282

A small plover with a single broad, normally complete, breast-band. Very like Semipalmated (87), but bill is proportionately larger, wingbar and breast-band more prominent, and rear white supercilium larger. Palmations clear only between outer two toes. Also compare Long-billed and Little Ringed Plovers (Plate 34).

a ADULT MALE BREEDING race *hiaticula* (NE Canada to W Europe) Sharp black-and-white head and breast pattern. Bill orange-yellow tipped black; legs orange-yellow. Race *hiaticula*, particularly in southernmost populations, averages slightly larger with paler grey-brown upperparts.

b ADULT MALE BREEDING race *tundrae* (N Scandinavia and USSR) Slightly smaller on average, and darker, more olive-brown above. White patch above and behind eye is often relatively small.

c ADULT FEMALE BREEDING: Breast-band less prominent in centre than on male, tinged slightly brown at sides. Ear-coverts more brownish. Race *tundrae* is depicted.

d ADULT NON-BREEDING: As breeding, but black is replaced by dusky-brown and brown-tinged supercilium is usually contiguous with pale forehead. Bare parts duller, bill sometimes all-black. On some, breast-band is broken in the centre.

e JUVENILE: Like palest, dullest non-breeding adult, but upperpart feathers show dark submarginal lines and extensive buffish fringes. Looks slightly scaly. Breast-band reduced in size in centre, sometime broken. Bill mainly blackish, legs dull orange-yellow.

f ADULT: In flight, wingbar is longer and clearer than on 87, fractionally more prominent on inner wing and on outer primaries. Clear wingbar is obvious distinction from 88 and 89.

g JUVENILE: Wing and tail patterns as adult.

h Underwing and axillaries look very white.

87 Semipalmated Plover *Charadrius semipalmatus*

Text page 283

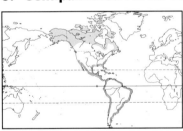

Very like 86, but averaging smaller, typically with a slightly narrower breast-band, less prominent white above and behind eye, and slightly stubbier bill. Generally more compact and rounded. Has clear palmations between all three front toes.

a ADULT MALE BREEDING: Sharp black-and-white head and breast pattern. Bill orange at base, black at tip. Legs orange-yellow. White patch above and behind eye typically very small on males, sometime absent. Narrow yellow eye-ring.

b ADULT FEMALE BREEDING: Differs in showing brownish tinge to black on head and breast.

c ADULT NON-BREEDING: Plumage pattern is like 86d. Black is replaced by grey- or olive-brown. Narrow supercilium joins pale forehead. Bill often all-black. Breast-band may be broken in centre

d JUVENILE: Like dull non-breeding adult, but upperpart feathers have narrow dark submarginal lines and buff fringes. Breast-band slightly more obscured, sometimes reduced to wide lateral breast-patches. Bill dusky, sometimes dull pinkish-yellow at base. Legs dull brownish, becoming dull yellow. Very similar to juvenile 86 pictured directly above.

e ADULT: In flight, shows long white wingbar, like 86 but with very slightly darker inner secondaries and white on shafts only of outer primaries.

f JUVENILE: Wing and tail patterns are like adult. Typically, both smaller and more compact in appearance than 86.

g Underwing very white, as on 86.

PLATE 34: Long-billed, Little Ringed and Malaysian Plovers

88 Long-billed Plover *Charadrius placidus*

Text page 284

The largest of the Palaearctic plovers with a single black breast-band. Unlike Ringed (86) or Little Ringed (89) Plovers, never shows a clear black eye-stripe. Proportionately longer-tailed than 86 or 89, with longish, slim, mostly-dark bill. In flight, shows very poor wingbar.

a ADULT BREEDING: White forehead; narrow white supercilium is interrupted above eye by edge of black frontal bar. Eye-stripe brownish-black. Breast-band black. Narrow yellow eye-ring visible at close range. Legs pale yellowish. Closed wings fall short of tail-tip. Body looks bulky. Fresh upperpart feathers tipped bright cinnamon

b ADULT NON-BREEDING: Briefly assumes a duller head and breast pattern.

c JUVENILE: As non-breeding adult, but lacks black on frontal bar and breast-band. Obscure brownish supercilium. Upperpart feathers neatly fringed warm buff.

d In flight, shows little white on wing, but greyish edges to secondaries and inner primaries form a poorly-contrasted pale wingbar. Wings longish; tail longish, with clear dark subterminal bar. Underwing-coverts and axillaries are white.

89 Little Ringed Plover *Charadrius dubius*

Text page 284

A small, slim plover with a single breast-band, pinkish legs, conspicuous yellow eye-ring, and mostly-dark bill. No obvious wingbar in flight. Actions more lively than Ringed Plover's (86). Head is proportionately smaller. Seen mostly inland.

a ADULT MALE BREEDING: Clear black head and breast pattern; differs from relatives in that dark frontal bar is separated from brown crown by a white line. Eye-ring very prominent, breast-band black

b ADULT FEMALE BREEDING: Slightly narrower eye-ring, and with a brownish tinge in breast-band.

c ADULT NON-BREEDING: Black is largely replaced by darkish brown, especially in breast-band. Buff infusion to supercilium and forehead. Bare parts slightly duller.

d JUVENILE: Brownish, poorly-patterned head, with very obscure buffish supercilia and forehead. Breast-band brown, usually broken into two lateral patches. Upperparts sandier-brown than adult, with dark submarginal lines and buff fringes. Eye-ring dull yellow, legs yellowish.

e In flight, shows hardly any pale wingbar; wing looks almost uniformly dark. Underwing-coverts and axillaries white, but underside of flight feathers is darker than in 86.

101 Malaysian Plover *Charadrius peronii*

Text page 294

A small coastal plover. Most like Kentish Plover (98), but easily distinguished by rufous breast-band or breast-patches of female and juvenile and black hindneck collar of male. Upperpart feathers show dark centres. Legs long, mid-grey, slightly paler than on most Kentish

a ADULT MALE: Frontal bar, lores, ear-covert spot and breast-band o large lateral breast-patches are clear black. Prominent white forehead and supercilium. Cap and nape washed variably with chestnut. Broad white and black hindneck collars. Black colours retained all year.

b ADULT FEMALE: Black on head and breast of male is replaced by bright rufous-brown, occasionally with black flecks. Less chestnut in cap than male. Hindneck shows much less white, never any black.

c JUVENILE: Very like adult female, but never shows blackish flecking in breast-band.

d ADULT MALE: In flight, long white wingbar is like 98.

e JUVENILE: Wing pattern is as on adult.

f Broad white sides to uppertail and tail are as on 98.

98 Kentish Plover *Charadrius alexandrinus*   Text page 292

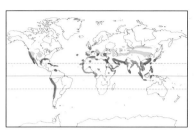

A small plover with a white hindneck collar. Breast-band is never complete: there are small dark lateral breast-patches. Five races of this widespread species are illustrated; a sixth occurs only on Java.

Nominate race (N Africa, W Europe to Korea)

a ADULT MALE BREEDING: Black frontal bar, eye-stripe from bill to ear-coverts, and sharply-defined patches at sides of breast. White forehead is continuous with short white supercilium. Rufous on cap is very variable: some show entirely-chestnut crown. Most individuals of this race have blackish legs.
b MALE ASSUMING BREEDING PLUMAGE.
c ADULT FEMALE BREEDING: Black areas of male are brown, uniform with rest of upperparts, or blackish-brown, contrasting poorly. No rufous on cap.
d ADULT NON-BREEDING: Non-breeding plumage of both sexes resembles breeding female. Some, like this individual, may become faded and worn in tropical winter quarters.
e JUVENILE: Like breeding female, but paler, with buff infusion to head and breast-patches. Coverts and scapulars show neat but narrow buff fringes.
f In flight, all races show a clear white wingbar and broad white sides to uppertail and tail. White on tail-sides is especially obvious on landing. Underwing-coverts and axillaries are white.

Race *seebohmi* (Sri Lanka, SE India)

g ADULT MALE BREEDING: No rufous cap. Frontal bar and mask may be obscure; on some, lores are completely white.
h ADULT FEMALE BREEDING: Resembles female of nominate race. Upperparts sometimes darker brown.

Race *dealbatus* (Japan, E China)

i ADULT MALE BREEDING: Very similar to nominate race, but averages longer-billed.
j ADULT FEMALE BREEDING: As in nominate race, some show blackish-brown mask and breast-patches.
k ADULT MALE NON-BREEDING: Some may retain a little rufous on cap.
l ADULT NON-BREEDING: As in all races, legs may be pale on some individuals.

Race *occidentalis* (coastal Peru and Chile). This race and *nivosus* (below) are together known as 'Snowy Plover'. Both are shorter-legged than Palaearctic races, and paler and greyer above. Breeding birds lack rufous on cap, and often show all-white lores.

m ADULT MALE BREEDING: Lores typically all-white. No rufous on cap.
n ADULT FEMALE BREEDING: Sexes are closely similar in this race.

Race *nivosus* (USA, Caribbean)

o ADULT MALE BREEDING: Resembles *occidentalis*, but eye-stripe is often narrower. Many breeding birds have all-white lores.
p ADULT FEMALE BREEDING: Lacks black on face and breast. Non-breeding plumage of both sexes is similar.
q JUVENILE: Plumage resembles juvenile of nominate race. Legs are shorter on average, and sometimes paler (as on this individual).
r Flight pattern of 'Snowy Plovers' does not differ from that of Palaearctic races.

PLATE 36: Lesser and Greater Sandplovers

107 Lesser Sandplover *Charadrius mongolus*

Text page 299

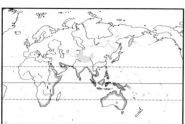

This and 108 have very similar plumage patterns and overlap almost completely in non-breeding range. Identification rests largely on structure: Lesser is smaller, shorter-legged and shorter-billed, with more rounded head sometimes suggesting Ringed Plover (86). Calls and leg colour are also helpful.

a ADULT MALE BREEDING race *stegmanni* (NE USSR): Forehead mostly white, bisected by vertical black line. This and similar race *mongolus* (inland E USSR) form the 'mongolus group'.

b ADULT MALE BREEDING race *atrifrons* (Himalayas, S Tibet): Forehead all-black or with tiny white patches. In the more southerly 'atrifrons' group', wings average shorter and bill and legs longer.

c ADULT FEMALE BREEDING: Black of male is replaced, often completely, by brown or rufous. Race *mongolus* is depicted.

d ADULT FEMALE BREEDING: Some show a little black, especially around eye. Race *mongolus* is depicted.

e ADULT NON-BREEDING: Breast shows lateral patches, sometimes joining narrowly across centre. No hindneck collar. Legs typically dark grey.

f JUVENILE: Breast-patches buffish. Bright buff fringes to scapulars and tertials.

g In flight, shows white wingbar and narrow white sides to rump and tail. Wingbar is variable and sometimes, as on bird to the right, much as on 108. On many individuals, the toes do not project beyond the tail-tip.

h Underwing-coverts and axillaries are white.

i Race *mongolus*: E Siberian birds (wintering Taiwan to Australia) are typically the shortest-billed.

j Race *atrifrons*: Typical of birds wintering between S Africa and Sumatra.

k Race *schaeferi* (E Tibet, wintering Thailand to Greater Sundas) averages longest-billed.

108 Greater Sandplover *Charadrius leschenaultii*

Text page 300

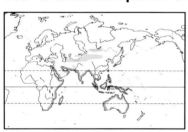

Separation from 107 requires care. Greater is typically larger, with broader, more angular head and relatively larger bill. Legs are longer and usually paler. Relative value of structural identification characters varies geographically in non-breeding range.

a ADULT MALE BREEDING: Eastern races are like 107; black and chestnut areas are typically narrower, but variable. Largest race *crassirostris* (Caspian to Lake Balkash) is depicted.

b ADULT MALE BREEDING race *columbinus* (west of Caspian): Extensively rufous above as well as on breast. Small bill of this race invites confusion with 107.

c ADULT FEMALE BREEDING: Less rufous than male, and sometimes lacking black in mask. Race *columbinus* is depicted.

d ADULT NON-BREEDING: Breast shows lateral patches, often joining narrowly in centre. Shape of head and bill and length and colour of legs are best distinctions from 107.

e JUVENILE: Buffish breast-patches and buffish fringes to upperparts.

f In flight, like 107 but typically shows more white on wing and on sides of rump and tail and a more contrasting dark subterminal tail-band. Toes project beyond tail-tip. Nominate race (easternmost) is depicted.

g Largest race *crassirostris* in flight.

h Underwing-coverts and axillaries are white.

i Race *columbinus*: Bill may be shorter than on longest-billed 107.

j Nominate race: Bill longer than on 107, head more angular.

109 Caspian Plover *Charadrius asiaticus*

Text page 301

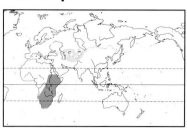

A fairly long-legged, long-winged plover of short grassland or bare ground. Plumages recall 110, but whitish underwing and narrow white wingbar provide constant distinctions. Legs usually greenish o brownish.

a ADULT MALE BREEDING: Dark brown crown and rear eye-stripe contrast with gleaming white supercilium, face and throat. Upper breast bright chestnut, bordered narrowly below by black.

b ADULT FEMALE BREEDING: Breast typically all grey-brown or with a very few white-tipped chestnut feathers. Never has neat black line on lower breast.

c ADULT NON-BREEDING: Head pattern like breeding, but browns are paler and white is mostly buffy. Breast always mottled grey-brown.

d JUVENILE: Very like non-breeding adult, but more scaled, with dark brown centres and bright rufous and buff fringes to upperpart feathers

e ADULT NON-BREEDING: Quite long, thin wings, with narrow but distinct white wingbar and inner primary flash. Toes project a little beyond tail.

f Underwing-coverts mostly white or almost white, axillaries pale brown.

g ADULT MALE: Can gain some chestnut prior to spring migration.

h Tail is broad and rounded, neatly fringed white.

110 Oriental Plover *Charadrius veredus*

Text page 302

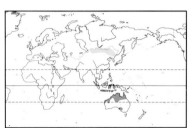

The long-legged and long-necked plover replacing' 109 in E Asia. Always has brown underwing, and never more than a trace of a white wingbar. Legs usually yellowish or pinkish.

a ADULT MALE BREEDING: Neck and legs are longer than on 109. The head and neck are much more extensively white and the brownish feather tips on the crown and ear-coverts may wear off, leaving a very pale-headed bird. Chestnut breast-band broadly bordered below by black.

b ADULT FEMALE BREEDING: Head darker than a, especially on crown and ear-coverts. Breast-band normally grey-brown, but sometimes with a little chestnut and black.

c ADULT NON-BREEDING: As b, but face and neck more suffused buff or pale brown. Fresh upperpart feathers show clear rufous or warm buff fringes.

d JUVENILE: As c, but the upperpart fringes are paler buff, giving a greater contrast, and breast is buff, mottled brown. Supercilium narrower than in 109.

e Effectively lacks a wingbar, although juvenile (depicted) has very narrow white tips to greater and inner primary coverts. Long-winged shape, like 109.

f ADULT NON-BREEDING: At a distance, almost uniform brown, often with slightly paler hindneck.

g Underwing and axillaries appear brown, but some flecks of whitish present. Underwing contrasts noticeably with white belly.

h Tail pattern is like that of 109.

120 **Eurasian Dotterel** *Eudromias morinellus*   **Text page 309**

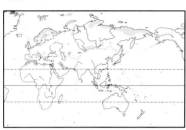

A chubby, medium-sized plover which always shows clear long supercilia, meeting in a 'V' on the nape, and a narrow whitish breast-band. Legs yellowish. Breeds mainly on montane plateaux and winters in stony or sandy sub-deserts.

a ADULT FEMALE BREEDING: Both sexes have similar patterns, but females tend to have uniform and very dark cap, sharp brilliant white supercilia, clean grey breast and a blacker belly.

b ADULT MALE BREEDING: Usually differs from female in slightly-streaked crown, browner breast and less black on belly.

c ADULT NON-BREEDING: Much duller, lacking black on crown and belly and chestnut on belly. Supercilia brown-buff, and forehead heavily streaked. White breast line less clear. Upperpart feathers completely fringed buff-brown or sandy-brown.

d JUVENILE: As c, but upperpart feathers darker brown with brighter buff fringes. On larger coverts, scapulars and tertials, the fringe is clearly interrupted at its tip. Neck and breast buff-cinnamon, and more clearly mottled brown. Underparts buffier.

e Always looks quite dark in flight. White tip to tail, especially on outer feathers, and white shaft of outer primary are surprisingly clear. Juvenile is depicted.

f Underwing-coverts and axillaries dull greyish-white, usually contrasting with the dark or dull flanks and belly (extent of contrast depends on season and age).

112 **Mountain Plover** *Charadrius montanus*   **Text page 303**

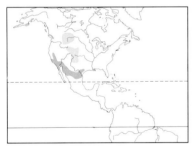

A pale brown, medium-sized plover of upland short grassland (not mountains). Winters in semi-deserts and on bare fields.

a ADULT BREEDING: The brilliant white forehead and supercilium contrast sharply with narrow black lores and black frontal bar. Underparts are mostly white, but sides of upper breast and neck are washed brown-buff. Never has black on breast.

b ADULT NON-BREEDING: Fresh plumage has quite rufous fringes. Black on head replaced by pale brown. Breast-patches are buffier and larger, sometimes joining in centre.

c ADULT NON-BREEDING: When worn, looks plainer brown above. Face is often very pale.

d JUVENILE: As non-breeding adult, but darker brown upperpart feathers have dark subterminal lines and bright buff fringes; more clearly scaly. Supercilium buff, breast flecked dark brown.

e In flight, looks long-winged with typically narrow white tips to greater coverts and white patch on inner primaries. Amount of white varies. Tail shows dark subterminal band and narrow white fringe.

f Underwing-coverts and axillaries white (compare 83).

120d

120f

120c

120a

120b

120e

112c

112e

112b

112a

112f

112d

90 Wilson's Plover *Charadrius wilsonia*

Text page 285

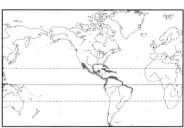

A coastal plover with a single breast-band and a heavy black bill.
a ADULT MALE BREEDING race *beldingi* (W Mexico to W Panama): Upperparts rather dark grey-brown. Male in all races has black in frontal bar, lores and breast-band. Race *wilsonia* (E USA to Belize and Leeward Is.) is similar, but paler above with narrower mask, longer supercilium and less rufous on crown.
b ADULT FEMALE BREEDING race *wilsonia*: Females of all races lack black. Breast-band typically all-brown in *wilsonia*, often conspicuously rufous in *beldingi*.
c MALE race *cinnamominus* (NE Colombia to NE Brazil): Crown and mask show much rufous; rufous is also admixed in breast-band.
d ADULT FEMALE BREEDING race *cinnamominus*: Mask, forecrown and breast-band strongly rufous.
e ADULT NON-BREEDING: Both sexes resemble breeding female, but generally lack rufous.
f JUVENILE: As non-breeding adult, but darker brown upperparts are neatly fringed buff and with dark submarginal lines. Looks scaly. Buff-and-brown-mottled breast-band may be almost broken.
g In flight, shows rather short white wingbar. Look for the heavy bill.
h Underwing and axillaries are white.

91 Killdeer *Charadrius vociferus*

Text page 286

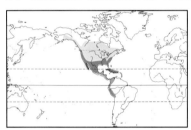

Very distinctive plover typical of inland pools and grasslands. Always has two prominent black or blackish breast-bands, blackish face mask, and a very long tail which extends beyond wing-tips. Rump and uppertail are uniquely bright orange-brown.
a ADULT MALE BREEDING nominate race (USA, Canada): Upperparts brown with a few rufous fringes. Face mask and breast-bands largely black. Eye-ring bright orange. Race *ternominatus* (West Indies) is similar, but averages paler and greyer.
b ADULT FEMALE BREEDING nominate race: Very like male, but usually shows more brownish on mask and breast-bands. Dull orange eye-ring. Non-breeding plumage in both sexes often has brown admixed in breast-bands.
c ADULT NON-BREEDING race *peruvianus* (Peru, NW Chile): As nominate race, but shows more extensive rufous fringes to upperparts.
d JUVENILE: Very like dull non-breeding adult, but all upperpart fringes are a slightly paler buff and have darkish submarginal lines. Tail-down may be retained for several weeks.
e In flight, shows long wings and long graduated tail. White wingbar is prominent. Orange-brown rump and uppertail obvious on landing.
f Underwing and axillaries are white.

92 Piping Plover *Charadrius melodus*

Text page 287

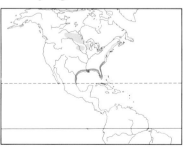

A small plover with a short, stubby bill, usually on sandy beaches.
a ADULT MALE BREEDING: Black frontal bar and breast-band. Bill orange at base, tipped black. Legs bright orange. Coastal nesters typically have incomplete breast-band. Female is very similar, but often brownish-black on forehead and breast-band.
b ADULT MALE BREEDING: Inland nesters typically have complete breast-band, though both patterns occur throughout range.
c ADULT NON-BREEDING: As breeding, but lacks black; looks extremely pale with prominent dark eye. Bill often all black.
d JUVENILE: Like non-breeding adult, but upperpart feathers fringed pale buff. Looks slightly scaly. Bill black, legs dull.
e In flight, shows long white wingbar and very pale upperparts. Longest uppertail-coverts form a small white patch at base of tail.
f Underparts entirely white except for breast-band or breast-patches

97 Forbes's Plover *Charadrius forbesi*

Text page 291

A smallish, long-tailed plover with two dark breast-bands. It is very like Three-banded Plover (96), but rather larger, distinctly darker brown, and with forehead darkish brown, never white or pale. Lacks wingbar and shows barred outer tail feathers. Usually seen on grassland or cultivated land.

a ADULT BREEDING: Supercilium and band on hindneck white. Breast-bands black, upper narrow band merging into darkish brown neck. Forehead brown. Longest undertail-coverts are barred with black. In non-breeding plumage, supercilium and band on hindneck infused with brownish-buff; breast-bands dull brown, upper one inconspicuous.

b JUVENILE: As non-breeding adult but duller, with feathers of upperparts narrowly fringed buffish. The dark feather centres make dark submarginal lines inconspicuous. Undertail-coverts show less barring.

c In flight, looks very dark, with virtually no trace of a wingbar. Wings and especially tail are relatively long.

d Underwing-coverts white, but with brown smudging on primary coverts and leading edge.

e Outer tail feathers are barred with blackish-brown and white.

96 Three-banded Plover *Charadrius tricollaris*

Text page 290

This smallish, fairly dark plover, typical of inland waters, has two black breast-bands. It is most easily distinguished from its close relative, Forbes's Plover (97), by its white or mainly-white forehead. As in 97, folded wings fall well short of tail-tip.

a ADULT race *tricollaris* (Africa): Forehead all-white. Sides of face and neck pale brown. Chin and throat often very pale.

b ADULT race *bifrontatus* (Madagascar): Forehead is bicoloured, with grey band over bill and white band above that. Face and neck rather dark greyish, with very little pale on chin or upper throat.

c JUVENILE: Very like adult, but in both races forehead is infused pale brown for a short period before assuming adult pattern. Upperpart feathers show dark submarginal line and narrow buff fringe. Often retains tail-down well after fledging.

d In flight, wings look dark, with a short white trailing edge and an inconspicuous narrow white wingbar.

e Underwing and axillaries are mostly white, smudged brown on outer coverts and narrowly on leading edge. Belly and undertail-coverts are also white.

f Sides and tip of tail are mostly unbarred white.

93 Black-banded Sandplover *Charadrius thoracicus*

Text page 288

Only in SW Madagascar, where found mainly on short coastal grassland. In all respects very like 94, but always shows a distinct da breast-band. Bill and legs dark.

a ADULT: Frontal bar and eye-stripe black, the latter merging into a complete black breast-band. Underparts white above breast-band but belly all cinnamon-buff, darkest at rear (perhaps paler on females). As in 94, upperpart feathers show contrast between dark brown centres and slightly paler fringes. Legs black.

b JUVENILE: Black-and-white head pattern is replaced by dull brow and pale buffish. As in 94, upperpart feathers are broadly fringed pal buff-brown. Underparts greyish-white, with distinct, complete greyish-brown breast-band. Legs grey.

c In flight, shows a faintly bolder white wingbar than 94, especially c outer wing. Contrast between dark lesser coverts and paler medians less than on 94. Tail as on 94. Toes project beyond tail-tip.

d Pattern of underwing is like that of 94.

94 Kittlitz's Sandplover *Charadrius pecuarius*

Text page 288

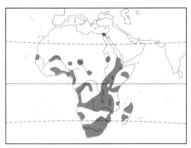

A small, long-legged, dark brown plover. Very like 93 but slightly smaller; never shows clear breast-band. Legs greenish-black when breeding, otherwise greyish tinged green or brown. Compare also with 95.

a ADULT BREEDING: White supercilia and black eye-stripes both meet at base of hindneck. Upperpart feathers with darkish brown centres and paler fringes. Throat white, breast and belly washed creamy-buff, rear belly and vent white. Depth of colour on breast very variable. Birds with brown tinge to black and with paler breas are probably females.

b ADULT BREEDING: An example from Madagascar.

c ADULT NON-BREEDING: Some birds become much duller, lacking black, and with brown and buff tinges to head pattern. Breast pale buff, with obscure lateral grey-brown patches.

d ADULT NON-BREEDING: Depth of colour is variable also in non-breeding plumage. An example from Egypt.

e ADULT NON-BREEDING: Paler individuals may appear almost pla brown above. Dark patch at bend of wing more obvious.

f JUVENILE: Like non-breeding adult, but upperpart feathers broad fringed buff-brown. Breast washed buff, with distinct brownish later breast-patches.

g In flight, shows dark leading edge to wing, narrow white wingbar, ar white sides to tail. Toes project well beyond tail-tip.

h Underwing is brownish on primary coverts and on leading edge, otherwise white.

95 St Helena Plover *Charadrius sanctaehelenae*

Text page 289

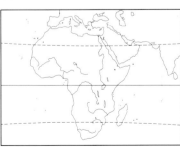

Only on remote island of St Helena. Very similar to 94, but larger wit longer legs and bill.

a ADULT: Face pattern distinctly blackish and white. Upperpart feathers darkish brown, with broad, brown fringes. Underparts almo white on most individuals.

b JUVENILE: In full juvenile, head pattern is dull brown and buffish lores whitish; brown feathers of upperparts narrowly fringed pale buff; breast washed dusky. Depicted example has already gained adult-like head pattern.

c ADULT: In flight, wings noticeably broad and rounded with virtual no wingbar. Lesser coverts contrastingly dark.

d JUVENILE: As adult, but coverts narrowly fringed buffish. This individual shows full juvenile head pattern.

e Underwing mostly dull, with brownish leading and primary coverts

99 White-fronted Sandplover *Charadrius marginatus*   Text page 293

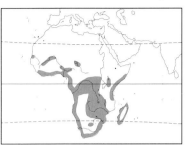

This small plover may recall Kentish (98), but has distinctly shorter and paler legs and a relatively longer tail which projects beyond folded wing-tips. Plumages are variable, but underparts are typically rufous and always lack sharply-defined lateral breast-patches. White forehead is large and conspicuous.

a ADULT MALE BREEDING: Much individual variation in colours not strictly related to geographical origin. Male has sharp black frontal bar and narrow black eye-stripe contrasting with brilliant white forehead and supercilium. Breast variably suffused with cream or rufous-buff; rufous may extend around hindneck. Occasionally has diffuse breast-patches, recalling 98, or complete rufous breast-band like 102. Depicted example is from Cape Province (nominate race).

b ADULT MALE BREEDING: An example from Kenya (race *tenellus*). Some individuals may be extensively rufous above as well as below

c ADULT MALE BREEDING: A bird from Madagascar (also race *tenellus*). In this population, rufous is typically concentrated onto neck and sides of breast.

d ADULT FEMALE BREEDING: As male, but black is less clear and breast suffusion sometimes paler or even absent.

e ADULT MALE NON-BREEDING: Black on frontal bar is replaced by dull brown. Many resemble breeding females.

f ADULT FEMALE NON-BREEDING: Some lose all trace of frontal bar Shape and breast pattern should always distinguish from 98.

g JUVENILE: Lacks black frontal bar, but has dark brown eye-stripe across lores. Underparts usually white. Upperpart feathers have broad sandy-buff fringes, some larger feathers distinctly tinged rufous

h In flight, shows long, distinct wingbar and clear white sides to rump and tail. Toes do not project beyond longish tail. Underwing-covert and axillaries are white.

102 Chestnut-banded Sandplover *Charadrius pallidus*   Text page 295

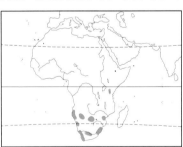

A comparatively small, short-tailed but quite long-legged plover associated mainly with strongly alkaline wetlands. Except in juvenile plumage, shows a narrow but complete chestnut breast-band.

a ADULT MALE race *venustus* (E African lakes): Upperparts grey-brown. Pale chestnut on forecrown and neck collar. Male has white forehead sharply outlined by black frontal bar and lores; chestnut breast-band usually flecked blackish on upper edge. Race *pallidus* (southern Africa) has paler and greyer upperparts, but male is otherwise similar; averages 15% larger.

b ADULT FEMALE race *venustus*: Lacks black; frontal bar and eye-stripe pale chestnut.

c ADULT FEMALE race *pallidus*: No black. Lacks chestnut on head, but has chestnut breast-band and very pale chestnut neck collar. Larger paler and greyer than *venustus*.

d JUVENILE: Lacks all black and chestnut. Breast-band greyish, but usually reduced to lateral patches. Wing-coverts and scapulars are fringed whitish; a few have dark submarginal lines. Taller, shorter-tailed shape should always distinguish from 99.

e In flight, shows narrow white wingbar and white sides to rump and tail. Toes project noticeably beyond short tail. Underwing-coverts and axillaries are white.

100 Red-capped Plover *Charadrius ruficapillus*

Text page 293

A small, dark-legged plover recalling Kentish (98), but always lacking a white hindneck collar and with tiny lateral breast-patches and a short supercilium.

a ADULT: Frontal bar, lores, eye-stripe and breast-patches black or blackish; extensive chestnut on crown and nape. On male, black areas lack brown tips, crown and nape often entirely chestnut.

b ADULT FEMALE: Sometimes duller than male, with centre of crown grey-brown.

c NON-BREEDING: Adult non-breeding and first-winter individuals may show only traces of adult head pattern. Breast white in centre. Supercilium extends only a little behind eye.

d JUVENILE: Chestnut and black of adults is replaced by brown. Lores and ear-coverts brown. Upperpart feathers show obscure dark submarginal lines and buff fringes.

e In flight, has distinct white wingbar and white sides to uppertail and tail, as on 98. Underwing-coverts and axillaries are white.

105 Double-banded Plover *Charadrius bicinctus*

Text page 297

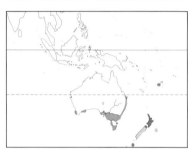

A smallish plover with pale greenish or yellowish legs and a slender bill. Compare with South American species on Plate 46.

a ADULT BREEDING nominate race (main islands, Chatham Is.): Two complete breast-bands, upper one narrow and black, lower broad and chestnut. Black frontal bar and dusky mask. Supercilium white. On male, black areas normally lack brown tinge.

b ADULT FEMALE BREEDING nominate race: Black often replaced by brown. Some breed in very dull plumage.

c ADULT BREEDING race *exilis* (Auckland Is.): Plumper and heavier than nominate race, warmer brown above but duller on breast-bands and on thighs.

d ADULT NON-BREEDING: Lacks all black and chestnut. Upper band brownish, lower band often very obscure. Supercilium creamy, indistinct. Upperparts have extensive rufous fringes when fresh.

e JUVENILE: As non-breeding, but lacks double breast-band. Longer and clearer buff supercilium. Broad dusky mark across breast and upper belly. Upperpart feathers have pale white-buff fringes. Compare Lesser Sandplover on Plate 36.

f In flight, fairly narrow white wingbar; rather dark tail with slightly paler outer feathers.

g Underwing and axillaries mostly white.

113 Black-fronted Plover *Charadrius melanops*

Text page 304

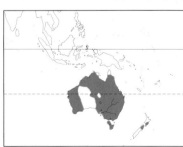

A smallish plover with a peculiar plumage pattern. Long dark mask and white head-band. Purplish scapular patch contrasts with pale coverts.

a ADULT: Forehead, face mask and V-shaped breast-band are black. Crown brown. Scapular patch deep purplish-chestnut, contrasting with whitish-streaked coverts. Longest undertail-coverts barred black. Legs pink-orange, and bill red with black tip.

b JUVENILE: Breast-band initially absent, but obscured brown band slowly appears. Eye-stripe dull brown, crown mottled white. Scapula patch brown, covert patch streaked brown and chestnut. Undertail-coverts white. Legs and bill brownish.

c In flight, pale covert patch contrasts with dark outer wing, leading coverts and scapulars, and dusky outer secondaries. Outer tail feathers and corners of tail white. Wings look broad and tail short.

d Seen from below, contrast of black and white is striking.

100b

100c

100e

100a

100

100d

100

105c

105a

105b

105

105

105f

105d

105g

105e

113b

113d

113a

113c

114 Red-kneed Dotterel *Charadrius cinctus* Text page 305

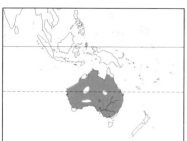

A medium-sized plover with a very distinctive wing pattern and long, bicoloured legs. In all plumages, dark cap contrasts with white chin and throat. Bill fairly long and slim. Found in freshwater marshlands.

a ADULT: Striking black hood and breast-band. Upperparts greenish-brown. Flanks black at front, splashed chestnut towards rear; upper flanks white, forming brilliant flash below edge of closed wing. Bill red, tipped black.

b JUVENILE: Cap greenish-brown, merging into rest of upperparts. Upperpart feathers dull green-brown with whitish-buff fringes. Underparts white, except for partly-obscured brownish breast-patches.

c IMMATURE: Juvenile quickly gains brownish breast-band and flanks; black of adult plumage appears later.

d In flight, dark upperparts contrast with brilliant white on secondaries and tips of inner primaries. Sides of rump and tail are also white. Toes project well beyond tip of tail.

e Underwing-coverts and axillaries are white. Dark band on flanks is obvious from below.

115 Hooded Plover *Charadrius rubricollis* Text page 305

A stocky, pale plover found mainly on sandy beaches. Disruptive patterning makes very good camouflage. Has a broad white hindneck collar and short orangey legs.

a ADULT: Entire head is black. Black lower hindneck collar extends into small lateral breast-patches. Bill pink, tipped black. Legs orange-brown to yellowish-pink.

b JUVENILE: Black on hindneck and cap is replaced by pale grey-brown, tipped buff-white; chin and throat whitish, washed pale grey. Upperpart feathers have distinct dark submarginal lines and buffish-white fringes; looks pale and scaly.

c In flight, shows broad and long white wingbar contrasting with blackish trailing edge and primary coverts. Sides of uppertail and base of tail broadly white, contrasting with blackish tail centre and subterminal tail-band.

d Entire underwing is very white.

119 Inland Dotterel *Peltohyas australis* Text page 308

A peculiar plover of Australian sub-deserts. Dark vertical mark through the eye is unique. Upperparts are streaked, with darker feather centres and sandy-buff fringes, recalling Eurasian Dotterel (Plate 38).

a ADULT BREEDING: Very striking black vertical band runs through the eyes and over the crown. Black band on hindneck is continuous with black Y-shaped breast-band. Upperparts strongly streaked.

b ADULT NON-BREEDING AND JUVENILE: In both these plumages, all black is lost and upperpart streaking is muted. Traces of dark face markings and collar are visible.

c In flight, wings lack white but show an indistinct, rich buffy bar or patch on inner primaries. Tail is darkish, narrowly tipped white.

d Underwing, axillaries and flanks are rich buff, contrasting with chestnut belly line, white rear belly and, in breeding adults, the black breast marking.

114d

114e

114a

114b

114c

115d

115b

115c

115a

119d

119a

119b

119c

85 New Zealand Dotterel *Charadrius obscurus*   **Text page 281**

A fairly large, heavy plover with a large black bill; shape recalls a short-legged Grey Plover (84). Restricted to New Zealand. Essentiall coastal.
a ADULT BREEDING: In both sexes, underparts, face and superciliur are whitish, variably washed with chestnut. Scapulars and tertials fringed tawny-chestnut when fresh.
b ADULT MALE BREEDING: Some males are extensively rich chestnu even on face, but vent and undertail always show some white.
c ADULT NON-BREEDING: Chin and throat white, upper breast obscurely smudged grey-brown; rest of underparts mostly white, slightly smudged on flanks. Upperpart feathers finely fringed white
d JUVENILE: Like adult, but upperpart feathers darker brown, fringe buff-tawny. Head has a dark-capped appearance. Underparts variably washed buff-tawny, with some darker flecking on breast.
e In flight, shows clear white wingbar, dark rump and whitish sides tc tail.
f Underwing-coverts and axillaries are white and undersides of fligh feathers very pale.

116 Shore Plover *Thinornis novaeseelandiae*   **Text page 306**

A distinctive wader, but now very rare and restricted to Southeast Islånd in the Chathams group. A smallish plover with shortish orange legs, a longish, slender bill and an encircling white head-band.
a ADULT MALE: Forehead, lores, chin, upper throat and sides of face black, extending around hindneck as a narrow collar. Bill has extensive orange-red base and a sharply-defined black tip.
b ADULT FEMALE: Black on head and neck is replaced by dusky-brown. Bill has a less extensive orange base which shades intc blackish tip.
c JUVENILE: Face is extensively whitish, with broad, dark brown eye-stripe. Bill brown, with orange tinge at base of lower mandible
d In flight, has clear white wingbar and white sides to tail and rump.
e Underwing-coverts and axillaries are mostly white, as underparts, bu under primary coverts show some brownish.

117 Wrybill *Anarhynchus frontalis*   **Text page 307**

A rather heavily-built plover with short, dark legs and plain greyish upperparts. The bill looks long and slim from the side, but from above shows a sharp curve to the right near the tip. Breeds on stony riverbeds, otherwise coastal.
a ADULT MALE BREEDING: Clear, prominent black frontal bar emphasises white forehead and supercilia. Well-defined black breast-band. Upperparts entirely plain greyish.
b ADULT FEMALE BREEDING: Frontal bar absent or obscure. Breast-band duller, browner and narrower. Axillaries and underwing-coverts white in all plumages.
c ADULT NON-BREEDING: Lacks frontal bar; supercilium indistinc Breast-band almost totally obscured in fresh plumage; later, a narrow grey or smudgy grey-and-black breast-band appears.
d JUVENILE: Breast-band absent, but some grey on sides of breast. Feathers of upperparts neatly fringed white.
e In flight, shows white wingbar which is strongest on inner primaries and broad grey tail with narrow white edges. Breeding male is depicted.

PLATE 46: South American plovers I

103 Collared Plover *Charadrius collaris*

Text page 296

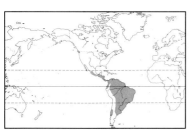

A small, slim plover with yellowish legs and relatively long, thin, dark bill. Does not have a white hindneck collar. Darker and browner above than 'Snowy Plover' (Plate 35).

a ADULT MALE: Sharply-defined black frontal bar, lores and breast-band. Chestnut wash on mid-crown, usually also pale chestnut wash over base of hindneck. Upperparts often with tawny-chestnut feather fringes.

b ADULT FEMALE: Very like male; a few are distinguishable by slight brown tinge to black areas and reduced chestnut on crown.

c JUVENILE: Breast-band is replaced by tawny-brown lateral patches. Lacks any black or dark brown on forecrown or lores. Upperparts have many pale tawny-buff feather fringes. Black steadily appears.

d MOULTING JUVENILE: May show blackish lateral breast-patches.

e In flight, shows narrow but clear white wingbar. Strongly contrasting white tail-sides are like 'Snowy Plover'.

f Underwing-coverts and axillaries are white.

104 Puna Plover *Charadrius alticola*

Text page 297

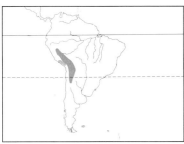

A fairly small plover of the high Andes. Neckless, rounded shape, pale face, and black legs and bill are distinctive. Compare with 105.

a ADULT MALE: Totally white face contrasts with broad black band on mid-crown from eye to eye. Crown and hindneck suffused pale chestnut. Small black lateral breast-patch, and broad chestnut lower breast-band.

b ADULT FEMALE: At least some are noticeably duller than males, with a slight brown infusion into black areas, and chestnut less extensive.

c ADULT NON-BREEDING: Some birds lose black and chestnut and show indistinct breast pattern.

d JUVENILE: Less white-faced than adult, and lacks all black and chestnut. Buff suffusion to forehead. Upperpart feathers fringed pale buff. Lacks breast-patches, and lower breast-band virtually absent.

e In flight, shows narrow white wingbar, most evident on inner primaries. Tail-sides are whitish. Toes do not project beyond tail-tip.

f Underwing-coverts and axillaries are white.

106 Two-banded Plover *Charadrius falklandicus*

Text page 298

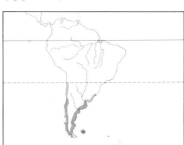

A smallish, dark-legged, mainly coastal plover, with two dark breast-bands, the upper one narrower and sometimes reduced to lateral patches. Recalls 104, but is a little larger and longer-billed.

a ADULT MALE BREEDING: White forehead and lores contrast with narrow black frontal bar. Crown and hindneck extensively washed chestnut. Breast-bands black; upper band sometimes complete, sometimes broken as in this Falkland Islands individual.

b ADULT FEMALE BREEDING: As male, but black areas are suffused with brown, upper breast-band is flecked white, and rufous on head is duller and less extensive.

c ADULT NON-BREEDING: All black is replaced by dusky-grey; chestnut on head is lost and a dull line appears on lores.

d JUVENILE: Like non-breeding adult, but much duller; face, except for creamy spots at bill-base, is washed with buffish; no frontal bar; breast-bands brown, flecked buff; upperpart feathers with dark submarginal lines and buff fringes.

e In flight, shows relatively short, narrow white wingbar, slightly shorter than on 104. White tail-sides are like those of 104. Tips of toes may project just beyond tail-tip.

f Underwing-coverts and axillaries are white. This individual is a breeding male with complete breast-bands.

111 Rufous-chested Dotterel *Charadrius modestus*   Text page 302

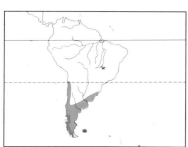

This small to medium-sized plover has distinctive white supercilia which meet on the forehead, and a richly-coloured lower neck and breast.

a ADULT BREEDING: Chocolate-brown cap almost encircled by brilliant white supercilia. Face, cheeks and throat clean ash-grey; lower neck and breast bright rufous, bordered below by fairly broad black band. Upperparts show gingery fringes when fresh. Rufous spots at ends of supercilia and on rearmost flanks.

b ADULT NON-BREEDING: Rufous and grey are lost. Forehead pale buff, speckled darker, supercilium creamy. Breast grey-brown, mottled paler.

c JUVENILE: As non-breeding adult, but upperpart feathers darker brown, fringed whitish-buff. Breast brownish, with buff mottling.

d In flight, wings look dark with a little obscured white in outer wing; white edges to dark tail and white supercilia are distinct.

e Underwing and axillaries mostly white, but primary coverts greyish.

118 Diademed Plover *Phegornis mitchellii*   Text page 308

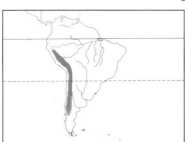

A tiny wader of river-valley gravel and grasslands of the high puna of the Andes. Peculiar longish, slightly drooping bill; yellowish legs.

a ADULT: Head blackish-brown with brilliant white supercilia meeting on forecrown. Chestnut hindneck obvious. Underparts finely barred, looking evenly grey except at close range.

b JUVENILE: Dull above and below, lacking well-marked head pattern. All of underparts darkish brown, with warm buff spots and fringes; supercilium buffish, obscure. Underparts paler than on adult and less clearly barred.

c In flight, the short, rather rounded wings and short tail are mostly dark. Mantle and tertials are darker than rest of upperparts. Wingbeats are stiff.

d Underwing and axillaries mostly white, contrasting a little with greyish belly.

121 Tawny-throated Dotterel *Oreopholus ruficollis*   Text page 310

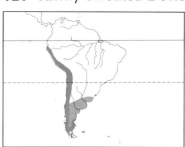

An unmistakably slim, upright plover of arid coastal and high Andean habitats. Has a long, slender, slightly drooping bill. Heavily-streaked upperparts and dark belly-patch are distinctive.

a ADULT: Dusky lores, white chin. Throat variably orange-tawny; grey of breast extends around hindneck. Scapulars and tertials show long dark and tawny streaks. Black central belly-patch. Legs dull pink.

b JUVENILE: Resembles adult, but head browner, throat buff and neck grey, fringed buff. Scapulars and coverts blackish-centred, small feathers with pale buff fringes. Underparts pale buff; belly-patch sooty-brown.

c In flight, wingbar clear, especially on outer wing. Tail greyish at sides with dark subterminal bar, but mostly hidden by long coverts.

d Underwing-coverts and axillaries contrastingly white.

111d

111e

111b

111a

111c

118a

118b

118c

118d

121c

121d

121a

121b

123 Black-tailed Godwit *Limosa limosa* Text page 311

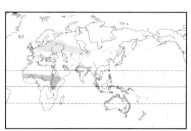

A tall, slender godwit with a relatively long, nearly straight, blunt-tipped bill. In flight, the combination of white wingbar and white underwing is diagnostic. Compare with Bar-tailed on Plate 49

a ADULT MALE BREEDING race *islandica* (Iceland, Lofotens, Shetlands): Mantle and scapulars blotched pale red, black and grey wing-coverts dull grey-brown. Throat to upper belly chestnut, barred dark brown on flanks and belly; rear belly lacks chestnut, unlike 12 or 125. Base of bill orangey.

b ADULT MALE BREEDING race *limosa* (W Europe to W Asia): As a but chestnut paler and less extensive on belly; bill and legs longer

c ADULT MALE BREEDING race *melanuroides* (E Asia): Much the smallest race. Plumage like *islandica*, but wing-coverts darker grey-brown.

d ADULT FEMALE BREEDING: As male, but chestnut paler and ofte heavily flecked white; scapulars retain many grey feathers. Some almost as bright as male. Bill averages longer.

e ADULT NON-BREEDING races *limosa* and *islandica*: Evenly grey neck, breast and upperparts. Base of bill flesh-pink. Diffuse pale supercilium. Female is depicted; male similar but shorter-billed.

f ADULT NON-BREEDING race *melanuroides*: Small; noticeably darker upperparts. Male is depicted.

g JUVENILE: Pale cinnamon wash over neck and breast; obvious near warm buff fringes to small brownish upperpart feathers.

h In flight, long brilliant white wingbar and large white flash on lower rump and uppertail are distinctive. Feet trail far behind tail. Non-breeding adult of one of western races is shown.

i Race *melanuroides* is darker with narrower wingbar and a little les white on uppertail.

j Underwing and axillaries are always conspicuously white.

124 Hudsonian Godwit *Limosa haemastica* Text page 312

A medium-sized, darkish godwit with a slightly-uptilted pointed bill Proportions are intermediate between those of 123 and 125. In flight, narrow white wingbar and mainly-black underwing diagnostic.

a ADULT MALE BREEDING: Whitish face with darkish eye-stripe contrasts with dark chestnut underparts. Upperparts mostly dark brown, spotted buff-white. Base of bill orangey. Male has belly mostl deep chestnut.

b ADULT FEMALE BREEDING: Usually noticeably paler below than male, with extensive white blotching; pale face and rear belly contrast less. Bill averages longer.

c ADULT NON-BREEDING: Darkish, even grey-brown upperparts like eastern race of 123, but has clearer white supercilium. Greater contrast between breast and belly. Base of bill pinkish-brown.

d JUVENILE: Upperparts very dark brown with neat buff fringes, more clearly notched buff on tertials. Neck and breast washed brown-buff.

e In flight, like 123 above but upperwing shows shortish white wingbar and uppertail a relatively narrow white band. Feet project less beyond tail. Non-breeding bird is depicted, with juvenile and breeding adul to the right.

f Underwing-coverts and axillaries black; flight feathers blackish with silvery bases forming a contrasting central bar. Axillaries contrast strongly with belly on non-breeding individuals.

125 **Bar-tailed Godwit** *Limosa lapponica*

Text page 313

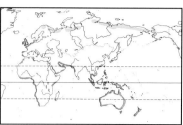

A relatively short-legged godwit. Compare 185, 123 and 124.

a ADULT MALE BREEDING: Underparts entirely unbarred, deep chestnut-red, often slightly flecked paler on rear flanks. Scapulars and mantle fringed deep chestnut. Bill relatively short.

b ADULT FEMALE BREEDING: Brightest individuals show some chestnut above and some dark barring and light chestnut blotches on underparts. Many show little change from non-breeding plumage. Bill averages longer.

c ADULT NON-BREEDING: Upperparts streaked pale grey-brown and pale buff-brown; most are browner than individual depicted.

d JUVENILE: Upperpart feathers and wing-coverts darkish brown, contrastingly edged bright buff. Neck and breast washed buff-brown

e In flight, race *lapponica* (Scandinavia and W USSR) shows prominent white back and rump; no obvious wingbar. Toes project a little beyond tail.

f In flight, race *baueri* (E USSR) shows dark back and rump, and pale uppertail-coverts heavily barred brown. The larger of the races.

g Underwing-coverts in race *lapponica* white, axillaries white narrowly barred brown.

h Underwing in race *baueri* is heavily barred dark brown.

185 **Asiatic Dowitcher** *Limnodromus semipalmatus*

Text page 362

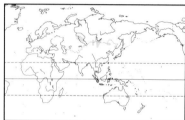

In all plumages resembles a small version of 125, but always has a heavy-based, straight, blunt-tipped, mostly-black bill. Compare with other dowitchers on Plate 72.

a ADULT MALE BREEDING: Face, neck and breast chestnut-red. Most of belly and flanks white, flanks prominently barred. Scapulars, tertials and mantle feathers blackish, neatly fringed pale brown and chestnut; looks streaked.

b ADULT FEMALE BREEDING: As male, but slightly duller and with more white flecks in chestnut. Bill averages longer.

c ADULT NON-BREEDING: Whitish supercilium; breast obscurely mottled grey-brown. Upperparts darkish grey-brown, slightly streaked paler.

d JUVENILE: Neck and breast strongly washed buff and slightly streaked. Scapulars, tertials and mantle blackish, narrowly and neatly fringed pale buff, contrasting with paler brown, buff-fringed coverts.

e In flight, heavily-barred rump and uppertail contrast little with back and tail. Paler band across secondaries and inner primaries distinctive. Toes project beyond tail-tip.

f Underwing and axillaries clearly white, sometimes lightly marked with brown.

126 **Marbled Godwit** *Limosa fedoa*

Text page 314

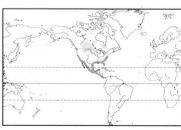

A large, fairly heavy godwit. In flight, cinnamon wingbar and underwing and lack of pattern on uppertail are distinctive.

a ADULT BREEDING: Upperparts speckled blackish and cinnamon. Underparts all pale cinnamon; neck, breast and flanks lightly streaked and barred (marbled) dark brown.

b ADULT NON-BREEDING: As breeding, but looks paler and plainer. Upperparts speckled and barred dark brown and cinnamon. Faded individuals may be almost as pale as 125, except on wings. In flight, flight feathers conspicuously cinnamon, with contrasting dark outer primaries and primary-covert patch. Feet project beyond tail-tip.

c JUVENILE: Very like non-breeding adult, but upperpart fringes more buff and underparts richer cinnamon-buff.

d Underwing and axillaries bright cinnamon.

125c

125a

125d

125e

125f

125b

125g

125h

185c

185d

185e

185a

185b

185f

185

126b

126c

126d

126a

127 Little Curlew *Numenius minutus*　　　Text page 315

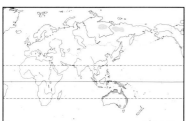

A tiny curlew with a distinctive dark eye-stripe, buff crown-stripe and a shortish, only slightly decurved bill. Has a strong buff tinge to plumage; lacks contrast on rump. Wing-tips fall roughly level with tail-tip, and tarsus is as long as or longer than bill. Occurs mainly inland.

a ADULT: Breast washed buff, finely streaked darker, forming a fairly sharp contrast with paler belly. Flanks at most lightly and irregularly barred. Scapulars and tertials with brown-buff notches. Coverts brown, edged paler.

b JUVENILE: Very like adult, but breast and flanks show only very few dark streaks. Neat pale buff fringes and spots on scapulars. Coverts brown, neatly fringed pale buff. (Painted to same scale as other curlews on Plates 51–53.)

c ADULT: In flight, looks dark above with slightly paler band across centre of wing. Flight feathers evenly dark, except for pale tips, unlike Whimbrel (129). Toes project beyond tip of tail. Pale buff flank feather is shown for comparison with 128.

d JUVENILE: Like adult in flight, but with neater buff fringes to coverts and scapulars.

e Underwing-coverts and axillaries buff, barred brown.

128 Eskimo Curlew *Numenius borealis*　　　Text page 316

This tiny curlew of the plains of the Americas is very close to extinction. Has buff crown-stripe, shortish decurved bill and dark rump area like 127, but is slightly larger, longer-winged, shorter-legged and more cinnamon in general tone.

a ADULT: Underparts washed buff-cinnamon, prominently streaked on breast and with clear Y-shaped marks on flanks (absent on 127). Upperparts notched and spotted brown-buff. Bill typically longer than tarsus; folded wings project well beyond tail.

b JUVENILE: Very like adult, but underparts more buff. Upperpart feathers have neat buff edges.

c ADULT: In flight, looks more uniformly dark above than 127; wings relatively longer. Unlike Whimbrel (129), the flight feathers are evenly dark except for pale tips to inners. Measurements indicate that toes do not project beyond tail-tip.

d JUVENILE: Narrow pale buff edges to scapulars and tertials; coverts fringed buff. Flanks tinged cinnamon and strongly barred.

e Underwing-coverts and axillaries strongly cinnamon, barred brown.

135 Upland Sandpiper *Bartramia longicauda*　　　Text page 322

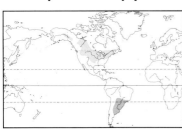

An odd-looking, brownish-streaked wader of short inland grasslands. Pot-bellied shape with long thin neck and tiny head, prominent dark eye, short bill, slightly drooping at tip, and long tail are highly distinctive. Legs yellowish.

a ADULT: Upperparts dull olive-buff, strongly barred dark brown and fringed pale brown-buff. Buff-washed breast is heavily streaked; flanks whitish with prominent dark chevrons. Tail projects beyond folded wing-tips.

b JUVENILE: Scapulars mostly dark brown, narrowly fringed pale buff, looks scaly. Wing-coverts paler brown, with narrow dark submarginal line and pale buff fringes. Flank marks less prominent.

c ADULT: In flight, looks dark with long tail and blackish rump; outer wing blackish, inner wing browner; some whitish often visible at sides of rump.

d JUVENILE: Like adult, but coverts and scapulars evenly fringed buff.

e Underwing-coverts and axillaries white, strongly barred dark brown. Wings often held aloft on landing.

127a

128a

127c

127d

128d

135a

128c

128e

127e

135c

135d

127b

135e

135b

127b

128b

129 Whimbrel *Numenius phaeopus*   Text page 317

A medium-sized curlew with a strongly-marked crown-stripe and face pattern. Rump pattern varies between races. Bill length overlaps with both smaller and larger curlew species.

a ADULT race *phaeopus* (Iceland to W USSR): Upperparts mainly dark olive-brown, variably notched and fringed whitish. Breast pale buff-white, streaked brown. Male's bill averages shorter. Race *alboaxillaris* (south of Urals) is similar but a little paler.

b ADULT race *variegatus* (E USSR): Similar to nominate race.

c ADULT race *hudsonicus* (Alaska, N Canada): Upperparts warmer brown than in other races; breast washed pale buff.

d JUVENILE nominate race: As adult, but upperpart feathers darker brown, with many neat buff spots, notches and fringes. Breast washed buff.

e JUVENILE race *hudsonicus*: Browner above and buffer below than nominate race.

f In flight, all flight feathers notched whitish on inner web. Races *phaeopus* and *alboaxillaris* have unbarred white back and rump, like other W Palaearctic curlews on Plate 52.

g Race *hudsonicus*: Upperparts buffish-brown; back and rump uniform with rest.

h Race *variegatus*: Back brown; rump whitish, barred brown. Often little contrast between back and rump.

i Race *phaeopus*: Underwing-coverts and axillaries white, variably but narrowly barred brown. Race *alboaxillaris* has an almost unbarred underwing.

j Race *hudsonicus*: Underwing-coverts and axillaries barred broadly brown and narrowly pale buff.

k Race *variegatus*: Underwing-coverts and axillaries barred broadly brown and narrowly white.

130 Bristle-thighed Curlew *Numenius tahitiensis*   Text page 318

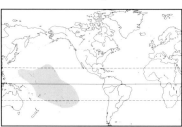

Size and head pattern as 129, but plumage more cinnamon above and below. In flight, shows distinctive bright cinnamon patch on rump and uppertail.

a ADULT: Upperparts spotted and notched cinnamon-buff. Underparts dull buff, tinged cinnamon; breast and flanks heavily streaked. Unique shining bristle-like feathers on thighs are rarely visible in the field.

b JUVENILE: As adult, but upperparts and coverts have bold, large buff-cinnamon spots. Breast buffish, often virtually unstreaked. In flight, shows white tips to all but outer 2 primaries.

c ADULT: In flight, has squarish area of unbarred cinnamon on lower rump and uppertail-coverts; outer four pairs of tail feathers deep cinnamon, barred brown. Flight feathers look dark.

d Underwing-coverts and axillaries deep cinnamon, barred brown; undertail-coverts uniformly pale creamy-cinnamon.

131 Slender-billed Curlew *Numenius tenuirostris*   Text page 318

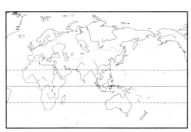

Smaller and paler than 132, with a shorter, slimmer, more pointed bill; compare also with Whimbrel (129). Shows more white than other curlews. No crown-stripe, but darkish cap and dusky eye-stripe contrast a little with streaked, pale supercilium.

a ADULT BREEDING: Breast whitish, streaked dark brown. Sides of lower breast and fore-flanks white, typically marked boldly with variable blackish ovals or heart shapes. Scapulars are sometimes tinged grey and rufous.

b ADULT NON-BREEDING: Very like breeding adult; flanks show fewer rounded or heart-shaped blackish marks. Female (lower) is longer-billed than male.

c JUVENILE: Very like adult, but flanks show brown streaks and lack blackish spots; some spots are gained during first winter. Inner 8 or primaries are narrowly tipped white.

d In flight, shows white from back to tail-tip; rump and uppertail are lightly marked with brown, and tail is barred dark brown. Extensive white notches on secondaries give paler inner wing than on 129 or 132. Dark outer primaries contrast strongly. On adult, only inner 6 to 7 primaries are tipped white.

e From below, shows almost pure white underwing and axillaries, continuous with white ground colour of flanks, breast and belly.

132 Eurasian Curlew *Numenius arquata*   Text page 319

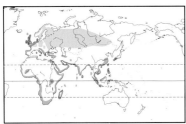

A large, brownish curlew with a mostly-white back and rump prominent in flight.

a ADULT BREEDING: Feathers of upperparts have dark, greyish-brown centres and paler fringes. Breast is washed buffish-brown. In smaller race *arquata* (Europe and Urals), flanks typically show irregular chevrons or cross shapes. Male has shorter bill than female (depicted).

b ADULT NON-BREEDING: Very like breeding adult, but grey-brown replaces buff on breast and upperparts.

c ADULT BREEDING race *orientalis* (Urals eastwards): Often paler than western race and averages larger; flanks typically strongly streaked.

d JUVENILE: Like adult, but with stronger buff infusion to breast, and flanks relatively lightly streaked. Upperpart feathers darkish brown with strongly contrasting buff notches and fringes. Newly-fledged individuals have very short bills, inviting confusion with 131 or 129.

e In flight, shows extensive white on back and rump. White on tail is lightly infused pale brown. Whitish notching on secondaries and inner primaries is less conspicuous than on 131.

f Race *orientalis*: Lower rump is barred more obviously than on nominate race, and inner wing is a little paler.

g Race *arquata*: Underwing-coverts and axillaries are white, with variable brown barring. Notching typically extends to outermost primaries. Some individuals, however, resemble 132h.

h Race *orientalis*: Underwing mostly unmarked white; axillaries contrast more with flanks.

i Palest individuals of *orientalis* lack brown markings on underwing, and may lack notching on up to 5 outer primaries.

131e

131c

131a

131d

129

131

131b

132b

132a

132e

132d

132i

132c

132h

132g

132f

133 Far Eastern Curlew *Numenius madagascariensis* Text page 320

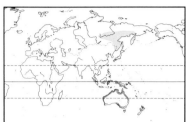

A very large curlew with a very long, heavy, decurved bill. Like Eurasian Curlew (132), but dark back, rump and underwing are distinctive in flight. Whole underparts are washed brownish, palest from rear belly to undertail.

a ADULT BREEDING: Upperparts have dark brown feather centres and rufous or brownish-olive edges and notches. Breast is extensively but finely streaked, flanks finely streaked. Primaries 7 and 8 diffusely tipped pale. Female has longest bill of any wader.

b ADULT NON-BREEDING: Like breeding adult, but duller grey-brown, lacking rufous tinge on upperparts.

c JUVENILE: Very like adult, but upperpart feathers neatly edged and notched buff-white, and streaking on underparts finer. Sharp white primary tips extend to primaries 7 and 8.

d In flight, looks dark above: never shows any white on back or rump. Secondaries and inner primaries are notched white.

e Underwing-coverts and axillaries are densely barred brown, appearing darker than rear belly.

134 Long-billed Curlew *Numenius americanus* Text page 321

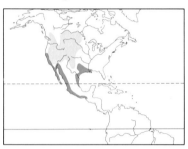

A large curlew which is distinctively cinnamon-coloured in all plumages. Compare carefully with Marbled Godwit (126).

a ADULT BREEDING: Mantle and scapulars are speckled black and cinnamon-buff. Tertials have strong barring and a narrow dark central line. Neck and breast slightly streaked, but most of underparts are unstreaked cinnamon. Female has much longer bill than male. Bill-tip is clearly drop-shaped.

b ADULT NON-BREEDING: Very like breeding adult, but upperparts are less strongly speckled.

c JUVENILE: Virtually identical to adult in the field. Scapulars and wing-coverts show slightly buffer notches and fringes. Tertials have a broader dark central line. During first few months of life, bill is distinctly shorter than adult's.

d In flight, looks dark above with secondaries and inner primaries cinnamon, notched brown. On adult (depicted), inner 7 primaries are mostly fringed pale cinnamon, while pale fringes on juvenile extend to primary 8.

e Underwing-coverts and axillaries virtually unbarred bright cinnamon.

136 **Spotted Redshank** *Tringa erythropus*

Text page 322

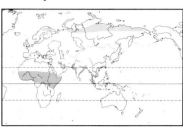

Black breeding plumage is unique. At other stages, long, dark red legs, long slim bill and more prominent white above lores are constant distinguishing features from 137. Red on bill is confined to lower mandible.

a ADULT BREEDING: Head, neck and underparts totally black; the re black, spotted and notched white. Underparts, especially on females often have obscure white fringes.

b ADULT IN MOULT: In early spring, may look blotched black and white as black replaces white of non-breeding plumage. In autumn may appear similar as white replaces black.

c ADULT NON-BREEDING: Pale. Upperparts brown-grey, neatly fringed and notched white; lores dark, contrasting with white supercilium. White underparts, undertail-coverts virtually pure white. Crown and hindneck darker than in Greenshank (139).

d JUVENILE: Fairly dark, with white-spotted and -notched upperparts clear supercilium in front of eye, and underparts densely barred wi grey.

e ADULT NON-BREEDING: In flight, wings are dark but the pale notches and bars on larger coverts and secondaries give a slightly paler trailing panel. Long, narrow, oval white patch shows on the back, but rump and tail are fairly darkly barred, appearing dull. Fee project well beyond tail.

f ADULT BREEDING: White back contrasts with black body.

g ADULT BREEDING: White underwing-coverts and axillaries contra with black belly.

h NON-BREEDING: Very white underwing, but flight feathers, even secondaries, darker than coverts.

137 **Redshank** *Tringa totanus*

Text page 323

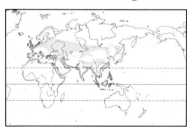

Fairly long, bright orange-red legs, fairly stout moderate-length bil and poorly-marked supercilium separate this from 136. See also 21C

a ADULT BREEDING race *totanus* (Ireland to W USSR): Very variabl but typically has quite strong dark brown streaking or spotting on head, neck, breast, flanks and belly. Upperparts may show some gre rufous or cinnamon feathers with dark brown markings.

b ADULT BREEDING race *ussuriensis* (E USSR to N China): These an *robusta* (Iceland, Faeroes) are typically more cinnamon than European birds, and show a higher proportion of breeding-plumag feathers.

c ADULT NON-BREEDING: Legs orange-red, bill-base duller; often shows clear white eye-ring. Upperparts quite plain grey-brown, wi some narrow whitish fringes. Breast finely streaked, but heavily washed grey-brown. Streaks on underparts extend along flanks an onto undertail-coverts.

d JUVENILE: Legs a paler yellow-orange, base of bill dull red-browr Upperparts generally warm brown, densely spotted and notched bu Underparts quite heavily streaked dark brown.

e In flight, easily identified by entirely-white secondaries and tips to inner primaries. These and the white back contrast with the generall dark upperparts. On landing, the whole back, rump and tail may loo white. Non-breeding adult is depicted.

f Apart from dusky primaries, the underwing is all-white. White secondaries and shorter projection of toes beyond tail separate fron 136.

136d

136a

136c

136b

136h

136g

136e

136f

137e

137b

137f

137a

137d

137c

139 Greenshank *Tringa nebularia* Text page 325

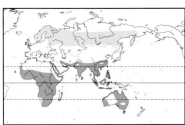

Larger size, stouter build, and quite stout and slightly-uptilted bill separate this from 138. See also Plate 56.

a ADULT BREEDING: Head, neck and upper breast fairly heavily streaked and spotted blackish-brown. Coverts dark grey, fringed white, but scapulars a mixture of black and grey feathers, fringed whitish.

b ADULT NON-BREEDING: Whole of head and neck looks pale, but with fine streaking over crown and hindneck. Underparts, including throat and foreneck, white. Coverts and scapulars grey, finely fringed white.

c JUVENILE: Upperparts browner than adult, with clear pale buff fringes especially on scapulars. Neck and breast slightly more heavily streaked than non-breeding adult.

d In flight, at all stages, shows very dark outer wings, fairly dark even-coloured inner wings and mantle. White flash on back and rump is prominent, not normally obscured by tertials. Tail pale, looks white at a distance. Toes project only slightly beyond tail. Juvenile is depicted.

e ADULT BREEDING: Underwing white but finely barred brown, contrasts with well-marked breast.

f Outside breeding plumage, breast also is white.

138 Marsh Sandpiper *Tringa stagnatilis* Text page 324

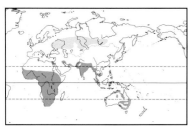

A distinctive, very long-legged bird with small body and quite long very fine bill. Usually shows clear supercilium. Long, slim neck makes belly look unusually deep and bulbous. Beware confusion with 139.

a ADULT BREEDING: Head and neck heavily streaked dark brown; lower breast and flanks show bars or chevrons. Upperparts, especially scapulars and tertials, are sharply patterned in greyish-cinnamon and dark brown. Legs frequently tinged yellowish.

b ADULT NON-BREEDING: The streaked crown and obscure eye-stripe emphasise the white supercilium; face, foreneck and centre of breast very white. Grey scapulars and mantle, fringed white, often contrast with darker coverts. Legs typically dull olive-green.

c JUVENILE: As non-breeding, but streaking on head and hindneck may be browner. Upperpart feathers brownish-grey, with narrow dark subterminal bars and pale buff fringes. Note that worn adults may also appear brownish.

d In flight, dark outer wing and fairly dark inner wing. Long white back and rump with pale tail are very like 139. Wingbeats, however, are faster and daintier, and whole length of toes is visible beyond tail-tip.

e Underwing-coverts and axillaries are mainly white, but with a small dark bar on median under primary coverts.

140 Spotted Greenshank *Tringa guttifer*
Text page 326

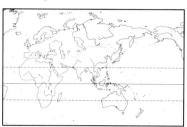

A stocky wader, closely resembling Greenshank (139), but with short stout, yellow or yellowish legs and a heavy, almost straight, distinctly two-toned bill.

a ADULT BREEDING: Some contrast between dark crown and lores and rest of head and upper neck, which are white with brown streaking. The most prominent feature is the intense, almost black, spotting on the lower neck, breast, flanks and, often, upper belly. Wing shows some contrast between dark shoulder and paler coverts. Most scapulars, tertials and mantle feathers are very dark brown, spotted and fringed whitish.

b ADULT NON-BREEDING: Head and hindneck much paler, washed grey and slightly streaked. Breast lacks spotting. Upperparts mostly dull grey, fringed whitish; scapulars contrast with dark brown lesser coverts, more so than in 139.

c JUVENILE: As non-breeding, but crown and upperparts are suffused pale brown; scapulars and tertials are spotted buff, coverts fringed pale buff. Breast lightly washed brown, faintly streaked at sides.

d In flight, shows white back and rump, very pale tail and contrasting all-dark upperwings. Very like 139 in plumage and in size and shape, but toes do not project beyond tail-tip.

e Underwing and axillaries are pure white (faintly barred brown in 139).

f Partial webbing between three front toes is unique in *Tringa*.

152 Tuamotu Sandpiper *Prosobonia cancellata*
Text page 337

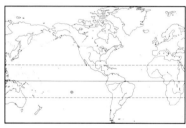

Very restricted island distribution and unique coloration make this species unlikely ever to be mistaken, but it is rarely seen and poorly known. See detailed distribution map on p. 338.

a Small, very dark brown wader with an unusually thin, pointed bill and greyish- or yellowish-brown legs. Has a faint creamy supercilium, and upperparts variably spotted and fringed dark buff and grey-brown. Breast, belly and undertail-coverts are usually entirely barred dark brown and pale cream.

b Minor colour variations may represent age, sex, seasonal or even inter-island variation.

c In flight, has very broad, rounded wings; looks very dark, with only a slightly paler patch on median coverts and a tiny pale line at tips of greater coverts. Tail pattern is especially variable.

d Underwings and axillaries mostly dull brownish-grey.

140c

140b

140a

139

140e

140d

139

140

140f

152a

152b

152c

152d

142 Lesser Yellowlegs *Tringa flavipes*

Text page 328

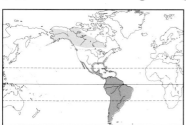

A slim, attenuated, medium-sized *Tringa* with a straight, slim bill; stands elegantly on long orange-yellow legs. Larger than Wood Sandpiper (145), and with longer legs and wings. Often confused with the larger and heavier 141.

a ADULT BREEDING: Strong brown streaks on head, neck and breast but relatively little streaking on flanks. Scapulars, tertials and mantle feathers mostly blackish with whitish spots and notches, often with some grey feathers mixed in. Coverts dull grey-brown.

b ADULT NON-BREEDING: Much greyer and paler; head, neck, mantle and scapulars grey or brownish-grey, often quite pale. Contrasting patch of pale notches on inner greater coverts and tertial Breast suffused brownish-grey; streaking is distinct only at close range.

c JUVENILE: As non-breeding, but upperparts brown with neat, bright buff spots and notches. Breast is washed brownish-grey and lightly streaked. Supercilium distinct, but shorter than on 145.

d In flight, shows neat square patch of white on uppertail-coverts and lower rump, darkish tail, dark outer wings and slightly paler coverts. Secondaries and inner primaries are dark, neatly and finely fringed whitish. Whole length of toes projects beyond tail-tip.

e Underwing-coverts and axillaries barred brown and white. Flight feathers dark.

141 Greater Yellowlegs *Tringa melanoleuca*

Text page 327

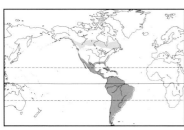

Compare relative size and bill shape very carefully with 142. Unlike Greenshank (139), appears spotted above, rather than streaked. Has long orange-yellow legs and a stout, almost straight or fractionally-uptilted bill.

a ADULT BREEDING: Head and neck very heavily streaked dark brown; on breast, flanks and even upper belly these streaks may form blackish spots and chevrons, more prominent than on 142. Scapular tertials and mantle very dark brown and boldly spotted white.

b ADULT NON-BREEDING: Upperparts grey-brown, finely spotted, notched and fringed white. Typically slightly darker than 142. Breast and flanks also show more dark streaking.

c JUVENILE: Brown upperparts are liberally spotted and notched bright buff. Distinct brown streaks on breast usually form a neat breast-band

d In flight, looks very similar to 142, but larger and more powerful. Outer wing is dark, but dark leading edge of wing contrasts slightly with paler coverts and secondaries. The latter are clearly notched whitish, unlike 142 or 139.

e Underwing-coverts and axillaries are barred brown and white. The darkest area is the outer primaries; the secondaries contrast less than on 142 owing to the pale notches.

142c

142b

142d

141e

142a

142e

141d

141c

142

141

141b

141a

141

142

143 Green Sandpiper *Tringa ochropus* Text page 329

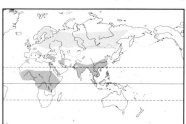

A blackish and white sandpiper found typically by inland fresh waters. Compare with 148 and 149 on Plate 60, as well as with 144 and 145.

a ADULT BREEDING: Larger and more rotund than 144 or 145. Quite distinct whitish spots above. Breast strongly streaked, more than in 144 or 145. White eye-ring and anterior supercilium contrast with dark lores and streaked crown. Legs dull greenish-grey.

b JUVENILE: Very dark greenish-brown above and on breast. Upperparts show poorly-contrasted buff spots. Breast finely streaked, with smudgy dark patches at sides. White eye-ring and supercilium in front of eye contrast strongly with crown and lores.

c ADULT NON-BREEDING: Much as juvenile, but spotting is smaller and less conspicuous, and breast is more strongly streaked.

d Broad, pointed dark wings contrast very strongly with white rump and uppertail. Toes project only very slightly.

e White underparts contrast brilliantly with almost black underwings and dark breast in flicking snipe-like flight.

144 Solitary Sandpiper *Tringa solitaria* Text page 329

The American counterpart of 143, but smaller, longer-winged and distinctively dark-rumped.

a ADULT BREEDING: Slim, long-winged and long-tailed. Upperparts dark, with pale spots; dull, finely-streaked head and breast show contrasting white eye-ring and darkish lores. Legs greenish.

b JUVENILE: Upperparts dark, with small pale spots. Breast washed dark, often forming lateral patches. Chin and foreneck narrowly whitish. Clear white eye-ring and supercilium in front of eye. Dark shoulder often evident. Primaries project farther beyond tertials and tail-tip than on 143.

c ADULT NON-BREEDING: As breeding, but head and neck washed dull grey and upperparts less spotted. White eye-ring clear. Upperparts duller, often fading to grey-brown.

d Upperparts all-dark, except for white bars on side of tail. Lesser coverts are marginally darker than medians. Fairly slim wings and longish tail; toes project slightly. All-dark from head to tip of tail.

e White belly contrasts with dark underwing; note strongly-barred tail. Outline differs noticeably from that of 143.

145 Wood Sandpiper *Tringa glareola* Text page 330

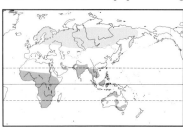

Longer-legged, paler and browner than 143 and 144, but occurs in similar habitats. Supercilium always relatively conspicuous. Compare also with 142 on Plate 57.

a ADULT BREEDING: Slim, quite elegant; quite long, yellowish legs. Upperparts boldly speckled. Conspicuous white supercilium; pale throat contrasts with streaked breast. Flanks slightly barred.

b JUVENILE: Upperparts warm brown, distinctly spotted buff. Clear supercilium. Breast washed buff, finely but clearly streaked brown. Buff fades to whitish in late autumn.

c ADULT NON-BREEDING: Upperparts brownish, less clearly spotted pale and dark, but supercilium distinct. Breast washed greyish, slightly streaked.

d Clear white patch on lower rump and uppertail is smaller and contrasts less with upperparts than on 143; body is slimmer and wings narrower. Note white shaft of outer primary. Feet project clearly beyond tail. Tail is fairly finely barred brown, contrasting with smallish white patch on rump.

e Longer and slimmer even than 144; white belly contrasts only slightly with whitish or greyish underwing.

143b

143a

143c

145a

144a

145c

144b

143d

145b

144c

144d

143

145

144

145e

143e

144e

145d

146 Willet *Catoptrophorus semipalmatus*

Text page 331

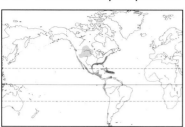

A tall, *Tringa*-like wader, with a straight, heavy, medium-length bi
and longish, thick, blue-grey legs. Pale eye-ring and short supercilia
give a spectacled appearance.

a ADULT BREEDING race *semipalmatus*, 'Eastern Willet': Neck, breas
and flanks heavily streaked and barred.

b ADULT BREEDING race *inornatus*, 'Western Willet': Much paler
underparts than in nominate race, with little flank barring. Fresh
plumage is depicted.

c ADULT BREEDING race *inornatus*: Individuals in worn plumage ma
appear relatively dark and brown, with obscure streaking on breas

d ADULT NON-BREEDING: Upperparts brownish-grey or grey,
feathers narrowly fringed white. Underparts white, with plain grey
wash on breast and flanks.

e JUVENILE: Like non-breeding, but slightly darker grey-brown;
upperpart feathers have darkish subterminal line, buff fringe and, or
tertials and rear scapulars, clear buff notches.

f A brilliant white wingbar crosses the entire wing, contrasting with
black on outer wing and grey coverts. The white rump contrasts onl
slightly with the grey-washed tail. Non-breeding adult is depicted.

g Underwing pattern of black/white/black contrasts with the pale body
White bar is much broader than on 124.

147 Terek Sandpiper *Xenus cinereus*

Text page 332

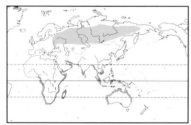

At all times of the year, the long, gently upcurving bill, short
yellow-orange legs and active feeding action are distinctive.

a ADULT BREEDING: Grey-brown above with a poorly-marked
anterior supercilium and clear blackish lines running along the
scapulars. Lateral grey breast-patches are finely streaked, and may be
lightly joined across centre of breast.

b ADULT NON-BREEDING: Plainer grey-brown than in breeding
plumage; blackish shoulder-patch becomes more obvious. Only a
trace of the black scapular lines.

c JUVENILE: As adult, but upperparts darker and browner; feathers
show indistinct dark subterminal bars and cinnamon-buff fringes.
Scapular lines present, but less prominent than on breeding adult.

d In flight, neat white trailing edge to secondaries contrasts with the
blackish bases to those feathers. Median coverts are paler than lessers
and greaters, forming a pale mid-wing panel. Back, rump and tail are
grey; whitish outer edge to tail is relatively inconspicuous.

e Note the dark bars on leading underwing-coverts and median unde
primary coverts. Wing-action is rather stiff.

146a

146b

146d

146c

146f

124

146g

146e

147d

147e

147c

147a

147b

148 Common Sandpiper *Actitis hypoleucos*   **Text page 333**

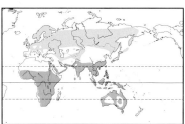

This and 149 are distinctive in their bobbing walk, flickering flight, and the white 'peak' in front of the wing. This species has browner upperparts than 149, duller and greyer legs, less contrast between base and tip of bill, and longer projection of tail beyond the folded primaries.

a ADULT BREEDING: Upperparts slightly glossy greenish-brown, faintly streaked darker and with dark bars on larger feathers. Sides o breast strongly infused brownish and streaked darker, almost forming a breast-band.

b ADULT NON-BREEDING: As breeding, but with plainer upperparts and smaller breast-patches, rarely joining in centre of breast. Juvenile Temminck's Stint (194) is shown for comparison.

c JUVENILE: Coverts brown, barred pale buff and dark as on 149, but unlike that species not contrasting strongly with the upperparts. Tertials have alternate pale and dark notches all along the outer webs Note relative lengths of wing and tail.

d JUVENILE: Some juveniles have yellowish legs like those of 149.

e In flight, shows a strong white wingbar from middle primaries to innermost secondaries, where quite prominent. Outer tail feathers tend to be whiter than on 149, but patterns are variable.

f Underwing shows two prominent dark bars, rather variable in pattern. Inner secondaries much whiter than on 149.

149 Spotted Sandpiper *Actitis macularia*   **Text page 334**

See 148 for shared features. This species differs at all times in smalle size, greyer upperparts, yellowish legs, bill with contrasting pale base and dark tip, wing pattern, and tail extending only a short distance beyond primaries.

a ADULT BREEDING: Upperparts greeny-brown, with distinct dark barring. Bill distinctly orange or pinkish at base, with black tip. Legs often pinkish. Unique spotted underparts. Male is depicted; spotting variable, but females tend to have larger and blacker spots.

b ADULT NON-BREEDING: Plainer upperparts. Underparts clean white, without spotting; white 'peak' between small lateral breast-patches and wing. Legs yellowish.

c JUVENILE: Mantle and scapulars strongly washed grey, with very fine buff fringes. Wing-coverts strikingly barred dark brown and pale buff, contrasting clearly with plainer scapulars and tertials. Pale and dark notches on tertials are normally absent or restricted to a small area near the tip; very rarely, however, they are as extensive as on 148. Note relative lengths of wing and tail.

d JUVENILE: Plainer tertials and more strongly-barred coverts are best distinctions from 148 at long range.

e In flight, wing shape and flight action are similar to 148, but the white wingbar is shorter and narrower, shows mainly in middle of wing (almost absent on inner secondaries). White in tail averages less.

f Underwing has longer trailing dark bar, crossing all of inner secondaries. Variable dark bars on underwing-coverts.

148e

149e

148

148

149

149

148

148f

149

149f

194

148

149

148d

149d

148b

149b

148a

149a

148c

149c

151 Wandering Tattler *Heteroscelus incanus*   Text page 336

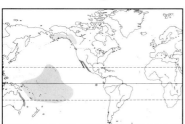

Compared with 150, this species is plainer and a shade darker above more barred below (breeding plumage only), has longer wings extending well beyond the tail, and is much more associated with rocky or coral coasts. Longer nasal groove and reticulated rear of tarsus are diagnostic when visible. Call is a rippling trill.

a ADULT BREEDING: In full plumage, all underparts (except for tiny area on belly) are heavily barred with dark grey—beware moulting birds, which may show larger unbarred belly-patch. Barred undertail-coverts are diagnostic. Uppertail and tail plain grey.

b ADULT NON-BREEDING: Plain, dark slate-grey upperparts, neck, breast and flanks. Supercilium obvious only in front of eye. Bill and legs are longer than in other rock-haunting sandpipers.

c JUVENILE: Upperparts rather plain, with indistinct pale fringes to scapulars, tertials and coverts. Uppertail-coverts and tail feathers lack distinct pale fringes and notches. Supercilium is slightly less prominent than on 150, mostly in front of eye.

d In flight, upperparts appear uniform dark slate-grey. Fractionally longer-winged and darker than 150.

e Underwing and axillaries very dark grey, contrasting with white belly in non-breeding plumage.

f In closest views, nasal groove can be seen to extend almost three-quarters of the way to the bill-tip. Extent of yellow on bill-base variable in both species.

150 Grey-tailed Tattler *Heteroscelus brevipes*   Text page 335

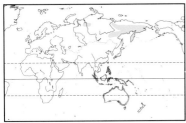

Very similar to 151 and often very difficult to separate. This species is fractionally paler and shorter-winged, and occurs more often on mudflats. Nasal groove is shorter; rear of tarsus scutellated. Call is a disyllabic upslurred whistle.

a ADULT BREEDING: Underparts are lightly streaked and barred with grey only on neck, breast and flanks; belly is always extensively white. Undertail-coverts show at most a few tiny markings. Uppertail-coverts in all plumages are finely fringed white, but this is rarely visible in field conditions.

b ADULT NON-BREEDING: Loses barring on underparts; neck, breast and flanks broadly suffused slate-grey. Supercilium typically quite long and prominent, often joining diffusely above the bill; lores more contrastingly dark.

c JUVENILE: Like non-breeding adult, but upperparts show small, neat whitish-buff spotting; edges of tail feathers are clearly notched whitish.

d In flight, upperparts lack white. Compared with 151, averages shorter-winged and may appear paler, especially on uppertail-coverts.

e Underwing-coverts and axillaries dark slate-grey, always contrasting with white belly and undertail.

f In closest views, it can be seen that nasal groove ends just over half-way to bill-tip.

151a

151b

150a

150b

150d

151d

150e

151e

150c

151f

150f

151c

154 Ruddy Turnstone *Arenaria interpres*　　　　Text page 339

A distinctive, chunky wader, found most often on rocky coasts. Dullest individuals may recall 155, but always show brighter legs and at least some white on chin and throat.

a ADULT MALE BREEDING: Sharply-patterned black and white on head and breast. Scapulars show extensive chestnut. Underparts are clean white from lower breast to undertail.

b ADULT FEMALE BREEDING: Head duller, typically with less white and more streaking on crown.

c ADULT NON-BREEDING: Much duller than in breeding plumage, lacking all chestnut on upperparts. Head mostly dark, but with buffish-white chin. Breast mostly dark grey-brown, but enclosing irregular brownish-white patches on sides and with white 'peak' extending centrally from lower breast towards throat.

d JUVENILE: Pale patches on head are more extensive than on non-breeding adult. Upperparts are more brownish, with neat buff or buffish-white fringes.

e In flight, strikingly patterned with dark and white on wings, back, rump and tail. Juvenile is depicted, but pattern is similar in all plumages. Paler head and upperparts, and slightly narrower wing are best distinctions from 155.

f Underwing-coverts, axillaries and much of body are noticeably white, contrasting strongly with dark breast-band and tail-band.

155 Black Turnstone *Arenaria melanocephala*　　　　Text page 340

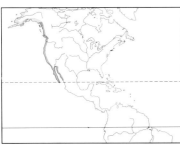

Similar to cosmopolitan 154, but with limited range on North American Pacific rocky coasts. Always looks darker and a little bulkier than 154, with dark chin and more solidly dark breast; legs are darker and more greyish. Darker also than 186, subtly different shape.

a ADULT BREEDING: Stunningly pied, with white spot at base of bill (larger on male) and fine white spots and streaks on breast, crown and greater coverts.

b ADULT NON-BREEDING: Upperparts and breast solidly dark slaty-grey, except for narrow white fringes to scapulars and coverts.

c JUVENILE: Like non-breeding adult, but browner, with neat buff or buffish-white fringes to scapulars, tertials and wing-coverts.

d In flight, shows a little less white than 154 on rump and on inner coverts, but white wingbar is slightly more prominent. Head, neck and breast look evenly all-dark. Wings slightly broader than on 154.

e Underwing-coverts, axillaries, and belly to undertail are clean white, sometimes with a little spotting on flanks. Head and breast are contrastingly dark.

186 Surfbird *Aphriza virgata*　　　　Text page 363

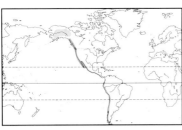

An unusual calidrid-like wader which is often found with turnstones or Rock Sandpiper (203) on rocky coasts. Has a short, blunt-tipped bill, with yellow on base of lower mandible, and yellowish legs.

a ADULT BREEDING: Strongly-streaked head, neck and upper breast. Lower breast and flanks boldly marked with brown chevrons. Very prominent, large, bright golden-buff ovals on larger scapulars.

b ADULT NON-BREEDING: Paler than 155, more like 203 in colour of upperparts and bare parts. Dull slate-grey above and on breast; flanks always show brownish-grey spots and 'V's.

c JUVENILE: As non-breeding adult, but upperparts slightly browner, most feathers fringed buff, with dark submarginal line. Breast mottled brown.

d In flight, white uppertail and tail-base contrast with broad black tail-band; long, prominent white wingbar.

e Underwing is mainly white, but with some greyish on primary coverts and on leading edge.

154b

154d

154a

154c

154f

154e

186d

155e

155c

155d

186b

186e

155b

186c

186a

155a

157 Red-necked Phalarope *Phalaropus lobatus*   Text page 341

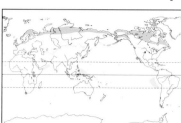

The smallest phalarope, always with a dark rump and needle-fine bill
This species and 158 are normally seen swimming.
a ADULT FEMALE BREEDING: Rich chestnut-red on neck. Sharp whit
  spot above eye. Scapulars fringed rufous-buff.
b ADULT MALE BREEDING: Duller than female, often with trace of
  pale supercilium.
c ADULT NON-BREEDING: White and grey with dark eye-patch
  ('phalarope-mark'). White fringes and dark feather centres on
  upperparts distinguish from 158.
d JUVENILE: Upperparts dark brown, fringed bright golden-buff; neck
  and breast suffused pink-buff. Forehead is initially dark.
e MOULTING JUVENILE: Most migrant juveniles have already
  moulted the head and neck feathers.
f In flight, has white wingbar and sides to rump like 158, but flies with a
  faster, more flicking and twisting action. Juvenile is depicted.
g MOULTING ADULT: Note lobed toes (but feet are not normally
  visible in flight).
h Underwing shows dusky markings on primary coverts and across
  median coverts.

158 Grey Phalarope *Phalaropus fulicarius*   Text page 342

Always separable from 157 by larger size and heavier, broader bill
a ADULT FEMALE BREEDING: Very striking white face and
  chestnut-red underparts. Upperparts appear streaked. Bill yellow
  with black tip.
b ADULT MALE BREEDING: Duller than female, with streaking on
  crown, buff suffusion to face, and often extensive white on belly.
c ADULT NON-BREEDING: Variable dark crown-patch and blackish
  eye-patch. Upperparts entirely pearly-grey with fine white fringes to
  feathers. Bill sometimes all-black.
d JUVENILE: Upperparts dark brown with broad brown-buff fringes,
  and initially with deep pink-buff suffusion over neck and breast.
e MOULTING JUVENILE: Most migrant juveniles have already
  moulted the head and neck feathers, and show much grey admixed in
  upperparts.
f In flight, bulkier and proportionately larger-winged than 157, but
  with similar white sides to rump and bright white wingbar. Wingbeats
  are slower.
g Underwing is white, contrasting strongly with belly on breeding
  female.

156 Wilson's Phalarope *Phalaropus tricolor*   Text page 340

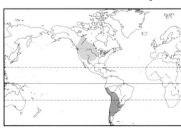

Longer-legged, longer-billed and more terrestrial than other
phalaropes, sometimes recalling a *Tringa* sandpiper. Unusual
pot-bellied appearance helps to distinguish from 142 and 208.
a ADULT FEMALE BREEDING: Pearly-grey, black and chestnut on
  neck and upperparts. Legs black.
b ADULT MALE BREEDING: Dark brown and dull orange-brown
  replace bright colours of female.
c ADULT NON-BREEDING: Ash-grey above and white below, with
  grey 'phalarope-mark'. Legs yellow.
d JUVENILE: Dark brown above, with broad buff fringes. Sides of breast
  washed buff. Legs pinkish-yellow.
e MOULTING JUVENILE: By Aug, most have already moulted head
  and most of upperpart feathers. Legs yellow.
f In flight, shows square white patch on rump and uppertail and dark,
  almost uniform wings. Toes project beyond tail-tip. White
  rump-patch is slightly obscured in breeding plumage.
g Axillaries and underwing-coverts are white.

159 Eurasian Woodcock *Scolopax rusticola*   Text page 343

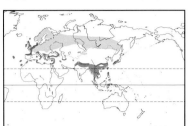

A chunky, heavy woodland wader with a fairly long, straight bill. Compare with 164, and also with other woodcocks on Plate 65. Transverse bars on crown and nape and silvery tail spots are common to all six species.

a ADULT: Brown, black, buff and reddish camouflaged plumage; all underparts lightly barred brown. Some show greyish lines at edges of mantle, like 164 (see Plate 65). No bare skin around eye: compare Amami Woodcock (160). On adults, the terminal bar on each primary covert is pale buff, narrower and also paler than the other pale markings on the feather.

b ADULT: Undersides of tail feathers are tipped bright silvery-white.

c In flight, wings appear broad but are longer and more pointed than those of other woodcocks. When flushed, twists rapidly away through trees. On juvenile (depicted), terminal bar on each primary covert is of similar width and colour to the other pale markings on the feather. Tail spots are slightly greyer than on adult.

d Roding (display) flight is with flicking wings low over treetops; individual flights may cover several kilometres. Bill points steeply downwards, but is raised when bird is calling. Whole underwing is barred, like rest of underparts.

e Short-billed individuals are being recorded with increasing frequency in W Europe (see text).

164 American Woodcock *Scolopax minor*   Text page 346

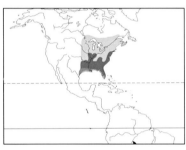

Fairly similar in proportions and in colours to 159, which occurs rarely in North America, but differs in being much smaller and in having orange-buff underparts which lack obvious barring. Grey on edges of mantle and scapulars is more prominent. Uniquely, has outer 3 primaries greatly reduced in length and width.

a ADULT: A rather small woodcock, with plain orange-buff underparts. Forehead and cheeks may also show some orange-buff. Neat, silver-grey 'V' on edges of mantle, and some grey also on outer scapulars. Juvenile is virtually identical.

b Undersides of tail feathers are tipped bright silvery-white.

c In flight, has broad, almost square-ended wings: small outer primaries cause a whistling or twittering noise, but are rarely visible in field conditions. Primaries and outer secondaries lack barring.

d Lesser and median underwing-coverts are plain orange-buff.

e MALE in display: At display stations, adopts peculiar upright posture and utters 'peent' calls. Also has circling flight high over display stations.

159d

159c

159a

159

159e

164a

159b

164e

164b

164d

164c

160 Amami Woodcock *Scolopax mira*

Text page 344

Only on one or two islands in Ryukyu group, south of Japan. Found i both evergreen forest and adjacent fields. Some Eurasian Woodcoc (159) winter on these islands, and must be distinguished carefully.

a Rather similar to 159, but differs in showing an area of pinkish ski around the eye. Forehead is flatter, forming a shallower angle with th bill. Middle secondaries are finely marbled as well as notched. Silve spots underneath tail are smaller and duller.

b In flight, broader-winged and shorter-tailed than 159. Uppertail-coverts pale sandy-rufous, contrasting more with back an tail than on 159.

c Very like 159 from below, except for broader-winged and shorter-tailed shape.

161 Dusky Woodcock *Scolopax saturata*

Text page 344

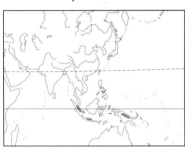

A small, dark woodcock with two well-separated races, found only i remnants of montane primary rainforest.

a Race *saturata* (Sumatra and Java): Chin buffish, supercilium brown-chestnut. Small white area on upper belly contrasts with brown-washed breast and rear belly; brown underpart barring is strong, but not conspicuous.

b Race *rosenbergii* (New Guinea): Chin and cheeks whitish; usually white spot above lores. Belly all whitish, becoming buffish toward rear, with strongly contrasting brown barring.

c In flight, has very dark upperparts and rather rounded wings.

d From below, race *saturata* looks very dark, with small whitish patch on upper belly.

e From below, race *rosenbergii* shows traces of whitish across whol belly.

162 Celebes Woodcock *Scolopax celebensis*

Text page 345

A large woodcock similar to Eurasian (159), but with longer bill an legs. Recorded only from montane forests on Sulawesi.

a Blackish upperparts with fairly small reddish-brown spots. Face an underparts ochre-buff with very few dark bars, except on flanks.

b In flight, looks large and dark with broad rounded wings. All fligh feathers are notched boldly with mid-buff.

c From below, the underwing-coverts and axillaries, which are black-brown with ochre-buff barring, contrast with plainer belly.

163 Obi Woodcock *Scolopax rochussenii*

Text page 345

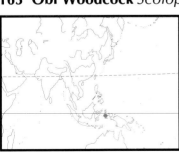

Known from only five specimens, the last obtained in 1902.

a A bulky woodcock with a deep bill. Upperparts show bold ochre-bu spots. Underparts bright ochre-buff; as on 162, only flanks are prominently barred.

b In flight, dark background to body and wings contrasts with bright buff spotting and notching. Wings are very broad and rounded.

c Underwing-coverts and axillaries are blackish-brown, barred ochre-buff, contrasting with unbarred belly. Buff notching on fligh feathers may be evident from below.

159

160

160a

161a

161d

161b

161

161e

162a

160c

162c

163b

163a

163c

162b

161c

160b

159

165 New Zealand Snipe *Coenocorypha aucklandica*   Text page 347

A small, 'neckless' snipe with a longish, slightly drooping bill and short legs, restricted to a few remote islands off New Zealand. All populations are severely threatened.

a ADULT race *aucklandica* (Auckland Is.): Relatively large and pale compared with other races, with large plain buff belly; flanks barred brown.

b ADULT race *meinertzhagenae* (Antipodes Is.): Upperparts rather dark. Ground colour of belly buff-yellow.

c ADULT race *huegeli* (Snares Is.): Underparts diffusely barred all over

d JUVENILE: Very like adult in all races. In *huegeli*, however, juvenile i described as greyer above and with greyish, not brown, base to the bill.

e Short, rounded wings and whirring flight are distinctive. Rarely flie during the day.

166 Chatham Islands Snipe *Coenocorypha pusilla*   Text page 348

Like 165, but even smaller and shorter-billed. Underparts mostly pale buff. Confined to Chatham Is.

a ADULT: Upperparts distinctly variegated in pattern. Base of bill brown; legs yellowish. Male is smaller and darker than female, and more brightly patterned above.

b JUVENILE: Upperpart markings are less well defined. Base of bill grey; legs duller than on adult.

c In flight, has short rounded wings and whirring wingbeats.

169 Wood Snipe *Gallinago nemoricola*   Text page 350

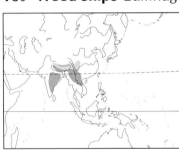

A heavy, dark snipe with broad, rather rounded wings. Recalls Eurasian Woodcock (159) in habitat choice and in pattern of underparts. Head and mantle patterns are typically snipe-like. Rarely seen except when flushed.

a ADULT: Upperparts blackish with rather dull buff-grey fringes. Coverts darkish brown, spotted and barred dull buff-grey. Crown-stripe is rather narrow, and belly completely barred.

b JUVENILE: Very like adult, but pale fringes to coverts and scapular tend to be narrower, giving a more scaly appearance.

c ADULT: In flight, broad, rounded wings and wavering flight are reminiscent of 159. Narrow, obscure, greyish trailing edge to secondaries.

d ADULT: Some individuals show rather more rufous uppertail-coverts. Very little white is visible in the spread tail.

e JUVENILE: Scapulars and coverts are more scaly, but difference is no likely to be discernible in flight.

f From below, shows whitish background to central belly, covered completely by heavy barring. Underwing looks all-dark.

165a

165b

165e

166a

165c

166b

165d

166c

169b

169a

169c

169d

169f

169e

170 Pintail Snipe *Gallinago stenura*

Text page 350

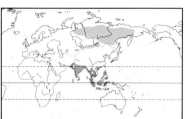

A medium-sized, short-tailed, relatively short-billed snipe, very similar to Swinhoe's (171). Very distinctive pin-shaped tail feathers rarely visible in field conditions. Face pattern differs from that of 171 in that pale supercilium is always broader than dark eye-stripe at base of bill.

a ADULT: Differs from 171 in that, on most individuals, tertials almost cover the primaries and tail only just extends beyond folded wings. Wing-coverts show brown-buff spots at tip. Prominent mantle lines.

b ADULT: Colours and patterns vary a little between individuals.

c JUVENILE: Very like adult, but mantle and scapulars show more vermiculations and less distinct pale edgings, and coverts are narrowly fringed pale buff.

d ADULT: In flight, indistinct greyish line on trailing edge of wing is immediate distinction from 175. Tail noticeably short, with toes protruding farther than in similar species.

e JUVENILE: Markings on upperparts finer than on adult. Spread tail shows less white than on 175.

f Underwing-coverts and axillaries dark, with broad brown and narrow white bars. Flanks heavily barred brown. Slightly smaller white central belly-patch than on 175.

175 Common Snipe *Gallinago gallinago*

Text page 354

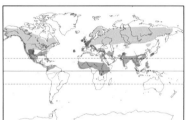

A rather pale snipe with a large white belly and a prominent white trailing edge to the wing. Outer tail feathers relatively broad.

a ADULT: Longish tail extends obviously beyond primary tips. Supercilium narrow at base of bill. Adult typically has prominent mantle lines, and wing-coverts with dull buff spots at tip.

b ADULT race *faeroeensis* (Iceland, Faeroes, Shetland, Orkney): Differ marginally from the two widespread races in more rufous plumage and finer barring on mantle.

c JUVENILE: Very like adult; coverts more neatly fringed pale buff.

d In flight, race *gallinago* (Eurasia) shows broad white trailing edge to inner wing; some white on corners of tail. Typically seven pairs of tail feathers.

e Race *delicata* (North America): Slightly narrower (but still prominent white trailing edge; typically eight pairs of tail feathers.

f Race *gallinago*: Underwing-coverts variable in pattern, but usually extensively white in central band. Narrow brown barring on axillaries.

g Race *delicata*: Underwing-coverts darker than on most *gallinago*. Brown bars on axillaries slightly broader than the white ones.

182 Jack Snipe *Lymnocryptes minimus*

Text page 359

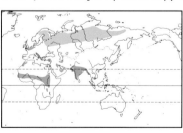

The smallest and narrowest-winged of the snipes. Uniquely among snipes, crown lacks central stripe, dark areas of upperparts are glossed green and purple, and tail is wedge-shaped.

a Small and short-billed compared with other snipes. Double supercilium encloses short dark line above eye. Bobs constantly while feeding. When disturbed, freezes and relies on near-perfect camouflage.

b Rarely seen in flight unless in display or flushed from underfoot. Wings show narrow white trailing edge like 175, but are narrower; flight is weaker and slower, rarely 'towering'. Tail all-dark.

c Underwing-coverts and axillaries are mostly dull greyish-white, with a little brown streaking.

167 Solitary Snipe *Gallinago solitaria*

Text page 348

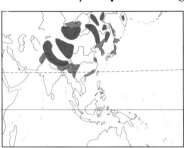

A large snipe rarely seen away from high mountains. Whitish edges to mantle and scapulars and gingery tone to breast and upperparts are distinctive.

a Gingery-brown of breast is not matched by any other snipe. Face contrastingly whitish. Whitish lines at edges of mantle and scapulars. Wings, tertials and tail all long.

b In flight, looks relatively large, slow and heavy. Clear pale panel across median coverts. Very narrow whitish trailing edge not obvious. Whitish face and chestnut on tail are often prominent.

c Spread tail is strongly graduated.

d Underwing and axillaries are barred roughly equally with brown and white. Flanks are heavily barred brown, but central belly is unbarred.

168 Japanese Snipe *Gallinago hardwickii*

Text page 349

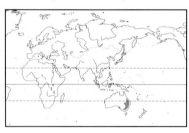

A large, strongly migratory snipe with relatively long wings and tail. Very similar to 171; both share face pattern with Pintail Snipe (170), which see.

a ADULT: Longish tail projects noticeably beyond folded wings; primaries are typically entirely covered by tertials. On adult, coverts have buff-brown spots at tip.

b JUVENILE: Very like adult, but coverts have more distinct pale buff fringes. Primaries show clearer and neater white fringes.

c In flight, like 171 but a little larger and relatively longer-winged. There is a clear, pale central wing-panel; narrow greyish trailing edge to wing is not conspicuous; some clear buffish is sometimes visible on tail-coverts on landing. Shaft of outer primary is whiter distally than on 171. Tail is relatively long and full, with slightly more white in outer feathers than on 171.

d Underwing-coverts and axillaries have brown bars just wider than white ones. Unbarred area of belly is larger than on 167.

171 Swinhoe's Snipe *Gallinago megala*

Text page 351

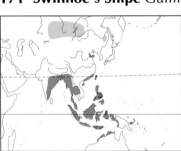

A medium-sized snipe, intermediate between 168 and Pintail Snipe (170) in size and tail structure. Like those species, distinguishable from Common Snipe (175) by broad supercilium, darker underwing and indistinct pale trailing edge to wing.

a ADULT: Tail extends obviously beyond folded wing-tips (unlike 170), and primaries project well beyond tertials (unlike typical 168). On adult, coverts have paired, dull buff spots at tip.

b JUVENILE: Very like adult, but wing-coverts and tertials are narrowly fringed whitish-buff.

c In flight, the narrow greyish trailing edge to wing is not conspicuous. Shaft of outer primary browner than on 168. Less white shows at corners of tail than on 168. Toes project less beyond tail-tip than on 170, and tail looks longer and fuller.

d Underwing and axillaries are dull brown, as on 168 and 170. Belly white, but flanks are barred dark brown.

173 Madagascar Snipe *Gallinago macrodactyla*   Text page 352

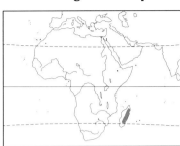

A rather large, heavy, long-billed snipe with a small and isolated range. Has a narrow greyish trailing edge to wing.

a ADULT: Wing-coverts have cold olive-brown spots at tip. Female ha on average longer bill than male. Face pattern is like that of Commor Snipe (175).

b JUVENILE: Wing-coverts show warm olive-buff fringes. Individual depicted still shows rufous down on head and neck.

c In flight, the narrow pale trailing edge to the wing is barely detectabl Looks large, heavy, and relatively slow.

d Tail has 16 feathers. Outer feathers show some white.

e From below, shows flank barring extending farther onto belly than o 175; underwing, with brown bars wider than white ones, looks darkish.

172 African Snipe *Gallinago nigripennis*   Text page 352

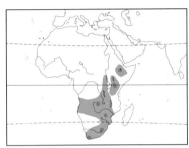

Very like Common Snipe (175), but with longer bill on average an slightly darker upperparts. Tail shows more white in flight.

a ADULT: Scapulars and mantle fairly dark, with many rufous markings. Wing-coverts have olive-buff spots at tip. White belly contrasts strongly with dark upperparts.

b JUVENILE: Very like adult, but wing-coverts are more narrowly fringed with whitish-buff.

c In flight, shows fairly narrow but clear white trailing edge to wing and extensive unbarred white at corners of tail. Wings look dark and are broader and more rounded than on 175. Flight action more fluttery

d Tail has 16 feathers. Outers are narrower than on 175 and are most unbarred white, with a few diffuse brown marks.

e Underwing and axillaries are variable in pattern. Depicted examp shows white central bar on coverts, but on other individuals covert are completely barred with brown. Wing is rather broader than or 175.

174 Great Snipe *Gallinago media*   Text page 353

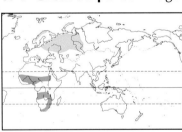

A bulky, medium-sized snipe with distinctive white spots on wing-coverts, much white in the tail and a heavily-barred belly. Ofte found in fairly dry habitats.

a ADULT: White spots on wing-coverts are very prominent, forming rows across closed wing. Only a little larger than Common Snipe (175), but clearly more bulky and relatively shorter-billed. Flanks an most of belly are strongly barred. Ridge of upper mandible often shows slight downward angle about half-way towards tip.

b JUVENILE: White tips to wing-coverts narrower and less clear.

c ADULT: In flight, shows characteristic blackish panel across greate coverts and greater primary coverts, bordered in front and behind with clear white bands. Narrow white trailing edge to wing. On landing, brilliant white outer tail feathers are prominent. Relativel slow, heavy and level flight.

d JUVENILE: As adult, but white bands are less prominent and some brown bars partly obscure the white tail-corners.

e ADULT: Outermost tail feather shows at least 15 mm of clear white a tip, and base colour to outer three pairs is very white.

f JUVENILE: Light brown barring extends to within 10 mm of tip on both webs of outermost feather.

g Only a small unbarred area on central belly; all of flanks and most belly heavily barred brown. Underwing rather dark. Compare Woo Snipe (169).

176 Magellan Snipe *Gallinago paraguaiae*

Text page 355

The only small snipe in South America, apart from migrant Commo
Snipe (175) in the north. There are three races, of which *andina* can l
distinguished in the field.

a ADULT nominate race (lowlands, N Argentina northwards):
Generally cold brown in colour, with prominent dark breast
streaking. Primaries are relatively short and are typically completel
hidden by tertials. Juvenile is very similar (see text).

b Race *andina* (puna zone, S Peru to N Chile and NW Argentina):
Smaller and shorter-legged. Legs are dull yellow.

c Race *magellanica* (central Chile and central Argentina southwards
Longer-winged than other races. Coloration is generally warmer an
more buff than on nominate race.

d In flight, shows obvious white on trailing edge of wing, like 175. I
nominate race (depicted), wings look shorter and broader than on
175.

e Race *andina* looks small and short-winged in flight. Toes may not
project beyond tail-tip. Outermost primary is extensively white on
outer web.

f Underwing of northern race *paraguaiae* is typically a little paler tha
on most migrant 175.

g Underwing of puna race *andina* often shows extensive unmarked
white.

177 Noble Snipe *Gallinago nobilis*

Text page 356

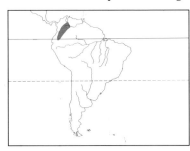

A bulky snipe of montane marshlands, mainly above 2000 m.
Plumage recalls 176, but bulk and wing shape approach those of
Andean (180).

a ADULT: Larger than 176 and usually darker, with a
disproportionately long, typically two-toned bill.

b In flight, wings lack obvious pale trailing edge and are relatively muc
broader than on 176.

c Axillaries and underwing-coverts are relatively dark. Extensive whi
belly and projecting toes are simple distinctions from 180.

d Tail is like that of 176, but lacks white on tail-corners of northern rac
of that species. Rump and uppertail are rather rufous.

178 Giant Snipe *Gallinago undulata*

Text page 356

Conspicuously larger than all other snipes. A lowland species foun
in tall, dense herbage, not always near water.

a ADULT: Very large, with bold blackish markings. Long bill is deep a
base and reaches high on forehead, giving a distinctive, flat-heade
profile. Juvenile is not known to differ. Larger race *gigantea* (souther
is depicted.

b Nominate race (Colombia to N Brazil) averages about 7% shorter
than southern race in wing and tarsus, and 16% shorter in bill
measurement. Plumage tends to be less boldly marked.

c In flight, shows broad, rounded wings like Eurasian Woodcock (159
Barred flight feathers are unique among snipes.

d Axillaries and underwing-coverts are evenly barred brown and whit
Central belly is unbarred white.

e Uppertail-coverts are almost unmarked tawny-chestnut. Tail is
obscurely barred, and shows no white on outer feathers.

179 Cordilleran Snipe *Gallinago stricklandii*

Text page 357

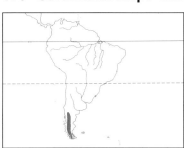

This species and its close relatives 180 and 181 differ most obviously from other South American snipes in lacking a clear white belly-patch and clear pale stripes on head and upperparts.

a ADULT: Darker and more bulky than Magellan Snipe (176), and much less clearly patterned. Differs from 180 in darker and warmer colours and smaller unmarked throat-patch; breast and flanks show obscure chevrons, and central belly is unbarred pale buff. Juvenile is indistinguishable in the field.

b In flight, looks obviously larger than 176, and broader, more rounded wings lack a white trailing edge.

c Underwing is evenly barred brown and pale buffish-brown.

d Tail of 14 feathers lacks chestnut on central feathers and white on outers.

180 Andean Snipe *Gallinago jamesoni*

Text page 358

A heavy, woodcock-like snipe, very like 179 but widely separated in range. Strictly montane, usually in grassy marshlands near the tree-line.

a ADULT: Like 179, but unbarred throat-patch is larger and central breast, whole belly and flanks are evenly barred brown on an almost whitish background. General coloration is colder brown. Juvenile is very similar, but with wing-coverts warmer buff and less clearly barred.

b In flight, superficially resembles Noble Snipe (177) but is shorter-billed, lacks pale lines on upperparts and rufous on tail, and shows almost no projection of toes beyond tail. 'Arm' is relatively longer than on 179. Juvenile is depicted.

c Underwing is mainly brown, with narrow whitish-buff barring. Fine barring on central belly may be difficult to see.

d Tail resembles that of 179.

181 Imperial Snipe *Gallinago imperialis*

Text page 358

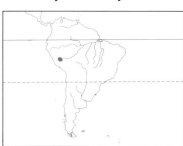

A rare snipe, thought extinct for a hundred years but recently rediscovered in Peru. It occurs above 3000 m, around the tree-line in damp, forested country, and draws attention by its loud calls.

a ADULT: Plumage is dark and richly rufous, except for lower belly, flanks and undertail which are strongly banded dark brown on a whitish background. Breast is obscurely mottled dark chestnut and blackish-brown. Juvenile is unknown.

b In flight, wings are short, very broad, and strongly rounded, and tail looks short. Upperparts all-dark.

c From below, banded belly contrasts with dark rufous breast and mainly-blackish underwing.

d Long uppertail-coverts (lifted aside) reach almost to tail-tip. There are only 12 tail feathers; all except central pair are plain brownish.

179d

179a

179b

179c

180c

180b

180a

180d

181

179

180

177

181b

181c

181a

181d

183 Short-billed Dowitcher *Limnodromus griseus*   Text page 360

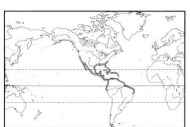

Dowitchers are typified by their snipe-like bill and feeding action and their rather godwit-like plumages. The American species differ obviously from each other in juvenile plumage, but less so when adult. Short-billed prefers intertidal habitats in winter; its usual call is a mellow 'tu-tu-tu'.

a ADULT BREEDING nominate race (E Canada): Belly remains white in centre, even in full plumage; undertail white or pale rufous. Breast and undertail are densely spotted or barred brown, and flanks barred often heavily. Narrow rufous edges above.

b ADULT BREEDING race *hendersoni* (central): Typically entirely rufous below, with brown markings confined largely to spotting on undertail and sides of breast. Relatively broad rufous edges above.

c ADULT BREEDING race *caurinus* (S Alaska): Underparts usually as nominate, but rather variable. Upperparts show narrow rufous edges and whitish tips like those of 184.

d ADULT NON-BREEDING: Rather plain greyish above and on breast. Pale supercilium contrasts with narrow dark eye-stripe. Most differ from 184 in that grey breaks into fine streaks or speckles on lower breast.

e JUVENILE: Very bright. Cap and upperparts are broadly edged chestnut-buff; larger feathers also show conspicuous submarginal markings, and tertials are irregularly barred or striped. Face and foreneck are washed buff, like breast.

f In flight, shows clear white on back, like Spotted Redshank (136), and a whitish trailing edge to the wing. Juvenile is depicted.

g Underwing-coverts and axillaries show light brown barring.

h Tail pattern is more variable than on 184, but juvenile and breeding adult typically show barred pattern, with white bars as broad as or broader than dark ones.

i Tail may lack barring, as on this non-breeding adult.

184 Long-billed Dowitcher *Limnodromus scolopaceus*   Text page 361

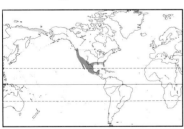

Separable from 183 on plumage characters, with care. Some are obviously longer-billed. Prefers fresh or brackish waters in winter; usual call is a high, thin 'keek'. Compare also with Asiatic Dowitcher (185).

a ADULT BREEDING: Underparts entirely red in full plumage, deeper in shade than on 183. Foreneck is spotted brown, breast spotted and barred, and flanks narrowly barred, but belly is unmarked. Upperparts show narrow rufous edges and whitish tips.

b ADULT NON-BREEDING: As 183, but breast is a little darker and more evenly greyish, lacking speckles along lower edge.

c JUVENILE: Duller than juvenile of 183. Many show contrast between grey head and neck and buff-washed breast. Upperparts show narrow, irregular chestnut edges, and typically no internal markings to the feathers. Tertials plain or with small internal markings near tip; on a tiny fraction of individuals, pattern may approach that of 183.

d In flight, shows white on back and secondaries like 183. Juvenile is depicted.

e Underwing is lightly barred, as on 183.

f Tail is always barred, with dark bars broader than, and often twice as broad as, white ones. Beware confusing tail-coverts with tail feathers. Rufous typically replaces white on tail in breeding plumage.

183a

183c

183

183b

184

184a

183d

183e

184b

183

183f

184c

184

183g

184d

184

184e

183i

183h

184f

187 Red Knot *Calidris canutus* Text page 363

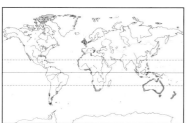

The second-largest calidrid. Always looks heavy, and rounded in shape, with relatively short, almost straight bill and rather short greenish legs. Breeding plumage suggests Curlew Sandpiper (205), while non-breeding plumage resembles that of 188. Strongly coastal

a ADULT MALE BREEDING race *canutus* (central Siberia): Extensivel deep chestnut below, with dark chestnut fringes on upperparts. Averages relatively long-billed. Females of all races show less evenly-coloured underparts and more extensive white on rear belly they average larger than males.

b ADULT MALE BREEDING race *rogersi* (E Siberia): Colours paler thar on nominate race. White typically more extensive on rear belly.

c ADULT MALE BREEDING race *rufa* (W Nearctic): This race shows palest chestnut underparts and most extensive white on rear belly.

d ADULT MALE BREEDING race *islandica* (NE Canada, Greenland): Underparts are as on *rogersi*, but upperparts show many yellowish fringes. Averages shorter-billed than *canutus*.

e POST-BREEDING ADULT: Mantle and scapulars become extensively blackish through wear, and races are no longer separable Head moults first into non-breeding plumage.

f ADULT NON-BREEDING: Rather plain grey above, with narrow whitish fringes to larger feathers. Underparts lightly marked and suffused with grey. Wings and tail fall roughly level.

g JUVENILE: Like non-breeding adult, but breast is washed pale buffish and upperparts are suffused brownish-buff. Coverts and scapulars show fine buff fringes and finely-marked dark submarginal lines, giving a scaly appearance. Legs more yellowish-green than on adult

h In flight, shows clear but narrow white wingbar. Lower rump and uppertail are whitish, with many grey bars, and look plain pale grey a a distance. Rump-patch is most heavily obscured in breeding plumage.

i Underwing-coverts and axillaries are mostly greyish or greyish-white

188 Great Knot *Calidris tenuirostris* Text page 364

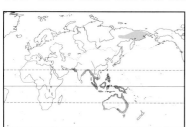

The largest calidrid. Breast is black-spotted in breeding plumage, never red as on 187. In other plumages, best distinctions are large size, longer bill, deeper chest and stronger contrast between breas and belly.

a ADULT BREEDING: Breast is heavily spotted black, sometimes solidly black in centre. Spots become chevrons on flanks and undertail. Large chestnut spots on scapulars are initially partly obscured by grey and black tips.

b ADULT NON-BREEDING: Upperparts more streaked than on 187, most evident on crown and hindneck. Breast-sides obscurely dark, usually with some grey or blackish spotting. Bill longer than on 187 body more tapering, with wings projecting noticeably beyond tail-tip; legs darker.

c JUVENILE: Upperparts show strongly-contrasted whitish-buff fringes centres of scapulars dark brown, and of coverts pale brown with dark shaft-streak and subterminal mark. Breast and flanks are spotted dar brown, and breast is suffused brownish-buff.

d In flight, wingbar is weaker than on 187 and primary coverts are more contrastingly dark. Lower rump and uppertail are white, sparsely marked with blackish; markings are strongest in breeding plumage

e Underwing-coverts are mainly white, and axillaries are white, slight sullied with grey-brown.

189 Sanderling *Calidris alba* Text page 365

A largish, thickset calidrid with a fairly heavy, shortish black bill. Typically coastal, especially on sandy beaches, and very active.

a ADULT BREEDING: Head, neck and upper breast are mostly chestnut, streaked brown, ending sharply against pure white underparts. Upperparts blackish, with variable amount of chestnut fringing.

b ADULT BREEDING: Brightest individuals are rich dark chestnut, inviting confusion with Red-necked Stint (192).

c MOULTING ADULT: Many migrant individuals in Apr/May show very little chestnut, owing to the broad grey tips to the breeding-plumage feathers. Upperparts appear mottled black and grey.

d ADULT NON-BREEDING: The palest calidrid; pale pearly-grey above and white below, with dark carpal patch sometimes evident

e JUVENILE: Variegated with blackish, white and pale buff. Mantle and scapulars blackish, with large paired buffish-white spots; tertials blackish, fringed buff; wing-coverts dull brown, with subterminal black patch and buffish-white fringe. Breast is washed buff and streaked at sides.

f MOULTING JUVENILE: By Oct, adults are all-grey but juveniles show some retained blackish feathers, especially tertials, wing-coverts and larger scapulars.

g In flight, shows strongest white wingbar of any calidrid: compare with Dunlin (204). Breeding adult is depicted.

h In non-breeding plumage, blackish lesser and primary coverts contrast strongly with pale grey median coverts. Tail-sides are pale grey.

i Whole underwing is very white, like belly.

206 Spoon-billed Sandpiper *Eurynorhynchus pygmaeus* Text page 382

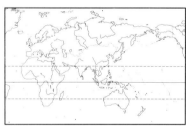

A rare, stint-sized wader with an extraordinary spatulate bill. Plumages recall 189 and Red-necked Stint (192). Feeding action is distinctive.

a ADULT BREEDING: Mainly-reddish head, neck and breast, streaked dark brown. Upperparts dark, with chestnut and whitish fringes. Bill swept from side to side while feeding.

b ADULT NON-BREEDING: Upperparts pale brownish-grey, with darker shaft-streaks. Wing-coverts grey, fringed white when fresh. Prominent white supercilium. Centre of foreneck and breast bright white.

c JUVENILE: Head shows contrasting brown crown and broad mask through eye. Mantle, scapulars and tertials blackish, fringed pale buffish. Coverts pale brown, fringed buff or reddish-buff. Breast washed buff, sometimes forming a faint breast-band, with streaking at sides. In a side view, bill shape is difficult to detect.

d In flight, white wingbar and sides to rump and uppertail are as on stints; white wingbar is relatively prominent. Non-breeding adult and (to the right) juvenile are depicted.

e Underwing-coverts and axillaries are white or whitish.

189b

189c

189h

189e

189a

189d

189f

189g

204

189i

206e

206b

206a

206c

206d

191 Western Sandpiper *Calidris mauri*   Text page 367

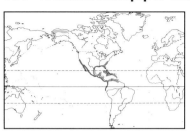

The westerly counterpart of 190, but ranges overlap broadly. Bill averages longer than on 190, and is finer-tipped and slightly drooping like that of Dunlin (204). Breeding and juvenile plumages are distinctive.

a ADULT BREEDING: Brighter than 190, with much rich chestnut in scapulars and chestnut patches on ear-coverts and sides of crown. Nape, mantle and wing-coverts are mostly greyish. Underparts whitish, marked with blackish spots or small chevrons from breast to flanks and upper belly and sometimes to undertail.

b ADULT PRE-BREEDING: Rufous is initially partly obscured by greyish feather tips.

c ADULT NON-BREEDING: Very like 190, but typically a slightly cleaner, colder grey. Head, neck and breast show finer dark shaft-streaks, typically extending right across upper breast.

d JUVENILE: Averages brighter than 190, and is always distinguishable by strong contrast of bright rufous on upper scapulars with greyish lower scapulars. Some, as depicted, show internal chestnut on upper scapulars like breeding adult. Compare also with Red-necked Stint (192).

e Closely resembles 190 in flight. Juvenile is depicted: note pattern of rufous on upper scapulars.

190 Semipalmated Sandpiper *Calidris pusilla*   Text page 366

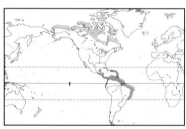

A relatively dull-plumaged, dark-legged stint. This and 191 are the only stints with partly-webbed toes, but webbing is very difficult to see. Compare also with Red-necked (192) and Little (193). Bill is typically blunt-tipped and rather deep at base; length overlaps with 191.

a ADULT BREEDING: Upperparts generally greyish or buff, never with extensive rufous. Dark centres to scapulars contrast strongly. Breast and fore-flanks streaked blackish.

b ADULT PRE-BREEDING: In fresh plumage, upperparts are mostly brownish-grey.

c ADULT NON-BREEDING: Rather plain grey-brown above, obviously greyer than Least (196). Breast-sides are washed grey and obscurely streaked.

d JUVENILE: Crown and upperparts have greyish-brown feather centres and buff or pale rufous fringes, giving a uniformly scaly pattern. Prominent supercilium, not 'split'; mantle lines faint or lacking. Lower scapulars have dark, anchor-shaped subterminal marks. Breast is washed buff and lightly streaked at sides.

e JUVENILE: On some, mantle and scapulars are brighter rufous, recalling 192. Rufous on upper scapulars is confined to fringes. Wear and fading quickly reduce rufous tones (birds to the right).

f JUVENILE: By Sept, buff may be very pale. Pattern may suggest Baird's (198), but note shorter wings and blunter bill.

g MOULTING JUVENILE: This individual, gaining grey but still showing rufous in scapulars, might be mistaken for 191.

h In flight, shows narrow white wingbar and white sides to rump and uppertail. Sides of tail are grey. Underwing-coverts and axillaries are white. Juvenile is depicted.

190d

191e

190

190

190

190

190

191

191

191

191

190h

191e

190

190e

190

191d

190

190f

191

190g

190a

190c

191a

191b

191c

190b

191

190

192 Red-necked Stint *Calidris ruficollis*

Text page 368

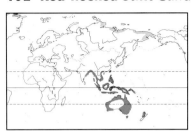

Structurally very like 193, but fractionally deeper bill-tip, shorter legs and longer wings give a subtly different outline. Dark legs; toes lack webbing. See also Plates 79 and 80.

a ADULT PRE-BREEDING: Broad pale grey tips to fresh upperpart feathers conceal rufous edges. Face and foreneck pale rufous.

b ADULT BREEDING: Unstreaked rufous or brick-red on cheeks, throat, neck and upper breast, but variable in both depth and extent of colour. Lower breast shows brown spotting overlying white. Wing-coverts and scapulars mostly grey, as in non-breeding plumage. Compare with Sanderling (189) and Spoon-billed Sandpiper (206).

c ADULT NON-BREEDING: Typically paler than 193, with less extensive dark feather centres. Never shows complete speckled breast-band; breast-patches usually clearly defined.

d JUVENILE: Supercilium duller behind eye than on 193, not usually 'split'. Pale mantle lines faint or lacking. Lower scapulars greyish at base, with drop-shaped dark subterminal area. Tertials greyish, with dark shaft-streak and narrow whitish edges. Dullest individuals may recall Semipalmated (190).

e WORN JUVENILE: Mantle may become very dark prior to moult.

f In flight, shows white wingbar and white sides to rump and uppertail. Some individuals show extensive white on inner primaries. Non-breeding adult is depicted.

g Most show wingbar like 193. Juvenile is depicted.

h Tail feathers 2–5, sometimes also 6 (outermost), typically shorter than on 193 (red outline); central pair projects farther.

i Tiny outermost primary typically shows obvious 'step' in dark centre. On 193, dark centre is evenly pointed and white fringe is of even width.

193 Little Stint *Calidris minuta*

Text page 369

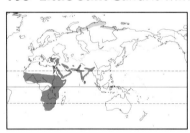

Very similar to 192, but subtly different in structure (see above). There are small differences in plumage patterns, but individuals not closely observed are best regarded as indeterminable between these two species. Compare closely with other stints on Plates 75 and 78. See also Plates 79 and 80.

a ADULT BREEDING: Face, cheeks, neck and upper breast orange-rufous, variable in shade, overlain by brown streaking; chin and throat always whitish. Yellowish or creamy lines at edges of mantle. Tertials and most wing-coverts brownish, fringed rufous.

b ADULT NON-BREEDING: Typically a little browner than other dark-legged stints, often with relatively broad dark feather centres. Grey areas of head and breast tend to be more streaked than on 192, some individuals show a complete breast-band of indistinct speckles.

c JUVENILE: Bright rufous ridge along centre of crown contrasts with whitish supercilium and lateral crown-stripe, and with greyish hindneck. Whitish lines at edges of mantle are conspicuous. Typically, centres of tertials, lower scapulars and wing-coverts are dark brown, and edges bright rufous, unlike on 192; some are a little greyer than individual depicted.

d In flight, shows clear white wingbar and white sides to rump and uppertail. Lacks extensive white on inner primaries present on some 192. Non-breeding adult is depicted.

e JUVENILE: Typically brighter than juveniles of other dark-legged stints.

192

192

193

193

193

192

193

192

192i

193

192f

193d

192g

193e

192c

193

192

192e

192b

193b

192d

192a

193a

193

192

192

193

193c

192h

194 Temminck's Stint *Calidris temminckii* Text page 370

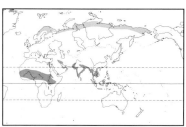

A dull-plumaged, pale-legged stint, found mainly in freshwater marshlands. Never shows strong pale supercilium or pale 'V's on mantle and scapulars. Legs usually dull greenish or yellowish. Bill thin, slightly drooping. White sides of tail distinguish it from all other stints. Tail projects noticeably beyond folded wings.

a ADULT BREEDING: Feathers of mantle and scapulars are centred blackish, fringed pale rufous and tipped grey when fresh; some grey-brown feathers are admixed, even in full plumage. Pale chin and throat contrast little with head and breast.

b ADULT NON-BREEDING: An even darkish grey-brown above. Breast dull grey-brown, palest in centre. Pattern recalls miniature Common Sandpiper (148). Legs sometimes quite bright yellow.

c JUVENILE: Upperparts show plover-like pattern of warm brownish feathers, each with dark submarginal line and deep buff fringe; look slightly scaly. Buff-brown breast-band, usually complete.

d In flight, shows relatively short and narrow white wingbar. Flight is fast and jinking; often 'towers' when flushed, like Common Snipe (175). Breeding adult is depicted.

e Broad white tail-sides, evident especially on take-off and landing, are unique among calidrids and recall Kentish Plover (98) and allies. Juvenile is depicted.

f Underwing-coverts and axillaries are mostly white, with some greyish across primary coverts.

207 Broad-billed Sandpiper *Limicola falcinellus* Text page 383

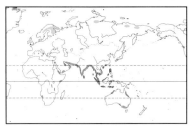

Looks like a large stint with a long bill. Bill is almost straight at base, but with a sharp downward angle near tip; breadth rarely visible in the field. Legs rather short, usually looking dark greyish. Supercilium is 'double' in all plumages. There are two poorly-defined races.

a ADULT BREEDING: Double supercilia join, narrowly, in front of eye. Whitish lines at edges of mantle and scapulars. Breast suffused brown and sharply streaked, divided neatly from white belly. Flanks show some streaks. Race *falcinellus* (Scandinavia and W USSR) is depicted. Worn individuals look very black above and strongly streaked on breast.

b ADULT BREEDING race *sibirica* (central and E USSR): Brighter rufous fringes; slight cinnamon tinge to breast; upper supercilium less clear.

c ADULT NON-BREEDING: Main supercilium and eye-stripe prominent, but upper supercilium often very hard to see. Grey-brown upperparts show clear dark shaft-streaks and dark centres to some larger feathers. Blackish carpal patch may be evident. Breast lightly streaked grey-brown.

d JUVENILE: Like fresh breeding adult, but fringes of upperparts pale buff and white. Wing-coverts broadly fringed buff. Breast washed buff-brown and lightly streaked brown; streaking does not extend onto flanks.

e In flight, has clear but narrow wingbar and white sides to blackish rump and uppertail. Breeding adult is depicted; juvenile (to the right) is similar.

f In flight, in non-breeding plumage, blackish leading edge to wing contrasts with grey-brown median coverts and scapulars.

g Underwing-coverts and axillaries mostly white or whitish.

194d

194e

194f

194a

194c

194b

207d

207e

207f

207b

207a

207g

207c

195 Long-toed Stint *Calidris subminuta* Text page 371

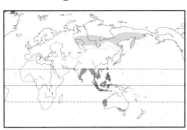

A pale-legged stint found mainly on inland marshes. Plumages are very similar to 196, but longish neck and relatively long legs and toes are unlike other stints. Feeding postures and plumages may recall Sharp-tailed Sandpiper (200) in miniature. Toe length is a difficult character to use in the field.

a ADULT BREEDING: Rufous cap contrasts with bright whitish supercilium; dark of forecrown extends to bill-base and may join dusky area of lores. Breast shows fine streaking and a rich creamy suffusion; streaking is sometimes absent from centre of breast. Upperparts are edged bright rufous. Tertial edges are typically of uniform width.

b ADULT NON-BREEDING: Upperparts are rather dark brownish-grey, with fairly clearly-defined broad dark feather centres. Breast is washed and streaked grey-brown.

c JUVENILE: Brightly patterned, with whitish lines at mantle edges recalling Little (193). Rufous cap contrasts with long whitish supercilia and greyish hindneck; typically shows whitish lateral crown-stripes. As on adult, dark of forecrown meets bill. Inner wing-coverts are usually greyer than the scapulars, with narrow whitish edges.

d In flight, shows clear white sides to rump and uppertail, but only a faint white wingbar which hardly extends to the outer wing. Only the outermost primary has a white shaft. Toes project a little beyond tail. Non-breeding adult is depicted.

e JUVENILE: Weak wingbar, but whitish mantle lines prominent.

f Underwing shows fairly prominent greyish bands across coverts.

196 Least Sandpiper *Calidris minutilla* Text page 372

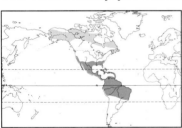

The smallest of the stints. Very like 195 in plumages, but more compact in structure; postures are typically hunched, almost crouching. Toes are shorter than on 195, but longer in relation to tarsus than on dark-legged stints. Occurs more often in intertidal habitats than does 195.

a ADULT BREEDING: A little darker and duller than 195. Head pattern differs in that lores are more solidly dark and supercilium runs into narrow pale band at base of forecrown. Breast streaking is broader and extends right across breast. Tertial edges are often slightly scalloped.

b ADULT BREEDING: Rufous edges wear rapidly from upperparts, and by late July some individuals become almost solidly dark above.

c ADULT NON-BREEDING: Distinctly browner than equivalent plumages of dark-legged stints. Compared with 195, dark feather centres are narrower and less distinct from paler fringes.

d JUVENILE: Head is less strongly patterned than on 195. Lores are typically solidly dark, contrasting with pale supercilium and base of forehead. Lateral crown-stripes are faint or absent. Pale mantle lines and scapular lines are usually less obvious than on 195. Inner wing-coverts are fringed buff or rufous, contrasting little with scapulars.

e In flight, shows narrow white wingbar and white sides to rump and uppertail. Wingbar is longer than on 195, and all primary shafts show some whitish. Toes do not project beyond tail-tip.

f JUVENILE: Smaller and more compact than 195, with stronger wingbar.

g Underwing-coverts show a little less dusky than on 195.

190 Semipalmated Sandpiper *Calidris pusilla*   Plates 75, 80   Text page 366

BARE PARTS: Bill black, almost straight, rather deep at base and with slightly-thickened tip; length overlaps with 191. Legs black; toes partly webbed.
PLUMAGE: Colours relatively dull. Mantle, scapulars and tertials are dull brown, with pale rufous and whitish fringes giving a scaly appearance. Pale lines on mantle and scapulars are faint or lacking. Dark-centred upper scapulars contrast a little with greyer lower scapulars, which show a dark anchor-shaped subterminal mark. Breast is washed buff and diffusely streaked at sides. Plate shows: a, fresh plumage (some are more rufous); b and c, worn plumage; d, partly faded.

191 Western Sandpiper *Calidris mauri*   Plates 75, 80   Text page 367

BARE PARTS: Bill black, typically longish, decurved a little near the tip, and less thickened at base and tip than bill of 190; bill shape often recalls the much larger Dunlin (204). Legs black; toes partly webbed.
PLUMAGE: Brighter rufous above than 190, particularly on central mantle and upper rows of scapulars. Bright upper scapulars often form broad, rufous 'V' bordering mantle and back, and contrast with lower scapulars which are greyer with dark shaft-streak and subterminal area. Breast is washed buff, with fairly extensive and well-defined streaking at sides.

192 Red-necked Stint *Calidris ruficollis*   Plates 76, 80   Text page 368

BARE PARTS: Bill black, slimmer than on 190 but faintly thicker at base and tip than on most 193. Legs black.
PLUMAGE: Upperparts show rufous and whitish fringes, but pale lines on mantle and scapulars are weaker than on 193, sometimes lacking. Rarely shows 'split supercilium' and dark central 'ridge' to crown as on 193. Rufous-fringed upper scapulars contrast with greyer lower scapulars, wing-coverts and tertials; lower scapulars show dark shaft-streak and subterminal smudge. Breast washed buffish, with diffuse, rather extensive streaking at sides. Plate shows: a, bright individual; b and c, partly faded and worn.

193 Little Stint *Calidris minuta*   Plates 76, 80   Text page 369

BARE PARTS: Bill black, finer than on 192, often slightly drooping. Legs black.
PLUMAGE: Bright above, with prominent pale 'V's on mantle and scapulars. Scapulars and tertials blackish, with deep rufous fringes. Wing-coverts brownish, fringed rufous. Crown shows dark 'ridge' along centre; lateral crown-stripes give 'split-supercilium' effect. Hindneck typically pale greyish. Sides of breast washed buff, with a little, rather sharply-defined streaking.

194 Temminck's Stint *Calidris temminckii*   Plates 77, 80   Text page 370

STRUCTURE: Tail extends noticeably beyond folded wing-tips.
BARE PARTS: Thin, slightly drooping, fine-tipped bill, blackish or brownish, tinged paler towards base. Legs variably yellowish, greenish or yellowish-brown.
PLUMAGE: Dull brownish upperparts and coverts show dark submarginal lines and narrow buff fringes. Diffuse breast-band or breast-patches. Sides of tail are white.

195 Long-toed Stint *Calidris subminuta*   Plates 78, 80   Text page 371

STRUCTURE: Longer-necked than other stints.
BARE PARTS: Bill fine and slightly drooping, blackish or brownish with paler brown or yellowish-green tinge at base. Legs variably yellowish-brown or greenish; toes are noticeably long-looking.
PLUMAGE: Brightly patterned, with obvious pale 'V' at edges of mantle. Inner wing-coverts greyer than scapulars, with narrow whitish edges. Rufous cap contrasts with greyish hindneck and long pale supercilia; 'split-supercilium' effect often striking. Dark of forecrown meets bill. Centre of breast is often unstreaked.

196 Least Sandpiper *Calidris minutilla*   Plates 78, 80   Text page 372

BARE PARTS: Very like 195, but bill averages darker and toes are shorter.
PLUMAGE: Very similar to 195, but with less contrasting pale hindneck, lateral crown-stripes and mantle lines. Wing-coverts are fringed rufous, contrasting less with scapulars than on 195. Supercilia typically meet narrowly above base of bill. Streaking usually extends right across breast.

206 Spoon-billed Sandpiper *Eurynorhynchus pygmaeus*
Plates 74, 80   Text page 382

BARE PARTS: Bill black, uniquely spatulate. Legs black; toes lack webbing.
PLUMAGE: Dark eye-stripe and ear-coverts give a masked appearance. Fringes to upperparts mostly pale buff. Rather narrow band of buff across breast, usually complete, with streaking at sides.

PLATE 80: Breeding plumages of adult stints and Spoon-billed Sandpiper

190 Semipalmated Sandpiper *Calidris pusilla*　　Plates 75, 79　Text page 366

General colour of upperparts is greyish-buff; rufous is sometimes present, but never extensive. Dark centres to scapulars are prominent. Underparts whitish, with dark streaking on breast and forward part of flanks.

191 Western Sandpiper *Calidris mauri*　　Plates 75, 79　Text page 367

Bright rufous forms conspicuous patches on sides of crown, ear-coverts and across scapulars. Underparts whitish, with blackish spots, triangles or small chevrons extending from breast onto belly, flanks and sometimes undertail. Plate shows: a, newly-moulted individual with rufous partly obscured by greyish tips; b, full plumage; c and d, worn plumage.

192 Red-necked Stint *Calidris ruficollis*　　Plates 76, 79　Text page 368

Typically shows extensive unmarked chestnut-red on face, foreneck and upper breast, but both shade and extent of colour are variable. Below red on upper breast is a narrow band, often complete, of brown spots or triangles on a white background. Lateral crown-stripes and pale mantle 'V' are faint or lacking. Wing-coverts and tertials often greyish as in non-breeding plumage. Plate shows: a, newly-moulted individual with extensive grey tipping above and white tipping obscuring spotting on breast; b, full plumage; c, late summer, rather worn and faded.

193 Little Stint *Calidris minuta*　　Plates 76, 79　Text page 369

Differs from 192 in that foreneck and breast are more orange-red in shade, and typically completely streaked or speckled with brown. Throat is always whitish, as well as chin, and there is no obvious brown speckling on white areas of breast. Pale lateral crown-stripes and lines at edges of mantle are typically clear. Wing-coverts and tertials are mostly edged bright rufous, contrasting less with scapulars than on 192.

194 Temminck's Stint *Calidris temminckii*　　Plates 77, 79　Text page 370

Generally rather dull, but a variable number of feathers show quite bright orange-chestnut edges once grey tipping of fresh plumage has worn off. Breast shows diffuse brownish band or lateral patches. Plate shows: a and b, fresh plumage; c, worn plumage.

195 Long-toed Stint *Calidris subminuta*　　Plates 78, 79　Text page 371

Bright rufous cap and fringes to upperparts. Mantle often shows strong pale 'V' as on 193. Breast shows fine streaking, especially at sides, on creamy background. Rufous edges to tertials are typically broad and of uniform width. Dark of forehead butts onto bill and may join dark of lores.

196 Least Sandpiper *Calidris minutilla*　　Plates 78, 79　Text page 371

Underparts are like those of 195, but streaking is broader, especially in centre of breast. Upperparts show narrower rufous and whitish edgings than on 195, and often wear to solid blackish-brown late in the breeding season. Tertial edges are often slightly scalloped. Pale of supercilia meets narrowly above base of bill. Plate shows: a, newly-moulted individual with extensive brownish-grey tips to feathers of upperparts; b, full plumage.

206 Spoon-billed Sandpiper *Eurynorhynchus pygmaeus*
Plates 74, 79　Text page 382

Face, foreneck and upper breast are bright chestnut-red as on 192, but red is spotted with brown on sides of neck and breast; spotting continues onto white zone of upper breast. Upperparts, particularly mantle and lower scapulars, show rather yellowish-chestnut fringes. Spatulate bill is diagnostic.

197 White-rumped Sandpiper *Calidris fuscicollis* — Text page 373

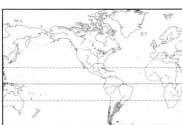

Like 198, a small calidrid, a little larger than the stints, with long wings extending well beyond the tail. Bill is short and slightly drooping, black with yellowish at base. In flight, shows white band on uppertail.

a ADULT BREEDING: Colours fairly subdued. Light chestnut-buff wash on crown, ear-coverts and scapular fringes. Clear, long, whitish supercilium. Throat, breast and upper flanks pale, neatly streaked brown; flanks show some blackish 'V's.

b ADULT MOULTING: Fresh brown-grey replaces worn blackish-centred feathers on upperparts. Some dark streaking may be retained on breast and flanks.

c ADULT NON-BREEDING: Dull brown-grey above, with dark shaft-streaks. Supercilium typically obvious. Breast suffused greyish and lightly streaked.

d ADULT NON-BREEDING: In fresh plumage, upperparts are clean grey with dark shaft-streaks or feather centres. (Larger-scale paintings are directly comparable with those of stints.)

e JUVENILE: Whitish supercilium separates dark-streaked, chestnut cap from rufous-washed ear-coverts. Hindneck greyish. Mantle and upper scapulars blackish, fringed chestnut, and lower scapulars greyish with whitish tips. Narrow whitish lines across scapulars and at edges of mantle. Neck, breast and upper flanks are infused grey or buffish-grey, and very finely streaked; a few streaks extend onto rear flanks. Bill shows yellowish-brown patch at base.

f In flight, appears long-winged with narrow, rather short white wingbar, and narrow band of white on uppertail-coverts which contrasts with darkish grey tail. Underwing-coverts and axillaries are white. Juvenile is depicted. In other plumages, uppertail may be lightly marked with grey or brown.

198 Baird's Sandpiper *Calidris bairdii* — Text page 374

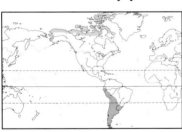

Very like 197 in size and shape, but slimmer and slightly more elongated, with a finer-tipped bill. Plumages are predominantly buffish-brown, always with complete, finely-streaked breast-band.

a ADULT BREEDING: Buffish above, with contrasting dark brown centres to scapulars. Short buffish supercilium; lores dusky. Streaked breast-band. Belly and flanks typically unmarked white.

b ADULT BREEDING: At end of breeding season, many appear rather blackish above.

c ADULT MOULTING: Upperparts show a mixture of worn, blackish feathers and fresh, greyish or buffish-brown non-breeding feathers.

d ADULT NON-BREEDING: Upperparts and breast-band buffish-brown or greyish. Scapulars may appear faintly scaly.

e ADULT NON-BREEDING: A rather rich brown individual, in fresh plumage, yet to replace two outermost primaries.

f ADULT NON-BREEDING: A few individuals are very plain greyish above, with only a faint brownish tinge to the plumage.

g JUVENILE: Upperparts are neatly and evenly fringed buffish or buffish-white, giving a clear scaly pattern. Chin and throat whitish, rest of head and breast washed buffish and streaked brown. Belly and flanks clean white.

h In flight, looks long-winged with short, very narrow, sometimes inconspicuous wingbar. Rump and uppertail noticeably broadly dark-centred; there are very narrow whitish sides to rump and buffish-grey sides to uppertail. Underwing-coverts and axillaries are white. Juvenile is depicted.

199 Pectoral Sandpiper *Calidris melanotos*

Text page 375

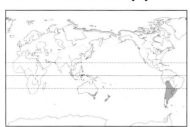

A medium to large calidrid with shortish, slightly-decurved bill and yellowish legs. Breast always has heavy streaks which end sharply against white of belly.

a ADULT FEMALE BREEDING: Relatively dull brownish; supercilium not conspicuous. Mantle, scapulars and tertials dark brown, fringed dull chestnut to brown-buff. Slight flank streaking.

b ADULT MALE BREEDING: Breast blackish-brown, mottled with whitish. Males are larger than females, with hardly any size overlap.

c ADULT NON-BREEDING: Plain brown above, with darker feather centres.

d JUVENILE: Relatively bright, with clear whitish supercilium, and feathers of upperparts fringed white, buff and chestnut; typically shows clear white 'V's on mantle edges and across scapulars. Breast finely streaked brown and variably washed with buff.

e In flight, wings look dark; very faint wingbar and whitish trailing edge to inner secondaries. Broad blackish centre to rump and uppertail. Juvenile is depicted. Compare with 200 and with Ruff (210).

f Underwing-coverts and axillaries whitish, contrasting with breast.

200 Sharp-tailed Sandpiper *Calidris acuminata*

Text page 376

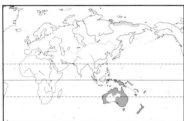

Similar to 199 in structure, but is slightly more angular, shorter-legged and shorter-billed, and lacks sharp demarcation on lower breast. Generally has capped appearance, with bright supercilium and prominent eye-ring. Juvenile is highly distinctive.

a ADULT BREEDING: Feathers of upperparts dark brown, extensively fringed chestnut and white-buff. Rufous cap. Supercilium broadens behind eye. Neck and breast heavily streaked brown; lower breast, upper belly and flanks marked with broad, very dark brown chevrons. Male is larger than female, with hardly any overlap in size.

b ADULT NON-BREEDING: Mainly dull brown above, with darker feather centres. Breast suffused greyish, finely streaked. Retains whitish supercilium and traces of rufous on cap.

c JUVENILE: Very bright. White supercilium; reddish cap; rufous lores and ear-coverts. Upperparts brightly fringed chestnut, white and bright buff. Foreneck and upper breast are washed bright orange-buff with narrow gorget of fine streaks across upper neck.

d In flight, very like 199 but wingbar is slightly more distinct. White lateral uppertail-coverts show dark shaft-streaks.

e All tail feathers are sharply pointed and tail is wedge-shaped.

f Underwing-coverts and axillaries are mostly whitish.

201 Cox's Sandpiper *Calidris paramelanotos*

Text page 377

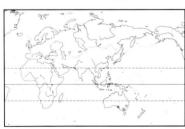

A poorly-known calidrid, first described in 1982. Has a fairly long, blackish, Dunlin-like decurved bill, sometimes with yellowish base, dull greenish legs, and tail shaped like 199. Closest resemblances are probably to 199 and to Dunlin (204).

a ADULT PRE-BREEDING: Moulting birds gain rufous suffusion to ear-coverts and breast. Fresh upperpart feathers have grey tips and buffy or pale chestnut fringes. Throat and breast heavily streaked, but lacking sharp demarcation on lower breast; some flank streaks. Full breeding and juvenile plumages unknown.

b ADULT NON-BREEDING: Upperparts brown-grey, with only slightly darker feather centres. Breast lacks rufous tinge. No flank streaking.

c In flight, shows white on sides (at least) of uppertail. Wingbar is slightly brighter than on 199 or 200, but weaker than on Curlew Sandpiper (205).

d Uppertail-coverts show more white than on 199 and 200. Central feathers are whitish, washed pale grey-buff, and marked with blackish-brown bars and chevrons.

199a

199c

199b

199d

200

200a

200b

201

199

200c

201a

200

199e

200d

201c

200

199

200e

200f

199f

201d

201

200f

199f

201c

199

200

201b

202 Purple Sandpiper *Calidris maritima*

Text page 378

A dumpy, fairly large calidrid with a longish, slightly drooping yellowish-based bill and short yellowish legs. Feeds typically on intertidal rocks. Very closely related to 203; many individuals indistinguishable on plumage, but ranges not known to overlap.

a ADULT BREEDING: Upperparts extensively fringed whitish and chestnut. Supercilium whitish. Breast and flanks heavily streaked brown; streaks may fuse to solid dark patch on lower breast.

b ADULT NON-BREEDING: Dark slate-grey on head, breast and upperparts. Mantle and scapulars show faint purplish gloss at close range. Wing-coverts fringed grey.

c JUVENILE: Feathers of upperparts smaller than on adults, fringed pale chestnut, white and buff. Wing-coverts neatly fringed pale buff. Foreneck and breast washed brown-grey and streaked brown. Compare with Sharp-tailed (200).

d FIRST NON-BREEDING: Some individuals retain juvenile wing-coverts for much of first winter.

e In flight, fairly bold white wingbar contrasts with dark upperparts. One or two inner secondaries are usually completely white. White at sides of rump and uppertail is also conspicuous.

f Underwing-coverts and axillaries mostly greyish-white. Primary coverts and underside of primaries darkish grey.

203 Rock Sandpiper *Calidris ptilocnemis*

Text page 379

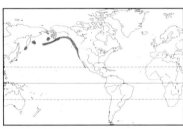

The Pacific equivalent of the Atlantic Purple Sandpiper (202). There are four races, of which three are extremely similar to 202 (and perhaps conspecific); the nominate race, however, is larger and paler, with a distinctive breeding plumage.

a ADULT BREEDING race *ptilocnemis* (Pribilof Is.): Distinctively pale (sometimes whitish) on head, neck and breast, with prominent blackish patches on lores, ear-coverts and lower breast. Mantle, scapulars and tertials fringed pale yellowish-chestnut; wing-coverts contrastingly greyish.

b ADULT BREEDING race *tschuktschorum* (E Siberia and W Alaska): All three more widespread races are more readily separable from nominate Rock than from 202. Best distinctions from 202 are darker chestnut fringes above and broader streaking below, typically forming an obvious dark patch on lower breast. Some show dark patches on lores and ear-coverts, like nominate race.

c ADULT BREEDING race *quarta* (Commander and Kuril Is.): Chestnut fringes are a little paler than on *tschuktschorum* and *couesi* (Aleutians and S Alaska).

d ADULT NON-BREEDING race *ptilocnemis*: Clear but short supercilium; breast off-white, slightly mottled; little streaking on flanks. Upperparts distinctively ash-grey, lacking purple sheen. Non-breeding adults of other races are very like 202, but with sharper spotting on lower breast and flanks, and more white on wing.

e JUVENILE race *ptilocnemis*: Scapulars brown, fringed pale chestnut and buff. Wing-coverts greyish, fringed pale buff. Breast and foreneck washed pale buff and finely streaked brown. Juveniles of other races are very like 202, differing in brighter buffish-brown foreneck and upper breast and in slightly sharper streaking on lower breast and flanks.

f In flight, widespread races show a slightly bolder white wingbar than on 202. Juvenile is depicted.

g Race *ptilocnemis* in flight shows strong wingbar with much white on inner primaries.

h Underwing is extensively white in race *ptilocnemis*, but in other races very similar to 202f.

204 Dunlin *Calidris alpina*

Text page 380

A rather variable calidrid in size, bill length, and in details of breeding plumage, but with distinctive hunched posture and decurved bill-tip. Black belly of breeding plumage is diagnostic. Races sometimes separable in field conditions.

a ADULT MALE BREEDING race *alpina* (N Scandinavia and NW USSR): Rufous upperparts and blackish belly-patch are present in all races. Nominate race is medium-sized, with rusty-red fringes above. Male (all races) shows paler, greyer hindneck than female, and shorter bill on average.

b ADULT FEMALE BREEDING race *alpina*: Hindneck contrasts less with mantle than on male.

c ADULT MALE BREEDING race *schinzii* (SE Greenland, Iceland, Britain, S Scandinavia): Smaller and shorter-billed than nominate race, with upperpart fringes more yellowish-red. Some individuals cannot be sexed on hindneck pattern.

d ADULT FEMALE BREEDING race *schinzii*.

e ADULT MALE BREEDING race *arctica* (NE Greenland): Smallest and shortest-billed race, on average, with pale reddish-yellow fringes above.

f ADULT FEMALE BREEDING race *arctica*.

g ADULT MALE BREEDING race *sakhalina* (NE USSR, N Alaska): Size and bill length as nominate race, but fringes to upperparts are a brighter and deeper red. Hindneck of female is as on American races.

h ADULT FEMALE BREEDING race *pacifica* (W Alaska): This and *hudsonia* (central Canada) are the largest, longest-billed and brightest races. Males show whitish hindneck as on *sakhalina*. In *pacifica*, streaking on underparts ends sharply, forward of black belly-patch.

i ADULT FEMALE BREEDING race *hudsonia*: In this race, breast streaking butts onto black belly-patch, without an intervening white band, and continues on the flanks and as fine shaft-streaks on the undertail-coverts.

j ADULT NON-BREEDING: Rather plain, dull grey-brown on head and upperparts. Wing-coverts fringed whitish. Breast suffused and lightly streaked grey-brown, especially at sides. Races are similar, except that on *hudsonia* grey-brown streaks extend finely to rearmost flank feathers. Race *sakhalina* is depicted.

k Largest, longest-billed individuals (females of races *pacifica* and *hudsonia*) suggest Curlew Sandpiper (205), but lack clear white supercilium and have less evenly-curved bill. Smallest, shortest-billed (males of races *schinzii* and *arctica*) are stint-like, but larger and plainer-plumaged.

l JUVENILE: Lines of blackish-brown spotting on flanks and sides of belly are diagnostic of this species. Breast suffused buff and streaked brown. Mantle and scapulars are fringed chestnut and whitish-buff, with whitish lines at edges of mantle. Coverts fringed buff or chestnut.

m MOULTING JUVENILE: Grey feathers appear first in scapulars and mantle. Belly spotting is retained to a late stage.

n In flight, shows clear white wingbar, white sides to rump and uppertail and grey sides to tail. Non-breeding adult is depicted.

o JUVENILE.

p ADULT MALE BREEDING race *pacifica*.

q Underwing is extensively white, in breeding plumage contrasting sharply with black belly.

208 Stilt Sandpiper *Micropalama himantopus*

Text page 384

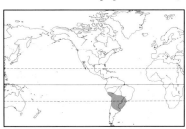

Like a fairly large, long-legged calidrid with a long, fairly thick, slightly drooping bill. Legs greenish. Feeding behaviour recalls that of American dowitchers (183, 184).

a ADULT BREEDING: Very distinctive. White supercilium contrasts with chestnut lores, ear-coverts and nape. Mantle, scapulars and tertials dark brown, edged rufous and whitish. Neck and upper breast strongly streaked brown, and entire lower breast, flanks, belly and undertail strongly barred.

b ADULT NON-BREEDING: Upperparts plain brown-grey, wing-coverts fringed white. Distinct white supercilium and darkish eye-stripe. Underparts white, clearly streaked grey on lower neck and breast.

c JUVENILE: Upperpart feathers mostly dark brown, fringed rufous or whitish-buff; wing-coverts grey-brown, fringed buff. Throat and breast washed buff, faintly streaked. Belly white.

d In flight, long wings, bill and legs form distinctive cross-shaped outline. Square white patch on lower rump and uppertail-coverts. Greater coverts are paler-tipped, but there is no clear wingbar. Juvenile is depicted.

e In breeding plumage, brown bars partly obscure the white rump-patch. Moulting adult, mostly in non-breeding plumage, is depicted.

f Underwing-coverts and axillaries white, slightly smudged grey; strong contrast with flanks in breeding plumage.

205 Curlew Sandpiper *Calidris ferruginea*

Text page 381

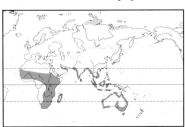

A largish, rather elegant calidrid with a long, decurved black bill and longish black legs. Clear wingbar and shorter, black legs always distinguish from 208; also, forehead is more rounded and bill more evenly curved.

a ADULT MALE BREEDING: Striking chestnut-red head, neck and most of underparts. Scapulars blackish, fringed dark chestnut and tipped grey. Wing-coverts mostly grey-brown. Male has underparts more evenly reddish.

b ADULT FEMALE BREEDING: Underparts slightly paler, with more white fringes and dark brown bars on belly. Bill averages distinctly longer.

c ADULT NON-BREEDING: Upperparts rather plain grey-brown, wing-coverts fringed whitish. Underparts white, with a little grey-brown suffusion on sides of breast. Distinct white supercilium and evenly-curved, fine-tipped bill distinguish from Dunlin (204).

d JUVENILE: Upperpart feathers mostly dark brown, with dark submarginal line and neat pale buff fringe; looks scaly. Foreneck and breast suffused pale buff, with only a little streaking.

e In flight, juvenile shows clear white wingbar and square white patch on lower rump and uppertail. Tips of toes project beyond grey tail.

f Rump-patch is clear also in non-breeding plumages, but on breeding adult (to the right) it is partly obscured by brown bars.

g Underwing-coverts and axillaries white, contrasting strongly with underparts on breeding adults.

209 Buff-breasted Sandpiper *Tryngites subruficollis* Text page 385

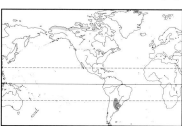

Distinctive, medium-sized wader, typically of grassy habitats. Face and underparts are strongly buff in all plumages. Short, dark bill; shortish, bright yellow-ochre legs. Males are larger than females, and sexes can be identified in the field by size.

a ADULT: Whole of underparts buff, paler towards rear. Upperpart feathers have fairly narrow dark brown centres, merging into buff-brown fringes. Note unusual, almost rectangular, head shape and dark eye isolated in pale face.

b JUVENILE: Very like adult; usually slightly paler on rear belly. Mantle, scapulars and wing-coverts have contrasting dark submarginal line, sometimes a subterminal spot, and sharp, whitish-buff fringe. Looks more scaly than adult, especially on coverts.

c In flight, shows no white above; dark outer wing contrasts with buff-brown inner wing. Sides of rump and uppertail contrast a little with darker tail. Pale bar at tips of greater coverts, clearer on juvenile (depicted), but no obvious wingbar.

d ADULT: In both sexes, mainly silky-white underwing shows blackish tips and subterminal zones of blackish spotting on primaries, secondaries and greater primary coverts. Male is depicted in display posture. Underwing of juvenile is similar, but blackish spotting of adult is replaced by finer speckling of dark brown.

210 Ruff *Philomachus pugnax* Text page 386

A large, calidrid-like wader with remarkable individual variability and sexual dimorphism in size and plumage. Despite variability, small head, shortish decurved bill, longish neck, pot-belly, hump-back and long legs are always distinctive.

a ADULT MALE BREEDING: Variably-coloured head tufts and neck plumes. Breeding colours often show also on flanks and upperparts. Bare parts are usually reddish or orange, sometimes yellowish; facial warts are occasionally greenish. Males do not overlap with females in size, and are usually separable by size alone.

b ADULT FEMALE BREEDING: Lacks tufts and ruff. Variable, but typically shows many black-centred feathers in upperparts, and prominent black blotching on breast and flanks. Obviously smaller than male.

c ADULT MALE MOULTING: When plumes are lost, may resemble breeding female. Some show extensive black or chestnut on flanks and may confuse unwary observers.

d ADULT NON-BREEDING: Grey-brown above, with extensive dark feather centres. Some have barred tertials. Mottled grey-brown on breast; belly whitish. Lores pale. Most show contrast between whitish sides of neck and darker hindneck. Male is depicted.

e ADULT NON-BREEDING: An appreciable proportion, almost always males, have conspicuous white on head and neck. On rare individuals, white extends to back and belly.

f JUVENILE MALE: Upperparts darkish brown, neatly fringed buffish; looks scaly. Lores, sides of face, and underparts buff, becoming whitish on belly. Legs initially greenish.

g JUVENILE FEMALE: Both sexes show similar variation in depth of buff coloration.

h In flight, looks long-winged and powerful. Narrow white wingbar. Clear white ovals, formed by white at sides of unusually long uppertail-coverts, reach almost to tail-tip. Non-breeding male is depicted.

i ADULT FEMALE NON-BREEDING: Smaller size of females is most evident in flight.

j Underwing-coverts and axillaries are white.

122 Magellanic Plover *Pluvianellus socialis*

Text page 311

A rare, somewhat turnstone-like wader, restricted to southernmost South America. Its relationships are uncertain, and it may be only distantly related to the true plovers. All plumages are soft grey and white.

a ADULT: Upperparts and breast are evenly pale grey, except for dusky lores and a brown suffusion to the lower breast. Size, shape and, to some extent, feeding habits recall Ruddy Turnstone (154). Bill has pinkish patches, and iris and legs are pinkish-red.

b JUVENILE: Upperparts are extensively spotted and fringed with white; inner wing-coverts fringed buffish-white. Dark line across lores is less clear. Breast lightly streaked. Bare parts duller; legs are more yellowish than on adult.

c In flight, shows a clear white wingbar, and dark centre and mainly-white sides to uppertail and tail. Lateral tail-coverts show faint shaft-streaks, and tail-corners are very finely vermiculated with grey.

d Underwing and axillaries are white.

211 Rufous-bellied Seedsnipe *Attagis gayi*

Text page 387

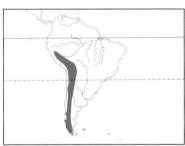

The largest of the four South American seedsnipes, found only in the high Andes. This and 212 look partridge-like on the ground, but more wader-like or sandgrouse-like in flight. No differences are known between the sexes.

a ADULT nominate race (Chile, Patagonia): Rufous above and below, richly patterned on upperparts and breast. Nominate race is palest. Upperpart feathers show many alternating light and dark bars. Race *simonsi* (Peru, Bolivia and NW Argentina) is similar, but a little darker.

b ADULT race *latreillii* (Ecuador): Underparts richer chestnut than on more southerly races, with bold blackish crescents on breast and flanks. Upperparts are darker and show less intricate barring.

c JUVENILE nominate race: Very like adult, but upperpart feathers even more finely barred or vermiculated. Outer 3 primaries show fine buffish fringes, absent on adult.

d In flight, upperparts look fairly uniformly rufous-brown. Adult of nominate race is depicted.

e Nominate race: Underwing-coverts and axillaries are mostly unmarked rufous, of a similar shade to the belly.

f Race *latreillii*: Underwing and axillaries rich chestnut.

212 White-bellied Seedsnipe *Attagis malouinus*

Text page 388

A little smaller than 211, and much more restricted in range. Best distinguished from 211 by bright white axillaries and underwing, strong contrast between breast and belly, and different call.

a ADULT: Barring on upperparts less intricate than on sympatric race of 211 (but quite similar to northernmost race *latreillii*). Breast brownish-white, boldly scalloped with dark brown, contrasting sharply with white belly. Juvenile is very similar, but looks paler and more scaly.

b In flight, looks rather dark above.

c Strikingly white underwing-coverts, axillaries and belly are diagnostic. Flanks and undertail show irregular brown chevrons.

122c

122a

122d

122b

211b

211a

211c

211f

212c

212b

211e

211d

212a

213 Grey-breasted Seedsnipe *Thinocorus orbignyianus*   Text page 388

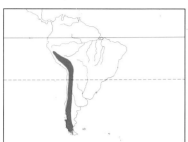

An upland seedsnipe, intermediate in size between the *Attagis* species (Plate 87) and 214. Many plumage features are shared with 214, but size and wing pattern are constant distinguishing characters.

a ADULT MALE: Extensive, clean blue-grey on face, neck and breast. White throat is outlined in black; some individuals show a trace of black bordering white belly, but none has vertical black line on breast as on 214.

b ADULT FEMALE: Lacks blue-grey of male. Indistinct throat-patch is, at best, only narrowly outlined in brown. In all plumages, upperwing is rather plain, showing only a narrow pale trailing edge, and tail has a pale buffish or whitish fringe.

c JUVENILE: Effectively indistinguishable from adult female, but covert pattern of broad tawny submarginal band, narrow dark subterminal line, and broad whitish-buff fringe may be indicative of juvenile.

d ADULT MALE: Black on axillaries and lesser and median underwing-coverts is a simple distinction from *Attagis* species (211, 212). Brown markings on flanks are more extensive than on 214.

e ADULT FEMALE: Females and juveniles show same underwing pattern as adult males. Some females have a trace of a brown line separating streaked breast from white belly.

214 Least Seedsnipe *Thinocorus rumicivorus*   Text page 389

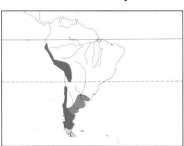

The smallest seedsnipe, rather similar in plumage to its congener (213). Unlike the other three seedsnipe species, occurs on coastal farmland and in semi-deserts as well as in mountains.

a ADULT MALE nominate race (mostly lowland, Tierra del Fuego to N Chile): Males of all races show ash-grey on face, sides and front of neck, and breast. Black border to white throat is joined to blackish line bordering white belly by a vertical black line in centre of breast. Nominate race is darkest in plumage.

b ADULT MALE race *bolivianus* (puna zone, N Chile, NW Argentina and SW Bolivia): The largest race on average. Plumage is paler than in nominate race, often tinged pinkish-brown.

c ADULT FEMALE: Lacks grey and black. Whitish throat is outlined in brown, usually strongly, and some also show a brown vertical line in centre of breast and a brown border to the streaked breast.

d JUVENILE nominate race: Very like adult female, but brown border to throat and brown lines on breast are absent or very poorly defined.

e JUVENILE race *bolivianus*: Relatively large and pale.

f In flight, shows faint whitish wingbar, and narrow but clear white trailing edge to the wing. Adult (depicted) has white at tips of inner 5 primaries only.

g JUVENILE: On juvenile, inner 8 or 9 primaries are pale-tipped. Smallest and palest race *cuneicauda* (mainly coastal, N Chile to Ecuador) is depicted.

h Tail is wedge-shaped, with bold white tips to all but central feathers. On some individuals, central feathers project slightly and are tipped buff (as depicted).

i Axillaries and lesser and median underwing-coverts are mostly black or blackish; pattern is sometimes less contrasting than on 213. Flank markings are less extensive than on 213.

213b

213a

213c

213

214

213d

213e

213

214f

214i

214g

214h

214b

214a

214c

214d

214e

1 LESSER JACANA *Microparra capensis*   **Plate 1**

Other name: Smaller Jacana
Much the smallest jacana, resembling an immature African Jacana (2) in miniature. Sympatric with African Jacana throughout its range, but much less common and much harder to see. A good example of neoteny in birds.

IDENTIFICATION Small size and long spidery toes and claws preclude confusion with any other wader species, except possibly a half-grown chick of African Jacana. Weight is only 20-25% that of the larger species. If size is not evident, best distinguished by chestnut-red nape, lack of bill-shield, contrasting pale brown wing-coverts, and conspicuous white trailing edge to the secondaries in flight. Note the mainly black underwing. Owing to small size and marshy habitat, perhaps most likely to be confused with crakes. No African crake is white-breasted, but the rare White-winged Crake *Sarothrura ayresi* of Ethiopia and South Africa also shows white on the secondaries in flight. **Bare parts:** Bill brown, paler and more pinkish on lower mandible. Iris dark brown. Legs and toes light greenish with olive-brown claws.
VOICE A sharp 'kruk'.
HABITS Found in densely-vegetated marshy areas around quiet lakes and rivers, usually in association with water-lilies, but also found in grassy swamps. Like other jacanas, walks across floating vegetation relying on its long toes and claws to spread its weight. Feeds on seeds and insects. Actions are more 'mouse-like' than related species. Flies readily and quite strongly; on landing often holds wings aloft briefly, showing black underwing. Nest is a simple clump of floating vegetation on which two to four eggs are precariously supported. Both parents incubate the eggs and tend the young.
MOVEMENTS Although a strong flier, appears to be a normally sedentary species. Found throughout the year in known breeding sites, and very rarely seen elsewhere, although often colonises new waterbodies before African Jacana. Some evidence of seasonal

wandering in coastal Kenya.
DESCRIPTION All plumages: Plumage always rather soft and downy. Small tuft of orange-brown feathers at base of bill; forecrown dark (variable in extent) but crown, nape and eye-stripe bright chestnut-red. Well-marked supercilium, chestnut-brown near bill but white above and behind the eye. Cheeks, throat, front of neck, breast, belly and undertail white; sides of neck suffused pale golden-yellow; flanks and axillaries rich chestnut-brown; underwing entirely black except for white trailing edge to secondaries. Hindneck and upper mantle, sometimes also back and rump, blackish-brown strongly glossed purple. Scapulars and tertials brown, sometimes with broad buff fringes. Wing-coverts plain pale brown; flight feathers black, with narrow (about 7 mm) but conspicuous white trailing edge to secondaries and inner primaries. Uppertail-coverts and tail reddish-chestnut, sometimes with purplish-brown feather centres or buffish barring.
AGE/SEX Even young juveniles are exceedingly difficult to distinguish from adults; in the hand, the feather structure may be even looser and more downy. Buff fringes to the scapulars and buff barring on the uppertail may indicate a juvenile. Females average slightly larger than males, but are similar in plumage.
RACES No geographical variation is known.
MEASUREMENTS Length about 160 mm (6¼"). Wing 85-100 mm; bill 14-18 mm; tarsus 31-37 mm; tail 29-36 mm.
REFERENCES Fry (1983b).

2 AFRICAN JACANA *Actophilornis africana*   **Plate 1**

Other name: Lily-trotter
The common and widespread jacana of sub-Saharan Africa.

IDENTIFICATION Adult's dark chestnut body, white on face and neck and blue bill and shield are unmistakable. Only African species remotely similar are Madagascar Jacana (3) which is closely related but allopatric, and Lesser Jacana (1) which may resemble half-grown chick of the present species. Adult easily distinguished from Madagascar Jacana by its dark hindneck and white foreneck, and in flight by its uniform rump and tail, lacking a white band. Juveniles are almost identical, but African usually has a browner crown, hindneck and eye-stripe, and the feathering bordering the base of the lower mandible is brown and white, not mainly blackish. Lesser Jacana is much smaller but, if size is not apparent, look for an incipient bill-shield and uniform brown crown and nape, which are diagnostic of juvenile African and Madagascar. Also, Lesser Jacana always shows contrasting pale brown wing-coverts and, in

flight, a white trailing edge to the secondaries. **Bare parts:** Bill and bill-shield bright pale blue; shield is horny like that of a coot *Fulica*. Iris brown. Legs and toes blue-grey. A short spur is present on the bend of the wing, but is rounded and barely breaks the surface of the feathering.
VOICE A whining 'kyowrr' and a coot-like 'kruk'; sometimes calls in duet. A peculiar husky rattling screech is sometimes given in flight.
HABITS Always found in association with fresh water with emergent or floating vegetation, but at times frequents quite small ponds; sometimes occurs on backwaters of rivers and streams. Feeds by walking daintily across floating vegetation, relying on its enormously long toes and claws to support it; also feeds among waterside plants or on dry land along the water's edge. Nest is a simple structure of plant material at the water's edge or on floating vegetation; in some

parts of the range nests all the year round. Both sexes are highly aggressive in territorial defence, but only the male incubates. When doing so, his wings are tucked underneath his body; the eggs are held between the wings and body and are not in contact with the nest. Later, chicks are brooded and often carried tucked two under each wing. The bone structure of the wings is specially modified to facilitate this. The chicks are highly precocial; when danger threatens, they can hide submerged beneath water plants with only the bill and nostrils above the surface. Adults and juveniles are strong fliers and capable of finding quite small patches of habitat remote from possible breeding sites. Occasionally gathers in large, loose flocks.

MOVEMENTS There is effective dispersal, bringing individuals to small and often temporary pools, but no regular migrations are suspected.

DESCRIPTION Breeding and non-breeding: Glossy black cap, hindneck, and eye-stripe from base of lower mandible, enclosing small white supercilium mainly in front of eye; supercilium is sometimes obscured by the bony shield covering the forehead. Throat, cheeks and neck white, becoming pale golden-yellow on the upper breast and sides of the base of the neck; longest golden-yellow feathers are barred black and tipped chestnut-red. Upperparts and underparts otherwise dark chestnut-red; small coverts, and feathers of scapulars and back are green-

ish at the base and in worn plumage may look more green than chestnut. Primaries and tips of greater primary coverts and outer secondaries are blackish, contrasting above and below with chestnut wing-coverts. **Juvenile:** Small bill-shield. Cap, hindneck and eye-stripe are dull brown. Supercilium is slightly longer than in the adult, but sullied with reddish-brown behind the eye. Upperparts greener than adult but rump, secondaries and outer greater coverts are contrastingly chestnut. Underparts white except for chestnut-red flanks, axillaries and underwing-coverts, and pale golden-yellow ruff at base of neck. The golden-yellow feathers never show black barring.

AGE/SEX Adults are always completely chestnut-red on the belly: any white indicates an immature. Females are considerably larger than males; they are probably separable on wing measurement, but, owing to apparent profusion of wrongly-sexed birds in museum collections, it is difficult to determine this. No plumage differences are known between the sexes.

RACES No geographical variation is known.

MEASUREMENTS Length about 305 mm (12″). Wing 139-172 mm; bill (from tip to top of frontal shield) 43-59 mm (adults), 41-49 mm (juveniles); tarsus 58-72 mm.

REFERENCES Cunningham-van Someren and Robinson (1962), Vernon (1973), Wilson (1974), Fry (1983a,b), Postage (1984).

3 MADAGASCAR JACANA *Actophilornis albinucha*   Plate 1

Very similar to the African Jacana (2) but restricted to Madagascar, where African does not occur. A little-studied species.

IDENTIFICATION Adult differs from African Jacana in its 'reversed' head and neck pattern: face and front of neck are black and crown and hindneck white. Also, there is a white patch on the uppertail-coverts extending around onto the thighs, showing as a narrow white rump-patch in flight. Juveniles are effectively identical to African Jacana, but the crown, hindneck and eye-stripe are usually blacker and the dark bar across the lores slightly broader; the feathering bordering the base of the lower mandible is mainly blackish. See African Jacana for differences between juvenile and Lesser Jacana (1). **Bare parts:** Bill and bill-shield pale blue. Iris brown. Legs and toes blue-grey. A short spur is present on the bend of the wing, but is rounded and barely breaks the surface of the feathering.

VOICE Often noisy. Calls are not known to differ from those of the mainland species.

HABITS See African Jacana. As in African, Comb-crested (4) and Bronze-winged (6) Jacanas, the radius is bowed and has a broad flange, enabling young to be brooded, even carried, between the adult's wings and body.

MOVEMENTS Found widely in the northern half of Madagascar, more commonly in the west (where recorded south to Tuléar). Apparently sedentary, but range may be slowly expanding eastwards as forests are replaced by ricefields.

DESCRIPTION Breeding and non-breeding: Crown mainly white but always shows a few black feathers.

Nape, hindneck and sides of neck white, tinged with golden-yellow bordering the shoulders. Lores black dappled with white. Tiny white chin-patch hidden beneath lower mandible; otherwise ear-coverts, throat and front of neck glossy black. Rest of upperparts and underparts rich chestnut-brown, except for white band across uppertail-coverts which extends across the rearmost flank feathers and onto the outside of the thighs. Wing-coverts above and below are chestnut-brown, but the primaries and outer secondaries are blackish. **Juvenile:** See African Jacana, from which differs only in blacker crown, hindneck and eye-stripe.

AGE/SEX Note the difference in head pattern between adults and juveniles. Birds in late post-juvenile moult may resemble adults but with some blackish dappling on the hindneck or white on the belly. Females average larger, but have similar plumage to males.

RACES No variation within its limited range.

MEASUREMENTS Length about 305 mm (12″). Wing 149-179 mm; bill (including shield) 46-56 mm (adults), 38-44 mm (juveniles); tarsus 61-68 mm.

REFERENCES Rand (1936), Benson *et al.* (1976), Fry (1983b).

4 COMB-CRESTED JACANA *Irediparra gallinacea*   **Plate 2**

Other name: Lotus Bird
The only jacana of Australasia, but overlaps in range with Pheasant-tailed Jacana (5) in the Philippines and SE Borneo.

IDENTIFICATION The fleshy reddish-pink comb is unique. The American species (7, 8) also have tall frontal wattles, but differ in adult plumage by their dark neck and breast and in all plumages by their bright greenish-yellow flight feathers. The adult African Jacana (2) is fairly similar in plumage pattern, but has a blue bill-shield and an entirely chestnut body. Pheasant-tailed in juvenile or non-breeding plumage is best distinguished by its narrow black band encircling the throat and its almost entirely white wings. In Indonesia and the Philippines, beware confusion with White-breasted Waterhen *Amaurornis phoenicurus*. **Bare parts:** A fleshy reddish-pink wattle arising from the base of the forehead overlies the blackish feathering of forehead and crown; a large vertical wattle of bulging profile, something like a cock's comb, joins this frontal wattle to the top edge of the bill. The bill is mainly reddish-pink, with a sharply-defined blackish tip. Iris pale brownish-white or yellowish. Legs dull greyish-green; toes and claws enormously long. Short, blunt spur on carpal joint.

VOICE Sometimes noisy. A thin, rather chick-like twittering call is given in flight; in alarm, a sharp, rather nasal call.

HABITS Found throughout the year around freshwater lakes and ponds with abundant floating and emergent vegetation, sometimes also on backwaters of rivers. Adult has the bone structure of the wing modified to produce a 'brood-chamber' between wings and body. Australian race nests Sept-Feb, but races in New Britain and probably Borneo nest Apr-June. Young birds may escape predators by submerging beneath water plants with only the bill and nostrils above water. Flies with rapid, shallow wingbeats; flights are usually short, and low above water surface, simply to take the bird to the next patch of vegetation. Usually seen singly or in pairs; on occasion, feeding territories are established from which others of species are excluded. Normally conspicuous owing to open, flat habitat and mainly blackish plumage, but may freeze, relying on disruptive patterning for concealment.

MOVEMENTS Appears to be a highly sedentary species. Rarely seen away from breeding sites, or even in prolonged flight.

DESCRIPTION Breeding and non-breeding: Highly conspicuous comb between bill and forehead. Feathering of forehead, crown, hindneck and upper mantle black, glossed with purplish-blue. Thin, dark line joining eye to base of lower mandible; rest of face, neck and upper breast, including supercilium, glossy pale golden-yellow, except for white chin and throat. Lower breast, upper belly, flanks and entire underwing are black, slightly glossed with purplish-blue. Lower belly, rear flanks and undertail are white tinged with golden-yellow. Lower mantle, back, scapulars and wing-coverts are dark greeny-brown (except on *novaeguinea*); rest of upperwing, rump and tail are glossy black. **Juvenile:** Frontal wattle and comb are small. Plumage differs from adult's in chestnut-red cap, extensive rufous-buff fringing to the greeny-brown feathers of the upperparts, and underparts entirely white except for black underwing and fore-flanks, and some tinges of yellow on the cheeks and the sides of the breast.

AGE/SEX Young birds gain a complete breast-band early in the post-juvenile moult, then lose the red cap, but the wattle and comb remain undeveloped until a late stage. No plumage differences are known between the sexes, but females are probably consistently larger than males.

RACES Three races are described: *gallinacea* (SE Borneo, Mindanao, Moluccas and Timor), *novaeguinea* (Misol I., Aru Is., N and central New Guinea) and *novaehollandiae* (S New Guinea, N and E Australia). There may be a gradual cline of increasing size from Mindanao to Australia, but this is difficult to determine owing to individual differences in size. Plumages are alike, except that in *novaeguinea* the upperparts are darker: the mantle, back, scapulars and coverts are all-black glossed with purplish-blue, and only the larger scapulars are greenish.

MEASUREMENTS Length 210-240 mm (9"). Wing 116-144 mm; bill (measured from bill-tip to point where wattle joins forehead) 26-35 mm; tarsus 52-68 mm.

REFERENCES Potter (1934), Hindwood (1940), Weston (1978), Fry (1983b).

5 PHEASANT-TAILED JACANA *Hydrophasianus chirurgus*   **Plate 2**

Other name: Water-pheasant
This extraordinary species is the only jacana to have a separate non-breeding plumage, and the only one with regular migrations. The assumption of a long tail in breeding plumage (as occurs in some passerines) is unique among waders. To a limited extent convergent with Long-toed Lapwing (58) in habits and plumage pattern.

IDENTIFICATION Sympatric with Bronze-winged Jacana (6) over much of its range, and also with Comb-crested (4) in the S Philippines and SE Borneo. Unmistakable by virtue of its largely white wings at all seasons, like Long-toed Lapwing (race *leucoptera*), and its dark body and pheasant-like tail in breeding plumage. Non-breeding and juvenile plumages are inconspicuous until the bird takes flight with rather slow, deliberate flaps of startlingly white wings; may recall a lapwing or Magpie *Pica pica* in flight. On landing, runs forward with raised wings until the floating vegetation supports its weight. **Bare parts:** Bill more slender than in Bronze-winged; slaty-blue with yellowish tip in breeding plumage, otherwise brown with yellowish basal half. Iris brown. Legs and toes pale blue-grey, duller greenish- or bluish-grey in non-breeding plumages. Strong, very sharp, whitish spur is present on the bend of the wing.

VOICE In the breeding season, has a distinctive, far-carrying mewing call 'me-e-ou' or 'me-onp' and shorter variants. A peculiar nasal 'tewn' is heard from winter flocks.

HABITS Breeds on large freshwater lakes and ponds with much emergent and floating vegetation, chiefly during the summer period Mar-July. In S India breeds mostly in the monsoon season, June-Sept; in Sri Lanka also breeds in Jan. Polyandry is the rule: in one season the female may lay up to ten clutches, to be incubated by several different males. A tame bird where unmolested. In winter, gathers at favoured sites, sometimes in flocks of 50-100; also may appear singly at small sites where does not breed. Swims readily, and often feeds while doing so, resembling an outsize phalarope. Flocks are often flighty. Unlike other jacanas, this is a strong and confident flier; sometimes mobs raptors, lapwing-like, high in the air.

MOVEMENTS Northern populations have a seasonal north-south migration. Withdraws completely from the upper Himalayas and from S China in the winter. In spring, may penetrate high into the Himalayas (has been recorded at 3800 m). Vagrants reach S Japan. In winter reaches Sumatra regularly, but is only a vagrant to Java. Regular but scarce Oct-Apr in Oman and South Yemen. There is also a recent sight record from Paraburdoo, NW Australia.

DESCRIPTION Breeding: Head is white except for variably-sized black patch on rear crown. A narrow black line extends down the sides of the neck from the nape to the upper breast, separating the white front of the neck from the bright glossy golden-yellow hindneck. Body feathering above and below is dark chocolate-brown, with some greenish and purplish gloss above, particularly on the scapulars. Wings are entirely white except for greenish-brown tertials, and black on the tips of the outermost secondaries and the primaries, on the edges of the outer 3 primaries (the outermost large primary is all-black including the shaft), and on the tips of the greater primary coverts and alula. The tips of the outer primaries are extraor-

dinarily elongated; the outermost primary (rarely, the outer 3 primaries) sports a spatulate, racquet-shaped extension about 20 mm long, while the seventh primary has a broader, parallel-sided protrusion, apparently to protect the racquets from breakage. Underwing-coverts and axillaries are white. The tail is blackish-brown and strongly graduated, with the two central pairs of feathers extremely elongated; the feathers are not very stiff and are usually downcurved, but blow in the breeze. Occasional individuals show some white in the tail. **Non-breeding:** Crown becomes blackish and hindneck brown, with area of golden-yellow reduced to small patches on the sides of the neck. Upperparts become paler, greenish-brown. A blackish-brown necklace from lores, through eye, and down sides of neck joins on the upper breast, but underparts are otherwise white. White on the lesser and median coverts is replaced to a variable extent by pale brown feathers or white barred with brown. Leading lesser coverts are always white, with a narrow black bar dividing them from the brown-barred coverts. Tail is shorter but still strongly graduated; central pair of feathers is greenish-brown, but others are usually all-white. **Juvenile:** As non-breeding, but with rufous rather than greenish-brown cap, pale buff rather than golden-yellow on sides of neck, and extensive rufous-buff fringing to the brown feathers of the upperparts including the wing-coverts. Initially, neck and upper breast are tinged buffish; the blackish necklace is indistinct, composed of brownish-black spots and streaks. When fresh, the outer 3 primaries show spatulate racquets.

AGE/SEX Rufous cap or rufous fringing on upperparts or wing-coverts is diagnostic of young bird. First-years may attain only a partial breeding plumage. Females are larger than males, but no differences are known in plumage. Sexing is probably possible by wing measurement for all but a few individuals, but the position is confused by wrongly-sexed birds in museum collections.

RACES No geographical variation is known.

MEASUREMENTS Length about 310 mm (12¼"), 390-580 mm (19") when breeding. Wing, including racquet but not spur, 190-244 mm (adults), 162-228 mm (juveniles); bill 23-30 mm; tarsus 45-58 mm; tail 194-376 mm (breeding plumage), 110-117 mm (two non-breeding adults).

REFERENCES Hoffman (1950).

6 BRONZE-WINGED JACANA *Metopidius indicus* Plate 2

A bulky, large-billed jacana of India and SE Asia, with highly glossy plumage.

IDENTIFICATION Adult is unmistakable by virtue of mainly blackish plumage contrasting with bright yellow bill, red wattle, white band behind the eye, and greenish mantle, scapulars and wing-coverts. Beware confusion with Moorhen *Gallinula chloropus* and with the much larger breeding male Watercock *Gallicrex cinerea*, both of which lack the white stripe on the head. Juvenile is best identified by its mainly greenish upperparts and the rich buff colour of the breast. Pheasant-tailed Jacana (5) is largely sympatric, but easily distinguished in non-breeding and juven-

ile plumages by the narrow blackish necklace on its whitish or pale buff breast, mainly pale brown upperparts, and startlingly white wings in flight. **Bare parts:** Bill strongly built for a jacana, bright yellow at tip, becoming greenish-yellow and then tinged reddish towards the base; mostly greenish-yellow in juveniles. Frontal wattle and base of culmen bright red; wattle is neatly rounded at the top. Iris brown. Legs and feet dark green. There is a short, blunt spur on the bend of the wing.

VOICE A short, harsh grunt is used as a contact call,

often in flight. In alarm or aggression, gives a wheezy piping 'seek-seek-seek'.

HABITS Found all year on lowland freshwater lakes and reservoirs with emergent and floating vegetation; also occurs in wet grasslands and overgrown paddyfields. More likely to be found in fragmented habitat than is Pheasant-tailed. If pressed, may hide by submerging or take refuge among vegetation away from the water. Males defend territories against each other with great vigour; they alone incubate the eggs and take care of the chicks. The larger females are often polyandrous. Nests are built on floating vegetation, in India normally in the monsoon season June-Sept. The male can run carrying the chicks between his wings and body. After breeding, sometimes gathers in mobile groups of a dozen or so. Flight is quite strong on broad, rounded coot-like wings, but considerably less agile than Pheasant-tailed.

MOVEMENTS Apparently largely sedentary with limited post-breeding dispersal. Perhaps now only a migrant to Sumatra; very rare in Java.

DESCRIPTION Breeding and non-breeding: Broad white band from eyelids to sides of upper neck. Rest of head, neck, underparts and underwing black with strong dark green gloss, except for dark rufous undertail and, on rear flanks, very dark rufous-brown with purplish gloss. Base of hindneck strongly glossed deep violet-blue. Mantle, scapulars, wing-coverts and outer webs of tertials glossy brownish-green, sometimes with narrow pale buff edges to the greater coverts, outer tertials and inner secondaries. Primaries, primary coverts, alula and secondaries blackish with dull greenish sheen. Back, rump, uppertail-coverts and tail deep rufous with purple gloss. **Juvenile:** Frontal wattle very small. Dull rufous-brown cap. Short white supercilium not extending beyond the eye. Narrow dark line across the lores. Dusky patch below ear-coverts. Throat and cheeks whitish, becoming deep buff on the front of the neck and pale yellowish-buff on the sides. Lower breast, belly and undertail whitish. Flanks and outside of thighs, axillaries and underwing black, glossed with dull greeny-blue. Hindneck sooty-black with dull greenish gloss becoming deep violet-blue at the base of the neck. Mantle, scapulars and wings as adult; occasionally a few rufous-fringed feathers in scapulars or violet-glossed mantle feathers. Back dull greenish-brown. Rump and uppertail sooty-brown, barred strongly with rufous and slightly glossed purple. Tail feathers mainly white, with rufous patches near the base and irregular blackish bars.

AGE/SEX Any white or buff on the underparts indicates young bird. Females are larger than males on average, but are not known to differ in plumage. Probably many birds can be sexed on measurements, but the position is confused by wrongly-sexed museum specimens.

RACES No geographical variation is known.

MEASUREMENTS Length 280-310 mm (11½″). Wing 150-197 mm (males mostly 150-180 mm, females mostly 167-197 mm); bill (from tip to top of frontal shield) 34-46 mm (adults), 32-38 mm (juveniles); tarsus 61-76 mm; tail 40-52 mm.

REFERENCES Mathew (1964).

7 NORTHERN JACANA *Jacana spinosa*   Plate 3

Other names: American or Middle American Jacana
Formerly treated as conspecific with Wattled Jacana (8); now known to be sympatric with it in W Panama, but hybrids are reported from there and also probably from Costa Rica.

IDENTIFICATION Dark coloration, bright greenish-yellow flight feathers, frontal wattle, enormously long toes and claws and jacana-like behaviour rule out all other Neotropical species except the very similar Wattled Jacana. Consistent differences from Wattled are a three-lobed, yellow frontal wattle, no rictal lappet hanging beside the bill, and a slight but distinct colour contrast between the blackish breast and the very dark maroon-chestnut belly. All races of Wattled are continuously blackish from breast to undertail, sometimes with an ill-defined tinge of chestnut or maroon on the belly; the race *hypomelaena*, which is sympatric with Northern, is normally black above as well as below. Juvenile Northerns may be distinguished from juvenile *hypomelaena* by their chestnut (not blackish) rump, uppertail and flanks; they are, however, effectively identical in plumage to juveniles of the widespread southern races of Wattled and can be identified only by the trifid (three-lobed) shape of the tiny frontal wattle. **Bare parts:** Bill mainly yellow, but edged with bluish at the base of the upper mandible and sometimes at the base of the frontal wattle. Frontal wattle bright yellow, clearly three-lobed. Iris brown. Legs and toes dull greyish-green. There is a long and sharply-pointed yellowish spur on the bend of the wing.

VOICE A noisy bird with rather complex vocalisations. Calls are generally hard and rasping and include single notes, chittering noises, and a typewriter-like clacking.

HABITS Like other jacanas, found around freshwater marshes and ponds with emergent and floating vegetation. Feeds chiefly on insects and seeds picked from the vegetation, but may feed on wet pastureland or on lawns adjacent to typical habitat. Polyandry and sex-role reversal are highly developed. Females have one to four mates for which they lay eggs, and they help to defend their offspring from potential predators; only rarely do the females brood the chicks. Only the males incubate, sitting on their wings with two eggs held between each wing and the breast. Breeding birds are highly territorial and aggressive towards their own sex and towards other species, but non-breeders often feed in loose groups. When approached, often take flight, displaying the vivid colouring of the wings. On landing, often hold wings aloft for a moment.

MOVEMENTS Almost entirely sedentary, but stragglers (usually young birds) occasionally reach the coastal plain of Texas almost as far as Houston, and may stay to breed. Also recorded as a vagrant or escape at Lake Okeechobee, Florida.

DESCRIPTION Breeding and non-breeding: Large wattle and spur. Entire head, neck, upper mantle and upper breast sooty-black glossed strongly with bottle-green. Rest of underparts including underwing dark maroon-chestnut; under primary coverts and carpal area dark brown. Rest of upperparts including coverts, tertials and tail brighter chestnut glossed with maroon; tail is loosely structured and largely hidden among long coverts above and below. Flight feathers bright greenish-yellow, with brown tips to all feathers and increasingly long and broad brown outer edges to primaries; primary coverts, alula and carpal area are all dark brown. Inner web of inner secondary sometimes has irregular brown markings. **Juvenile:** Wattle and spur small. Cap and nape dark brown. Long, whitish supercilium from bill to sides of nape. Narrow, blackish eye-stripe from bill extends backwards to join blackish hindneck. Underparts off-white, except for quite bright buff suffusion to the breast and dark maroon-chestnut flanks. Underwing as adult, except for whitish dappling on the leading lesser primary coverts. Mantle, scapulars, wing-coverts and tail feathers dull brown strongly glossed green and with some chestnut and buff fringes, par-

ticularly to coverts and scapulars. Rump and upper-tail initially dark brown with broad chestnut fringes. Flight feathers as adult's, but brown on inner secondary may extend submarginally along outer web.
AGE/SEX Any whitish in the plumage indicates young bird. Feathers of rump, uppertail and outer median coverts of juvenile are quickly replaced by adult-type feathers; replacement of nape, breast and belly feathers follows; the chin is normally the last area to show retained white feathers. Females are considerably larger than males, averaging 77% heavier in the breeding season, but are not known to differ otherwise.
RACES Three: nominate *spinosa* (W Panama to Guatemala and Belize), *gymnostoma* (Mexico, occasionally S Texas), and *violacea* (Cuba, Isle of Pines, Jamaica and Hispaniola). All are very similar.
MEASUREMENTS Length 170-230 mm (7¾"). Wing 113-141 mm; bill (measured to the angle at the base of the shield) 28-36 mm; tarsus 48-62 mm; tail 38-49 mm.
REFERENCES Jenni and Collier (1972), Jenni et al. (1974), Jenni and Betts (1978), Stephens (1984a, b).

8 WATTLED JACANA *Jacana jacana*   Plate 3

Other name: South American Jacana
The only jacana of South America, but sympatric with the very similar Northern Jacana (7) in W Panama. Hybrids are known from Panama, and probably also Costa Rica.

IDENTIFICATION See Northern Jacana for a full discussion of the distinctions between these two species. Behaviour, black or chestnut-and-black body plumage with bright greenish-yellow flight feathers, and enormously long toes and claws quickly eliminate all other Neotropical species. Consistent specific characters are the two-lobed, dull red frontal wattle, well-developed rictal lappets, and lack of colour contrast between the breast and the belly. A black back also indicates this species, but occurs only in the northernmost race. Juveniles of most races can be distinguished from Northern Jacana only by the shape of the developing frontal wattle. **Bare parts:** Bill yellow, sometimes brownish. Two-lobed frontal wattle and lappets overhanging the base of the bill are dull red, sometimes with a tinge of blue on the top of the wattle. Legs and toes dull greyish-green or pale pinkish-yellow. There is a long and viciously sharp, thorn-like spur on the bend of the wing, averaging over 1 cm long in adult females.
VOICE Varied cackling calls, apparently similar to those of Northern Jacana.
HABITS Much as Northern Jacana. As in that species the sex-roles are reversed and polyandry occurs, at least in areas of high density. In seasonally-variable sites, more likely to breed in pairs at low density. Mainly a lowland bird, but nests as high as 720 m in Venezuela. Breeding season is chiefly June-Feb. Nests are sometimes built over shallow water in ricefields and wet grassland. This species has been recorded grooming ticks from capybara *Hydrochoerus hydrochaeris*.
MOVEMENTS Proliferation of races suggests that this species is highly sedentary. The single record from

Chile was possibly of a vagrant from across the Andes. An apparent hybrid with Northern Jacana in Costa Rica raises the possibility of occasional penetration beyond Panama.
DESCRIPTION See Identification and Races sections for differences from Northern Jacana.
AGE/SEX Any whitish in the body plumage indicates young bird. Normally, the chin is the last area to retain any white feathers. Females are considerably larger than males and with practice can be identified in the field. The sexes are not known to differ in appearance, except that on the female the top of the frontal wattle is tinged with blue, while on the male it usually is not.
RACES Six: *hypomelaena* (W Panama to N Colombia), *melanopygia* (W Colombia, W Venezuela), *intermedia* (N Venezuela), nominate *jacana* (Trinidad, the Guianas to E Bolivia and N Argentina), *scapularis* (apparently isolated in W Ecuador), and *peruviana* (E Peru). The nominate race, covering most of the range, has chestnut upperparts like Northern Jacana. Only *hypomelaena* and *scapularis* differ noticeably. In *hypomelaena* all chestnut of upperparts, flanks and underwing of both adult and juvenile is replaced by black, normally completely. In *scapularis* the upperparts are rufous but some black feathers are admixed among the upper scapulars; also, in both adult and juvenile, the yellow in the outer 1-2 primaries is so pale as to be almost white. The northern races are marginally the smallest, but considerable variation precludes separation on measurements.
MEASUREMENTS Length 170-230 mm (7¾"): average nominate male 192 mm, female 213 mm. Wing 113-143 mm; bill (measured to the angle at the base

of the shield) 29-33 mm; tarsus 51-62 mm; tail 37-52 mm.

REFERENCES Betts (1973), Osborne and Bourne (1977), Osborne (1982).

9 PAINTED SNIPE *Rostratula benghalensis*   Plate 4

Other name: Greater Painted Snipe
This is a very strange bird, more closely related to the jacanas than to other waders including the true snipes. A similar species (10) replaces it in South America. Sexual dimorphism is strongly developed.

IDENTIFICATION Like a large, short-billed snipe in size and proportions, but plumage pattern is unmistakable. Most conspicuous features are the white or yellowish eye-ring and streak behind the eye, white 'harness' across the shoulders, and whitish belly and flanks, contrasting with the dark greenish and brownish of the rest of the bird. In flight, like a large snipe in size and with broad and rounded wings like Eurasian Woodcock (159); legs often dangle and wingbeats are rather slow and erratic. South American Painted Snipe is much smaller and has a more strongly-curved bill, a whiter crown-stripe, and white spots in the scapulars and on the wing-coverts; both sexes are darker than Painted Snipe and lack rufous and olive-green colours. **Bare parts:** Bill pale reddish-brown with greenish basal third, distinctly down-curved over terminal third. Iris dark brown. Legs dull yellowish-green, sometimes tinged brownish or grey.

VOICE Female in display has a soft hooting 'koh, koh, koh' like blowing across the top of an empty bottle, heard mainly at night; also various hisses and growls; her trachea, unlike the male's, is highly convoluted. When flushed, both sexes are normally silent but may utter a loud, explosive 'kek'.

HABITS Exclusively a wetland species, chiefly crepuscular. Nests among emergent vegetation in shallow water, building a mound of vegetation to keep the eggs above water; usually nests in extensive swamps and marshes, occasionally in overgrown paddyfields. Incubation is almost entirely by the male; the larger, brighter female is often polyandrous and may lay several clutches, each for a different male. Female gives display call chiefly at dusk and at night, either on the ground or from 'roding' flight like Eurasian Woodcock's. There are also remarkable spread-wing displays, given by both sexes. Feeds singly or in loose groups, sometimes up to 25. Body is bobbed rhythmically downwards as the bird walks and probes. When disturbed, usually freezes; groups may form a motionless tableau, each bird holding a different attitude. When approached, often does not flush until observer is very close, then flies only a short distance. At dawn and dusk, may leave the marshland to feed on open plough or grassland.

MOVEMENTS No regular migrations, except in NE China, where it appears to be only a summer visitor, and perhaps also in Australia. Elsewhere, mainly sedentary but performs irregular movements in response to conditions of rainfall or drought; occurs sporadically outside normal range, and sometimes remains to breed. A 900-km movement has been recorded in N India. Vagrant Israel, Somalia, Zanzibar and Pemba.

DESCRIPTION Breeding and non-breeding plumages are alike. **Female:** Crown greenish-brown with golden-buff crown-stripe; white patch around the eye

display

extending backwards a short distance; rest of head and neck dark rufous-brown, usually paler around the bill and sometimes with some whitish on chin and throat. Broad complete blackish-brown breast-band bordering rufous neck, also extending around base of neck as a complete collar. Bright white breast-band below the blackish band, then below that a blackish-brown patch each side of the breast, forming a broken band on the lower breast. Belly and undertail white suffused creamy-buff, flanks more or less smudged with brown. Axillaries, median and greater underwing-coverts bright white; underside of flight feathers and leading coverts mainly grey, with buffish spots and brown bars. Mantle, back, rump, tertials and most scapulars mainly greyish-green with intricate but sober patterning of dark brown and rufous; more or less hidden in the centre of the scapulars are several narrow and lanceolate pure white feathers. Wing-coverts dark olive-green with regular fine blackish barring. Primary coverts, primaries and secondaries, uppertail-coverts and tail mainly ash-grey patterned with blackish bars and large, rounded golden-buff spots, each outlined in blackish. A conspicuous feature of the spread wing is a narrow, fairly discrete black bar which crosses the base of the primaries and secondaries. There is also a very narrow white trailing edge to the secondaries. **Male:** Plumage is much duller. Rufous on head and neck is replaced by finely-patterned ash-grey on hindneck and by mottled grey and brown on the neck and breast, becoming paler, almost whitish, on the chin and throat. Patch around and behind eye is golden-buff. Black on breast is replaced by mottled brown. Both the white breast-band and the belly are suffused with buff. Mantle as female, but there is a more conspicuous golden-buff 'V' mark formed by the mantle edges and the inner scapulars. Some white is hidden in the scapulars, but no feathers are pure white. Wing-coverts differ dramatically from female in pattern, being basically greenish-gold and spotted rather than barred; there are conspicuous paired golden-buff spots near the tip of each feather, and ash-grey hidden at the base. **Juvenile:** Juveniles of both sexes are very similar to the adult male, but differ slightly in the pattern of the wing-coverts. Juvenile coverts show paler buff spots and initially a whitish-buff tip; the grey at the base of the feather largely replaces the greeny-gold of the adult male, particularly on the inner web. Initially there is some down at the tips of the tail feathers.

AGE/SEX Sexes are dimorphic in both plumage and size. For African birds, wing >134 mm indicates female, <133 mm male. As soon as post-juvenile moult starts, young can also be sexed using the wing-covert patterns described above. Beware confusion between juvenile and adult male.

RACES Two. Australian birds *australis* are considera-

bly larger, but there are no noticeable differences in plumage. Within the nominate race, which covers the whole of the rest of the range, Chinese examples average about 3 mm shorter in the wing than African ones.

MEASUREMENTS Length 230-260 mm (9½"). Wing: *benghalensis* 125-135 mm (males), 135-150 mm (females); *australis* average 146 mm (males), 156 mm (females). Bill 39-54 mm; tarsus 40-51 mm; tail 41-51 mm.

REFERENCES Beven (1913), Lowe (1963), Muller (1975), Komeda (1983).

10 SOUTH AMERICAN PAINTED SNIPE   Plate 4
Nycticryphes semicollaris

Much smaller and plainer than its Old World relative and virtually lacking in sexual dimorphism.

IDENTIFICATION Not likely to be confused with any other South American wader. Smaller and shorter-billed than true snipes and with a much weaker, more fluttery flight. Diademed Plover (118) also has rounded wings and may look similar in flight, but is found only at high altitude. Apart from smaller size, differs from Painted Snipe (9) in its darker plumage, white spots on the scapulars and wing-coverts, and more sharply-decurved bill. **Bare parts:** Bill straight for most of its length but sharply downcurved at tip; rather variable in colour, usually greenish or yellowish-brown but often reddish-brown over the outer two-thirds. Iris brown. Legs and feet green; there is a small area of webbing between the middle and outer toes.

VOICE Silent when flushed. May give a plaintive whistle, also a hoarse 'wee-oo' as a contact or alarm call.

HABITS Found throughout the year in open swampy areas and wet grassland in lowland regions, often with Magellan Snipe (176) and Pectoral Sandpiper (199). Breeding season may last from July to Feb, the timing depending on local conditions. Both sexes incubate the clutch, normally of two eggs; the nest is a simple structure of grasses and reed-stems on swampy ground close to the water's edge. Nesting is often semi-colonial. There is no proof of polyandry in this species. When flushed, flies usually only a short distance, rarely rising above about 10 m; wingbeats are strong but rather erratic and bat-like.

MOVEMENTS No regular migrations, but performs short-distance movements in response to local conditions; of regular seasonal occurrence in some localities.

DESCRIPTION Breeding and non-breeding plumages are similar. **Adult:** Head, neck and breast dark sooty olive-brown, except for blackish cap with central whitish-buff crown-stripe from bill to nape, and inconspicuous fine buffish supercilium backwards from eye. Bright white patch on sides of lower breast. Sharp division between dark breast and off-white belly and vent. Flanks and undertail suffused creamy-brown. Axillaries and underwing-coverts bright white. Mantle dark brown with fine grey barring; a conspicuous golden-buff line at the edge of the mantle forms a contrasting 'V' on the upperparts. Scapulars strongly marked blackish, grey and rich brown; a large bright white patch shows half-way along outer edge of scapulars. Rump and uppertail-coverts paler, dull brown with fine vermiculations. Tail graduated; tail feathers are similar to coverts and rump in pattern and very loosely structured. Wing-coverts dark brown with fine grey and brown markings; longer medians show conspicuous, large, rounded white spots. Greater coverts, also primary coverts, primaries and secondaries, brown with small, rounded buffish spots. **Juvenile:** Similar, but throat and breast are pale buff with dark brown spotting and streaking. White in scapulars is replaced by creamy-buff. Wing-coverts lack white spots, and are mainly dark brown with broad pale buff fringes and bars. Only a small white patch on the sides of the breast.

AGE/SEX Streaky breast and lack of white on upperparts indicates juvenile. Female averages a shade larger, but is not known to differ in plumage.

RACES No geographical variation is known.

MEASUREMENTS Length 190-215 mm (8"). Wing 101-111 mm (males), 107-115 mm (females); bill 36-42 mm; tarsus 31-38 mm; tail 46-56 mm.

REFERENCES Johnson (1965), Höhn (1975).

11 CRAB PLOVER *Dromas ardeola*   Plate 9

An extraordinary species, restricted to the coasts of the Indian Ocean. Its tunnel-nesting habit, its pure white egg and its nidicolous young are unique among waders.

IDENTIFICATION The mainly pied plumage coupled with a massive black bill makes this bird unmistakable. Juveniles are less contrasty, mainly grey and white above, but are more likely to be mistaken for a gull than for any other sort of wader. Confusion with Pied Avocet (27) is most unlikely, even at long range, owing to the huge bill of Crab Plover, which is always obvious, and the difference in gait between the species: the avocet walks steadily and delicately, head down while feeding, and the Crab Plover has a stop, run, dip forward action like a plover. Beware the real possibility of confusion with the much smaller-billed, plainer Grey Plover (84), which may become very pale, almost whitish-grey, in tropical areas. **Bare parts:** Bill very large, very deep at gonys but tapering to a pointed tip, solidly black. Iris dark brown. Legs pale greyish or greyish-blue; toes and part of tarsus project beyond tail-tip in flight.

VOICE Usual call in winter quarters is a falsetto 'ka', not unlike that of Bar-tailed Godwit (125) in quality, usually repeated rapidly. Noise from a dense flock is a constant rising whinney. On the breeding grounds, gives a variety of sharp whistles, 'kew-ki-ki', 'ki-tewk' etc. Incubating females may hiss at intruders from the back of the burrow. Young beg noisily for food, even well into the winter.

HABITS Nests Apr-Aug in dense colonies on sandy islands or extensive coastal dunes. The single large white egg (rarely two) is laid in a chamber at the end of a tunnel at least 1.5 m long. Tunnels are excavated by the birds themselves and may honeycomb very large areas, extending up to about 1 km from the sea. The chick is nidicolous, relying on food carried in by the adults. Activity at the colonies is largely crepuscular and nocturnal. Even when fledged, the chick is highly dependent on the adults for food; food-begging behaviour persists well into the winter. Adults and young feed almost exclusively on crabs, which are hunted on the beaches and mudflats with a stealthy plover-like action. When prey is spotted, the bird advances in a rapid run which ends with a stab of the bill. Small crabs may be consumed whole, while larger ones are crushed and eaten piecemeal. Usually feeds singly or in small loose groups, but individuals gather from a wide area to roost communally at high tide. Flight is fairly slow, with rather stiff wingbeats, usually quite low above the water. Flocks fly in dense packs or in lines or 'V's. The head is sunk back into the shoulders in flight, but the long legs trail behind. Both flocks and single individuals are often fairly approachable.

MOVEMENTS Known to breed only in the Gulf of Oman, the Gulf of Aden, and the southern Red Sea; other breeding areas may yet remain to be discovered. In much of its range occurs throughout the year, but bulk of population shifts southwards in Aug-

Nov, after breeding, returning northwards in Mar-Apr. Normally absent from southern part of African range and from areas east of breeding range (except N Sri Lanka) during the breeding season. Sometimes moves south in family parties (two adults plus one juvenile). Winter range includes oceanic islands; regular in numbers on some isolated island groups, but no records from others nearby. Vagrant Malaysia, W peninsular Thailand (perhaps regular).

DESCRIPTION Breeding and non-breeding: Head is white with small blackish marks just before and behind the eye, and a variable amount of grey suffusion and blackish streaking on rear crown; some birds of both sexes are completely white-headed. Underparts and underwing-coverts are white. Lower hindneck and mantle are black. Long black feathers from the sides of the rear mantle lying alongside the inner scapulars form a black wedge each side of the white back and rump. Uppertail-coverts, tail, scapulars and tertials are variable in colour, white on some individuals but pale silvery-grey on others. Lesser and median coverts are white, greater coverts and secondaries black. Lesser and median primary coverts are white. The alula, greater primary coverts and primaries are essentially black, but with white on the feather shafts; there is also some whitish at the bases of the primaries. The white areas on the primary coverts and the primary bases form two small whitish bars across the otherwise black outer half of the wing. On the underwing, the primaries and secondaries show as white, with a blackish trailing edge particularly to the outer primaries. **Juvenile:** As adult but black of mantle is replaced by dark silvery-grey, and white of wing-coverts is replaced by pale grey. Scapulars and tertials pale grey. Lower rump, uppertail and tail are a darker grey than in any adult. Head always shows a strong grey suffusion and darker streaking on rear crown.

AGE/SEX Juveniles remain distinct in plumage until the start of the following breeding season. One-year-old birds may be diagnosed later, in the hand, by their heavily-worn primaries. Sexes are similar in plumage and in size, except that males tend to have a slightly longer and heavier bill than females.

RACES No geographical variation is known.

MEASUREMENTS Length about 380-410 mm (15½"). Wing 200-226 mm (adults), 191-219 mm (juveniles); bill 41-64 mm, depth 14-17 mm; tarsus 84-102 mm; tail 62-70 mm.

REFERENCES Penny (1971), Neelakantan *et al.* (1980).

12 EURASIAN OYSTERCATCHER *Haematopus ostralegus* Plate 5

Other names: Oystercatcher, European Oystercatcher

A very familiar and easily-identified wader within its wide range; it is the only pied oystercatcher found in Europe, Asia and Africa. This, Magellanic (19) and South Island Pied Oystercatcher (20) are the only oystercatchers that habitually occur inland.

IDENTIFICATION A large black-and-white wader with a prominent long orange bill, red eye and eye-ring, and stout pinkish legs. The whitest of the pied oystercatchers. In flight, identified easily by its white back and long wingbar; the white wingbar extends to at least the middle primaries, and often to the outers. Non-breeding birds have a white bar across

the throat; the three races of the present species are the only oystercatchers that show this interesting feature. No overlap in range with other pied oystercatchers has been recorded. Eurasian is most similar to the Pied Oystercatcher (20) of Australasia, but latter has the white wingbar restricted to the secondaries (sometimes the inner primary) and its white rump-patch ends squarely on the lower back. Pied Oystercatcher shows more black on the breast and never has a white throat-band. American Oystercatcher (13) has a clear contrast between brown upperparts and black head and neck, yellow eyes, a shorter wing-bar, and white above the tail restricted to a narrow band on the uppertail-coverts. **Bare parts:** Bill orange in adults, slightly paler at tip, slightly duller in winter; in young juveniles, dull yellowish-pink at base and dark brownish at tip, becoming steadily brighter with age. Iris red in adult, reddish-brown in immatures, and mud-brown in juveniles; eye-ring scarlet in adult, dull reddish-yellow in immatures, almost lacking in juveniles. Legs medium-pink in adults, greyish in juveniles becoming brighter with age; feet do not project beyond tail in flight.

VOICE Most of the calls are based on the high, sharp 'kleep' contact note; there is a disyllabic 'kle-eap', a quiet 'weep' and, when agitated, a repeated sharp 'kip' or 'pick'. Display on the ground includes a trilling piping call, slowing and tailing off at the end; in aerial display a more melodic 'tee-teeoo', repeated rhythmically.

HABITS Nests Apr-July in a variety of coastal habitats (saltmarshes, sandy or rocky beaches, dunes, short-grass cliff tops) and also widely inland, mainly along shingle river valleys but also around reservoir and lake edges and on grass or cereal fields, often some distance from water. The nest is often raised above the surrounding land on an earth-bank, a rooftop, or even a hollowed fence-post. There is a slow, deep-flapping butterfly display flight, strikingly different from the normal flight. Almost exclusively coastal when not breeding; occurs in large concentrations in favoured estuaries, also on open sandy or rocky shores. May occur in unexpected sites inland on migration. Winter roosts are dense and may number several thousand individuals. Birds with a blade-like tip to the bill feed chiefly on mussels and cockles, opened skilfully by inserting the bill-tip inside the shell or by hammering through; those with more pointed bills probe for worms on the intertidal flats or in nearby pasture fields. Diet influences bill shape, which is not constant for any individual. Best feeding sites on mussel-beds are vigorously defended by dominant birds, chiefly adults; young feed more often in loose flocks on mudflats or pasture. Flight is strong and direct with shallow wingbeats; groups often fly in ragged lines. Noisy piping display, in which birds run parallel with downward-pointing bills, is heard all year.

MOVEMENTS The most migratory oystercatcher. Some western birds (nominate race) are almost sedentary, but others winter south to Mauretania or in smaller numbers as far as Nigeria, where records are apparently increasing. Vagrants have reached Greenland, Spitsbergen, the Azores, Madeira, Canary Is., and Cape Verde Is.; birds ringed in Britain on migration have been found on Bear I. (June 1977) and in Greenland (Apr 1979). The central race *longipes* winters on the coasts of the Middle East, India and Sri Lanka, also NE Africa; occurs more rarely southwards in E Africa, but has reached South Africa (21 records by 1980). Most arrivals in S Africa are in Dec. Vagrants (probably *longipes*) have occurred inland in Kenya, Uganda and NE Zaire (Oct 1913). Vagrants in Namibia (four records by 1980) are of

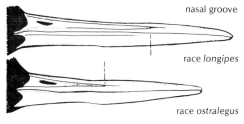

nasal groove

race *longipes*

race *ostralegus*

indeterminate race. The eastern race *osculans* winters in SE China, vagrant Japan and south to peninsular Burma. Vagrant Commander Is. Some individuals may not attempt to breed until five years old, and many immatures remain on the wintering grounds all year. Vagrants are often long-stayers.

DESCRIPTION Adult breeding: Head, neck, breast and upperparts glossy black, contrasting brilliantly with long white wingbar formed by inner secondaries, base of outer secondaries and base of most primaries. Back, rump, uppertail-coverts and base of tail white. Broad black terminal tail-band, broadest on central feathers. Belly, flanks and undertail white. Underwings almost entirely white. **Adult non-breeding:** As breeding, but for short period in autumn and early winter adult may show white bar across the throat, sometimes a triangular patch with apex pointing towards bill-base. **Juvenile:** As non-breeding adult, but upperparts and wing-coverts brownish-black with brownish-buff fringes. Uppertail-coverts barred brown and tipped buff. Looks rather dirty at a distance. Bare-part colours are extremely useful characters. Initially bill is always pointed. **Immature non-breeding:** Early non-breeding plumages are rather browner than those of adult and white throat-bar is usually broader (but sometimes may be absent). Adult breeding plumage is not attained until at the earliest second season after hatching.

AGE/SEX Brownish plumage of juvenile distinct but is normally lost, except for a few inner median coverts, by Nov-Jan. Bare-part colours allow separation into three age-classes: first-year (bare parts very dull), immature (iris brownish-red, eye-ring dull orangey-yellow, legs sullied with grey), and adult (bright colours). Sexes differ in bill length and depth, and up to 90% can be sexed by length:depth ratio; separating values, however, differ locally. Females' bills are longer and thinner than those of males, averaging about 8 mm longer. Male has on average a 5% broader black tail-band, measured on central feathers.

RACES Three: nominate *ostralegus* (Europe, coastal W USSR), *longipes* (central USSR) and *osculans* (Kamchatka to N China). Bill length increases from west to east. The race *longipes* differs in being rather browner above than the other two races; the nasal groove extends more than half-way along the bill (less than half-way in *ostralegus*). The race *osculans* lacks white on shafts of outer 2-3 primaries, and shows no white on the outer webs of the outer 5.

MEASUREMENTS Length 400-460 mm (17"). Wing 235-284 mm; bill 62-102 mm; tarsus 45-60 mm; tail 88-112 mm.

REFERENCES Harris (1967), Heppleston (1971, 1972), Dare and Mercer (1973, 1974), Hockey and Cooper (1982).

13 AMERICAN OYSTERCATCHER *Haematopus palliatus*   Plate 6

The American equivalent of the Eurasian Oystercatcher (12) but less numerous and less migratory, breeding only at the coast.

IDENTIFICATION American is the only pied oystercatcher with a strong contrast between brown back and wings and black head and neck, and is the only one with the combination of yellow eye and red eyering; it shows less white above than any of the other pied species. It is the only pied oystercatcher normally found in the Americas except for Magellanic Oystercatcher (19) in the extreme south; Eurasian Oystercatcher could reach Atlantic North America or the Aleutians as a vagrant. Differs from Eurasian in its browner upperparts, yellow eye and paler legs (adults only), shorter wingbar, darker tail, and dark back and upper rump. Never shows a white throatbar. Like Magellanic, shows only a narrow band of white across the uppertail-coverts in flight. Differs from Magellanic in browner upperparts, red eye-ring, dark-tipped secondaries and whiter under primary coverts. Populations in W Mexico, Galapagos Is. and E Argentina, and occasional individuals of other races, are like the Variable (17) and Chatham Islands (18) Oystercatchers of New Zealand in showing a smudgy lower border to the black breast rather than a neat division between black and white. The W Mexican population *frazari* is known to interbreed with American Black Oystercatcher (14) on occasion, and may be in effect a hybrid population. Northern *frazari* often have a considerable amount of black flecking on the belly. **Bare parts:** Adult has bill orange-red, paler at the tip, iris lemon-yellow, eye-ring orange-red, and legs pale pink. Young bird initially has bill dull pinkish-brown, tipped darker, iris brownish, eyering narrow and dull reddish, and legs dull greyish; it gains adult colours over a two-year period.
VOICE Its shrill piping 'kleep' and piping display are virtually identical to Eurasian Oystercatcher's.
HABITS Strictly coastal at all seasons, only a vagrant inland; nests and feeds on rocky coasts, as well as on sandy or shell beaches. Breeding and feeding behaviour are generally similar to Eurasian Oystercatcher's. Does not occur in such large concentrations; normally seen in scattered pairs or small flocks. Nominate race feeds almost entirely on mudflats and beaches, while *frazari* shows strong preference for rocky coasts.
MOVEMENTS Mainly sedentary, but wanders occasionally outside the breeding season. Nominate race is only a summer visitor to recently re-established breeding grounds in New England, and spreads southwards into Central America in winter. Vagrant

north to New Brunswick and Nova Scotia, once Lake Ontario, Canada (May-July 1960). In California, singles have wandered northwards as far as Point Reyes between Oct and Apr, and are occasionally resident (one was present on Anacapa I., off Oxnard, from May 1964 to late 1981); also three together inland at Salton Sea (Aug 1977).
DESCRIPTION Breeding and non-breeding: Head, neck and breast black. Upperparts warm dark brown except for black primaries, black tips of secondaries and tail, white wingbar and white band across uppertail. The wingbar comprises inner secondaries, bases of outer secondaries and generally the bases of innermost primaries. The white uppertail-coverts form a narrow curving white patch. Belly and underwings white, although the under primary coverts are variably washed dark brown. **Juvenile:** As adult but all dark feathers of upperparts, including head, are extensively spotted pale buff; the spots are bordered by narrow dark brown lines. Bare-part colours are distinctive.
AGE/SEX Juvenile plumage is distinct in the field for two to four months. Bare-part colours, however, are useful for at least one, probably two years. Sexes similar in plumage, except that male tends to be blacker-backed and redder-billed (at least in nominate race); females average larger, and 8-10 mm longer in bill length.
RACES Five, but their status is uncertain: nominate *palliatus* (E United States, E Mexico, Colombia to Uruguay, West Indies, Bahamas), *frazari* (W Mexico), *galapagensis* (Galapagos Is.), *pitanay* (W Panama to Chiloe I., Chile) and *durnfordi* (Argentina). The three Pacific populations have no white, or very little, in the primaries. The isolated *galapagensis* has disproportionately large legs and toes. The race *pitanay* is the smallest in wing measurement, *frazari* the largest; *durnfordi* is the shortest-legged. Three races, *frazari*, *galapagensis* and *durnfordi*, are browner above, and have a mottled lower breast rather than a sharp division. Baker (*in litt.*) speculates that there are no valid subspecies, and that the observed pattern has resulted from clinal variation and hybridisation with black oystercatchers.
MEASUREMENTS Length 400-440 mm (16½"). Wing 232-275 mm; bill 64-95 mm; tarsus 49-68 mm; tail 90-112 mm.
REFERENCES Tomkins (1947), Kenyon (1949), Cadman (1979).

flight patterns

(a) Eurasian Oystercatcher
    (race *ostralegus*)

(b) American Oystercatcher
    (race *palliatus*)

(c) Eurasian Oystercatcher
    (race *osculans*)

a   b   c

14 AMERICAN BLACK OYSTERCATCHER   Plate 8
Haematopus bachmani

Other name: Black Oystercatcher
A strictly coastal all-black oystercatcher of the North American Pacific coast.

IDENTIFICATION An all-black oystercatcher with yellow eyes and a slightly brownish tinge to the upperparts. The only oystercatcher within its range, except for a small overlap with American Oystercatcher (13) in the extreme south. Almost identical to the Blackish Oystercatcher (21), which however has a heavier bill; in practical terms, the two can be separated only by distribution. The wings are relatively broad and rounded for an oystercatcher, and the flight is heavy and direct, usually low. **Bare parts:** Long, straight orange bill, tending towards yellowish at the tip. Iris clear lemon-yellow, eye-ring orange-red. Legs strong, pale pink. All bare-part colours are duller in juveniles and sub-adults.
VOICE Similar to other oystercatchers. A rapid piping 'peep-peep-peep' or disyllabic 'pee-up', also a slower, repeated 'peep' when alarmed. Typical oystercatcher piping display in which birds run side-by-side with heads forward and bills pointing downwards.
HABITS Found on exposed rocky coasts and outlying islands, flying to feed on rocky reefs exposed at low tide. Occasionally on adjacent sandy or shingle beaches, exceptionally on mudflats. Fairly tame but watches intruders alertly. Usually found singly or in small groups, often very difficult to spot against the dark rocks. Sometimes associates with Surfbirds (186), Black Turnstones (155) and Rock Sandpipers (203).
MOVEMENTS Distribution somewhat patchy, particularly in the south. Essentially sedentary, but spreads in autumn and winter to sites where it does not breed. Vagrant (once) to Pribilof Is.
DESCRIPTION Breeding: Head, neck and upper breast virtually black, shading into brownish-black on the belly and undertail. Upperparts brownish-black, sharply demarcated from the black at the base of the hindneck. Wings and tail entirely brownish-black. **Non-breeding:** Some birds show a few paler tips to the belly feathers. Legs may become slightly dusky. **Juvenile:** As adult, but upperparts have many narrow brown edgings; coverts are brownish with black subterminal bands and buffish tips. Eye-ring dull orange, iris orange-brown, bill orange-brown with dark outer half, and legs initially brownish.
AGE/SEX Young birds can be distinguished by brownish fringes above and by dull bare parts. Later steadily become brighter and are almost as adult by the end of the first 12 months. Females average slightly larger, tend to have longer and thinner bills, and are more likely to show pale tips to the belly feathers.
RACES No geographical variation is known. Rarely, may interbreed with American Oystercatcher in the extreme south of its range.
MEASUREMENTS Length 430-450 mm (17¼"). Wing 254-266 mm; bill 71-81 mm; tarsus 52-56 mm.
REFERENCES Webster (1941, 1942), Eley (1976), Hartwick (1974, 1976, 1978a, b).

15 AFRICAN BLACK OYSTERCATCHER Haematopus moquini Plate 5

Other names: Black Oystercatcher, African Oystercatcher
This is a scarce bird with a population of only about 4,800 adults, restricted to the coasts of southern Africa.

IDENTIFICATION A black oystercatcher with red eyes and glossy black upperparts. As the only black oystercatcher in southern Africa, it can safely be identified on range. Differs from American Black (14) and Blackish (21) Oystercatchers in having red not yellow iris, blacker upperparts, and deeper pink legs; virtually identical to the Sooty (22) and Variable (17) Oystercatchers. The shorter-winged and longer-billed (probably extinct) Canarian Black Oystercatcher (16) is similar except that it may have a whitish flash on the inner primaries. African Black has the lowest bill:tarsus ratio of any oystercatcher. **Bare parts:** Colours and sequence of colour changes are not known to differ from those of Eurasian Oystercatcher (12).
VOICE Calls similar to those of Eurasian Oystercatcher, but slightly flatter in tone; distinguishable with practice.
HABITS Typically a bird of rocky coasts, often abundant on offshore islands. Nests chiefly Dec-Feb, in dense colonies in some localities. Especially at island colonies, may be susceptible to predation by introduced mammals and to human disturbance. In display has a slow butterfly-flight like most oystercatchers. Immatures especially also occur on estuarine sandbars, sandy beaches, less frequently muddier estuaries, lagoons or even saltpans. On rocky substrates feeds mostly on limpets and mussels, but in sandy habitats a wider range of molluscs and worms is taken. Fairly wary when on sand, but on dark rocks relies more on its good camouflage. Tamer than vagrant Eurasian Oystercatcher, which may occur alongside.
MOVEMENTS Adults are sedentary, moving only locally to exposed islands and sandy beaches to breed and to more sheltered areas after breeding. Juveniles disperse farther, but rarely more than 160 km. Vagrant north to Lobito, Angola, in the west and Dawson's Rock, Natal, in the east; there are also possible records for Senegal (Canarian Black?), Gabon, Mozambique, and the Dahlak Is., Red Sea.
DESCRIPTION Breeding and non-breeding: All-black, noticeably glossy above when breeding. **Juvenile:** Browner, with extensive buffish fringes to upperparts and wing-coverts. Bare-part colours are a useful distinction.

AGE/SEX Juvenile distinctly browner, but after a few months very difficult to tell from adult except by bare-part colours. Sexes similar, but females have noticeably longer bills (average 71.6 mm against 63.2 mm for males).

RACES No geographical variation is known.
MEASUREMENTS Length 420-450 mm (17"). Wing 269-301 mm; bill 58-89 mm; tarsus 53-56 mm; tail 102-110 mm.
REFERENCES Hockey (1981, 1983a, b).

16 CANARIAN BLACK OYSTERCATCHER   Plate 5
Haematopus meadewaldoi

Other names: Meade-Waldo's Oystercatcher, Canarian Oystercatcher
This oystercatcher, previously known from the eastern Canary Islands, is almost certainly extinct. There has been no firm sighting since 1913. Records of black oystercatchers from Tenerife (western Canaries) in July 1968 and Feb 1981, and unexplained records in Senegal in 1970 and 1975, however, raise the possibility that this species still exists. It has previously been treated as a subspecies of either Eurasian (12) or African Black Oystercatcher (15).

IDENTIFICATION Black plumage and red iris and eye-ring render this oystercatcher almost identical to African Black, dark Variable (17) and Sooty (22), but at least some Canarian Black show a more distinct white patch on the bases of the inner primaries, visible in flight, especially from below. Compared with African Black, it is shorter-winged and may average longer in bill length. **Bare parts:** Probably identical to Eurasian Oystercatcher.
VOICE Probably as Eurasian or African Black.
HABITS The few reports indicate that it is similar to other black oystercatchers in its ecology. It occurs chiefly singly or in pairs well scattered around the rocky coastlines, sometimes on sandy beaches. There are confirmed records from Lanzarote, Fuerteventura and the minor islands lying just to the north of these.

No nesting records have ever been described.
MOVEMENTS Believed to be sedentary, except for movements between islands; conceivably migrates to the African coast.
DESCRIPTION Adult: Differs from African Black only in showing a larger white patch at base of inner primaries, visible beyond coverts at least on underwing. It is not known, however, whether this is a constant feature. **Juvenile:** Unknown.
AGE/SEX Nothing is known.
RACES Monotypic.
MEASUREMENTS Two specimens examined. Length probably about 430 mm (17"). Wing 260-264 mm; bill 72-81 mm; tarsus 53-54 mm.
REFERENCES Bannerman (1969), Hockey (1982), Collar and Stuart (1985).

17 VARIABLE OYSTERCATCHER Haematopus unicolor   Plate 8

Other names: New Zealand Black or New Zealand Sooty Oystercatcher
This is the only species of oystercatcher with both pied and black forms. These forms have been considered as subspecies, even as distinct species, but are probably the two extremes of a single polymorphic population. There are only 2,000-3,000 individuals, of which about 70% are black, 20% pied and 10% intermediate.

IDENTIFICATION The black form 'unicolor', normally dominant, is the only black oystercatcher in New Zealand; it is very similar to the Sooty Oystercatcher (22) of Australia, but averages slightly smaller. The pied form 'reischeki', commonest in northern North Island, might be confused with the smaller SIPO (Pied Oystercatcher, 20), but is easily distinguished in flight by its shorter wingbar and narrow white band across the base of the tail, and at rest by its more extensive black breast with a smudgy lower border. The white peak between the black breast and the folded wing of SIPO is absent in this species. In addition, Variable is a slightly larger and bulkier bird. Intermediates between the two forms are frequent and are known as 'smudgies'; the majority are more black than pied, usually with some white around the vent and on the wing. Chatham Islands Oystercatcher (18) is almost identical in plumage to 'reischeki' but does not overlap in range. **Bare parts:** Bill is slightly deeper than that of Pied Oystercatcher. Colours and sequence of colour changes of bare parts are apparently as in Eurasian Oystercatcher (12).

VOICE Typical of oystercatchers. Very similar to that of SIPO, but slightly huskier and less piercing.
HABITS Unlike SIPO, this species is a coastal breeder, nesting chiefly on sandy beaches and among sand-dunes. Breeding season is mainly later, Dec onwards, but sometimes begins as early as Oct. Also unlike SIPO, it is mostly non-migratory and remains on its breeding areas all year. Avoids competition with SIPO by feeding chiefly on rocky shores and sandy ocean beaches, taking mainly mussels and limpets. Occasionally gathers in single-species flocks, up to 150 birds; often joins larger flocks of SIPO in estuaries and harbours.
MOVEMENTS Normally sedentary. A few individuals wander from the breeding areas, but probably only locally.
DESCRIPTION Black phase adult: Usually sooty-black, but some are a glossy black. **Pied phase adult:** Head, breast and most of upperparts black, usually slightly glossy. White wingbar covers bases of outer secondaries, whole of inner secondaries and the tips to the greater coverts. Squarish white patch on

uppertail-coverts, variably obscured by black feather tips. Lower breast has a broad zone where the black breast merges into the white belly. **Juvenile:** Black areas are noticeably browner than on adult, and there are small buffish-white tips to the coverts and scapulars.

AGE/SEX Once the juvenile plumage has been lost, young may still be separable from adults by bare-part colours. Sexes are alike but females average slightly larger, particularly in bill length.

RACES The forms 'unicolor' (coasts of North, South and Stewart Islands) and 'reischeki' (North Island, W and NE South Island) are sometimes considered as separate races or subspecies. Interbreeding is common, and intermediates of a variety of plumage patterns are frequent. Percentage of 'unicolor' increases southwards: 34-39°S, 43%; 39-44°S, 85%; 44-48°S, 94%. Both pied individuals and 'smudgies' decline in frequency southwards.

MEASUREMENTS Length 470-490 mm (19"). Wing 257-296 mm; bill 72-98 mm, average 81.7 mm (males) and 90.6 mm (females); bill depth 10-13 mm; tarsus 50-57 mm; tail 93-100 mm.

REFERENCES Stidolph (1973), Baker (1973, 1974a, 1975, 1977), Jones (1979).

18 CHATHAM ISLANDS OYSTERCATCHER   Plate 8
Haematopus chathamensis

Restricted to the Chatham Is. group, 640 km east of New Zealand. This is a rare and endangered bird, at one time numbering about 50 individuals, but presently there are about 70. It appears to be very closely related to Variable Oystercatcher (17), and may be an isolated population of that species in which the pied type of plumage has become genetically fixed.

IDENTIFICATION This is the only oystercatcher found on the Chathams; it occurs nowhere else. In plumage it is virtually identical to the fully-pied phase of Variable ('reischeki'), but the zone of the breast in which black and white are intermixed is slightly broader, and the white rump is slightly smaller and more obscured. In addition, it is slightly smaller with a noticeably shorter bill, but with stouter legs and feet. See Variable for distinctions from the South Island Pied Oystercatcher, race finschi (20). **Bare parts:** Colours and sequence of colour changes of bare parts are similar to those of Variable Oystercatcher.

VOICE Not known to differ from that of Variable Oystercatcher.

HABITS Generally very similar to Variable and other rock-dwelling oystercatchers. Widely distributed around the Chatham Is. coasts, but more numerous in the south. Strongly territorial throughout the year; rarely seen in groups of more than family size, but occasionally up to nine together. Predation by feral cats and Wekas Gallirallus australis has restricted nesting to offshore islands and cliff ledges. Reduced disturbance by domestic stock and man on the small islands since their declaration as reserves has increased breeding success. On the main islands of the group the problems persist.

MOVEMENTS Entirely sedentary within the group, but marked birds have moved between islands.

DESCRIPTION See Identification section for minor differences from pied phase ('reischeki') of Variable Oystercatcher.

AGE/SEX Young birds can be distinguished initially by plumage, and later only by bare-part coloration (see Variable Oystercatcher). Males and females have similar plumages, but females are larger in size and average 9 mm longer in bill measurement.

RACES This is a tiny population with no racial variation.

MEASUREMENTS Length 470-490 mm (19"). Wing 260-272 mm; bill about 60-85 mm, average 67.8 mm (males) and 76.8 mm (females); tarsus 50-52 mm; tail 91-98 mm.

REFERENCES Baker (1974a), King (1981).

19 MAGELLANIC OYSTERCATCHER Haematopus leucopodus Plate 7

This southern South American species, with its yellow eye-ring and unique wing pattern, is perhaps the most distinctive oystercatcher.

IDENTIFICATION Like all American oystercatchers, and unlike all others, the eyes are yellow; uniquely, however, the eye-ring is also yellow. Overlaps at northern extremities of its range with American Oystercatcher (13), and also sympatric with Blackish Oystercatcher (21). Differs in pied plumage having blackish rather than brownish upperparts; also lacks the black-tipped outer secondaries of American Oystercatcher. Unmarked white secondaries, a unique feature among oystercatchers, and white-tipped greater coverts form an extremely conspicuous white triangular patch on the inner half of the wing. As in the sympatric races of American Oystercatcher, no white is visible on the primaries in flight. Uniquely among pied oystercatchers, the under primary coverts and lesser coverts are black, contrasting with white in the central and trailing part of the underwing. A similar pattern, but with less extensive black areas, is shown by Pied Oystercatcher (20) of Australasia. At rest, the black extends farther down the breast than in American and Eurasian species, also recalling Pied Oystercatcher. **Bare parts:** Bill orange-red, rather slim and long-looking, much thinner than that of Blackish Oystercatcher; brownish with a reddish base in juveniles. Eye-ring and iris bright lemon-yellow, dull brownish in juveniles. Legs pale pink, greyish in juveniles; toes rather short and slender compared with those of Blackish Oystercatcher. All juvenile colours brighten steadily during the first year or more.

VOICE Display call is typical of oystercatchers, a repeated piping 'pee-pee'. Contact and alarm calls include the standard 'peep', but the most frequent note is a distinctive disyllabic whistle 'hoo-eep' or 'pee-you', unusually soft and plaintive.

HABITS During the breeding season, many move well inland to short grassy areas near inland pools or even semi-desert areas; especially on the southernmost islands, they also breed coastally on sandy beaches. They have a typical head-down piping display but, unlike other oystercatchers, also have a strongly-developed display in which the tail is held vertically. Substantial flocks may gather on sandy beaches and stony mussel-beds, which are the main non-breeding habitats. The longish, slim bill is used chiefly for feeding on sand-worms, but mussels and limpets are also taken. The flight is strong and low; like other oystercatchers, can swim well if necessary.

MOVEMENTS Largely sedentary. There is a post-breeding movement to the coast and some north-ward movement of the southernmost breeders from Tierra del Fuego.

DESCRIPTION Breeding and non-breeding: All upperparts black apart from the white base of tail, tips of longest uppertail-coverts, secondaries and most of the greater coverts. Black under primary coverts and lesser coverts contrast with median and greater underwing-coverts and axillaries, which are white. Head, neck and breast black, rest of underparts white. **Juvenile:** Bare parts duller, upperparts much browner with narrow buff fringes.

AGE/SEX Juvenile feathers of mantle and scapulars are replaced fairly quickly by black feathers which contrast with the brownish coverts. Older immatures may be distinguished only by their dull bare parts. Little sexual difference; males have slightly shorter but deeper bills than females, often slightly pinker in shade.

RACES No geographical variation is known.

MEASUREMENTS Length 420-460 mm (17¼"). Wing 237-267 mm; bill length 68-85 mm, depth at gonys 9-11 mm; tarsus 43-51 mm; tail 93-108 mm.

REFERENCES Humphrey *et al.* (1970), Woods (1975), Miller and Baker (1980).

20 PIED OYSTERCATCHER *Haematopus longirostris*　　Plate 8

This oystercatcher is restricted to Australasia. The population in New Zealand, South Island Pied Oystercatcher (SIPO for short), is often treated as a separate species or as a race of Eurasian Oystercatcher (12).

IDENTIFICATION The only pied species of oyster-catcher over most of its range; in New Zealand sympatric with Variable Oystercatcher (17) but has not yet occurred alongside Chatham Islands Oystercatcher (18). Like Eurasian, but unlike the four American species, it has glossy black upperparts and adult has a red iris. It differs from all races of Eurasian, however, in having a shorter white wingbar, less white on the back, a black leading edge to the underwing including black median under primary coverts, and black coming very slightly farther down the breast. Also, it never shows the white bar across the throat found to varying degrees in the Eurasian races. In New Zealand, differs from the pied form of Variable and from Chatham Islands Oystercatcher most obviously in having less black on the breast, a sharper division between the black and the white on the breast, and more white on the rump and lower back. At rest, SIPO is easily distinguished from Variable by the white 'peak' between the breast and folded wing, obvious in both front and side views. In flight, the wingbar is longer and broader, and white extends as a large patch across the rump, ending squarely on the lower back. **Bare parts:** Colours and sequence of colour changes appear to be the same as in Eurasian Oystercatcher.

VOICE Typical piping 'kleep' call and noisy piping display, similar to Eurasian Oystercatcher.

HABITS Differs from other Australasian species in habitat preferences and flocking behaviour. When not nesting, gathers on estuaries, sometimes in flocks of hundreds, to feed on worms and molluscs. In Australia, nests mainly on sandy beaches or among sand-dunes. Most numerous in SE Australia and Tasmania, elsewhere very scattered and often scarce. SIPO nests Sept-Nov, chiefly inland on riverine shingle-banks, ploughed or grass fields; regularly feeds on arable land. It is a thriving race; numbers wintering in the North Island harbours have undergone a spectacular explosion since about 1940, and there is a recent breeding record for North Island.

MOVEMENTS Nominate race apparently performs only short movements to reach favoured estuaries fairly close to the breeding site. New Zealand race *finschi* moves quickly to the coast after breeding and may be found on estuaries on Stewart I. (Paterson Inlet), the north and east coasts of South Island, and throughout coastal North Island. Arrivals in the north begin in late Dec and peak in Jan-Feb. Spring migration southward starts in early July and continues to late Aug. Young birds tend to move farther north than adults. Immature non-breeders summer in the wintering areas.

DESCRIPTION See Identification section for differences from Eurasian Oystercatcher.

AGE/SEX Brownish plumage identifies the juvenile, but this is quickly replaced by adult-type black feathering. Bare-part coloration enables the separation of four categories: juveniles, first-years, older immatures, and adults. Sexes are similar in plumage, but the female averages slightly larger, especially in bill length.

RACES Two: nominate *longirostris* (Australia, Tasmania, S New Guinea and Aru Is.) and *finschi* (New Zealand). In the nominate race, the wingbar is confined to a narrow strip at the bases of the secondaries and tips of the greater coverts, while in *finschi* the bar is broader across the secondaries and greater coverts, with usually two of the inner secondaries completely white, and may spill over onto the inner

2-3 primaries. The race *finschi* is smaller on average and may have a proportionately slightly longer bill. Within *longirostris* there is a slight cline of increasing size towards the north.

MEASUREMENTS Nominate race: length 480-510 mm (19½"); wing 263-295 mm; bill 69-89 mm, depth 9-11 mm; tarsus 53-60 mm. SIPO (four specimens examined): length about 460 mm (18"); wing 256-268 mm; bill 84-95 mm; tarsus 50-52 mm.

REFERENCES Sibson (1966), Baker (1973, 1974a, 1975, 1977).

21 BLACKISH OYSTERCATCHER *Haematopus ater*   Plate 7

Other name: Black Oystercatcher
Almost identical to the American Black Oystercatcher (14) and safely identifiable only on range.

IDENTIFICATION The only black oystercatcher in South America. Differs from the partly sympatric American and Magellanic Oystercatchers (13,19) in all-dark plumage, much deeper bill, slightly larger size, and more solitary habits. The toes are longer than those of Magellanic Oystercatcher and have more webbing. Effectively identical to the American Black Oystercatcher, but the bill is typically deeper and has an obvious 'step' along the lower edge. Brown back and yellow eyes distinguish the two American species from other black oystercatchers. **Bare parts:** Bill orange-red, becoming slightly more yellowish towards the tip; very broad and blade-shaped over distal three-quarters in all but a few individuals, broadening just beyond the nostril, with a small 'step' on the lower mandible. Iris initially brown, becoming bright lemon-yellow in full adults; eye-ring brownish initially, becoming orange-red in adults. Legs pale pink; toes longish with a substantial web between the outer and middle ones.
VOICE Not known to differ from American or American Black Oystercatchers.

HABITS A strictly coastal bird of essentially rocky habitats, sometimes seen on adjacent sandy beaches. Widely distributed, but generally occurs singly or in parties of up to four or five, rarely in larger flocks. Has hybridised on occasion with Magellanic.
MOVEMENTS Essentially sedentary. Range may extend northwards to Uruguay outside the breeding season.
DESCRIPTION All plumages are as described for American Black Oystercatcher.
AGE/SEX Juveniles can be distinguished by their duller bare parts. In addition, the brownish-tipped coverts are normally obvious well into the first winter — only a few are replaced by June. Females average larger, particularly in bill length. Only females show whitish fringes to the belly feathers in adult non-breeding plumage.
RACES No geographical variation is known.
MEASUREMENTS Length 430-455 mm (17½"). Wing 253-276 mm (juveniles), 262-282 mm (adults); bill 65-84 mm; tarsus 52-58 mm; tail 93-108 mm.
REFERENCES Johnson (1965), Jehl (1978).

22 SOOTY OYSTERCATCHER *Haematopus fuliginosus*   Plate 8

The black oystercatcher of Australian coasts, generally much scarcer than Pied Oystercatcher (20) but a common bird in the Bass Strait.

IDENTIFICATION The all-dark plumage and range are sufficient to preclude confusion with the sympatric Pied Oystercatcher and other black oystercatchers. It is very similar to African Black Oystercatcher (15) and black phase of Variable Oystercatcher (17), and effectively separable only by range. Its relatively long tail, extending past wing-point and longer than in all similar species, provides the only real difference. The two black American species (14,21) both differ in showing a brownish mantle and yellow eyes. Rather a heavy flier, but wings appear slightly less rounded than other black oystercatchers. **Bare parts:** Bill orange-red, sometimes yellowish towards the tip; duller brownish in juveniles. Eye scarlet; brown in young juveniles, later becoming dull red. Eye-ring orange, narrow and pale in juveniles. Legs relatively bright pinkish-red, dull greyish in juveniles. Colours of all bare parts steadily assume those of adults over the first year or two of life.
VOICE Typical of oystercatchers, with a loud 'kleep' contact and alarm call and a constantly-repeated piping 'pit' or 'pee' as display. Some calls are softer and more plaintive than similar calls of Pied Oy-

stercatcher.
HABITS Found on rocky and stony beaches, reefs and headlands throughout Australia, but relatively scattered in the northern part of its range. Often feeds on dark rocky areas, where well camouflaged, but also forages conspicuously along tidelines of sandy beaches and in sandy harbours. Usually in ones or twos, rarely in small groups. More wary than Pied Oystercatcher. Usually nests among boulders on rocky promontories or offshore islands. Single birds occasionally associate with Pied Oystercatcher, with which has interbred.
MOVEMENTS Sedentary, with limited dispersal.
DESCRIPTION Breeding: Uniform sooty-black, slightly glossed greenish above and below. **Non-breeding:** Rather duller, with a few small whitish tips to the belly feathers immediately after the moult. **Juvenile:** Duller and browner, with pale buffish or whitish tips and fringes to most feathers. Bare parts duller. The retained body feathers on mantle, coverts and underparts soon bleach, but are then replaced by adult-type feathers.
AGE/SEX Pale tips to feathers of upperparts are a clear indication of a juvenile; bare-part colours are help-

ful. Females tend to be slightly larger, but there is much overlap.

RACES Two are described: nominate *fuliginosus* (most Australia) and *ophthalmicus* (Gulf of Carpentaria, Cape York). Differences are marginal, latter having a fractionally fleshier eye-ring and longer bill, and the species is probably better considered monotypic.

Most individuals cannot be assigned to either race, and intergrading undoubtedly occurs.

MEASUREMENTS Length 460-490 mm (18½"). Wing 275-296 mm; bill 64-84 mm, depth at gonys 10-13 mm; tarsus 50-56 mm; tail 98-117 mm.

REFERENCES Baker (1977).

23 IBISBILL *Ibidorhyncha struthersii*　　　　　　　Plate 9

A very unusual wader of mountain riverbeds of central southern Asia. It is unique in both appearance and habits, but may be distantly related both to oystercatchers and to stilts and avocets.

IDENTIFICATION Strikingly unlike any other wader. It is fairly large with a longish, strongly-decurved bill reminiscent of Whimbrel (129) in shape, but differs in its reddish bare parts and grey, black and white plumage. Restricted to rocky riverbeds. Flies with flicking, rounded wings which show a brilliant white flash towards the tip of the primaries both above and below. Flight and wing pattern are like Stone-curlew (31), but latter is brown not grey and has a short, straight bill. Beware River Lapwing (61), which is strongly patterned in similar colours and occurs in similar habitat. **Bare parts:** Bill strongly decurved; bright red in breeding adults, reddish-brown otherwise, but dull sepia in juveniles at first. Iris dark red, paler yellowish-red in juveniles. Legs bright red in most breeding adults, pinkish-grey otherwise, but tinged greenish in young juveniles.

VOICE A repeated ringing 'klew-klew', reminiscent of many larger *Tringa* sandpipers, but slightly higher and longer; also a rapid loud Whimbrel-like 'tee-tee-tee-tee'.

HABITS A bird of wide, high-altitude valleys with flat stony floodplains, breeding between 1700 m and 4400 m. Nests on shingle-banks and islets during late Mar-early June. Four eggs are laid in a scrape lined with tiny pebbles. Behaviour is strongly territorial and there are circling displays on the ground between rival birds. Outside breeding season some descend as low as 100 m in the foothills. An inconspicuous bird when resting or feeding quietly among stones or in shallow water, but the penetrating calls may attract attention. Feeds by probing among stones and boulders of riverbed, sometimes wading deeply, and by pecking; sometimes rakes the bill through gravel to dislodge prey. Food consists of aquatic and terrestrial invertebrates, also small fish. In flight it usually holds its head outstretched and slightly high, this and the rather rounded wings suggesting an ibis rather than a Whimbrel. Found in scattered pairs or small groups, quite frequent in some valleys but very scarce in many.

MOVEMENTS Sedentary, but some move to lower elevations in winter.

DESCRIPTION Breeding: Crown, front of face, chin and upper throat black, outlined by narrow white line from lower throat up to the eye; above the eye the white broadens and sweeps backwards under black cap, but it does not meet on nape. Back and sides of neck, mantle, upper back and breast bright bluish-grey. Breast is bordered below by a narrow white line, then a broad black band. Rest of underparts white. Lower back, most wing-coverts, scapulars and tertials are an even brownish-grey, although the tertials are tipped dusky. Outermost greater and median coverts and all primary coverts are blackish. Outer primaries are black with small white subterminal spot, inner primaries white narrowly tipped black. Outer 2 secondaries white with broad black tip, rest of secondaries greyish-brown, but the next five outers are washed dusky at tip. Rump grey-brown, obscurely barred blackish. Tail as rump, but outer webs of outer feathers whitish barred black. Underwing-coverts are pale greyish-brown; white and black flight-feather pattern shows through. **Non-breeding:** As above, but black face is partially obscured by white-tipped feathers. **Juvenile:** As adult in pattern, but face is whitish or dark brown with many white-tipped feathers. Breast-band is also dark brown; white upper breast-band is lacking. Upperparts rather browner than on adult with extensive buffish-orange fringes when fresh, giving obscurely-scalloped appearance.

AGE/SEX Juvenile distinguishable in the field until about Nov, but after the post-juvenile moult very similar with just slightly whiter throat. Sexes similar in plumage; females average slightly larger.

RACES No geographical variation is known.

MEASUREMENTS Length 380-410 mm (15½"). Wing 230-247 mm; bill 60-83 mm; tarsus 44-52 mm; tail 113-120 mm.

REFERENCES Phillips (1945), Bates and Lowther (1952), Stepanjan (1979), Pierce (in prep.).

display posture

back of black cap raised in display

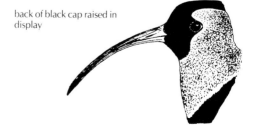

Other names: Black-necked Stilt, Pied/White-headed Stilt, Hawaiian Stilt

This almost cosmopolitan species has developed leg length to its extreme among waders, but remains a remarkably elegant bird. We include all the pied stilts in this species despite there being three major groups with distinct plumages, each perhaps warranting treatment as a full species. Black Stilt (25) is also often included as a race of this species.

IDENTIFICATION All races are rendered unmistakable by almost grotesquely long pink legs, a thin, black, almost straight bill, black wings and white underparts. Apart from Black Stilt, the only remotely similar species are Andean Avocet (30), which has a strongly-upturned bill and broader, more rounded wings, and immature Banded Stilt (26), which has a white mantle and is much shorter-legged. Immature Black Stilt is very similar, but shorter-legged and, except in young juveniles, always has at least some black smudging on the underparts. Hybrids with Black Stilt (which see) are frequent. The subspecies fall into three groups which are readily distinguishable in the field by the pattern of the head and neck (see Table on page 391). **Bare parts:** Bill black, thin and straight or fractionally upcurved; juvenile may show some reddish at base of lower mandible. Iris red, yellow-brown in juveniles. Legs pinkish-red in adults, brighter when breeding, dull fleshy-pink or greyish-pink in juveniles; in flight, almost the whole tarsus is visible beyond the tail-tip.

VOICE Vocabulary is fairly wide, but most calls are based on a sharp bark, 'kek', a continuous, irritating, high-pitched 'kikikikik', and a yelping 'kee-ack'. In the Australasian race *leucocephalus* barking calls are softer and more nasal, rather like a toy trumpet.

HABITS Breeds in a wide range of wetland habitats, mainly in tropical and subtropical regions, including coastal saltmarshes and commercial saltpans and inland lakes (fresh or salt), sewage-farms and marshes. Nests singly on occasion, sometimes far outside normal range, but mostly in loose colonies. Young remain dependent on their parents for a period after fledging, and share feeding territories which are defended by the adults against other birds. Stilts feed in areas ranging from dry mud to belly-deep water, but most often in water about knee-depth. Feeding techniques include picking from mud or water surfaces, probing in soft mud, chasing fast-moving prey in the water, and a sort of avocet-like scything. Normal gait is a steady walk, resembling a large *Tringa* but more graceful; only when running or in a strong wind do they look ungainly. When approached, bobs head and scolds, then takes flight. Flight is swift and easy on long, pointed wings.

MOVEMENTS Northern populations in North America and Eurasia are migratory, leaving Aug-Nov and returning Mar-Apr; *mexicanus* winters in USA only in the extreme south, and *himantopus* mainly south of the Mediterranean. Many Eurasian stilts winter in sub-Saharan Africa, but probably do not penetrate much beyond the equator. Has wintered in England. Spring overshoots of *mexicanus* have been seen in British Columbia, Alberta (bred), Saskatchewan (bred), New Brunswick and Newfoundland; there is also an autumn record from Ontario (Sept 1955). Nominate race is vagrant north to Ireland, Britain (has bred twice), Sweden and Japan (bred), and

west to the Azores, Madeira and Canary Is. Tropical and southern populations are mainly sedentary but dispersive. The race *leucocephalus* is also migratory, reaching islands as far north as the Philippines as a non-breeding visitor; has recently bred in Papua New Guinea. It has expanded enormously in New Zealand this century; most winter in the North Island harbours but some in South Island; vagrant to offshore islands, to the Chathams (has bred), and to Tasmania.

DESCRIPTION Breeding: Crown, nape and hindneck variably black, white or greyish (see Races). Wing-coverts and flight feathers black. Mantle, scapulars and tertials are usually black, but can be brown or blackish-brown in female. Back, rump, uppertail-coverts and base of tail are white; some central tail feathers are washed very pale grey. Underparts white, except for black underwing-coverts and flight feathers; inner lesser and median underwing-coverts are white, forming a narrow wedge of white on the otherwise black underwing. Some breeding males may show a pinkish flush to the underparts in fresh plumage. **Non-breeding:** In some birds of nominate race, greyish becomes more extensive on the crown, nape and hindneck. **Juvenile:** As non-breeding, but crown and hindneck greyish or blackish, never white. Mantle, scapulars, tertials and coverts dull brown with buffish or dull reddish-buff fringes and subterminal dark sepia lines. Inner primaries and secondaries are clearly but narrowly tipped white.

AGE/SEX Juvenile plumage is distinct for several months. After the post-juvenile body moult, back is brown or blackish-brown, and there is usually a greyish wash on head or neck. Wings remain more worn than on adult; any white on trailing edge indicates young bird. Males are about 6% longer-winged than females, and also average larger in other measurements. Mantle, scapulars and tertials are black in male, but can be brown or blackish-brown in female, contrasting with the wings. In nominate race sexing by head pattern is hazardous owing to individual and geographical variation; in most populations breeding male is likely to be whiter-headed than female.

RACES Five: nominate *himantopus* (S Eurasia, India, Sri Lanka, Africa), *leucocephalus* - 'Pied or White-headed Stilt' (SE Indonesia, Australasia), *knudseni* - 'Hawaiian Stilt' (rare and endangered, Hawaii), *mexicanus* - 'Black-necked Stilt' (USA to Peru and N Brazil, Galapagos Is.), and *melanurus* (Peru and N Brazil to central Chile and Argentina). Their characters are summarised on page 391. All three American races have black on hindneck and sides of head. The races *knudseni* and *mexicanus* are closely related, although the former has very long legs and bill, more black on forehead and sides of neck and a smaller post-ocular spot. The races *mexicanus* and *melanurus* intergrade in Peru; *melanurus* is larger, and has a white crown and a white band across the base of the hindneck. The race *leucocephalus* has

NEW ZEALAND BLACK AND PIED STILTS

This plate shows the plumage sequence of immature Black Stilts and the observed plumage patterns of hybrid Black X Pied; this information is based upon a detailed study by R.J. Pierce (1984b).

The taxonomic status of birds within the genus is obscure, being partly limited by the lack of spirit material from which full anatomical comparisons can be made (see p.36).

The Australian, New Zealand and adjacent Pacific populations vary in certain proportions, especially in the lengths of the tibia *and* tarsus. This trend extends north to *knudseni* in Hawaii which has the longest tarsi of all.

The Pacific populations are characterised by having a broader wing chord than nominate *himantopus*.

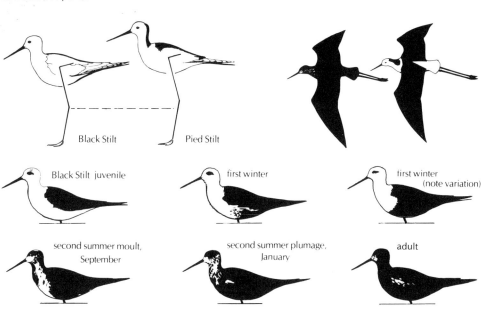

Black Stilt   Pied Stilt

Black Stilt juvenile   first winter   first winter (note variation)

second summer moult, September   second summer plumage, January   adult

HYBRID PATTERNS The tarsus length decreases in relation to increasing amounts of black in the plumage.

a mainly-white head and neck, but with a ridge of slightly longer black feathers on nape and upper hindneck, sometimes forming an almost complete black collar around base of neck. Head and neck pattern of nominate race is variable, but never resembles that of other races; some individuals have head and neck entirely white. Within nominate race, there are clines of decreasing size from north to south and (less marked) from east to west. Within *leucocephalus*, New Zealand birds are longer-winged, longer-

billed and shorter-legged, probably through interbreeding with Black Stilt; they also show slightly more black on the hindneck.
MEASUREMENTS Length 350-400 mm (14¾"). Nominate race: wing 206-255 mm; bill 56-69 mm; tarsus 100-137 mm; tail 72-86 mm. The averages for other races are shown on page 391; most populations show wide ranges.
REFERENCES Schwartz and Schwartz (1951), Hamilton (1975), Goriup (1982), Espin *et al.* (1983).

25 BLACK STILT *Himantopus novaezelandiae*　　　　Plate 11

An endangered and decreasing species found only in New Zealand, possibly the rarest wader in the world. Formerly bred commonly in North and South Islands, but now only 10-15 pure breeding pairs remain, nesting in inland riverbeds of S Canterbury and N Otago, South Island. Interbreeds commonly with Pied Stilt (24); indeed, there may be few if any genetically pure Pied Stilts in New Zealand.

IDENTIFICATION The slender build, long thin bill and very long pink legs easily identify this bird as a stilt. Adults are entirely black with a greenish gloss to hindneck, mantle and wings, and present no identification problem. Juveniles and immatures show varying amounts of white below and are difficult to separate from hybrids between Pied and Black. At fledging, juvenile Black has entirely-white underparts, like hybrid and Pied juveniles, and is best identified from its parents (which will probably be nearby). Soon after fledging, black patches develop on the flanks and belly; this plumage is kept until a moult into largely-black plumage in the spring. One-year-old and even some older Black Stilts may show small white patches around the bill or on the breast or belly. Hybrids show more white on face and on belly than Black Stilts; typical adult hybrid has a black hindneck, upper mantle (white in Pied) and breast-band, with a variable amount of black on crown, ear-coverts, neck and underparts. Black markings on underparts, but no black hindneck or breast-band, is indicative of immature Black Stilt. Some hybrids are so black, and immature Blacks so variable, that it is not safe to identify one-year-old Black Stilts as pure-bred. **Bare parts:** Bill thin, straight and black, slightly longer and broader than in Pied Stilt. Iris bright red. Legs bright pink, shorter than in Pied Stilt. Immatures have duller iris and leg colours, and often some pinkish on the base of the bill.
VOICE Yapping calls like those of Pied Stilt but slightly louder and higher-pitched.
HABITS Rather different breeding habits have helped pure Black Stilts to survive the huge expansion of Pied Stilts in New Zealand over the past century, but also make Blacks more vulnerable than Pied to predatory introduced mammals (cats, ferrets and brown rats). They nest singly, rather than in colonial groups, on riverine shingle and associated marshlands. These areas are often not only readily accessible to predators, but also vulnerable to flooding. Anti-predator distraction displays are poorly developed and rarely used; the young remain flightless longer than young Pied Stilts and are especially vulnerable. Nesting season is Sept-Feb. In contrast to Pied Stilt, family parties stay together all winter. Territorial Blacks are dominant and aggressive towards Pieds. Closely adapted to riverbed foraging: probes in river shin-

gle, also scythes and pecks. Sometimes feeds in fields, probing soil for worms and grubs. Behaviour is generally more confiding than in Pied Stilt.
MOVEMENTS Most pairs and families of Black Stilts remain inland and close to the breeding grounds all year, in contrast to the Pied Stilts from nearby breeding areas which all migrate northwards for the winter. Some immature Blacks, as well as some unmated and interbreeding adults, join the migration and occur regularly in small numbers at Kawhia Harbour in North Island, and rarely elsewhere. Most dark stilts wintering in the north are, however, hybrids. Differences in migration strategy also help to maintain the Black Stilt as a species: they are mostly in pairs and on territory before the Pied Stilts and hybrids return.
DESCRIPTION Breeding: Mantle and coverts are glossy black with a slight greenish sheen; rest of bird is dark sooty-black. Birds up to 18 months old may retain some white flecking on underparts. **Non-breeding:** During wing moult, may gain a greyish or off-white forehead and chin. **Juvenile:** Fresh juvenile has completely-white forehead and underparts. Crown, sides of face, and hindneck are variably marked with grey. Wings and mantle are greyish-black, lacking pale feather edges of juvenile Pied. Rump and tail are whitish with an ill-defined broad greyish terminal tail-band. **First-winter:** As juvenile, but with a variable amount of black on underparts, chiefly on belly and flanks. Breast normally remains completely white, but in some birds blackish markings extend forward to breast.
AGE/SEX Young immatures are distinctly different from adults, but beware confusion of immatures with hybrids. Sexes do not differ in plumage, but females average slightly shorter-legged.
RACES No geographical variation.
MEASUREMENTS Length 370-390 mm (15"). Wing 221-255 mm; bill 59-68 mm; tarsus 81-92 mm; tail 76-81 mm.
REFERENCES Pierce (1980a, 1982, 1984a,b).

26 BANDED STILT *Cladorhynchus leucocephalus*   Plate 11

An Australian endemic, highly distinctive in its appearance. Its remarkable breeding biology is similar in some respects to that of flamingoes.

IDENTIFICATION The pied pattern of the plumage, sometimes with a chestnut-and-black band on the underparts, precludes confusion with any other species. Differs from the Black-winged Stilt (24) in its relatively shorter legs and wings, and in the white back and secondaries; the wings fall roughly level with the tail-tip at rest. Individuals lacking a breast-band may resemble Red-necked Avocet (29), but have brighter legs, a straighter bill and always a white head and neck. In flight the wingbeats are flickering, considerably faster than those of other stilts and avocets, and the white secondaries on the otherwise black wings are distinctive. **Bare parts:** Bill black, slender and slightly upturned. Iris dark. Legs long, bright orangey-pink (peach-coloured), toes partially webbed.
VOICE A soft barking 'chowk' or 'chowk-uk', cacophonous when given from a dense flying flock.
HABITS Found on salt-lakes, commercial saltpans, and sometimes estuaries. Usually in large dense single-species flocks, but when feeding often associates with Red-necked Avocet and Black-winged Stilt. Immatures are sometimes seen singly in association with estuarine waders. Typically feeds by swimming, avocet-like, but also wades in shallows. Brine-shrimps are the chief food. Breeds opportunistically in huge colonies on low islands in large inland salt-lakes. The first nests were not found until 1930. The nesting season is apparently governed by rainfall and availability of food. A recently-abandoned colony found in 1980 contained an estimated 179,000 nests at densities as high as 18 per square metre. It appears that the colonies remain active for long periods, and that new nests are added as the young birds leave. The young can swim and feed themselves from a very early age, and form crèches like those of flamingoes; it is not known whether the adults ever feed them.The

pure white down of the newly-hatched chick is unique among waders. If conditions deteriorate, flightless young are abandoned and may be discovered walking in open country far from water.
MOVEMENTS Large numbers appear at coastal salt-pans when conditions are unsuitable inland, chiefly during the southern summer. Lone vagrants have appeared in Tasmania, coastal New South Wales and Queensland.
DESCRIPTION Breeding: Entirely white except for black on scapulars and folded wing, and broad chestnut band across lower breast joining a blackish-brown belly-patch. Upperwing entirely black, except for pure white secondaries and whitish near the tips of the inner 5 primaries; underwing mainly white, but with black leading underwing-coverts and under primary coverts. Tail white sullied with grey-brown. **Non-breeding:** Breast-band and belly-patch may become poorly defined and paler with the admixture of white and brown-tipped feathers. **Juvenile:** As adult except for complete absence of breast-band and belly-patch. There are fine white tips to the inner 8 primaries when fresh, more clearly defined than those of the adult.
AGE/SEX The full sequence of plumages is unknown, but apparently only juveniles and immatures totally lack a breast-band. Clear (but narrow) white tips to the primaries indicate juvenile, but these feathers may be replaced before the appearance of a breast-band. No differences are known between the sexes.
RACES No geographical variation is known.
MEASUREMENTS Length 360-450 mm (16"). Wing 185-210 mm; bill 64-77 mm; tarsus 74-89 mm.
REFERENCES McGilp and Morgan (1931), Jones (1945), Burbidge and Fuller (1982).

27 PIED AVOCET *Recurvirostra avosetta*   Plate 12

Other name: Avocet
The most widespread avocet. Strongly pied in all plumages, always with a dark cap and nape.

IDENTIFICATION As in all avocets, the bill is slender and strongly upcurved. Differs from American Avocet (28) chiefly in black or blackish-brown cap and nape, whiter wings and shorter legs; ranges even of vagrancy, however, are not known to overlap. In Pied Avocet, as in Red-necked Avocet (29), the white primary coverts and alula isolate the black area of the outer primaries. At rest, the white band across the outer scapulars is usually broader than the black bands which border it. The most similar species within its range is Crab Plover (11); this is easily distinguished by its massive black bill (not slender and upcurved), white or pale grey nape, black back, and mainly black wings in flight. **Bare parts:** Bill slender, black, strongly upcurved, slenderer than in American Avocet. Iris brown. Legs normally blue-grey, but both pink and orange have been recorded in single individuals; tarsus and toes extend well past tail in

flight.
VOICE A clear 'kluit', normally melodic and soft but harsher and shorter when alarmed. Also gives other similar calls. Noisy when breeding.
HABITS Breeds in saline or brackish areas with short vegetation, usually in large colonies with nests as close together as 1 m. In W Europe, colonies are chiefly within specially-protected areas. When breeding, very noisy and aggressive; capable of driving off birds as large as Shelduck *Tadorna tadorna*. Lowers head and neck and chases intruders approaching the nest or, later, entering the brood territory. Outside breeding season also found on muddy coasts and estuaries. May gather to roost in large flocks, 45,000 or more on some Kenyan lakes. Feeds on soft exposed mud or in water, often swims and up-ends like a dabbling duck. Feeds by picking or with strong sideways sweeps of the bill, even when up-ending.

Flies on rather stiff, straight wings with black-and-white pattern flashing, often in dense flocks. On migration seen in loose lines, usually flying quite low.

MOVEMENTS Mainly migratory, although present all year in much of African range and in parts of W Europe. Eastern birds are the strongest migrants. First-years do not breed and may remain in the wintering range. Vagrants have been recorded in E Atlantic islands from Iceland south to Cape Verde Is.; vagrant also in Japan.

DESCRIPTION Adult: No seasonal variation except for slight bleaching of blackish colours, particularly on crown, and appearance of whitish fringes on freshly-moulted feathers. Black patch covers crown down to just below eye, nape and upper hindneck. Scapulars and sides of mantle black; outer lesser coverts, median coverts black; outer 6 primaries black; tertials and largest scapulars darkish mottled grey; central tail feathers often washed pale grey. Otherwise brilliant white. **Juvenile:** As adult, but black areas are all dull brownish or grey-brown. Most of white upperparts initially heavily mottled and have sepia, grey-brown and buff fringes.

AGE/SEX After post-juvenile moult, some coverts and retained brownish primaries may be visible at close range or in the hand. Females are very slightly duller blackish than males, but many pairs can be sexed in the field by bill shape: males have longer, straighter-based bills, while females' bills are shorter and more strongly curved.

RACES There is a slight cline of increasing size from Atlantic across Europe and Asia, but no races are described.

MEASUREMENTS Length 420-450 mm (17"). Wing 206-240 mm; bill 82-93 mm (males), 72-85 mm (females); tarsus 85-98 mm (males), 77-92 mm (females); tail 66-90 mm.

REFERENCES Makkink (1936), Cadbury and Olney (1978).

28 AMERICAN AVOCET *Recurvirostra americana* Plate 12

The longest-legged avocet, and the only one with distinct breeding and non-breeding plumages.

IDENTIFICATION Easily identified by black-and-white plumage, strongly-upturned bill, mainly-white scapulars, and pale orange or pale grey head and neck. Taller than other avocets. In flight is broader-winged and shows less white than Pied or Red-necked Avocets (27, 29), and at rest the black bar across the folded wing usually looks broader than the white bar across the scapulars. **Bare parts:** Bill black, relatively broad at the base, strongly upturned. Iris brown. Long blue-grey legs.

male   female

VOICE A penetrating 'kleet' or 'kluit', which sounds more disyllabic when made as a contact call but sharper and almost monosyllabic when repeated rapidly in agitation.

HABITS Breeds around saline, usually alkaline, lakes on the prairies of W and central USA and central S Canada, usually in loose groups but forming large colonies in a few places. Also nests at some W coast estuaries; has bred on the Atlantic coast. Wider selection of habitats outside breeding season, often on estuaries and coastal flats or by fresh water. Feeding actions similar to other avocets; swims well. Outside the breeding season, may gather in flocks of several hundred and feed in quite dense groups, forming a spectacular mass of black and white.

MOVEMENTS Migrates to winter in southern part of breeding range, adjacent coasts and N Central America, returning in late Apr or May. Regular on Atlantic coast north to Delaware. Occasionally occurs as far north as New Brunswick; has been recorded on Caribbean islands (Cuba, Jamaica, Barbados, Tobago and Bonaire, Netherlands Antilles), but not yet on South American mainland. Has bred farther north in Canada and as far east as the Atlantic coast. Vagrants are recorded from Greenland and Baffin I.

DESCRIPTION Breeding: Breeding plumage appears in Jan-Mar. Head and neck are palish orangey-brown, whitish around eye and base of bill; the colour becomes more pinkish on upper mantle and upper belly and then shades into white. Outer 8 primaries, primary coverts and alula blackish-brown; secondaries mostly white, but outers have brown tips. Greater coverts are brown, tipped white, and tertials are pale brownish-grey. Outer scapulars form a white band above closed wing, while the dark brown inners form a dark 'V' bordering the back. Rump and tail are mainly white, with central tail feathers washed pale grey. **Non-breeding:** Orange-brown colour is lost during July-Sept and replaced on crown, sides of head, nape and hindneck with pearly-grey. Rest of head, neck and breast become white. Appears strikingly pale-headed at a distance. **Juvenile:** As adult, but dark browns of coverts, scapulars and tertials clearly paler; feathers initially have pinkish-buff tips. Crown is pale brownish, washed pinkish-buff, contrasting with darkish chestnut on nape and back of neck which merges again into pinkish on upper mantle. Pattern of white on primaries differs from adult: outer 5 primaries are all-dark, while inner 4 show some white.

AGE/SEX Sexes are similar in plumage, but dimorphic in bill shape and length; males have longer, straighter-based bills, while those of females are shorter but much more strongly upcurved. Young birds may be distinguished until the primary moult by the pattern of white on the primaries and by the greater degree of wear on the flight feathers. Most attain breeding plumage in the first year.

RACES No geographical variation is known.

MEASUREMENTS Length 400-500 mm (17¾"). Wing 213-242 mm; bill 84-99 mm (males), 78-86 mm (females); tarsus 85-103 mm; tail 76-90 mm.

REFERENCES Gibson (1971), Hamilton (1975).

29 RED-NECKED AVOCET *Recurvirostra novaehollandiae*   Plate 12

Other name: Australian Avocet
A particularly colourful avocet restricted to Australia, where it is widespread and fairly common.

IDENTIFICATION Easily identified as an avocet by its slender, strongly-upcurved bill, white underparts, pied upperparts, long bluish legs, and feeding habits. Very similar to American and Pied Avocets (28, 27), differing chiefly in range, dark chestnut-red head and neck (paler and browner in juveniles), and the amount of black on the wings, which is intermediate between the two but closer to Pied. The coloured head and neck recalls American Avocet, but the colour is darker, sharply defined from the white base of the neck, and present in all plumages throughout the year. In flight, the white alula and inner primaries are further distinctions from American Avocet. Wings are long and narrow, and project clearly beyond tail-tip at rest. **Bare parts:** Bill black, upcurved and fairly slender. Iris reddish-brown. Legs long, with feet projecting beyond tail-tip in flight, pale blue-grey.
VOICE Similar to other avocets. A clear, ringing, fluty 'tuut' or 'kluut' serves as the contact call. A shorter, sharper version is repeated as the alarm call.
HABITS Nests in loose colonies, sometimes singly, on the edges of shallow saline or brackish lakes or lagoons. Eggs have been found in July and Sept. Non-breeders sometimes appear on estuarine mudflats. Feeding habits typical of avocets: forages mainly using sideways sweeping action of the bill, frequently swimming and sweeping the surface layers or up-ending for food.
MOVEMENTS Occurs almost throughout Australia, but only rarely near the N and E coasts of the continent, and only a vagrant to Tasmania. Fairly sedentary, but inland birds move towards coastal areas in

response to dry weather. Between 1859 and 1878, perhaps 1892, was established as a breeding bird at several New Zealand localities, chiefly on South Island; now only an extremely rare vagrant (last reported 1912 and 1968-70).
DESCRIPTION Breeding and non-breeding: Head and most of neck deep chestnut-red, with some whitish around bill and a white ring around the eye. Base of neck white, also entire underparts. Mantle and scapulars white, except for blackish-brown inner large scapulars and outer mantle feathers which form a pair of blackish stripes on the upperparts. Outer 7 primaries and their coverts, and a band covering the median coverts, tertials and bases of the greater coverts, form two separate blackish-brown areas on the upper surface of each wing. Tail is washed very pale grey. **Juvenile:** Similar to adult but head is paler and browner. Dark areas of upperparts are paler brown and fringed initially with buffish-white. Some of the white scapulars and mantle feathers show brownish-buff fringes. The innermost of the black primaries show whitish tips when fresh, broader than those of the adult, but these wear rapidly.
AGE/SEX A difficult species to age once post-juvenile moult has started, but look for retained juvenile median coverts. Apparently shows less sexual dimorphism in bill shape than American and Pied Avocets.
RACES No geographical variation is known.
MEASUREMENTS Length 430-460 mm (17½"). Wing 215-238 mm; bill 81-98 mm; tarsus 79-94 mm.
REFERENCES Bryant (1947, 1948).

30 ANDEAN AVOCET *Recurvirostra andina*   Plate 12

While the other three avocets all frequent estuaries and low-level lakes, this species is found almost exclusively at high altitude. It also differs from the other avocets in its stilt-like plumage pattern, orange eye, rather short legs, very bulky body and broad wings.

IDENTIFICATION Similar in appearance to Black-winged Stilt (24), but is bulkier and has the typical upturned bill of an avocet. Head and neck are always all-white, not black-and-white as in the sympatric race of Black-winged Stilt. In flight, wings are much broader than those of a stilt, and the tail is blackish (not pale grey). All-blackish wings and mantle and more strongly-upcurved bill distinguish it from non-breeding American Avocet (28). **Bare parts:** Bill black. Iris orange (dark brown in other avocets); eye-ring yellow. Legs blue-grey.
VOICE Similar to the other avocets. Typically a di-syllabic barking 'kluut-kluut', repeated rapidly when agitated.
HABITS Breeds at high altitudes, mainly above 3500 m, in the Puna zone of S Peru, W Bolivia, N Chile and NW Argentina. Lays eggs in Jan and perhaps also in Sept-Oct. Found particularly around alkaline lakes. Feeds with lateral sweeping movements of the bill, as do other avocets, or by swimming and up-ending.

MOVEMENTS Little known: seems to be essentially sedentary, although there is some movement to slightly lower altitudes, particularly in Apr-July. Has been recorded as low as 330 m in N Chile, and even on the Peruvian coast near Mollendo (Mar-Sept).
DESCRIPTION Breeding and non-breeding: Whole of head, neck, upper mantle and underparts pure white. White lower back and rump. Rest of mantle and scapulars dark chocolate-brown; wing-coverts and tertials slightly darker brown. Longest uppertail-coverts and tail chocolate-brown. Underwing silvery-black with contrastingly white coverts and axillaries. **Juvenile:** Unknown.
AGE/SEX No differences are known between the sexes. The juvenile plumage is undescribed.
RACES No geographical variation is known.
MEASUREMENTS Length 430-480 mm (18"). Wing 236-258 mm; bill 68-84 mm; tarsus 77-84 mm; tail 97-106 mm.
REFERENCES Johnson (1965).

31 STONE-CURLEW *Burhinus oedicnemus* **Plate 13**

Other names: Stone Curlew, Thick-knee, European Stone-curlew
The most widespread *Burhinus* species, and the only one with regular migrations.

IDENTIFICATION Easily identified as a *Burhinus* by large size, brown-streaked upperparts and breast, thick yellowish legs, and bold face pattern with large staring yellow eye. In most of its range it is the only stone-curlew, but it overlaps with Great Thick-knee (38) in India and with three other species in Africa, where identification may not always be easy. Great Thick-knee differs obviously in its larger size, greyish, unstreaked plumage and massive, upturned bill. In Africa, most likely to be confused with Senegal Thick-knee (32) and Water Dikkop (33). Separation from these two species depends chiefly on close observation of the pattern of the wing-coverts and of the proportions and colouring of the bill. In Stone-curlew, a clear white bar across the wing-coverts is bordered above and below by black. Spotted Dikkop (34) is conspicuously spotted and lacks white on the wing-coverts. **Bare parts:** Bill small in proportion to other stone-curlews, blackish with extensive yellow at the base, normally including the base of the culmen (less often in *indicus*). Eye very large with bold yellow iris. Legs dull yellowish-brown.

VOICE Named from its chiefly arid habitat, and from its call (which may be reminiscent of Eurasian Curlew (132)). Vocal mainly at night, when its powerful calls may carry several kilometres in calm conditions. Most calls are variants on a 'cur-lee' which has accent on the higher-pitched second syllable. Typical territorial call starts with slurred whistles, which build up in pitch and volume to a series of clear, loud 'cur-lee' calls, then die away. Beware confusion with Eurasian Oystercatcher (12).

HABITS Found in a variety of dry, open, flat or rolling habitats, including sandy or stony semi-deserts in the south, short grasslands and heathlands, and well-drained arable farmland in the northwest. Eggs, normally two, are laid in a poorly-lined scrape, chiefly Apr-July, but Feb-June in Canary Is. and India. Spends much of day resting, often in shade, becoming active and sometimes noisy at dusk and at night. May fly several kilometres from the nesting area at night to feed in unexpected habitats, such as intertidal zone in some coastal areas. Food is chiefly insects and other invertebrates, but also takes small lizards and small rodents, occasionally eggs of other birds. Feeding action is stealthy, plover-like. When approached, squats flat on ground, relying on camouflage for concealment, and flushes at close range, or slinks furtively away. Behaviour is normally very timid, but in some localities nests on the outskirts of villages. After breeding, may gather into pre-migratory flocks at traditional sites, sometimes over a hundred individuals together.

MOVEMENTS Southern breeding birds are largely sedentary, although may (except the island races) perform limited seasonal movements. Records from Thailand and, less regularly, Kampuchea may represent a small resident population or perhaps wandering birds from farther west. Northern birds of the nominate race and probably also *harterti* are migratory, leaving southward in Sept-Oct and returning to the breeding grounds in late Mar or Apr; in the northern winter they are thinly distributed in N Africa south to N Kenya and N Uganda. Vagrants occur farther south in Kenya and once in the Serengeti National Park, N Tanzania (Jan 1971). There is one record from Sierra Leone (Jan 1982): this bird had been ringed as a chick in S England the previous June.

DESCRIPTION Breeding and non-breeding: Crown, nape, hindneck and upperparts brown, sometimes greyish, gingery or sandy in tone, streaked with darker brown or with broader dark centres to the feathers. Strong face pattern of whitish lores and cheeks and mark above and behind the eye, contrasting with dark brown malar stripe joining lower mandible to hindneck and dark brown line below the eye. Chin and throat are whitish. Neck, breast and flanks are suffused brownish and heavily marked with long dark brown streaks. Belly and vent are whitish; undertail is washed strongly with cinnamon-buff. Underwing is mainly whitish, but strongly contrasted with black on the tips of median and greater primary coverts and the outer primaries, and with brown along the leading edge. On the upperwing, the lesser coverts are brown becoming black bordering the median coverts; the median coverts are white bordering the lesser coverts, then black, then grey bordering the greaters; and the greater coverts are grey with a black subterminal band and a white tip. The alula, greater primary coverts and secondaries are black; the primaries are black with a white flash across the outer 2-3, the middle ones having a smaller less conspicuous white patch at the base and a white tip. The tail is longish and strongly graduated; the central feathers are patterned like the rest of the upperparts, but all feathers except the central pair show a broad black tip and a broad white subterminal band. **Juvenile:** Very like adult in pattern, but median coverts and tertials tend to show dark subterminal bars and bright buff edges; tertials are rather pointed in shape. Greater coverts tend to show broader white tips than on the adult. Tail feathers, particularly the central pair, initially show obvious streamers of down at the tips.

AGE/SEX Juveniles are very difficult to distinguish from adults, except in the hand. Retained inner median coverts may be present until mid-winter. They show greater primary wear than adults throughout the first winter. The presence of down streamers at the end of the central tail feathers indicates juvenile; these may be present for two to three months after fledging. Sexes are now known to differ in plumages but not in measurements.

RACES Six: nominate *oedicnemus* (Europe, and east to the Caspian Sea), *distinctus* (W Canaries), *insularum* (E Canaries), *saharae* (N Africa, N Arabia, SW Turkey, S Greece, most or all Mediterranean islands), *harterti* (south and east of the Caspian Sea) and *indicus* (Pakistan to Sri Lanka and peninsular Burma). The northern races *oedicnemus* and *harterti* are the largest, while *insularum* and *indicus* both average roughly 8% shorter-winged than these; the other races are intermediate. Compared with the nominate race, *distinctus* is slightly smaller and more contrastingly marked, *insularum* is smaller, paler, more rufous and less heavily streaked, *saharae* is slightly smaller and more sandy and more rufous in colour, *harterti* is paler, greyer, less heavily streaked, and more diffusely patterned on the wing-coverts, and *indicus* is smaller, darker, browner, and more heavily streaked. The race *indicus* tends to have slightly less yellow on the bill than the other races.

MEASUREMENTS Length 400-440 mm (16½"). Wing 224-255 mm (nominate), 203-226 mm (*indicus*); bill 33-41 mm; tarsus 67-83 mm; tail 113-129 mm (nominate).

REFERENCES Vaurie (1963), Glue and Morgan (1974), Christen (1980), Westwood (1983).

32 SENEGAL THICK-KNEE *Burhinus senegalensis*   Plate 13

This stone-curlew of chiefly riverine and lakeshore habitats in the Nile valley and a band just south of the Sahara is replaced to the south by Water Dikkop (33), a species of similar habits; both occur in parts of W Africa.

IDENTIFICATION Very similar to both Water Dikkop and Stone-curlew (31) in general appearance, both on the ground and in flight, but slightly smaller; overlaps with Water Dikkop in W Africa, while Stone-curlew can occur anywhere in its range. Of these three species, Senegal Thick-knee has the longest and heaviest bill, but identification rests chiefly on the distribution of colour on the bill and the pattern of the wing-coverts. In this species, there is no white at all in the lesser or median coverts: the leading lessers are dark brown, butting against the pale greyish of the median coverts. At long range, the grey may look palest bordering the dark lesser coverts, but unlike in Stone-curlew and Water Dikkop this never stands out as a white bar. The upperparts always lack Water Dikkop's cross-bars and vermiculations. Spotted Dikkop (34) has conspicuously-spotted upperparts and no contrasting covert pattern. **Bare parts:** Bill proportionately quite long and heavy, blackish with yellow at base; culmen and most of cutting edge are dark. Iris yellow. Legs pale yellowish-brown.
VOICE Much as Stone-curlew, but calls are more nasal and metallic.
HABITS Generally very similar to Stone-curlew. Habitat choice differs in that it avoids open deserts and is rarely found farther than 2-3 km from water. May be seen on riverbanks or even on rocks in midstream, but rarely wades. Often tamer and more approachable, sometimes seen in gardens or other open areas in towns and villages. In some places nests semi-colonially: there is a record of 21 nests found on the flat roof of a house in Egypt. Still nests on rooftops in central Cairo.
MOVEMENTS Apparently sedentary in the Nile valley, but south of the Sahara performs more or less regular short-distance movements in response to conditions of drought and flood. During rains becomes less common in N Nigeria but more common in Zaire. In Kenya, breeds only in NW but wanders southwards regularly to Lake Baringo and once to Lake Kanyaboli (Nov 1969).
DESCRIPTION All plumages: As corresponding plumages of Stone-curlew, except in covert pattern. Lesser coverts are dark brown. Tips of longest lesser coverts, median coverts, and bases of greater coverts are pale brownish-grey, with dark brown shaft-streaks on some feathers. Greater coverts are narrowly tipped white and have a black subterminal band.
AGE/SEX Juveniles are very difficult to distinguish. Look for down-streamers on the central tail feathers, or excessively-worn and narrow primaries. Sexes are not known to differ in plumage or measurements.
RACES Two, not very distinct and with a broad zone of intergradation: nominate *senegalensis* (Senegal to Nigeria) and *inornatus* (Egypt, Sudan and Ethiopia to Kenya). The race *inornatus* tends to be darker, and northern birds in particular average longer-winged.
MEASUREMENTS Length 320-380 mm (13¾"). Wing 203-222 mm (nominate), 208-231 mm (*inornatus*); bill 39-45 mm; tarsus 67-78 mm; tail 89-115 mm.

33 WATER DIKKOP *Burhinus vermiculatus*   Plate 14

Other name: Water Thick-knee or Thicknee
A close relative of the Stone-curlew (31) and Senegal Thick-knee (32), but found largely to the south of those species' ranges.

IDENTIFICATION Similar in appearance to Stone-curlew and Senegal Thick-knee, but differs from both in pattern of upperpart feathers, pattern of coverts, and distribution of yellow on the bill. This species has the smallest and dullest patches of yellow on the bill, which is distinctly heavier than that of Stone-curlew. The fine cross-bars and vermiculations on the upperpart feathers are unique among *Burhinus* but can be seen only at close range. On the coverts there is a clear pattern of dark brown, then white, then grey. The white bar across the lesser coverts is a conspicuous feature; unlike in Stone-curlew, there is no blackish lower border to this bar. **Bare parts:** Bill fairly heavy, mainly blackish with small areas of yellowish-green on the sides at the base; dark of culmen broadens markedly at the base of the bill. Iris yellow. Legs dull yellowish-brown, sometimes greyish or greenish; toes project beyond tail-tip in flight.
VOICE Like other stone-curlews in tone. Vocal mainly at night. Usual calls are a loud trisyllabic whistle 'kwa-lee-vee', and a harsher 'whee'.
HABITS Much as Senegal Thick-knee, but even more restricted to waterside habitats; never found far from water. Unlike other African *Burhinus*, widespread at the coast on the shores of creeks and islands. Sometimes wades. Reputed to associate with crocodiles

in some localities. Nest-scrape is occasionally lined; may nest on small islets. Often very tame and approachable. Usually seen in pairs or small groups. **MOVEMENTS** Apparently entirely sedentary; can always be found in traditional sites.

DESCRIPTION All plumages: Essentially as corresponding plumages of Stone-curlew but rather darker brown. Upperpart feathers differ from those of other stone-curlews in having irregular concentric or parallel brown barring across the feathers in addition to the dark shaft-streaks. Covert pattern resembles Senegal Thick-knee's, except that a clear white band divides the dark brown leading lessers from the brownish-grey of the median coverts.

AGE/SEX Young are very difficult to distinguish from adults; look for down-streamers on the central tail feathers or excessively-worn and pointed primaries. No plumage differences are known between the sexes.

RACES Two: nominate *vermiculatus* (Zaire, S Uganda and Kenya to S Africa) and *büttikoferi* (Liberia to Gabon and N Uganda). The race *büttikoferi* differs in being darker brown, less grey, above; at least some individuals have longer bills than the nominate race. **MEASUREMENTS** Length about 380-410 mm (15½"). Wing 193-216 mm; bill 37-44 mm (nominate), 47-48 mm (two specimens of *büttikoferi*); tarsus 70-82 mm; tail 96-114 mm.

34 SPOTTED DIKKOP *Burhinus capensis*   Plate 14

Other names: Spotted Thick-knee or Thicknee, Cape Dikkop
The dry-country stone-curlew of southern Africa. Its range overlaps widely with Water Dikkop (33), also with Stone-curlew (31) and Senegal Thick-knee (32) chiefly north of the equator.

IDENTIFICATION Easily separated from all other *Burhinus* species by conspicuously-spotted pattern of the upperparts, and lack of a contrasting pattern on the wing-coverts. The dark central shaft-streak of each feather is expanded into a bar or bars at the base of the feather and a more or less rounded subterminal spot near the tip. The whitish areas of the lores, cheeks and above the eye are smaller than in other African stone-curlews, giving a darker and less contrasted face pattern; the lores typically show more brown than whitish. In size and in proportions of bill, most resembles Stone-curlew. In flight, distribution of black and white on the flight feathers similar to other African *Burhinus*; look for the covert pattern, and for strong barring on the central tail feathers shown only by this species. The underwing pattern differs in that greater primary and secondary coverts are broadly tipped blackish to form a striking dark central bar along the underwing, lacking in the other species. **Bare parts:** Bill blackish with yellow base; distribution of yellow most like that in Senegal Thick-knee, but the bill is less heavy. Iris yellow. Legs bright yellow or brownish-yellow, sometimes darker along the front of the tarsus.

VOICE Vocal mainly at night. Usual calls are a distinctive, plaintive 'tche-uuuu', gradually dying away, and a rapid 'pi-pi-pi-pi' when alarmed.

HABITS Similar to other stone-curlews. Habitat includes open dry country, bushy or wooded grassland, rocky riverbeds, and the vicinity of towns and villages. May even nest locally in suburban gardens. Does not show a particular preference for water, at least in the north of its range. Display postures usually show the strongly-patterned underwing to full advantage. Like other dry-country burhinids, for example Stone-curlew and Bush Thick-knee (37), often encountered on dirt roads at night. Usually seen in pairs, sometimes in small groups.

MOVEMENTS Apparently mostly sedentary, but may appear occasionally in areas where it is not known to breed.

DESCRIPTION Breeding and non-breeding: Head, neck and breast mostly buffish-brown with dark brown shaft-streaks, broad on crown, nape and sides of breast; small whitish area above eye, narrow bar from bill across cheeks, and unmarked whitish chin and throat. Belly and flanks are off-white, narrowly streaked dark brown except on the lower belly and vent. Undertail-coverts are rich cinnamon-brown. Underwing and axillaries mainly whitish except for brown leading edge, blackish tips to the flight feathers, and a narrow blackish bar at the tips of the greater primary and secondary coverts. Upperparts, including wing-coverts and central tail feathers, warm buffy-brown strongly barred with dark brown; last bar on most feathers is a rounded subterminal spot. Flight feathers are black, except for a white flash across the outer primaries and a white basal patch and white tip on the middle primaries. Tail is strongly graduated; all feathers except central pair have a black tip and a white subterminal band. **Juvenile:** Differs only in covert pattern. Wing-coverts show a dark brown shaft-streak or indistinct submarginal bar rather than the spotting of adults.

AGE/SEX Juvenile is identical to the adult except in covert pattern; initially it shows rather loose downy feathering, particularly on the hindneck and rear flanks, and down-streamers on the tips of the tail feathers. The streamers are likely to be present for at least a month or two after fledging. No plumage differences are known between the sexes.

RACES Four: nominate *capensis* (Kenya to South Africa), *maculosus* (Senegal to Eritrea, Somalia, N Kenya and Uganda), *dodsoni* (coastal Somalia, Dahlak Is., SW Arabia), and *damarensis* (Namibia, W Botswana and NW Cape Province). Compared with the nominate race, *damarensis* is paler and *maculosus* is warmer, more tawny, above. In *dodsoni*, the pattern differs slightly in that the feathers of the mantle and scapulars show a bar near the tip rather than a subterminal spot; these areas, but not the wing-coverts, appear barred and streaked rather than spotted. The races *dodsoni* and *maculosus* average about 5% shorter in wing length than the nominate race. **MEASUREMENTS** Length about 430 mm (17"). Wing 222-245 mm (nominate); bill 33-41 mm; tarsus 85-103 mm; tail 110-123 mm.

REFERENCES Broekhuysen (1963).

35 DOUBLE-STRIPED THICK-KNEE *Burhinus bistriatus*   Plate 15

Other names: Double-striped Stone-curlew, Mexican Thick-knee
The more widespread and northerly of the two American stone-curlews. Around South American homesteads, sometimes kept in semi-domesticity to control insects.

IDENTIFICATION A rather large and long-legged stone-curlew, with proportions recalling the Australian Bush Thick-knee (37). As in Peruvian Thick-knee (36), there is a long and striking white supercilium bordered above by a neat black band. Range is separated by 1000 km from the Peruvian species; differs from it in slightly larger size, darker and proportionately much heavier bill, darkish crown, darker and more streaked upperparts, a clear division between the dark breast and the white belly, and less contrast between the wing-coverts and the secondaries in flight. **Bare parts:** Bill black with dull greenish-yellow base, rather heavy. Large eye with yellow iris. Long greenish-yellow legs.
VOICE Short, chattering but strident calls, given mostly at dusk or at night.
HABITS Much as other *Burhinus* species. The nest is a simple depression in the soil, sometimes a hoofprint. Eggs have been found in Costa Rica in Jan and Mar. Found in arid open grassland and savannas, also agricultural country; often encountered on dirt roads at night. Essentially crepuscular and nocturnal, resting inconspicuously during the day. Seldom flies, relying on crouching behaviour and camouflage for concealment. Not gregarious, but sometimes in small scattered groups. Not particularly shy. The habitat available for this species is increasing as the forests are converted to pasture.
MOVEMENTS Essentially sedentary, but dispersing individuals have reached Curaçao (July 1934) and Texas (shot in Dec 1961).
DESCRIPTION Breeding and non-breeding: Forehead creamy-brown, streaked dark brown; crown and nape dark brown with pale brown feather edges. Strong off-white supercilium from in front of eye to sides of nape, bordered above by brownish-black bands at sides of crown. Upperparts, including wing-coverts and rump, darkish brown with tawny-buff edges giving a strongly-streaked appearance. Two white wing-flashes: one subterminally on outer 2 primaries, often poorly defined, and the other, bolder, on the bases of the middle and inner primaries. Tail graduated; central two pairs of feathers are patterned as upperparts, rest pale brown with brownish-white subterminal bar and black tip. Chin white; sides of face, neck and upper breast whitish-buff finely streaked brown; lower breast greyish-brown with fine brown streaks forming a neat division against the whitish underparts. Underwing and axillaries white. Undertail-coverts tawny-brown.
Juvenile: As adult, but feathers of upperparts have broader buff edges, and the head, neck and breast are strongly tinged buff.
AGE/SEX Juveniles are very difficult to distinguish from adults. No differences are known between the sexes.
RACES Four, but difficult to separate owing to considerable individual variation. Nominate *bistriatus* (S Mexico to Costa Rica) is the largest, especially in wing and tarsus, and tends to be rather dark with a greyish breast; *pediacus* (N Colombia) is rather pale, with pale cinnamon-buff edges to feathers of upperparts; *vocifer* (Venezuela to N Brazil) is rather dark, with a brownish breast; *dominicensis* is rather small and is confined to Hispaniola.
MEASUREMENTS Length 430-480 mm (18"). Wing 236-273 mm; bill 37-46 mm; tarsus 101-128 mm; tail 111-139 mm. One specimen of *dominicensis*: wing 226 mm; bill 40 mm; tarsus 97 mm; tail 108 mm.
REFERENCES Freese (1975).

36 PERUVIAN THICK-KNEE *Burhinus superciliaris*   Plate 15

The smaller of the two South American species, this rather pale stone-curlew has a very restricted range.

IDENTIFICATION A typical stone-curlew in size and proportions. It shares with Double-striped Thick-knee (35) the white supercilium bordered by black above, but is smaller and greyer and has a proportionately much weaker bill which shows more extensive colour at the base. The face and crown are paler, the upperparts are less heavily streaked, and the coverts are contrastingly clean grey. In flight, shows two white flashes in the primaries, as does Double-striped, but there is greater contrast between the coverts and the flight feathers. It is the only stone-curlew in its range, being well separated from range of Double-striped.
Bare parts: Bill black, with yellowish-green on basal half of cutting edge and lower mandible; bill-base greenish-grey in juveniles. Large eye with yellow iris. Legs quite long, yellowish-green, but more brownish in juveniles; toes project less beyond the tail than in Double-striped.
VOICE Noisy at night, as are other *Burhinus*. Also gives a chattering scolding cry (hence the onomatopoeic local name of 'Huerequeque').
HABITS Much as other stone-curlews. Inhabits poor agricultural land, semi-desert, arid grasslands, and bush-country in the coastal lowlands and westernmost Andean foothills; mainly crepuscular and nocturnal. The only documented nest of this species, found in 1978, contained two eggs on 5 June. Often seen in pairs, but flocks of up to 35 have been recorded.
MOVEMENTS Appears to be entirely sedentary. Only once recorded across the border in Chile, in 1851, but it is not clear whether this bird was a vagrant or whether the breeding range has since contracted northwards.
DESCRIPTION Breeding and non-breeding: Lores and sides of forehead whitish with very fine darker streaks. Crown brownish-grey finely streaked brown. Blackish-brown lateral crown-stripe from above eye

to side of nape. White supercilium from side of forehead to side of nape, in some bordered below by blackish beneath eye and on the rear of the ear-coverts. Upperparts grey-brown finely streaked brown and slightly mottled buff; on closed wing, lesser coverts form brown bar along leading edge of wing which is continued backwards by the darkish outer scapulars. Rest of coverts grey, faintly mottled buffish-white when fresh. Flight feathers blackish, with two white flashes in primaries; there is a white band across the outer 3 primaries, and the bases of the middle and inner primaries are white. Bases of secondaries are greyish. Tail graduated; central tail feathers are patterned as upperparts, others show broad subterminal whitish bar and black tip. Chin white; sides of face, neck and upper breast buffish, finely streaked

brown, this colour gently merging into greyish-white on lower breast, flanks and upper belly. Central belly white, undertail-coverts buffish-tawny, sometimes mottled brown. **Juvenile:** As adult, but upperparts rather darker with warmer tawny and buff fringes. Grey coverts show buff fringes and irregular brown submarginal lines. Supercilia may be almost joined by a palish band across the nape.

AGE/SEX Juvenile coverts with submarginal lines are distinctive and may be visible at close range in the field. No differences are known between the sexes.
RACES No geographical variation is known.
MEASUREMENTS Length 380-430 mm (16"). Wing 221-232 mm; bill 29-34 mm; tarsus 84-96 mm; tail 107-116 mm.
REFERENCES Williams (1981).

37 BUSH THICK-KNEE *Burhinus magnirostris*   Plate 16

Other names: Bush or Southern Stone-curlew
The largest member of the genus *Burhinus*, although smaller-bodied (but lankier) than the two *Esacus* stone-curlews (38,39). Its bill and leg proportions are much closer to those of its South American congeners than to its African and Eurasian ones.

IDENTIFICATION Differs from the Beach Thick-knee (38) most obviously in its chiefly inland habitat, streakier plumage and less sharply-defined head pattern. Also has smaller, all-dark bill and much longer, greenish legs. In flight, shows mainly black flight feathers, and the feet project well beyond the tail. The two species may be found together on coasts and small islands. No other Australasian wader is similar. The widespread Stone-curlew (31) of Eurasia and North Africa occurs as close as Burma, but is considerably smaller and shorter-legged, has a bolder face pattern, and white bars across the wing-coverts.
Bare parts: Bill all black, lighter at base of lower mandible, shortish and evenly tapered in comparison with Beach Thick-knee. Eyes large, iris yellow mottled dark brown towards the outer edge. Legs dirty yellowish-green, feet slightly darker.
VOICE Well known for its eerie nocturnal wailing song: a series of mournful whistling notes, starting low and slowly, quickening and rising in pitch, then descending and ending with staccato notes. Sometimes several birds in chorus. Rarely vocal during the day. This song gave rise to the Aboriginal name 'Willaroo'.
HABITS Found throughout the year in open woodland, along dry watercourses, fringes of mangrove and coastal sandy scrub; in northern parts of the range more frequent near habitations, on golf-courses, and even wasteland in towns (e.g. Cairns, N Queensland). Wary and largely inactive during the day. If approached, may freeze and flush only at close range, or run furtively towards cover. Becomes active at night and is often met with on country roads. Predatory on small vertebrates and on insects and other invertebrates.
MOVEMENTS Sedentary throughout its range, but apparently only a vagrant to S New Guinea.
DESCRIPTION All plumages: Crown, hindneck, mantle, back and rump clean grey with dark brown shaft-streaking, forming a continuous grey band down the central upperparts. Small patch of chestnut-brown by base of lower mandible, and from beneath eye

down sides of nape bordering the grey band. Forehead, lores, supercilium, throat and cheeks clean whitish. Underparts light creamy with dark brown shaft-streaks, very broad across breast but narrower on neck and flanks; belly white, undertail-coverts buff sometimes with a few brown markings. Scapulars blackish or dark brown with bold buff edges, forming dark areas which usually meet across the grey band running down the upperparts. Lesser coverts dark brown fringed dark chestnut. Medians mainly whitish, but suffused brown and with bold dark shaft-streaks. Greater coverts brown with some white fringing on inner feathers. Secondaries are black; primaries are black with a large white flash formed by a white band right across each of the outer four feathers (sometimes a white spot on primary 6) and a smaller white flash (sometimes bold, sometimes almost absent) at bases of the inner primaries. Tail mainly grey, somewhat mottled and barred with brown, strongly graduated; most outer feathers are black-tipped and have a white subterminal area. Axillaries and underwing-coverts are largely white.
AGE/SEX Juveniles are extremely similar to adults, but first plumage has rather loose feathering and shows dirty-brownish nape and upper back, and buff fringes to the rump (these are also present on a minority of adults). Medians show less white, and undertail never has brown markings. After post-juvenile body moult, look for narrow and pointed outer primaries (broader and blacker in adults) and retained buff-tipped rump feathers among new all-grey adult-type feathers. Sexes are not known to be separable.
RACES Three races are described, but they hardly differ in appearance or measurements and probably intergrade since no discontinuities are known in the range: *rufescens* (NW Australia, Northern Territory), *ramsayi* (N Queensland), and *magnirostris* (most of range, S Queensland to SW Australia).
MEASUREMENTS Length 550-580 mm (22"). Wing 264-309 mm; bill 43-53 mm; tarsus 112-145 mm.
REFERENCES Bedggood (1977).

38 GREAT THICK-KNEE *Esacus recurvirostris*

Plate 16

Other names: Great Stone Plover, Great Stone-curlew
A massive thick-knee of the coasts of the Indian subcontinent. Forms a species pair with the Australian Beach Thick-knee (39).

IDENTIFICATION Partly sympatric with Stone-curlew (31) but easily distinguished by larger size, unstreaked greyish upperparts, massive uptilted bill, strongly-patterned face, and almost exclusively waterside habitat. In flight, there is a large pale area across the coverts; the wings are broad and clearly 'fingered' at the tip, recalling a bustard (Otididae) rather than a wader. Very similar to Beach Thick-knee in plumage pattern, but slightly smaller with a slimmer, strongly-uptilted bill, and with less black on the sides of the head. The black areas on the sides of the crown, ear-coverts and moustache are all largely separate, although on some individuals the first two are joined by a narrow black line in front of the eye. Lores are mostly white (mostly black in Beach). Neck and breast lack streaking. In flight, shows less white on inner primaries and an unbroken dark trailing edge to the underwing. **Bare parts:** Bill black, with yellow along sides of inner third of upper mandible and a smaller patch on lower mandible near base; culmen is angled slightly upwards from half-way along its length, and lower mandible is strongly uptilted at the gonys. Iris yellow, eye very large. Legs yellowish- or greyish-green; feet barely project past tail in flight.
VOICE Territorial note is a wailing whistle of two or more syllables given with a rising inflexion, most frequent at night. Alarm call is a loud harsh 'see-eek'.
HABITS Typically a bird of shingle-banks along larger riverbeds or by large lowland lakes, but found also on coastal beaches and intertidal flats; sometimes visits nearby grasslands, especially during rains. Mainly crepuscular and nocturnal, but occasionally seen feeding, plover-like, during the day. Takes mainly crabs and other invertebrates; has been observed eating eggs of Kentish Plover (98). Rather wary, relying initially on camouflage but later walking away or flying if approached too closely. Flight strong and powerful. Generally solitary or in pairs, sometimes in family groups, but occasionally gathers in flocks of up to 20 or so. Nests Jan-Aug, mainly Feb-Apr in India and Apr-July in Sri Lanka. Both sexes incubate and tend the chicks.
MOVEMENTS Mainly sedentary, but performs local movements presumably in response to changes in feeding conditions.
DESCRIPTION Breeding and non-breeding: Forehead white. Crown, mantle and scapulars grey-brown, slightly streaked darker. Short black moustachial stripe. Blackish-brown mask around eye, curving down side of neck; white supercilium in the centre of the dark mask, sometimes joining the white of the forehead. Lores white, or mainly white with a blackish-brown line in front of the eye. Cheeks and throat white. Wings and tail much as Beach Thick-knee except for distribution of white on the flight feathers. White band across the outer 3 primaries; inner primaries tipped white and with some white at base; secondaries blackish with white bases. Underwing mainly white, but with dark trailing edge to secondaries, dark subterminal band across inner primaries, and mainly dark outer primaries. Neck and breast suffused grey-buff with very indistinct (sometimes absent) streaking. Belly almost white, not contrasting with underwing. **Juvenile:** As adult in pattern, but upperparts show buffish fringing and spotting when fresh.
AGE/SEX Young birds are distinguishable only at close range. No differences are known between the sexes.
RACES No geographical variation is known.
MEASUREMENTS Length 490-540 mm (20"). Wing 257-271 mm; bill 68-74 mm, depth at gonys 15-17 mm; tarsus 78-88 mm.

39 BEACH THICK-KNEE *Esacus magnirostris*

Plate 16

Other names: Beach Stone-curlew, Australian Stone Plover
A massive thick-knee of tropical coasts from Australia north to Malaysia, forming a species pair with the closely-related Great Thick-knee (38).

IDENTIFICATION Large size, enormous bill and strong patterning on head and wings serve to identify this species. The head pattern is very striking: a broad black band curves from the forehead down the side of neck, enclosing a sharply-defined, narrow but drooping, brilliant white posterior supercilium; this contrasts with the white cheeks, chin and throat and short black moustachial stripe. This pattern, virtually unstreaked upperparts, relatively short legs, and huge bill with yellow patches at the base are simple features to distinguish it from Bush Thick-knee (37). In flight, an amazing area of flashing white on the inner primaries, extensive pale grey across the inner wing, and slow heavy beats of broad 'fingered' wings suggest a bustard (Otididae) rather than a stone-curlew. Only the toes extend beyond the tail-tip. Great Thick-knee is very similar in plumage and build, but differs obviously in smaller size, relatively slimmer and strongly-upcurved bill, and less extensive black areas on the sides of the head. The lores are mostly white (mostly black in Beach Thick-knee). In flight, Great Thick-knee shows less white on the inner primaries and an unbroken dark trailing edge to the underwing; the upperparts are a slightly paler brown than in the present species, and the neck and breast are unstreaked. **Bare parts:** Huge bill, very long and deep; black, with yellow spot near base of lower mandible and yellow patch at base of upper mandible, extending back from the nostril. Large eye with bright yellow iris. Yellows of bill and eye duller in juveniles. Legs brownish or greenish-yellow, heavily built.

VOICE Territorial call is harsh wailing 'wee-loo', higher-pitched and less fluty than Bush Thick-knee. The alarm call is a weak yapping 'quip' or 'peep', somewhat oystercatcher-like but much less penetrating; sometimes a rising 'quip-ip-ip'.

HABITS In contrast to Bush and Great Thick-knees, a strictly coastal bird. Found throughout the year on sandy beaches, especially where large mangrove-backed sandflats or reefs are exposed at low tide. Essentially crepuscular and nocturnal, resting in shade during the day unless disturbed, and rarely seen feeding. Despite vast bill, takes mostly relatively small items such as crabs and other marine invertebrates. Slow, stalking, rather plover-like feeding technique. Generally seen singly or in pairs, occasionally in small groups.

MOVEMENTS Appears to be entirely sedentary.

DESCRIPTION Breeding and non-breeding: Black or blackish-brown patch on sides of head, covering most of forehead and lores and extending down to sides of upper neck. Short and thick black moustachial patch. Curving white supercilium from just in front of eye to side of nape. Chin and throat white. Crown, hindneck and mantle olive-brown, very finely flecked darker; neck and upper breast finely streaked. Breast strongly suffused grey, becoming whitish or pale buffish-grey on belly; contrasting tawny-cream vent and undertail. Closed wing shows white carpal patch, horizontal blackish-brown lesser-covert bar, narrowly white along the lower edge, and broad area of greyish coverts. Wing pattern dramatically black-and-white. Isolated white patch subter-

minally on outer 3 primaries, otherwise outer 5 primaries black. Inner primaries and their primary coverts brilliant white. Bases and outer webs of all secondaries, and all of inner secondaries white. Dusky trailing edge to middle and outer secondaries. Greater coverts, also outer median and lesser coverts, very pale grey. Underwing shows translucent white triangular patch on the inner primaries, white band across the outer primaries, and a dark trailing edge to the secondaries. Back and rump olive-brown, as mantle. Tail olive-brown, with central pair of feathers darker and slightly mottled. Outer five pairs of tail feathers show dull brown terminal bar, whitish subterminal band, then another darkish bar. **Juvenile:** Very similar to adult, but upperparts slightly paler with buff fringes. Leading lesser coverts pale brown fringed buff, median and greater coverts grey-brown with obscure subterminal blotches and fine buffish-white fringes.

AGE/SEX Juveniles are very difficult to distinguish, but show duller bare parts and a somewhat obscured covert pattern. No differences are known between the sexes.

RACES As would be expected in a sedentary species scattered over many islands, there is some geographical variation. In the past, four races have been described, but the differences between them appear to be inconsistent. None is now recognised.

MEASUREMENTS Length 530-570 mm (22"). Wing 264-285 mm; bill 70-79 mm, depth at gonys 19-22 mm; tarsus 83-90 mm.

40 EGYPTIAN PLOVER *Pluvianus aegyptius*   Plate 14

A most unusual wader, with strikingly-patterned plumage and with methods of incubation and chick-care unique among birds. It is reputed to pick food and parasites from the teeth of crocodiles (it is probably the 'crocodile bird' of Herodotus), but this behaviour has never been properly documented.

IDENTIFICATION Quite unlike any other wader. An unmistakable, chunky, short-legged bird with deep blue-grey upperparts, peach-buff underparts and striking black bands (glossed green) on head, sides of neck, breast and mantle, contrasting with bright white throat and supercilia. In flight the mainly white wings, outlined in black and crossed by a broad diagonal black bar, are spectacular; the wings are short, but broadly based and somewhat triangular. **Bare parts:** Bill longish for a courser-like bird, sharply pointed, black with a slightly paler base. Iris dark brown. Legs blue-grey, rather short.

VOICE High-pitched but harsh syllables rapidly repeated, 'cherk-cherk-cherk' or 'krrr-krrr-krrr', at times run together, serve as the alarm call in a variety of contexts. Also a 'wheep', and a shorter 'whup' call to the young.

HABITS Breeds territorially on sandbars along the middle stretches of large rivers, thus highly locally within its wide range. The bold wing pattern is featured in displays. The clutch is not incubated in the normal sense, since the eggs are rarely warmed by the adult's body. They are kept buried in the warm sand, usually to a depth of about 3 mm, and cooled by the adult sitting above them and periodically wetting the sand with water carried from the river in the

belly feathers. The eggs hatch 'underground'. The chicks are precocial and leave the nest-site within the first day; if danger threatens, they crouch in a hollow while the adult buries them completely by throwing sand over them with its bill. Buried chicks may also be wetted with water from the river. Chicks up to three weeks old may be treated in this way. The unusual incubation strategy allows this bird to nest in a habitat where the eggs would otherwise become overheated or dehydrated. When not breeding, or particularly when the rivers are in spate, may be found in other wetland habitats or even, rarely, away from water. Usually seen in pairs, sometimes in small flocks. Generally very tame and approachable. Feeds by deliberate pecking, also by chasing flying insects, scratching at the sand by jumping with both feet together, or digging with the bill. Normal gait is plover-like. Flight is fast and low with flicking wingbeats.

MOVEMENTS Mostly sedentary, but nomadic when displaced by high water-levels, particularly June-Oct. Single vagrants have been recorded in Libya, Israel and Canary Is.

DESCRIPTION Breeding and non-breeding: Forehead, crown and nape are glossy black, outlined by fine white supercilia running from bill to meet in a

'V' on the lower nape. Lores black, becoming a broad black line across the ear-coverts which merges into the black hindneck. Chin and throat white, rest of underparts peach-buff, deepest on vent and under-tail and palest bordering the narrow black breast-band and the black of the face and neck. Underwing and axillaries are white. Mantle is black, with long black feathers from lower mantle overlying the back and rump and reaching almost to the uppertail-coverts. Black areas of head and body are all faintly glossed with green. Sides of back and upper rump are white, but are completely overlain by the blue-grey scapulars. Coverts and tertials are blue-grey; greater coverts are broadly tipped white. Outer pri-mary is mostly black, other primaries are white with a narrow black tip and a broad black band near the base. Primary coverts are white with narrow black tips; leading primary coverts, also alula, are black but tinged blue-grey. Secondaries are white, with broad diagonal black band from middle of outermost feather to tips of inner four feathers; outer secon-daries are white at base and at tip. Tail is blue-grey tipped white, with a narrow black subterminal band on outer feathers. Rump and uppertail are blue-grey. **Juvenile:** Like adult in pattern, but duller and with much rusty-brown admixed in black areas of head; breast-band is dull and thin. Leading lesser and median coverts, also rump feathers, are rusty-brown. **AGE/SEX** Juvenile is distinct at close range, but after a few months indistinguishable in the field. Sexes are similar in appearance, size and voice.
RACES Normally considered monotypic, but a race *angolae* is sometimes separated (N Angola and W Zaïre).
MEASUREMENTS Length 190-210 mm (7¾"). Wing 127-144 mm; bill 16-20 mm; tarsus 32-37 mm; tail 59-67 mm.
REFERENCES Howell (1980).

41 TWO-BANDED COURSER *Rhinoptilus africanus*   Plate 17

Other name: Double-banded Courser
A small courser typical of open arid country in E and S Africa.

IDENTIFICATION This species is typified by strongly-scaled upperparts, buffish face and breast with pat-tern of fine streaking, and two narrow but complete blackish rings around the upper breast and the base of the hindneck. The markings on the upperparts are more distinct than in the much larger Heuglin's Courser (42), which also has a more striking head pattern; all other African coursers have plain backs in adult plumage. In flight, there is a striking broad chestnut band on the trailing edge of the wing which contrasts with the blackish outer primaries, and an inconspicuous narrow white patch across the uppertail-coverts. **Bare parts:** Bill black, short, thin and only slightly decurved; some individuals show a tinge of brown at the base of the lower mandible. Iris dark brown. Legs ivory-white or very pale yellowish-white; in flight, feet project beyond tail-tip. **VOICE** Not very vocal. Usual call is a thin plover-like 'peeu-weee', falling in pitch during the first syl-lable then rising again; often heard on moonlit nights. Also a sharper 'kik-kik' when flushed; seldom calls in flight. When anxious, delivers one or two longish whistles then a burst of staccato piping. Various other quiet calls are given when breeding.
HABITS Found in a variety of open, dry habitats on sandy and stony substrates; prefers stony areas, avoids dense scrub and long grass. Upperpart colour matches habitat; usually relies on camouflage, often presenting back to intruder. If approached, prefers to run, but may fly short distance with fast, flicking wingbeats. Well scattered but not uncommon in suitable habitats. Rarely seen in groups of more than three. Chiefly nocturnal, but feeds also at dawn and dusk and sometimes active during the day. Does not normally drink. Feeds probably entirely on small insects. Bill is short for a courser and is not used for digging. Nests all year in some localities. Lays a sin-gle egg, usually among mammal droppings; no scrape is made.
MOVEMENTS Largely sedentary, but wide fluctua-tions in counts at particular localities suggest that at least local seasonal migrations occur.
DESCRIPTION Breeding and non-breeding: Base colours vary considerably (see Races). Crown brown with dull buff fringes slightly darker than the long buffish supercilium. Narrow brown eye-stripe from bill continues behind the eye. Upperparts, includ-ing wing-coverts and tertials, are brown with broad dark brown submarginal bands and large pale sandy-buff fringes. Outer 2-4 primaries dark brown with pale inner webs, next three have mainly darkish outer webs with chestnut on inner webs and at the tip; inner primaries and secondaries mostly pale chest-nut, may be variably whitish-tipped or -mottled sub-marginally. Uppertail-coverts narrowly white. Outer tail feathers white (sometimes washed buffish), rest dusky-brown mottled buff-brown towards tip and nar-rowly tipped white or buffish. Whitish chin and buffish throat, neck and upper breast are all finely streaked dark brown. Breast shows two neat black bands which continue around base of hindneck; rest of underparts buffish or buffish-white. Underwings and axillaries mainly buffish-white, with small dark brown spots at carpal and on primary coverts; there is great contrast with dark leading primaries. **Juven-ile:** As adult but rather sandier; all of upperparts have sandy-buff feathers with narrow, finely-pencilled, dark submarginal lines and narrow whitish fringes. Outer primaries are neatly fringed buff-white at tip. Upper breast-band is initially absent; lower one is irregu-lar, brown, and partly obscured.
AGE/SEX A young juvenile can be told in the field by its poor breast pattern; older birds can be sepa-rated, but least easily in northern populations where adult submarginal dark bands on upperparts are nar-rowest. In the hand, look for retained inner coverts and buff-fringed or very worn primaries. Sexes simi-lar, although in Kalahari one sex (thought to be female) tends to be darker and more rufous.
RACES Eight are described, largely on the basis of

local colour variation: *raffertyi* (central Ethiopia), *hartingi* (Somalia), *gracilis* (central Kenya, N Tanzania), *illustris* (central Tanzania), *bisignatus* (Angola), *sharpei* (Namibia), nominate *africanus* (S Namibia, W Cape Province), and *granti* (Transvaal, central Cape Province). In essence, northernmost populations tend to have sandiest upperparts, and underparts with pale buffish wash and fine streaking, grading southwards through greyer, paler individuals with almost white underparts to darker, dull buff-brown or earth-brown birds in southern Africa; these last have strongly-streaked deep buff-brown underparts, sometimes streaked below the breast-bands. Northern *hartingi* and *raffertyi* are medium-sized (wing 134-148 mm); central three races are smallest (wing 130-137 mm); while southern *sharpei*, *africanus* and *granti* are largest (wing 143-163 mm).

MEASUREMENTS Length 200-240 mm (8½"). Wing 130-163 mm; bill 11-14 mm; tarsus 44-59 mm; tail 49-67 mm.

REFERENCES Maclean (1967), Uys and Underhill (1977).

42 HEUGLIN'S COURSER *Rhinoptilus cinctus*　　Plate 17

Other name: Three-banded or Treble-banded Courser
A widespread but local courser of tropical E Africa, rarely seen because of its mainly nocturnal habits.

IDENTIFICATION A fairly large-headed and long-legged courser with strongly-blotched upperparts, a dark brown crown, long clear white supercilia, and a distinctive breast pattern like a fancy V-necked pullover. The three bands of the alternative name are a chestnut 'V' across the sides of the neck and the lower throat, a narrow chestnut line across the lower breast, and between these a broad zone of heavy brown streaking bordered below and partly also above by a narrow brown line. Two-banded Courser (41) is the only other courser which has non-uniform upperparts; it is smaller, lives in more open habitats, has shorter, less conspicuous, buff supercilia, lacks chestnut markings on the breast, and has a finely-streaked throat and a palish crown. The Violet-tipped Courser (43) is much darker and has uniform upperparts, as do the other coursers of the region, Burchell's (46) and Temminck's (48). In flight, the wings are mostly very dark but the wing-coverts form a paler patch; the uppertail-coverts and outer tail feathers are white. **Bare parts:** Bill black with yellowish base. Iris light brown. Legs pale brownish-yellow or dull yellowish; toes and part of the tarsi project past tail in flight.
VOICE Heard mainly at night; has in the past been mistaken for the voice of a nightjar *Caprimulgus*. Both alarm call and song are based on repetitions of evenly-pitched 'kui' or 'wicky' syllables at rates of two to five per second. In the song, which lasts about three seconds, the rate of delivery accelerates, the volume rises then falls, and the pitch decreases very slightly towards the end.
HABITS A bird of dry, fairly open grassy scrub or sparse woodland. Nests on the ground, often in the shade. Mainly nocturnal, spending the day resting under bushes and emerging at night to feed on insects; often seen on dirt roads at night. May freeze, relying on camouflage when initially disturbed. It will fly if pushed, running rapidly on landing to find a new hiding place. Occasionally seen in groups of up to six.
MOVEMENTS Probably mainly sedentary. Odd sightings away from main range in Tanzania, and recently South Africa (two, Kruger National Park, Oct 1983), indicate that longer movements do occur.
DESCRIPTION Breeding and non-breeding: Crown is dark chocolate-brown with an indistinct buffish central stripe on the forehead and front part of the crown. Long supercilia from forehead meet squarely on the nape, mostly white but buffish in front of the eye. The white on the nape is often obscured by long feathers from the rear crown. Obscure dark line across lores and upper edge of ear-coverts. Ear-coverts pale chestnut-buff, bounded below by a short dark brown moustachial line. Mantle, back, rump, scapulars, tertials and wing-coverts are centred dark brown and fringed bright buff, rather more narrowly reddish-buff on back and rump. Inner primaries and secondaries are brown fringed with buff; outer primaries are blackish. Uppertail-coverts white, forming a narrow band above the tail. Middle four pairs of tail feathers are brown, washed blackish subterminally and tipped white; there is more white on fifth pair, and outer feathers are mostly white, slightly smudged brown on inner web. Underparts are white, except for pale buffish wash on chin and throat and a complex breast pattern: narrow chestnut 'V' on throat, broad zone of heavy brown streaking across upper breast, bordered below and partly above by narrow brown bands, and narrow chestnut band across lower breast. Streaked zone is washed buffish-brown, particularly at sides. Underwing is mostly white with a black leading edge, two isolated black bars at the tips of the greater and median under primary coverts, and blackish undersides to the outer 2 primaries. **Juvenile:** Superficially as adult, but duller; initially the chestnut bands are dull buff-brown. The supercilium is buffish and less well defined. The upperpart feathers each have a broad, rounded brown centre, a thin dark submarginal line and a wide pale buff fringe. On the larger scapulars, tertials and inner secondaries, there are broad buff submarginal blotches and whitish-buff fringes. The tips of all the primaries initially have neatly-defined buff fringes. The tail feathers are sometimes faintly mottled with buff and dark brown.
AGE/SEX Juveniles can be easily distinguished at first, but soon lose the upperpart pattern by wear and gain the chestnut lines of the adult plumage; later may be separable only in the hand. Only juveniles show neat pale tips to the outer 3 primaries, although these may wear off rapidly. No differences are known between the sexes.
RACES Two are currently recognised: nominate *cinctus* (most of range) and *seebohmi* (southern fringe in Zimbabwe and Namibia). They are very similar, but in *seebohmi* the chestnut is a pinker colour and the throat line is buffy-pink rather than chestnut.

Within *cinctus*, southern populations have less clear upperpart patterning of dark feather centres and duller olive-buff fringes, and may lack the central crown-stripe. A third subspecies *'emini'* has been described from the area of Lake Victoria, but these birds are usually included in the nominate race.

MEASUREMENTS Length 250-275 mm (10½"). Wing 156-173 mm; bill 15-17 mm; tarsus 58-71 mm; tail 74-89 mm.

REFERENCES Dowsett *et al.* (1977).

43 VIOLET-TIPPED COURSER *Rhinoptilus chalcopterus*   Plate 17

Other name: Bronze-winged Courser

A rarely-seen courser of tropical and southern Africa which has extraordinary violet iridescence at the tips of the inner 9 primaries. It is not known whether this has a display function or is a strategy for reducing the rate of abrasion of the wing-tips.

IDENTIFICATION A rather large, heavy-headed courser with mainly darkish brown plumage and an unusual head pattern of short supercilia and crown-stripe and a whitish line behind the eye. The broad malar stripes, almost meeting across the whitish throat, and the greyish-brown breast-band bordered below by a black line are distinctive. Most likely to be first seen in flight, when it shows brown coverts contrasting with blackish flight feathers, separated by a narrow whitish wingbar across the tips of the greater coverts and the bases of a few outer secondaries. The tail is mainly blackish-brown, with a broad white tip (adults only) and white uppertail-coverts. Beware confusion with *Vanellus* species, particularly Black-winged Plover (66). Burchell's (46) and Temminck's Coursers (48) are much paler and have no dark breast-band or pattern on the throat. Heuglin's (42) and Two-banded Coursers (41) both have strongly-patterned upperparts. The diagnostic violet tips to the primaries are normally covered by the tertials, and thus not easily visible in the field. **Bare parts:** Bill black, with red on gape and at base of lower mandible. Eyes large, with iris dark brown and a narrow red eye-ring. Legs dull purplish-red; the toes and part of the tarsus project beyond the tail in flight.

VOICE Vocal mainly at night; beware confusion with stone-curlews, particularly Spotted Dikkop (34). A penetrating trisyllabic 'gee-kew-eee' with a rising inflexion, also a harsher 'grorr-raang'.

HABITS Found in open patches among fairly dense scrub and open woodland, often in recently-burnt areas or areas where bare earth has been exposed. Spends the day resting in the shade, and rarely encountered unless flushed. Normal posture when resting is apparently standing up, but if approached will lower gradually into a crouching position facing the observer, when it becomes very hard to spot. Individuals may roost in the same small area on successive days. Emerge at night to feed plover-like on insects, particularly grasshoppers. Seen most often in headlights along dirt roads at night, occasionally in groups of up to six.

MOVEMENTS An intra-African migrant; found in most parts of its range throughout the year, but in seasonally-variable numbers. Movements are not yet understood. Occurs in extreme south of its range only between Sept and May, apparently as a non-breeding visitor. In Kenya may be chiefly a non-breeding migrant from the south. In the north of the range it appears to be only a breeding visitor.

DESCRIPTION Breeding and non-breeding: Crown dark brown with creamy feather edgings; forehead creamy, and short creamy crown-stripe from forehead to mid-crown. Creamy-white supercilia from forehead to just behind eye, becoming dark rufous-brown on the sides of the nape. Whitish mark from eye to rear of ear-coverts. Lores, cheeks and ear-coverts blackish-brown flecked pale chestnut. Chin and throat white with variable blackish or brownish malar stripes, square-ended against lower throat, sometimes very broad and almost meeting in centre of throat. On some individuals, blackish flecking on the front of the neck joins the dark malar areas to the breast-band. Breast-band is broad, an even greyish-brown with a narrow blackish lower border; in centre of breast, above the black border, there is a large but variably-sized buffish-white area. Rest of underparts, including axillaries, pale buffish- or creamy-white. Underwing-coverts mostly creamy-white, but with white greater coverts which border white on the bases of the secondaries and inner primaries. Under primary coverts mainly creamy-white, but with black on leading edge and at tips to lesser, median and greater coverts forming separate black bars. Hind-neck, mantle, back, rump, scapulars, tertials and coverts all even brown, sometimes with narrow pale rufous fringes. Greater coverts and outer tertials are edged and tipped off-white. Carpal coverts mostly off-white. Alula, primary coverts, primaries and secondaries are black, with a small amount of white visible at the bases of the outer secondaries. Primaries 1-9 have a broad violet sheen covering the exposed part of each feather tip; the violet is bordered proximally by iridescent narrow green and then blue bands meeting the black of the rest of the feather. The outer primary, slightly shorter than primary 9, is browner and paler, particularly towards the tip, and lacks iridescence. The uppertail-coverts are white, forming a narrow band between the brown rump and slightly darker brown base to the tail. The tail becomes blacker subterminally, contrasting strongly with a conspicuous white fringe, broadest on the outer feathers. **Juvenile:** Resembles adult in pattern, but breast-band is finely mottled and fringed with buff and the upperpart feathers show brownish-buff fringes and fine, dark subterminal lines. Primaries are narrower and more pointed and show some green iridescence, bordered proximally by blue, but very little violet. Tail feathers lack broad white tips of adult, and may show a brownish-buff fringe and a dark subterminal line.

AGE/SEX Juveniles progress rapidly through a complete moult, but may be identified in the hand if they retain any juvenile outer primaries. These are much

247

narrower and more pointed than the adult-type primaries and are almost lacking in iridescence at the tip. No consistent differences are known between the sexes.

RACES Probably best regarded as monotypic, although a southern race 'albofasciatus' (Angola and Tanzania to Cape Province) has been described.

MEASUREMENTS Length 250-290 mm (10¾"). Wing 167-191 mm; bill 16-19 mm; tarsus 67-78 mm; tail 73-88 mm.

REFERENCES Wilson (1977), Verschuren (1977).

44 JERDON'S COURSER *Rhinoptilus bitorquatus*   Plate 18

Other name: Double-banded Courser

Prior to 1986, the last authentic record of this Indian species was in the Penner valley in 1900. In mid-January 1986, it was rediscovered in the same area owing to the efforts of Bharat Bhushan of the Bombay Natural History Society. It is the only *Rhinoptilus* outside central and southern Africa.

IDENTIFICATION Verging on extinction. If seen, would be easily identified by the lucky observer. It is the only courser with white on the wing-tips: there is a brilliant white flash subterminally on the outer primaries, and a narrow but clear white bar across the bases of the secondaries and tips of the greater coverts. On the ground, shows broad creamy-white supercilia and uniform pale grey-brown upperparts. The chestnut throat-patch, and breast pattern of two dusky brown lines separated by a white one are diagnostic. Only the Indian Courser (47) is sympatric. **Bare parts:** Bill black, with pale yellowish-flesh basal half. Iris brown. Legs pale pinkish-cream; toes and part of tarsus project beyond tail-tip in flight.

VOICE Described only as a 'plaintive cry'. Apparently not very vocal.

HABITS Recorded only in the Penner and Godavari valleys in E Andhra Pradesh, from Anantapur to Nellore in the Penner valley and at Bhadrachalam on the Godavari River. The habitat was rocky, hilly country with light forest or patches of scrubby jungle, unlike the flatter and more open habitat of Indian Courser. Found in pairs or small parties. Flight was described as faster than that of Indian Courser. It now appears that this is a mainly nocturnal species like its three African congeners.

MOVEMENTS Thought to be entirely sedentary. The rather rounded wing suggests it is not a migratory species.

DESCRIPTION Breeding and non-breeding plumages probably similar; juvenile plumage never described. **Adult:** Narrow, irregular creamy crown-stripe; crown and nape otherwise dark chocolate-brown, flecked creamy on forehead. Long supercilia from bill past ear-coverts, creamy from bill to behind eye but the rear third white. Sides of face and ear-coverts warm brown flecked dark brown. Chin and upper throat creamy-white; lower throat has a broad chestnut band and an irregularly dark-flecked area separated by a whitish band. Lower neck is warm grey-brown; upper breast has two dusky brown lines separated by a narrow white line; lower breast is washed pale grey-brown. Belly, flanks, axillaries and undertail are white. Underwing shows black undersides to flight feathers except for white band across outer primaries, and creamy coverts except for lesser coverts which are black and under primary coverts which are blotched whitish-buff and black. Hindneck warm grey-brown; mantle, back, rump, scapulars and tertials paler grey-brown. Leading lesser coverts dark brown and greater coverts tipped white; coverts otherwise grey-brown, faintly fringed buffish. Primary coverts and primaries black with broad white flash subterminally across outer 3-4 primaries; secondaries black with white bases. Wing is rather rounded with wing-point at primaries 8 and 9, 10th -2 mm and 7th -4 mm. Tail is mostly dark brown, with white at the base, on the uppertail-coverts and on extreme tail-tip.

AGE/SEX No differences are known between the sexes. The juvenile plumage is unknown.

RACES No variation within its limited range.

MEASUREMENTS Length about 270 mm (10½"). Two specimens examined, both males. Wing 164-171 mm; bill 17-19 mm; tarsus 65-68 mm; tail 54-65 mm.

45 CREAM-COLOURED COURSER *Cursorius cursor*   Plate 18

A superbly-camouflaged desert species but with a striking wing pattern in flight; the widest-ranging and most migratory courser. We diverge from standard nomenclature by including the E African races, normally treated as this species, with Burchell's Courser (46) of southern Africa. Superficially, at least, they have far more in common with that species. Some authorities recognise only one species. Detailed behavioural studies are needed to clarify the situation.

IDENTIFICATION The pale sandy-cream upperparts, paler cream underparts (lacking a darker belly-patch), brilliant black and white 'V's on the nape, and the grey rear crown provide easy separation from all species except Burchell's Courser. In flight, wings are very long and pointed for a courser, and the lazy, flicking wingbeats recall a large pratincole. The wing pattern of black outer wing and dusky secondaries contrasting with the creamy forewing and upperparts, and very striking jet-black axillaries and underwing with a narrow white trailing edge to the secondaries, is highly distinctive. Burchell's Coursers in E Africa are considerably smaller and shorter-winged, sandy-brown rather than creamy in colour, and show a fairly clear division between the pale sandy-brown chin to upper belly and the whitish lower belly, vent and undertail. In Burchell's, axillaries and underwing-coverts are brownish-grey not black, and there is a broader but less well-defined white trailing edge. Juvenile Cream-coloured is sandy-cream with irregular wavy darkish lines over its upperparts, including central tail feathers, unlike juvenile Burchell's Courser which is darker sandy-brown, extensively blotched dark brown above and with barred central tail feathers. Temminck's Courser (48) is obviously smaller and darker, and has a black belly-patch, rufous lower breast and rufous (not grey) rear crown. Indian Courser (47), which may occur alongside in NW India, is similar size to Cream-coloured but is patterned like Temminck's and has diagnostic black lores.

Bare parts: Bill longish and decurved, almost black but with paler dark horn base, more extensively yellowish-brown at base in juveniles. Iris brown. Legs creamy or ivory-white; toes project beyond tail in flight.

VOICE Many calls are based on a short whistled 'quit', sometimes repeated. Also a harsh 'praak-praak'. In display 'quit-quit-whow'.

HABITS Nests Feb-July in N Africa, May-July in S USSR, laying typically two eggs in a shallow scrape. Typically a bird of open, arid, sparsely-vegetated plains, including the fringes of cultivation. Poorly-developed circular or gliding flights occur in display. Except on Socotra, only rarely found breeding south of the Sahara. Vagrants usually appear on farmland or among coastal dunes. Runs vigorously while feeding; often digs for concealed food using bill. If approached, often prefers to run but may take flight with leisurely but powerful wingbeats. Generally found in pairs or small groups, although at times is fairly gregarious.

MOVEMENTS A partial migrant; northern and particularly northeastern populations are most migratory, while island birds are sedentary. Eastern birds move to NW India, where present Aug-Apr, and probably also Arabia. Some N African birds apparently winter on the S Saharan fringe Aug-Mar. Limits of southward movements appear to be Gambia, Mali (Niger inundation zone), Chad and Somalia. After breeding, gathers into mobile groups which occasionally appear in Mediterranean countries or farther north into Europe. Has occurred north to Ireland, Scotland, Norway, Finland and European USSR. Most N European records are in Sept-Oct, including a flock of ten in the Netherlands in Sept 1969.

DESCRIPTION Breeding and non-breeding: Crown, forehead and lores sandy-cream; rear crown grey, tapering to a black triangle. Clear white supercilia and black eye-stripes start at eye and both meet in a double 'V' below the black lower nape. Upperparts even sandy-cream; primaries, primary coverts and alula black; secondaries are black on inner webs, sandy on outer webs, and have a narrow white trailing edge which contrasts strongly below, less so above. Tail feathers sandy-cream, all except central pair with variable blackish subterminal band and narrow white tip. Chin, belly and undertail very pale creamy, rest of underparts slightly darker. Underwing-coverts and axillaries black, except for narrow sandy leading edge of lesser coverts. **Juvenile:** Like adult, but supercilium is creamy, and grey and black on crown are absent; there is only a faint brownish eye-stripe. Head and breast show obscure brownish spotting. Sandy upperparts and central tail feathers have fine, irregular and often-obscured dark subterminal lines. All primaries are clearly fringed with buff.

AGE/SEX Juvenile plumage, including primaries, is lost rapidly. Birds in late stages of post-juvenile moult show clear buff fringes on unmoulted primaries and perhaps a few spots or bars on head or upperparts. Sexes similar; males average slightly larger.

RACES Four are described, but with plumage variations which almost certainly reflect local variations in substrate colour: *exsul* (Cape Verde Is.), *bannermani* (Canary Is.), nominate *cursor* (Morocco to SW Iran, Socotra) and *bogolubovi* (N Iran to S central USSR). The race *bogolubovi* tends to be more pinkish than *cursor*, and *exsul* and *bannermani* more sandy. The island races are similar in size, and smaller than the other two. The race *bannermani* is often lumped with *cursor; exsul* has declined and may face extinction.

MEASUREMENTS Length 210-240 mm (9"). Widespread races: wing 153-172 mm; bill 20-25 mm; tarsus 51-63 mm; tail 56-64 mm. Island races: wing 145-166 mm; bill 19-23 mm; tarsus 49-57 mm; tail 51-59 mm.

46 BURCHELL'S COURSER *Cursorius rufus*   **Plate 18**

Previously, this name has been applied only to those populations in southern Africa. Here, however, we also include the coursers in Somalia and Kenya which have conventionally been considered as races of Cream-coloured Courser (45); at least superficially, they have much more in common with Burchell's Courser. Some authorities recognise only a single species. A detailed field study is clearly required.

IDENTIFICATION The curving white supercilia bordered below by black eye-stripes, meeting in a double 'V' on the nape, and the grey rear crown show this to be a close relative of the larger Cream-coloured Courser. On the ground, it is distinguished by its brown rather than cream infusion above and below and by the clear separation of its brownish breast and fore-belly from its whitish rear belly. In flight, the pale sandy-grey or grey-brown underwing-coverts and axillaries and the largely white secondaries contrast strongly from below with the black outer wing; on Cream-coloured Courser the underwing and axillaries are, dramatically, all-black, with just a narrow white trailing edge to the secondaries. The juveniles are strongly blotched dark brown and pale, and have barred central tail feathers, compared with very lightly-marked feathers on Cream-coloured. Overlaps widely with Temminck's Courser (48), which is even smaller, more rufous (even than the nominate *rufus*) especially on the crown and breast, lacks the grey rear crown and has a large chestnut-and-black area on the lower breast and belly compared with the narrow dark line right across the belly in nominate *rufus*. On Temminck's, the white trailing edge to the secondaries is also narrow. **Bare parts:** Bill longish, decurved, mainly blackish with dull horn at base. Iris brown. Legs creamy or ivory-white; feet project past tail in flight.

VOICE Like Cream-coloured Courser: a repeated lowish grunt, 'whick', and a triple 'whit-whit-which'.

Juvenile plumages and underwing characteristics of Cream-coloured (45) and Burchell's Coursers (46)

Burchell's Courser
(S Africa)

Burchell's Courser
(E Africa)

Cream-coloured
Courser

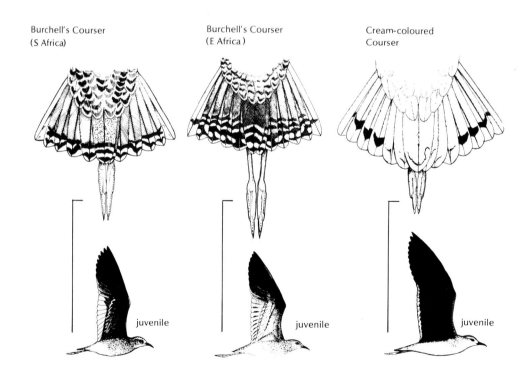

Burchell's Courser
(S Africa)

Burchell's Courser
(E Africa)

Cream-coloured
Courser

juvenile

juvenile

juvenile

Often calls in flight.

HABITS Although occurs in semi-arid areas, especially in E Africa, found mainly in dry savanna or better grassland than Cream-coloured Courser. Otherwise not known to differ markedly in general habits. Nominate *rufus* differs from sympatric Two-banded Courser (41) in more open habitat, including saltpans, more gregarious behaviour, and wider diet. The longer bill is used for digging, and seeds are eaten as well as insects. Two eggs are laid; in S Africa breeding is more seasonal than is Two-banded's, chiefly Aug-Nov.

MOVEMENTS Fairly sedentary, but with seasonal appearances and disappearances in some parts of its range. Probably moves only locally.

DESCRIPTION Like Cream-coloured. See Identification and Races for discussion of major differences. **Breeding and non-breeding:** Upperparts washed brown, northern birds very sandy-brown. Primaries and primary coverts black. Secondaries greyish to sandy-grey with substantial white tips and fringes. Tail greyish or greyish-sandy, with subterminal dark bar and white tips to the outer feathers, outer pair edged white. Chin whitish; breast and upper belly washed a variable shade of grey or sandy-brown; rear belly contrastingly white. Outer half of underwing black, underwing-coverts and axillaries grey-brown to pale sandy-brown; secondaries mainly white. **Juvenile:** Upperparts, including crown, have a strongly barred-and-notched pattern of dark brown and palish buff; upperwing-coverts have mid-brown centres and broad buff fringes. Tail clearly barred buff and brown, at least at tip. Breast buff-brown extensively blotched mid-brown. Primaries fringed buff.

AGE/SEX As for Cream-coloured.

RACES Three: nominate *rufus* (S and SW Africa), *littoralis* (Kenya, S Somalia), and *somalensis* (N Somalia). In E Africa both adults and juveniles are paler and lack the dark line on the belly; *rufus* has chestnut forecrown, dark earthy-brown upperparts, grey central tail feathers, grey-brown breast, blackish belly line, grey-brown underwing-coverts and axillaries, whitish flecks on uppertail-coverts and very white secondaries. The race *littoralis* is generally dull grey-brown above, paler below; centre tail brown-grey, underwing-coverts pale brown-grey. The race *somalensis* is paler still, brownish-sandy above and below; under primary coverts dark grey-brown, rest of underwing-coverts and axillaries pale sandy- or creamy-brown. All are similar in size, although *rufus* has noticeably shorter legs (averages 47.1 mm, against 54.7 mm for E African individuals) and bill (20.8 mm, against 23.3 mm).

MEASUREMENTS Length 200-225 mm (8¼"). Wing 123-145 mm; bill 19-24 mm; tarsus 43-58 mm; tail 45-53 mm.

REFERENCES Maclean (1967).

47 INDIAN COURSER *Cursorius coromandelicus*   Plate 18

A beautifully-marked courser which is widespread but patchily distributed in the Indian subcontinent. Not uncommon in suitable habitat.

IDENTIFICATION Resembles Cream-coloured Courser (45) in size and structure, although slightly smaller and with proportionately broader wings. In plumage, however, it is more like the much smaller African Temminck's Courser (48). Diagnostic features are black lores, long brilliant white supercilia starting well in front of eye, and white uppertail-coverts. Also differs from Cream-coloured in grey-brown (not black) underwing and entirely deep-chestnut crown (lacking grey). Its general coloration is also much darker and warmer than in that species, with cinnamon-chestnut throat and breast, even grey-brown upperparts, and a dark grey-brown mid-belly line which develops centrally into a blackish patch. Juveniles differ from those of Cream-coloured in having upperparts strongly blotched dark brown and creamy-buff and in white uppertail-coverts. The third courser in India is Jerdon's (44), now probably extinct but still to be looked for; this shows large white areas in the wing, and a strongly-patterned breast. Beware confusion with pratincoles in flight. **Bare parts:** Bill black, clearly decurved. Iris brown. Legs long, ivory-white; toes project past tail in flight.

VOICE A low 'gwut' or 'wut' is the contact and alarm call.

HABITS Generally very similar to Cream-coloured, with which it may occur in Pakistan and NW India, but prefers less arid habitat. Avoids the scrubby, hilly country once inhabited by Jerdon's Courser. Nesting occurs mainly Mar-Aug. Flies powerfully on flick-ing beats of long wings, like Cream-coloured.

MOVEMENTS Mainly resident, but performs poorly-understood nomadic movements or local migrations. No records outside the Indian subcontinent.

DESCRIPTION Breeding and non-breeding: Crown deep rich chestnut with black wedge at rear. Long white supercilia from in front of eye meet on nape. Lores broadly black, continuing in broad eye-stripes which meet on nape. Lower hindneck rich cinnamon. Mantle, back, rump, scapulars, tertials and upperwing-coverts are an even grey-brown. Primaries, primary coverts and alula are black. Outer secondaries black narrowly tipped white, becoming increasingly grey-brown with larger white tips towards innermost. Uppertail-coverts white. Outer tail feathers white, central pair as upperparts, rest with greyish base, blackish subterminal bar and broad white tip. Sides of face and chin are whitish; throat pale cinnamon, becoming darker and richer on breast and shading to deep chestnut on upper belly. Mid-belly darkish brown-grey with black central patch. Rear belly and undertail-coverts contrastingly white. On underwing, primaries are black, contrasting with brownish-grey secondaries, underwing-coverts and axillaries and with the white trailing edge. **Juvenile:** As adult, but crown dark brown, flecked cream. The supercilium is cream in front of eye, then whitish to nape, and is bordered below by irregular dark brown blotches. The lores are pale. The upperparts are strongly but irregularly barred and blotched mid-brown and cream; the upperwing-coverts are pale grey-brown with slightly darker submarginal bands and fringed pale buff. Primaries are all neatly but narrowly fringed buff. Underparts pale chestnut-brown, blotched brown; belly is initially white, but dark central patch appears before upperparts are completely moulted.

AGE/SEX Juveniles are very distinct, but once upperparts are moulted in Sept-Oct they become difficult or impossible to separate. Sexes similar; females may average fractionally larger.

RACES Monotypic. Sri Lankan individuals are slightly smaller; there may perhaps be a cline of increasing size northwards.

MEASUREMENTS Length about 230 mm (9"). Wing 144-163 mm; bill 18-22 mm; tarsus 49-59 mm; tail 51-57 mm.

REFERENCES Phillips (1942).

48 TEMMINCK'S COURSER *Cursorius temminckii*   Plate 17

The smallest courser, widespread on short grasslands over much of sub-Saharan Africa.

IDENTIFICATION Plain upperparts and small size distinguish this species readily from all except Burchell's Courser (46), but only in S Africa does Burchell's have dark on the belly. Temminck's is more rufous below than Burchell's, has a chestnut not grey rear crown, and always a large central blackish belly-patch contrasting with white on the flanks. In flight, Temminck's has only a small amount of white on the secondary tips, rarely visible from above, while Burchell's has a broad white trailing edge. In E Africa, Burchell's is also much paler above and below than Temminck's. Plumage of Temminck's is strikingly similar to that of Indian Courser (47), which however is much larger, has black lores, longer white supercilia, mainly-grey flanks and in flight shows a clear white trailing edge to the secondaries and a white patch above the tail. In Temminck's, lores are pale brownish and both white supercilium and black eye-stripe start at the eye. **Bare parts:** Bill quite long-looking, very dark brown, base of lower mandible often paler horn. Iris warm brown. Legs whitish, often tinged greyish or creamy, relatively long; toes project beyond tail in flight.

VOICE Relatively quiet, but contact note is a high, sharp, twittering 'perr-perr' or 'err-err'.

HABITS Frequents short grassland and open bush-country, particularly burnt areas, more rarely thicker bush or even glades among taller trees; seen on airfields. Breeds in every month, but season varies locally. In Zambia, nests only in the dry season. Two eggs are laid, normally on bare ground. Like others of the genus *Cursorius*, runs very fast and bobs head when agitated. Often stands very upright, displaying the black-and-white pattern of the underside. Wingbeats are rather jerky and flickering, faster than in larger coursers. When not breeding, gathers into small flocks.

MOVEMENTS Mainly resident, but variable in numbers or seasonal in occurrence at some localities, suggesting some regular migrations as well as local searching for attractive sites. Southern tip of range is occupied only Feb-Aug.

DESCRIPTION Breeding and non-breeding: Forehead and chin are pale cinnamon; crown is chestnut mottled brownish bordering forehead, while rest of crown is rich dark chestnut except for a black wedge at the rear. White supercilium starts at the eye, bordered below by a curving black eye-stripe; both eye-stripes and supercilia meet in 'V's on the nape. Hindneck is brownish. Wing-coverts, scapulars, mantle, back, rump, uppertail and tertials are grey-brown, sometimes quite warm in tone. Primaries, primary

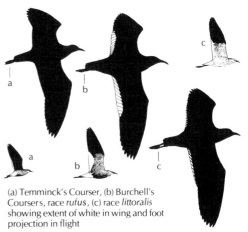

(a) Temminck's Courser, (b) Burchell's Coursers, race *rufus*, (c) race *littoralis* showing extent of white in wing and foot projection in flight

coverts and outer secondaries are an even, slightly bluish black; rest of secondaries are increasingly grey towards body, with small white tips to inner webs. Central pair of tail feathers is plain grey-brown, outer pair is white; rest have grey-brown base, blackish subterminal spot and white fringe. Throat is a brownish-chestnut, becoming brighter on the breast and deep chestnut on the upper belly; rear flanks and lower belly are white but with a black central patch. Underwings dark; grey-brown axillaries and coverts contrast little with black flight feathers. **Juvenile:** As adult, but crown is dark brown flecked buffish-chestnut, supercilia are buffish-cream, and eye-stripes dark brown. Upperpart feathers are irregularly barred and notched dark brown and brownish-buff, and tipped whitish. Wing-coverts are broadly fringed pale buff; all primaries and outer secondaries are neatly fringed deep buff. Most tail feathers are mottled buff and dusky towards tip. Underparts paler than adult's, with breast variably spotted dark brown; lacks bright cinnamon on belly. There is a poorly-defined blackish-brown belly-patch.

AGE/SEX Juvenile is initially very distinct, but once mottled upperparts are lost can be separated only in the hand by buff-fringed or very worn primaries. Sexes are similar in plumage and in size.

RACES Two are described: nominate *temminckii* (most of range) and *damarensis* (Namibia). The latter is paler, but is not a well-defined race.

MEASUREMENTS Length 190-210 mm (8"). Wing 117-131 mm; bill 16-19 mm; tarsus 39-44 mm; tail 41-44 mm.

49 AUSTRALIAN PRATINCOLE *Stiltia isabella*

Plate 21

Other name: Australian Courser

A pratincole in appearance and behaviour, but structurally rather different from the other species, showing some features in common with coursers. Although based in Australia, it is a regular visitor to the Oriental region.

IDENTIFICATION Differs from Oriental Pratincole (51), which might occur anywhere in same range, in smaller size, longer legs and short, slightly-rounded tail, as well as in colour and patterning. All other pratincoles have forked tails; this, however, is the only one whose feet project beyond the tail in flight and, if poorly seen, these might be mistaken for tail-streamers. At rest, the posture is usually more upright than Oriental Pratincole and the legs are obviously much longer. The tail reaches to just beyond the pale brown tertials on the folded wing, well short of the wing-tip. Flight is less graceful than Oriental Pratincole's, with rather stiff wingbeats more like one of the smaller terns *Sterna* than an outsize swallow *Hirundo*. Note the black underwing-coverts, dark chestnut 'waistcoat' and especially the strong contrast between the inner wing and the black outer primaries. **Bare parts:** Bill orange-red at base, with a sharply-defined blackish-brown tip; in young birds, mainly blackish with some yellowish along the cutting edges. Iris brown. Long dark grey legs, sometimes brownish or even dark red.

VOICE Usual call is a highly distinctive shrill sweet 'hoo-wee-too', like a human whistle, with slight accent on the higher-pitched middle syllable, or 'hoo-wee'. Far-carrying, and often heard from flying birds long before they can be seen.

HABITS Feeds more on the ground than does Oriental Pratincole, running then stopping and dipping forward like a plover, or darting after flying prey. Bobs head and tail. Also hawks insects high in the air. Flies quite frequently on moonlit nights, and call may be heard on nocturnal migration. Usual habitat black-soil plains and other open grassy areas, often seen on airfields; breeds chiefly in semi-desert habitats well inland. Breeding biology is unique among waders: the eggs are laid on open ground and the chicks, as soon as they can leave the 'nest', adopt a particular burrow, usually a rabbit burrow, and use it as an underground refuge whenever danger threatens; the adults, however, feed them outside (there are no records of adults entering burrows). The breeding season is very long overall, May-Dec, but the timing varies locally depending on weather conditions. When not nesting, often forms loose flocks of up to a few hundred birds. At times very tame and approachable.

MOVEMENTS There are regular north-south movements, bringing birds to the south of their range only in the southern summer, but the northern parts of the breeding range are occupied all year. Migrates regularly as far as Java, Borneo, N Sulawesi and S New Guinea. May occasionally cross into the northern hemisphere. Breeding is documented only for Australia.

DESCRIPTION Breeding: Bright sandy-rufous head, breast and upperparts in fresh plumage, quickly becoming paler and browner through wear. Outer primaries, underwing and axillaries black, with pale silvery trailing edge to the secondaries and inner primaries showing from below. Outer primary remarkably long and attenuated. Tail white, with broad black subterminal bar not reaching outer feathers; extreme tip brownish, with white spots visible on spread tail. Broad chestnut band across lower breast and belly. Vent and undertail white. **Non-breeding:** Upperparts usually browner, sometimes a mixture of worn brown and fresh sandy-rufous feathers. Breast-band concentrated into two patches at the sides, meeting narrowly in the middle like a waistcoat. Some individuals may perhaps become streaky on the neck and breast. **Juvenile:** As adult, but upperpart feathers brown fringed sandy-buff, with a suggestion of a brown shaft-streak and often a thin subterminal line. The inner 8 primaries are tipped buff. Tail-tip buff, often with thin brown lines on the last 1-2 mm. Bill mainly blackish, lacking orange-red. Outer primary not attenuated. **First non-breeding:** Darker above than juvenile, with bright fringes worn away to leave brown feather centres, and duller feathers of similar pattern moulted in. General impression delicately scaly. Neck and upper breast streaked brown, with sometimes a concentration of streaks around the unstreaked pale throat, recalling *Glareola* species.

AGE/SEX Sexing is not known to be possible, but lores vary in shade and this character may be of value. Before the post-juvenile wing moult, young birds can be distinguished by pale tips to the primaries, visible beyond the tertials on the folded wing, and by the lack of an attenuated outer primary; unlike in adults, the outer primary projects less beyond the second outer than the second outer beyond the third outer. It is not clear how useful bill colour and neck streaking are as characters for ageing.

RACES No geographical variation is known.

MEASUREMENTS Length 220-240 mm (9"). Wing 178-221 mm (adults), 170-181 mm (juveniles); bill 15-17 mm; tarsus 41-49 mm. Difference between outer and second outer primary 18-33 mm (adults), 3-10 mm (juveniles).

REFERENCES Maclean (1973, 1976a), Hopkins (1976).

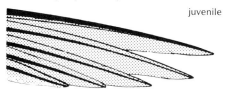

juvenile

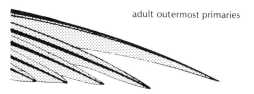

adult outermost primaries

50 COMMON PRATINCOLE *Glareola pratincola*

Plate 19

Other names: Pratincole, Collared Pratincole

The most widely distributed pratincole. The name 'Collared' is unhelpful, since the feature referred to is not a collar and is present also in its close relatives.

IDENTIFICATION This is one of the larger pratincoles. In flight, it shows reddish-chestnut or chestnut-and-brown underwing-coverts and axillaries, a narrow white trailing edge to the wing (sometimes difficult to see), white on uppertail and a deeply-forked black-tipped tail. Oriental and Black-winged Pratincoles (51,52) are closely similar to Common in appearance and habits, but note that in flight Oriental differs in lack of white trailing edge and much shallower tail fork, while Black-winged differs in all-black underwing and axillaries and in lack of white trailing edge. White-tipped secondaries are diagnostic of Common, but beware juveniles of Oriental and Black-winged which have very narrow buffish-white secondary tips (rarely visible in field conditions). In Africa particularly, Common may almost lose its white tips through excessive wear. The three species are difficult to distinguish on the ground, but Common is palest above and on breast, has most red on bill, and in adults has tail-streamers normally roughly equal to or a little longer than the folded wings. Slightly shorter-legged than Black-winged Pratincole. Other pratincoles are much smaller, except Madagascar Pratincole (53) which also has a chestnut underwing but is much darker above and below and lacks creamy bib, white on secondaries and tail-streamers.

Bare parts: Bill short and decurved, black, with red at base extending across side of bill as far as the nostrils and usually meeting narrowly underneath the bill-base; in juveniles, the coloured area is paler and less extensive. Iris brown. Legs brownish-black; claw of middle toe long (10-12 mm) and rather irregular in shape.

VOICE A variety of high, harsh tern-like calls based on 'kik' and 'kirrik', sometimes a rolling trill 'kikki-kirrik-irrik'. Calls are higher-pitched and less emphatic than those of Black-winged. Noisy at colonies.

HABITS Nests in large colonies on flat areas with short or patchy vegetation, often around margins of fresh or alkaline wetlands or on dried mud, sometimes in ploughed fields. Season is mainly May-Aug in migratory Palaearctic race, Mar-May in Pakistan, and Apr-Sept (locally variable) in E Africa. Similar habitats are used all year, but on migration may appear on coasts, at reservoirs or at desert oases. Feeds chiefly on swarming insects in graceful, rapid, swallow-like flight, particularly at dawn and dusk; also often feeds from ground by running or lunging forward after flying or grounded insects. Highly gregarious throughout the year; flocks of several thousand may gather to feed or perform aerial evolutions. Associates freely with Oriental and Black-winged in zones of overlap. Interbreeding with vagrant Black-winged has been recorded in France.

MOVEMENTS Palaearctic breeders are strongly migratory; after moult at intermediate sites in July-Sept, all move to sub-Saharan Africa, returning Mar-early May. Few if any penetrate beyond 5° N. Vagrant most European countries north to Norway and west to Ireland, also Madeira, Canaries and Cape Verde Is. At least some of the small Pakistan population moves into W India for the winter and mingles with Oriental Pratincole; vagrant S Sri Lanka. African races are mainly resident or locally dispersive; in E Africa there are few localities where the species is found all year. Vagrant S Cape Province.

DESCRIPTION Breeding: Lores blackish or brownish; narrow buffy-white eye-ring from which a sharp black line encircles creamy chin, cheeks and throat. Crown, neck, upper breast, flanks, mantle, back, upper rump, scapulars, tertials and upperwing-coverts are an even grey-brown. Primaries and secondaries contrasting brownish-black, the latter with clear but narrow white tips. Lower rump, uppertail-coverts and most of outer webs of outer tail feathers white; rest of tail black or blackish. Lower breast washed creamy-buff; belly and undertail-coverts white. Underwing-coverts and axillaries reddish-chestnut, sometimes admixed with brownish feathers. **Non-breeding:** Lores are paler, black throat-band is replaced by a string of dark vertical streaks which partly extend into the creamy throat, and the breast becomes a mottled grey-brown. This plumage is kept for only a short period during wing moult. **Juvenile:** As non-breeding, but crown and nape slightly streaked darker; feathers of upperparts, including secondaries, are greyer and have a clear blackish subterminal bar and a broad buffish-white fringe. Throat outline is even less distinct; neck and breast whiter, with clear brown streaks and blotches. Tail fork is shallower.

AGE/SEX Juvenile distinct, but almost immediately moults into an adult-type plumage when can be identified only in the hand if some juvenile secondaries have been retained. Sexes alike, but breeding male has black lores, female brownish. Males average about 3% larger in wing length than females; tail-streamers of male average about 5% longer.

RACES Three: nominate *pratincola* (Palaearctic, Pakistan), *erlangeri* (S Somalia and N Kenya) and *fuelleborni* (rest of African range). African races are slightly smaller (*erlangeri* smallest), darker brown above and on breast, and have less chestnut on underwing-coverts, sometimes admixed with brown.

MEASUREMENTS Length 235-265 mm (9¾"). Wing 171-203 mm; bill (exposed culmen) 12-15 mm; tarsus 28-33 mm; tail 100-118 mm (adults); tail difference, longest to shortest, 48-69 mm (adults), 29-35 mm (juveniles).

REFERENCES Sterbetz (1974).

middle claw

Common Pratincole   Black-winged Pratincole   Oriental Pratincole

51 ORIENTAL PRATINCOLE *Glareola maldivarum*

Plate 21
(see also Plate 19)

Other names: Large Indian, Eastern or Eastern Collared Pratincole

The Oriental equivalent of the W Palaearctic and African Common Pratincole (50), but also shows plumage and structural similarities to the Black-winged Pratincole (52). Previously treated as a race of Common Pratincole.

IDENTIFICATION Very similar to Common and Black-winged Pratincoles in all aspects, but with the unique combination of wholly-dark secondaries (except in the juvenile) and chestnut underwing-coverts. Adult has entirely-dark upperwing surfaces, like Black-winged; juvenile has a very narrow buffish-white trailing edge to the secondaries, narrower than that of juvenile Common. Tail-streamers are much shorter than on either species; the closed wings extend well beyond the tail. In all plumages, tends to have more extensive orangey-buff on the lower breast than Common Pratincole. Occurs with Common Pratincole and Little Pratincole (56) in India, and with Australian Pratincole (49) from Java and Sulawesi south to Australia. Differs from Australian in larger size, darker colours, shorter legs, forked tail and more graceful, swallow-like flight. **Bare parts:** Bill black with some red on the gape in post-juvenile birds, but red is less extensive than on Common Pratincole. Iris dark brown. Legs brownish-black.

VOICE Apparently not unlike Common. Sharp 'kyik', 'chik-chik' or 'chet' calls, particularly in flight, also a loud 'cherr' and a rising 'trooeet'.

HABITS Not known to differ from Common Pratincole. In Australasia, sometimes associates with Oriental Plover (110) or, more rarely, Australian Pratincole.

MOVEMENTS Indian populations are mainly resident, but are breeding visitors to some areas and apparently nomadic in others. Those breeding in E Asia are mostly migratory, spending the northern winter in Indonesia and N Australia; small numbers are recorded in S New Guinea. Irregular in occurrence in southern parts of Australia. Vagrants have reached South Island and Stewart Island in New Zealand, Christmas I., Cocos Is., Mauritius, and the Seychelles. There is a single W Palaearctic record (still pending acceptance), from SE England in June-Oct 1981.

DESCRIPTION Plumages and plumage sequence as Common Pratincole. **Adult:** Flight feathers dark, with no trace of white on the secondaries. Red on the bill becomes brighter when breeding. **Juvenile:** Very narrow buffy-white tips to the secondaries, less than 3 mm broad.

AGE/SEX Narrow pale tips to the secondaries are indicative of juvenile or first-winter individual. The extent of first-winter wing moult is very variable, but usually a few juvenile secondaries are retained throughout the first 12 months. Sexing might be possible by the colour of the lores in breeding plumage (see Common Pratincole). Males have a slightly deeper tail fork on average, but sexual dimorphism in size is very slight.

RACES No geographical variation is known.

MEASUREMENTS Length 230-240 mm (9¼"). Wing 170-200 mm; bill (exposed culmen) 12-15 mm; tarsus 30-37 mm; tail 71-85 mm (adults); tail fork 22-33 mm (adult males), 17-30 mm (adult females), 8-25 mm (juveniles).

52 BLACK-WINGED PRATINCOLE *Glareola nordmanni*

Plate 19

A close relative of the previous two species, originally thought by many to be just a colour-phase of Common Pratincole (50) but the distinctions are now much better understood. A powerful migrant.

IDENTIFICATION Generally very similar to Common and Oriental (51) but slightly larger, darker in plumage, darker-billed, longer-legged and with diagnostic black (not chestnut) underwing and axillaries. Lacks Common's white trailing edge to the wing, and shows less contrast between wing-coverts and flight feathers; looks broader-winged than Common. Tail length is intermediate between the other two species. On breeding Black-winged, lores are blacker and black may extend slightly forward over bill-base and backwards over eye. Experienced observers can distinguish Black-winged by voice. Note that Common and Oriental also show strong contrast between dark underwing and whitish belly, and may seem to have black underwing if seen poorly or in bad light. Beware confusion with Cream-coloured Courser (45) if seen from below. **Bare parts:** Bill black, with a small area of red on sides at gape, not reaching nostril. Iris brown. Legs brownish-black, slightly longer than on related species; claw of middle toe curved and fairly short (6-7 mm).

VOICE Lower-pitched and more strident than Common Pratincole's, distinguishable with practice. When breeding, a low 'chrr-chrr', 'ketteck' and a distinctive falcon-like 'pwik-kik-kik'. At other times also 'kritt', 'krip' and 'kikiip'.

HABITS Very similar to Common. Nests in large colonies on open steppes May-July. Sites are always near water and sometimes in slightly taller vegetation than tolerated by Common. Highly gregarious at all seasons, often in flocks with Common; has rarely interbred, while pairs of Black-winged have nested in Common Pratincole colonies in E Europe. Recently, a pair nested in W Germany. In winter, habitats include sandbanks along large African rivers, which are rarely used by Common. Like Common, wanders widely following insects and often gathers at locust swarms.

MOVEMENTS After breeding, gather to moult in July-Aug, then migrate to Africa during Aug-Oct. Unlike Common, most cross the equator; the bulk of the population winters in Botswana and S Africa. Return movement occurs Mar-May. The paucity of records at intermediate sites suggests that they attempt a rapid, high, non-stop migration. Most probably enter Africa across Arabia and the Red Sea, but then take a western route through Africa. Only two records for Kenya (Oct 1953, Oct 1969). Vagrants, mostly singles, have occurred across Europe as far as Iceland, Ireland, Scotland and Norway; most in W Europe are in Aug-Sept. Vagrant Cape Town. No vagrancy yet recorded east of breeding grounds.

DESCRIPTION Adult: See Identification section for differences from Common Pratincole. **Juvenile:** Very narrow buffy-white tips to the secondaries, less than 3 mm broad. Underwing-coverts and axillaries black, sometimes narrowly tipped chestnut-buff.

AGE/SEX Juvenile is initially very distinct, but many moult almost completely in early autumn; subsequently can be distinguished only if some juvenile

inner secondaries are retained. Sexes similar in plumage, except that breeding male has larger, blacker patch on lores than female. Males average nearly 6% longer in wing length and about 10% longer in tail-streamers.

RACES No geographical variation is known.

MEASUREMENTS Length 230-260 mm (9½"). Wing 180-216 mm; bill (exposed culmen) 12-15 mm; tarsus 34-41 mm; tail 89-117 mm (adults); tail difference, longest to shortest, 39-57 mm (adults), 23-36 mm (juveniles).

REFERENCES Hayman (1956), Walmsley (1970, 1976), Becker (1976).

53 MADAGASCAR PRATINCOLE *Glareola ocularis* Plate 20

This pratincole is confined as a breeding bird to E Madagascar, and thus has the smallest range of any of the species. Outside the breeding season it migrates to E Africa.

IDENTIFICATION A rather heavy-looking, dark brown pratincole with a chestnut patch on the belly and long, dark wings which are rufous below; its dark-capped appearance is emphasised by two whitish marks below the eye. In proportions and size it most resembles the three larger pratincoles (50-52), but compared with Common Pratincole (50) is slightly smaller in body size, shorter-tailed, but proportionately longer-winged. In flight, it differs most obviously from Common in its shallowly-forked tail, with only a small amount of white at the base and on the uppertail-coverts, and in the lack of a white trailing edge to the wing. Similar to Rock Pratincole (54) in breeding habits and general appearance, but is much larger, has a chestnut belly-patch and underwing, and lacks a collar on the hindneck. **Bare parts:** Bill rather deep and heavy, mainly blackish with a little blood-red at the gape. Iris dark brown. Legs greyish-black, short for the size of the bird.

VOICE A harsh and sharp repeated 'wick-wick-wick'.

HABITS Like Rock Pratincole, nests on rocks in fast-flowing perennial rivers. Breeding season is probably late Sept-Mar. When not nesting, also seen in wet grassy areas and on coastal beaches. In E Africa essentially a coastal bird, found near river mouths and nearby sand-dunes and scrub; rarely around inland rivers and lakes. Feeds mainly in flight, which is more tern-like than in its smaller relatives, graceful yet powerful, with sharp jinking turns. Stance is rather more hunched than Common Pratincole's, with a rather protruding breast. Gregarious; flocks of up to 9,000 have been recorded.

MOVEMENTS Breeding has been proved only in E Madagascar, but the species occurs also in the west (south to the Mangoky River) as a non-breeding visitor. Most, perhaps all, leave the island to spend the southern winter locally on the coasts of tropical E Africa between N Mozambique and S Somalia.

Vagrant away from the coast in Kenya and Tanzania, normally only in very small numbers, but hundreds were once recorded on the Kenyan shores of Lake Victoria (Aug 1920). Once recorded in Ethiopia (Oct 1973). Normally absent from E Africa Oct-Mar. Recorded on passage in the Comoro Is.; vagrant Mauritius and Réunion.

DESCRIPTION Breeding and non-breeding: Forecrown and lores very dark chocolate-brown; rest of crown dark warm brown, becoming dark grey-brown, slightly paler, over the rest of upperparts. Lesser coverts are darker, the same shade as the crown, and the primaries, primary coverts and secondaries are blackish-brown. Uppertail-coverts white, forming a narrow white band above the tail. Tail is black, with a little white centrally in the outer two pairs and narrow white tips to the second and third pairs of feathers; tail is only slightly forked and the outer feathers are noticeably rounded. Chin is pale greyish-brown, with some blackish feathers bordering the bill; face, throat, breast and flanks are grey-brown. There is a round white spot between the gape and the eye, below the lores, and a smallish white streak beneath and behind the eye bordering the dark cap. Upper belly rich chestnut; lower belly and undertail-coverts are white. Underwing-coverts and axillaries are rich chestnut. **Juvenile:** Not yet described.

AGE/SEX Males are similar to females in plumage, but slightly longer-winged on average. Nothing is known about ageing this species.

RACES No geographical variation is known.

MEASUREMENTS Length 230-250 mm (9½"). Wing 186-202 mm; bill 13-16 mm, bill depth 6.5-7.5 mm; tarsus 25-28 mm; tail 65-73 mm, depth of fork 8-18 mm.

REFERENCES Appert (1971), Benson *et al.* (1976), Britton (1977).

Madagascar Pratincole   Common Pratincole   Black-winged Pratincole

54 ROCK PRATINCOLE *Glareola nuchalis* Plate 20

Other name: White-collared or Collared Pratincole
A small, dark pratincole of tropical Africa, typically found by fast-flowing rocky rivers.

IDENTIFICATION Plumage mostly dark ash-grey and grey-brown. Adults show a white line beneath the eye and a white or chestnut collar across the hindneck. In flight, the wings are all-dark except for a distinctive whitish patch in the centre of the underwing, the tail is slightly forked, the belly is contrastingly whitish, and there is a narrow white band across the uppertail-coverts and base of the tail. Grey Pratincole (55) is similar in size, but easily distinguished by its pale plumage, buffish breast and nape, dark bar across the ear-coverts, and very striking wing pattern. Madagascar Pratincole (53) is similar in general colour, but much larger, with rufous-chestnut belly and underwing and dark grey legs; it has no collar. Common and Black-winged Pratincoles (50, 52) are again much larger, are paler above, have strongly-forked tails and chestnut or black on the underwing-coverts. **Bare parts:** Bill black with bright red base, duller in juveniles. Iris brown. Legs conspicuously bright coral-red in adults, more orangey in juveniles.
VOICE Contact call is a faint, whistled 'kip' or 'killip'. In display, both sexes give a musical purring trill. Also has a hoarse 'kek-kek-kek'. Noisy and aggressive in defence of the nest.
HABITS Occurs chiefly in traditional, often widely-scattered sites. Strongly associated with emergent rocks in rivers or sometimes lakes. When water-levels are high, perches on branches, tree-trunks or fence-posts in flooded meadows; sometimes seen perched on semi-submerged hippopotamuses. Spends most of the day resting, sometimes in dense groups, but feeds by hawking flying insects over the river at dawn and dusk; also feeds during the day in overcast conditions. In some locations, flocks leave the river at dusk to feed around nearby streetlamps. Occasionally feeds with Grey Pratincole, and may perch with them on sandbanks. Odd records away from rivers and breeding lakes presumably refer to migrants. Western birds sometimes resort to coastal lagoons and beaches after breeding. Strongly gregarious for most of the year, but, when breeding, pairs defend individual territories. There is a buoyant courtship flight with wings held high over the back. In ground displays the feathers of the hindneck are flared to emphasise the collar. The clutch of one or two eggs is laid into a crack or depression in the bare rock; nest-sites are always on rocks surrounded by deep, sometimes fast-flowing water. Young chicks are well camouflaged and can swim strongly if necessary.
MOVEMENTS Seasonal in occurrence in many parts of its range, but its movements are not yet understood. Non-breeding ranges of the two subspecies overlap to some extent — certainly in Togo and Cameroun. Breeding season is mainly May-July in Togo (*liberiae*) and the species is scarce or absent in Nov-Dec. In Zambia, species is present only during Aug-Mar (varying between sites) and absent at other seasons. Apparently sedentary at breeding sites in Kenya and NE Gabon. Records at Berber, Sudan, and in the Ethiopian highlands may refer to vagrants.
DESCRIPTION Breeding and non-breeding: Crown and nape dark grey-brown, outlined from beneath eye and onto nape by sharply-defined white or white-and-chestnut line. Blackish patches on lores and on chin. Upperparts dark brownish-grey, apart from black flight feathers, white uppertail-coverts and some white on sides and base of tail. Front of neck and breast ash-grey, becoming paler towards legs; rear belly and undertail-coverts are whitish. Underwing dark grey, apart from small central silvery patch on outer coverts and bases of inner primaries and outer secondaries. **Juvenile:** Similar in pattern to adult, but lacking pale collar and eye-stripe. All grey-brown feathers of upperparts, head, neck and breast are neatly marked at the tip with a pair of lateral pale buff or brownish spots outlined by narrow black lines. The inner 6 primaries and also the inner secondaries are tipped pale buff with subterminal dark line. Tip of tail shows a narrow buff subterminal bar.
AGE/SEX Once buff spotting is lost, young can be distinguished (but only in the hand) by retained pale-tipped inner primaries or secondaries. No differences are known between the sexes.
RACES Two: *nuchalis* (Gabon to Kenya and Mozambique) and *liberiae* (Sierra Leone to W Cameroun). The race *liberiae* differs in that collar on hindneck is chestnut, shading to white towards the eye; *nuchalis* has a white collar. Also, juveniles of *liberiae* have slightly browner spotting than those of *nuchalis*, and *liberiae* is faintly shorter- and blunter-winged.
MEASUREMENTS Length 175-195 mm (7¼"). Wing 143-160 mm; bill 10-12 mm; tarsus 19-21 mm; tail 55-60 mm.
REFERENCES Brosset (1979), Penry (1979), Cheke (1980, 1982).

55 GREY PRATINCOLE *Glareola cinerea* Plate 20

Other name: Cream-coloured Pratincole
A small pale pratincole of W and central Africa with a very striking black-and-white pattern in flight.

IDENTIFICATION Small size and pale dove-grey upperparts immediately distinguish it from the other African pratincoles. In flight, the brilliant and extensive white wing-panel and mainly-white underwing are totally distinctive. The Rock Pratincole (54) is similar in size and may overlap in habitat, but is very much darker above and below; in flight it shows completely-dark wings except for a silvery patch on the underwing. Other African pratincoles, Common (50), Black-winged (52) and Madagascar (53), are much larger and darker and have dark legs. Overlap with the Oriental region Little Pratincole (56) is most unlikely; latter species has a rather plain face pattern, mainly-black primaries and black underwing-coverts. **Bare parts:** Bill orange-red at base with a black distal half. Iris brown. Legs bright orange-red.

VOICE Contact note, frequently given while feeding, is a liquid 'prrrp'. Also a hoarse 'kree-kree-kree'. There is a trilling song like that of Rock Pratincole.

HABITS Like Rock Pratincole essentially a riverside bird, but found chiefly on broader stretches with extensive sandbanks. Difficult to see when sitting on pale sand. Often very tame. At times hawks insects over nearby grassland or woodland. Flight is buoyant and graceful on long, narrow wings; deep wing-beats are interspersed with glides. Highly gregarious, and a colonial nester. Breeding season is mostly Apr-Aug. Two eggs are laid in a simple depression in the sand.

MOVEMENTS Little known, but movements seem governed by water-levels. Some movement to the coastal belt occurs after breeding and when the rivers are high.

DESCRIPTION Breeding and non-breeding: Crown medium-grey; long white supercilium from bill to side of nape; neat black eye-stripe from bill to just behind eye joining black vertical smudge from rear of ear-coverts to sides of neck. Throat and ear-coverts white. Broad pale chestnut collar around hindneck. Mantle, back, rump, scapulars, tertials and most of the wing-coverts are pale dove-grey. Primary coverts, outer primaries, trailing edge of secondaries and primaries are black; flight feathers otherwise white. Rump, uppertail-coverts and tail white, but with subterminal black bar. Tail is only slightly forked, but the fork is emphasised by the pattern of black. Breast and upper belly washed pale cinnamon to chestnut; lower belly and undertail are white. Axillaries and most underwing-coverts are white; under primary coverts are mostly black. **Juvenile:** As adult, but lacks black-and-white head pattern. Crown sandy-grey, streaked sandy-buff; supercilium pale buff mostly behind the eye. Collar across the hindneck is sandy-grey. Upperparts grey, but obscured by wide buffish fringes; the larger scapulars and tertials also have dark subterminal bars. Tail as adult, but washed buffish and speckled dark at the tip. Breast is washed with pale cinnamon.

AGE/SEX Juveniles are easily distinguished by their buffish fringes and poor head pattern. Young birds are not separable from adults after their post-juvenile moult. No differences are known between the sexes.

RACES Two: nominate (most of range) and *colorata* (upper Niger River). The race *colorata* differs marginally in having a wider pale collar on the hindneck and a slightly deeper breast colour.

MEASUREMENTS Length 180-200 mm (7½"). Wing 139-153 mm; bill 10-12 mm; tarsus 21-25 mm.

56 LITTLE PRATINCOLE *Glareola lactea*   Plate 21

Other names: Milky, Small or Small Indian Pratincole
A highly distinctive, small, pale pratincole of India and SE Asia.

IDENTIFICATION Much smaller and greyer than the other pratincoles of this region. In flight, shows highly-distinctive broad white panel across the secondaries, more black than white in the primaries, and a startling black-and-white pattern on the underwing, with black axillaries and coverts. Other sympatric species, Common (50) and Oriental (51), are obviously larger and lack a conspicuous white wing-panel. The Grey Pratincole (55) of Africa is a similar size and colour with extensive white in the wings, but is easily distinguished by range, white wing-linings, more white than black in the primaries, paler grey mantle, orange-red legs and, in adults, a long black eye-stripe and white supercilium. **Bare parts:** Bill largely black, with a small red patch at the base. Iris brown. Legs dark brownish or blackish-grey.

VOICE A rather high-pitched, rolled 'prrip' or 'tiririt' in flight, frequently uttered when feeding. Also short calls such as 'tuck-tuck-tuck' and other calls when nesting.

HABITS Similar to Grey Pratincole. Essentially a bird of larger rivers where banks of sand or shingle are exposed, also feeding over nearby marshy ground or cultivation. Penetrates up to 1800 m in suitable habitat in the Himalayas. When not breeding, often occurs at estuaries or coastal lagoons, sometimes in large swarms. Particularly active towards dusk, flying almost until dark with quick, angular, swallow-like flight. Feeds mostly by hawking insects in flight, but may chase them on the ground like a plover. When resting, well camouflaged against a background of sand or shingle. Gregarious throughout the year; nests colonially on riverine sandbanks. False-sitting and broken-wing displays are used to lure intruders away from the eggs and chicks.

MOVEMENTS Present in many breeding areas only between Apr and Aug. Moves downstream in winter, when more frequent in estuaries and coastal marshlands. Also undertakes local movements in response to changing water-levels in the rivers. Vagrant Arabian Gulf and Oman.

DESCRIPTION Breeding: Crown darkish, varying from dark chocolate-brown on forecrown, through grey-brown, to pale grey-brown on hindneck. A black line crosses the lores from gape to eye; ear-coverts are pale greyish-buff. Upperparts, including coverts, scapulars and tertials, an even brownish-grey; primary coverts black. Outer primaries are black, but the inner 1 or 2 are white and the next 2 or 3 have white inner webs; on most individuals there is also a small white patch towards the base of the middle primaries, but this is completely absent on some. Secondaries are white, with a fairly broad black tip to all except innermost forming a contrasting trailing edge. Rump and uppertail white; tail is slightly forked, white with subterminal black bar, broadest on central feathers. Throat is pale buff, infused salmon-pink, breast buffish-grey and belly white. On underwing, the coverts, axillaries, most primaries and trailing secondary bar show as black, contrasting with white over most of the secondaries, and whitish on the inner primaries and central-primary patch (if present). **Non-**

breeding: Briefly during wing moult, becomes duller with paler greyish-brown forecrown, and very pale throat variably spotted and streaked with pale brown. The black line across the lores is lost. **Juvenile:** As moulting adult, but crown extensively spotted buff; upperwing-coverts are obscurely washed buffish at tip with a pale brown subterminal bar, more pronounced on the scapulars and tertials. The chin is whitish, but the throat and upper breast are ringed by small pale brown spots. Tail tipped buffish-brown and mottled subterminally by irregular brown lines.

Primaries are narrowly fringed buff at tip.
AGE/SEX The juvenile is distinct for about two months, and then can be separated only in the hand by retained buff-tipped primaries. Sexes are not known to differ in plumage, but males average about 3% longer-winged.
RACES No geographical variation is known.
MEASUREMENTS Length 165-185 mm (7"). Wing 146-163 mm, average 155.4 mm (males), 150.7 mm (females); bill 8-10 mm; tarsus 19-22 mm; tail 50-57 mm.

57 NORTHERN LAPWING *Vanellus vanellus* Plate 22

Other names: Lapwing, Peewit, Green Plover
A common and familiar Palaearctic species. It is the shortest-legged lapwing in proportion to its size, and also the broadest-winged.

IDENTIFICATION Easily identified by its long crest, dark glossy green upperparts, white underparts, black or pied breast, and orange-brown undertail-coverts. Looks chiefly black and white at a distance. Very distinctive deep-flapping flight on broad, rounded wings; often in large dense flocks. Wings are normally entirely dark above, except for whitish spots near the tips of the outer 3 or 4 primaries, but beware moulting birds which may show the white bases to the secondaries (normally hidden by the greater coverts); most other vanellids show a bold white band or patch on the wings in flight. The only other waders with upstanding crests, Black-headed Plover (62) and Southern Lapwing (74), are both brown above and have a white undertail. **Bare parts:** Bill short, black. Iris dark brown. Legs rather short, dull reddish-flesh, not projecting beyond tail-tip in flight.
VOICE Thin, plaintive, mainly disyllabic calls are given in flight and also constantly from excitable grounded flocks: usually 'wee-ip', at a variety of intonations and pitches. The territorial song, typically given in flight, is a prolonged medley of 'coo-wee-ip' and 'wee-willuch-coo-wee-ip'.
HABITS Breeds mainly Apr-July and is single-brooded. Nests chiefly at low altitude, favouring short grass, but also nests on bare ground and among crops. Male has spectacular flight display, twisting and turning with great speed and agility, detectable at night by the quiet creaking of the wings. On the ground has a bowing display, revealing the orange-brown undertail, accompanied by wheezing calls. Found on grasslands and farmland throughout the year, also on estuaries especially in cold weather. Widespread in winter, often in flocks of thousands. Feeds nocturnally when conditions allow; during full moon, feeds more at night and roosts more during the day.
MOVEMENTS In western parts of range, a westward migration begins in late June, and large numbers moult in W Europe during July-Sept. Onward migration continues after moult. Typically a diurnal migrant, usually in flocks of several dozen, sometimes hundreds or thousands. In winter, freezing weather provokes strong diurnal movements. Vagrants have occurred in E America from Baffin I. south to Barbados, particularly during severe weather in Europe. In Africa normally penetrates only as far as Canaries and Egypt, but a Polish-ringed individual has been

display flight

recovered in S Africa. Occasionally nests in Iceland.
DESCRIPTION Breeding: Forehead, crown and long, wispy crest are black. Face is mainly white, with irregular blackish mark around eye and across cheeks and ear-coverts. Underparts white, except for black or largely black chin, throat and breast, and orange-brown undertail. Mantle to rump, also scapulars, tertials and coverts glossy green, with some purple sheen on the scapulars. Lesser coverts are glossed blue or greenish-blue. Primaries and secondaries are black, with brownish-white markings near tips of the outer 3 primaries. Underwing-coverts mainly white, contrasting strongly with the black flight feathers, but median and greater under primary coverts are black. Tail white with a broad black, almost-terminal band, but outer feathers are almost entirely white; tail-tip and longest rump feathers are orange-brown. **Non-breeding:** As above, but mantle and covert feathers are broadly tipped deep buff after the autumn moult. Throat and upper breast become white, leaving a blackish breast-band which is more or less dappled with white. **Juvenile:** Similar to non-breeding adult, but showing some buff spotting on the feather tips in addition to complete buff fringes. Before the post-juvenile moult, the breast-band is dull and has many greyish tips.
AGE/SEX After adults complete their autumn wing moult, the species is very difficult to age. Buff spotting at the edges of some large scapulars (in addition to the buff bars) indicates juvenile. Breeding males have solid black throat and long crest, while females usually show a variable amount of white speckling on the throat, a duller face and a shorter crest. The sheen on the lesser coverts is blue in adult males, green in young females, and blue-green at other stages. Adults and males have more bulging primaries than first-years and females; differences between individuals are obvious in flying flocks. There are also

small differences in the primary patterning: adult female has larger, but more diffuse whitish patches on outer feathers than adult male.

RACES There is apparently no geographical variation in this species, owing to considerable mixing in winter of birds from different breeding grounds and subsequent abmigration.

MEASUREMENTS Length 280-310 mm (11½"). Wing 215-237 mm (males), 210-234 mm (females); bill 22-28 mm; tarsus 43-50 mm; tail 88-112 mm.

REFERENCES Klomp (1954), Bagg (1967), Imboden (1974), Dabelsteen (1978).

58 LONG-TOED LAPWING *Vanellus crassirostris* Plate 24

Other names: White-faced Lapwing, Long-toed or White-winged Plover
This lapwing is extraordinary in that it shows ecological and structural similarities to the jacanas.

IDENTIFICATION A typical lapwing in appearance and shape, although rather long-legged and with an upright stance. Easily distinguished from other vanellids by entirely-white face and front of neck, contrasting with black on rear crown, hindneck and breast; and in flight by extensive white along the forewing, including the entire carpal area and the primary coverts. In the southern race *leucoptera*, the secondaries and all but the outer 3 primaries are also white, recalling Pheasant-tailed Jacana (5). Heavy flight and deep wingbeats are like Crowned Lapwing's (67); extensively white wings and large trailing feet may suggest a pond heron *Ardeola*. Beware confusion with White-headed Lapwing (64), which also has mostly-white wings. **Bare parts:** Bill quite heavy, pinkish-red with solid blackish tip. Iris red or reddish-brown; narrow pinkish-red eye-ring. Legs long, dark pinkish-red, with brighter tibia, 'knee' joint and soles; longer toes than other lapwings, central toe about 67% of tarsus length. There is a short, sharp carpal spur, just breaking the feathering.

VOICE A metallic clicking 'kick-k-k-k', often repeated, and a plaintive 'wheet'. Aggressively noisy when breeding.

HABITS This species is restricted to marshlands and freshwater pools with much emergent and floating vegetation. It feeds mostly, and sometimes nests, on floating vegetation, like a jacana. Nest may occasionally be on dry land up to 100 m from the water's edge. The water surface is not used by other African lapwings, but bordering areas of waterlogged grassland are contested vigorously with Blacksmith Plovers (59). Long-toed, usually the aggressor, is also highly aggressive towards African Jacana (2) but not successful in excluding adults from its breeding territory; also attacks herons and other potential predators. Less conspicuous and often rather shy when not breeding. Often encountered singly, rarely in more than family-sized groups. Like African Jacana, feeds largely on aquatic insects; also takes small molluscs.

MOVEMENTS A sedentary species, rather patchily distributed.

DESCRIPTION Breeding and non-breeding: Head and neck white, except for bluish-black nape and hindneck. Black extends around sides of neck to join broad bluish-black band across breast and central upper belly. Underparts, axillaries and underwing-coverts otherwise white, except sometimes for some blackish in the longest central undertail-coverts. Mantle, scapulars, back and rump light grey-brown. Uppertail-coverts blackish bordering the rump, but rear feathers are white forming a narrow white band at the base of the tail. Tail feathers entirely blackish, except for white at the base particularly of the outer two pairs. Tertials as scapulars in colour but darker, and sometimes glossed greenish-blue. Wing-coverts white, although nominate race may show black admixed in greater primary and secondary coverts. Flight feathers all-black with greenish-blue gloss in nominate race, all-white except for outer primaries in *leucoptera*, or intermediate. **Juvenile:** Similar to adult in pattern, but black of nape and breast-band is browner and shows buff tipping, and coverts, tertials, mantle and scapulars show a mottling of brown and buff.

AGE/SEX Juvenile primaries, narrower and browner than those of adults, may be used to distinguish young birds after post-juvenile body moult. Sexes are not known to differ in plumage or measurements.

RACES Two: southern *leucoptera* (S Tanzania and Malawi southwards) differs in that secondaries and inner 7 primaries are white, not black as on the nominate northern race. On *leucoptera*, the wing is slightly shorter and the tarsus longer. Intermediate birds, with secondaries and inner primaries silvery-grey or white with black markings, occur in Tanzania and Malawi.

MEASUREMENTS Length about 310 mm (12"). Wing 201-221 mm (nominate), 197-214 mm (*leucoptera*); bill 30-35 mm (nominate), 71-85 mm (*leucoptera*); tail 90-100 mm.

REFERENCES Saunders (1970), Walters (1979).

59 BLACKSMITH PLOVER *Vanellus armatus* Plate 24

A conspicuously-patterned lapwing of southern African wetlands, named for its distinctive alarm call.

IDENTIFICATION Easily identified by the bold contrasts of its black, white and grey plumage. In the adult the white patches on the cap and hindneck, each surrounded by black, are highly distinctive; the juvenile is patterned less clearly, but also shows a conspicuous white hindneck. The adult's wings show mostly grey at rest, with a conspicuous black area across the lower scapulars. In flight, primaries and secondaries are all-black (except for some white at the bases of the inner secondaries), and coverts are

contrastingly grey on upperwing and white on under-wing. Unique plumage pattern should preclude confusion, but compare other African *Vanellus* species.
Bare parts: Bill black. Iris deep carmine-red. Legs black, longish; toes and part of tarsi project beyond the tail-tip in flight. Sharp blackish spur on the bend of the wing.

VOICE A distinctive metallic 'tink-tink', like the sound of a blacksmith's hammer on an anvil. Single calls may be repeated at varying rates of up to about two or three per second, depending on the degree of alarm or arousal, or strung together into a rapid 'tink-tink-tink-tink...'. Also, may give a screeching call and an excited 'kerweek'.

HABITS Typically a waterside species, almost always nesting in a few metres of the water's edge. Can be found beside both fresh and saline lakes. Sometimes wades in shallow water. Defends large nesting territories against other Blacksmiths and sometimes against neighbouring Long-toed Lapwings (58). Often travels a kilometre or two from water to feed, and may be found in open country alongside Crowned Lapwing (67) or even in small grassy patches among thorn-scrub. Nesting birds are noisy and conspicuous, mobbing intruders with characteristic calls. When not nesting often gathers in parties, sometimes of several dozens; behaviour is sometimes quiet and relatively placid.

MOVEMENTS Mostly sedentary, apart from non-breeding flocking in good feeding areas and dispersal to breed in well-scattered pairs. Capable of finding quite small temporary pools.

DESCRIPTION Breeding and non-breeding: Forehead and crown pure white ending sharply just above the eye. Face, nape, upper hindneck and underparts from chin to lower breast continuously black, contrasting sharply with the white cap, belly, flanks and

undertail. Axillaries and underwing-coverts white; underside of primaries and secondaries black, except for white bases to inner secondaries. Lower hindneck pure white. Mantle, back and rump are black. Upper scapulars, bordering the mantle, are grey, divided sharply from the black of the lower scapulars which overlie the back and rump; grey continues from the upper scapulars across the wing-coverts and tertials. Primaries, primary coverts and secondaries are all-black, except for white at the bases of the inner secondaries which forms a narrow white wedge between the grey coverts and black flight feathers. Lower rump, uppertail-coverts and base of tail are white. Tail has a broad terminal black band; this is narrowest on the outer pair of feathers, which also show a narrow white tip. **Juvenile:** Like adult in pattern, except that crown is dark, chin to centre of upper breast is whitish, and the upper scapulars have some blackish feathers admixed. All black feathers are tipped buffish initially, and the scapulars also show buff spotting at the sides. The grey coverts show a dark brown subterminal line and a buff fringe. The tertials are brownish-grey with irregular buff edgings and dark brown barring.

AGE/SEX Juveniles apparently moult rapidly into adult-type plumage and quickly become inseparable from adults in the field. Some may be distinguished in the hand by retained inner median coverts or by rather pointed and worn primaries. The spur is very small in young birds; in adults, males have longer spurs than females. The sexes are alike in plumage and measurements.

RACES No geographical variation is known.

MEASUREMENTS Length 280-310 mm (11½"). Wing 193-224 mm; bill 25-28 mm; tarsus 67-80 mm; tail 84-92 mm.

REFERENCES Hall (1959, 1964), Thomas (1983).

60 SPUR-WINGED PLOVER *Vanellus spinosus* Plate 23

Other name: Spur-winged Lapwing
This is one of the several lapwings with a sharp spur on the carpal joint. It is closely related to River Lapwing (61) and sometimes treated as conspecific.

IDENTIFICATION Easily recognised by the brown upperparts and the distinctively-pied pattern of the underparts: the entire breast and upper belly are black, the crown is black and slightly crested, and the neck is mainly brilliant white with a black stripe from bill to breast. The white hindneck is conspicuous when the bird presents its back to the observer. In flight, shows brown coverts and black flight feathers divided by a diagonal white band from carpal to inner secondaries. The tail shows a very broad black terminal band, almost as broad as the white band across the uppertail. Overlaps in Iraq with Red-wattled Lapwing (77), but latter easily distinguished by red wattles, yellow legs and black hindneck. In Africa, both Blacksmith Plover (59) and Long-toed Lapwing (58) have pied head patterns, but both have white crowns. River Lapwing is allopatric, but is similar in structure and many elements of plumage pattern; it, however, shows grey-brown on the neck and breast, a longer crest, black encircling bill, an isolated black belly-patch, a black wedge on the carpal area, and

more white in the inner secondaries.**Bare parts:** Bill black. Iris dark crimson or reddish-brown. Legs and feet brownish-black; feet project beyond tail-tip in flight. Long, sharp, curved black spur on carpal joint, shorter and blunter in juveniles.

VOICE Noisy in alarm, repeating a sharp metallic 'pitt' or 'tick' which is reminiscent of Blacksmith Plover. Territorial call is a loud rhythmic 'did-ye-do-it' or 'ti-ti-ter-el', less raucous and measured than similar call of Red-wattled Lapwing. Often calls at night.

HABITS Usually found at or near fresh or saline wetlands, including open coasts (rarely), estuaries, coastal saltpans, marshes, irrigated farmland, lake edges and larger rivers. Nests Mar-Sept around E Mediterranean and in W Africa. Has complex displays on ground featuring the pied patterning and wing-spurs. Aggressive near the nest. Feeds on adjacent dry grassland or farmland as well as in waterside vegetation; feeding action is rather slow and deliberate, often with rather hunched posture. Usually well scattered when breeding, but otherwise may gather in small groups, sometimes in flocks of a hundred or more at favoured sites.

MOVEMENTS Those breeding in Greece and Turkey are summer visitors, present only between mid-Mar and early Oct. Occurs on passage in Cyprus and Crete. It is not known how far these individuals penetrate into the African range of the species. Breeding in Greece was first noted in 1959, but the species is now well established; there is no evidence of further northward expansion. Vagrants have reached Spain, Belgium, W Germany, Czechoslovakia, Iran, Oman, Malta and Black Sea coasts north to Odessa. African breeders are largely sedentary, but perform local movements in response to rainfall and drought. Does not breed south of Kenya, but wanders south to central Tanzania; there is also a record from Vryburg, NE Cape Province.

DESCRIPTION Breeding and non-breeding: Forehead, crown and nape black; long feathers of rear crown form a small pointed crest overlying white feathers of hindneck; black vertical band from chin to join black breast; rest of face and neck brilliant white. Entire breast, flanks and upper belly are black, forming a 'waistcoat', contrasting with white lower belly, vent and undertail. All of underwing-coverts and axillaries are white; flight feathers entirely black from underneath. Upperparts from mantle to upper rump and across wing-coverts are plain pale brown. Inner primary coverts and outer median and greater coverts are white or white-tipped. Primaries and secondaries black, except for some white on inner secondaries and bases of outer secondaries. Lower rump and uppertail white; tail is mostly black, but with white base broadest on outer feathers. **Juvenile:** As adult in pattern, but black areas of head and underparts are tinged brownish and flecked with white (chin is especially pale); and upperparts, especially coverts, show broad buff fringes.

AGE/SEX Juveniles are difficult to distinguish after Oct, except in the hand by retained coverts and worn primaries. Sexes are similar in plumage, but males average larger. Spurs measure 5-10 mm in adult females, 8-12 mm in adult males. Iris tends to be redder in males, less sullied with brown.

RACES Monotypic. African populations may be slightly shorter in wing and tarsus than Mediterranean ones.

MEASUREMENTS Length 250-280 mm (10½"). Wing 190-220 mm; bill 26-33 mm; tarsus 60-78 mm; tail 86-98 mm.

REFERENCES von Helversen (1963), Ferguson-Lees (1965).

61 RIVER LAPWING *Vanellus duvaucelii*   Plate 23

Other names: Asian Spur-winged Plover/Lapwing
A strongly-patterned lapwing of Indian and SE Asian rivers, very similar in structure to Spur-winged Plover (60) and quite similar in plumage. Sometimes treated as conspecific.

IDENTIFICATION Easily distinguished from other lapwings by its plumage pattern. Rarely seen far from riparian habitat. Of the three breeding lapwings in the Oriental region, this has the most white in the wing, most black in the tail, and is the only one with a belly-patch and dark legs. The distinctive broad, helmet-like black crest is not always evident as it normally lies against the hindneck, but note that black is continuous from nape to upper breast, including a broad area around the bill. In flight, a white band crosses the wing from just beyond the carpal to the inner secondaries; on the leading edge of the wing, the white band is flanked by black primary coverts and a black wedge extending back from the carpal joint. Plumage pattern is most similar to that of Sociable Plover (71) but latter has a larger, more diffuse belly-patch (breeding plumage only), a conspicuous supercilium, a pale face and throat, and entirely-white secondaries. Structurally very similar to the allopatric Spur-winged Plover, but with breast, hindneck and cheeks mainly grey-brown, underparts mainly white (not mainly black) with isolated belly-patch, black crest, black lores, black wedge on carpal area, and more white on inner secondaries. **Bare parts:** Bill black. Iris dark crimson or reddish-brown. Legs and feet brownish-black; in flight, feet project beyond tail. Long, curved, sharp black spur on carpal joint, shorter and blunter in juveniles.

VOICE Like Spur-winged Plover. A sharp positive 'tip-tip' or a longer 'dip-dip-to-weet', distinguishable with practice from similar but more measured and raucous call of Red-wattled Lapwing (77).

HABITS Generally very similar to Spur-winged, but normally seen only near rivers and adjacent farmland; rarely occurs by still water. Nests typically on sandbar or shingle exposed in river, Mar-June. Has complex displays in which crest may be raised. Not gregarious, not often seen in groups of more than family size. Most often encountered singly or in pairs. Food is chiefly insects, worms, crustaceans and molluscs. Disruptive plumage pattern is effective camouflage against a background of sand or shingle.

MOVEMENTS Appears to be entirely sedentary, even at quite high altitude (900 m) on northern edge of range in Nepal.

DESCRIPTION Breeding and non-breeding: Crown, nape, face, chin and throat black: black is sooty on face, but becomes glossy towards rear crown. Black is outlined by white narrowly behind eye, more broadly on the sides of throat and upper breast. Sides of neck and hindneck are pale grey. Mantle, back, rump, scapulars, tertials, and most of wing-coverts are pale sandy-brown. Carpal area and outer lesser and median coverts are black, forming a curving wedge-shaped patch. Greater coverts tipped white, broadly on outers. Inner secondaries white, outers with white bases and black tips. Primaries black, but bases of inner primary coverts are white. Uppertail-coverts white; tail white at base, but with broad terminal black band. Breast is medium-grey, darker on lower breast and often slightly tinged pinkish; rest of underparts white, except for small, sharply-defined black central belly-patch. Underwing-coverts and axillaries white, contrasting with black primaries and outer secondaries. **Juvenile:** As adult in pattern, but black partly obscured by brownish tips; coverts sandy-brown, each with irregular, slightly darker submarginal mark and buff fringe.

AGE/SEX Juvenile initially distinct, but by Oct very difficult to tell in the field; in the hand, the short blunt spur and worn pointed primaries of the first-winter

bird are distinctive. Sexes similar, but males average slightly larger.
RACES No geographical variation is known.
MEASUREMENTS Length 295-315 mm (12"). Wing 187-214 mm; bill 24-30 mm; tarsus 61-72 mm; tail 88-94 mm.
REFERENCES Hingston (1932).

62 BLACK-HEADED PLOVER *Vanellus tectus*   Plate 24

Other names: Black-headed Lapwing, Crested Wattled or Blackhead Plover
The only regular African wader south of the Sahara that sports an upstanding crest; Northern Lapwing (57) is very rare south of the Sahara.

IDENTIFICATION Easy to identify by virtue of its unique combination of crest, black-and-white head, and brown upperparts. Note the small, pink 'head-lights'. The bright white nape, sandwiched by black, is a conspicuous feature at all ages. In flight, shows a large white wingbar and area on the forewing which covers the carpal area, primary coverts and base of the primaries; only Long-toed (58) and White-headed Lapwings (64) show more white on the outer half of the wing. Northern Lapwing shares a wispy crest, but is easily distinguished by its shorter legs and dark green upperparts and in flight by its exceptionally broad wings, lacking white above except at the wing-tips. At a distance, Crowned Lapwing (67) is not dissimilar, but Black-headed is conspicuously black on the sides of the neck and the central breast. **Bare parts:** Bill pinkish-red, with black outer third. Iris bright golden-yellow. Small, oval, pink wattles above lores cover the area between the eye and forehead, and may almost meet across the forehead. Legs bright pinkish-red, sometimes tinged brownish.
VOICE Mobbing calls are a loud 'kwairr' and a shriller 'kiarr'. When highly alarmed or when flushed, utters a piercing, whistled 'kir'.
HABITS Found all year in dry plains, particularly on bare ground or very short grass, sometimes in lightly-bushed grassland. Fairly tame, often nesting close to buildings and paths. Usually seen singly or in pairs, rarely in flocks of up to about 40 individuals. Often largely inactive during the day, feeding mainly at night. Flight is rather slow.
MOVEMENTS Mostly sedentary. The race *latifrons* has been recorded once in N Tanzania (Aug 1962), the southernmost record of the species. Nominate race occurs north to Ennedi in E Chad. In 1869, one was shot in Wadi Araba (Israel-Jordan border); other Mediterranean reports are now generally discredited.
DESCRIPTION Breeding and non-breeding: Head and neck mainly black, with wispy crest from rear crown, but forehead is white, as is a patch on the

chin and throat and lines from the back of each eye which meet broadly on the nape. Long black feathers in the centre of the breast continue the black down-wards from the neck in a central vertical line. Sides of breast are washed with brown. Rest of underparts and underwing-coverts are immaculate white. Mantle, back, rump, scapulars, tertials, and lesser and median coverts are evenly medium-brown. Greater coverts are tipped white. Primary coverts, alula and basal third or so of all primaries and secondaries are bright white; flight feathers are otherwise black. Uppertail-coverts and base of tail are white; tail is mostly black, with a narrow white tip. Juvenile: As adult in pattern, but black of head and brown of upperparts are strongly fringed with buff. Larger scapulars and tertials are strongly barred with buff. Crest and elongated black feathers of the upper breast are shorter and browner than those of adults, and wattles are smaller. Tail is tipped buffish. Primaries are narrower and more pointed than those of adults. Bill-base and legs are brownish-pink.
AGE/SEX Juveniles are initially clearly distinct from adults, but soon moult into adult-type plumage. The last buff-fringed feathers to be replaced are likely to be the inner median coverts. No differences are known between the sexes; possibly the males may have a slightly longer crest and a slightly longer and heavier bill.
RACES Two: nominate *tectus* (Senegal to Ethiopia and NW Kenya) and *latifrons* (S Somalia to E Kenya). The race *latifrons* is slightly shorter-winged and has a broader white forehead, just broader than the distance from bill-base to eye. In the nominate race the white may be mostly hidden by the wattle. The races apparently do not intergrade; there is a zone in N Kenya where neither has occurred.
MEASUREMENTS Length about 250 mm (10"). Wing 180-201 mm (nominate), 173-193 mm (three specimens of *latifrons*); bill 22-26 mm; tarsus 53-62 mm.
REFERENCES North (1937).

63 YELLOW-WATTLED LAPWING *Vanellus malabaricus*   Plate 28

This lapwing is the only one which is restricted to the Indian subcontinent.

IDENTIFICATION A medium-sized, predominantly brown lapwing with yellow legs and large yellow wattles. The black cap is bordered narrowly below by white. Chin and throat are black, while the brown neck and upper breast are divided from the white

underparts by a narrow blackish line. In flight, shows a subterminal black tail-band (not reaching the outer feathers) and a white wingbar across the inner half of the wing. The most similar species in the region is Grey-headed Lapwing (76) but this is noticeably larger, has smaller yellow wattles, a pale greyish-brown head, a much greyer breast with a less distinct black line and all-white secondaries. The White-tailed Plover (72) lacks a dark cap, is much paler overall and has a white tail, while the Sociable Plover (71) has a prominent supercilium, a much paler face and breast, dark legs and white secondaries. Red-wattled Lapwing (77), the other widespread breeding lapwing in the Indian region, is larger and darker and has a conspicuous black-and-white pattern on the neck and breast, as well as red 'headlights' and bill-base.

Bare parts: Bill yellow at base, sometimes tinged greenish, and black at tip, rather more slender than Red-wattled's bill. Bright yellow wattles above and below each side of bill-base, joining narrow yellow eye-ring. Iris greyish-white or pale lemon-yellow. Longish yellow legs. Tiny yellow carpal spur.

VOICE A plaintive drawn-out 'tchee-it' is the normal contact call; when alarmed also calls 'chit-oo-eet', and when very agitated a repeated sharp 'whit-whit-whit'. Much less vociferous than Red-wattled.

HABITS Occurs in a variety of lowland habitats, including the fringes of wetlands, dry grassland and agricultural country; generally in drier areas than Red-wattled, although the two species are occasionally seen together. Nests Mar-Aug, holding large exclusive territories inside which both adults and chicks always feed. Both sexes share incubation. Like many tropical lapwings, carries water in belly feathers to cool eggs. Much less demonstrative than Red-wattled, but will attack intruders near the nest; often raises crown feathers in display. Flight is buoyant but rather slow. Outside the breeding season may gather in small parties, but these rarely reach double figures.

MOVEMENTS Mainly sedentary, but performs local movements away from wettest areas during monsoon, and in some areas is only a dry-season visitor. Longer movements have been recorded, but has not yet been seen much beyond breeding range. Only an occasional visitor to the Katmandu valley in Nepal.

DESCRIPTION Breeding: Forehead, crown and nape black, bordered from above eye backwards by narrow white band; these bands do not quite meet on the nape. Large yellow wattles above and below lores. Chin and throat blackish; rest of face, neck and upper breast mid-brown. Mantle to upper rump, also wing-coverts, uniform, dull sandy-brown, but with white wingbar formed by white inner secondaries, bases to rest of secondaries, and tips of greater coverts. All but inner secondaries are tipped black; primaries black, although bases of inner webs of inner primaries are whitish. Lower rump and uppertail are white; tail is white, with a fairly narrow blackish subterminal band across the central four pairs of feathers and a slight buffish infusion around this blackish bar. Upper breast mid-brown, occasionally tinged greyish, bordered below by sharp, narrow, black breast-band. Rest of underparts white. Underwing including coverts, axillaries, and bases of primaries and secondaries is white, contrasting with mainly-black primaries and black secondary tips. **Non-breeding:** During moult, especially Nov-Dec, adults may have brown feathers in the black crown or, exceptionally, an entirely dark brown crown. Latter individuals are always distinguishable from juveniles by their brown, not whitish, chin and throat. **Juvenile:** As adult, but crown is brown, slightly flecked paler, the sandy-brown upperparts are extensively marked with dark brown subterminal bars, the median coverts and tertials have pale buff edges, and the chin is white. Primaries are noticeably pointed.

AGE/SEX Juveniles are distinguished by brown crown, white chin and bars on upperparts. They can sometimes be identified in the field at close range as late as Jan. Sexes are similar in plumage, but males average slightly longer in the wing and tarsus.

RACES Monotypic. There is a slight cline of increasing size from south to north.

MEASUREMENTS Length 260-280 mm (10½"). Wing 192-211 mm; bill 23-26 mm; tarsus 57-66 mm; tail 71-84 mm.

REFERENCES Jayakar and Spurway (1965a,b, 1968), Johns and Thorpe (1981).

---

64 WHITE-HEADED LAPWING *Vanellus albiceps*　　　Plate 25

Other names: White-headed Plover, White-crowned or Black-shouldered Wattled Plover/Lapwing
A very strongly-marked African lapwing, perhaps similar in ecology to the River Lapwing (61) of India.

IDENTIFICATION One of the easiest lapwings to identify, since it has several striking diagnostic characters and is strictly a waterside bird. Most obvious features are a brilliant white stripe along centre of crown from bill to nape, very long pendant greenish-yellow wattles from base of bill, a broad white band above the folded wing, and contrasting black wing-coverts. In flight, wings are mainly white above except for the outer 3 primaries, which are black, and a large squarish black area formed by the outer coverts; the underwing is strikingly white. The tail shows a broad terminal black band. At a distance might be mistaken for race *leucoptera* of Long-toed Lapwing (58), which also has mainly-white wings but lacks the black wrist-patches and white on the scapulars. **Bare parts:** Bill yellow, with black outer third. Long, pointed, greenish-yellow rictal wattles. Iris yellow. Legs yellowish-green. Very long and sharp black carpal spur, often over 2 cm.

VOICE Very noisy and aggressive when breeding. Usual note is a rapidly-repeated piping 'keep' or 'peep' recalling Eurasian Oystercatcher (12); also a loud 'whit-whit' in alarm.

HABITS Restricted in habitat largely to mud or sand-banks along larger rivers and the immediate vicinity. Avoids estuaries and coasts. Rarely seen away from water, but may remain if river dries up; in flood conditions more likely to be seen on margins of still water. Nests usually on a sandbank or exposed shingle in the river during dry seasons: Feb-May in Nigeria, but July-Oct in Zambia. Nests on lakeshores in some localities. Highly aggressive behaviour and displays of boldly-pied wings are normally sufficient to prevent trampling by hippos and buffaloes. Adults carry water to the nest, by soaking their belly feathers, to cool the eggs. Well scattered and territorial when nesting, but gathers in small parties at other seasons, up to 30 together. Behaviour is generally nervous; takes flight readily and rarely allows close approach.

MOVEMENTS Mainly sedentary, but locally migratory during flood conditions, moving upriver or retreating to wetlands on higher ground.

DESCRIPTION Breeding and non-breeding: Head and neck clean ash-grey, except for bold white forehead and central crown-stripe (sometimes narrowly bordered blackish), small white spot below and in front of eye, and narrow white stripe from chin to breast. Grey continues from sides of neck onto sides of upper breast, but underparts otherwise white. Entire underside of wing is white except for black tips to outer 3 primaries. Upper mantle is grey, continuous with hindneck, then narrowly blackish, then white, then brown on lower mantle. Back feathers, normally overlain by the mantle and scapulars, are curiously silvery-white; lower back shows a short black bar. Rump, uppertail and base of tail are white, but tail-tip shows a broad black terminal band. Scapulars and tertials are brown like lower mantle, but outer scapulars are broadly white bordering wing-coverts.

Inner lesser, median and greater coverts show a mixture of black and white, with brown suffusion on some larger feathers; outer coverts are solidly black with slight bluish gloss. Secondaries, primary coverts and primaries are white, except for the outer 3 primaries which from above are largely black. **Juvenile:** Like adult in pattern, but with less white on crown and throat. Outer coverts are brownish, not black, and show buffish-white fringes. The upperparts are mottled indistinctly with pale buff and brown. Spurs and wattles are initially very small. Primaries are paler and more pointed than those of adult.

AGE/SEX Juveniles quickly undergo post-juvenile body moult and subsequently differ from adults only in worn and pointed primaries. The carpal spur grows rapidly to adult length. Sexes are similar; the breadth of the dark border to the crown-stripe has been suggested as a distinguishing character, but seems variable in both sexes.

RACES No geographical variation is known.

MEASUREMENTS Length about 280-320 mm (11¾"). Wing 205-230 mm; bill 30-35 mm; tarsus 70-81 mm; tail 90-105 mm.

REFERENCES Reynolds (1968), Begg and Maclean (1976), Tarboton and Nel (1980).

65 SENEGAL PLOVER *Vanellus lugubris*   Plate 26

Other name: Lesser Black-winged Plover
The common name invites confusion with Senegal Wattled Plover (68), but closest affinities are clearly with Black-winged (66). A plains plover.

IDENTIFICATION This and Black-winged Plover are rather plain lapwings with plumage pattern somewhat like an oversized Common Sandpiper (148). Head and upperparts are brownish. Breast is brown, rest of underparts white with a white 'peak' between breast and folded wing. Small size, darker upperparts and plain crown are ready distinctions from Crowned Lapwing (67), with which it often occurs. Caspian Plover (109) is smaller and slimmer, with an obvious supercilium and no white peak. At rest, easiest distinctions from Black-winged are slimmer outline, longer legs, and slight green tinge to the upperparts; white above bill usually forms a small discrete patch, less broad than the eye-to-bill distance, as opposed to Black-winged's larger, more diffuse one. Senegal Plover never shows more than a small patch of white towards rear of folded wing. In flight, note that white bar is on trailing edge of wing, coverts being all-brown and secondaries all-white; also, edges of tail are white not black. Both species have underwing mostly white, but Senegal has under primary coverts brown.
Bare parts: Bill black, shorter and stouter than in Black-winged Plover. Iris orangey-yellow. Legs reddish-brown.
VOICE A clear melodious whistle 'kitti-kooee', or a shorter 'thi-wit' with accent on the second note. Easily distinguishable with practice from similar calls of Black-winged.
HABITS Typically a bird of dry open areas and agricultural country, often in same areas as Crowned Lapwing; it is attracted to recently-burnt ground, and also shows some preference for the vicinity of water. Nests Sept-Oct in S Africa. Rather scarce in most parts of

range, most often seen in pairs or small groups. In Kenya occurs mostly below 1500 m. Often tame and approachable.
MOVEMENTS Strictly seasonal in occurrence at many localities within its wide range, but the movements are not yet understood. Occasionally appears in Kenyan highlands and other places where it does not breed. Often heard overhead on nocturnal migration.
DESCRIPTION Breeding and non-breeding: Forehead white, chin and throat whitish, rest of head, neck and breast dull brownish-grey; crown is slightly darker grey, and centre of breast cleaner, less brownish. Lower edge of breast is blackish bordering the white of the rest of the underparts; blackish band is less than 1 cm broad. Underwing and axillaries are white, except for brown under primary coverts (lessers show white wedges at the tips). Mantle to upper rump, scapulars, tertials and wing-coverts dark brown with faint greenish sheen; greater coverts are very narrowly tipped white. Secondaries are all-white, except for brown bases to extreme inners and black bases to outers. Primaries black, but with white tips to inner 3-4. Lower rump and uppertail are white. Tail white, but with broad black terminal band on central pair of feathers which becomes much narrower and just subterminal on next three pairs; outer two pairs are almost unmarked white. **Juvenile:** Head and breast pattern less well defined. Upperparts, particularly coverts and tertials, show extensive buff spotting around feather edgings; tertials may be barred with buff at tips. Primaries are browner, narrower and more pointed than on adult, and show fine buff fringes extending to all except outer two feathers.

AGE/SEX After post-juvenile moult, young birds are distinguishable only in the hand by retained buff-fringed inner coverts or worn and pointed brownish primaries. Sexes are similar in plumage and in size.

RACES No geographical variation is known.
MEASUREMENTS Length about 220-260 mm (9½″). Wing 174-186 mm; bill 20-23 mm; tarsus 57-69 mm; tail 66-77 mm.

66 BLACK-WINGED PLOVER *Vanellus melanopterus* Plate 26

Other name: Black-winged Lapwing
A very close relative of Senegal Plover (65), often difficult to distinguish.

IDENTIFICATION This and Senegal Plover are readily distinguished from other African plovers by their plumage colour and pattern, which at rest may recall Common Sandpiper (148). Head, breast and upperparts are brownish, and underparts white with a white 'peak' between breast and folded wing. Crowned Lapwing (67) is similar, but always has a strong and distinctive head pattern. Caspian Plover (109) is a smaller, slimmer bird with an obvious supercilium and no white peak. Separation from Senegal Plover requires care, especially since head and breast patterns of Black-winged are rather variable. Most useful feature is the white on the outer coverts, visible as a white line the full length of the folded wing and as a diagonal white bar across the inner wing in flight. Also note in flight that secondaries (except inner 3) are black-tipped, black of tail extends to edges, and under primary coverts are white not brown. Black-winged is the larger but shorter-legged bird, typically with more black on the lower breast and more white on the forehead; upperparts lack greenish tinges. **Bare parts:** Bill black, fairly slender. Iris yellow; narrow reddish eye-ring. Legs dark reddish.
VOICE Usual call 'kuk-kuk-kooee' or 'che-che-cheereek', rather harsher and more strident than similar calls of Senegal Plover. Noisy when breeding, often alerting game animals to presence of observer.
HABITS Generally similar to Senegal Plover, but in most regions shows a preference for higher altitudes. Has recently been found nesting on the coastal plain of Zululand. Frequently feeds near game animals or domestic cattle, often in loose association with Crowned Lapwing. Much less nervous than Crowned and remarkably tolerant of vehicles or approach on foot. Locally common as a breeding bird, sometimes several pairs together, and may gather in large non-breeding flocks (occasionally thousands). Flight is more agile and delicate than in most African lapwings; flying flocks are tightly grouped and may be mistaken for smaller plover species.
MOVEMENTS Probably less migratory than Senegal Plover, and recorded all year in many E African localities. Performs limited altitudinal movements to adjacent lowlands, reaching coastal plain in Natal and Zululand; vagrant Dar-es-Salaam, coastal Tanzania.

A record in Arabia (the type specimen) is probably erroneous.
DESCRIPTION Breeding and non-breeding: Head, neck and upper breast mainly clean ash-grey, sometimes brown-tinged, but cap is darker, chin and throat white; there is a variable, often diffuse, patch of white above bill, usually broader than the eye-to-bill distance and often merging into whitish lores or a short white supercilium. On lower breast, a black band, often 2-3 cm broad, divides the grey from the white of the rest of the underparts. Underwing-coverts including primary coverts are all-white; the extreme bases of the inner webs of the primaries are also white. Mantle to upper rump, also scapulars, tertials and most of wing-coverts are plain darkish brown. Outer median and greater coverts are white; coverts bordering these are white-tipped, and have a narrow blackish line dividing the white from the brown base. The inner 3 secondaries are almost unmarked white, while the others have increasingly broad black tips. Primaries are black above (the white on the bases of the inner webs is not visible on upperwing surface). Some white may be visible on bases of primary coverts. Lower rump and uppertail are white. Tail is white with broad subterminal black band, becoming slightly narrower towards outer edge of tail; on outer three pairs of feathers, black is often broader on the outer web. **Juvenile:** Head, neck and breast rather pale brown, faintly mottled with buff; darker lower breast-band initially absent. Upperparts show broad buffish fringes to coverts, larger scapulars, and tertials, giving a scaly appearance. Primaries are rather pointed.
AGE/SEX After post-juvenile moult, look for retained buff-fringed coverts or worn and pointed primaries which separate young birds. Sexes are similar in plumage and in size.
RACES Two: nominate *melanopterus* (Ethiopia, Somalia) and *minor* (Kenya to E Cape Province). The race *minor* is smaller, but apparently similar in appearance.
MEASUREMENTS Length about 260-270 mm (10½″). Wing 215-228 mm (nominate), 200-221 mm (*minor*); bill 23-28 mm; tarsus 55-64 mm; tail 68-76 mm (*minor*).
REFERENCES Cyrus (1982), Allan (1983).

Black-winged Plover   Crowned Lapwing   Caspian Plover   Senegal Wattled Plover

67 CROWNED LAPWING *Vanellus coronatus* **Plate 25**

Other name: Crowned Plover
One of the commonest and most widespread of breeding waders in eastern and southern Africa.

IDENTIFICATION An easy lapwing to identify by virtue of its distinctive crown pattern: forehead and supercilia are black, meeting in a sharp 'V' low on nape, and crown centre is black encircled by a brilliant white 'head-band'. A steep, rather bulging forehead enhances the flat-topped appearance of the head. At a distance, the black forehead and horizontal black line above the eye are the most conspicuous features. The pattern is similar but more muted in the juvenile. Apart from crown, the plumage pattern of brown head, breast and upperparts, blackish lower breast-band and white underparts with long white 'peak' between breast and folded wing is similar to that of Senegal and Black-winged Plovers (65, 66), with which it often associates. Both of these, however, are smaller, darker brown and have duller bill and legs. In flight, shows diagonal white bar across secondaries and coverts, like Black-winged and Senegal Wattled (68), but primary coverts and extreme bases of primaries are also white. Flight is considerably slower and heavier than in Senegal or Black-winged. Beware confusion with Violet-tipped Courser (43), especially at night. **Bare parts:** Bill pinkish-red with blackish outer half. Iris orangey-yellow, often dusky bordering the pupil. Legs quite bright pinkish-red.
VOICE A noisy species, with constantly-repeated 'yik' or 'kee-weet' in alarm and a raucous, slow 'kree-kree-kree-kreeip' flight call.
HABITS Typically a bird of arid and semi-arid grasslands, with or without scrub, often seen on cultivated land. Recently-burnt ground is ideal. Avoids the lusher coastal fringe in SE Kenya, but does occur coastally in S Africa. Breeds mostly July-Dec, but June-Mar in S Africa. This lapwing is not strongly territorial and often nests in loose groups; the distance between nests is often less than 50 m, and adults from nearby nests mix freely at all stages of the nesting cycle. Parties of up to ten indulge in prolonged, noisy display flighting over the nesting grounds, particularly towards evening. Sometimes active at night. Sometimes seen singly, but usually in pairs or small flocks, up to 40 or more together. Mixes freely with other plains plovers, notably Black-winged; sometimes seen with wetland lapwings, for example Blacksmith Plover (59).
MOVEMENTS Mainly resident, but performs local movements particularly after breeding. Moves to drier areas during rains.
DESCRIPTION Breeding and non-breeding: Centre of crown black, ringed by a white band; forehead, lores adjacent to bill, and supercilia solidly black. Both white head-band and black supercilia form 'V's on the nape. Chin and throat whitish; rest of face and neck pale fawn brown, becoming darker on breast and ending in a narrow black line on the lower breast. Rest of underparts white, including axillaries and underwing-coverts. Hindneck to upper rump, also scapulars, tertials and inner wing-coverts are fawn-brown. Lower rump and uppertail-coverts white; tail white with black, almost terminal band, which becomes much narrower towards edges of tail. Greater coverts and some outer medians are white-tipped; primary coverts are mostly white, but outers are edged and tipped black; alula is mostly brown. Primaries and secondaries are black, with white at base just visible beyond coverts on most feathers. **Juvenile:** Forehead and forward part of white head-band are heavily marked buffish-brown, so that white 'U' on rear crown is most conspicuous feature of head. Otherwise as adult, but brown of upperparts, wing-coverts and breast is heavily marked with buffish fringes and notches and narrow dark subterminal lines. Primaries 5-9 often have sharp but narrow buffish fringes when fresh.
AGE/SEX Ageing is especially difficult owing to long breeding season in most parts of range. After post-juvenile moult, look for retained median and lesser coverts or pale-edged or heavily-worn and pointed primaries. Sexes are similar in plumage, but males measure about 3% larger on average.
RACES Two are widely accepted: nominate *coronatus* (Ethiopia to S Africa) and *demissus* (Somalia). The race *demissus* is paler and faintly more reddish above, and averages slightly smaller. Namibian breeders are paler and greyer and have been described as a third race *'xerophilus'*.
MEASUREMENTS Length about 300-310 mm (12"). Wing 187-216 mm (nominate), 187-207 mm (*demissus*); bill 26-32 mm; tarsus 60-78 mm; tail 82-101 mm.
REFERENCES Symmes (1952), Skead (1955), Ade (1979).

68 SENEGAL WATTLED PLOVER *Vanellus senegallus* **Plate 25**

Other name: Wattled Plover/Lapwing
A large, widespread lapwing of damp African grasslands.

IDENTIFICATION Mainly stone-brown at rest, but with conspicuous white forehead-patch, whitish lower belly and undertail, black chin and throat, yellowish legs and bicoloured wattles. In flight, has a diagonal white band across the inner wing. Rather larger than other African plovers with similar wing pattern. Note contrast between brown flanks and white axillaries. The only other African wader with pendant wattles is White-headed Lapwing (64), which also has a white forehead, but it is easily distinguished by its much whiter plumage and conspicuous black wrist-patches. Plumage is unlike any other African vanellid, but beware confusion with stone-curlews, particularly Spotted Dikkop (34). Yellow-wattled Lap-

wing (63) of India and Masked Lapwing (80) of Australasia show similarities, but both have a whiter breast and a neat black cap. **Bare parts:** Bill yellow with black at tip: a solid black tip on southern race *lateralis*, but on other races black is restricted to the ridge of the upper mandible. Large wattles between eye and bill, mainly yellow but red above the level of the eye; fleshy yellow eye-ring joins wattle. Iris pale yellow, with a variable inner band of pale grey bordering the pupil; sometimes the grey and yellow are separated by a blackish ring giving a 'roundel' or 'bull's-eye' effect. Legs bright yellow, sometimes tinged greenish. Sharp black spur on carpal joint. **VOICE** Commonest calls are based on a shrill, piping 'peep-peep'. In alarm, 'kee-weep' or a repeated 'yip-yip'. Often calls at night.
HABITS Typically, a bird of soggy grasslands on the fringes of marshes or river floodplains. Always breeds near water, but may feed in drier habitats nearby including cultivated land, burnt grassland or rocky slopes. Nesting season is Mar-June in northern part of range, Sept-Dec in south. Territorial behaviour is strong and pairs are normally widely scattered. Parties rarely reach double figures. Not a shy bird, often allowing close approach, even nesting near busy roads.
MOVEMENTS Apparently sedentary in some areas, but strictly seasonal elsewhere, depending on rains. An occasional visitor to parts of Kenya and Tanzania east of breeding range. In Transvaal, arrives at breeding areas in early Sept and departs in late Mar. Vagrant south to Port Elizabeth, E Cape Province.
DESCRIPTION Breeding and non-breeding: Forehead and forecrown white bordered blackish-brown. Chin, throat and front of neck solidly black, rest of face and neck streaked blackish-brown on a pale brownish background. Breast, flanks and upper belly darkish fawn-brown. Lower belly, vent and undertail whitish. Race *lateralis* has blackish-brown band across belly and rear flanks. Axillaries and underwing-coverts white. Mantle to upper rump, also scapulars and tertials, darkish brown with faint greenish tinge. Lesser coverts and inner medians as mantle, but greater coverts and outer medians rather paler; greaters and outermost medians are white-tipped. Secondaries black, with white at base; primaries and primary coverts black, although primaries show some white at bases of inner webs (not visible from above). Lower rump and uppertail-coverts white. Tail white at base and tip, but with a broad black band which is edged brownish proximally and at tips of central feathers. **Juvenile:** Almost exactly as adult, except for small wattles and striking differences in head pattern. White on crown heavily obscured with brownish streaking. Black throat-patch completely lacking: this area is white with faint brown streaks. Streaking on neck much paler and browner than in adult. This species is unusual in that juvenile shows hardly any buff fringes on the upperparts and wing-coverts; a few narrow fringes are present initially on the median coverts, but disappear rapidly. Primaries slightly narrower than on adults.
AGE/SEX Obscured white crown and whitish throat are diagnostic of young birds, but after the post-juvenile body moult latter become virtually impossible to distinguish from adults. Sexes are similar in plumage and in size.
RACES Three are generally recognised: nominate *senegallus* (Senegal to Sudan and N Uganda), *major* (Ethiopia) and *lateralis* (E Zaire, S Uganda and W Kenya to N Namibia and Natal). The first two are effectively identical, although *major* may average slightly larger. The race *lateralis* differs in having a blackish-brown bar across the belly and a solid dark bill-tip. The population breeding in the western half of the range of *lateralis* has recently been referred to a fourth race '*solitaneus*'.
MEASUREMENTS Length about 340 mm (13½"). Wing 222-252 mm; bill 30-37 mm; tarsus 75-96 mm; tail 96-107 mm.
REFERENCES Little (1967).

69 SPOT-BREASTED PLOVER *Vanellus melanocephalus*   Plate 27

Other name: Spot-breasted Lapwing
A beautifully-marked lapwing restricted to the northern and central Ethiopian highlands.

IDENTIFICATION At rest, easily distinguished by unique spotted breast-band combined with black cap and throat-patch, yellow wattles and bill-base and shortish yellow legs. Black crest normally overlies hindneck. In flight, shows a broad diagonal white band across the wing, dividing brown coverts from black flight feathers, but a rather narrower black tail-band than other Ethiopian lapwings of similar wing pattern: Spur-winged (60), Black-winged (66) and Senegal Wattled (68). Most unlikely to be encountered away from its upland habitat and restricted range. **Bare parts:** Bill black; yellow patch at base of upper mandible, triangular viewed from above, covering almost half the culmen ridge and broadening at base to reach cutting edges. Small, oval, pale yellow wattle above and in front of eye, joining dull yellow eye-ring. Iris pale yellow or yellowish-grey. Legs shortish, clear pale yellow. Carpal spur short, does not break the feathering.
VOICE Calls are reported to include a 'pewit' not unlike Northern Lapwing's (57). Also a longer 'kree-kree-kre-krep-kreep-kreep'.
HABITS Found on marshy grasslands and moorlands, mostly above 3000 m. Not particularly rare within its range. Breeding is reported for Apr and for Aug; nest was undescribed until 1972. After breeding, may gather in flocks of up to 40. Actions generally recall Northern Lapwing's. Often tame and approachable.
MOVEMENTS Apparently entirely sedentary.
DESCRIPTION Breeding and non-breeding: Forehead to lower nape solidly black with faint bluish sheen; long feathers of lower nape form a loose crest which overlies the feathers of the hindneck. White supercilium from just in front of eye to sides of nape. Chin, throat and front of neck solidly black. Lores, sides of face and neck, also hindneck, pale greyish-

brown. Breast grey-brown at sides, but most feathers white with bold black shaft-streak forming a spotted breast-band. Rest of underparts white, including underwing. Mantle to upper rump, also scapulars, tertials and inner wing-coverts brown, slightly darker than neck, with faint greenish tinge. Lower rump and uppertail-coverts white, tail white with narrow black subterminal band across all feathers. Greater coverts, also outermost medians and lessers are white. Secondaries black, with white bases broadening rapidly towards body; inner secondaries almost all white. Primaries and primary coverts black. **Juven-**

ile: No information is available.
AGE/SEX Since juvenile plumage has never been described, no information can be given about ageing; techniques for related species may be useful. Sexes are similar in plumage and probably also in size.
RACES No geographical variation is known.
MEASUREMENTS Length about 340 mm (13½"). Wing 227-246 mm; bill 25-27 mm; tarsus 58-63 mm. Only five specimens measured.
REFERENCES Urban *et al.* (1972).

70 BROWN-CHESTED PLOVER *Vanellus superciliosus*　　　Plate 27

Other names: Brown-chested Wattled Plover, Brown-chested Lapwing
A small, rather uncommon lapwing, the only one with well-defined intra-African migrations.

IDENTIFICATION Combination of yellow wattles and rufous forehead and breast-band is diagnostic. No other lapwing has a rufous breast-band, but beware confusion with Caspian Plover (109), which has breast rufous in breeding plumage but lacks wattles and black cap and has face mainly white. In flight, Brown-chested shows a short, white, diagonal bar across the wing, not reaching the leading edge, and a broad black tail-band which tapers rapidly towards the outer feathers; size and wing pattern recall Black-winged (66), but these two species are not known to overlap in range. **Bare parts:** Bill black, with small yellowish patch at base of lower mandible. Small yellow wattle on lores, extending upwards slightly above eye. Iris yellow. Legs darkish grey or reddish-brown.
VOICE Calls are shrill and penetrating. Usual flight call is described as like the squeaking of a rusty hinge.
HABITS Breeds in dry grassy W African savannas during Dec-Apr, including bushed 'orchard bush' country. Eggs are laid often on burnt ground where nest will be safe from fire. After breeding, gather in flocks of up to 50 and gain weight for migration. Off-season, July-Dec, is spent in central or E Africa, on grasslands or lakeshores; burnt ground is attractive to feeding birds. Often in small flocks, sometimes singly or with Senegal Plover (65).
MOVEMENTS Apparently a strong migrant, departing entirely from W African breeding grounds by early June, returning early Dec. E African records are all for July-Dec, especially Aug-Oct, except for one Apr vagrant in S coastal Tanzania. No Kenyan records east of Lake Victoria basin. Vagrant recently to Mwinilunga, NW Zambia.
DESCRIPTION Breeding and non-breeding: Fore-

head and short supercilia pale chestnut. Crown and nape black with faint bluish gloss; longish feathers on nape overlie upper hindneck. Chin whitish; rest of face, neck and upper breast ash-grey, sometimes tinged brownish. Central and lower breast shows variable rich chestnut-brown breast-band, broadest in centre of breast; sometimes sides of breast or extreme lower fringe of breast-band are ash-grey. Rest of underparts, including underwing, are clean white. Mantle to upper rump, also scapulars, tertials and wing-coverts greenish-brown; larger feathers show irregular rufous edgings when fresh. Lower rump and uppertail-coverts white. Tail white with black terminal band, which becomes narrower and just subterminal towards edges of tail and may not reach outer feathers. Greater coverts and outer median coverts are white-tipped. Secondaries black with white bases; primaries and primary coverts black. **Juvenile:** Wattles small. Iris dull brown. Black cap absent, but replaced by brown which is slightly darker than rest of head. Grey and chestnut of head and neck largely replaced by dull grey-brown, although some feathers of lower breast may be tipped chestnut. Rufous fringes on upperparts and coverts are much more extensive than those of adult; brown cap may also show rufous fringes. Primaries rather pointed.
AGE/SEX Juvenile may still be recognisable after migration in Aug or later. Sexes are similar in plumage and in size.
RACES No geographical variation is known.
MEASUREMENTS Length about 230 mm (9"). Wing 184-199 mm; bill 19-22 mm; tarsus 53-60 mm.
REFERENCES Serle (1956).

71 SOCIABLE PLOVER *Vanellus gregarius*　　　Plate 22

Other name: Sociable Lapwing
This is a strongly migratory lapwing in which the breeding and wintering ranges are entirely separate. It is one of the few with separate breeding and non-breeding plumages. It is listed in the *Red Data Book* of the USSR as a declining species.

IDENTIFICATION A rather plain, pale brown bird for most of the year, but striking in breeding plumage. Bold supercilia may suggest an outsize Eurasian Dotterel (120) rather than a lapwing; also like former, has

a black-and-chestnut belly-patch in breeding plumage. Confusion is possible with Caspian Plover (109) and with Eurasian or Pacific Golden Plovers (81, 82). More obviously a vanellid in flight, when shows fairly broad wings with contrast of black primaries and unmarked white secondaries, and mainly white tail with black subterminal band (not reaching outer feathers). Closest relative is probably White-tailed Plover (72), which has longer, conspicuously yellow legs, much less obvious supercilia, and no black in tail. Vagrants in flocks of Northern Lapwing (57) can be picked out at long range by faster wingbeats, smaller size and proportionately longer and narrower wings; when closer, note white secondaries, lack of breast-band, projection of feet beyond tail, and absence of white near primary tips. **Bare parts:** Bill black, rather short and slender. Iris dark brown. Legs black, sometimes tinged greyish or brownish.

VOICE Noisy when breeding, mainly an aggressive, harsh, trisyllabic 'krech-krech-krech' or monosyllabic 'reck' or 'kjek'; when mobbing, these notes may run together into a sharp rattle. In winter relatively quiet.

HABITS Nests Apr-July, chiefly in ecotone between grassland and *Artemisia* scrub, often but not always near water. Nests sometimes singly, but usually in loose semi-colonial groups of up to two dozen pairs with nests 20-50 m apart; each pair defends its own small territory. No aerial display is known, but males in early spring indulge in prolonged group displays on the ground. During post-nuptial moult, gathers into large flocks, sometimes over a thousand. In winter, feeds on grassland, ploughed and stubble fields, sometimes near water; occurs rarely in intertidal habitats. Usually seen in flocks. Vagrants in Europe associate with Northern Lapwing.

MOVEMENTS Leaves all parts of breeding area during Aug-Nov, spending Oct-early Apr in winter quarters. There are three separate wintering areas, but relatively few reach NE Africa, probably via Iraq and Arabia. Return passage begins in early Mar. Westward vagrancy across Europe is frequent; there are at least 75 separate records, mostly in spring and autumn passage periods (autumn vagrants often spend the winter). There are records for most European countries west to Spain and Ireland, but none yet from Scandinavia; vagrant also Morocco, Malta, E Mediterranean, Somalia (once), Masirah Is., Kuwait, S India,

Maldive Is. and Sri Lanka.

DESCRIPTION Breeding: Forehead and long supercilia white or creamy-white; supercilia are broadest behind the eye and just meet on nape. Lores narrowly blackish, prominent dark posterior eye-stripe. Crown blackish; ear-coverts and sides of face and upper neck yellowish-buff. Mantle to upper rump, scapulars, tertials and wing-coverts plain grey-brown; coverts initially have pale sandy fringes. Primaries black, secondaries white. Lower rump and uppertail-coverts are white; tail is white, with blackish subterminal band on central four pairs of feathers. Chin and throat are pale yellowish-buff; breast and base of neck brownish-grey or greyish; belly extensively black, but becoming dark chestnut towards rear belly; undertail-coverts white. Underwing-coverts and axillaries are white, contrasting with black primaries. **Non-breeding:** Crown is dull grey-brown, supercilia dull buffish, and loral line less distinct. Upperparts initially broadly edged dull sandy-brown, but this soon wears off. Throat is white and sides of face pale buffish; breast feathers have pale greyish-brown centres and are fringed paler, giving a mottled appearance. Belly white. **Juvenile:** As non-breeding, but upperparts show grey-brown feather centres, darkish brown subterminal bars and buff fringes; these give a strongly-streaked appearance to the crown and a rather scaly mantle and wings. The breast feathers are similarly patterned; the darker subterminal bars form distinct 'V' marks.

AGE/SEX Juvenile becomes virtually indistinguishable from adult after Nov. First-years normally do not attain full breeding plumage: belly is often white with dark flecks. Sexes similar, but males in breeding plumage tend to have more solidly-black crown and belly, more chestnut on belly and a greyer infusion to the breast. Males average faintly larger.

RACES No geographical variation is known.

MEASUREMENTS Length 270-300 mm (11¼"). Wing 194-221 mm; bill 25-33 mm; tarsus 54-64 mm; tail 75-91 mm.

REFERENCES Chekmenev (1961), Riley and Rooke (1962), Khrokov (1978), van den Berg (1984).

72 WHITE-TAILED PLOVER *Vanellus leucurus* Plate 22

Other name: White-tailed Lapwing
A remarkably elegant, long-legged lapwing which often feeds in deep water. Winter distribution is like that of its close relative, the Sociable Plover (70), but the breeding areas are more southerly.

IDENTIFICATION This medium-sized, slim lapwing is easily identified by its very pale whitish face, greyish breast, pale brown crown and upperparts, and very long yellow legs. In flight, it shows a large white band from the secondaries across to the primary coverts and, uniquely for a plover, a pure white tail. Upright stance and pale face are good fieldmarks. This is the only lapwing likely to be seen feeding persistently in deep water or submerging its head while feeding. May be confused with non-breeding or juvenile Sociable Plover, but latter, apart from preferring drier habitats, has a well-marked dark eye-stripe and pale supercilium, a black tail-band, no white on carpal area, and black legs. **Bare parts:** Bill black, relatively long and slender. Iris reddish-brown or brown; nar-

row reddish or pinkish eye-ring. Legs very long, bright yellow; part of tarsus as well as toes projects beyond the tail in flight.

VOICE Noisy when breeding, but rather silent for much of year. Spring calls include a loud, mellow 'pet-oo-wit', the second syllable starting lower but rising in pitch, not unlike part of spring song of Northern Lapwing (57). In winter, 'pee-wick' or 'kwie-wuk', again recalling Northern Lapwing but quieter, less strident.

HABITS Rarely found far from margins of shallow, still or slow-flowing water. Nests Apr-June, often in semi-colonial groups of up to two dozen (USSR) or several hundred pairs (Iraq); nest-spacing may be only a few metres. Often nests in loose association with other colonial waterside birds such as Black-winged Stilt (24) and Common Pratincole (50). Feeds on land at times, but mostly in shallow water; usually pecks at items on surface, but in deeper water occasionally submerges its head. Walks rather delicately, but is less graceful than a stilt. Gregarious; seen mostly in small flocks, sometimes with stilts or *Tringa* sandpipers. Vagrants in Europe may associate with Northern Lapwings, but choose largely different feeding areas.

MOVEMENTS Iraqi and Iranian breeders are probably mostly sedentary, but northern parts of Iraqi range are vacated in winter. Populations in USSR are migratory, leaving during Aug-Sept to spend Sept-Mar in winter quarters in NE Africa, Middle East or Pakistan/N India; occasional individuals winter in S USSR. Return passage occurs in Mar-Apr. Compared with Sociable Plover, routes to and from Africa are probably more westerly, and is more frequently seen around Persian Gulf. Less given to westward vagrancy, but has occurred across Europe north to Finland and west to England, Sweden and France. Vagrant also Cyprus, Malta, Libya, Tunisia and once Nigeria (six on shore of Lake Chad, Jan 1969). Has nested recently in Syria, Turkey and Azerbaydzhan, perhaps indicating some westward spread.

DESCRIPTION Breeding and non-breeding: Crown and nape pale brownish-grey; forehead, lores, chin, supercilia (indistinct) and sides of face whitish; ear-coverts and hindneck pale creamy-grey. Upperparts greyish-brown with a lilac sheen, but median and greater coverts greyer; there are black subterminal bands and broad white tips to outer median and all greater coverts. Similar markings are present, but less prominent, on the largest scapulars. Alula and primary coverts white. Primaries mostly black, but bases of inner feathers are white; secondaries are white, but outers are tipped black. Lower rump, uppertail-coverts and tail white. Breast strongly grey, often slightly infused brown; lower breast and upper belly are washed rosy-buff. Rest of underparts white. Underwing-coverts and axillaries white, contrasting with black primaries. **Juvenile:** Crown is mottled with dark brown feather centres and bold bright buff fringes. On mantle and scapulars, very dark feather centres or broad subterminal bars contrast strongly with yellowish-buff fringes and blotches. Upperwing-coverts rather greyer than on adult, with buff fringes and dark subterminal bars. Tail white, with tiny pale brownish subterminal band and narrow buffish tip. Neck is paler than on adult; both neck and breast are mottled brownish-grey and whitish.

AGE/SEX Juvenile is very difficult to distinguish after Oct, except in the hand. Sexes are identical, except that males tend to have breast more uniformly grey; male averages slightly larger than female.

RACES No geographical variation is known.

MEASUREMENTS Length 260-290 mm (10¾"). Wing 168-187 mm; bill 26-32 mm; tarsus 63-78 mm; tail 67-81 mm.

REFERENCES Dean *et al.* (1977), Pettet (1982).

73 PIED PLOVER *Vanellus cayanus*   Plate 30

Other names: Pied Lapwing, Cayenne Plover
A strongly-patterned South American plover of uncertain affinities. It is usually placed with the lapwings, but many features are similar to those of the ringed plovers *Charadrius*. Sometimes given its own genus, *Hoploxypterus*.

IDENTIFICATION The broad black forehead, white throat and neck, black breast-band and white belly form a pattern unique among South American plovers. Some individuals may show a trace of white on the forehead, thus recalling Semipalmated and Collared Plovers (87,103), but are easily distinguished by their long reddish legs, white ring surrounding the brown centre to the crown, black and white 'V' across the upperparts, and lapwing-like pattern in flight. Much smaller than the other two South American lapwings, Southern and Andean (74,75), and quite different in plumage pattern. **Bare parts:** Bill black, tinged pinkish at base. Iris grey or pinkish; eye-ring bright pinkish-red. Legs quite long, bright orange-red or pinkish-red; toes project beyond the tail-tip in flight. Adults have a sharp carpal spur.

VOICE A pleasant disyllabic whistle, 'kee-oo', with the second syllable lower in pitch; when flushed, may give a slightly sharper and shorter call. During the undulating display flight a short version, 'kiee', is repeated frequently.

HABITS Found throughout the year in savannas and low ground around rivers in the forested zones of South America. Often seen on sandbars in rivers or sandy riverbanks, normally singly or in pairs but occasionally gathers in small flocks. Feeds plover-like on insects and small molluscs.

MOVEMENTS Appears to be entirely sedentary.

DESCRIPTION Breeding and non-breeding: Top of crown greyish-brown, completely encircled by a white band. Forehead, lores, whole of side and back of head, hindneck, upper mantle and breast-band black with slight purplish gloss; ear-coverts faintly tinged brown. Some individuals show a trace of white above the bill. Chin, throat and upper breast form a clear white area completely encircled by black. Mantle and back greyish-brown, bounded laterally by a narrow white 'V' on the outer mantle and inner half of the scapulars; the black outer half of the scapulars forms another, broader, 'V' outside the white one. White rump, uppertail, base of tail, and sides to lower back contrast with a broad black terminal tail-band; there is some brown at the junction of the black and white on the tail. Tail-band decreases in width towards the edges of the tail, and the outermost tail feathers are usually all-white. Lesser coverts, inner median and greater coverts, and tertials are brown; this colour contrasts with a large white central patch in wing formed by white outer median and greater coverts, most of the secondaries, bases of the inner primaries, and inner primary coverts. Outer primaries and primary coverts are black. On the closed wing, the white forms a broad curved band. Underparts and underwing-coverts are white. **Juvenile:** As adult, but face mask is strongly tinged brown, the black scapular lines are obscured, and the breast-band is dusky-grey. Coverts and scapulars are brown, with pale cinnamon-buff fringes.

AGE/SEX Immatures can be distinguished initially by their poorly-marked scapulars and breast-band. Later,

they may resemble adults except for a few retained buff-fringed inner median coverts. No differences are known between the sexes.

RACES No geographical variation is known.

MEASUREMENTS Length 210-240 mm (8¾"). Wing 138-153 mm; bill 20-25 mm; tarsus 43-47 mm; tail 55-71 mm.

REFERENCES Friedmann and Smith (1955).

74 SOUTHERN LAPWING *Vanellus chilensis*   Plate 30

Other name: Chilean Lapwing
The most familiar and widespread of South America's endemic waders. One of the world's three lapwings with upstanding crests.

IDENTIFICATION The only crested wader in South America. The four races vary somewhat in plumage details, but all are easily identified by black or blackish crest, face, throat and breast-band. Larger than Pied Plover (73) and Andean Lapwing (75) and considerably more abundant and widespread. Avoids forested zones and the high Andes, where the other lapwings are based. In flight, has deep beats of broad, rounded wings, showing extensive white across the inner half; best distinguished from Andean by broad black breast-band contrasting with white underwing, and broader black tail-band. Legs are longer than Andean's; toes project beyond the tail-tip in flight. **Bare parts:** Bill blackish at tip, with purplish-pink basal half. Iris and eye-ring pinkish-crimson. Legs longish, deep purplish-red. A sharp reddish spur on the carpal joint.

VOICE A very noisy bird, quick to raise the alarm with characteristically penetrating and strident calls: these are based on a harsh barking 'tee-ow' and a shorter 'pi-up', often rapidly repeated. When flushed, a loud harsh 'parp-peup-peup-peup' is almost always given. Calls of southern and southwestern races are slightly harsher and higher-pitched than those of northern birds.

HABITS Breeds in lowland grassland throughout tropical and temperate zones. Reaches high densities on Argentinian pampas and on seasonally-flooded grassland in the tropics. Also nests on ploughed fields. Breeding season is chiefly Apr-July in Venezuela, but in southern latitudes nests during the austral summer. There is a slow-flapping display flight. Highly aggressive in defence of eggs and chicks. Normally monogamous, but at high density may indulge in co-operative breeding in which groups of three or four birds defend a single territory; Southern Lapwing is the only wader in which two individuals of the same sex have been found caring for the same clutch of eggs. When not breeding, range of habitats extends to include inland and coastal wetlands, where often gathers in flocks of up to 200. Feeds almost exclusively on insects, worms and other soil invertebrates.

MOVEMENTS Largely sedentary in the tropics, although with some post-breeding dispersal. Vagrants have reached Trinidad on occasion, also W Ecuador. The southern races *chilensis* and *fretensis* are partly migratory, withdrawing from the colder parts of the range during the southern winter. A vagrant to the Falkland Is. in spring and autumn (seen most years) and to the Juan Fernandez Is.

DESCRIPTION Breeding and non-breeding: For racial variations see below. Crest blackish; forehead and throat blackish, variably outlined by white. Rest of head evenly coloured bluish- or brownish-grey. Broad blackish breast-band, rest of underparts white. Mantle grey-brown with bronzey sheen, strong on some. Rump and uppertail-coverts show fairly narrow band of white, tail mostly black with distinct but narrow white tip. Wing pattern complex: outer lesser coverts purple, forming dark patch on anterior part of closed wing; inner median coverts and inner greater coverts greenish-brown; scapulars brown, tertials brownish-grey; white patch on outer median and greater coverts, extending as a silvery band across inner secondaries; rest of secondaries, primaries and primary coverts black. **Juvenile:** As adult, but patterning less distinct. Forehead is browner with feathers tipped pale, and throat line is indistinct; the white areas around these are tinged buff. The crest is slightly shorter, and the spur short and blunt. The breast-band is sooty-brown, and the coverts, mantle, scapulars and tertials are brown, fringed buff and indistinctly barred towards their tips with sepia and dull buff. Central tail feathers are tipped buff, not white.

AGE/SEX After post-juvenile body moult, immatures can still be distinguished by worn, pale and pointed primaries and rather worn tail feathers. Males are slightly larger than females on average, but no consistent differences are known between the sexes.

RACES Four are commonly recognised: *cayennensis* (N South America, south to Amazon River), *lampronotus* (most of range, from Amazon south to northernmost Argentina and N Chile), nominate *chilensis* (Argentina and Chile south to the line joining Chiloe I. and Comodoro Rivadavia) and *fretensis* (southernmost Chile and Argentina). The race *tretensis* differs from *chilensis* only in being slightly smaller, and may not warrant subspecific status. Three groups can be distinguished on head pattern.

1) *cayennesis*: head cinnamon-brown, black throat does not join breast-band, white extensive on crown and face. 3) *lampronotus*: head brownish-grey, black stripe on throat joins breast-band, only a faint whitish band on crown. 3) *chilensis/fretensis*: head blue-grey, full throat stripe, narrow but clear white band on crown, short crest. Southern breeders are longer-winged but shorter-legged than those in the north.

MEASUREMENTS Length 310-380 mm (13½"). Wing 217-237 mm (*cayennensis*), 226-240 mm (*lampronotus*), 238-267 mm (nominate), 232-252 mm (*fretensis*); bill 26-35 mm; tarsus 70-85 mm (*cayennensis*), 66-77 mm (*lampronotus*), 60-80 mm (nominate), 57-67 mm (*fretensis*); tail 89-130 mm.
REFERENCES Myers (1978), Walters and Walters (1980).

75 ANDEAN LAPWING *Vanellus resplendens*   Plate 30

A pale-headed lapwing with strongly glossy plumage, found at high altitude in the central and northern parts of the Andes.

IDENTIFICATION Slightly smaller than the Southern Lapwing (74), which it replaces at high altitude. Easily distinguished by contrastingly pale head and neck, lacking Southern's black crest, face and breast-band. In addition, has very glossy green upperparts, a conspicuous purple patch on the wing-coverts and, in flight, white confined to a diagonal bar across the inner half of the wing. **Bare parts:** Bill rather slender and pointed, dark brown with reddish basal half. Iris pink. Legs pink, rather short for a lapwing, and toes do not project beyond tail-tip in flight. Small spur on carpal joint, projecting 2-3 mm beyond the feathering.
VOICE A soft querulous call. In alarm, a sharp 'wik', or similar disyllabic call, often repeated rapidly and noisily as a group mobs a raptor or human intruder near the nest.
HABITS Rather poorly known. In the breeding season, chiefly Nov-Apr, common in open grassy areas of the temperate and puna zones of the Andes, usually near freshwater lakes and rivers. Avoids saline lakes and marshes. Nests among grasses or on barren stony areas, chiefly from 3000 m to 4500 m. During the austral winter, may be found at much lower altitudes and even on the coast.
MOVEMENTS Almost sedentary in some areas, but performs altitudinal migrations, descending during the southern winter. Records at low altitude are few, but has been seen at 300 m in E Ecuador Feb-July, and on the Peruvian coast May-Sept.
DESCRIPTION Breeding and non-breeding: Whole head and neck pale creamy-brown with just a hint of grey; nape and hindneck greyer; lores, area around eye and ear-coverts dusky-brown, forming an indistinct mask. Breast grey, merging into creamy throat above but bordered below by a sharp, slightly darker grey line against the white of the lower breast, belly and flanks. Mantle and scapulars strongly glossed green; leading lesser coverts are also green, but rest of lesser coverts are strikingly purple. Median coverts mostly white; greater coverts, inner secondaries and bases of outer secondaries brilliant white, contrasting with black triangle of primaries, primary coverts and distal parts of outer secondaries. Tertials brownish-green, with less of a metallic sheen. On the closed wing, this pattern results in a sharp, dark purplish and clear white band separating the green mantle from the white breast. A squarish white patch covers the rump, uppertail-coverts and the base of the tail, contrasting with a broad brownish-black subterminal band and a narrow white tip to the tail. The central tail feathers are tipped buff-brown. **Juvenile:** Shows a pale creamy head like the adult, but the breast is creamy with only a slight grey wash. Breast feathers are initially buff-tipped. All feathers of wing-coverts, mantle, scapulars and tertials dull brownish-green, with narrow pale buff fringes and a dark greenish submarginal band. Tertial tips show a small, irregular, pale buff spot inside the submarginal band.
AGE/SEX Immatures are not known to be distinguishable from adults after post-juvenile body moult. No differences are known between the sexes.
RACES No geographical variation is known.
MEASUREMENTS Length 330-360 mm (13½"). Wing 210-233 mm; bill 27-32 mm; tarsus 47-56 mm; tail 94-117 mm.
REFERENCES Johnson (1965).

76 GREY-HEADED LAPWING *Vanellus cinereus*   Plate 23

This is the largest of the Palaearctic lapwings and is a strong migrant.

IDENTIFICATION A large, heavily-built lapwing with conspicuously bicoloured bill and bright yellow legs, but rather plain grey and brown plumage. The head and neck are entirely grey or brownish-grey, the breast grey often with a darker band across the lower part, the upperparts brown and the underparts otherwise white. In flight, shows a bold white wing-patch encompassing carpal area and entire secondaries; white tail has a fairly narrow black subterminal band. Not likely to be confused with other lapwings, except possibly White-tailed Plover (72), with which it might overlap in NE India. White-tailed is smaller, slimmer and paler and has a longish black bill and no wattles; in flight, it has white primary coverts, black-tipped outer secondaries, and no tail-band. **Bare parts:** Bill yellow with sharply-defined black terminal third. Small yellow wattles above bill-base. Iris conspicuously red; narrow yellow eye-ring. Legs bright yellow; in flight, toes project only partly (about two-thirds of middle toe) beyond tail-tip. There is a very short carpal spur.
VOICE A plaintive 'chee-it' is normal contact call;

when disturbed or agitated, a rasping 'cha-ha-eet' and a sharp 'pink'. Often not very vocal in winter.

HABITS Nests Apr-July in marshland edges, swampy grassland and rice-paddies. Strongly territorial, noisy and aggressive when breeding. Uses same habitats in winter, but sometimes occurs on drier agricultural land or short grass. Gregarious outside the breeding season; often in mixed groups with other lapwings or smaller plovers. Feeds often in shallow water, mainly on insects, worms and molluscs.

MOVEMENTS Whole mainland population departs southward to spend Sept-Apr in NE Oriental region, west to Calcutta and Katmandu. Those breeding in Japan leave northern parts of range, but many winter in S Honshu; extent of mixing with continental populations is unknown. Vagrant northward in USSR to Transbaikalia and Vladivostoc, westward to Kashmir, and south to Andaman Is., Malaysia, Philippines, Borneo and Sulawesi.

DESCRIPTION Breeding: Head and neck plain pale slate-grey, sometimes tinged brownish. Mantle to upper rump, scapulars and tertials uniform brown, but outer medians white and greater coverts tipped white. Secondaries white. Primaries black. Lower rump and uppertail-coverts white; tail white, but with blackish subterminal band which is broadest on central pair and just reaches inner webs of outer feathers. Breast slate-grey, bordered below by blackish band; rest of underparts white. Underwings totally white, except for contrasting black primaries. **Non-breeding:** Head and neck brown, tinged grey; chin and throat whitish, streaked brown; breast grey, at lower border merging into partly-obscured blackish breast-band. Upperwing-coverts show very narrow paler tips. **Juvenile:** As non-breeding, but brown of upperparts extensively fringed buff; the breast-band may be initially absent, or brownish and poorly defined.

AGE/SEX Juvenile is difficult to distinguish in the field after Nov. Sexes are similar in plumage, but males average slightly larger.

RACES No geographical variation is known.

MEASUREMENTS Length 340-370 mm (14"). Wing 231-257 mm; bill 34-40 mm; tarsus 69-84 mm; tail 93-112 mm.

REFERENCES Sakane (1957, 1958), Okugawa *et al.* (1973).

77 RED-WATTLED LAPWING *Vanellus indicus* Plate 28

Other name: Red-wattled Plover

A large lapwing, well known for its strident calls, occurring from Iraq eastwards to Indochina and Malaysia.

IDENTIFICATION Easily identified by combination of red wattles and bill-base and yellow legs, and by the strong black-and-white patterning of the head and breast. Cap, hindneck, face, throat and central breast are black, ear-coverts and sides of breast always white. The Australian Banded Lapwing (79) shows similar patterning, but always has a white throat and is much smaller and shorter-legged. In flight, Red-wattled shows a narrow white wingbar, mostly-black secondaries, and a rather narrow black subterminal tail-band. The most similar sympatric species are Spur-winged Plover (60) and River Lapwing (61): Spur-winged has underparts extensively black, while River has brownish-grey across the breast and a small black belly-patch, and both have dark-coloured bare parts; in distant flight, both show more white across the wing and more black in the tail. Yellow-wattled (63) is smaller, paler brown above and on upper breast, and lacks white on the neck, as well as showing conspicuous yellow wattles. Northern (57) is crested, darker green above, much shorter-legged, lacks wattles, and has duller bare parts. **Bare parts:** Bill red, with blackish outer third. Small red wattle above lores, joining narrow red eye-ring. Iris red, browner in young birds. Legs pale yellow, sometimes washed greenish or greyish. Short, dark spur on carpal joint.

VOICE Very noisy, often heard at night. Pairs sometimes call in duet. Usual call is a strident, rhythmic 'did-he-do-it', often with the first syllable repeated, or a similar 'kree-dee-dee'. When mobbing, repeats a sharp 'trint' incessantly. There is a well-developed song given in display flight.

HABITS Typically a waterside bird, but found extensively on cultivated land or grassland where there are small pools and ditches, sometimes in damp woodland glades. More widespread during the monsoon. Nests during Mar-Sept, but season varies locally; strongly territorial, and vigorous in defence of eggs or young. May nest close to human habitation; has been recorded nesting on a rooftop in New Delhi. Flight is powerful, with regular deep wingbeats; shows considerable speed when pressed. In display flight, performs rapid tumbling dives. Appears to feed much at night, especially during full moon. Not gregarious, normally seen in pairs or family groups, but may form flocks of up to 30 when not breeding. Behaviour is generally wary and alert, but may allow close approach at times.

MOVEMENTS Mainly sedentary over most of its range, but dispersive in response to rainfall or drought. Vagrant to west coast of upper Persian Gulf, Masirah Is. and W Oman. Those in S USSR are breeding visitors only, arriving Apr (rarely end Feb). In Himalayas, those nesting at highest altitudes (up to 1800 m) winter in the foothills.

DESCRIPTION Breeding: Forehead, crown, nape and hindneck black; ear-coverts, sides of neck and breast white (but see Races); chin, throat and central breast black. Underparts, including axillaries and underwing, are otherwise white. Mantle to upper rump, also scapulars, tertials and most of wing-coverts pale brown with greenish gloss; median and lesser coverts show purplish gloss. Tips of greater coverts and outer medians are white. Secondaries black, with white at base more extensive towards body; inner secondaries wholly white. Primaries and primary coverts black. Lower rump and uppertail-coverts white. Tail white with black subterminal band; black is bordered brown on central feathers. **Non-breeding:** During wing moult, black crown is tinged browner and throat shows variable amount of white speckling. **Juvenile:** As non-breeding, but chin and throat almost all-white, while cap, face and breast are dark grey-brown rather than black. Wing-coverts are less

274

glossy and are obscurely fringed buffish. Bare-part colours are muted.

AGE/SEX Juveniles initially distinct, but difficult to distinguish in the field once post-juvenile moult has started. In the hand, look for comparatively-worn primaries; juvenile inner medians may be retained all winter in *aigneri* , but are usually all replaced by Dec in other races. Sexes are similar in plumage, but male averages about 5% longer-winged than female and tends to have a longer carpal spur.

RACES Four: *aigneri* (Iraq to W Pakistan), nominate *indicus* (E Pakistan to Bangladesh, including all India), *lankae* (Sri Lanka) and *atronuchalis* (Assam and Burma to Vietnam and N Malaysia). The first three show no clear distinctions and are somewhat arbitrary divisions; there are clines of decreasing size

and of darker and more glossy upperparts running from west to east and from north to south. The race *lankae* is the smallest, darkest and most glossy, but is effectively indistinguishable from southernmost nominate birds. The race *atronuchalis* is like *lankae*, but has a complete black ring around neck, isolating a white patch on the side of the head, and a white band across the base of the hindneck dividing the black from the brown upperparts.

MEASUREMENTS Length 320-350 mm (13"). Wing 208-247 mm for whole range, means about 235 mm (Iraq), 223 mm (N India), 218 mm (S India) and 217 mm (Sri Lanka, SE Asia); bill 31-36 mm; tarsus 70-83 mm; tail· 104-128 mm.

REFERENCES Naik *et al.* (1961).

78 JAVANESE WATTLED LAPWING *Vanellus macropterus*   Plate 28

Other name: Sunda Lapwing

Very probably extinct following man's intensive agricultural and hunting activities in its limited range. Recorded with certainty only from Java (possibly also Timor and Sumatra), but has not been reported since 1939.

IDENTIFICATION A very distinctively-dark long-legged lapwing with conspicuous wattles. The plumage is mostly blackish-brown, with a glossy black crown, blackish head and neck, and large glossy black belly-patch which contrasts with the white vent. In flight, a narrow white patch covering the uppertail-coverts contrasts strongly with the dull plumage; although there is some pale colour underneath the inner secondaries, white is absent on the upperwing. Seen overhead, the white wing-linings, vent and undertail contrast dramatically with the black belly-patch. **Bare parts:** Bill black, with a small amount of flesh-pink or yellowish at the base of both mandibles. Large pale creamy wattles protruding upwards and downwards from the lores. Iris dark brown. Legs long, greenish-yellow to orangey-yellow; toes projecting past tip of tail in flight. Long curved black spur on the carpal joint. ·

VOICE Nothing is known.

HABITS Found on open areas near freshwater ponds, perhaps also on agricultural land. Present near Jakarta in the 1920s; last seen at Meleman on the south coast of E Java in 1939. May still exist in some remote area.

MOVEMENTS There are reports suggesting that this species once migrated between Timor and Sumatra,

but these may be erroneous. One report concerns several said to have perched on a ship's railing off the Javanese north coast.

DESCRIPTION Breeding and non-breeding: Crown and hindneck glossy blue-black; rest of head and neck blackish-brown, sharply divided from grey-brown base of neck. Breast grey-brown, bordered below by large glossy black belly-patch. Thighs, vent and undertail white. Mantle, scapulars, tertials and coverts are grey-brown. Flight feathers are black from above, but inner secondaries show greyish-white inner webs when seen from below. White uppertail-coverts and base of tail feathers; broad black sub-terminal tail-band, narrowly tipped white on outer five pairs of feathers and buffish on central pair. Under primary and secondary coverts white, axillaries brownish-grey. **Juvenile:** This plumage has never been described.

AGE/SEX Nothing is known.

RACES Monotypic.

MEASUREMENTS Length about 270-290 mm (11"). Wing 237-249 mm; bill 36-43 mm; tarsus 87 mm. Few specimens are available.

REFERENCES Kuroda (1936), Temple (1979).

79 BANDED LAPWING *Vanellus tricolor*   Plate 29

Other name: Banded Plover

An Australian endemic plover, medium-sized and rather fast-flying for a vanellid.

IDENTIFICATION The only large plover found in Australia apart from the Masked Lapwing (80). Banded is considerably smaller, always has a dark breast as opposed to a white one, and shows a broad white bar on the upperwing in flight (showing as a translucent bar on the underwing when flying overhead). The U-shaped breast-band is diagnostic. The legs are relatively shorter than on Masked Lapwing and do not project beyond the tail in flight. The wing-beats are often faster and more clipped than is typical of the genus, and may suggest one of the smaller

plovers. Usual stance rather upright, emphasised by the vertical black-and-white patterning on the neck. **Bare parts:** Bill canary-yellow, often with a dusky nail (tip of upper mandible). Iris and eye-ring bright canary-yellow, with a small oval red wattle in front of each eye. Legs shortish, dark purplish or bluish-black, redder above the joint.

VOICE The alarm call, a querulous 'er-chill-char, er-chill-char', recalls that of Masked Lapwing in character, but is faster and slightly less raucous. Also a strident 'kew-kew, kew-kew'.

HABITS Much as other *Vanellus* plovers. Found typically on short grassland in bare grazed fields, plains and airfields, but may occur on stony ground and even mudflats. Sometimes near water, but seldom wades. Usually in small wary parties, but occasionally gathers into large non-breeding flocks far from cover. Often uses foot-tapping to dislodge insects from grassland. Breeds June-Nov, often socially. The nest is a sparsely-lined scrape in open grassland.

MOVEMENTS No regular migrations, but appears to be nomadic when not breeding, depending on local conditions.

DESCRIPTION Breeding and non-breeding: Distinctive head pattern formed by glossy black crown, red wattle, white band behind eye, and black band from lores and across cheeks which continues broadly down the sides of the neck and into a broad breast-band. Throat, front of neck and upper breast form a white oval surrounded by black. Rest of underparts are white. Nape, mantle, coverts, tertials and scapulars brown with a faint purplish gloss. Upperwing shows mainly-brown coverts, some medians and greaters dark brown tipped white forming a diagonal white band; inner secondaries are also largely white, but primaries and outer secondaries are black. Underwing is white, except for black undersides to the primaries. Rump and base of tail are white; white-tipped tail has a broad black subterminal band. **Juvenile:** Differs chiefly in that crown is brown with buff fringes, and band on neck and breast is blackish-brown with broad buff feather tips forming irregular bars. Upperparts have broad pale buff fringes; tertials have irregular buff bars. Bare parts are duller in colour, and the wattles are smaller than in the adult.

AGE/SEX Juveniles can be distinguished for almost a full year. Individuals in post-juvenile moult may show a mixture of glossy black and worn brown feathers in the cap, mask and breast-band. The last feathers to be replaced are the buff-fringed lesser and median coverts. Sexes are not known to differ, although males may average slightly larger.

RACES No geographical variation is known.

MEASUREMENTS Length 250-280 mm (10½"). Wing 183-204 mm; bill 21-24 mm; tarsus 44-52 mm.

REFERENCES Dann (1981).

80 MASKED LAPWING *Vanellus miles*   Plate 29

Other names: Spur-winged Lapwing, Spur-winged or Masked Plover
A large, conspicuous and successful vanellid plover of Australia and, recently, southern New Guinea, which has established itself in New Zealand since 1932. Its spread seems to coincide with scrub clearance and the provision of water for livestock.

IDENTIFICATION An unmistakable Australasian lapwing characterised by large size, black crown, white underparts and a ludicrously large bright yellow wattle around the eyes, across the forehead and hanging down beside the chin. The entirely-white chin, throat and central breast are unique among lapwings. Only the Banded Lapwing (79) overlaps in range, but it is smaller, has a complete black U-shaped breast-band and in flight shows a narrow, but clear, diagonal white bar across its upperwing; there is no white in Masked's upperwing. **Bare parts:** Bill bright yellow, paler at the tip (sometimes greenish), with nail of upper mandible dusky. Wattles bright yellow, size variable between races. Iris yellow. Legs dull red, long, with feet extending fully beyond tail-tip in flight. Long sharp wing-spur, yellow with blackish tip.

VOICE A very noisy bird, often calling at night in townships. Typically, a grating staccato 'keer-ki-ki-ki' or 'krik-krik-krik', a sharp 'kek', or a more slurred repeated 'kreerk-kreerk', often on descending scale.

HABITS Breeds in a very wide range of open habitats with low vegetation. It has become common in areas altered by man, liking pasture and ploughed land, preferably near water. Often breeds in towns, even taking to flat roofs; may feed on grassy areas close to busy traffic. Even in the south of the range, the breeding season is long, and may extend from Apr to Jan. It is aggressive, dive-bombing and screaming overhead when its chicks are threatened. When not breeding, more frequently found on lakeshores, wet flashes and muddy intertidal zones, but can be found almost anywhere; often in small or moderately-sized flocks. Flaps quite slowly and deeply on broad rounded wings. Feeds in typical plover manner, often using foot-tapping when feeding on grass.

MOVEMENTS The frequency of extralimital records suggests a substantial post-breeding dispersal. This has probably accounted for the colonisation of New Guinea and New Zealand, and the occurrence of both races as visitors to SW Australia. Also a visitor, and potential colonist, to N New Zealand, presumably from South Island. Otherwise, apart from concentrating around wetlands outside the breeding season, there is no regular migration. Vagrants have reached the Moluccas, Christmas I. (south of Java), Norfolk I. and Campbell I.

DESCRIPTION Breeding and non-breeding: Crown black. In *novaehollandiae* (but not in *miles*), the ear-coverts, hindneck, sides of lower neck and sides of breast are also black. Sides of face are covered by huge yellow wattles. Underparts white, except for lateral black breast-patches in *novaehollandiae*. Upperparts plain olive-brown. Primaries, primary coverts and tips of secondaries blackish. Alula and outer greater coverts tinged grey. Longest uppertail-coverts and base of tail white. Broad black subterminal band and narrow white terminal fringe on tail. Underwing-coverts white, contrasting with blackish primaries and tips to outer secondaries. Inner secondaries silvery-grey underneath. **Juvenile:** As adult, but head blackish-brown obscured by many buffish tips. Feathers of mantle, tertials, scapulars and coverts show central olive-brown area but are irregularly mottled or barred dark brown and fringed buff. Tail feathers have narrow buffish tips.

AGE/SEX After post-juvenile moult, young birds may show some retained juvenile coverts. Spur usually much shorter and blunter than on adults. No differences are known between the sexes.

RACES Two, each of which has in the past been given specific status: nominate *miles*, Northern Masked Lapwing (S New Guinea, NE Australia to approx 25° S), and *novaehollandiae*, Southern Masked Lapwing (New Zealand, SE Australia south of 25° S). Northern race has little or no black on the hindneck, lacks black on upper mantle and breast, and has very extensive yellow wattles reaching to well behind the eye. The longer-winged southern race has black breast-patches, a black collar, and the wattle narrowly surrounding the eye but prominent only in front of it. There is a broad intergrade zone in which intermediates are frequent.

MEASUREMENTS Length 330-370 mm (13¾"). Wing 216-233 mm (northern), 230-260 mm (southern); bill 30-37 mm; tarsus 71-86 mm; spur 12-20 mm (adults), 5-14 mm (juveniles and immatures).

REFERENCES van Tets *et al.* (1967), Thomas (1969), Barlow (1972), Barlow *et al.* (1972), Dann (1981).

81 EURASIAN GOLDEN PLOVER *Pluvialis apricaria* Plate 31
(see also Plate 32)

Other names: Golden Plover, Greater Golden Plover
The most southerly nester and the shortest-distance migrant of the genus, rare south of 30° N.

IDENTIFICATION Intermediate size, bulky shape, relatively narrow pointed wings, and black underparts in breeding plumage distinguish this genus from *Charadrius* and *Vanellus* plovers. Grey Plover (84) differs from the golden plovers in larger size, black axillaries, large white rump and uppertail, stronger wingbar and much greyer plumage (except in fresh juvenile), but the three golden plovers, Eurasian, Pacific (82) and American (83), may cause considerable identification problems. Eurasian is the largest, plumpest and shortest-legged, and is the only one with axillaries and most of underwing-coverts clean white. In breeding plumage, shows a broad but irregular white line along the flanks between black belly and folded wing, and white undertail even in full plumage; some, mostly southern breeders, show almost no black on face, throat and sides of neck. Pacific and American show solid black on face, mostly black undertail, and a broken or absent flank line. In non-breeding and juvenile plumages, Eurasian shows a relatively poor supercilium; it is generally more golden-brown than American in corresponding plumages, but beware occasional Eurasian which are very grey. Wing-tips of Eurasian fall about level or just beyond the tail-tip (well beyond tail-tip in Pacific and American). For a summary of characters, see Table on page 392. **Bare parts:** Bill black, relatively short and slim. Iris dark brown. Legs dark grey, sometimes tinged greenish; toes do not project beyond tail-tip in flight.

VOICE Call is a pleasant, penetrating whistle 'tloo' or 'too-ee' often heard well before the bird can be seen. Territorial song, sometimes heard in winter quarters, is a rather melancholy 'per-peeoo', the second note longer and initially slightly higher in pitch.

HABITS Nests mainly May-Aug (from late Mar in extreme south of range) in a variety of habitats, from upland moorland to coastal tundra; strictly an upland breeder in S Britain. Territorial, but pairs are often clumped in best habitat; in Britain, late-nesting pairs may use territories vacated by early nesters. There is a high, circling display flight. Strongly gregarious on migration and in winter. A high proportion of the population, probably about half a million birds, winters in Britain and Ireland, where permanent grassland is the preferred feeding habitat; also occurs on cultivated farmland, lakeshores, saltmarsh and intertidal mud. Behaviour generally wary and alert; quick to take flight, and often circles for many minutes before landing. Still hunted in many areas. Often feeds with Northern Lapwing (57), but species quickly segregate in flying flocks.

MOVEMENTS Northern nesters are strongly migratory. Adults leave breeding grounds July-Aug, juveniles later; begin to arrive in southern parts of winter range mainly Oct-Nov, after adults have moulted. Northward passage peaks in Apr-early May, and northernmost breeding areas are re-occupied by early June. Icelandic population visits mainly Ireland, Scandinavian and Russian ones W Europe and W Mediterranean; origin of Caspian and E Mediterranean birds is presumably easternmost breeding range. British breeders winter mostly in lowlands adjacent to breeding sites; return to breeding grounds begins in Feb if weather allows. Vagrant southward to Gambia (Dec-Feb, occasionally in small parties), Azores, Madeira, Canaries, Mauretania, Iraq and Kuwait; records in Nigeria and the Gulf of Guinea probably refer to Pacific or American species. In spring, vagrant to Newfoundland (Apr), S Greenland, Spitsbergen, Bear I. and Jan Mayen.

DESCRIPTION Breeding: Crown, hindneck and upperparts blackish, strongly spotted with bright gold. A white band from forehead runs across supercilium, down sides of neck and along flanks; underparts in area enclosed by this band are black or blackish, although many individuals show little or no black on face and neck. Undertail-coverts and vent whitish, slightly marked with pale brown chevrons. Axillaries white, underwing-coverts mostly white but with variable amount of greyish smudging. Upperwing rather plain, but shows narrow but clear whitish wingbar, formed by narrow white tips to greater coverts and narrow white edgings to primaries. **First breeding:** Some birds show a black-spotted breast and belly, with black restricted to small wedges at tips of feathers. **Non-breeding:** Rather plain golden-brown above and below. Upperparts are brownish, spotted with bright yellow (fading to dull yellow). Breast rather dark grey-brown, spotted yellowish. Belly is whitish. **Juvenile:** Superficially very like non-breeding adult, but spotting is finer and a little paler and duller in colour. Feathers of breast, tertials, scapulars and wing-coverts show a broad central dark wedge at the tip; belly and flank feathers have a thin dark terminal bar.

AGE/SEX Dark-tipped belly and flank feathers may be retained until mid-winter, as may juvenile tertials and scapulars, but ageing is difficult even in the hand. Sexing is only rarely possible even in breeding plumage owing to the wide geographical variation, but may be clear in nesting pairs. Male is blacker, while female often shows brown tinges below and an admixture of white feathers; in 'northern' birds, male shows a solid black bar above bill, while female lacks this and has ear-coverts mainly golden-brown.

RACES Monotypic, but shows wide variation in breeding plumage of which the extremes were formerly treated as races: 'southern' (nominate) and 'northern' ('altifrons'). Southern form (dominant from mid-Scandinavia and Estonia southwards) shows less black on face and neck and, in female, throat and sides of neck may be whitish. Northern form (dominant in Iceland, N Scandinavia and USSR) is mainly black or blackish on face. Both forms occur throughout range; proportions at a single locality may change between years. Many individuals are intermediate. Mean wing length decreases from west to east.

MEASUREMENTS Length 260-290 mm (10¾"). Wing 170-203 mm; bill 19-26 mm; tarsus 38-45 mm; tail 60-80 mm.

REFERENCES Ratcliffe (1976), Byrkjedal (1978), Parr (1980), Fuller and Lloyd (1981), Edwards (1982).

82 PACIFIC GOLDEN PLOVER *Pluvialis fulva*   Plate 32

Other names: Asian Golden, Eastern Golden or Asiatic Lesser Golden Plover
Until recently, considered by most authorities conspecific with American Golden Plover (83), but new studies show that there is no evidence of interbreeding where the two forms overlap in Alaska.

IDENTIFICATION Often not easy to distinguish from Eurasian Golden (81) and American Golden Plovers: see Eurasian Golden and the Table on page 392 for fuller discussion of the differences. Spangled upperparts, dark legs and pale area around bill-base are useful for separation from *Charadrius* plovers. It is the smallest and slimmest of the three golden plovers, but shares many characters, including smoky-grey underwing, with American Golden. Many individuals cannot be separated from American Golden, even as museum specimens, and should remain indeterminate; distinctions are clearest in juvenile and non-breeding plumages, when Pacific Golden is basically yellowish-buff, American Golden brownish-grey. In breeding plumage, Pacific Golden shows more white on flanks and undertail, a narrower black band above the bill, and often more gold spotting on the upperparts. Measurements will separate more than 90%, but using all characters Connors (1983) was unable to identify 7% of North American breeders. **Bare parts:** Bill black. Iris dark brown. Legs greyish-black; tips of toes may project beyond tail-tip in flight. Both bill and legs are proportionately longer than in other golden plovers.

VOICE A range of loud monosyllabic or disyllabic calls, sharper and less mellow than similar calls of Eurasian Golden. A rapid 'tu-ee' or 'chu-wit' recalling Spotted Redshank (136) and a plaintive 'kl-ee' or 'ki-wee', almost like Northern Lapwing (57), are the most useful for separation from Eurasian Golden. Overlap in calls with American Golden is apparently complete, but a full study of this is lacking.

HABITS Nests June-July on well-drained tundra, often on hillsides, ridges or raised polygons. In Alaska, may nest alongside American Golden; in central Siberia, breeding grounds are generally more northerly and more open than those of Eurasian Golden in the zone of overlap. Non-breeding habitat is generally intertidal mud, beaches and reefs around the Indian and Pacific Oceans, even on quite small oceanic islands, but extensive use is also made of short grasslands, such as airfields, and freshwater pools where available. Occurs by shores of lakes and rivers on migration in USSR. Some individuals defend winter feeding territories, while others are non-territorial. In con-

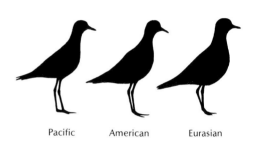

Pacific   American   Eurasian

trast to Eurasian Golden, many are tame and approachable. They may feed on urban grasslands and, where coastal or grassland roosting sites are unavailable, may roost on the flat roofs of buildings.

MOVEMENTS A powerful migrant. Many Alaskan breeders migrate direct to Hawaii across 4500 km of open ocean—accurate navigation is important here! First migrants reach Pacific islands in Aug-Sept, rarely late July in Hawaii, and New Zealand in Oct. Northward movement begins in Mar and breeding grounds are re-occupied from early May. Normal winter range includes NE Africa, northern and eastern fringes of Indian Ocean, SE Asia, Australasia, islands of W and central Pacific, and coastal California (small numbers only). Vagrant E Africa south to Cape Town and inland to Lakes Nakuru and Turkana, Europe westwards to E Britain, New England, Galapagos and Chile.

DESCRIPTION Breeding: See Identification and Table on page 392 for differences from Eurasian Golden and American Golden. Plumage of underparts is intermediate between these two species, while upperparts are similar to Eurasian Golden. **Non-breeding:** Upperparts pale brown, spotted and fringed bright yellow. Supercilium washed yellow-buff. Breast suffused buffish-brown and mottled bright yellow. **Juvenile:** Upperparts brownish, spotted and fringed bright yellow. Supercilium prominent, yellowish-white. Breast very strongly buffish, mottled bright yellow; the mottling extends a short distance along flanks, but central belly and undertail-coverts are unmarked whitish.

AGE/SEX Juveniles are initially distinct at close range, but after Nov very difficult to tell in the field; a good clue is dark mantle and upper scapulars (yellow spots and fringes worn away) contrasting with paler and brighter lower scapulars and wing-coverts. Adults moult chiefly in winter quarters and may retain traces of breeding plumage throughout southward migration. Most one-year-olds do not attain full blackish underparts of breeding plumage. Sexes similar except in full breeding plumage, when female has more white feathers admixed in black underparts: males show typically less than 10% of feathers white, females often 25% or more, but both sexes are variable.

RACES No geographical variation is known.

MEASUREMENTS Length 230-260 mm (9¾"). Wing 152-173 mm; bill 18-24 mm; tarsus 39-46 mm; tail 54-70 mm. Wing:bill x tarsus gives best separation from American Golden.

REFERENCES Johnson and Macfarlane (1967), Pym (1982), Connors (1983).

83 AMERICAN GOLDEN PLOVER *Pluvialis dominica*   Plate 32

Other name: previously part of Lesser Golden Plover
Very closely related to Pacific Golden Plover (82) and, until recently, usually considered conspecific. Normal migration routes and wintering areas are very different.

IDENTIFICATION This is the greyest of the three golden plovers in juvenile and non-breeding plumages, and the blackest below in breeding plumage, but is intermediate in body size and proportions of bill and leg. See Eurasian Golden (81), Pacific Golden and the Table on page 392 for a full discussion of differences. In breeding plumage, look for black flanks with little or no white bordering the folded wing, and almost solidly black undertail. When not breeding, greyer than corresponding plumages of other golden plovers, but beware occasional Eurasian Golden which are equally grey, and confusion with Grey Plover (84). Constant features of separation are smaller size, clearer supercilium and smoky-grey axillaries and underwing: Eurasian Golden shows white axillaries and Grey Plover black. Also differs from Grey in darker crown (emphasised by paler supercilium), long wings projecting well beyond tail-tip at rest, and slightly smaller and slimmer bill. Grey Plover is further distinguished by white rump and stronger white wingbar. In juvenile, golden spotting on upperparts is smaller and paler than in Pacific Golden. Spotting on the mantle and upper scapulars wears quickly to form an almost solidly dark area contrasting with paler back, lower scapulars and wing-coverts. Dark streaking and tipping on breast feathers is broader than in Pacific Golden, and forms a mottled or almost a barred pattern. Particularly in breeding plumage, some individuals cannot be assigned with certainty to either species, even using a combination of measurements and plumage characters, and should be left unidentified. Bare parts: Bill black. Iris dark brown. Legs greyish-black.

VOICE Not known to differ from that of Pacific Golden.

HABITS Nests late May-July on well-drained arctic tundra, usually in drier areas than Grey Plover. Nesting habitat is apparently identical to that of Pacific Golden, and at several Alaskan localities the two species breed side-by-side. Outside breeding season, found in a variety of habitats from coastal mud or sandflats to fringes of inland rivers and marshes and grassland up to 1200 m, but in contrast to Pacific Golden most winter on inland grasslands. Many defend feeding territories. Generally tamer and much more approachable than Eurasian Golden. Vagrants in Europe frequently join flocks of Eurasian Golden.

MOVEMENTS Many migrate in autumn over W Atlantic on a Great Circle, oceanic route; some may migrate non-stop from James Bay, Canada, to S America. A smaller number of southward migrants, chiefly juveniles, use east or west coasts or inland route across Great Plains. Migrants are evident in USA Aug-early Nov, but many reach Argentina by late Aug. Absent from N America early Dec-late Feb. Northward migration begins late Feb, following an inland route through S America, crossing central America or Gulf of Mexico to Texas, to reach breeding grounds by late May. Common in Texas late Mar and in Canadian prairies mid-May. Vagrants are frequent in W Europe in Sept-Oct, particularly in SW England; owing to uncertain identification, eastern limit of vagrancy is unknown. Some have wintered. Also vagrant in autumn or winter to the Gambia, Sierra Leone, and probably Ghana. Records of golden plovers in Nigeria and the Gulf of Guinea perhaps refer to this species. In Australia, has reached Victoria and probably Queensland. In spring or summer, has reached Greenland and E Siberia.

DESCRIPTION Breeding: Forehead, lores, sides of face, central underparts and flanks black; undertail-coverts mainly black, blotched whitish. The black is outlined above by a white band from forecrown, across supercilia and sides of neck to join large white patches on sides of breast; latter are prominent and can almost meet across the breast. Upper flanks may show a narrow whitish line. Crown, central hindneck, mantle, rump, scapulars and tertials mottled blackish and golden. Wing-coverts largely brownish-grey with faded spotting, but with a few brighter breeding-plumage feathers admixed. Primaries and secondaries dark brown, with an obscure paler wash on middle primaries and a very narrow whitish wingbar formed by the tips of greater coverts. Underwing-coverts and axillaries are plain smoky-grey with fine whitish fringes. Non-breeding: Much duller and greyer. Upperparts greyish-brown, fringed and notched pale or dull yellowish and whitish. Prominent off-white supercilium, emphasised by dusky spot on ear-coverts and mark in front of eye. Breast washed pale greyish, initially with dull yellowish fringes; belly paler. Juvenile: As non-breeding, but upperparts darker blackish-brown with neat, small spots of off-white or pale yellow; supercilium long and noticeably whitish; breast, upper belly and flanks strikingly mottled grey and white.

AGE/SEX Adults often retain breeding plumage until late Oct/Nov. Mottled grey breast of juvenile is distinctive at moderate range until about Dec. One-year-olds usually gain little or no black on underparts. Sexes similar except in full breeding plumage: differences then as in Pacific Golden.

RACES No geographical variation is known.
MEASUREMENTS Length 240-280 mm (10¼"). Wing 169-193 mm; bill 20-27 mm; tarsus 39-44 mm; tail 56-78 mm. Wing:bill x tarsus gives best separation from Pacific Golden.
REFERENCES Myers and Myers (1979), Pym (1982), Connors (1983).

84 GREY PLOVER *Pluvialis squatarola*   **Plate 31**

Other names: Black-bellied Plover, Silver Plover
This is the largest of the plovers outside the *Vanellus* group, and is the only truly cosmopolitan plover. In breeding plumage it is one of the most striking waders.

IDENTIFICATION The black axillaries contrasting with the white underwing-coverts are always present and form a consistent and unique fieldmark. When feeding, hunched stance and lethargic behaviour give the species a characteristic dejected appearance. Large white rump and bold white wingbar, contrasting with blackish primary coverts and carpal area, show well in flight. In breeding plumage the belly and flanks are black, contrasting with pure white vent and undertail. The three species of golden plovers (81, 82, 83) are similar in proportions and plumages, but are smaller, browner (except juvenile American Golden), more often in inland or dry habitats, and lack Grey Plover's white rump and black axillaries. Confusion is possible between Grey and American Golden in non-breeding plumages, but look for larger size, plumper outline, paler plumage, poorer supercilium and shorter wings (projecting only slightly beyond tail-tip at rest) to identify Grey. In distant flight, parties may be mistaken for other similarly-sized waders, particularly Red or Great Knot (187, 188) or Bar-tailed Godwit (125). More variegated above than other basically grey waders. In the tropics, first-year individuals in particular may become very whitish through wear and fading. **Bare parts:** Rather heavy-looking black bill. Large eyes, iris dark brown. Legs dark grey or blackish.

VOICE The usual call is a very distinctive, loud, far-carrying, slurred whistle 'tlee-oo-ee', the second syllable lower in pitch: a characteristically flat and melancholy sound. A triple whistle is given on the breeding grounds.

HABITS Nests late May-Aug on lowland tundra north of the tree-limit, often but not always in damper areas than used by golden plovers. Sometimes nests near coast, but avoids most of the smaller arctic islands. Preferred non-breeding habitat is intertidal mudflats and beaches. On migration, and sometimes also in winter, found around inland lakes and pools or on grassland; in Europe, occasionally seen on farmland with flocks of Eurasian Golden. Many individuals defend feeding territories in winter quarters, to which they may return in subsequent years, while others are more mobile. Feeds as much at night as by day in some localities. Forms large communal roosts, often joining with other waders. Strong, swift flight; often flies in loose flocks, typically in irregular-line formation.

MOVEMENTS Adults leave breeding grounds late July-Sept, juveniles mainly Sept-mid Oct. Southward movement continues into Nov or later. In South Africa, first arrivals are in Sept and first departures in Feb. Northward passage peaks during May, and first returns to breeding grounds are in late May or early June. Scarce inland in USSR during northward passage, suggesting that most fly direct from southern coasts, but perhaps less so in North America (migrates up the Mississippi valley). There is evidence from museum specimens that females have a far more southerly winter distribution than males. Young birds typically remain south during their first breeding season; thus present all year in many parts of non-breeding range. Almost cosmopolitan, but records in Greenland, Iceland, Faeroes, Spitsbergen, Madeira and Macquarie I. can be treated as vagrants. Scarce in Tasmania and New Zealand.

DESCRIPTION Breeding: Underparts black, except for white rear belly and vent, mainly-white undertail, and a broad white band from forehead above eye and down neck, ending on the side of the breast. Axillaries black. Underwing-coverts are white, except for greater primary coverts which are dusky-grey. Upperparts including coverts are spangled with silvery-white and blackish-grey. Crown is strikingly pale. Squarish white area on rump and uppertail-coverts, often obscurely barred. Tail white, barred grey. Primary coverts blackish; primaries and secondaries blackish, except for bold white wingbar across primaries, bases of secondaries and tips to greater coverts. **Non-breeding:** Upperparts and coverts pale brownish-grey, spotted and notched whitish. There is a diffuse mark through the eye and a dusky patch on the ear-coverts. Breast and flanks white, well streaked with brownish-grey. Axillaries remain black. **Juvenile:** Upperparts and coverts greyish-brown, with margins spotted pale gold or yellowish-white. Underparts white, but with buff-brown barring and streaking covering breast and flanks. Otherwise as non-breeding.

AGE/SEX Fine dark tips to the underpart feathers are diagnostic of juveniles; during Oct-Dec, the bars at the feather tips wear off to leave a streaked pattern like that of the adults. Some inner median coverts usually show brownish spotting throughout the first year. One year-olds usually remain in non-breeding plumage, but may gain some black-spotted or black-tipped feathers on the underparts; some show worn juvenile feathers as late as Mar-Apr. Sexing is possible only in full breeding plumage. The male has almost solid black underparts with a few feathers

showing whitish fringes, while the female has a brownish tinge to the underparts and many whitish feathers even in full plumage. Contrast between the white 'head-band' and the dark underparts is less marked in the female, which (at least in the Nearctic) has browner upperparts than the male.
RACES Monotypic, but there are clines of increasing size from Atlantic to Pacific across both continents.

MEASUREMENTS Length 270-300 mm (11¼"). Wing 178-215 mm; bill 24-34 mm; tarsus 42-52 mm; tail 66-83 mm.
REFERENCES Branson and Minton (1976), Hussell and Page (1976), Stinson (1977), Townshend *et al.* (1984).

85 NEW ZEALAND DOTTEREL *Charadrius obscurus*   Plate 45

Other name: Red-breasted Dotterel
This plover is the largest and bulkiest of the genus. It is restricted to New Zealand, and is an endangered species with a population of perhaps around 1,400 individuals.

IDENTIFICATION A large, rather plain brown plover, sometimes with rufous underparts in breeding plumage. In non-breeding plumage is most likely to be confused with Greater Sandplover (108) and Oriental Plover (110), but these are smaller and much less bulky. Shape is similar to Pacific Golden Plover (82) and Grey Plover (84), but upperparts are never spotted. Legs are shorter and darker than those of Oriental, and bill is heavier than on both Oriental and Pacific Golden. Flight pattern resembles that of Greater Sandplover; note white underwing and axillaries, clear white wingbar, and dark rump. Differs from Greater Sandplover in larger size, greater bulk, broad brown band across the lores, extensively brown breast (never completely white in the centre), and brown smudging on flanks (absent in Greater). Underparts become variably chestnut-red in breeding plumage, but white is always present on vent and undertail and very few attain completely-red breast, flanks and belly; most show very little red. **Bare parts:** Heavy black bill. Iris dark brown. Legs grey.
VOICE Typically a reedy 'trrt'; on the breeding grounds a sharply rising 'tweet' and a rolling 'turr'. Birds chasing in display give a complex buzzing 'whreeerwhreet', surging up and down in pitch.
HABITS Last century, bred widely in South Island, but now there are two distinct populations, separated by about 1000 km. The Stewart I. group, thought to number about 200, nests on exposed mountain ridges above the tree-line, and among coastal dunes; they gather on the coast in the winter, Mar-Aug. A second population nests exclusively on the coast around northern North Island. It prefers broad sandy beaches, particularly near brackish or flowing fresh water. Territories are widely spaced and vigorously defended; eggs are laid Aug-Jan. A long-running colour-marking study has already recorded a 31-year-old male. There are estimated to be 1,000-1,200 individuals in the winter months, but a complete census has not yet been made. Many gather in small flocks Feb-May and visit estuaries; sometimes seen on grazed fields a little way inland. Some remain in pairs all year. Food includes relatively large items such as small mussels and small fish.
MOVEMENTS The Stewart I. population is sedentary, except for short post-breeding movements towards favoured winter flocking sites. Small winter flocks occur in southern South Island. Colour-marking has revealed that some of the northern population may

Grey Plover
New Zealand Dotterel   Greater Sandplover

move considerably within their limited range, while others are sedentary. There are rare sightings away from breeding areas, but no evidence of any interchange between the two populations. A few birds of unknown origin are regularly recorded at Farewell Spit, the northwest tip of South Island. No colour-marked individuals have been seen beyond North Island.
DESCRIPTION Breeding: Forehead and short, narrow supercilium are white (but chestnut in some full-plumaged males). All upperparts, including lores and ear-coverts, grey-brown; feathers of head, mantle, scapulars and tertials show tawny-chestnut fringes. Wing-coverts fringed white. Inner primaries have small areas of white on bases of outer webs; these plus white greater-covert tips and bases of secondaries form a distinct white wingbar. Secondaries are also narrowly tipped white, forming a thin white trailing edge. Rump grey-brown; central pairs of tail feathers dark brown, darker towards tip, outer two pairs paler brown, fringed white. Underparts show a highly variable amount of chestnut-red and white; any red is usually an irregular patch or suffusion, mainly on belly and extending to lower breast and flanks. Vent and undertail always show some white. Underwing and axillaries white, contrasting strongly with chestnut-red (if present) on belly and flanks. **Non-breeding:** Mainly Mar-May. Upperparts slightly paler, with fringes pale grey rather than chestnut; longest scapulars and tertials are neatly but narrowly fringed white. Chin and throat white; partially obscured zone on upper breast, washed and spotted with grey-brown. Rest of underparts white, but some grey-brown smudging on flanks. **Juvenile:** As non-breeding, but upperparts rather darker brown with feathers fringed warm buffish-tawny. Pale sides of head and neck and dark crown give more of a capped appearance than in the adult. Breast shows darkish brown spots, fringed tawny. Rest of underparts variably washed with warm buffish-tawny.

AGE/SEX After post-juvenile body moult, first-winter birds closely resemble adults. Breeding plumage is normally attained in the first summer. Both sexes vary considerably in the depth of colour on the underparts, but only males (a minute proportion) ever become completely rich chestnut from throat to belly. Within individual pairs, the male is normally the redder, but late in the season the male and female can be similarly coloured.

RACES Monotypic: the two populations are only recently separated.

MEASUREMENTS Length 260-280 mm (10¾"). Wing 154-174 mm; bill 25-28 mm; tarsus 37-41 mm.

REFERENCES Edgar (1969), Phillips (1980), Reed (1981).

86 RINGED PLOVER *Charadrius hiaticula*   Plate 33

Other names: Common Ringed or Greater Ringed Plover
This is a common and familiar Palaearctic species which also nests in Greenland and NE Canada, where its range overlaps that of the very similar Semipalmated Plover (87).

IDENTIFICATION This is a rather bulky, small plover with a single black breast-band, a narrow white hind-neck collar, and orangey legs and bill-base. In flight, it shows a strong white wingbar and a blackish sub-terminal tail-band. In juvenile plumage, black is lacking and the brown on the breast may not quite form a complete band. There is considerable range overlap with Little Ringed Plover (89) and in places the two species breed side-by-side. Little Ringed is distinguished most easily by lack of a clear wingbar and by the thicker, brighter eye-ring which is more conspicuous at all ages than on Ringed. In addition, Little Ringed is smaller, has a different voice, duller, pinker legs, slightly faster feeding actions, and faster wingbeats; it can be distinguished at long range by its subtly different profile, the head appearing relatively smaller and less rounded and the body longer and slimmer. Semipalmated Plover is difficult to distinguish from Ringed (particularly of the race *tundrae*), unless the bird calls or gives views of the amount of webbing between the toes. Ringed has visible webbing between the outer and middle toes, but not (except under closest scrutiny) between inner and middle; Semipalmated has obvious webbing between both inner and middle and outer and middle. Also, Semipalmated is smaller than Ringed, with a shorter and narrower wingbar; in breeding plumage it usually shows a slightly narrower, more parallel-sided black breast-band, and much less white above and behind the eye. Long-billed Plover (88) has, like Semipalmated, sometimes been considered conspecific with Ringed; it differs chiefly in long, mainly-black bill, longer paler legs, longer darker tail, and very weak wingbar. **Bare parts:** Bill black, with conspicuous orange-yellow over basal two-thirds, duller when not breeding; in juveniles, bill mostly blackish-brown, with base of lower mandible dull yellow. Iris dark brown; narrow dull yellowish-orange eye-ring. Legs bright orange-yellow in adult, duller and more yellowish in juveniles.

VOICE Normal contact note is a highly distinctive mellow whistle with a rising inflection, 'too-li'. Other calls include a sharper and higher 'tooee' or 'wip' when alarmed, a low 'tooweep' warning call and a loud 'telee-telee'. The song, often given in display flight, is a repeated 'teeleea' or 'leea'.

HABITS Nests mainly coastally in south of range, sometimes inland along rivers or at lakes or gravel-pits, but extensively inland on arctic tundra; season is late Mar-early Sept in W Europe, but much shorter farther north. Often nests on shingle beaches, sometimes at quite high density in undisturbed areas. Displays include a slow-flapping flight around the territory, and a well-developed injury-feigning distraction display to lead predators away from eggs or young. In winter range, occurs in a variety of coastal habitats, and also inland along rivers and lakeshores; sometimes feeds away from the water on grassland or cultivated ground. A gregarious species; often forms flocks of a few hundred at high-tide roosts. Normally wary and alert, but allowing fairly close approach.

MOVEMENTS Mainly a migratory species, but some W European birds may remain close to the nesting territory all year and start to display in Feb or earlier. Nearctic breeders all migrate across N Atlantic, mostly via Iceland and Greenland, passing through W Europe chiefly in second half of May and returning mid-Aug to mid-Sept; most probably winter in W Africa. Those breeding in the N Palaearctic also winter largely in Africa, and migrate through Europe on a similar schedule. A small number appear in Japan and China on migration and in winter. Vagrant Azores, Alaska (bred 1970), Sakhalin, Tibet, Korea, Maldive Is., Pakistan, N India, Burma, Malaysia, Singapore, Brunei, New Guinea, Australia and New Zealand.

DESCRIPTION Breeding: Black lores, ear-coverts, frontal bar and base of forehead surround a white band across the forehead; ear-coverts may be brownish-black. There is a white streak above and behind the eye. Underparts and narrow hindneck collar are white, but underparts are crossed by a black or brown-and-black breast-band which continues narrowly around base of hindneck. Underwing and axillaries are white. Crown, mantle to uppertail, scapulars, wing-coverts and tertials are plain brown; sides to rump and uppertail are white. Greater coverts are white-tipped; rest of wing-coverts may show narrow whitish fringes when fresh. Primaries and secondaries are blackish, with white on shafts and on webs (even of the outer primaries) forming a strong wing-bar; inner 2 secondaries are almost wholly white. Tail brown at base, but with a strong blackish subterminal bar and a white tip to most feathers; central pair lacks white tip, and outer pair is virtually all-white. Non-breeding: All black is replaced by dusky-brown. White forehead is contiguous with a short whitish supercilium. Breast-band is often concentrated into brown patches at sides of breast, barely meeting across the centre. Bare parts become duller: bill may be mainly blackish, with only a trace of colour at base. Breeding plumage is sometimes regained after only three or four months. **Juvenile:** As non-breeding, but brown feathers of upperparts show clear pale buffish fringes and a narrow dark subterminal line. Bill may be entirely blackish for a few months after fledging.

AGE/SEX Buffish fringing is diagnostic of juveniles, but is lost quickly and by Jan first-year birds are very difficult to separate from adults. Some young birds gain only partial breeding plumage. In full breeding plumage, males are usually distinguishable quite easily by blacker ear-coverts, broader blacker breast-band, and brighter eye-ring: female typically has brownish ear-coverts and retains brown in breast-band all year, especially at sides.

RACES Two: nominate (NE Canada to W Europe) and *tundrae* (N Scandinavia and USSR). The race *tundrae* is smaller and darker than the nominate race. This division is unsatisfactory in that there are clines in both size and upperpart colour which run north-south rather than east-west: the largest, palest individuals are in S Britain and France, and are much more distinct from *tundrae* than are nominate birds from Greenland. Most of NW Europe probably falls in a zone of dynamic secondary intergradation, and it is not possible to draw the dividing line.

MEASUREMENTS Length 180-200 mm (7½"). Wing 120-144 mm; bill 12-16 mm; tarsus 22-27 mm; tail 54-68 mm.

REFERENCES Väisänen (1969), Taylor (1974, 1978, 1980), Pienkowski (1984).

87 SEMIPALMATED PLOVER *Charadrius semipalmatus* Plate 33

The American counterpart of the Ringed Plover (86); these two are sometimes considered conspecific in view of reported interbreeding in Baffin I., Canada.

IDENTIFICATION A small, fairly dark plover with a single, usually complete, breast-band. In all respects very similar to Ringed Plover, particularly the smaller, darker race *tundrae* which breeds in N Scandinavia and N USSR. The only certain distinctions from Ringed are a greater degree of webbing between the toes, a shorter and narrower wingbar, and call. In general, Semipalmated is smaller, shorter-billed and more compact. In breeding plumage it shows a smaller white area above and behind the eye, and black breast-band is often narrower, especially in the centre (but width is variable in both species). In flight, the white wingbar is slightly less prominent; adults have the inner web of the second innermost secondary washed with brown, while on Ringed Plover it is virtually white. Similarly, on the outer 3 primaries the white is restricted sharply to the primary shaft, while in Ringed it extends slightly onto the outer webs. On juveniles of both species, the wingbar may be more extensive. Many individuals can be identified by measurements, but palmations are the most useful character for live birds in the hand. On American coasts, Semipalmated is most likely to be confused with Wilson's (90), but is easily distinguished (with practice) by proportions of head and bill and by leg colour: Wilson's always has heavy head, thick bill and pinkish legs. Other bright-legged small plovers in the Americas are Piping (92) and Collared (103): note pale upperparts and white uppertail-coverts of Piping, and lack of white on hindneck of Collared. **Bare parts:** Colours and sequence of colour changes as in Ringed Plover. Bill averages slightly shorter. Toes have substantial webs, distinctly larger than those of Ringed Plover: web between inner and middle toes is obvious in Semipalmated, very small and rarely visible in Ringed; both species show a web between outer and middle toes, larger in Semipalmated.

VOICE Flight call is sufficiently distinct from that of Ringed to allow confident identification on call alone: a clear, fairly sharp whistle with a rising inflection 'chee-wee' or 'chuwit', less mellow and fluty than similar call of Ringed. When anxious, gives a sharp 'chip-chip' or 'tup-tup'. In display flight, a regularly-repeated, slightly harsh 'kerr-ree'.

HABITS Breeding habits and habitat much as Ringed Plover. In tiny area of overlap on Baffin I., mixed pairs have been reported but there is apparently no zone of intergradation. Non-breeding habitat is also similar to that used by Ringed, including coastal mud and sand, and margins of inland lakes and pools.

MOVEMENTS Many winter coastally in USA and Central America, but most perform long-distance movement to South America. In autumn, many migrate via James Bay, the Maritime Provinces and New England, and the W Atlantic Ocean to make landfall in Antilles or northern South America, but others are seen throughout USA. More common in interior USA on spring passage. Occurs on Bermuda in autumn. Vagrant to Tierra del Fuego (May 1929), Azores (Sept 1972, an adult ringed two months earlier in the Gulf of St Lawrence), and Isles of Scilly, SW England (Oct-Nov 1978).

DESCRIPTION Breeding: Differs from *tundrae* race of Ringed Plover as follows. The white post-ocular patch is small, but variable, sometimes almost absent. Black breast-band is slightly narrower, especially in the centre. Wingbar comprises white shafts to all primaries, obscure white on outer webs of middle primaries, extensive white on inner webs of middle and inner primaries, and white-based secondaries (particularly inner webs). White on inner secondaries is much reduced and shows a grey-brown wash. **Non-breeding:** Black on head and breast is replaced by grey-brown. White post-ocular patch larger, sometimes joined to white forecrown to form a supercilium. Coverts are very narrowly fringed whitish when fresh, but this colour is soon lost. Breeding plumage is regained well before breeding season. **Juvenile:** As non-breeding, but more extensively white, especially on supercilium, inner secondaries and rest of wingbar. Upperpart feathers, including coverts, have narrow dark subterminal bands and extensive buff fringes.

AGE/SEX The juvenile upperpart fringes are detectable at close range to Nov, but beware similar fringes on fresh coverts of non-breeding adult. Dull bare parts are a helpful indication of a young bird. Females average slightly larger, and in breeding plumage have a substantial number of brown feathers in black of mask and breast, which in males are virtually all-black. Some breeding males show virtually no white above the eye. Sexes are distinguishable only at close range or in the hand.

RACES No geographical variation is known.
MEASUREMENTS Length 170-190 mm (7"). Wing 113-131 mm; bill 11-14 mm; tarsus 22-26 mm; tail 54-60 mm.
REFERENCES Sutton and Parmelee (1955), Smith (1969), Dukes (1980).

88 LONG-BILLED PLOVER *Charadrius placidus* Plate 34

Other name: Long-billed Ringed Plover
A bird of S and E Asia, yet to be recorded out of this region, which has plumage features in common with Little Ringed Plover (89) and Killdeer (91).

IDENTIFICATION Head pattern and single complete breast-band are similar to Ringed (86), Semipalmated (87) and Little Ringed Plovers, but Long-billed is a slightly larger bird with a longish dark bill; fairly long legs and tail give a long and tall appearance rather different from those species. Black frontal bar is broader; ear-coverts are always suffused brown or grey-brown, and are never completely black. White above black frontal bar recalls Little Ringed, as do yellowish eye-ring and legs, but black bands across lores are narrower and do not meet above the base of the bill. In flight, shows a very weak wingbar like that of Little Ringed, but relatively broader wings; tail is longish and graduated, with little white at sides and an unusually clear dark subterminal bar. Tail shape and rufous fringes to fresh upperparts recall Killdeer, but uppertail is plain brown and there is only a single breast-band. **Bare parts:** Bill long and slim, black; at close range, yellowish-orange is visible at base of lower mandible. Iris dark brown; narrow yellowish-orange eye-ring. Legs long, pale yellowish or pinkish-yellow.
VOICE Usual call is a clear penetrating 'piwee' with a rising inflection; when breeding, also a pleasant 'tudulu'.
HABITS Nests mainly on pebble beaches and spits on lakeshores and in stony riverbeds at altitudes of up to 1000 m; avoids areas of pure sand and large stones. Occurs in similar habitats when not nesting, also in cut ricefields and coastal habitats including mudflats. Not gregarious, normally scattered when feeding, but sometimes gathers into loose groups.
MOVEMENTS Most migrate south or southwest after breeding, but apparently resident in parts of S China and in Japan from Honshu southwards. Winter range extends from Nepal and Bengal to northern parts of SE Asia. Vagrant Malaysia and recently Brunei (singles) and Bali (flock of five).

DESCRIPTION Breeding: Forehead white adjoining bill, with broad black frontal bar which narrows noticeably towards the eye. Narrow white above frontal bar broadens into white patch above and behind the eye. Black or blackish-brown eye-stripe from bill to behind eye; ear-coverts brown or grey-brown. Underparts are white except for breast-band, rather narrow in centre, black or blackish often suffused grey-brown at sides; blackish continues around base of hindneck below white collar. Underwing-coverts and axillaries white. Upperparts, including crown and wing-coverts, are fairly warm greyish-brown with bright cinnamon fringes when fresh, but rapidly becoming uniform; greater coverts have narrow white tips. Flight feathers are dark brown, but with narrow whitish or greyish edges to inner primaries and outer and middle secondaries which contribute to the weak wingbar; outer primary lacks white on shaft. Central tail feathers are uniform brown, but others show grey-brown at base, clear white at tip and a blackish subterminal bar; on outer pair, subterminal bar extends to outer web. **Non-breeding:** Plumage may become duller for a short period during wing moult.
Juvenile: Frontal bar is lacking and forehead is connected to an indistinct supercilium. Breast-band lacks black. Upperparts are fringed neatly with warm buff.
AGE/SEX Juvenile plumage is lost very rapidly, so that ageing is rarely possible in the field. Sexes are similar in plumage and in size.
RACES No geographical variation is known.
MEASUREMENTS Length 190-210 mm (8"). Wing 135-154 mm; bill 18-21 mm; tarsus 30-34 mm; tail 76-78 mm.
REFERENCES Panov (1963), Taylor (1979).

89 LITTLE RINGED PLOVER *Charadrius dubius* Plate 34

This plover has a very wide distribution, but is rather restricted in its habitat. It has spread westwards in recent decades.

IDENTIFICATION A small plover with plumage pattern similar to Ringed (86), Semipalmated (87) and Long-billed Plovers (88), but readily distinguished by diagnostic call, smaller size and rather different shape. Best distinctions from Ringed in adult plumage are the bold yellow eye-ring, pinker or more yellowish legs, the lack of obvious colour on the bill-base, and the lack of an obvious wingbar. Shape is less bulky, with a proportionately smaller and less bulbous head; stance is rather furtive, and feeding actions are faster than in Ringed. At close range, adult also differs in showing a narrow white line above the black frontal bar. Juveniles are best distinguished by shape and size, more conspicuous eye-ring than in Ringed of similar age, usually duller legs, call, and lack of wingbar. Distinctions from Semipalmated are similar, but note that Semipalmated is slightly smaller and more dainty than Ringed, with more obvious webbing between the toes than in other small plovers. Long-billed shares a number of features with Little Ringed, but is clearly larger and also has proportionately longer bill, legs and tail; both show a weak wing-bar (formed chiefly by white at covert tips), a conspicuous eye-ring, white above black frontal bar, and duller bill and legs than Ringed Plover. Long-billed differs in absence of black at base of forehead, brownish ear-coverts in all plumages, and slightly-graduated tail with strong subterminal bar extending to the outer web of the outer feathers. **Bare parts:** Bill thinner than in Ringed Plover, blackish with some yellow at base of lower mandible. Iris dark brown; eye-ring broad and bright yellow in adults, dull yellow in juveniles. Legs usually dull pinkish in breeding birds, but, exceptionally, pinkish-red or dark greyish; juveniles tend to have yellower legs, sometimes dull orange-yellow.

VOICE A clear, descending 'pee-oo' is the usual call, readily distinguishable from Ringed Plover's call which rises in pitch; it is exceptionally far-carrying for a bird of its size. Also gives a shorter 'peeu' or 'cru', and an insistent 'pip' in alarm. Song is a repeated 'cree-ah', heard most often early in the season.

HABITS Nests in a wide variety of inland habitats, chiefly along gravelly rivers or lakeshores but has adapted well to industrial sites such as gravel-workings and even rubbish-tips. The nest itself may be well away from the water's edge, even on adjacent farmland. Normally defends a territory against conspecifics and other small plovers, but may nest semi-colonially with nests as little as 9 m apart. Breeding season in Europe is Apr-Sept, in S India Dec-June. When not nesting, also occurs on muddy shores inland or on coast. Often solitary, rarely joining with mass flights or roosts of other waders, but sometimes occurs in small flocks of a dozen or so. Behaviour is wary, but may freeze and allow close approach.

MOVEMENTS A migratory species over the bulk of the range, but present in southern breeding areas all year. The race *curonicus* is entirely migratory, visiting Africa, India and SE Asia (where it mixes with the resident *jerdoni*) and the Indonesian region; some winter around the Mediterranean. Most leave breeding areas by late Sept and return during Mar. In Africa, most winter between the Sahara and the equator, but slightly farther south in E Africa; vagrant central Zambia. Vagrant also to Ireland (only three records by 1979), Azores, Madeira, Cape Verde Is., Australia (12 records by 1981), and W Aleutians (June 1974).

DESCRIPTION Breeding: Plumage differences from Ringed are as follows. Black band above base of bill narrower, sometimes incomplete. Black frontal bar has a narrow white line above. Flight feathers lack conspicuous white, but greater coverts and greater primary coverts are narrowly tipped white. **Non-breeding:** Black of head is replaced by brown or blackish-brown, and breast-band has extensive brown suffusion. White of forehead and supercilia is tinged buff. Breeding plumage is often regained quickly. **Juvenile:** As non-breeding, but upperparts are sandy-brown with warm buff fringes and clear dark subterminal lines. Dark crown; obscure buffish supercilia; breast-band brown, flecked buff, forming patches at sides of breast which barely join in centre.

AGE/SEX Juvenile fringes are distinctive, but most feathers are replaced within about three months of fledging. Older birds are distinguishable in the hand by retained juvenile inner medians and more worn and pointed primaries. In breeding pairs, male is often distinguishable by thicker eye-ring, and female by brown tinges to black areas.

RACES Three: nominate (Philippines, New Guinea, New Britain and New Ireland), *jerdoni* (India and SE Asia) and *curonicus* (N Africa, Eurasia from Britain to Japan). All are very similar, differing chiefly in length and colour of the bill. Both *jerdoni* and nominate show more yellow at base of bill than *curonicus*, but of the three races *jerdoni* has the shortest bill and *dubius* the longest. The race *jerdoni* is also rather short-winged. In *jerdoni* and nominate, non-breeding plumage hardly differs from breeding.

MEASUREMENTS Length 140-170 mm (6"). Wing 105-117 mm (*jerdoni*), 109-123 mm (*curonicus*); bill 11-12 mm (*jerdoni*), 12-14 mm (*curonicus*), 14-16 mm (nominate); tarsus 22-26 mm; tail 51-64 mm.

REFERENCES Simmons (1956), Jaensch (1982).

90 WILSON'S PLOVER *Charadrius wilsonia* Plate 39

Other name: Thick-billed Plover

This American species is another small plover with a single breast-band, but is remarkably large-billed and more sexually dimorphic than most ringed plovers.

IDENTIFICATION A small to medium-sized plover, brown above and white below, with a white hind-neck collar and a single, rather broad, black, rufous or grey-brown breast-band. Readily distinguished from similar species by its disproportionately large and heavy black bill. The black frontal bar of the male often does not reach the eye, so that white forehead is contiguous with a short supercilium. Pinkish legs are like those of Killdeer (91), but colour is unique among American plovers which have a single breast-band. Female lacks black, and may be distinctly rufous or gingery on mask and breast-band. A more difficult species to identify in flight, but is larger than Semipalmated Plover (87): look for distinctive bill. Beware confusion with half-grown Killdeer. See also Ringed (86), Piping (92), Kentish (98) and Collared Plovers (103). **Bare parts:** Bill black, deep at base and rather long, both mandibles curving evenly to a dagger-like pointed tip. Iris dark brown. Legs pinkish or pinkish-grey, brighter when breeding.

VOICE The call is a high, rather weak, whistled 'whit', less melodic than calls of other small plovers. In alarm, gives a repeated sharp 'quit' or 'quit-it', lower in pitch.

HABITS Normally a strictly coastal species and only a vagrant inland, but has bred inland (once) at Salton Sea, S California. Breeds typically on sandy beaches and sandbars or the edges of coastal lagoons; when not breeding, also occurs on estuarine mud-flats and near fresh waters a short distance inland. Usually feeds on higher, drier parts of beach; feeding action is remarkably slow and deliberate for a bird of its size. Crabs form a substantial portion of the diet. Behaviour is generally alert, but often allows quite close approach. A fairly gregarious bird, often in small flocks or with other small plovers.

MOVEMENTS A partial migrant, found all year in many parts of range. Nominate race withdraws from E USA (except S Florida) in the northern winter, and occurs south to Brazil. Vagrant Bermuda, and north to Nova Scotia on the east coast; inland, there are several records from the Great Lakes region May-July and one from Oklahoma. On the Pacific coast, *beldingi* is also migratory to some extent, reaching central Peru in winter; it occurs as a vagrant in S California; two records of flocks at airstrips in E Ecuador in Sept may be of this race.

DESCRIPTION Note racial variations. **Breeding male:** Forehead extensively white, normally contiguous with white supercilium. Front of crown black; rest of crown, nape and ear-coverts grey-brown, variably tinged rufous. Blackish line across lores. Underparts white except for fairly broad black breast-band. White collar around hindneck; upperparts otherwise even grey-brown with paler feather edgings. Lesser coverts often darker than median coverts, forming a paler panel in the mid-wing. Greater coverts tipped white. Primaries blackish with narrow white bases to inners, decreasing towards outer primaries, but all show white on shaft. Secondaries dark, with slightly paler bases. Central tail feathers as upperparts, but with subterminal darker patch; others white-tipped and progressively whiter towards edge of tail. **Breed-**

ing female: As male, but with less white on forehead, and supercilium tinged pale brown. Black on head and breast is replaced by brown or rufous. **Non-breeding:** Both sexes are as female, but head and breast markings are grey-brown and usually lack rufous. **Juvenile:** As non-breeding but breast-band less distinct, sometimes almost broken in the centre. Upperpart feathers grey-brown, with dark sepia subterminal lines and broad buff fringes giving a strongly scaly pattern.

AGE/SEX Juvenile can be distinguished in the field by scaly upperparts for only a few months after fledging. Sexes are dimorphic in breeding plumage: male is black on lores, frontal bar and breast-band, female brown or rufous.

RACES Three: nominate (E USA, E Mexico, Belize, Bahamas, Greater Antilles, Leeward Is.), *cinnamominus* (NE Colombia to NE Brazil, including the Dutch Antilles, Venezuela islands, Trinidad, Grenada and Mustique), and *beldingi* (Pacific coast, central Baja California south to Panama). The nominate race generally lacks rufous except on the ear-coverts; West Indian individuals, however, sometimes separated as '*rufinucha*', are strongly rufous on crown. In *cinnamominus*, crown is strongly rufous, males show mixed rufous and black in the breast-band, and females are strongly gingery on mask and breast-band. The race *beldingi* is darker above than nominate, and has a broader mask, less white on forehead, a shorter, narrower supercilium, typically a narrower breast-band, and more rufous on crown and nape and (in female) on breast-band.

MEASUREMENTS Length 165-200 mm (7¼″). Wing 111-128 mm; bill 19-22 mm; tarsus 27-32 mm; tail 42-50 mm.

REFERENCES Tomkins (1944), Bergstrom (1982).

91 KILLDEER *Charadrius vociferus* Plate 39

A familiar Nearctic and tropical American species found widely inland on grass and farmland, even among habitations, as well as on coasts.

IDENTIFICATION Very distinctive; it is the largest of the ringed plovers and the only double-banded plover within its (currently recorded) range. The two black or brownish-black breast-bands are present in all post-fledging plumages. Its unique bright orange-brown rump and uppertail and strong white wing-bar complete the identification. The other plovers with two black breast-bands, Three-banded (96), Forbes's (97) and Two-banded (106) are all smaller, plain-rumped, and with less black on the face than Killdeer. At rest, folded wings fall well short of tail-tip. In flight, wing-action is easy and graceful, rather different from its congeners and even recalling a Ruff (210). **Bare parts:** Bill black. Iris dark brown; eye-ring bright orange. Legs pinkish-grey (occasionally yellowish).

VOICE Penetratingly loud, shrill calls, usually given rapidly and repeatedly. Typically 'kill-dee' and mono- or multisyllabic variants such as 'twill-wee-wee-wee' and 'twee-il'.

HABITS Breeds in savannas and agricultural land, mainly in the lowlands, sometimes at high density.

Also occurs in a wide range of other grassy or wetland habitats, including estuaries (especially on migration and in winter). Common close to habitation and sometimes even nests on the flat roofs of houses. There is a striking aerial display in which male (often accompanied by the female) hovers high in the air or performs a butterfly-flight on stiff, slowly beating wings, calling repeatedly. A well-developed distraction display features the bright rump and tail. Typically a noisy and conspicuous species, often the first among a mixed group of waders to take wing and give the alarm. Typical plover feeding habits, including frequent foot-pattering, even on grass. Usually seen singly or in pairs, sometimes in small flocks when not breeding.

MOVEMENTS The nominate race is migratory, leaving more northerly and more inland areas of North America during July-Nov, sometimes later, and returning Feb-Apr. Winter range includes West Indies, where mixes with the resident race. Late-autumn storms may carry vagrants northwards up the Atlantic coast. Vagrant Hawaii, Galapagos, Labrador,

Iceland, Faeroes, Norway, Britain, Ireland, France, Switzerland and the Azores. W European records are mostly Nov-Apr, in contrast to Sept-Oct peak for other American birds.

DESCRIPTION Breeding: White of forehead extends narrowly underneath eye. Short blackish eye-stripe behind eye is just contiguous with narrow black frontal bar. Black line from bill crosses cheeks to join brown or blackish-brown patch on ear-coverts. Short white supercilium above and behind the eye. Crown and nape are brown. Underparts and hindneck collar are white, except for broad black upper breast-band, continuing around base of hindneck, narrower lower breast-band, and a brownish suffusion on the sides of the breast between the two bands. Upperparts brown, sometimes with rufous fringes. Greater coverts are white-tipped. Flight feathers are blackish-brown, crossed by broad and long white wingbar. Lower back, rump and uppertail bright orange-brown, contrasting with rest of upperparts. Tail is long and graduated, with orange-brown at base, a broad blackish-brown subterminal area, broadest on central feathers, and a white edge and tip. **Non-breeding:** As above, but adults after autumn moult show exten-sive rufous and buffish-brown fringes on mantle and coverts. Black areas may show some admixed brown. Eye-ring is duller. **Juvenile:** Closely resembles adult once fledged, but mantle and coverts all have buff fringes and indistinct dark subterminal markings. Down-streamers may be visible on the end of the tail for several weeks.

AGE/SEX Buff fringes and tail-down identify juven-ile, but after the post-juvenile moult ageing is possi-ble only in the hand. Since the timing of the breeding season varies with latitude, juveniles may be pres-ent at a variety of times of year. Sexing is not usually possible, but some breeding females show much brown admixed with the black on the face.

RACES Three: nominate race (USA, Canada) is the largest; *ternominatus* (resident in West Indies) is smaller and greyer; and *peruvianus* (Peru, NW Chile) resembles the nominate race, but is smaller and with more pronounced rufous feather edgings.

MEASUREMENTS Length 230-260 mm (9¾"). Wing 147-175 mm (nominate), 151-165 mm (*peruvianus*); bill 18-23 mm; tarsus 32-38 mm; tail 88-98 mm.

REFERENCES Demaree (1975), Mace (1978), Lening-ton (1980), Mundahl (1982).

92 PIPING PLOVER *Charadrius melodus*   Plate 39

A distinctive ringed plover of central and E North America which is currently declining in numbers. Prairie populations are small, but have never been censused; there are fewer than 20 pairs in the Great Lakes area and fewer than a thousand pairs on the Atlantic coast.

IDENTIFICATION The combination of orange legs and bill-base, like Semipalmated Plover (87) but brighter, and very pale sandy-grey upperparts, even paler than 'Snowy' Plover (98), is diagnostic. In addi-tion, Piping never shows black on ear-coverts, and little on lores, so that dark eye stands out boldly from a pale face; it is also the only small plover with a white patch across the uppertail-coverts. Black breast-band is often incomplete. Piping is a larger bird than Snowy, and with stubby bill and plump outline more simi-lar to Semipalmated in shape. In flight, it shows a long and prominent white wingbar, and the white uppertail-covert patch is conspicuous. **Bare parts:** Bill bright pale orange with a sharply-defined blackish tip, rather short and stubby; in non-breeding and juvenile plumages, bill may be all-blackish. Iris dark brown. Legs orange, sometimes tinged yellowish, duller on young and non-breeding birds.

VOICE The species is named after its distinctive call, a penetrating, plaintive, somewhat ventriloquial whis-tle 'peep' or a descending 'peep-lo'. Series of descending whistles is given in display. Calls of females are slightly shriller than those of males.

HABITS Nests on sandy beaches on coasts or inland lakeshores, preferring areas with scant vegetation. This habitat choice has brought conflict with human leisure interests, and there has been a considerable decline and some range contraction during recent decades. Breeding distribution lies to the south of that of Semipalmated. Strictly coastal in winter, again preferring sandy habitats. Feeding action is rather steady and deliberate. Territorial when breeding, but often seen in small flocks in winter and on migration.

MOVEMENTS Prairie, Great Lakes and N Atlantic populations are entirely migratory; spring arrivals begin in late Mar and last departures are in late Aug. Present all year on coasts from N Carolina south-wards. Usual winter range extends to NE Mexico and the Greater Antilles, but there are two reports for Belize. Vagrant California (has wintered), NW Mexico, Ecuador (Oct 1955) and Lesser Antilles (Jan 1977). A few non-breeders summer south of breeding range.

DESCRIPTION Breeding: Forehead white, with black frontal bar which virtually reaches the eyes. Small whitish patch above and behind the eye. Lores, ear-coverts, crown and nape very pale sandy-grey; in males, lores may be dusky near bill. Underparts and hindneck collar are white, except for rather narrow black or brownish-black breast-band which continues around base of hindneck and is often broken or obscure in the centre of the breast. Mantle to rump, also scapulars, tertials and wing-coverts are pale sandy-grey; greater coverts are white-tipped. Flight feathers are darker, crossed by white wingbar; bases of all primaries and secondaries are white, and inner secondaries are entirely white. Uppertail-coverts are broadly white at tip, and base of tail is white, form-ing a squarish white patch. Outer two pairs of tail feathers are white, others sandy-grey, darker towards tip. **Non-breeding:** All black on head and breast is lost. Face is very pale; white forehead is contiguous with whitish supercilium. Breast-band is reduced to greyish patches at sides of breast. **Juvenile:** As non-breeding, but with upperparts broadly fringed pale buff, giving a faintly scaly pattern.

AGE/SEX Juveniles are distinct in the field until about Oct. After post-juvenile moult, young may be distin-guished in the hand by rather worn and pointed primaries and by retained juvenile inner medians. First-year birds are rather dull in breeding plumage. Sexes can be separated only in full breeding plumage: males then show brighter bare parts and a broader frontal bar, while females may be brownish-black on frontal bar and breast. Bill of male is faintly larger. Extent of breast-band shows similar variability in both sexes.

RACES Monotypic. Two races have previously been described on the basis of the extent of the breast-band: nominate (coastal), band usually broken; and *circumcinctus* (Great Lakes and Prairies), band usually complete. Both groups, however, show a wide range of variation in this character; moreover, individuals may change either towards or away from a complete breast-band between seasons.

MEASUREMENTS Length 170-190 mm (7¼"). Wing 114-127 mm; bill 12-14 mm; tarsus 21-24 mm; tail 48-57 mm.

REFERENCES Wilcox (1959), Cairns and McLaren (1980), Cairns (1982), Russell (1983).

93 BLACK-BANDED SANDPLOVER *Charadrius thoracicus*   Plate 41

Other names: Madagascar Plover, Black-banded Plover
A small plover very closely related to Kittlitz's Sandplover (94), restricted to Madagascar (where Kittlitz's has arrived relatively recently as a nesting species). Recent records are all from the southwest coastal strip and indicate that possibly fewer than a thousand individuals now remain. At present, it is not clear whether competition with Kittlitz's may account for the decline.

IDENTIFICATION Shares head pattern, darker lesser coverts, and dark centres to upperpart feathers with Kittlitz's, but adult has a black breast-band and deeper cinnamon on lower breast and belly. Juvenile is like Kittlitz's, but with a greyish-brown breast-band. Black-banded is slightly larger than Kittlitz's on average, but measurements overlap considerably. Wingbar is bolder. Most unlikely to be seen away from Madagascar, but may well occur outside presently-known range. See also St Helena Plover (95). **Bare parts:** Bill black. Iris dark. Legs black, greyish in juveniles.

VOICE Usual call is 'pit' or 'pirds', very similar to that of Kittlitz's but hoarser; also a hoarse 'twitwitwi'. In distraction display, adult calls 'tui' or 'twiz'.

HABITS Generally very similar to Kittlitz's, with which it frequently occurs on grassland, but does not penetrate far inland. Preferred habitat is coastal grazed grassland, often very dry. Often visits the margins of shallow brackish marshes and ponds; less often, occurs on sandy ocean beaches and sandy or muddy estuarine flats. Nesting season appears to be chiefly Nov-Jan, but there is a record of a chick in Aug. Fairly common in Mangoky region (NW part of known range); at times, gathers into single-species roosts of as many as 33 birds. Commonly seen with other coastal waders such as Ringed Plover (86) and White-fronted Sandplover (99), but tends not to join communal roosting flocks.

MOVEMENTS Believed to be entirely sedentary. The species was described in 1896 from a specimen collected at Loholoka, about one-third of the way up the east coast, but all subsequent records are from the SW coastal strip between Morondava and Androka (21-25° S). The breeding range may not yet have been fully described.

DESCRIPTION Adult: Differs from Kittlitz's as follows. Fairly broad black breast-band, contiguous with black of eye-stripe and hindneck collar. Underparts from chin to breast-band pure white; below breast-band, lower breast and belly are washed with cinnamon-buff, most deeply on lower belly, vent and undertail-coverts. Brown of upperparts is slightly paler; lesser coverts are dark, but contrast less than in Kittlitz's. Wingbar is bolder: white is present on shafts of all primaries, and the inner 6 show white on the webs. **Juvenile:** Underparts greyish-white crossed by greyish-brown breast-band; otherwise as Kittlitz's. Legs and feet grey.

AGE/SEX Ageing methods described for Kittlitz's may perhaps apply. Differences in depth of colour on underparts may be related to sex, females being paler. **RACES** No geographical variation is known.

MEASUREMENTS Length about 130-140 mm (5¼"). One specimen measured: wing 108 mm; bill 16 mm; tarsus 30 mm; tail 47 mm.

REFERENCES Appert (1971), Dhondt (1975), Collar and Stuart (1985).

94 KITTLITZ'S SANDPLOVER *Charadrius pecuarius*   Plate 41

Other name: Kittlitz's Plover
A widely-distributed but rather local African plover, common at many inland wetlands.

IDENTIFICATION A rather long-legged small plover with dark brown, rather variegated upperparts, a blackish leading edge to the wing, and black-and-white patterning on head and hindneck but not on breast. Breast is often strongly suffused creamy-buff. In flight, it shows white tail-sides, a short white wing-bar concentrated on the outer greater coverts and inner primaries, and dark lesser coverts with a distinctive pale panel formed by the median coverts;

most unusually for a small plover, the toes project well beyond the tail-tip. Juvenile Kittlitz's lacks black and white on head, sometimes has well-marked breast-patches, and may resemble other small plovers, particularly Lesser (107) and White-fronted (99); best distinctions are longer legs, blackish lesser coverts (often visible on folded wing), well-defined buffish collar, and dark feather centres which give a more variegated appearance to the upperparts (some Kittlitz's, however, are almost plain). See Black-banded Sandplover (93) and St Helena Plover (95), which are closely related. In Madagascar, Black-banded is easily distinguished at all ages by breast-band, but note that Kittlitz's often shows brown patches at sides of breast. **Bare parts:** Bill black. Iris dark brown. Legs greenish-black in breeding adults, otherwise paler greenish- or brownish-grey.

VOICE Often silent, but may give a hard 'trip' or 'tric', or a plaintive 'pip-ip', in alarm or when flushed. A short trilling call is sometimes given in flight.

HABITS Essentially a waterside species, but often occurs in cultivated ground or grasslands or on dried mud some distance from the water's edge. Found mainly around inland lakes and rivers, but also occurs on coastal sandy beaches and intertidal mud. Often gathers into flocks, sometimes over a hundred, and may join roosts of other small waders. Nest is usually fairly close to water's edge; adjacent nests may be as little as 20 m apart. Breeds all year in some parts of range. Not a shy bird and may tolerate consider-able disturbance near the nest.

MOVEMENTS Almost entirely sedentary, but seasonal appearances and disappearances in some locations show that at least local movements do occur. The only record beyond the breeding range is of a female apparently collected in S Norway in May 1913.

DESCRIPTION Breeding: Forehead white, enclosed by black frontal bar and lores. Black from bill con-tinues through eye and down sides of neck to meet in a half-collar at base of hindneck. Very narrow white line above frontal bar. White supercilia from eye backwards meet in a broad white half-collar above black on hindneck. Crown and nape, also mantle, scapulars, tertials, median and greater coverts, are dark brown with variable buffish edges and fringes giving a rather variegated appearance; paler edges often wear off to leave feathers lanceolate. Lesser coverts, lower back, rump and uppertail are blackish-brown with a few narrow buffish fringes. Primary coverts and alula are blackish. Primaries and secon-daries blackish, with a narrow white trailing edge to the secondaries; a short wingbar comprises fine white tips to the greater coverts, white on the webs of (typi-cally 5) inner primaries, and white primary shafts (sec-ond and third outermost primaries often lack white on shaft). Central tail feathers blackish-brown, dark-est at tip, others brown with increasing amounts of white on edges and tip; outer pair normally pure white. Underparts white with wash of creamy-buff across breast and upper belly, variable in extent and in depth of colour; some individuals also have small patches of dark brown feathering on the sides of the breast. Axillaries white, underwing-coverts mainly white but sullied with brown along leading edge and on primary coverts. **Non-breeding:** In some, not all, black of frontal bar and eye-stripe becomes brownish, white of supercilium and half-collar becomes duller, colour on underparts fades, and sides of breast become sullied with brown. **Juvenile:** Like a dull non-breeding individual, but all feathers of upperparts, including wing-coverts, broadly fringed pale buff-brown. Forehead, supercilium and hindneck collar are dull buffish-white. Underparts are whitish, usually with a buffish wash and brown patches at sides of breast. Some show a narrow and irregular necklace of brown spots.

AGE/SEX After post-juvenile moult, young birds may be identified in the hand by retained juvenile feathers on inner medians and rump and by worn and pointed primaries. In full breeding plumage, males tend to have blacker facial markings and deeper colour on the breast, but sexing is extremely difficult.

RACES Now considered monotypic, although those in Nile valley and in Madagascar have previously been treated as separate races. Equatorial populations average slightly smaller than those in north and south of range.

MEASUREMENTS Length 120-140 mm (5"). Wing 98-112 mm; bill 15-18 mm; tarsus 28-33 mm; tail 41-46 mm.

REFERENCES Hall (1958), Clark (1982a), Taylor (1983).

95 ST HELENA PLOVER *Charadrius sanctaehelenae* Plate 41

Other names: Wirebird, St Helena Sandplover
An endemic to the remote Atlantic island of St Helena, 2800 km west of S Angola. It is very closely related to Kittlitz's Sandplover (94) and sometimes treated as conspecific. The total population is probably about 200-300 pairs. Habitat change poses a threat to several of the breeding areas.

IDENTIFICATION Fairly common on St Helena, but most unlikely ever to be encountered elsewhere. Shares dark centres to upperpart feathers, blackish lesser coverts, and head pattern with Kittlitz's and Black-banded (93), but is conspicuously larger, longer-billed and longer-legged. The upperparts show less conspicuous buffish feather edges than on Kit-tlitz's, and the underparts are whiter, lacking creamy-buff. The wings are relatively shorter, broader and more rounded, and show a weaker wingbar: the primary shafts lack white except on the outer primary. The webs of the primaries are broader than on Kit-tlitz's. Feathering at the base of the upper mandible is more extensively black than on the mainland species; black of lores often almost meets above bill. On the underwing, entire leading edge is dusky and there is less white on the under primary coverts. **Bare parts:** Bill black. Iris dark brown. Legs black; look spindly and probably gave rise to the local name of Wirebird; chicks have olive-green legs.

VOICE Similar to Kittlitz's; no differences are known.

HABITS Forages on grassy plains, upland pastures, ploughed fields, even in remote gardens, but is never seen on the shore. Widely distributed, particularly in flatter areas and around the edges of the island. When breeding, withdraws to open plains in more remote areas; 11 separate breeding areas were known in 1952. Nests mostly in dry season, but breeding sea-son spans all year except July-Sept. One or two eggs are laid in a simple scrape. Feral cats and the

introduced Indian Myna *Acridotheres tristis* are occasional predators of eggs or young and rats may also present a problem. Usually seen in pairs, more rarely in groups of up to six. Often very reluctant to fly.
MOVEMENTS Entirely sedentary.
DESCRIPTION Adult: See Identification section for differences from Kittlitz's. **Juvenile:** Brown feathers of crown and upperparts are fairly narrowly fringed with whitish or pale buff, and lack the broad pale edges of the adult feathers; some median coverts show a faint darker brown subterminal line. There is a dusky wash on the breast. Lores are whitish; black

is lacking on head and neck.
AGE/SEX After post-juvenile moult, some young birds retain old inner median coverts which will distinguish them in the hand. Primaries may become very worn. Sexes are similar in plumage and in size.
RACES Monotypic.
MEASUREMENTS Length around 150 mm (6"). Only 15 specimens measured: wing 112-118 mm; bill 21-22 mm; tarsus 38-41 mm; tail 51-56 mm.
REFERENCES Harting (1873), Pitman (1965), Collar and Stuart (1985).

96 THREE-BANDED PLOVER *Charadrius tricollaris*   Plate 40

Other names: Treble-banded Plover, Three-banded Sandplover
A common and familiar small plover of inland wetlands throughout E and S Africa. A distinct race is found in Madagascar.

IDENTIFICATION Easily identified by conspicuous white 'head-band', white on forehead, and 'sandwich' pattern on breast with two black bands separated by a white one. The two black breast-bands are present in all plumages. In flight, shows very narrow white wingbar, visible only at close range, and long tail with extensive white on outer feathers; wingbeats are characteristically jerky and erratic. Forbes's Plover (97) of W Africa is similar, but larger and darker and without white on forehead. Both species have long wings and very long tail which give an elongated appearance unlike that of other small plovers. Forbes's also differs in darker wings, barred pattern on sides of tail and on longest undertail-coverts, and usually in choice of habitat. See also Killdeer (91) and Two-banded Plover (106), which also have two black breast-bands. **Bare parts:** Bill bright pinkish-red with dark brownish outer half. Iris pale walnut-brown; obvious orange-red eye-ring. Legs pinkish-brown.
VOICE When flushed, usual call is a plaintive piercing whistle with a rising inflection 'piuu-eet', sometimes repeated; also a shrill 'wick-wick'.
HABITS Found throughout the year around the margins of inland fresh waters, including rivers, muddy pools and large lakes; more rarely seen at coastal lagoons and estuaries, even on the beach, or in brackish habitats inland. Usually nests on shingle; season is chiefly Mar-June in tropics, later farther south, but will nest opportunistically if conditions are suitable. Often solitary, but mixes freely with other small waders; occasionally forms loose flocks of up to 40.
MOVEMENTS Mainly sedentary, but more widespread when not breeding, often occurring on temporary pools. Occasional records in E Nigeria, outside the known breeding range, suggest that longer movements sometimes occur.
DESCRIPTION Nominate race. **Breeding and non-breeding:** Forehead white; narrow white supercilia, just joining white forehead, meet across upper hindneck; crown and nape dark brown. Lores, sides of neck and hindneck are pale brown, becoming whitish on chin, throat and front of neck. Narrow black band across upper breast is bordered below by a broader white band; both black and white bands extend well around base of neck and virtually join across base of hindneck. Below the white band is a

Three-banded Plover

Forbes's Plover

second, broader, black breast-band. Rest of underparts are white; underwing is mainly white, but marked with brownish along leading edge and across greater primary coverts. Mantle, centre of back, rump and uppertail, scapulars, tertials and most wing-coverts are plain dark brown; greater coverts and sometimes some median coverts are tipped white. Alula, also median and greater primary coverts, are blackish with white tips. Flight feathers are dark brown, with white tips to secondaries, broadening strongly towards body, and to most primaries except the longest. Sides of lower back, rump and uppertail are white. Central pair of tail feathers is plain brown, narrowly tipped white when fresh, next pair brown with blackish subterminal band and large white tip; towards outer edge, brown and blackish are replaced progressively by white, so that outer pair is white with blackish subterminal band across inner web only. **Juvenile:** Black breast-bands are present before fledging; head pattern is also like adult's but initially with brownish forehead. All dark brown feathers of upperparts show narrow but clear buff fringe and dark subterminal line. Central tail feathers may retain long streamers of down (up to 15 mm) until well after fledging.

AGE/SEX Buff fringes are a clear indication of young bird, but beware white-fringed median coverts of some adults. After post-juvenile moult, most young retain some buff-fringed inner lesser and median coverts, easily visible in the hand. Primaries of young birds are narrower and wear faster than those of adults. Sexes are not known to differ in plumage or in size.

RACES Two: nominate (African continent) and *bifrontatus* (Madagascar). The race *bifrontatus* differs distinctly in dark greyish rather than pale brown face and neck, smaller whitish area below bill restricted to chin and upper throat, and bicoloured forehead: grey of lores extends across lower forehead, while white is restricted to a narrower band, higher on forehead than in nominate race. The grey face is already present in newly-fledged juveniles. Also, there is less white in the wing, particularly at the tips of the median and greater primary coverts and on the inner secondaries. It averages faintly larger in bill and tarsus measurements, but ranges overlap almost completely.

MEASUREMENTS Length about 180 mm (7"). Wing 106-117 mm; bill 15-17 mm; tarsus 24-26 mm (nominate), 25-27 mm (*bifrontatus*); tail 58-69 mm.

REFERENCES Tyler (1978), Clark (1982b).

97 FORBES'S PLOVER *Charadrius forbesi*   Plate 40

Other name: Forbes's Banded Plover
A close relative of Three-banded Plover (96) and sometimes considered conspecific. The ranges of the two species are largely separate.

IDENTIFICATION The bold 'sandwich' pattern on the breast of two black or brownish bands separated by a white one is always present, and precludes confusion with all other African plovers except Three-banded. Forbes's is an obviously larger, darker bird than Three-banded, more likely to be seen in dry country; the best distinction, however, is the absence of white on the forehead. Forbes's often has brownish breast-bands, while in Three-banded they are always black. In flight, Forbes's shows almost uniformly brown wings, with even less white than Three-banded, and blackish barring on the outer tail feathers; as in Three-banded, the flight is curiously jerky and erratic. Ringed Plover (86) is similar in size to Forbes's, but relatively shorter in wing and tail, with a bold white wingbar in flight and just a single breast-band. Killdeer (91), a potential vagrant to W Africa, also shows two black breast-bands, but is a much larger bird with a rufous uppertail, bold white wing-bar and neck collar and strongly-pied face pattern. South American Two-banded Plover (106) has mainly-white face, shorter tail, and black legs. **Bare parts:** Bill dark brown, with some pinkish at base of lower mandible. Iris pale walnut-brown; narrow orange-red eye-ring. Legs yellowish- or pinkish-brown.

VOICE A plaintive piping 'pee-oo', sometimes repeated, and a sharper 'pee-pee-pee-pee'.

HABITS Differs markedly from Three-banded in showing much less attachment to waterside habitats. Nests during the wet season, Mar-Sept in Nigeria, in rocky upland areas. The nest is usually near the summit of a granite outcrop, where surface-water run-off can be avoided; two or three eggs are laid in a scrape lined with tiny pebbles. Newly-fledged broods appear in nearby cultivation and ricefields. During the dry season, breeding grounds are deserted and the species moves to grassland habitats including airfields, golf-courses and even quite small open areas in forested regions, often close to habitation. May be seen in cultivated areas or at pools or reservoirs, but not often near streams. Like other grassland plovers, attracted to burnt ground. Not gregarious, but occasionally seen in small loose flocks.

MOVEMENTS Local movements are known between breeding and dry-season habitats, but it is likely that longer movements occur. In E Africa, a scarce migrant to western parts of Uganda and Tanzania, and recently Kenya, chiefly Apr-July. Not yet recorded south of Kabwe, central Zambia.

DESCRIPTION Breeding: Differences from Three-banded are as follows. Forehead, lores, neck and sides of face are brown, with only a small whitish patch on the chin; some individuals show a whitish spot before the eye. White band across upper hindneck is narrower. Brown of crown and upperparts is even darker than in Three-banded. Lower black breast-band is broader; upper band shades into brown of neck, and lacks a distinct upper border. Brown markings on leading edge of underwing and on under primary coverts are more extensive. Longest undertail-coverts are strongly barred with blackish-brown. White on upperwing is reduced: white tips to primary and greater coverts are very small, median coverts lack white, and white trailing edge to secondaries is much narrower. Outer three pairs of tail feathers are strongly notched or barred blackish-brown and white. **Non-breeding:** At least on some birds, breast-bands become dark brown, and supercilium and band across hindneck sullied with brownish-buff. **Juvenile:** Like a dull non-breeding adult, but dark feathers of crown and upperparts are fringed buffish and some also show a dark subterminal line. White at tips of middle tail feathers is replaced by buff. Undertail-coverts show less barring.

AGE/SEX Ageing is more difficult than in Three-banded, owing to less obvious subterminal lines on coverts and more variable adult plumages, but same methods probably apply. Sexes are not known to differ in plumage or in size.

RACES No geographical variation is known.

MEASUREMENTS Length about 200 mm (8"). Wing 123-135 mm; bill 16-19 mm; tarsus 29-33 mm; tail 61-75 mm.

REFERENCES Brown (1948).

98 KENTISH PLOVER *Charadrius alexandrinus*   **Plate 35**

Other name: Snowy Plover

Kentish is often considered conspecific with White-fronted Sandplover (99) and Red-capped Plover (100), sometimes even other small plovers, but these three are probably best considered together as a superspecies.

IDENTIFICATION This is a rather elegant small plover with relatively long dark legs, a slim dark bill, a white hindneck collar and dark lateral breast-patches (never a complete breast-band). In flight it shows a clear white wingbar and broad white sides to the tail. Breeding males have sharply-defined black breast-patches, and frontal bar not reaching the eyes. In the Americas, upperparts are obviously paler than in all similar species except the bright-legged Piping Plover (92), which also differs in stubby bill and white uppertail-coverts. Collared Plover (103) is paler-legged than Kentish, with darker upperparts, no white on hindneck and usually a complete breast-band. In Africa, Kentish overlaps in winter with White-fronted, but is readily distinguished by lack of creamy or rufous wash to underparts, whiter hindneck, clearer breast-patches, less obvious white forehead, and by shape: Kentish is rounder-bodied and shorter-tailed, with folded wing-tips level with or reaching beyond the tail-tip. Lesser Sandplover (107) is larger, lacks white on hindneck, and has more diffuse breast-patches. In the Indonesian region, Malaysian Plover (101) is similar, but has a more variegated appearance to the upperparts, and females have rufous breast-band. Kentish occurring within range of Malaysian are likely to be in non-breeding plumage and lack the black or rufous on head and breast always present on Malaysian. Red-capped Plover is easily distinguished by rufous cap and hindneck bordered by black on sides of neck. Beware confusion with juvenile or non-breeding Ringed (86), Semipalmated (87) or Little Ringed (89) Plovers, which may have a broken breast-band. **Bare parts:** Bill black, fairly long and slender. Iris dark brown. Legs dark grey, sometimes tinged brownish or yellowish, or pale yellowish-brown; pale legs seem more prevalent in less migratory populations.

VOICE In Palaearctic races, usual flight call is a soft 'pit' or 'twit'; sometimes single notes are run together into a rattle. Alarm calls are a hard 'prrr' and a plaintive 'too-eet'. Song is a rhythmic repetition of a rattled 'tjekke'. In the Americas, calls include a low 'krut' and a soft whistle 'ku-wheet'.

HABITS Nests chiefly on sandy beaches, either at coast or by brackish or saline inland wetlands; relatively uncommon at fresh water, even on migration. Both sexes incubate, but one parent, usually the female, often deserts the brood shortly after hatching and may mate again. Mainly coastal outside breeding season, but also regular at some brackish or saline lakes. Feeding action is faster than in Ringed and Semipalmated Plovers, and this often draws attention to it in mixed groups. Generally cautious, but sometimes allows close approach. Sociable, often in fairly small single-species flocks or mixed with flocks of other small waders.

MOVEMENTS Inland and northern coastal populations are migratory, present on breeding grounds

chiefly Mar-Oct, but present all year in southern parts of breeding range. In America, vagrant north to S British Columbia, Saskatchewan and Ontario and south to Panama. Records in SW Ecuador may refer to largely sedentary South American race. Palaearctic birds are vagrant north as far as Ireland and Poland and south to N Zaire and S Kenya.

DESCRIPTION Breeding male: White forehead and supercilium; black frontal bar not reaching eyes; blackish ear-coverts. Colour of crown and nape, also lores, is variable: see Races. Underparts white, with distinct black patches at sides of breast; white hindneck collar. Upperparts fairly uniform grey-brown, pale in American races. Primary coverts and flight feathers are blackish, with a white wingbar formed by tips of primary and greater coverts, bases of inner primaries, bases of most secondaries, and white inner secondaries. Sides of rump, uppertail and tail are white; tail centre is brown at base, slightly darker towards tip. **Breeding female:** See Races. Areas of black in male may be blackish-brown, or just brown, uniform with upperparts. **Non-breeding :** Both sexes lack black and resemble dull female. Breast-patches are brown, but sharply defined. **Juvenile:** As non-breeding, but white of forehead and supercilia is washed buffish, breast-patches are pale buffish-brown and more diffuse, and upperparts show distinct and neat buff fringes giving a scaly appearance at close range.

AGE/SEX Juvenile is distinct initially, but bleaching soon makes ageing difficult. First-year birds are duller than adults in breeding plumage. Sexes are distinct in breeding plumage, except in South America. Male has black on head and breast, female has these areas blackish-brown or brown; in W Palaearctic, male sometimes has a rufous cap.

RACES Six: nominate (Eurasia east to Korea, N Africa), *dealbatus* (Japan, E China), *seebohmi* (Sri Lanka, SE India), *javanicus* (Java), *nivosus* (USA, Caribbean), and *occidentalis* (coastal Peru and Chile). The last two, known collectively as 'Snowy Plover', have paler upperparts, shorter legs, typically white lores (at least in breeding birds), and generally lack rufous on cap; sexual dimorphism is less in *occidentalis* than in other races. Nominate and *dealbatus* are darker than Snowy, with breeding male showing black lores and often bright rufous crown and nape; *dealbatus* is longer-billed, but intergrades with the nominate race over a broad zone. The race *seebohmi* differs from Eurasian races in lacking rufous cap of male. Status of *javanicus* is obscure; some authors have treated it as a full species.

MEASUREMENTS Length 150-175 mm (6½"). Wing 102-123 mm; bill 13-19 mm; tarsus 23-30 mm; tail 42-50 mm.

REFERENCES Rittinghaus (1961), Purdue (1976), Jonsson (1983), Lessells (1984).

99 WHITE-FRONTED SANDPLOVER *Charadrius marginatus* **Plate 42**

Other name: White-fronted Plover
With Kentish (98) and Red-capped Plovers (100), this plover forms a group of closely-related but allopatric species; White-fronted is the African representative of the group.

IDENTIFICATION Size, habitat, wingbar and white sides to the tail all recall Kentish, with which it overlaps along the northern edge of its range. It is, however, shorter-legged and shorter-winged than Kentish, with wing-tips falling short of the tail-tip. Plumages are variable, but typically more rufous above and below and always lacking Kentish's sharply-defined black or brown breast-patches. Some White-fronted show rufous or buff breast-patches, sometimes centred brownish, most also have underparts broadly washed with creamy- or rufous-buff, a feature never shown by Kentish. At a distance, most White-fronted show a conspicuous, brilliant white triangle covering the forehead and the short supercilia, extending almost onto the crown. Juveniles lacking black on head might be mistaken for Kittlitz's (94), but are paler, often more rufous, shorter-legged and lack contrastingly dark lesser coverts. Beware confusion between rufous adults and Chestnut-banded Sandplover (102). **Bare parts:** Bill black. Iris brown. Legs greyish, usually tinged greenish or yellowish, rarely black.

VOICE Normal contact calls are a hard 'pwut' and a quiet low-pitched 'twit' or 'kewi'; also calls 'chuit' and a dry, trilling 'trrr' in anxiety or alarm.

HABITS Widely distributed along sandy coasts and larger rivers; also common at some larger lakes, both fresh and alkaline. Nests typically in sand, a short distance from water; adults often bury the eggs and carry water to the nest in the belly feathers. Feeds actively, often with very fast runs in which the body seems to drift sideways; may chase receding waves in the manner of Sanderling (189). Sometimes forms single-species flocks of up to 70 or more. Often gathers with other small waders at roost.

MOVEMENTS Mostly sedentary, but with seasonal influxes and departures at some localities suggesting that regular movements do occur. Some birds move to the coast or to larger lakes after breeding.

DESCRIPTION Breeding: Forehead broadly white, contiguous with white supercilium extending to rear of ear-coverts. Black or blackish frontal bar very high on forehead, virtually on crown. Black or blackish eye-stripe from bill to rear of ear-coverts. White underparts and collar around hindneck, with variable creamy- or rufous-buff wash on breast, sometimes also belly and flanks or collar; in some, the colour is restricted to distinct patches on the sides of the breast. Underwing and axillaries white. Crown, nape, mantle, scapulars, tertials, wing-coverts and the central back, rump and uppertail are medium-brown, often with broad rufous or buff feather edgings, sometimes tinged greyish. Greater coverts and greater primary coverts are tipped white. Flight feathers brownish-black; primaries all have white on shaft, and inners have extensive white on webs; inner secondaries are whitish, especially at tips. Sides of lower back, rump and uppertail are white. Tail is blackish-brown in centre, but outer two pairs of feathers are unmarked white. **Non-breeding:** Black on head may become brownish. Rarely, frontal bar may be lost in females. **Juvenile:** Lacks black on head, but shows large white forehead and a strong dark line across the lores. Underparts white, sometimes with a creamy wash. Brown feathers of upperparts show broad pale sandy-buff fringes, with tinges of rufous particularly on nape and in scapulars; some are strongly rufous above.

AGE/SEX Individuals lacking a distinct frontal bar are almost always juveniles. Older immatures may be separable in the hand by retained juvenile coverts or by very worn and pointed primaries. Males tend to be blacker on head and to have stronger underpart coloration than females.

RACES Five: nominate (S Angola to Cape Province), *tenellus* (Natal to Ethiopia and Sudan, also Madagascar), *pons* (S Somalia), *mechowi* (Cameroun and N Angola to central Africa and Zaïre), and *hesperius* (W Africa to central Africa). Some authors restrict *tenellus* to Madagascar, assigning the continental population to *mechowi*. Racial divisions are blurred by intergradation and individual variation. Collar is usually white in nominate race and *pons*, usually pale rufous in other races. The race *tenellus*, particularly in Madagascar, often has a concentration of rufous on the sides of lower neck and upper breast, but W African birds also may show this pattern. The nominate race averages slightly larger than the others, is rather paler above, and shows very little suffusion of colour on underparts.

MEASUREMENTS Length about 180 mm (7"). Wing 99-113 mm (nominate), 97-107 mm (others); bill 14-17 mm; tarsus 22-26 mm; tail 46-52 mm (nominate), 41-47 mm (others).

REFERENCES Maclean and Moran (1965), Summers and Hockey (1980), Kieser and Liversidge (1981), Taylor (1983).

100 RED-CAPPED PLOVER *Charadrius ruficapillus* **Plate 43**

Other name: Red-capped Dotterel
A small plover endemic to Australasia which is part of the Kentish Plover (98) superspecies; some systematists still consider it a race of Kentish Plover, but there are sufficient consistent characters to warrant treatment as a full species.

IDENTIFICATION The small size and relatively leggy appearance of this tiny plover clearly separate it from all resident and migrant plovers in its range. In flight, shows a strong white wingbar and broad and conspicuous white sides to the rump, uppertail and tail. The tiny breast-patches and, especially, the lack of a white collar across the hindneck are the easiest distinctions from Kentish Plover; note also the shorter supercilium extending only a short way behind the eye. The mainly-white breast and black legs preclude confusion with the larger Ringed and Little Ringed Plovers (86, 89). Lesser Sandplover (107) is often confused with Red-capped, but is larger, with diffuse brown lateral breast-patches, no red cap, a quite different tail pattern and slightly darker upperparts. Lessers gaining breeding plumage usually show extensive black on the face and at least some chestnut on the breast. **Bare parts:** Bill black, fairly fine. Iris brown. Legs dark greyish-black, slightly tinged greenish in juveniles.

VOICE A wide range of calls, mostly similar to those of Kentish Plover. Usual flight notes are a quiet but positive 'wit', often repeated rapidly, and a slightly buzzing 'pzzt'. When flushed, may give a sharper variant, 'kittup'. When breeding, a more melodic 'poowit' and purring short trills are given.

HABITS Found in a variety of coastal habitats, especially shell or sandy beaches near muddy or sandy flats, also widely inland at brackish permanent lakes. Less commonly seen on freshwater pools and rivers, and other wetlands such as sewage-farms. During the breeding season, defends relatively small breeding territories; otherwise often in flocks, sometimes of hundreds. Runs very fast, and feeds actively in typical plover style. Flight is fast and jinking, often in tight flocks. In New Zealand, usually found with the abundant Double-banded Plover (105); interbreeding has been reported. Relatively tame and approachable.

MOVEMENTS Essentially sedentary, with some postbreeding dispersal. A vagrant to New Zealand, has been found breeding in South Island riverbeds (has not bred in recent years) and wintering in the northern harbours.

DESCRIPTION Breeding and non-breeding: Black or blackish frontal bar; black line from bill through eye and ear-coverts extends down the side of neck and curves forwards slightly onto the sides of the breast to form tiny lateral breast-patches. Forehead, short supercilium and entire underparts are clean white. Crown and nape bright chestnut-red or reddish, butting onto grey-brown mantle; centre of crown is sometimes grey-brown like the mantle. Upperparts all plain grey-brown, rather darker than on all races of Kentish Plover. Central tail feathers darker brown, contrasting with broad white sides of tail. Clear but narrow white wingbar across tips of greater coverts and bases of inner primaries. **Juvenile:** Brown where adults are reddish and black. Upperparts generally buffish-brown, individual feathers with rather obscure darker subterminal bands and buff fringes. Crown feathers tipped buffish. Breast-patches mid-brown. Compared with Kentish Plover, shows rather darker upperparts, more positively marked lores and ear-coverts, and no white collar.

AGE/SEX Juveniles and first-winter birds can be distinguished by duller colours and retained juvenile inner medians. There is little sexual dimorphism: the female is often well marked with black and chestnut, but in some the black is replaced by blackish-brown; on male whole of crown and nape is chestnut-red (female is more likely to show greybrown in centre of crown).

RACES No geographical variation is known.

MEASUREMENTS Length 140-160 mm (6"). Wing 98-107 mm; bill 12-14 mm; tarsus 24-28 mm.

REFERENCES Hobbs (1972), McKenzie (1980), Davis (1980).

101 MALAYSIAN PLOVER *Charadrius peronii* Plate 34

Other name: Malaysian Sandplover
A close relative of the Kentish Plover (98) and may be difficult to distinguish from migrants of that species.

IDENTIFICATION Like Kentish, a small sandplover with white wingbar, white sides to the tail, and white collar around the neck. The breeding male has a black frontal bar, mask and breast-patches, and chestnut on the cap. There is, however, no equivalent to Kentish's plain non-breeding plumage. Constant differences from Kentish Plover are slightly smaller size and shorter but broader-based bill; range of leg colours is slightly paler. Upperparts are usually more variegated, with dark feather centres and a mixture of faded and fresh (darker brown) feathers. Male differs from male Kentish in more extensive black on the breast, sometimes almost forming a complete breast-band, which continues around base of hindneck as a solid black band bordering the mantle; also, tends to have a brownish centre to the crown rather than a complete chestnut cap, and black on earcoverts reduced to a roundish spot, often separated by white from the dark lores and eye. Females and juveniles are distinct from Kentish in that breast-band and base of hindneck, also lores and cap, are bright pale rufous-brown. Breast-band is usually complete, recalling Chestnut-banded Sandplover (102). In some females and juveniles, the white collar on the hindneck is very narrow, even incomplete. Red-capped Plover (100) differs most obviously from male Malaysian in lacking black and white on the hindneck. **Bare parts:** Bill black, often with a small brownish area at the base of lower mandible; rather broadly-based. Iris brown. Legs yellowish-grey to greyish-slate.

VOICE A soft 'whit' or 'twik' like Kentish Plover.

HABITS Rather little is known, but probably similar to Kentish in most respects. Scarce over most of its range, usually found in isolated pairs or family groups in traditional sites. Occasionally found on mudflats, but most frequent on sandy or coral beaches. Nests Mar-June in Malaysia; recently recorded nesting July-Aug on Bali.

MOVEMENTS Apparently sedentary.

DESCRIPTION Breeding and non-breeding plumages are similar. **Male:** Large white area on forehead extends into a short supercilium. Black frontal bar, neat line across the lores, and black at rear of earcoverts. Cap and nape pale grey-brown, washed rufous-brown except in centre of crown. Clear but narrow white collar. Large black breast-patches, sometimes almost joining in the centre; black extends around base of hindneck and upper mantle, forming a broad band below white collar. Upperparts grey-brown, often strongly variegated owing to dark feather centres and differential bleaching and wear. Primaries dark brown, with wingbar formed by white across webs of the inner 5 and the tips of their primary coverts; secondaries have white bases, and greater coverts are tipped white. Tail dark brown in the centre, outer two or three feathers white; white sides also to rump and uppertail-coverts. Underparts white. **Female:** As male, but black of head and breast is replaced by pale rufous-brown; well-marked birds may have some blackish-brown feathers on breast and on forecrown, forming a dark frontal bar. Crown

less gingery, mainly pale sandy-brown. White on hindneck is reduced and collar is sometimes incomplete. **Juvenile:** Young of both sexes are like adult female, but never show any blackish-brown.

AGE/SEX Juveniles and immature males are very difficult to distinguish from adult females; immature males usually gain some blackish feathers on forecrown, ear-coverts and breast by Aug (Malaysia), but some not until Jan or Mar. Adult males lack rufous in breast-band. Adult females may show blackish in breast-band, mask and frontal bar, but not on hindneck.

RACES Geographical variation is apparently small.
MEASUREMENTS Length 140-160 mm (6"). Wing 95-105 mm; bill 13-15 mm; tarsus 26-30 mm.
REFERENCES Hoogerwerf (1966), Smythies (1968), Medway and Wells (1976).

102 CHESTNUT-BANDED SANDPLOVER *Charadrius pallidus* Plate 42

A very neatly-marked small plover with a restricted range in E and S Africa.

IDENTIFICATION Upperparts are more greyish than on other small African plovers, very pale grey in S African race. Adult is easily identified by conspicuous chestnut breast-band, while juveniles have greyish patches on the sides of the breast or a narrow greyish breast-band. Short tail, with long white undertail-coverts often protruding alongside, and longish legs are also distinctive. The E African race is restricted to saltflats at a handful of favoured Rift Valley lakes. Both Kittlitz's (94) and White-fronted (99) Sandplovers may show a concentration of colour on the sides of the breast, but never such a strong contrast between chestnut breast-band (broadest in the centre) and white underparts; both also show white or buffish on the nape or hindneck. Lesser and Greater Sandplovers (107, 108) and Caspian Plover (109) show chestnut on breast in breeding plumage, but are larger and are also differ in likely habitat. **Bare parts:** Bill black, rather slender and pointed. Iris brown. Legs dark grey or greenish-grey; toes project slightly beyond tail-tip in flight.
VOICE Calls include a quiet 'chup' or 'pip', a dry 'trrp' or 'trr-eet', and a plaintive 'hweet' when anxious. At least in E African race, there is also a remarkable, most un-plover-like call, best written 'je-weeew' ('j' is soft): the second syllable rises sharply in pitch then falls away.
HABITS The E African race *venustus* is known from only seven localities between Lake Magadi, S Kenya, and Bahi Swamp, central Tanzania. It occurs at alkaline lakes, commonly at several places. Nesting season is May-Sept. Feeds chiefly in water or soft mud, on aquatic larvae, often wading quite deeply; may also catch adult insects. It is aggressive towards other waders feeding nearby. Often takes short flights on rather short, slightly-rounded wings; rarely flies long distances. Generally a tame species, allowing close approach even sometimes at the nest. The S African nominate race normally occurs only on saltpans on or near the coast, where it nests often at high density, but vagrants sometimes appear by fresh water. Nesting season may last almost all year. Habits are generally similar to those of *venustus*.

MOVEMENTS The E African race is thought to be entirely sedentary, although there may possibly be some interchange between sites. Vagrancy has not been recorded; claims at Kenyan sites other than Lake Magadi are thought to be mistaken. The nominate race may have regular movements: some sites are vacated after breeding, while winter increases occur at others. Vagrants have appeared as far from breeding range as Zambia.
DESCRIPTION Breeding and non-breeding plumages are similar. **Male:** Forehead white, bounded by black frontal bar and black eye-stripe from bill to behind eye. Black of frontal bar and eye-stripe is narrowly fringed pale chestnut above; the chestnut continues across hindneck as a narrow collar, and joins narrow chestnut band across upper breast. Some black feathers may be admixed in breast-band, sometimes forming an anterior black border to central part. Underparts, including underwing, are otherwise white. Long undertail-coverts reach almost to tip of rather short tail. Upperparts, including crown and nape, are grey-brown or very pale brownish-grey; feathers are tipped greyish-white when fresh. Median coverts are slightly paler than lessers and greaters; greater coverts are white-tipped. Inner primaries show white on webs, and all primaries have white on shaft. Secondaries are narrowly white-tipped. Sides of lower back, rump and uppertail are white, central areas as mantle. Tail is dark in centre, but outer two pairs of feathers are white except for subterminal brownish smudge. **Female:** As male, but lacks black on head and breast-band. In E African race, female has chestnut frontal bar and eye-stripe, while in S Africa these areas are mostly grey-brown, uniform with the crown. **Juvenile:** Black and chestnut are lacking. Underparts are white, with obscure greyish patches on the sides of the breast which sometimes meet to form a breast-band. Wing-coverts show whitish fringes and, on some feathers, dark subterminal lines.
AGE/SEX Retained coverts or grey feathers in breast-band indicate young bird. Primary-wear is also helpful, but moult strategy of adults seems very variable

in this species. Sexing appears to be straightforward, although occasional females may show a tiny trace of black in the frontal bar.

RACES Two well-marked races: nominate (S Angola to Port Elizabeth, Cape Province), and *venustus* (soda-lakes around Kenyan/Tanzanian border). The race *venustus* is distinctly smaller, and is grey-brown above as opposed to very pale brownish-grey of nominate race. Nominate females generally lack chestnut on

head. Bill of nominate race is proportionately rather smaller.

MEASUREMENTS Length about 150 mm (6"). Wing 99-106 mm (nominate), 85-94 mm (*venustus*); bill 12-15 mm; tarsus 24-27 mm; tail 39-43 mm (nominate), 35-40 mm (*venustus*).

REFERENCES Jeffery and Liversidge (1951), Richards (1980), Taylor (1983).

103 COLLARED PLOVER *Charadrius collaris*   Plate 46

A small, slim, rather dark plover of South and Central America. It is poorly named, since it is notable for the *absence* of a hindneck collar.

IDENTIFICATION In size and proportions quite similar to the slightly larger Kentish Plover (98), but Collared is easily distinguished by paler legs, darker upperparts, and (in adults) a complete black breast-band. Also, as in Red-capped Plover (100), white does not extend in a collar around the base of the hind-neck: the brown of the nape is contiguous with the lower hindneck and mantle. Other South American 'ringed' plovers, Puna (104) and Two-banded (106), also lack a white collar, but show at least a partial second breast-band and are more portly in shape. Semipalmated Plover (87) shares the features of a single breast-band, a dark line across the lores, a small pale spot above and behind the eye and yellowy or orangey legs, but is larger, has a white neck collar, and never shows chestnut on the crown. Compared with Semipalmated, Collared has a longer, thinner bill, never with extensive orange at the base. The chestnut on the head is often inconspicuous, except in a close view. **Bare parts:** Bill black, with a trace of orange at the base of the lower mandible; rather long and slender. Iris dark brown. Legs yellowish-orange or yellowish-flesh.

VOICE Calls rather sharp and metallic, based on 'chit' or 'pit'. Most are mono- or disyllabic, but less frequently several notes are run together.

HABITS Found throughout the year in a wide range of wetland habitats, including sandy beaches on the coast, estuarine mud, and the banks of rivers and ponds inland; also occurs in open sandy savannas. Nesting season varies with latitude but, surprisingly, those nests found in W Mexico have been in Nov-Dec. There is a ground display in which the male fluffs out his breast and chases the female, but no aerial display has been described. Outside the breeding season usually seen well scattered or in pairs, but may form small loose flocks.

MOVEMENTS Apparently sedentary, but the species has not been studied in detail. Appears to be commoner in central Chile during Apr-Sept than in the nesting season.

DESCRIPTION Breeding and non-breeding: White forehead is outlined by a broad, sharply-defined

black frontal bar and a narrow black line across the lores; the frontal bar extends down to the eye, dividing the small white supercilium into two. Ear-coverts dull blackish, with reddish tinge at rear. Top of crown has a chestnut wash bordering the frontal bar, merging into warm grey-brown on the rear crown. Most have a pale chestnut wash around the base of the neck, sometimes extending into the sides of the black breast-band. All upperparts are grey-brown, with a variable amount of tawny or dull chestnut edging, especially evident on wing-coverts and longer scapulars and tertials; during wing moult all coverts, scapulars, tertials and some mantle feathers broadly fringed and edged this colour, but most feathers lose their fringes quite rapidly. Outer three pairs of tail feathers are almost completely white; central two pairs are dark, almost blackish-brown towards the tip. White wingbar extends over middle and inner primaries and tips of greater coverts. Underparts are white, except for sharply contrasting black breast-band which is broader at the sides than in the centre. **Juvenile:** At first shows tiny lateral tawny-brown breast-patches, and no black or even dark brown on forecrown or lores. Upperparts are pale grey-brown obscured by many pale buff or tawny fringes. After a few weeks black starts to appear in breast-patches, then dusky or blackish head markings, and later the complete breast-band.

AGE/SEX Following the post-juvenile moult, immatures may be recognised in the hand by their more worn and pointed primaries; retained buff-fringed inner median coverts may be difficult to separate from new, adult-type feathers. Sexes differ only very slightly and are not usually distinguishable: female tends to have less chestnut on the head and the black areas less well defined and fractionally browner.

RACES Some authors have assigned the rather shorter-winged northern individuals (Mexico to N Brazil) to a separate subspecies *'gracilis'*.

MEASUREMENTS Length 140-150 mm (5¾"). Wing 94-110 mm; bill 14-16 mm; tarsus 23-27 mm; tail 40-53 mm.

REFERENCES Widrig (1983).

Semipalmated Plover

Collared Plover

104 PUNA PLOVER *Charadrius alticola* Plate 46

A smallish plover found chiefly in the puna zone of the high Andes. It is closely related to Two-banded Plover (106), and possibly a high-altitude representative of that species.

IDENTIFICATION Adult is easily distinguished by its rather steep white forehead, black breast-patches, chestnut band across lower breast (if present), and black legs. Double-banded Plover (105) of Australasia also has black and chestnut breast-bands, but both are always complete, and lores and forehead show much less white. Two-banded Plover is similar, but larger and longer-billed and its lower band is black not chestnut; ranges are not known to overlap. Semipalmated Plover (87) and Collared Plover (103) both have a single (normally complete) breast-band, dark lores and pale legs. Kentish Plover (98) has paler upperparts, a white supercilium, and underparts entirely white except for small black or brown breast-patches. In juvenile plumage may be confused with juvenile Two-banded, but note smaller size and single indistinct band across lower breast. In flight, shows a narrow white wingbar and narrow white sides to the tail. **Bare parts:** Bill black, short and stubby compared to Two-banded Plover. Iris dark brown. Legs black.
VOICE Not particularly vocal; a whistled, far-carrying 'weep'.
HABITS Found throughout the year in the puna zone of flat, saline grasslands between 4000 m and 5000 m high in the Andes, nesting at low density among pebbles and short grass near saline or freshwater lakes. Food includes small crustaceans. Recent observations of parties of up to 30 on the coast, particularly June-Oct, suggest that the estuarine habitat may be regularly used by some individuals in winter.
MOVEMENTS Probably mainly sedentary. Recent records in several areas of coastal S Peru suggest a regular coastward migration by part of the population.
DESCRIPTION Breeding: Forehead and lores white; broad black band across forecrown from eye to eye. Dusky blackish-brown patch from below eye over ear-coverts. Small, indistinct creamy spot behind eye. Mid-crown and hindneck brown-grey, suffused pale chestnut except on rear crown. Mantle and scapulars grey-brown, with some feathers edged pale ginger. Wing-coverts grey-brown, but lesser coverts rather darker brown forming slightly darker band on closed wing. Tertials rather long, uniform grey-brown. Fairly narrow white wingbar, formed by bases of inner and middle primaries and white-tipped greater coverts. Tail mostly brown, with outer one or two pairs of feathers whitish; central tail feathers darker than lower back. Underparts white, with small black patch on sides of upper breast and a much broader, complete, chestnut lower breast-band partly obscured with white. **Non-breeding:** For a short period during the moult, the lower band becomes brownish. **Juvenile:** Less white-faced than adult, with forehead suffused buffish; head lacks all chestnut and blackish and shows fine buffish fringes. Coverts are fringed with pale whitish-buff. No sign of upper breast-patches; and lower breast-band very indistinct, pale buff, with slightly darker feather centres especially towards sides.
AGE/SEX Juvenile gains adult-type pattern after one or two months, but colours are dull. Chestnut on head is restricted to immediate rear of frontal bar and ear-coverts. Breast-patches and breast-band are composed of mostly dull brown feathers with white fringes. Pale-fringed juvenile inner median coverts are retained. Sexes are alike, but female tends to have less extensive chestnut on the head, and black parts of plumage tinged brown.
RACES No geographical variation is known.
MEASUREMENTS Length 165-175 mm (6¾"). Wing 118-125 mm; bill 13-15 mm; tarsus 24-28 mm; tail 47-54 mm.
REFERENCES Hoy (1967), Graves (1981).

105 DOUBLE-BANDED PLOVER *Charadrius bicinctus* Plate 43

Other names: Banded or Double-banded Dotterel
Part of the population has a unique migration pattern for a wader: breeding in New Zealand and migrating to S Australia. Probably New Zealand's second most numerous breeding wader after South Island Pied Oystercatcher (20).

IDENTIFICATION The breeding adult is the only plover with two breast-bands found in Australasia. The South American Puna Plover (104) also has one black and one chestnut breast-band, but the black band is always incomplete and the lores and entire forehead are white. Winter-plumaged birds resemble Lesser and Greater Sandplovers (107, 108), but are smaller-billed and brighter-legged with more buffish-brown plumage, particularly on sides of head and neck. The normal stance is more upright than in other small plovers. The white throat and front of neck separate Double-banded from the much larger New Zealand Dotterel (85) and the Rufous-chested Dotterel (111) of South America, both of which have chestnut on the breast when breeding. **Bare parts:** Bill black, rather slender. Iris dark brown. Legs pale grey-green to yellowish-green, with tendency for juveniles to have a stronger yellowish tinge.
VOICE Principal flight and anxiety call is a clear incisive 'chip', often repeated three or four times; during the display flight, notes are run together to give a slow trill. There is also a longer 'tweep' or 'twilt', and a repeated 'whee-chedlet' by males in aggressive encounters.
HABITS Nominate race nests Aug-Feb in a wide range of habitats from ocean beaches to sandy and especially stony riverbeds, including lakeshores, ploughed fields, arid ground and high mountain slopes. Breed-

ing males have sparkling colour contrasts and strongly developed territorial and sexual displays. There is a rather fast 'butterfly' display flight. Post-breeding flocks favour short grass and the fringes of marshland where available. Most winter coastally in sandy or muddy harbours or inland by fresh or brackish wetlands. Often found in small loose feeding flocks, sometimes on dry ground well away from water, and large communal roosts. Auckland Islands race differs in breeding entirely in alpine zone of highest hills and wintering on rocky coast; these often wade into rock pools to capture prey.

MOVEMENTS The nominate race migrates from its breeding grounds to winter in sandy and muddy harbours, chiefly in N North Island (especially Manukau Harbour) and in SE Australia; few winter in South Island. Most leave breeding areas in Feb or Mar and return by Aug. Only occasional individuals summer in Australia. Vagrants, presumably of the nominate race, have occurred on New Caledonia, New Hebrides, Fiji, Lord Howe I., Campbell I., and Norfolk I. The race *exilis* of the Auckland Is. is virtually sedentary; it breeds on the highest hilltops of the larger islands, but almost the whole population winters on Derry Castle Reef at the northernmost tip of the islands.

DESCRIPTION Breeding: Forehead and supercilium white; supercilium narrow and inconspicuous behind eye. Black frontal bar. Lores black, merging below eye into blackish-brown line running down side of neck and into narrow black band across upper breast. A white line separates the upper breast-band from a broad chestnut-brown lower one. Rest of underparts white, occasionally flecked dark on the front of the thighs. Ear-coverts, crown, hindneck and rest of upperparts rich grey-brown. Wings grey-brown with contrasting dark flight feathers; a small white wingbar is formed by white bases to inner primaries and narrow white on the tips of the greater coverts and bases of the secondaries. Narrow white sides to rump. Tail rather dark, slightly paler towards sides. **Non-breeding:** This plumage is of short duration in the nominate race, covering the primary moult and a short period afterwards, but lasts much longer in *exilis*. Black and chestnut on head and breast are lost. Upper breast-band becomes a strong dusky-brown wash, and the lower band greyish and even less distinct. Supercilium creamy, infused brown, indistinct behind eye. Wing-coverts, scapulars and tertials gain extensive warm reddish-brown fringes. **Juvenile:** As non-breeding, but supercilium longer and rather more pronounced. A dark zone across the breast (spanning both breast-bands), formed by grey-brown spots, is often relatively indistinct and broken. Back and scapulars show many whitish-buff tips; coverts darkish-brown with narrow sepia subterminal line and whitish-buff fringe.

AGE/SEX First-summer birds gain breeding plumage, but show worn primaries and retained juvenile inner median coverts. Males tend to be brighter than females, but there is wide variation; black areas, especially frontal bar, are replaced by dark brown in some females.

RACES Two: nominate *bicinctus* (mainland New Zealand, Chatham Is.) and the recently-described *exilis* (Auckland Is.). The nominate is rather smaller, especially in tarsus and toe lengths, and in breeding plumage has slightly paler and colder brown upperparts, brighter breast-bands and whiter thighs. The race *exilis* is plumper and heavier. Differences are relatively slight, but the sedentary nature of *exilis* generally precludes confusion (although the nominate race has recently been reported from the Auckland Is.). The total population of *exilis* is thought to number about 160 individuals in winter.

MEASUREMENTS Length 175-190 mm (7¼"). Wing 122-137 mm; bill 15-19 mm; tarsus 28-32 mm (nominate), 32-37 mm (*exilis*); central toe 21-24 mm (nominate), 26-30 mm (*exilis*). Weight 57.7g (mean of six nominate males in Nov), 81.8g (mean of four *exilis* males).

REFERENCES Cunningham (1973), Bomford (1978), Pierce (1980b), Phillips (1980).

106 TWO-BANDED PLOVER *Charadrius falklandicus* Plate 46

A South American endemic plover with two breast-bands, although the upper one is often incomplete. A close relative of the upland Puna Plover (104), but chiefly coastal in habitat.

IDENTIFICATION Birds with an incomplete upper breast-band are very similar in plumage pattern to Puna Plover, but are distinguished by black or blackish (not chestnut) lower breast-band, less white on the forehead, larger size, and proportionately longer and slimmer bill. Double breast-band recalls Killdeer (91) but Two-banded is much smaller and not known to overlap in range; the mainly-white face, narrow wingbar, shorter tail (lacking rufous coloration), and black legs are further distinctions from this species, and from Three-banded Plover (96) and Forbes's Plover (97) of Africa, which also show two black breast-bands. Kentish Plover (98) is often black-legged, but is smaller and much slimmer, with no trace of a band across the lower breast. See also Double-banded Plover (105). **Bare parts:** Bill black. Iris brown. Legs black or blackish-grey.

VOICE Normal contact note on the ground is a thin 'tseet'. In flight has a rather plaintive, liquid whistle, 'whiit' or 'prit'. In the display flight, less plaintive calls are uttered in rapid succession, forming a loud twittering whistle.

HABITS When breeding, chiefly Sept-Feb, these plovers are found on coastal beaches, riverbanks, and the shores of small fresh or brackish pools on flat ground a short distance inland. The display flight is dramatic, with solo irregular dashes in all directions and aerial chases. Flocks of 150 or more may gather on sandy beaches or intertidal mudflats outside the breeding season; some establish winter feeding territories. Feeds along the edge of the surf, on beds of rotting kelp, on short grass and around the edges of freshwater pools.

MOVEMENTS Colour-ringing studies have shown that

the Falkland Is. population is sedentary, apart from short movements between breeding grounds and favoured winter feeding sites. In contrast, the mainland South American population is strongly migratory, most vacating the southern part of the breeding range in the austral winter and extending northwards on the Chilean coast and as far as Uruguay and S Brazil on the Atlantic coast.

DESCRIPTION Breeding: Forehead white with black frontal bar; dusky patch below eye and over most of ear-coverts, often extending down sides of neck to join upper breast-band. Small pale spot behind the eye. Behind the frontal bar the forecrown is washed light chestnut, and the back of head is medium grey-brown with a few rufous tips; the hindneck is also washed chestnut. Rest of upperparts an even grey-brown, except for dark brown centre to the tail and white outer tail feathers. Narrow white wingbar is slightly shorter than on Puna Plover. Underparts white with a narrow black upper breast-band, sometimes complete, sometimes forming pointed lateral breast-patches, and a complete broad black band across the lower breast and upper belly. **Non-breeding:** As breeding, but briefly during moult the black on the crown and breast-bands becomes a dusky-grey, the chestnut head colour is lost and a

dull line appears across the lores. **Juvenile:** Similar to non-breeding adult, but head is duller; small creamy spots on sides of forehead and behind eye, cap mid-brown with buff-fringed feathers. All coverts, scapulars and mantle feathers show darkish brown centre, thin darker submarginal line, and buff fringe. Underparts white, with breast-bands dark brown flecked buff.

AGE/SEX Immatures resemble adults after post-juvenile moult, but are duller and retain some juvenile inner median coverts. Females are slightly duller than males: the black areas of the head and the breast-bands are infused with brown, the upper breast-band is more obscured with pale tips, and the ginger on the head is duller and more restricted in extent. In extreme cases, males may have bright rufous crowns, while females may show only a trace of rufous.

RACES Many Falkland Is. breeders have incomplete upper breast-bands, but they have not been described as a separate subspecies.

MEASUREMENTS Length 170-185 mm (7"). Wing 124-132 mm; bill 16-19 mm; tarsus 26-30 mm; tail 46-55 mm.

REFERENCES Humphrey *et al.* (1970), Woods (1975), Myers and Myers (1979).

107 LESSER SANDPLOVER *Charadrius mongolus*   Plate 36

Other names: Mongolian Plover/Sandplover/Dotterel
This species is very similar in all plumages to Greater Sandplover (108), and there is virtually complete overlap in non-breeding range: identification requires care, and birds not seen well are best left unidentified.

IDENTIFICATION A small to medium-sized plover, rather plain brown with breast-patches for much of the year but with bright chestnut-and-black head and breast in breeding plumage. In flight, it shows a clear white wingbar and a narrow white fringe to the tail. Best features to separate from Greater are leg length and colour, relative proportions of bill, head and body, call, extent of white on wing and tail, and size. Lesser has shorter, dark grey legs, with toes about level with tip of tail in flight; in Greater, leg colour is more variable but almost always paler, and legs are relatively longer with toes projecting beyond tail-tip in flight. Proportions of Lesser, particularly head and bill, suggest a longer-legged, longer-billed Ringed Plover (86), while Greater has a heavier-looking and clearly longer bill, often emphasised by a rather flat sloping forehead. In flight, wingbar of Lesser is of fairly even width, while in Greater it broadens on the primaries; Greater also shows slightly more white at edges and tip of tail. Size is a useful feature, provided there are other species to provide a comparison, but there is a small degree of overlap between the two in wing length and in weight. See Table on page 393. Ringed Plover and Kentish Plover (98) are not dissimilar in non-breeding and juvenile plumages, but both are smaller and show at least some whitish on the hindneck. Also note bright legs and stubby bill of Ringed, and sharp breast-patches and white sides to tail in Kentish. See also Double-banded Plover (105). **Bare parts:** Bill fairly stout, black; length about equal to the distance between bill-base and rear edge of eye. Iris dark brown. Legs dark grey, sometimes tinged

greenish; may look black at a distance.
VOICE Normal calls can be distinguished from those of Greater by experienced observers; most frequent are a short hard 'chitik' or 'chiktik', often likened to call of Ruddy Turnstone (154).
HABITS Nests May-Aug discontinuously across E Asia from Himalayas to NE Siberia (rarely Alaska). Breeding grounds are entirely above or beyond tree-limit: at altitudes up to 5500 m in Himalayas, but on coastal shingle or sand-dunes in Siberia and Commander Is. May be seen at inland wetlands after breeding or on cultivated ground after breeding or on migration. Winters on coasts and estuaries, mostly around Indian Ocean and SW Pacific, often in large numbers. Joins freely with Greater Sandplover and other small waders.
MOVEMENTS Strongly migratory. See Races for breeding and winter ranges. Perhaps only a migrant in Mongolia, where first recorded in 1972. Last adults depart Africa in early May, and return is mainly Sept onwards. Many stay in winter quarters all year. Vagrant Spain, Norway, Poland, Austria, E Mediterranean, E African lakes (particularly Lake Turkana), central Zambia, W Alaska, Yukon Territory, Ontario, Oregon, California and Louisiana.
DESCRIPTION Breeding: Black or brownish mask extends across forehead, lores and ear-coverts. In males, forehead varies between all-black and mainly white with a central black dividing line. Crown pale brownish-chestnut, with paler bar on forecrown which continues as a pale supercilium, whitest in a patch behind the eye. Nape and hindneck pale chestnut. Upperparts and wing-coverts greyish-brown; pri-

mary coverts darkest. White wingbar is formed by tips to greater coverts, bases of secondaries and outer webs of inner 5 or 6 primaries; rest of primaries show white on shaft. White sides to rump. Tail has outer two pairs of feathers with white on outer web; otherwise mainly grey-brown, with an only slightly darker subterminal bar and a narrow pale tip. On underparts, chin and throat are white sharply outlined by chestnut on breast and sides of neck. The breastband, which may be outlined narrowly above by black, extends slightly onto anterior flanks and upper belly; rest of underparts white, including underwing-coverts and axillaries. **Non-breeding:** As breeding, but loses all black and chestnut. Forehead is whitish, extending backwards as relatively narrow white supercilia. Lores are pale grey-brown; crown, hindneck and upperparts grey-brown; wing-coverts narrowly fringed dull white, forming a paler area. Underparts white with large brown-grey lateral breast-patches, sometimes almost joining in the centre. **Juvenile:** As non-breeding, but upperparts and upperwing-coverts extensively fringed sandy-buff, especially bright on scapulars and tertials. Breast-patches buffish, with grey feather centres.

AGE/SEX Juveniles become very difficult to separate in the field after Oct. Sexing is possible in breeding

plumage: on females, black of males is replaced by brown or rufous, except sometimes near eye.

RACES Five: *pamirensis* (S central USSR, winters Africa to W India), *atrifrons* (Himalayas, S Tibet, winters India to Sumatra), *schaeferi* (E Tibet, winters Thailand to Greater Sundas), nominate *mongolus* (inland E USSR), and *stegmanni* (Kamchatka, Commander Is., Chukotsk Peninsula). Both *mongolus* and *stegmanni* ('*mongolus* group') winter Taiwan to Australia; they differ from the southern races ('*atrifrons* group') in larger size, and in breeding male having white forehead, bisected vertically by a black line, and a blackish upper border to the rufous breast. In the southern races, male has forehead black, sometimes with small white 'headlights'. There are irregular clines of increasing darkness and wing length, and decreasing bill length and leg length, running from southwest to northeast.

MEASUREMENTS Length 190-210 mm (7¾"). Wing 118-145 mm; bill 15-21 mm; tarsus 27-38 mm; tail 44-52 mm. The *mongolus* and *atrifrons* groups can be separated by wing:tarsus ratio of 4.1 (adults; for juveniles add 3 mm to wing length): above this = *mongolus* group, below = *atrifrons* group.

REFERENCES Sinclair and Nicholls (1980), Taylor (1982).

108 GREATER SANDPLOVER *Charadrius leschenaultii*   Plate 36

Other names: Large Sand Dotterel/Plover, Geoffroy's Plover
This large, long-billed *Charadrius* nests in the deserts of S Eurasia, but is a coastal bird when not breeding. Its non-breeding range is very similar to that of its close relative the Lesser Sandplover (107).

IDENTIFICATION A rather long-legged, large-billed, chunky sandplover, lacking a white neck collar and typically having palish grey-green legs. In all plumages it requires great care to separate from Lesser Sandplover. See latter species and Table on page 393 for a summary of the most useful characters. Note that, owing to geographical variation in both species, the value of the separating characters probably varies with location: body size should differ most in India and SE Asia, and bill length most in Australia. See also Caspian (109) and Oriental Plovers (110). **Bare parts:** Bill long, fairly stout, black; length greater than the distance between bill-base and rear edge of eye. Iris dark brown. Legs longish, variable in colour from dull orange-yellow to almost black, but on most pale greenish-grey often with darker toes and joints.

VOICE Usual call is a short soft trill 'trrri' in which individual notes are not discernible; distinguishable from Lesser's call with practice. Song is a repeated melodious whistle 'pipruirr'.

HABITS Nests Mar onwards in west of range, but June onwards in central Asia; nesting habitat is normally in vicinity of water, usually at much lower altitudes than Lesser. Coastal when not nesting, occurring commonly on sandy beaches as well as on estuarine mud. Rarely seen inland, except on migration, but sometimes feeds on coastal grassland. Gregarious, often mixing with other small waders and often forming mixed flocks with Lesser. Feeding methods include probing.

MOVEMENTS Mainly migratory, but some winter on shores of Caspian Sea close to breeding grounds.

Wandering flocks form in breeding area from mid-July. First arrivals of adults in E Africa are in Aug (earlier than Lesser Sandplover) and juveniles arrive from late Sept-Nov. Main departure is in late Apr (also earlier than Lesser). Many young birds remain in winter quarters throughout the first year. Winter range differs from Lesser's only in more widespread records from Indian Ocean islands; Lesser is unrecorded as yet from Madagascar and surrounding islands. Scarce but regular at Lake Turkana, Kenya, especially at passage times, Japan and Korea on passage, and New Zealand. Westward vagrancy more frequent than in Lesser: vagrant across Europe as far as France, N Scotland, Sweden and Finland, and N Africa to Tunisia and Morocco. Vagrant also Lake Chad (Nigeria), central Tanzania and Entebbe (Uganda).

DESCRIPTION Chief differences from Lesser Sandplover are as follows. **Breeding:** Forehead and breast patterns are variable, as in Lesser, but black and chestnut areas are usually narrower. Crown and nape are grey-brown strongly washed pale chestnut, which infuses the supercilium. Hindneck chestnut; rest of upperparts grey-brown, fairly pale, often with strong rufous edges on mantle, and sometimes also scapulars and tertials. White wingbar as Lesser, but slightly narrower across inner wing, also shorter, rarely extending beyond middle primaries; narrow on innermost primary but broader, extending more towards tip, on the next 4 primaries. Tail shows slightly more white than Lesser on sides and tip; subterminal bar is more contrastingly darker. **Non-breeding:** See Lesser Sandplover. Lacks black and chestnut. Breast-band reduced to lateral brown-grey patches, often very narrowly joining in centre. **Juvenile :** As non-breeding, but upperparts and upperwing-coverts pale brown extensively fringed buff; supercilium washed buff and often poorly marked. Breast-patches clearly buffish, with grey-brown feather centres.

AGE/SEX Juvenile can be distinguished in the field only for a few months. Sexes differ only in breeding plumage: female has mask dark grey-brown instead of black (although there may be some black in front of eye), and less rufous on crown, nape and sides of breast-band.

RACES Three: *columbinus* (Turkey and Jordan east to Caspian), *crassirostris* (Caspian east to about Lake Balkash) and nominate *leschenaultii* (W China, Mon-golia and adjacent USSR). The race *columbinus* is shortest in bill length, with bill shape fairly similar to that of western Lesser Sandplovers; in breeding plumage both sexes show extensive rufous fringing on upperparts and rufous of breast extending onto flanks. The race *crassirostris* is the largest in wing, bill and tarsus lengths, while the nominate race is intermediate in bill length but has on average the deepest bill.

MEASUREMENTS Length 220-250 mm (9¼"). Wing 132-153 mm; bill 20-28 mm; tarsus 34-41 mm; tail 49-56 mm.

REFERENCES Cheltsov-Bebutov (1976), Kitson *et al.* (1980), Sinclair and Nicholls (1980), Taylor (1982).

109 CASPIAN PLOVER *Charadrius asiaticus*　　　　　Plate 37

A close relative of Oriental Plover (110) and previously treated as conspecific; Caspian is the more westerly species, wintering in S and E Africa.

IDENTIFICATION A small to medium-sized plover with slim outline, longish legs, a slim bill, a well-marked supercilium and a broad dark zone across the breast. In flight, it shows long, pointed wings with a short white wingbar centred on the inner primaries, whitish underwing-coverts , brownish axillaries, and a broad, rather short and square, white-fringed tail. In breeding plumage, breast (at least in male) becomes chestnut with a blackish lower border, and face becomes very white. Oriental is similar, but larger and proportionately longer-legged and longer-necked, with no obvious wingbar and whole under-wing brownish. In breeding plumage, Oriental often has very pale creamy head and a broader dark lower border to the breast. Confusion is possible in winter with Lesser (107) or Greater Sandplovers (108), but note that these are chiefly coastal species and Caspian a bird mainly of inland grasslands. In addition, both these sandplovers show thicker bills, dark lateral breast-patches rather than a broad dark zone, and less clear supercilia; their shape is more compact, with wing-tips and tail-tip about level (in Caspian, folded wings extend well beyond the tail). See also Rufous-chested Dotterel (111), Mountain Plover (112) and Brown-chested Plover (70). **Bare parts:** Bill black, longish and rather slim. Iris dark brown. Legs long-ish, variably pinkish-yellow, yellowish- or greyish-green, pale brown or slate-grey; on most, legs are yellowish-brown in winter; tips of toes project beyond tail-tip in flight.

VOICE Most frequent call is a loud sharp 'tyup' or 'tup'; also a long rattling 'tptptptptp', a soft piping 'tik', and a shrill whistled 'kwhitt'. In display, male gives repeated ringing trisyllabic calls.

HABITS Nests Apr-July in dry steppes, often some distance from water. Non-breeders summer nearby, often on muddy fringes of lakes or rivers or on culti-vated land. In Africa, found chiefly inland on short dry grasslands, but also on dried mud of lakeshores, ploughed fields, shallowly-flooded areas and even rarely in intertidal habitats with other waders. Often quite tame and approachable. Gregarious, often seen in large feeding groups or dense flying flocks.

MOVEMENTS Flocks gather on breeding grounds during July-Aug; first flocks arrive in E Africa in early Aug but main arrival is not until Oct. Spring departure from Africa spans late Feb-Apr. Relatively scarce at intermediate sites, especially in autumn, and migration may be normally direct and non-stop. Vagrant across Europe to Norway, England, France, Italy and Malta, also to Nigeria, Cameroun, NW India, Sri Lanka, Maldive Is., and once N Australia (Sept 1896).

DESCRIPTION Breeding: Forehead, long super-cilium, lores, chin, throat and cheeks are white; crown, nape, a small patch in front of eye, and ear-coverts are brown. Hindneck is whitish-brown, upperparts otherwise brown. Flight feathers and pri-mary coverts are contrastingly dark. A short white wingbar is formed by white tips to outer greater coverts and inner primary coverts and white on webs of inner 4 or 5 primaries. There are narrow white sides to rump, but not to uppertail. Tail is brown, slightly darker towards tip, with narrow whitish edge and whitish V-shaped tips to all feathers. Underparts are white, with broad chestnut breast-band, often with blackish lower border. Axillaries are brownish and underwing-coverts whitish. **Non-breeding:** White of head is washed more or less buffish. Upperparts including hindneck are brown, with broad rufous-buff edgings when fresh. Breast is entirely grey-brown. **Juvenile:** As non-breeding, but upperpart feathers and coverts have darker centres and bright rufous-buff or buff fringes. Breast-band buffish, mottled grey-brown.

AGE/SEX Juvenile is difficult to distinguish after Oct. Female attains much less breeding plumage than male: many lack chestnut entirely and show a pale grey-brown breast, others show some white-tipped chestnut feathers; the darker lower border to the breast is indistinct or absent, never completely black.

RACES No geographical variation is known.

MEASUREMENTS Length 180-200 mm (7½"). Wing 140-157 mm; bill 18-22 mm; tarsus 36-43 mm; tail 46-61 mm.

REFERENCES Poslavski (1978), Taylor (1983), Nielsen and Colston (1984).

110 ORIENTAL PLOVER *Charadrius veredus*

Plate 37

Other names: Oriental Dotterel, Eastern Sandplover
A large *Charadrius* with long migrations. This is the eastern replacement of Caspian Plover (109), previously treated as conspecific.

IDENTIFICATION Similar to Caspian, but roughly 14% larger in body length and proportionately longer-legged and longer-necked. Outside breeding plumage, best distinguished by darker wings above and below. Upperwing lacks clear wingbar, although outer greater coverts are narrowly tipped white and some individuals show traces of white on the outer webs of up to 4 inner primaries; underwing browner than in Caspian, and axillaries are brown with narrow white fringes. Breeding birds are usually much whiter on the head, neck and upper back than Caspian, some being completely whitish or creamy except for brown rear crown. Oriental always has a broader supercilium, and a broader black breast-band. The legs are usually more brightly coloured. Greater and Lesser Sandplovers (107, 108) both have similar non-breeding plumages, but are smaller and more compact, have narrower breast-bands, and are usually found only on shores. Beware confusion with Pacific Golden Plover (82), which is similar in size but has proportionately shorter legs and wings, dark legs, strongly-patterned rather than plain upperparts, a darker face and, generally, brighter yellow-buff coloration. **Bare parts:** Bill black. Iris brown. Legs yellow to orange, tinged fleshy or greenish.
VOICE Flight call a sharp whistled 'chip-chip-chip'; also has trilling calls and a short, piping 'klink'.
HABITS Habits generally very similar to Caspian Plover's. Breeds Apr-July in arid inland of N China and Mongolia. Forms large winter flocks on dry grassland and thinly-vegetated plains in inland areas, especially N Australia, but single birds or migratory flocks may be found on dry mud near fresh water, on richer grassland, or rarely at the coast on saltfields, estuarine mud and ocean beaches. Often far from water, in Australia sometimes with Inland Dotterel (119). Rather wary; bobs head in alarm, runs very fast and tall or sometimes stealthily with legs flexed. Flight powerful, usually fast and high, often with erratic turns.
MOVEMENTS Long-distance migrant from breeding grounds, wintering chiefly in Indonesia and N Australia. Occurs on migration in China and Japan and has occurred on Andaman and Cocos Is. Present in Australia Sept-Mar, but rare except in north; vagrants have penetrated to S Australia, Raoul I. (1908), and on several occasions to New Zealand.
DESCRIPTION Breeding: Brightest individuals show broad, rich chestnut breast-band with black lower border, and forecrown and nape conspicuously creamy or whitish. Otherwise as non-breeding. **Non-breeding:** Brown crown and mark backwards from eye contrast with pale buff forehead, throat, cheeks and supercilium. Upperparts brown, in fresh plumage with bold rufous or buffish edgings to the scapulars and wing-coverts emphasising the lanceolate shape of the larger feathers. Underparts whitish with broad, poorly-defined, smooth brownish breast-band. Axillaries brown with narrow whitish fringes, underwing mostly brown but with some whitish feathers among the coverts. Upperwing uniform with brown back and scapulars; no clear wingbar, but outer greater coverts are narrowly tipped white and there may be traces of white on the outer webs of the inner 4 primaries. The shaft of the outer primary is always contrastingly white. The tail has a narrow white fringe to the sides and tip. **Juvenile:** As non-breeding adult, but upperpart and covert fringing is more extensive and paler buff. Breast-band is buff, mottled with darkish brown.
AGE/SEX Fresh juveniles show extensive pale buff fringing on the wing-coverts; on the inner medians this is retained sometimes until the following breeding season, contrasting with the richer chestnut fringes to the feathers grown during the post-juvenile moult. In this plumage, young also differ in their rather worn and pointed primaries; those of the adults are only slightly worn by the start of the next breeding season. In breeding plumage, only males show a solid chestnut-and-black breast-band and a creamy or whitish forecrown and collar. Some females attain chestnut in the breast-band, but most resemble non-breeding birds. First-year males usually attain only a dull, pale chestnut, buff-fringed breast-band and may be difficult to distinguish from adult females.
RACES No geographical variation is known.
MEASUREMENTS Length 220-255 mm (9¼"). Wing 156-178 mm; bill 20-25 mm; tarsus 43-50 mm; tail 59-64 mm.
REFERENCES Larkins and McGill (1978), Close (1982), Pedler (1982), McCrie (1984).

111 RUFOUS-CHESTED DOTTEREL *Charadrius modestus*

Plate 47

A handsome South American species which bears a strong resemblance to the Caspian and Oriental Plovers (109, 110) of the Old World. It also shows more similarity to the Mountain Plover (112) of North America.

IDENTIFICATION Distinctive by virtue of its almost plain brown upperparts, rufous or grey-brown breast, and white belly. In flight, shows no wingbar but conspicuous white sides to the blackish-brown rump and tail; there is a narrow white trailing edge to the secondaries. Flight is rapid and direct. Tawny-throated Dotterel (121) is larger, has a long, slim bill and long legs, and has a dark belly-patch in all plumages. American Golden Plover (83) is fairly similar in non-breeding plumage, but larger and stronger-billed, with strongly-mottled upperparts, grey axillaries, a poor wingbar and no white in the tail. No other South American species is similar. Strikingly similar in size, proportions and plumage to Caspian Plover; it can always be distinguished from Caspian and from Mountain by lack of white wingbar and by blackish

302

rump and central tail with strongly-contrasted white outer tail feathers. Differs from Oriental Plover in smaller size, bright white (not dark brown) underwing, and pattern of rump and tail. In breeding plumage, differs from all these species in grey face and throat, supercilia meeting narrowly across forehead, and broader black band across lower breast. **Bare parts:** Bill slender, black, sometimes with a little dull yellow at base of lower mandible. Iris dark brown. Legs grey-brown, in juveniles slightly duller or tinged yellowish.

VOICE Normal call is a disyllabic, tremulous 'peeoo' with a falling inflexion; when very agitated, this is shortened to a repeated 'peu-peu-peu', or lengthened to 'pee-ooo' when a predator is in the territory. Also utters a wheezy 'whee-ar' during territorial defence. During high aerial display flight, gives 'pic-pic-pic' and rattling calls.

HABITS Breeds Sept-Jan on inland grassland, sometimes in boggy lowlands or dry stony upland areas. Noisy and conspicuous when breeding. Often gathers in post-breeding flocks prior to northward migration. Outside the breeding season mainly a grassland species, but also occurs on coastal mudflats and beaches, sometimes with Two-banded Plovers (106). Inconspicuous and often rather wary in winter.

MOVEMENTS Most southern breeders migrate north in Mar-Apr after breeding and return in late Aug-Sept. Some, however, remain close to the breeding grounds, even in Tierra del Fuego. Many Falklands birds migrate to the mainland in winter, but an unknown proportion is resident. Winter stragglers have reached Tristan da Cunha (May 1952) and Peru (June 1972, Aug 1984).

DESCRIPTION Breeding: Forehead, lores, earcoverts, chin and throat are pale ash-grey. Brilliant white supercilia meet on the forecrown and end with a small chestnut spot on the sides of the nape. Crown is dark chocolate-brown. Upperparts darkish-brown, with slight gingery fringes on many feathers when fresh. Outer secondaries are narrowly, and inners broadly, tipped white. Primary shafts are brownish-white distally. Rump and central tail feathers are dark sooty-brown, but sides to rump and outer two pairs of tail feathers are white. Under primary coverts are greyish, secondary coverts and axillaries bright white. Breast rich rufous, with sharp black band across the lower breast. Rest of underparts white, except for small patch of tawny-buff behind each thigh. **Non-breeding:** Mainly Mar-July. Upperparts slightly paler brown, with many whitish fringes on scapulars and tertials. Head very much paler, forehead and forecrown pale whitish-buff, speckled darker; supercilium creamy and relatively diffuse, mostly behind the eye. Small whitish area on chin and throat. Neck and breast all grey-brown, slightly mottled. **Juvenile:** As non-breeding, but all upperparts dark brown speckled or fringed whitish-buff; on tertials, fringes are often interrupted by dark brown shaft-streak. Coverts rather pale brown, broadly fringed brownish-buff. Breast with pale buff fringes, paler but more mottled than on adult.

AGE/SEX Upperpart pattern of juveniles is distinctive. One-year-old birds may show retained juvenile inner median coverts. Sexes are not known to differ in size, but females tend to be slightly duller in breeding plumage.

RACES None is described, but Falkland Is. birds average larger in wing and tarsus measurements.

MEASUREMENTS Length 190-220 mm (8"). Wing 143-155 mm (Falklands, mean 149 mm), 137-151 mm (mainland, mean 144 mm); bill 17-19 mm; tarsus 31-38 mm (Falklands, mean 35.4 mm), 27-37 mm (mainland, mean 30.9 mm); tail 57-69 mm.

REFERENCES Humphrey *et al.* (1970), Johnson (1965), Woods (1975).

112 MOUNTAIN PLOVER *Charadrius montanus*   Plate 38

This exclusively North American bird is not a mountain species, but nests in dry upland grassland and winters in semi-deserts or on agricultural land. Its numbers have decreased markedly this century, but there may still be more than 300,000 breeding individuals.

IDENTIFICATION A pale brown plover of inland fields, grasslands and dried mud. For much of the year it is very plain, with buffy-brown on sides of breast and a poorly-marked supercilium, but in breeding plumage both sexes gain black lores and a black frontal bar, contrasting with the white forehead and supercilium, and a mainly white breast. In flight, there is a narrow but clear white wingbar, and tail shows a distinct white fringe and a dark subterminal bar; underwing and axillaries are white. Breeding plumage is distinctive (other American plovers with a black frontal bar also show black on the breast); at other seasons best distinguished by relatively large size, longish yellowish-brown legs, pale buffy-brown plumage, and inland habitat. American Golden Plover (83) is slightly larger, darker-legged, and has darker, greyer plumage conspicuously spotted and notched on upperparts. In flight, best distinctions are underwing colour and tail pattern (American Golden has dull brownish underwing and axillaries, and lacks white in the tail). Wingbar on Mountain is more sharply defined than on American Golden, and contrasts strongly with very dark secondaries and tips to inner primaries; wingbeats are faster. Eurasian Dotterel (120) in non-breeding plumage has more contrasting supercilia, a white line across the brownish breast, and no wingbar. Closest affinities may be to latter species and to Caspian and Oriental Plovers (109, 110), which also see. **Bare parts:** Bill slim, blackish or brownish-black. Iris dark brown. Legs fairly long, pale brown or brownish-yellow.

VOICE A variety of penetrating, drawn-out whistles, and a harsh shrill 'kip'. In display, gives a clear 'wee-wee-wee'.

HABITS Nests on the short-grass prairies late Apr-July, particularly in association with blue grama-buffalo grass communities. Ungrazed areas and land once ploughed grow taller species of grass and are unsuitable for nesting; much habitat has been altered in this way, or lost to cereal production. Female often leaves her first clutch for the male, then lays a second clutch which she incubates. Flocks form on the breeding grounds from mid-June onwards. The winter is spent chiefly in flocks, sometimes of several hundred, in semi-desert or dry agricultural country. May join other waders and gulls following the plough. Often very tame and approachable.

MOVEMENTS Present on breeding grounds late Mar-Sept, and in wintering areas chiefly mid-Oct to Feb, rarely from mid-July. Vagrants have reached Washington, Oregon, Alabama, Florida, Virginia, and Massachusetts.

DESCRIPTION Breeding: Brilliant white of forehead extends into a longish supercilium. Black frontal bar; rest of crown greyish-brown. Lores are crossed by neat black line, but eye-stripe is inconspicuous behind the eye. Ear-coverts and sides of neck and upper breast pale brownish-buff; underparts otherwise white, including underwing and axillaries. Upperparts greyish-brown, with narrow dull cinnamon fringes. White wingbar is formed by neat tips of greater coverts, white primary shafts, and white bases to inner primaries. Tail as upperparts at base, but shading to brown over outer third and narrowly fringed white. **Non-breeding:** As breeding, but black on crown and lores is replaced by pale brown, ear-coverts are slightly browner, upperparts show slightly more extensive dull rufous fringes, and patches on sides of breast are buffier, cover a more extensive area and sometimes join in centre. **Juvenile:** As non-breeding, but upperparts slightly darker brown with narrow dark subterminal bars and bright buff fringes. Crown appears speckled or finely striped. Supercilium is buffish; sides of breast are flecked darkish brown.

AGE/SEX Young are easily distinguished from moulting adults in post-breeding flocks, but resemble adults by Nov. Sexes are similar in plumage and in size.
RACES No geographical variation is known.
MEASUREMENTS Length 210-235 mm (8¾"). Wing 144-159 mm; bill 19-23 mm; tarsus 38-42 mm.
REFERENCES Graul (1975), Graul and Webster (1976), Wallis and Wershler (1981).

113 BLACK-FRONTED PLOVER *Charadrius melanops* Plate 43

Other name: Black-fronted Dotterel
A highly distinctive Australasian endemic plover. It is common in continental Australia, scarce in Tasmania and locally common in New Zealand. Its ecology, behaviour and bare-part coloration are similar to those of the Three-banded Plover (96) of Africa.

IDENTIFICATION The vertical black bar on the forehead, the black 'V' on the white breast, and the contrastingly dark scapulars are all features unique among small plovers. In short flights, wingbeats are jerky and the flight low and dipping, recalling a short-tailed passerine, but the wing-action can be easier over longer distances. Flight pattern shows a whitish panel across the inner wing, and a white-fringed tail. **Bare parts:** Bill bright pinkish-red, with a sharply-defined black outer third. Iris dark brown; eye-ring scarlet. Legs dull pale orange or pinkish.

VOICE An explosive high-pitched 'dip' repeated at one- or two-second intervals, a soft 'tink-tink', and other clicking, buzzing and churring calls. Often not very vocal.

HABITS Usually seen on mud, gravel or shingle at edge of fresh or brackish water; rarely on open seashores. Frequently on isolated small pools, even in cities. Feeds mainly by picking, but occasionally probes. Foot-trembling is sometimes used while feeding. Nests Aug-Jan on river shingle, sand or sometimes bare ground among leaf-litter up to 300 m from water; in New Zealand often in same areas as Double-banded Plover (105), but riverside territories are frequently more enclosed by high banks or vegetation. There is a well-developed distraction display which features the reddish rump and uppertail, as in Killdeer (91). Usually feeds singly or in pairs; not a flocking species but, when conditions are poor, larger numbers, rarely up to 100, may be seen feeding in close proximity.

MOVEMENTS No evidence of regular migrations, but certainly capable of long flights. Many remain on or near breeding grounds all year. Has colonised New Zealand since 1954: first proved breeding was in 1961, and there were over 300 pairs by 1967. Found once outside Australasia: said to have been collected near Madras, India, in June.

DESCRIPTION Breeding and non-breeding: Crown brown; white supercilia from just in front of eye meet on nape; a black vertical bar from mid-crown to forehead joins black lores and broad black eye-stripes, which also meet on nape. Underparts white except for bold black V-shaped breast-band, and longest undertail-coverts which have broad black bars. Underwing white, except for blackish from carpal area to median under primary coverts; dark undersides to flight feathers contrast strongly. Mantle, tertials and coverts brown; feathers have darker centres, giving a variegated pattern when worn. Small scapulars all purplish-chestnut, forming a solid dark patch. Rump and uppertail-coverts dark-brown, broadly tipped chestnut. Tail has central two pairs of feathers all-dark, outer pair all-white, and others mainly white with dark subterminal bar. Upperwing largely dark, but with pale panel (varying in intensity) formed by whitish edges to longest coverts and some white on inner secondaries. Folded wing shows pronounced whitish streaking. Primaries rather blacker than outer secondaries; lesser coverts contrastingly brown. When fresh, broad white tips to greater coverts may form a narrow wingbar. **Juvenile:** Head pattern poorly defined; forehead is white and lacks black bar, crown is mottled with white. Coverts have bright chestnut fringes, rather than the broad pale edges of the adult. Scapulars all-brown. Undertail-coverts all-white. Breast-band initially completely obscured by white tips, but becomes more evident as wear reveals the brown bases to the feathers. Bill and legs are brownish, eye-ring absent.

AGE/SEX Before post-juvenile moult, juveniles most easily distinguished by white breast or brown breast-band (partially obscured by white) and lack of chestnut scapulars. After moult, most look like adults in the field, but some chestnut-fringed inner medians are retained for almost a full year, enabling easy age-ing of birds in the hand. In juveniles primaries are paler and narrower, and wear faster, than in adults. Sexes are similar in plumage and in size.

RACES No geographical variation is known.

MEASUREMENTS Length 160-180 mm (6¾"). Wing 102-118 mm; bill 15-18 mm; tarsus 21-27 mm.

REFERENCES Maclean (1977), Heather (1973, 1977).

114 RED-KNEED DOTTEREL *Charadrius cinctus*   Plate 44

This endemic plover of Australia and New Guinea is unusually aquatic in its feeding and breeding habits. Unusually for a southern hemisphere small plover, there are normally four eggs in a clutch.

IDENTIFICATION A medium-sized plover with rather long legs but, unusually, a stance which is horizontal or even with protruding breast inclined downwards. At all times its black or brown cap, white chin, throat and sides of neck, and greenish-brown upperparts are distinctive. At a distance, the head and breast pattern of the smaller, shorter-legged Black-fronted Plover (113) may appear similar, but latter is easily distinguished at closer range by the white posterior supercilium and grey-brown cap. Red-kneed's long bicoloured legs, with feet which project beyond the tip of the tail in flight, and lack of a white hindneck collar are additional features to aid identification. In flight, the white secondaries and tips to inner primaries, and the broad white sides to the rump and tail, form an obvious and unique flight pattern. Flight is swift and dashing on rather rounded wings. **Bare parts:** Bill fairly long and thin, pinkish-red with black tip; on juvenile, duller with more extensive, brownish-black tip and brown also along upper mandible. Iris brown. Legs pinkish-red from body to just below 'knee' joint, becoming brownish-green or grey-blue on lower tarsus.

VOICE Main flight and alarm call is a double, rather sharp but clear 'wit-wit' or 'chet-chet'. During display or in threat, it has a short melodious trill 'prr prip-prip'.

HABITS A freshwater species which occurs down to the coastal fringe. It is typical of well-vegetated wetlands and is unusual in building a substantial nest, often on a wet substrate and under overhanging vegetation. Semi-colonial breeder and, in larger wetlands, often in small flocks throughout the year. This is the most aquatic member of the genus, capable of swimming quite well and often feeding while wading into water. Unusually for a plover, it frequently submerges its head or probes into wet mud. It rarely feeds on dry ground. No display flight is described, but there are displays in which the white areas of wing, tail and breast are prominent. Often relies on disruptive camouflage among vegetation or stones when initially disturbed, then jerkily bobs its head before flying.

MOVEMENTS No regular migrations, but there is some post-breeding dispersal and also movements in response to rainfall and drought. Numbers vary enormously through the year at many inland and coastal localities. Recently recorded as a vagrant in New Zealand (Mar 1976).

DESCRIPTION Breeding and non-breeding: Whole of top of head including lores, ear-coverts and hind-neck black, sometimes washed greenish-brown, forming a well-defined cap. The white chin, throat and sides of neck are outlined in black, merging into a broad black breast-band which extends down the upper flanks; black is replaced on the rear flanks by chestnut, which breaks into spots behind the legs. Undertail spotted brown. Rest of underparts white. Upperparts glossed metallic green-brown. The upper fringe of the flanks is white, at rest showing as a white bar separating the upperpart colour from black and chestnut on breast and flanks. Primaries blackish, inners tipped white; secondaries broadly tipped white. Central pair of tail feathers blackish-brown, others mainly white. Broad white sides also to rump and lower back. **Juvenile:** Dark-capped appearance as in adult, but cap is dark brown and merges into upperparts. Wing-coverts and tertials duller than adult's and with fairly broad whitish-buff fringes; there are a few fringes also on the mantle and scapulars. Underparts white, apart from partially obscured, brownish lateral breast-patches.

AGE/SEX A brownish breast-band is steadily gained; later, this and cap become blackish. Any brown on cap or breast indicates young bird, while only adults show the chestnut flank-patches. No differences are known between the sexes.

RACES No geographical variation is known.

MEASUREMENTS Length 175-195 mm (7¼"). Wing 109-120 mm; bill 19-22 mm; tarsus 36-42 mm.

REFERENCES McGill (1944), Maclean (1977).

115 HOODED PLOVER *Charadrius rubricollis*   Plate 44

Other name: Hooded Dotterel

A stocky plover endemic to southern Australia and as yet enigmatic in its affinities. Especially common on Tasmanian beaches.

IDENTIFICATION Its sturdy, rather neckless appearance with a horizontal stance and protruding breast separate this from all other plovers in Australia except the Red-kneed Dotterel (114). However, its short pale legs and conspicuous white band across the hind-neck distinguish it at all times. Rarely seen away from

ocean beaches, except in W Australia. In adult plumage the black head, white nape and pale sandy-grey upperparts provide a unique pattern, while the pale brown head and white neck collar of the juvenile are also good identification features. It has a very striking broad white wingbar in flight. Larger size, paler colour and lack of a breast-band provide separation from vagrant Ringed Plover (86). **Bare parts:** Bill pinkish at base, distal third black; on juveniles, blackish with a small area of dull fleshy-pink at base of lower mandible. Iris brown; eye-ring deep pinkish-red, paler orange in juveniles. Legs rather short, pale orange-brown to yellowish-pink, paler in juveniles.
VOICE A fairly deep, repeated 'kew-kew' is the main flight note, although a higher-pitched 'kseep' is sometimes given when agitated.
HABITS For a plover, it moves rather slowly and deliberately, although can run fast if pressed. Often seen pecking and probing in drifted material like a Ruddy Turnstone (154), especially on the upper tidewrack zone of sandy beaches. Rarely occurs on rocky coasts or on margins of saltmarsh. Typically a bird of exposed ocean beaches, but also occurs around saline lakeshores in Western Australia. These two habitats are used all year. When disturbed, its reaction is to move slowly away, keeping its inconspicuous pale back towards the intruder but bobbing its head. The upperpart colour and the disruptive patterning of the head make very good camouflage. Although not especially wary, does not allow close approach, flying off to settle farther along the shore. Rarely found in flocks of more than family size, but some favoured beaches may hold flocks of up to 50. Breeds Aug-Jan, laying two or three eggs in a simple scrape in the sand.
MOVEMENTS Little is known, but the same beaches are normally occupied throughout the year. There is some post-breeding dispersal, particularly of young birds. Despite its breeding inland in Western Australia, there are apparently no records from similar habitats inland in South Australia and Victoria.
DESCRIPTION Breeding and non-breeding: Whole of head and neck black or brownish-black, except for white band across hindneck. Black collar across base of hindneck narrowly joins black on throat, and also extends onto sides of breast to form small black breast-patches. Underparts otherwise white. Upperparts pale brownish-grey, slightly darker on upper back, sometimes with some blackish feathers among the scapulars. Primary coverts and primaries blackish, with broad white wingbar extending to the outermost primary; inner secondaries wholly white, outer secondaries blackish with white at base and, narrowly, at tip. Central tail feathers blackish, merging with broad blackish oval patch towards tip of tail; outer two pairs of tail feathers and bases of outer five pairs are white. **Juvenile:** Completely lacks blackish of adult; head and collar dull grey-brown tipped whitish-buff, with indistinct buffish-white spot above the lores. Bright white collar. Throat almost white, but faint grey-brown tipping forms a wash of colour. All feathers of upperparts are pale brown-grey with narrow dark subterminal band and whitish fringe, giving a scaly appearance.
AGE/SEX Worn juveniles may become very bleached and faded. Juvenile steadily gains dark head, collar and shoulder-patches. After post-juvenile moult, may be identified only by retained inner coverts and worn primaries. No differences are known between the sexes.
RACES No geographical variation is known.
MEASUREMENTS Length 190-205 mm (7¾"). Wing 139-145 mm; bill 16-18 mm; tarsus 25-27 mm.
REFERENCES Lane (1982), Newman (1982).

116 SHORE PLOVER *Thinornis novaeseelandiae*   Plate 45

Other name: New Zealand Shore Plover
Formerly widely distributed in New Zealand, but now confined to Southeast I. in the Chatham archipelago, 640 km east of the main islands, and one of the rarest waders. There were an estimated 70 pairs in 1937, and 82 individuals in Mar 1972; in 1982, there were about 40 breeding pairs and a post-breeding total of about 140. Sometimes placed in the genus *Charadrius*.

IDENTIFICATION A rather thickset small plover, of turnstone-like proportions and coloration. The black mask extending from the forehead to the throat, contrasting with white underparts, is diagnostic. Juveniles lack this, but show a bold dark patch through and behind the eye. A strong white-wingbar is visible in flight; innermost 2-3 secondaries are entirely white. There are white sides to the rump and tail. **Bare parts:** Bill rather fine and pointed for a plover, slightly drooped, black with variable amount of dull orange or orange-red at base (depending on age and sex). Iris dark brown; adults have narrow reddish eye-ring. Legs orange, rather short and thick.
VOICE Highly vocal, with loud, ringing calls recalling Chatham Islands Oystercatcher (18). Contact calls 'kleet' or 'pip'; when flushed, a louder 'kleet' or 'splew'. Calls of adults may accelerate into a loud ringing rattle during aggressive encounters. Calls of juveniles and females are noticeably higher-pitched than those of adults and males.
HABITS Frequents mainly the intertidal and splash zones around the edges of the island, but also found on barren ground inland, even under trees. Feeds chiefly on wave-washed rock platforms, with rapid pecking action rather atypical of plovers; sometimes uses foot-trembling. Apparently feeds extensively at night. Usually very tame and easy to approach. The nest is unlike in *Charadrius* in being rarely open to the sky. The eggs are laid Oct-Feb, at the end of a short horizontal tunnel in thick vegetation or among stones; sometimes a deserted petrel burrow is used. The vicinity of the nest is defended against neighbouring birds, but the feeding grounds are communal. There is a slow-wingbeat 'butterfly' display flight around the territory.
MOVEMENTS Certainly capable of long flights, but

only occasional stragglers now reach other islands. A record of one collected in 1841 on the Auckland Is. is probably erroneous.

DESCRIPTION Adult: Crown brown, completely encircled by white band. Black or blackish wedge encompasses forehead, throat and sides of face, joining below the white band on the nape. Upperparts brown, with variable amount of whitish edging on coverts and tertials. Longest scapulars are edged greyish-white, forming a short silvery line above the folded tertials. Clear white wingbar. Underparts and underwing white, with some brown smudging on the sides of the breast. White sides to rump and tail. **Juvenile:** Black wedge across head is absent. Forehead, lores and throat are white, but there is a dark brown band from in front of the eye across the ear-coverts. Bill mostly brownish, with some orange at the base of the lower mandible.

AGE/SEX Juveniles are readily distinguished by their mainly-white faces. Sexes can also be easily told by the colour of the mask — black in males and paler and more brownish in females — and by the extent of orange-red on the bill-base: in males, it extends more than half-way down the bill and is sharply divided from the black tip, while in females it covers less than half the bill and shades into the black tip.

RACES There is no evidence that the extinct populations were any different from that still extant.

MEASUREMENTS Length about 200 mm (8"). One adult male: wing 123 mm; bill 25 mm; tarsus 22 mm.

REFERENCES Phillips (1977).

117 WRYBILL *Anarhynchus frontalis*   **Plate 45**

Other name: Wry-billed Plover
This small plover, confined to New Zealand, is one of very few bird species with a laterally asymmetrical bill. The total population has been estimated at 5,000-7,000.

IDENTIFICATION The sideways-bent bill is diagnostic when visible. Rather greyer above than other small plovers in New Zealand, and more heavily built; the neck is rather short and thick. There is a narrow black breast-band in breeding plumage, obscured in winter, but juveniles show a completely white breast. In flight, shows a clear white wingbar and a short, broad, white-fringed tail. Larger and greyer than Red-capped Plover (100), which is rare in New Zealand, and with less white on tail-sides. **Bare parts:** Bill black, tapering to a point, straight when viewed from side, but from above shows a slight bend to the left at base and a tight curve to the right, usually of about 14-23 degrees, near the tip. Iris dark brown. Legs short, similar in proportion to those of turnstones (154, 155), greenish-black.

VOICE A shrill 'weet' or 'peep', similar in tone to Ringed Plover (86). Flocks make chittering noises at times. Courtship song is a bubbling trill.

HABITS Breeds only on some larger stony riverbeds in South Island, present Aug-Jan. Lays two eggs on open shingle near water. Winters in large flocks in favoured muddy harbours on North Island. The bill is perfectly designed for extracting prey items such as mayfly larvae and fish eggs clinging to the underside of stones; such foraging sites are not accessible to other riverbed plovers which have thicker-tipped bills. Typically, prey are captured by clockwise sweeps beneath the stones in riffles. In the non-breeding habitat, Wrybills feed by ordinary pecking and probing and by sweeping the bill through the mud. Often runs fast with head tucked in. May rest on one leg for long periods. Before spring migration, flocks perform complicated aerobatics *en masse*.

MOVEMENTS Found in certain North Island harbours (mainly the Firth of Thames and Manukau and Kaipara Harbours) throughout the year, but the bulk of the population leaves between July and Oct for the South Island breeding grounds, returning from late Dec onwards. Migration is chiefly coastal; small flocks are seen on passage on the Canterbury coast, Farewell Spit, and southern coasts of North Island. Rare inland migrant in North Island: there are records from Lake Rotorua and Lake Hatuma.

DESCRIPTION Breeding: Grey crown, nape, lores and ear-coverts, sometimes with a black frontal bar; there is a clearly-defined white bar across the forehead joining the supercilia, which extend to just behind the eye, and a small whitish smudge below the eye. The rest of the upperparts are plain grey, with a narrow white wingbar and sides to the tail evident in flight. The wingbar is strongest on the inner primaries and outer greater coverts. In fresh plumage, there are a few white fringes to the wing-coverts. The underparts and underwing are white, with a narrow, almost parallel-sided black breast-band. **Non-breeding:** The black breast-band is effectively absent, since the black bases of the feathers are obscured by broad white tips. Males show no black on the forehead. **Juvenile:** Lacks breast-band. All grey feathers of the upperparts are initially white-fringed.

AGE/SEX Young may retain white-fringed juvenile inner median coverts throughout the first year. Only males show a prominent black frontal bar in breeding plumage. The breast-band is usually duller and narrower in females.

RACES No geographical variation.

MEASUREMENTS Length 200-210 mm (8"). Wing 120-128 mm; bill 26-30 mm; tarsus 27-30 mm.

REFERENCES Sibson (1963), Pierce (1979, 1983).

118 DIADEMED PLOVER *Phegornis mitchellii*

Plate 47

Other names: Diademed Sandpiper-plover, Mitchell's Plover
A most unusual plover-like bird of the high Andes, local in distribution and often difficult to find. The calidrid-like bill has led to uncertainty as to its true taxonomic position.

IDENTIFICATION An unmistakable bird. No other wader, except perhaps Shore Plover (116), is remotely similar in plumage pattern. Only slightly larger than a Western Sandpiper (191) and with a longish, gently drooping bill recalling Western or Dunlin (204). The blackish face is outlined in brilliant white, and the underparts are finely barred like those of Tuamotu Sandpiper (152). At a distance, looks dark brown above and pale grey below. The wings are rather short and rounded; in flight, resembles South American Painted Snipe (10), a lowland species. **Bare parts:** Bill longish, slender and drooping, black. Iris dark brown. Legs yellowish-flesh to orangey-yellow, perhaps greenish-yellow in juveniles.
VOICE A clear, penetrating, plover-like whistle, rather low-pitched. In anxiety, a lower and more plaintive note.
HABITS Breeds mainly Oct-Jan, in the puna zone of the high Andes, frequenting gravelly and grassy areas by freshwater lakes and streams. Not shy, allowing fairly close approach, but very inconspicuous owing to small size, slow movements and disruptive camouflage. Occurs at low density on nesting grounds, and not gregarious in winter; rarely seen in groups of more than half a dozen. Flies with peculiarly stiff beats of wings, held mostly below the horizontal, and with head held high. May occur as low as 2000 m in the south of the range but in the north not below 3300 m.
MOVEMENTS Southern breeders descend from top parts of range in Mar after breeding, but still a high-altitude species in winter; return to breeding sites in Oct. There may also be limited northward migration along the Andes in autumn and return in spring.
DESCRIPTION Breeding and non-breeding: Head blackish-brown, paler around base of bill, with long brilliant white rear supercilia joined by white band across the top of the crown. Small white crescent beneath the eye. Half-collar at base of hindneck and upper mantle bright deep chestnut; some individuals also show some chestnut in crown. Mantle and tertials dark grey-brown; rest of upperparts an even, mid grey-brown. Flight feathers all-dark, except for narrow white fringes and tips on inner secondaries, more extensive on innermost feathers. Bright creamy-white line of carpal coverts on closed wing is distinctive, but often hidden by overlapping flank feathers. Central pair of tail feathers dark brown, next four pairs brown with white spots at and near tip, outer pair barred brown and white. Underwing and axillaries white. Bright white band across base of throat, rest of underparts white, narrowly barred dark brown on breast; the barring becomes broader on belly, but paler and more widely spaced. **Juvenile:** Lacks black-and-white head pattern and chestnut collar of adult. Head is plain dull brown, with a pale buffish posterior supercilium. All upperparts are darkish brown, slightly obscured with warm rufous-buff bars, spots and fringes; coverts are tipped or barred buff and have a darkish subterminal bar. Underparts are pale brownish-white, with brownish barring only on the breast and flanks.
AGE/SEX Some buff-fringed coverts may be retained until at least Oct, enabling first-year birds to be distinguished in the breeding season. Sexes are similar in plumage pattern, but the female is slightly duller.
RACES No geographical variation is known.
MEASUREMENTS Length 165-190 mm (7"). Wing 110-117 mm; bill 22-26 mm; tarsus 21-24 mm; tail 47-52 mm.
REFERENCES Johnson (1965, 1972), Zusi and Jehl (1970).

119 INLAND DOTTEREL *Peltohyas australis*

Plate 44

Other names: Australian Dotterel, Australian Courser
An uncommon small wader of the arid interior of the Australian continent. It has sometimes been placed with the coursers, but recent studies confirm that it is a true plover.

IDENTIFICATION The only wader with a conspicuous vertical black line through the eye. Usually it is the only small plover found in its desert or semi-desert habitat. In size and shape it most closely resembles Eurasian Dotterel (120), with which it shares a cryptically-patterned brown-streaked mantle. When facing the observer, the buffish-white face and upper breast contrast strongly with the bold black 'Y' across the chest and form a striking pattern. **Bare parts:** Bill black, rather short and fine. Iris dark brown. Legs dull yellow-ochre, feet darker.
VOICE Not very vocal. A quiet gruff 'kr-root' when flushed; a brisk 'quick', sometimes repeated, is the usual flock contact and alarm call.
HABITS Usually encountered on bare, arid, stony or sparsely-vegetated plains or uplands, but occasion-ally on ploughed land; seldom seen near water. Often met with at night on favoured stretches of outback dirt road. Parties feed on plant material during the day, but species is more active and more likely to be solitary at night, feeding largely on nocturnal invertebrates. Fairly tame.
MOVEMENTS Nomadic, but found throughout the year in some parts of the range, while regular north-south movements have been reported from NW Victoria. Once recorded east of the Great Dividing Range, at Sydney NSW.
DESCRIPTION Breeding: Face and foreparts are white suffused buff; a broad black frontal bar extends downwards through the eye, leaving a whitish eye-ring. There is a complete black ring around the base of the neck and a black mid-ventral line, forming a

'Y' on the breast. Flanks, axillaries and underwing are plain rich buff, becoming deep chestnut bordering the white rear flanks, belly and undertail. On some individuals, the undertail is lightly suffused buff. Upperparts are entirely brown and buff, all feathers having a lanceolate dark brown centre and long buff edges. The tail is dark brown, with small white tips and edges to the outer feathers. The flight feathers are dark brown, boldly edged and tipped buff across the secondaries and inner primaries; buff on the outer webs of the inner primaries forms a short, poorly-contrasted wingbar. **Non-breeding:** An eclipse non-breeding plumage occurs, probably during wing moult. All black is lacking, although a trace of the

dark facial bar and the dark collar is visible; the dark centres to the crown and mantle feathers are paler. **Juvenile:** As non-breeding.
AGE/SEX Young birds are not known to be distinguishable from adults in non-breeding plumage. There are no known plumage differences between the sexes.
RACES No geographical variation is known.
MEASUREMENTS Length 190-230 mm (8¼"). Wing 132-149 mm; bill 17-19 mm (exceptionally 14 mm); tarsus 31-35 mm.
REFERENCES Bock (1964), Maclean (1973, 1976b), McNamara (1980).

120 EURASIAN DOTTEREL *Eudromias morinellus*   Plate 38

Other name: Dotterel
This bird is unique among plovers in that the female has brighter plumage than the male. It is often placed in the genus *Charadrius*, with which it has very strong affinities.

IDENTIFICATION A smallish, stocky, yellowish-legged plover of dry, mainly inland habitats. In all plumages, the bold supercilia meeting in a 'V' on the nape and the pale line crossing the darker breast are distinctive and diagnostic. In flight, shows no white on the wing (except for shaft of outer primary), a dull greyish-white underwing, and a narrow white or buffish tail-tip; flight is fast and direct. Breeding plumage shows highly-contrasted white supercilia and breast line, dark cap, mainly-grey upper breast, chestnut lower breast and flanks, black belly, and white vent and undertail. Non-breeding plumage resembles that of Caspian (109) and Oriental (110), but in these species the supercilia start on the forehead and do not extend to nape, the upperparts are plainer and the legs longer. Juvenile is boldly scalloped and spangled with bright buff on upperparts, and may be mistaken for Pacific Golden Plover (82); latter, however, is darker-legged and longer-billed, has no pale line on the breast, and has shorter supercilia which do not meet on the nape. Compare supercilium with that of juvenile Cream-coloured Courser (45). **Bare parts:** Bill rather short and slim, black but sometimes tinged greenish or greyish at base of lower mandible. Iris dark brown. Legs dull yellow or yellowish-brown.
VOICE Not very vocal, mostly silent in winter. Usual calls are a soft 'pweet-pweet-pweet' and 'kwip-kwip'; variants on these include tinkling trills, and a trilling 'skeer' on take-off.
HABITS Nests May-Aug on arctic coastal and inland tundra and in montane areas widely scattered across temperate Eurasia. Sometimes nests at sites used mainly as migration stop-overs, such as Pyrenees and Caucasus. Exceptionally, nests in temperate lowlands, regularly below sea-level in recently-reclaimed Dutch polders. In mountains, prefers well-drained plateaux with short vegetation. Female usually takes little part in incubation of her first clutch, and may lay more clutches for subsequent mates; she rarely assists in brood-care, but may rejoin the family once well grown. Well scattered when nesting, but gathers into flocks towards end of season and is gregarious in winter. Often abundant in winter quarters, found chiefly

in dry sandy or stony areas on high plateaux, avoiding richer areas of cultivation. Remarkably tame at all seasons.
MOVEMENTS Birds from all parts of breeding range winter in a narrow zone from Morocco to Iran; at least 10000 km distant from E Siberia. Present in winter quarters mainly Sept-Apr; spring departures begin late Feb. Ringing studies indicate considerable mixing in winter of birds from different areas, and subsequent abmigration. Usually migrates in small parties (known as 'trips'), which stop at traditional intermediate sites. In Palaearctic, vagrant to Canaries, Madeira, Iceland, Faeroes, Spitsbergen (bred 1974) and Bear I., also Japan (regular in autumn). Elsewhere, recorded only in Bermuda, Hawaii and W USA: scarce but regular in NW Alaska in summer (probably breeds), and very rare Sept vagrant to Washington and California.
DESCRIPTION Breeding: Forehead dark brown, strongly speckled whitish, crown and nape dark brown; long white supercilia start above eye and meet in a 'V' on nape. Lores are dusky, and ear-coverts blackish bordering the supercilium, but most of sides of face, chin and throat are white. Neck and upper breast dull greyish, sometimes with fine brownish streaks. Upperparts from mantle to rump and uppertail, also tertials, scapulars and wing-coverts are darkish grey, edged narrowly with dull rufous-buff, especially on scapulars and tertials. Outer primary has clear white shaft. Tail has central feathers darkish-grey shading to black and narrowly tipped cinnamon, rest with blackish subterminal bar and broad white tip. Grey of upper breast is divided from the deep chestnut of upper belly and flanks by a neat but narrow white band; this is bordered above by a narrow blackish line, and below by a more irregular dusky one. Central belly is black; vent and undertail-coverts white. Underwing-coverts and axillaries dull greyish-white. **Non-breeding:** Black, grey, white and chestnut are lost. Crown becomes streaked dark brown and buffish, supercilia brownish-buff. Upperparts as breeding, but slightly browner and duller. Lower neck and breast are mottled greyish-brown and crossed by obscure narrow whitish breast line; belly notice-

ably whiter. **Juvenile:** As non-breeding, but with dark brown feather bases on crown, mantle, scapulars and tertials contrasting strongly with their pale buffish fringes. On most coverts there is a darker subterminal area, and the buff fringe is broken by a brown shaft-streak. Neck and breast bright buffish-cinnamon, streaked brown at sides, crossed by unstreaked buffish-white breast line; belly white, washed buffish.

AGE/SEX The distinctive juvenile scapulars and tertials are usually easy to see, and may be retained well into the winter. Female averages slightly larger, but is separable only in full breeding plumage: typical female has almost solid blackish-brown cap, a clean grey breast and sides of neck, and very sharp white supercilia and breast line; typical male has more extensive whitish flecks on forehead, brownish tinge to neck and breast, white lines less sharply defined, and less black on belly. Some are intermediate and should not be sexed.

RACES No geographical variation, in spite of very wide range.

MEASUREMENTS Length 200-220 mm (8¼"). Wing 143-163 mm; bill 14-19 mm; tarsus 33-40 mm; tail 62-73 mm.

REFERENCES Nethersole-Thompson (1973), Nielsen (1975), Burnier (1977), Kålås and Byrkjedal (1984).

121 TAWNY-THROATED DOTTEREL *Oreopholus ruficollis*   Plate 47

This South American endemic plover breeds both coastally and in the high Andes. There are superficial resemblances to the smaller Eurasian Dotterel (120).

IDENTIFICATION Plumage pattern similar to Eurasian Dotterel's with dark crown, whitish supercilia, rufous and buff edges to the dark brown mantle feathers, and dark belly-patch; differs in orange-chestnut face and throat, lack of white breast-band, strongly-streaked scapulars and wing-coverts, and in flight by narrow but clear white wingbar and blackish subterminal band to mainly-grey tail. Proportions of bill, neck and legs recall Upland Sandpiper (135), but lacks the long tail of that species. Upright stance, rufous throat and dark belly-patch are simple distinctions from other South American waders.In overhead flight, differs from American Golden Plover (83) in conspicuous pure white underwing and axillaries and dark belly-patch. **Bare parts:** Bill black, long and slender, slightly drooped at tip. Eye large, iris dark brown. Legs long, dull pinkish, in juveniles dusky-grey; toes blackish, short and rather stout.

VOICE Generally silent on the ground, but calls loudly when flushed, a distinctive, tremulous, reedy note with a falling inflexion, often repeated (frequently heard from flocks flying overhead). Also, a plaintive whistled 'whees-tur-tur'.

HABITS Found in semi-arid and poor grassland from the coastal plain to 4500 m in the central Andes. A summer breeder, at least in southern parts of the range, but little is known of the breeding biology. When not breeding, often gathers in feeding flocks. Flies fast, high and directly, like American Golden Plover, often in loose flocks. A frequent target for hunters, and population in some areas has decreased markedly owing to persecution.

MOVEMENTS Lowland, northern populations are sedentary. Those in high Andes descend to lower altitudes after breeding, and those in the southernmost areas mostly migrate north in Mar-Apr to grasslands as far as 30° S, returning late Aug-Sept. Vagrant to the Falkland Is. (two in Aug 1961).

DESCRIPTION Breeding and non-breeding: Forehead and supercilium creamy-white, often tinged tawny-red. Narrow, often sharply-defined blackish eye-stripe from bill to behind eye, ear-coverts dusky grey-brown. Crown quite dark grey-brown, slightly streaked paler; a pale reddish wash extends the line of the supercilia across the nape. Often a pale creamy patch below the eye. Chin creamy-white; throat, ear-coverts and front of neck a variable shade of tawny-red, often with whitish flecks. Breast, sides of neck, hindneck and upper mantle clean grey-brown, tinged rufous. Lower mantle, scapulars and coverts centred blackish and edged bright tawny-buff, forming a streaky pattern. Tertials show dark brown centres and narrow dull tawny edges. Rump and uppertail-coverts plain brownish tinged rufous, some feathers with warm buff tips. Longest uppertail-coverts reach almost to tip of tail. Tail essentially grey, with a narrow blackish bar about 1 cm from the tip and a very narrow buff tip; outer feathers have tawny-buff at the base. Flight feathers dark, with strong white wingbar across bases of primaries and secondaries and the tips of the greater coverts. Narrow white trailing edge to the secondaries. Entire underwing and axillaries contrastingly white. Grey on breast becomes buffish-grey on upper belly and buffish on rest of underparts, except for small black patch in centre of belly. **Juvenile:** As adult in pattern, but throat is warm buff, and brown cap and greyish breast are obscured by buff fringes. Mantle feathers, scapulars and coverts are small, blackish-centred, and fringed neatly with buffish-white, giving a scaly rather than streaked appearance to the upperparts. Longer scapulars and tertials also show a dark subterminal fringe. Uppertail-coverts show a dark subterminal bar and a whitish-buff tip. Underparts very pale buff, with brownish-black belly-patch.

AGE/SEX Some juvenile inner median coverts may be retained after the post-juvenile moult. No differences are known between the sexes.

RACES Two: the apparently isolated population of the N Peruvian coast is usually separated as *pallidus*. These birds are smaller, paler and greyer, with slightly more white on the inner webs of the outer tail feathers.

MEASUREMENTS Length 250-290 mm (10½"). Wing 146-152 mm (*pallidus*), 160-183 mm (nominate); bill 27-31 mm; tarsus 45-53 mm; tail 69-90 mm.

REFERENCES Hudson (1920), Johnson (1965), Humphrey *et al.* (1970).

122 MAGELLANIC PLOVER *Pluvianellus socialis* Plate 87

A rare and beautiful soft grey-and-white wader found only around the southern tip of South America. It is unusual in a number of respects, not least its habit of feeding its young by regurgitation, which is unique among waders. Its relationships are uncertain, and it may not be a plover at all.

IDENTIFICATION The short thick legs, stout toes, uniform dove-grey upperparts and breast-band, as well as range, provide an easy distinction from all other shorebirds. It has a rather long body, with short legs set well back, and a rather upright stance. The usual gait is an inelegant shuffle or waddle, although it can run quickly. In flight, it has a strong white wing-bar and broad white sides to the rump and base of tail. **Bare parts:** Bill black, with a small area of pinkish at base of culmen and another at base of lower mandible; these patches are yellowish and more extensive in juveniles. Bill quite strong and rather pointed, recalling turnstones' (154, 155). Iris pink-red in adult, orangey in juvenile. Legs pinkish-red in adult, dull yellowish in juvenile, also recalling turnstones' in proportions.

VOICE Most frequently a ringing 'coo' or 'ceu', intermediate between a dove and a plover. The alarm call is 'pip-wheet'.

HABITS Breeds in early spring (Nov), mostly around freshwater or brackish lagoons and lakes; territories are strongly defended. Displays on the ground include an upright pose with breast puffed out. Both sexes incubate the two large eggs; in most broods, only one chick survives and is fed by the adults until after fledging, apparently sometimes by regurgitation. A few remain throughout the summer in the coastal wintering areas of sheltered bays and river mouths. Extremely inconspicuous when standing still against shingle, even its shadow being difficult to see because of its short legs. Feeds by pecking, but will turn over small stones with its strong bill like a turnstone and even, uniquely, scratch or dig for food into the substrate with its powerful legs. The flight is quite strong and fast, often erratic. Habits outside the breeding season have not yet been described.

MOVEMENTS Most are sedentary, apart from post-breeding dispersal to the coast. Some move a very short distance northwards in the winter, when the range extends from the Straits of Magellan northwards to Santa Cruz and Chubut provinces of Argentina.

DESCRIPTION Breeding and non-breeding: All of upperparts pale grey, with whitish-grey forehead, quite well-marked dusky loral line and a slightly dusky ear-covert patch. Chin and throat white. Upper breast clean pale grey, becoming darker and infused with brownish on lower breast. Belly, undertail, underwing and axillaries white. Flight feathers greyish-brown, with clear white wingbar extending across the bases of all primaries; inner 2 secondaries wholly white, others white-based; greater coverts white-tipped. Rump grey, with bright white sides. Central pair of tail feathers blackish-brown, others white, but with a unique pattern of faint grey vermiculations across corners of tail. **Juvenile:** Whole upperparts extensively tipped, spotted and fringed white; inner coverts are fringed buffish-white. Breast-band streaked grey; feathers show dark grey shaft-streaks and broad white edges. Lacks adult's dark lores. Upper mandible shows extensive yellowish patch covering more than half of the culmen.

AGE/SEX Retained juvenile feathers differ markedly from adult-type feathers, and are a clear indication of young bird. Sexes are apparently similar.

RACES No geographical variation within its tiny range.

MEASUREMENTS Length 195-215 mm (8"). Wing 132-142 mm; bill 14-16 mm; tarsus 17-20 mm; tail 58-65 mm.

REFERENCES Johnson (1965), Humphrey *et al.* (1970), Jehl (1975).

123 BLACK-TAILED GODWIT *Limosa limosa* Plate 48

The tallest and most elegant of the four godwits. It breeds in temperate climates, as well as boreal and low-arctic zones.

IDENTIFICATION A relatively large wader, simple to identify in flight owing to its combination of long and broad white wingbar, white axillaries and underwing, broad white band across the lower rump and uppertail, and black tail-band; long bill and legs give it a much elongated appearance, even in comparison with other godwits. The American Hudsonian Godwit (124) is similar, but differs most obviously in black axillaries and underwing-coverts (contrasting with white on undersides of flight feathers), much narrower wingbar on the upperwing, and narrower white band across the uppertail (not so broad as the black tail-band). At rest, confusion is possible with both Bar-tailed (125) and Hudsonian Godwits, but Blacktail is separable both on plumage characters and on structure. In breeding plumage, Blacktail always shows a white rear belly and heavy, irregular barring on lower breast and belly; both Bartail and Hudso-nian often have red on belly (at least in males), almost unbarred in Bartail but heavily barred in Hudsonian. In non-breeding plumage, Blacktail shares with Hudsonian rather evenly grey-brown upperparts, but is slightly paler (except in eastern race *melanuroides*) and has a less contrasting supercilium; Bartail differs in its more variegated upperparts, with broad dark brown feather centres forming a streaked pattern. In shape, Blacktail is rather longer-legged and longer-necked than Bartail, with a rather flatter forehead. Bill shape is also a guide, being slightly blunter and less upcurved in Blacktail. These differences are to some extent obscured by sexual dimorphism in both species; beware also Hudsonian, which is intermediate in proportions but closer to Bartail. Overall size is a useful character, but note geographical variation: Blacktail is generally the larger species, but Bartail averages larger than Blacktail in E Asia and Australasia. **Bare parts:** Bill long, almost straight or faintly upcurved, often distinctly bicoloured; distal third or more blackish, and base flesh-pink or more orange during breeding. Iris dark brown. Legs long, dark grey or blue-grey; toes and part of tarsus extend beyond tail-tip in flight.

VOICE Noisy when breeding, but otherwise relatively quiet. Display calls include a slightly growling 'grutto', a sharp repeated 'wick-a-wick-a-wick-a' or 'tititit', and a hoarse 'wee-eeh' recalling Northern Lapwing (57). Contact calls are a short quiet 'tuk' or 'kek', often repeated.

HABITS Nests Apr-Aug in damp grassy moorland, blanket-bog, reclaimed land, or lowland grasslands adjacent to freshwater wetlands. Male has a switch-back display flight including spectacular rolling and tumbling. Often forms loosely colonial groups. Intruding predators are mobbed aggressively. When not breeding, favours the upper reaches of muddy estuaries, muddy inland lakeshores, and nearby farmland or flooded grassland; inland wintering is common in Africa, India and parts of Australasia. Feeds by picking and by forward-angled probes; food is swallowed by upward flicks of bill and head. A gregarious species, occurring in flocks of thousands in favoured places. Populations in Iceland and W Europe have increased in recent decades.

MOVEMENTS Southward movements span late June-Oct. Icelandic race winters largely in Britain, Ireland and W France; W Palaearctic nominate race winters chiefly in sub-Saharan Africa and N India; eastern race is found from E India eastwards to Australasia. Return passage occurs Feb-Apr. Many non-breeders remain in winter quarters all year. Vagrant Atlantic USA, Newfoundland, Spitsbergen, Jan Mayen, Cape Verde Is., South Africa, Seychelles, Tasmania, New Zealand, Auckland Is., Aleutians and W Alaska.

DESCRIPTION Breeding: Crown brownish, infused chestnut; supercilium creamy, becoming chestnut behind eye; lores broadly dusky; eye-stripe much narrower behind eye. Hindneck mostly chestnut, flecked dark brown. Mantle, scapulars and tertials blackish, blotched pale cinnamon and chestnut; usually some grey non-breeding feathers are retained. Wing-coverts are mostly worn grey-brown, edged paler, but a few bright feathers may be gained. Primaries black, all but outers with broad white bases. Secondaries white at base, with broad black tips. Rump and uppertail-coverts form a square white patch. Tail mostly black, but all feathers except central pair have white bases, broader towards edges of tail. Chin is whitish; throat, foreneck and breast bright chestnut with dark brown crescents on sides of lower neck and of breast. Upper belly is white, blotched with chestnut and barred with brown. Lower belly and vent are white. Underwing white, outlined narrowly by black leading coverts and tips to flight feathers; axillaries white. **Non-breeding:** As breeding, but with upperparts an even grey-brown; wing-coverts are edged whitish. The supercilium is whitish, fairly prominent in front of the eye where it contrasts with dark lores. Foreneck and breast are grey; rest of underparts white, with some grey mottling on the flanks. **Juvenile:** As non-breeding, but crown streaked brown and cinnamon; neck and breast initially washed with dull reddish-buff. Feathers of mantle, scapulars and wing-coverts are dark grey-brown, fringed dull chestnut on the mantle and scapulars but cinnamon-buff on coverts.

AGE/SEX Small, neatly-fringed scapulars and coverts of fresh juveniles are very distinct. Ageing is difficult after Dec. Breeding pairs can usually be sexed on plumage characters, female having typically more retained grey or whitish feathers in upperparts, breast and belly; difference is often very marked, but single individuals of unknown race may be difficult to sex. The female averages larger in all measurements; bill length is the best guide and is of value in the field.

RACES Three: *islandica* (Iceland, recently also Lofotens and Shetland), nominate *limosa* (W Europe to W Asia) and *melanuroides* (E Asia). Nominate race is largest, and increases in size from W Europe eastwards; *islandica* is intermediate in body size, with longish wings but short bill; *melanuroides* is very much the smallest. In breeding plumage, *islandica* and *melanuroides* show more extensive and darker red below than the nominate race. In non-breeding plumage, *melanuroides* is darker above than the others.

MEASUREMENTS Length 360-440 mm (15¾"). Wing 201-240 mm (*islandica*), 188-231 mm (nominate), 168-210 mm (*melanuroides*); bill 74-100 mm (*islandica*), 79-123 mm (nominate), 67-93 mm (*melanuroides*); tarsus 60-76 mm (*islandica*), 64-96 mm (nominate), 59-73 mm (*melanuroides*); tail 67-88 mm (nominate and *islandica*).

REFERENCES Haverschmidt (1963), Mülder (1972).

124 HUDSONIAN GODWIT *Limosa haemastica*

Plate 48
(see also Plate 59)

A scarce bird, once thought to be very rare but now known to occur in sizeable numbers in favoured places: more than 10,000 pass through the James Bay area, Canada, in late summer and over 7,000 winter in Bahia San Sebastian, Tierra del Fuego.

IDENTIFICATION Like Black-tailed Godwit (123), this godwit has a black-and-white pattern on the wings and tail which is very striking in flight. Hudsonian differs, however, in black axillaries and underwing-coverts, rather than brilliant white as in Blacktail, and in showing less white on upperwing and on rump. On Hudsonian, the wingbar is narrower and reaches only to the inner primaries, while on Blacktail a broad wingbar reaches the outer primaries; Hudsonian shows a relatively narrow band of white at the base of the tail, slightly narrower than the black band at the tail-tip, while on Blacktail the white extends from the uppertail onto the lower rump and is obviously broader than the black on the tail. Compare wing and tail patterns carefully with Willet (146). In shape, Hudsonian is distinctly shorter-necked and shorter-legged than Blacktail, with proportions perhaps closer to Bar-tailed Godwit (125). All plumages are rather dark compared with other godwits. In breeding plumage, males show completely red belly as in Bartail, but overlain by heavy barring; head is normally contrastingly pale. In non-breeding plumage, upperparts are rather plain dark grey-brown, not unlike eastern race *melanuroides* of Blacktail. Hudsonian differs, however, in shape and in its narrow, contrastingly whitish supercilium from bill to behind eye. **Bare parts:** Bill long and pointed, slightly upcurved as on Bartail, dark brown with basal third of lower mandible pinkish-brown; when breeding, colour more extensive and brighter or more orangey. Iris dark brown. Legs blue-grey or darker grey; toes project beyond tail-tip in flight.

VOICE Rather silent on migration, but noisy when breeding. Most calls are variants on a clear, high 'toe-wit' or 'whit'; song is a repeated 'toe-whit-ta'.

HABITS Nests end May-July in sedgey lowland marshlands near coasts or rivers. Males have elaborate, noisy, wide-ranging display flights. Wings are often held aloft on landing, displaying the pied underwing. On migration and in winter, occurs on muddy estuaries, coastal pools, flooded grassland and ricefields, less frequently on sandflats and beaches. Gregarious, often in large flocks. Flight is swift and powerful.

MOVEMENTS A spectacular migrant, both in distances travelled and apparent accuracy (transatlantic vagrancy is relatively very unusual). After breeding, almost the whole population gathers along S Hudson Bay and James Bay in July-Aug (adults) and mid-Sept to early Oct (juveniles), but only small numbers are seen between there and South America in autumn, and route must cross W Atlantic. There is presumably a staging-post in N South America, but records are few north of the wintering concentrations in S Argentina. Spring migration is more westerly, passing through Texas and the Great Plains on a broader front, chiefly in late Apr-May. Occurs on passage in small numbers in E USA and West Indies in autumn. Vagrant Britain (first record in 1981), Falklands (not since 1860), New Zealand (almost regular in tiny numbers), Fiji, Norfolk I., Galapagos, Pacific Mexico and W USA and Canada.

DESCRIPTION Breeding: Crown dark brown, streaked cinnamon; long whitish supercilium; lores are crossed by narrow blackish line, continued rather indistinctly behind eye. Side of face and chin whitish, variably streaked dark brown. Upperparts dark brownish-black, with pale chestnut and whitish-buff

notches; upperwing-coverts mostly dark grey-brown, retained from non-breeding, but some brighter feathers are gained. Wingbar is formed by narrow white bases to outer secondaries and inner 5 primaries, but bases of outer primaries are silvery-grey with white shaft-streaks, continuing the wing-bar more faintly; flight feathers otherwise black, as are primary coverts. Rump is greyish-brown; uppertail-coverts and bases of outer tail feathers are white, forming a white band above the mostly-black tail; tail-tip is very narrowly white. Underparts are strongly infused deep chestnut, variable in extent, but undertail-coverts and rear belly are always whitish; superimposed in dark brown on this colour, throat is streaked, sides of breast narrowly and irregularly barred, and rear flanks, belly and undertail-coverts strongly barred. Some individuals, chiefly females, have little chestnut and show strong barring on a dull brownish background. Secondaries and inner primaries show more white below than above; bases of outer primaries are strikingly silver. Underwing-coverts and axillaries are black, and under primary coverts blackish. **Non-breeding:** As breeding, but upperparts are uniform dark grey-brown with darker forecrown and narrow whitish supercilium. Wing-coverts are grey-brown, narrowly fringed white. Underparts show an even grey-brown wash to neck, breast and upper belly, but a whitish rear belly. **Juvenile:** As non-breeding, but upperparts very dark brownish, fringed pale buffish, and wing-coverts fringed buff. Scapulars and tertials are dark brown, with deep buff notches which almost form bars. Neck, breast and upper belly are faintly washed with brownish-buff.

AGE/SEX Juveniles when fresh are distinctly neater and more buff than adults, but very difficult to distinguish in the field after Dec. Female averages larger than male, but measurements overlap considerably. In breeding plumage, male has much more extensive red on underparts, with head and rear belly contrastingly paler; females have large white bases to red feathers, and appear paler or more blotched.

RACES No geographical variation is known.

MEASUREMENTS Length 370-420 mm (15½"). Wing 200-229 mm; bill 64-96 mm; tarsus 52-72 mm; tail 67-82 mm.

REFERENCES Hagar (1966).

125 BAR-TAILED GODWIT *Limosa lapponica*   Plate 49

This godwit nests in the Arctic from Scandinavia to Alaska, and is widespread on coasts (almost everywhere except the Americas) as a non-breeding visitor.

IDENTIFICATION A fairly large, long-billed and long-legged wader, but compared with other godwits appears rather dumpy and short-legged; on males, bill is also often rather short. In flight, absence of white wingbar and of black on tail are ready distinctions from Black-tailed and Hudsonian Godwits (123, 124); wings and tail are grey-brown, quite unlike the bright cinnamon of Marbled Godwit (126). Confusion is most likely with curlews, particularly Whimbrel (129) which matches Bartail in its geographical variation of back and rump colour; in both species, back and rump are mainly white in W Palaearctic,

while in E back is brown and rump strongly brown-barred. Slightly-upcurved bill is an easy distinction from Whimbrel; long bill and lack of wingbar are the best features to separate from Grey Plover (84) and knots (187, 188), which may also look similar in distant flight. At rest, Bartail can easily be confused with other godwits. Compared with Blacktail, Bartail is more dumpy and shorter-legged, with a slightly more pointed and upcurved bill and a steeper forehead. In breeding plumage, male differs in largely unbarred underparts, which may be red from chin to under-tail. In non-breeding plumage, Bartail differs further from Blacktail and Hudsonian in its browner, more heavily-streaked upperparts. See also Asiatic Dowitcher (185). **Bare parts:** Bill longish, pointed and slightly upcurved; distal half blackish and base pinkish-flesh or yellowish-flesh. Iris dark brown. Legs dark grey, sometimes tinged greenish or bluish; only part of toes extends beyond tail-tip in flight.

VOICE Contact and alarm calls throughout the year are a barking 'kak-kak', a deep 'kirruc', and variants of these; generally not very vocal, except when breeding. Song is more melodic than in other godwits, with striking variations of speed and pitch; phrases include 'a-wik-a-wik' and 'ku-wew'.

HABITS Nests end May-Aug, mainly on lowland tundra but also in rolling uplands; sometimes among scattered trees. Nesting grounds are well north of those of Blacktail. Song flight of male includes complex aerobatics. Occurs at inland wetlands on migration, but essentially an estuarine species when not breeding. Feeds typically along tide edge, the longer-billed females in deeper water than the males. Often flies in large flocks, which sometimes perform aerial manoeuvres like those of smaller waders. Numbers may be huge at favoured sites; recent Mauritanian counts are of over half a million birds.

MOVEMENTS After breeding, adults move rapidly south to favoured coastal moulting sites; dispersal or onward movement continues in Oct-Nov. Often observed migrating just offshore. Nominate race winters Europe, Africa and W India, intermediates in E India, and eastern race from S China south to Indonesia and Australasia. In Mar-Apr, adults may return to moulting sites for pre-breeding moult, then depart for breeding grounds during May. Many immatures remain in non-breeding range all year. Vagrant Atlantic USA and Canada, Iceland (possibly annual), Spitsbergen, Madeira, Maldive Is., Sri Lanka, Campbell I., Auckland Is., Macquarie I., and Pacific North America south to California.

DESCRIPTION Breeding male: Whole head, neck and underparts are deep chestnut-red, although crown has dark brown streaking, chin and supercilium are slightly paler, and underparts may be slightly mottled grey-brown and whitish. Mantle feathers and scapulars are centred blackish-brown and extensively fringed dark chestnut with a little whitish. Upperwing-coverts mostly dark grey-brown,

fringed paler; median and greater coverts especially are also tipped whitish. Secondaries obscurely fringed whitish, primaries and outer wing mostly dark. Back, rump and uppertail variably white or brown-barred (see Races). Tail feathers evenly barred white and darkish brown. Underwing-coverts and axillaries white, variably barred brown. **Breeding female:** As male, but only rarely with chestnut-red on underparts, mantle or scapulars; the colour is replaced by pale chestnut or cinnamon. Some show entirely greyish-white underparts, barred dark brown. **Non-breeding:** Crown and upperpart feathers brownish-grey, with darker brown central streaks. Supercilium whitish, contrasting with dark lores and narrow eye-stripe behind the eye. Neck and breast slightly washed pale brown and finely streaked darker. Rest of underparts whitish. **Juvenile:** As non-breeding, but crown and upperpart feathers have brown centres and broad bright buff edgings, giving a strongly-streaked appearance. Breast and neck are washed buffish-brown, finely streaked darker.

AGE/SEX Juvenile is easily distinguished at close range by bright buff, or when faded whitish-buff, fringes to coverts; some coverts may be retained until Jan. One-year-old birds do not return to breeding grounds and remain largely in non-breeding plumage. Females are noticeably larger and longer-billed. In breeding plumage, only males have deep chestnut-red underparts.

RACES Two: nominate *lapponica* (Scandinavia and W USSR) and *baueri* (E USSR and Alaska). These intergrade, and some authorities recognise an intermediate race *menzbieri* (central USSR). They can be distinguished by colour of axillaries, rump and lower back: nominate race has white axillaries narrowly barred brown, white lower back with a few brown bars, and white rump; *baueri* has brown axillaries narrowly barred white, a dark lower back and upper rump, and lower rump and uppertail heavily barred brown and white. The race *baueri* averages larger.

MEASUREMENTS Length 370-410 mm (15¼"). Wing 190-231 mm (nominate), 199-256 mm (*baueri*); bill 75-108 mm (nominate females), 61-85 mm (nominate males), 95-119 mm (*baueri* females), 72-94 mm (*baueri* males); tarsus 46-63 mm; tail 66-89 mm (nominate).

REFERENCES Smith and Evans (1973).

126 MARBLED GODWIT *Limosa fedoa* Plate 49

The predominantly cinnamon colour of this bird is unique for a godwit, but is matched by three American curlews, most noticeably the sympatric Long-billed Curlew (134).

IDENTIFICATION A rather large and heavily-built godwit, easily distinguished from all other waders by its largely cinnamon wings, tail and underparts, combined with a long, bicoloured, slightly-upcurved bill. Long-billed Curlew is very similar in plumage pattern, although the cinnamon flight feathers are more heavily marked with brown, but its larger size and particularly the very long downcurved bill are always obvious. Among the godwits, Bar-tailed (125) is closest to Marbled in structure; faded Marbled may be mistaken for eastern Bartail *baueri*, but is rather longer-legged and longer-billed, and in flight always

lacks white on rump and shows extensive cinnamon on flight feathers and underwing. Other godwits (123, 124) have boldly black-and-white wings and tail. **Bare parts:** Bill long, upcurved and pointed, often distinctly bicoloured; base broadly pink, sometimes pinkish-grey or yellowish-pink, and distal third or more blackish. Iris dark brown. Legs longish, grey or blue-grey; toes and part of tarsus project beyond tail-tip in flight.

VOICE Noisy when breeding. Contact call is a distinctive, loud, rather harsh 'cor-ack'; variants of 'ger-whit' and a barking 'rack-a' are repeated in display;

alarm call is a sharp 'wik-wik'.

HABITS Nests early May onwards, chiefly in wet meadows and grassy areas near pools on the prairies; an isolated population breeds on coastal marshland on James Bay. Male has a high circling display flight which ends in a steep dive. Often nests in semi-colonial groups with no clear territorial boundaries. Both sexes tend the young, but males may flock once young are well grown. At other seasons, essentially a coastal bird; found chiefly on muddy bays and estuaries, but also feeds on saltmarshes and coastal pools. Moves rather slowly, with sedate picking and probing feeding action. Normally found in small flocks. Often fairly tame for a godwit.

MOVEMENTS A relatively short-distance migrant, wintering on the Pacific coast from Oregon south to Panama, less frequently on Gulf coasts, Florida to Belize, and more rarely in S Atlantic USA. Non-breeders often remain in winter range all year. Vagrant Colombia, Pacific S America south to N Chile, Galapagos, West Indies (regular in small numbers), and Atlantic coast north to Nova Scotia.

DESCRIPTION Breeding: Supercilium, chin and sides of face pale cinnamon-buff; crown dark brown; neat dark eye-stripe across lores and upper ear-coverts. Hindneck cinnamon, streaked dark brown, extensively towards base of neck. Mantle, scapulars and tertials have brownish-black feather centres, with extensive whitish-buff and pale chestnut-buff notch-ing giving a speckled appearance. Upperwing-coverts have brown centres and are edged warm cinnamon-buff. Primary coverts dark brown; outer 4 primaries are darkish brown, contrasting with almost unmarked bright cinnamon inner primaries and outer secondaries. Rump and uppertail dark brown, spotted dull buff and cinnamon; tail is barred cinnamon and brown. Apart from pale, almost whitish-buff foreneck, underparts are pale cinnamon, finely and clearly barred brown on breast, and more obscurely barred on flanks and undertail. Underwing-coverts and axillaries are bright cinnamon. **Non-breeding:** Very similar to breeding plumage. Upperparts still look speckled, but background colour is paler brown. Underparts also are paler, and show very little brown barring; sometimes underparts are slightly mottled with whitish. **Juvenile:** As non-breeding, but with wing-coverts buff-brown edged paler buff, and underparts a richer cinnamon-buff colour.

AGE/SEX Juvenile difficult to separate, even at close range; after Oct ageing is virtually impossible in the field, but primary wear is useful for birds in the hand. Sexes similar in plumage, but females average substantially larger, especially in bill length.

RACES No geographical variation is known.

MEASUREMENTS Length 420-480 mm (17½"). Wing 205-255 mm; bill 82-122 mm (males), 88-130 mm (females); tarsus 60-83 mm; tail 77-95 mm.

REFERENCES Nowicki (1973), Ryan (1982).

127 LITTLE CURLEW *Numenius minutus*   **Plate 50**

Other name: Little Whimbrel

This, the world's tiniest curlew, is a little-known species with a relatively small population. It forms a species pair with the nearly extinct Eskimo Curlew (128).

IDENTIFICATION Obviously a curlew, but not much larger in body size than Pacific Golden Plover (82) or a male Ruff (210). The plumage is generally buffish-brown, including the rump and back. There is a striking head pattern with a quite broad pale buffish crown-stripe, dark brown sides to the crown, buffish supercilia, and a dark eye-stripe formed by a small dusky triangular patch in front of the eye and a dark line starting below the eye and curving up to the rear ear-coverts. In flight, its size may suggest a large plover or a Ruff rather than a curlew, but it shows deep-chested shape and long decurved bill as other curlews. There is a pale panel across the outer median coverts, contrasting with rather darker brown primary coverts, the rump is dark, and the underwing is buff barred with brown. Careful comparison is needed with Eskimo Curlew, which is also tiny and has a patterned crown. Eskimo, however, is slightly larger and darker; plumage is less buff and has cinnamon tinges, particularly to the underwing. Breast and flanks of Eskimo are more heavily barred, often with Y-shaped flank markings. In the hand, the pattern of scaling on the legs is diagnostic. Little has a more rounded wing, with the two outermost primaries differing by less than 4 mm; in Eskimo the outermost primary is 4-11 mm longer, extending well past the tail. Upland Sandpiper (135) is similar in size and plumage pattern, but has shorter, yellowish legs, a short bill, and a very long tail extending well past folded wing-tips.

Bare parts: Bill shortish for a curlew, almost straight over basal half but evenly decurved towards tip; blackish-brown, with base, particularly of lower mandible, pinkish-brown. Iris dark brown. Legs yellowish or bluish-grey; scaling on tarsus is scutellated; tips of toes often just project beyond tail-tip in flight.

VOICE Usual flight call is a soft whistle 'te-te-te', composed of usually three notes, each rising slightly in pitch. Variants on this include a rough 'tchew-tchew-tchew' in alarm; also in alarm, gives a harsh 'kweek-ek' recalling Northern Lapwing (57). Noisy when breeding. Songs include a rising 'corr-corr-corr' followed by 'quee-quee-quee' on level pitch.

HABITS Nests May-Aug in loose colonies in open burnt areas or grassy clearings in larch woodland, chiefly along river valleys. Breeding localities so far discovered account for only a fraction of the known population. Male has a remarkable high display flight in which he sings, then dives steeply producing a whistling sound apparently from wings and tail. When not breeding, found on inland grassland, bare cultivation, freshwater margins and similar habitats; gathers in dense flocks of several hundred, sometimes thousands, on blacksoil plains of N Australia. Occurs more rarely on coasts. Feeds mostly by picking. Often quite tame and approachable.

MOVEMENTS Post-breeding flocks gather from late July, and most leave breeding grounds by early Sept. Occurs on passage in Japan, Philippines, and E

Indonesia. Winter quarters in S New Guinea and N Australia are occupied mid-Sept to Mar (rarely to May). Movements within Australia depend largely on rainfall; in some years, reaches southern coasts and Tasmania. Rare New Zealand. Vagrant Wales (Aug-Sept 1982), Norway (July 1969), Kazakhstan (Sept 1928), Seychelles (Oct 1972-Apr 1973), Hong Kong (Oct) and California (Sept-Oct 1984).

DESCRIPTION Breeding and non-breeding: Bold buff-and-brown head pattern (see Identification). Upperparts darkish brown, liberally spotted and fringed pale buff; tertials have deep buff notches or brown and buff barring. Flight feathers, primary coverts, and leading lesser coverts are dark brown, contrasting with rather paler median coverts; bases of primaries are slightly paler. Tail is barred dark brown and dull grey-brown. Chin and upper throat are pale creamy-buff. Breast is suffused buff, with fine and distinct brown streaking ending fairly sharply against creamy-white belly; flanks have some irregular brown barring. Underwing and axillaries are buff, barred darker brown. **Juvenile:** As adult, but breast streaking and especially flank barring less pronounced. Upperparts show pale buff spots on scapulars and tertials; wing-coverts are broadly fringed pale buff.

AGE/SEX Juveniles are distinguishable at close range by buffier plumage, at least up to Oct. Some first-winter birds renew outer primaries before return migration. Sexes are similar in plumage, but females average slightly larger.

RACES No geographical variation is known.

MEASUREMENTS Length 290-320 mm (12"). Wing 176-193 mm; bill 38-48 mm; tarsus 46-54 mm; tail 62-77 mm.

REFERENCES Crawford (1978), Labutin *et al.* (1982), Moon (1983).

128 ESKIMO CURLEW *Numenius borealis*   Plate 50

Once abundant, this small American curlew was greatly reduced in numbers by relentless shooting between 1850 and 1890, and perhaps also by habitat change. By 1929 it was thought to be extinct, but it is still seen in tiny numbers on migration. Recent claims include a party of 23 in Texas in May 1981.

IDENTIFICATION Curlew-like in proportions and bill shape, but much smaller than any other curlew likely in the Americas. About 25% shorter than Whimbrel (129) in body length, and differs further in rich cinnamon ground colour to underparts and underwing. In the hand, Eskimo Curlew has the inner web of the outer primaries evenly dark brown, while in Whimbrel there are bold buffish notches. Bristle-thighed Curlew (130) is Whimbrel-sized, but with diagnostic cinnamon rump and uppertail. The most similar species to Eskimo Curlew is Little Curlew (127), recently recorded in California. Eskimo differs in slightly larger size, relatively longer and more pointed wings (extending well beyond tail-tip at rest), in cinnamon coloration (absent in Little, replaced by pale buffish), shorter legs, and more heavily-barred breast and flanks; flanks of Eskimo show bold Y-shaped markings, but Little has at most only light brown barring. In the hand the rear of the tarsus shows a reticulate pattern of scaling, while in Little the whole tarsus is scutellated. Extreme care should be taken to eliminate Little if a sighting of Eskimo Curlew is suspected. See also Upland Sandpiper (135).**Bare parts:** Bill decurved, short for a curlew, fleshy-brown at base and blackish towards tip. Iris dark brown. Legs quite short, bluish-grey; toes do not project beyond tail-tip in flight.

VOICE Poorly known. Reportedly a rippling 'tr-tr-tr' and a soft whistle 'bee-bee'; some calls similar to Upland Sandpiper's.

HABITS Nests on arctic tundra, but breeding biology has not been studied; no breeding sites are currently known. Wintering habitat is pampas grassland in S South America. On migration, formerly occurred in large flocks on the prairies and on coastal grassland. It is not known to what extent the conversion of the pampas and prairies to agricultural land has affected the population.

MOVEMENTS Previously nested in NW Northwest Territories in Canada, perhaps also in Alaska, and migrated to South America via SE Canada or New England and the Atlantic Ocean. Chief wintering grounds were between S Brazil and central Argentina, occasionally west to Chile. Return migration took a more westerly route via Central America, Texas and the Great Plains. Recent sightings are in keeping with this migration schedule. Previously a vagrant to Baffin I., Bermuda, Greenland, Ireland, Britain, Falkland Is., Pribilofs, and extreme E USSR.

DESCRIPTION Breeding and non-breeding: Dark brown head-stripes and indistinct pale central crown-stripe. Upperparts including rump and uppertail dark brown, mottled brown and buff. Primary coverts dark brown, sometimes with greaters clearly tipped white. Primaries and secondaries dark, inner 6 primaries white-tipped. Tail brownish-grey barred brown. Underparts strongly washed buffish-cinnamon, with breast strongly barred and flanks with brown Y-shaped markings as well as brown streaks. Axillaries and underwing-coverts strikingly cinnamon, barred brown. **Juvenile:** Very similar, but tertials and scapulars have narrow pale buff edges, and coverts much broader ones. Primary coverts tipped buff; inner 7 primaries are tipped whitish. Underparts more buffish than on adult, but with strong brown streaking on breast, fine streaking on upper belly and 'Y' marks on flanks.

AGE/SEX Ages very difficult to distinguish. Sexes similar in plumage, but female averages larger.

RACES Monotypic.

MEASUREMENTS Length 290-340 mm (12¼"). Wing 187-226 mm; bill 42-60 mm; tarsus 42-46 mm; tail 76-84 mm.

REFERENCES Weston and Williams (1965), Banks (1977), Farrand (1977).

129 WHIMBREL *Numenius phaeopus*   **Plate 51(see also Plate 52)**

This is the only curlew which breeds, albeit with four races and a broken distribution, all around the high northern latitudes; it also has the widest non-breeding range.

IDENTIFICATION The most widespread of the four curlews which have strong head markings, and most familiar of the three medium-sized curlews. The distinctive call is a valuable identification feature. The central crown-stripe may be difficult to see, but the contrast of the pale supercilium with the dark eye-stripe and sides to the crown is usually obvious. This head pattern is a simple distinction from three larger curlews and from the similarly-sized Slender-billed (131), all of which have diffuse eye-stripes and lack head-stripes and crown-stripe. Size is readily apparent if seen with other curlews, but may be difficult to judge on lone individuals. Whimbrel is dwarfed by Eurasian Curlew (132) and especially by Far Eastern and Long-billed (133, 134), and in turn is much larger than Little and Eskimo Curlews (127, 128). Further distinctions from Eurasian Curlew are the relatively shorter bill, the rather dark upperwing, contrasting more with the white on the back and rump (if present), and the typically more heavily-barred underwing. Where range overlaps with Far Eastern, Whimbrel shows a small amount of white on the rump (except for vagrant *hudsonicus*) and is always proportionately much shorter-billed. Long-billed Curlew shows bright cinnamon colours in plumage, markedly different from Whimbrel's drab brown. Among curlews, the most similar species is the rare Bristle-thighed (130), which is best distinguished by its slightly thicker bill and in flight by its bright cinnamon on rump and tail. In flight, confusion is also possible with Bar-tailed Godwit (125) unless the bill shape is visible. **Bare parts:** Bill blackish-brown, paler brown or fleshy at base; longish, almost straight at base, but strongly decurved over distal two-thirds. Iris dark brown. Legs dull bluish-grey, sometimes tinged greenish.

VOICE Most frequent call is a highly distinctive, far-carrying rippling titter 'bibibibibibibi...' composed of a series of flat-toned, evenly-emphasised notes. Various shorter calls are given, some resembling those of Eurasian Curlew. Song is a prolonged bubbling like that of Eurasian Curlew, accelerating and rising in pitch.

HABITS Nests May-Aug, typically in boreal or low-arctic moorland and tundra not far from tree-line. Male has high circling song flight. Both parents incubate the eggs and tend the brood. Occurs widely inland on migration, often around wetlands but also on short dry grassland and farmland. Essentially coastal in non-breeding range, on exposed reefs and sandy or rocky beaches as well as estuaries; often visits inland grassland to feed, including mown grass in parks and on golf-courses. May roost in trees where no more suitable sites are available. Probes frequently, but feeds more by picking than do larger curlews; often eats crabs. Gathers in large flocks at roost and on migration, but feeds generally singly or in small parties; individuals sometimes defend feeding territories. Flies strongly, with faster wingbeats than those of larger curlews.

MOVEMENTS Southward passage begins in July, and first arrivals in southernmost part of non-breeding range are in Sept. American race winters widely on coasts from Oregon and North Carolina south to Tierra del Fuego and S Brazil; vagrant New Guinea, Australia, New Zealand (almost annual), Falkland Is., Greenland, W Europe and Sierra Leone. W Palaearctic races winter on coasts of SW Europe, Africa, Persian Gulf and India, including E Atlantic islands, and Malagasy region; vagrant Atlantic USA and Canada, and Maldive Is. E Palaearctic populations visit SE Asia and Australasia; vagrant NE India and W Alaska. Return passage is chiefly Mar-May. Many non-breeders are present all year in winter range.

DESCRIPTION Breeding and non-breeding: Head pattern shows contrasted brown and buffish stripes (see Identification). Upperparts including upperwings dark brown, variably spotted, notched and fringed whitish and buffish. Back, rump and uppertail variably white, brown or barred (see Races). Tail grey-brown, barred brown, with ground colour whiter towards sides of tail. Neck and underparts whitish or buffish-white, suffused and streaked brown on neck, breast and flanks; undertail shows some brown bars. Underwing-coverts and axillaries vary from largely white to heavily barred brown and buff (see Races). **Juvenile:** As adults, but wing-coverts, scapulars and tertials show clearer buff spots and notches. Breast is more buff, with slightly finer streaking.

AGE/SEX Fresh buffish plumage of juvenile may be distinct until Nov. Primaries are often much more abraded on first-winter birds than on adults. Sexes are similar in plumage, but females average larger.

RACES Four: nominate *phaeopus* (Iceland-W USSR), *alboaxillaris* (probably breeds south of Urals, winters E Africa), *variegatus* (E USSR) and *hudsonicus* ('Hudsonian Curlew', Alaska and N Canada). W Palaearctic races show white lower back and rump, *variegatus* a brown back and a barred white rump, and *hudsonicus* a brown back and rump uniform with the rest of the upperparts; *hudsonicus* is also rather more buffish-brown above and below. W Palaearctic races average larger than the others. The race *alboaxillaris* is whiter above and below, but may be just a colour morph.

MEASUREMENTS Length 400-460 mm (17"). Wing 214-278 mm; bill 54-99 mm; tarsus 52-68 mm; tail 86-103 mm.

REFERENCES Skeel (1983).

Eurasian Curlew   Whimbrel

130 BRISTLE-THIGHED CURLEW *Numenius tahitiensis*   Plate 51

A rare and poorly-known curlew, which breeds only in W Alaska and winters on oceanic islands in the Pacific. The nest was not discovered until 1948.

IDENTIFICATION A medium-sized curlew with pale crown-stripe and supercilia contrasting with dark head-stripes and eye-stripes. In these respects it resembles Whimbrel (129), but Bristle-thighed differs in its conspicuous bright cinnamon-chestnut rump and uppertail, cinnamon tinges to underparts, and slightly thicker and blunter-tipped bill. The tail feathers, especially the outer four pairs, are bright cinnamon-chestnut, barred dark brown. The axillaries are cinnamon, barred brown; undertail-coverts are unbarred creamy-cinnamon. Wing-coverts often show rather large, round, pale cinnamon-buff spots. Cinnamon colours may recall Eskimo Curlew (128) or Long-billed Curlew (134), but Bristle-thighed is much larger than Eskimo, and bill shape and striped head pattern differ from Long-billed. Marbled Godwit (126) is brighter cinnamon on the wings, but has an upcurved bill. In flight, contrastingly bright rump, tail and underwings of Bristle-thighed are diagnostic. Its unique long, shiny bristles on the thighs do not provide an identification character except in the hand. **Bare parts:** Bill rather heavy, longish and downcurved; base fleshy-coloured and tip dark brown. Iris dark brown. Legs bluish-grey, proportionately rather short and thick.

VOICE Strikingly different from that of Whimbrel. Calls include a long whistle 'chi-u-it', reminiscent of Grey Plover (84), a short rippling whistle 'whe-whe-whe-whe' and a ringing 'whee-wheeoo'.

HABITS Nests on barren tundra in mountainous regions of Alaska; eggs have been found in June. After breeding, in early Aug, adults and juveniles gather on the Alaskan coast prior to migration. Remarkably, this species winters only on remote, often tiny, oceanic islands. It feeds on exposed reefs, on dry ground well away from the shore, and among seabird colonies where it feeds largely by stealing eggs, even on occasion from underneath incubating birds. Eggs are broken by spearing them with the bill or by dropping them onto a hard surface. Food also includes vegetable matter, crustaceans, insects, and even scorpions. Usually seen singly or in groups of up to five or six. When roosting, often perches in trees or on roofs of houses.

MOVEMENTS Southward movement occurs from late Aug; it is likely that adults and young migrate together. Winter quarters on Polynesian islands are occupied chiefly Sept-May; a few non-breeders remain all year. Normal range apparently extends from Caroline Is. south and east to Fiji and through E Polynesia to Pitcairn and Ducie Is. Occurs on passage in Hawaii (sometimes in winter) and on the Marquesas Is. Very rare on continental shores; vagrant Japan, Bonin Is., Norfolk I., Kermadec Is., Washington, S Alaska and Vancouver I. B.C.

DESCRIPTION Breeding and non-breeding: Head shows pale buffish crown-stripe, broad dark brown head-stripes, long buffish supercilia, and a solid dark brown eye-stripe. Ear-coverts and neck are buff, slightly streaked brown. Mantle, scapulars and tertials are dark brown, spotted and notched cinnamon-buff; wing-coverts often show bold olive-buff spotting. Primary coverts are dark brown, narrowly edged whitish-buff. Flight feathers mainly dark brown; inner 2 primaries show clear white tips, and next 5 diffuse pale tips. Underparts dull buffish, sometimes with a cinnamon tinge; breast and upper flanks are heavily streaked brown. Undertail-coverts are a paler unbarred creamy-cinnamon. Underwing-coverts and especially axillaries are more strongly cinnamon, barred with brown. **Juvenile:** As adult, but upperparts and coverts show larger, more obvious buffish-cinnamon spotting. Primary coverts show broader white tips; inner 8 primaries are boldly tipped white. Underparts are more buffish, with much less streaking; breast may be virtually unstreaked.

AGE/SEX Juvenile is separable, but to some extent differences are obscured by individual variation. In the hand, primary pattern and degree of wear are useful. Sexes are not known to differ in plumage, but female averages heavier, longer-winged and shorter-billed.

RACES No geographical variation is known.

MEASUREMENTS Length 400-440 mm (16½"). Wing 225-260 mm; bill 70-95 mm; tarsus 51-62 mm; tail 86-102 mm.

REFERENCES Allen and Kyllingstad (1949), Lacan and Mougin (1974).

131 SLENDER-BILLED CURLEW *Numenius tenuirostris*   Plate 52

A medium-sized curlew lacking a crown-stripe, the palest member of the genus. Now very rare and probably still dwindling in numbers.

IDENTIFICATION Similar in size to Whimbrel (129) and Bristle-thighed Curlew (130) but lacks a crown-stripe. Most closely resembles a Eurasian Curlew (132) in miniature, especially the paler eastern race of latter *orientalis*. Differs chiefly in its smaller size, whiter plumage (particularly on breast and tail), bill shape, face pattern, and the shape of the flank spots. Look . for sharply-defined dark brown breast streaking against an almost white background (sometimes lightly suffused with brown); Eurasian Curlew and

Whimbrel both show a strong brownish or buffish-brown suffusion across the breast and poorly-defined streaking. The supercilium is bolder than on Eurasian Curlew, tending to isolate the dark cap, and there is a fairly narrow dark bar crossing the lores in place of Eurasian Curlew's diffuse rounded dark area. All plumages except the juvenile show bold blackish spots on the white flanks, usually described as heart-shaped but may also be lozenge-shaped, rounded triangular, or almost oval; spotting is less extensive in non-breeding plumage. In flight shows white from upper back to tail-tip, more extensive than in Eurasian Curlew and Whimbrel, and an almost pure white underwing. **Bare parts:** Bill dark brown, nearly black at tip, with pinkish-brown at base of lower mandible; on average shorter than Eurasian Curlew's (but many Eurasian show a similar bill length in proportion to body size), and tapers to a fine point with virtually no lateral expansion or pitting at tip. Iris brown. Legs and feet bluish- or slate-grey, more delicately built than in Whimbrel or Eurasian Curlew.

VOICE Calls are like Eurasian Curlew's, but higher-pitched and shorter. Most usual calls are short 'cour-lee', less guttural than Eurasian Curlew, and in flight or alarm a shrill 'kew-ee' which may be almost monosyllabic.

HABITS Generally very little known. Breeds in the Siberian taiga zone, apparently mainly in extensive marshlands and peat-bogs but also in marshes within steppe woodlands. Non-breeding birds are found chiefly on shallow, fresh or brackish inland waters, but at times also on dry grassland or estuarine mud. Available records suggest that the species prefers to gather in large winter flocks at favoured sites. Vagrants often join flocks of Eurasian Curlew.

MOVEMENTS Post-breeding migration is in a direction just south of due west, to reach wintering grounds in the Mediterranean basin (mainly Tunisia and Atlantic Morocco). Recent winter records have been very few, and no sites are currently known which regularly hold migrant or wintering birds. The population has probably been dwindling throughout this century. The range of vagrancy includes Oman in the south, the Canaries and Azores in the west, and the Netherlands, Germany and Poland in the north. In about 1925, one was collected at Crescent Beach on the Canadian shore of Lake Erie. There are also two undated specimens from Japan. Poorly-substantiated records exist for Aldabra, Chad and Somalia, but there are as yet no good records south of the Palaearctic.

DESCRIPTION Breeding: Ground colour of head, neck and underparts basically white, sullied and lightly streaked with brown on cap, ear-coverts and hindneck, and more lightly also on neck and breast. Dark bar across lores contrasts slightly with paler supercilium and cheeks. Side of lower breast and fore-flanks marked with bold blackish spots. Rear flanks, belly, undertail and underwing unmarked white. Upperparts and upperwing brown, with brownish-white feather edgings and notches. Lower back, rump, uppertail and tail white; uppertail has some brown streaking, and tail is barred dark brown. **Non-breeding:** Underparts have more streaks, and flank spots are present but less distinct. **Juvenile:** Similar to other plumages, but flanks have brown streaks instead of bold blackish spots.

AGE/SEX Juveniles attain some heart-shaped spots by the end of the first winter. In addition, there are white tips to the inner 8 (sometimes 9) primaries on juveniles, but only to the inner 6 (rarely 7) on adults. Female averages larger than the male, especially in bill length.

RACES No geographical variation is known.

MEASUREMENTS Length 360-410 mm (15¼"). Wing 243-259 mm (males), 248-275 mm (females); bill 68-78 mm (males), 76-96 mm (females); tarsus 59-66 mm (males), 62-69 mm (females); tail 82-108 mm.

REFERENCES Brosselin (1968), Kistyakovski (1980), Marchant (1984).

132 EURASIAN CURLEW *Numenius arquata* Plate 52

Other names: Curlew, European or Common Curlew
The common large curlew of Eurasia, Africa and the Oriental region; farther east in Siberia, and in Australasia in winter, it is replaced by Far Eastern Curlew (133).

IDENTIFICATION Large size, long downcurved bill, plain head pattern, whitish underwing and white back and rump are the main identification features. Both the other large curlews, Far Eastern and Long-billed (134), show darker underwings (brown in Far Eastern, cinnamon in Long-billed) and lack white on back and rump. Whimbrel (129) may cause confusion if its smaller size is not apparent; look for contrasting head pattern, dark brown upperparts, breast and usually underwing, and relatively shorter bill of the smaller species. In flight, wingbeats of Eurasian Curlew are gull-like, and those of Whimbrel faster, recalling Bar-tailed Godwit (125). Note that race *alboaxillaris* of Whimbrel can have underwing and axillaries as white as Eurasian Curlew's. Small, short-billed Eurasians may be confused with Slender-billed Curlew (131), which see; Slender-billed resembles a miniature Eurasian, but is always whiter, particularly on breast and tail, and except in juvenile plumage has bold, rounded, blackish spots on flanks. Flank markings on Eurasian are often prominent, but are cross-shaped or anchor-shaped rather than rounded.

Bare parts: Bill brownish-black, with pinkish base to lower mandible. Iris dark brown. Legs bluish-grey, sometimes tinged greenish; toes project partly beyond tail-tip in flight.

VOICE Well known for its far-carrying calls. Usual contact call is a rising 'cour-loo', with accent on the first syllable, from which the bird is named. Other calls include a low 'whaup', and a rapid 'tyuyuyuyu' in alarm. Song, often heard in winter quarters, is a beautiful sequence of bubbling phrases, accelerating and rising in pitch.

HABITS Nests Apr-Aug in wide range of mainly temperate habitats, including upland moorland, grassy or boggy open areas in forests and damp grasslands; in some areas has adapted well to non-intensive farmland, particularly in river valleys. Male has a shallow gliding display flight. Territories are large and often poorly defined. Chiefly coastal when not breeding, but occurs in small numbers at inland wetlands; gathers in large numbers at favoured estuaries. Less often seen on open shores than Whimbrel. Feeds largely by deep probing in intertidal mud or damp soil, but also by picking; varied diet includes worms, crabs, molluscs, berries and sometimes eggs. Generally rather wary.

MOVEMENTS Gathers on coasts from July onwards, after breeding; southward movement continues until Nov. Some European breeders may not move far, but range includes Mediterranean and W Africa; remarkably, winters regularly in Iceland and Faeroes, where not known to breed. Eastern birds are more migratory; non-breeding range includes Gulf of Guinea, S and E Africa, E Mediterranean and coasts east to Philippines and Japan. Return to breeding areas begins in Feb in W Europe, but not until late Apr in N USSR. Many non-breeders remain in winter quarters all year. Vagrant Massachusetts, New York, Greenland, Jan Mayen, Bear I., Borneo, and N and W Australia.

DESCRIPTION Breeding: Fairly variable in shade of background colour and intensity of streaking. Head, neck and breast washed pale buffish-brown and streaked dark brown; supercilium poorly contrasted; lores show a diffuse dusky spot; chin is whitish. Upperparts show greyish-brown feather centres with paler greyish-brown fringes; tertials have more clearly darkish brown centres with large olive-brown notches. Lower back and rump are white. Uppertail-coverts and base of tail are white with a little brownish streaking; rest of tail is washed olive-brown and barred darker. Belly is whitish; flanks are quite prominently streaked as far as legs, and often lightly on rear

belly. Underwing-coverts and axillaries are white with a little brown barring or flecking. **Non-breeding:** As breeding, but less bright; buffish is replaced by duller brown. **Juvenile:** As breeding, but more buff, and lacking bold streaking on breast and flanks. Upperparts show extensive buff fringes; wing-coverts, scapulars and tertials have contrasting brown feather centres and buff notching.

AGE/SEX Juvenile is separable at moderate range in the field up to Nov by bright buff fringes and notches; later, only in the hand, with primary wear the most useful character. Sexes are similar in plumage, but female averages larger, especially in bill length.

RACES Two: nominate *arquata* (Europe and Urals) and *orientalis* (Urals and central USSR), but variation is clinal and there is no sharp division between the races. The race *arquata* is typically smaller, has a whiter rump, underwing and axillaries slightly barred brown, and buffer underparts frequently with four-pointed spots on flanks. The race *orientalis* is typically larger, its lower rump has some obvious brown barring, the underwing is virtually unmarked white, and the flanks are streaked rather than spotted. Owing to intergradation and individual variation, it is rarely possible to identify racial origin of individuals.

MEASUREMENTS Length 500-600 mm (21½"). Wing 268-326 mm; bill 83-164 mm (males), 123-192 mm (females); tarsus 67-94 mm; tail 103-119 mm.

REFERENCES Bainbridge and Minton (1978).

133 FAR EASTERN CURLEW *Numenius madagascariensis*   Plate 53

Other names: Eastern or Australian Curlew
This is the largest of the curlews. It migrates between Siberia and Australia; despite its scientific name, it has never been recorded from Madagascar. There is recent evidence that it may be decreasing in Australia.

IDENTIFICATION In flight the large size, dark rump, strong dark brown markings on the otherwise white underwings, buffish-brown belly, and brown flight feathers mottled with white are sufficient to distinguish this from the two other large curlews, Eurasian and Long-billed (132, 134). The eastern race of Eurasian, *orientalis*, may overlap with Far Eastern in SE Asia; former differs in having an extensive white on the rump and lower back, obvious in flight, and virtually unmarked white axillaries and underwing-coverts. At rest, the plumage of both races of Eurasian is whiter, particularly on the lower belly, vent and undertail (these areas are buffy-brown in Far Eastern). Far Eastern tends not to show a contrastingly dark patch on the lores, present as a roundish spot on most Eurasians. Range has not yet overlapped with that of the American Long-billed; latter is also dark-rumped, but its underparts, underwings and flight feathers are extensively bright cinnamon. Plumage pattern is similar to the American race *hudsonicus* of the Whimbrel (129), which however is much smaller and shorter-billed and shows a strongly-marked crown and face pattern. **Bare parts:** Bill dark brown, fleshy towards base, very long and often rather heavy. Iris dark brown. Legs dull blue-grey; toes protrude beyond tail-tip in flight.

VOICE Similar to Eurasian Curlew's, but normal contact call is a flatter, less fluty 'coor-ee'. When disturbed

or agitated, gives a strident 'ker ker-ee-ker-ee'. There is a wide range of other calls based on these. Bubbling song is slightly sharper and less melodic than that of Eurasian.

HABITS Breeds territorially in damp bogs and peaty marshes. There is a gently gliding display flight on still, slightly-downcurved wings, during which the bird gives its bubbling song. In winter, is found mostly coastally on beaches and sandy or muddy estuaries, occasionally inland near large wetlands. Feeds by picking from the surface, but chiefly by probing deeply with its long bill for burrowing invertebrates; usually feeds singly or in loose flocks, but at high tide may gather in large flocks to roost. Flocks often fly in lines or 'V' formations.

MOVEMENTS A long-distance migrant through Australasia and eastern parts of SE Asia. Most winter in Australia and migrate via the Philippines and New Guinea. More frequent in New Zealand in recent years. Many spend the northern summer in the non-breeding range. Few records of vagrancy, although since 1961 a fairly regular spring vagrant in W Alaska and the Aleutians, and also reported recently in Afghanistan (May 1975) and Thailand. There is also a record from Iran early this century.

DESCRIPTION Breeding: As non-breeding, except for a slightly rustier infusion on the upperparts and tail. **Non-breeding:** Head is buffish-brown, streaked dark brown; crown is slightly darker, but supercilium only slightly paler; ear-coverts, throat and neck buffish-brown streaked darker; lores dusky but not contrastingly dark, giving bland facial appearance. Slightly paler feathering around eye. Upperparts, including rump and tail, show dark brown feather centres with pale brownish-olive fringes and notches. Flight feathers brown, secondaries and inner primaries notched with brownish-white; pale fringe on primaries 7 and 8 not obvious and not clear-cut. Underparts are washed darkish brownish-buff, palest on rear belly, streaked finely but quite extensively on breast, less so on flanks and upper belly. Underwing-coverts and axillaries whitish, very extensively barred dark brown, making the underwing look contrastingly dark against the belly. **Juvenile:** Simi-lar, but upperparts and coverts with extensive, neat buffish-white notching. Primaries 7 and 8 are neatly tipped white. Underpart streaking is finer.

AGE/SEX Juveniles can be identified in the field up to Nov by their paler and fresher appearance, after then only in the hand. Sexes are similar in plumage. Females average larger, especially in bill length: males average 155 mm and females 184 mm; bill >180 mm indicates female, <150 mm male. Beware juveniles, which have shorter bills than adults for the first few months of life.

RACES No geographical variation is known.

MEASUREMENTS Length 600-660 mm (25"). Wing 290-338 mm; bill 128-201 mm; tarsus 77-95 mm.

REFERENCES Vinter (1980), Tolchin (1980), Close and Newman (1984).

134 LONG-BILLED CURLEW *Numenius americanus*　　Plate 53

The common large curlew of North America. Its breeding range has contracted westwards during the present century, but the species now benefits from full protection.

IDENTIFICATION A cinnamon or a rich, deep buff infusion to the plumage, brightest on the underwing and belly, and a very long downcurved bill are sufficient to identify this species. Neither of the large Palaearctic curlews, Eurasian or Far Eastern (132, 133), shows any cinnamon, and Eurasian additionally shows a whitish underwing and a conspicuous white back and rump in flight. Whimbrel (129) is the other common curlew in North America, but is much smaller than Long-billed and is browner with a conspicuously-striped head pattern; vagrant Whimbrels of other races additionally show at least some white on the rump. Bristle-thighed (130) is Whimbrel-sized and also has a striped head pattern; it differs from Long-billed also in its contrastingly bright rump and tail. Marbled Godwit (126) is smaller than Long-billed Curlew, but similar in plumage and proportions; its bill is curved slightly upwards rather than downwards, and the cinnamon secondaries and inner primaries are brighter and less heavily marked with brown. Note that the relatively short bills of some Long-billed, particularly juveniles and males, may lead to confusion with other curlews. **Bare parts:** Bill downcurved, very long and slim; tip dark, and base of lower mandible pinkish or greyish-brown. Iris dark brown. Legs dull bluish-grey.

VOICE Noisy when breeding. Normal contact call is a loud, rising 'cur-lee'. In alarm gives a sharper 'kee-he-he-he', and 'pill-will' recalling Willet (146). Song is a prolonged rolling 'cur-leeeeeeeu' and variants.

HABITS Nests Apr onwards in remnants of original prairie habitats, including damp meadowland and drier short-grass areas, particularly on gravelly soils. Holds large territories which male advertises by slow-flapping and gliding song flight. After breeding, moves chiefly to estuaries, but some winter on farmland inland. Often occurs in flocks, feeding on intertidal flats or nearby grasslands. Generally rather shy.

MOVEMENTS A relatively short-distance migrant, moving to coasts of California, Louisiana, Texas and Central America, regularly south to Honduras.

Arrivals in non-breeding range span July-Nov, and departures Mar-early May. Many non-breeders spend all year in winter range. Vagrant Fort Simpson (Northwest Territories), James Bay, New Brunswick, Atlantic USA (more regular south of Virginia), West Indies, Panama and recently NE Venezuela.

DESCRIPTION Breeding and non-breeding: Crown fairly heavily streaked dark brown and cinnamon, forming a slight contrast with paler buff-cinnamon supercilium; lores are indistinctly dusky and ear-coverts pale. Mantle and scapulars are quite extensively blackish, with cinnamon spots and fringes; rump and tail are slightly more spotted and barred with cinnamon. Inner primaries and outer secondaries are strongly washed cinnamon and barred brown; tertials are more greyish-brown. Neck, breast and belly are cinnamon of varying shade; neck and breast have fine brown streaks, and flanks show some vertical bars, but belly is virtually unmarked. Underwing-coverts and axillaries are a striking uniform cinnamon, with a few brown streaks on under primary coverts and occasionally axillaries. **Juvenile:** Very like adult, but upperparts, especially wing-coverts, show buffer spotting; tertials have broader dark central bars and are notched buffish. Inner 8 primaries show clear pale tips (inner 7 in adults).

AGE/SEX Ageing is always very difficult in the field. In the hand, primary wear is the easiest character to use: primaries of first-winter birds are more abraded than those of adults. Sexes are similar in plumage, but females average larger and noticeably longer-billed (males average 139 mm, females 170 mm).

RACES Two: nominate *americanus* (south of about 43° N in USA) and *parvus* (farther north in USA and S central Canada). The race *parvus* averages smaller, but differences are slight and apparently clinal.

MEASUREMENTS Length 500-650 mm (22½"). Wing 257-308 mm; bill 113-219 mm; tarsus 72-92 mm; tail 104-136 mm.

REFERENCES Stenzel *et al.* (1976), Fitzner (1978), Allen (1980).

135 UPLAND SANDPIPER *Bartramia longicauda*   Plate 50

Other names: Upland Plover, Bartram's Sandpiper
A most unusual sandpiper which shows similarities to the curlews and to the 'shanks', but is probably only distantly related to these groups.

IDENTIFICATION A very distinctive species of chiefly dry inland habitats. It resembles a tiny curlew in plumage, but has a short *Tringa*-like bill and a very long tail which protrudes well beyond the folded wingtips. The head is rather small in proportion to the body, and is often held high on a longish and remarkably thin neck. Buffy plumage, intricately patterned with brown, and contrasting crown-stripe and supercilia recall Little Curlew (127), but short-billed, long-tailed shape and yellowish legs are obvious differences; the very rare Eskimo Curlew (128) is more cinnamon in plumage tone. Distant birds might also be mistaken for golden plovers (81-83) or juvenile Ruff (210). In flight, brown with blacker primaries and long tail and wings; dark underwing and flanks contrast with paler belly and undertail, and there is a narrow whitish trailing edge to the wing. **Bare parts:** Bill thin and short, very slightly decurved towards tip; sides yellow or yellowish-brown, tip and culmen dark brown. Iris dark brown; eye is large and prominent. Legs dull yellow, often tinged brownish or greenish; feet do not project past tail in flight.

VOICE Usual flight call is a measured piping 'quip-ip-ip-ip' with the last syllable pitched lower than the first three, or 'pulip-pulip', but vocabulary is wide, especially when nesting. Song includes longer versions of the flight call and 'willa-willa-willa' followed by a vibrant 'rrrrrpheeleoo'; also 'qua-a-ily'.

HABITS Nests end Apr-Aug, chiefly on prairie grasslands (primary or restored), sometimes in loose colonial groups. One of the commonest breeding waders in the centre of its range, but scarce and declining in the east. Aerial displays are given close to the ground and at great height; may fly with flicking wingbeats recalling Spotted Sandpiper (149). Often holds wings aloft on landing; perches freely on fence-posts or telegraph poles. Or migration and in winter appears on pasture, alfalfa fields, rough grasslands, and short grass such as airfields and golf-courses, even on suburban lawns. Feeding action is sometimes plover-like. Usually seen singly or in small groups apart from other waders. Often tame, migrants sometimes exceptionally so.

MOVEMENTS A long-distance migrant to pampas of central South America; rarely, winters farther north.

Southward movement mostly through Great Plains, Mexico and N South America spans late Aug-Nov. Returns by a similar route Mar-May, reaching southernmost breeding grounds by early Apr. Occurs more rarely on passage in West Indies. Vagrant California (12 records by 1984), Australia, New Zealand, Chile, Falklands, South Shetlands, Tristan da Cunha, Azores, Iceland and SW Europe east to West Germany and Malta (38 in British Isles up to 1984).

DESCRIPTION Breeding and non-breeding: Crown dark brown, lightly streaked buffish; the buffish crown-stripe is often indistinct. Lores, supercilium, chin and most of sides of face are pale buffish; ear-coverts slightly darker. Wing-coverts and tertials are dull olive-buff, barred dark brown; ground colour to scapulars is a richer paler brown. Primary coverts and primaries are blackish-brown, secondaries slightly paler with narrow whitish trailing edge. Back, rump, uppertail-coverts and central pair of tail feathers are mainly blackish-brown, with some whitish at sides of rump; other tail feathers are pale orange-buff at base, barred brown and tipped white. Throat, breast and upper belly are washed buffish and show strong brown streaking, forming chevrons on lower breast and upper belly; rest of underparts whitish, but with strong brown chevrons on flanks. Underwing-coverts and axillaries are heavily barred whitish and brown. **Juvenile:** As adult, but upperparts look scaly. Wing-coverts have clear buff fringes and dark submarginal lines; the scapulars are very dark and uniform, with narrow, neat buffish-white fringes; tertials are notched pale buff.

AGE/SEX Scaly pattern of juvenile is distinct at close range, but difficult to see after Nov. Sexes are similar in plumage, but females average very slightly larger in wing and tail.

RACES None is described. Average size decreases slightly from west to east.

MEASUREMENTS Length 280-320 mm (11¾"). Wing 156-191 mm; bill 26-35 mm; tarsus 44-53 mm; tail 73-92 mm.

REFERENCES Higgins and Kirsch (1975), Bowen (1977).

136 SPOTTED REDSHANK *Tringa erythropus*   Plate 54

Other name: Dusky Redshank
This Palaearctic 'shank' has the most dramatic plumage changes in the genus, from largely black when breeding to largely white and grey.

IDENTIFICATION A rather elegant *Tringa* with longish legs and a relatively long and slender bill. This species and Redshank (137) share a red base to the bill and conspicuously bright red or orange-red legs; compare carefully with Ruff (210), which may have similar colours and is quite like Redshank in proportions. Spotted is slightly larger than Redshank, and

differs in shape in its longer, slightly droop-tipped bill, proportionately smaller head and longer neck, and slightly longer legs. In breeding plumage, combination of black underparts and red legs is unique among waders except for Black Stilt (25), which is restricted to New Zealand; moulting birds are blotched black and white below. In non-breeding plumage, paler grey above than other shanks and very white-faced and white beneath; the dark line across the lores contrasts strongly with white supercilia and cheeks. In flight, white back and upper rump form a white slit enclosed by the scapulars and tertials, as in American dowitchers (183, 184); feet, however, project farther beyond the tail. Wing lacks Redshank's broad white trailing edge, but secondaries and inner primaries are heavily notched with white and are paler than the rest of the wing. Compare with Marsh Sandpiper (138) and Greater and Lesser Yellowlegs (141, 142), all of which can have orange legs. **Bare parts:** Bill blackish, with base of lower mandible deep red when breeding, at other times orange-red; slender, straight except for faint droop at tip. Iris dark brown. Legs rich red when breeding, otherwise orange-red; toes plus a little tarsus project beyond tail-tip in flight.

VOICE A distinctive sharp, rapid whistle 'chu-it', falling then rising in pitch, is the usual flight call; a shorter 'chip' is given in alarm. Flocks have a short conversational 'uck'. Song, given usually in flight, is a complex series of creaking or grinding whistles.

HABITS Nests late May-Aug, mainly in lightly-wooded tundra but also in more open habitats. Female leaves the nesting area early, often before eggs hatch, leaving male to tend the brood. When not breeding, prefers freshwater lakeshores or brackish lagoons, but also occurs on sheltered muddy coasts. May occur singly, but in favoured sites forms flocks which often feed in deep water as dense packs, sometimes swimming and up-ending like a raft of Pied Avocets (27). Feeds also by picking or probing in muddy substrates, and in water by sweeping the bill from side to side. Rather shy; if flushed, flight is direct and very fast.

MOVEMENTS Females appear south of breeding range from mid-June onwards, males from late July, and juveniles mainly Aug. Adults moult, sometimes in large flocks, before onward movement. Arrivals in Africa begin in Aug but peak in Oct. Return passage spans Mar-May. A few remain in tropics all year, but many non-breeders summer just south of breeding range. Vagrant E North America,

Barbados, Madeira, Africa south to Cape Province, Seychelles, Cargados Garajos Is., Borneo, W Aleutians, Pribilofs, British Columbia, Oregon and California.

DESCRIPTION Breeding: Head, neck and entire underparts are sooty-black, except for narrow white eyelids, and undertail-coverts which are barred dark grey and white; some show whitish fringes on breast, flanks and belly. Mantle is also largely blackish; scapulars, wing-coverts and tertials are blackish, with contrastingly white spotting and fringing. Tertial edges are boldly notched with white. Flight feathers mostly blackish, but secondaries and inner primaries are notched and barred whitish. Back and upper rump are unbarred white; lower rump and uppertail barred white and dark grey. Tail is mainly dark grey, with narrow whitish bars. Underwing-coverts and axillaries are white. **Non-breeding:** Sharp dark line across the lores contrasts with white supercilium, extending to just behind eye, and whitish cheeks. Upperparts from forehead to mantle and scapulars are an even pale brownish-grey, with narrow whitish fringing on larger scapulars. Wing-coverts and tertials pale grey-brown, spotted and notched whitish. Underparts are white or greyish-white, except for even grey wash on sides of breast and upper flanks, and light barring on rear flanks and undertail. **Juvenile:** Upperparts as non-breeding, but slightly browner in tone; wing-coverts, scapulars and tertials are brownish-grey, spotted and notched off-white. Underparts, except whitish chin and throat, are pale greyish, lightly barred with brownish-grey.

AGE/SEX Juvenile underpart barring is distinct in the field until Nov. Females average slightly larger, and in breeding plumage are less black below than males; vent may be largely white, and some crown feathers pale-edged.

RACES No geographical variation is known.

MEASUREMENTS Length 290-320 mm (12"). Wing 158-180 mm; bill 52-65 mm; tarsus 52-64 mm; tail 60-69 mm.

REFERENCES Hildén (1979).

137 REDSHANK *Tringa totanus* Plate 54

Other name: Common Redshank

A familiar and noisy wader which nests in a broad band across the Palaearctic. Tunisian nesters are the only sandpiper-like birds to breed in Africa.

IDENTIFICATION A medium-sized mainly grey-brown wader with fairly long orange-red legs and a reddish-based bill a little longer than the distance from bill-base to nape. In flight, it is easily recognised by its white back and upper rump, showing as a white slit enclosed by dark scapulars and tertials, and its unmarked white secondaries and tips to inner primaries which form a broad and conspicuous trailing edge to the wing; no other wader shows this combination, but compare Terek Sandpiper (147), which is grey on back and rump, and the American dowitchers (183, 184), which show only a narrow whitish trailing edge. The most similar species is Spotted Redshank (136), which in flight shows greyish-mottled secondaries slightly paler than the rest of the wing. At rest, Spotted is distinguished by its longer legs, and longer, thinner, slightly droop-tipped bill with red-based lower mandible; in non-breeding plumage, Spotted has a paler face crossed by a contrasting dark eye-stripe, a whiter breast, and paler grey upperparts with whitish spotting and notching on wing-coverts and tertials, while its mainly-black breeding plumage is highly distinctive. Ruff (210) may also cause confusion, especially males in non-breeding plumage which often have orange-red legs and bill-base and, like Redshank, may feed in loose flocks on flooded grassland. Separation is simple in flight; at rest, Ruff differs in its broad-bodied, smaller-headed proportions, shorter bill, and rather browner upperparts with broad dark feather centres. See also

Greater and Lesser Yellowlegs (141, 142). **Bare parts:** Bill medium length, straight, dark brown, with basal third or more extensively orange-red. Iris dark brown. Legs longish, bright orange-red on adults, becoming darker red when breeding; young initially have orange-yellow legs, which may remain orange for some years before gaining adult colours.

VOICE A noisy bird, often the first of a group of waders to take panic and give alarm calls. Vocabulary is wide, but most usual flight call is 'teu-hu-hu' with first syllable longer and more accented; this call and variants are delivered much more rapidly in alarm. Usual alarm call on the ground is a long, mournful 'tyuuuu'. Songs are a repeated 'tyoo' in display flight and a yodelling repetition of 'taludl' on alighting.

HABITS Nests Mar-Aug in a wide variety of inland and coastal wetlands, often at high density in coastal saltmarshes or inland damp grasslands; not strongly territorial. Male has rising and falling song flight in which the wings are vibrated below the horizontal. Adults may gather from a wide area to join communal mobbing of predators. Mainly coastal when not nesting, but small numbers winter at some inland wetlands. Feeds on rocky, muddy or sandy shores, using an easy, continuous, quite fast walk and a regular pecking action; probes infrequently. May feed in flocks, particularly on open mudflats or flooded grassland, but some adults defend feeding territories on shores or saltmarshes. Large flocks gather with other waders at roost. Generally nervous and wary.

MOVEMENTS Less migratory than other *Tringa* species. Some in W Europe and Iceland may be virtually sedentary; other populations move farther, but very few penetrate beyond the equator. Departure and southward passage span June-Oct, and return northwards is chiefly Feb-Apr. A few regularly oversummer in non-breeding range. Regular in small numbers in Africa south to Cape Town and Tanzania, and in Indonesia south to Timor. Vagrant Greenland, Bear I., Spitsbergen, Cape Verde Is., E South Africa, Botswana, Seychelles, Maldive Is., Cocos Is., Christmas I., N Australia, and recently Adelaide.

DESCRIPTION Breeding: Extremely variable in grey, brown, pale cinnamon or dark cinnamon basic colour and in proportion of breeding plumage feathers

attained in each population (see Races). Most populations show light and dark morphs. Head shows an indistinct dark line from bill to eye, and a narrow whitish eye-ring. Upperparts are mainly brownish or cinnamon, with variable blackish or warm brown notching and barring. Wing-coverts grey-brown, some with narrow white fringes. Primaries mostly blackish, but inners are white-tipped; secondaries white. Lower back, rump and uppertail-coverts white; lower rump and uppertail lightly barred brown. Tail white, strongly barred brown, central feathers infused grey-brown. Underparts whitish, infused with brownish or cinnamon on breast and variably streaked and spotted dark brown. Underwing mostly whitish, contrasting with dark wedge formed by outer primaries. **Non-breeding:** As breeding, but upperparts are plainer and greyer with much-reduced dark brown spotting and streaking. Underparts are white, with breast strongly infused brownish-grey and finely streaked brown, and flanks and undertail lightly streaked brown. **Juvenile:** As non-breeding, but upperparts warm brown with extensive buff notches and fringes. Breast is suffused buff-brown, and breast, flanks and undertail lightly streaked darker. Central tail feathers are suffused dark cinnamon.

AGE/SEX Extensive buff markings of juvenile may remain distinct in the field until Oct. Later, ageing is possible in the hand by retained inner medians or worn primaries of young birds. Sexes are very similar; females average slightly longer-winged.

RACES Six now recognised, but many populations are intermediate: nominate *totanus* (Ireland to W USSR), *robusta* (Iceland, Faeroes), *ussuriensis* (E USSR, Mongolia, N Manchuria), *terrignotae* (E China), *craggi* (NW Sinkiang) and *eurhinus* (Kashmir, W China). There are minor variations in size and colour, but these are compounded by individual variation. The race *robusta* is largest; this and *ussuriensis* are typically more cinnamon, and show a higher proportion of breeding plumage feathers than European birds.

MEASUREMENTS Length 270-290 mm (11"). Wing 149-176 mm; bill 34-50 mm; tarsus 41-55 mm; tail 56-78 mm.

REFERENCES Goss-Custard (1969), Hale (1971, 1973), Hale and Ashcroft (1982).

138 MARSH SANDPIPER *Tringa stagnatilis*   Plate 55

A rather delicate *Tringa*, the smallest of the seven 'shanks'. In many ways it resembles a small Greenshank (139).

IDENTIFICATION A sandpiper with long, usually greenish legs, a slim body, a rather small head on a slender neck, and a longish, fairly slim bill. In flight it shows dark wings and extensive clear white on back, rump and uppertail. Plumage patterns and leg colour are very similar to those of Greenshank and Spotted Greenshank (140), and these species are easily confused; Marsh is the smallest and slimmest of the three, but is best identified by its proportionately longer legs, slimmer (usually straight) bill which typically shows colour only near the base, whiter face in non-breeding plumages, and more delicate proportions of head and neck. Toes project farther beyond tail-tip in flight. Greyish-buff patterning of upperparts

in breeding plumage is also distinctive. Lesser Yellowlegs (142) differs in flight in dark back and upper rump, and at rest is longer-winged, shorter-billed and yellower-legged. Compare also Wood Sandpiper (145) and Wilson's Phalarope (156). **Bare parts:** Bill longish, rather slender and pointed, usually straight but sometimes noticeably droop-tipped or upcurved; brownish-black, with greenish-grey at base not usually extending beyond basal third. Iris dark brown. Legs dull greyish-green or yellowish-green, rarely more yellowish, in spring may even be orange-yellow; in flight, toes plus a little tarsus project beyond tail-tip. **VOICE** Usual call when flushed is a loud 'yip', often rapidly repeated, or 'plew'; not unlike Greenshank in tone, but higher-pitched and thinner. Song is a repeated 'tu-ee-u' and alarm call on breeding grounds a sharp 'chip'.

HABITS Nests late Apr-Aug in steppe and boreal wetlands; prefers open freshwater marshland with lush grassy vegetation, but will tolerate brackish water. Nests solitarily, or in loose colonies with nests sometimes less than 10 m apart; both sexes incubate and tend the brood. When not breeding, occurs typically at inland wetlands, fresh or brackish, sometimes in large numbers; more rarely feeds on sheltered coasts. Feeds much in water, walking briskly and steadily, pecking mainly from water surface; may feed in tight co-ordinated groups. Fairly wary.

MOVEMENTS Present on breeding grounds Apr-Sept. Departures begin early July, and first arrivals in winter quarters are in Sept. Generally scarce at passage sites, and many may overfly wide areas. Common in African and Indian parts of range, scarcer in SE Asia and Australia. Return passage spans Mar-May. Many non-breeders spend all year in winter quarters or summer at intermediate sites. Vagrant W Europe west to Sweden and Britain, Cape Verde Is., Madagascar, Seychelles, Providence I., New Zealand, and W Aleutians.

DESCRIPTION Breeding: Crown and hindneck buffish-brown, streaked darker; supercilium indistinct; lores show a dusky triangle in front of eye; ear-coverts are lightly streaked. Upperparts show a striking pattern of dark brown feathers broadly edged, notched or barred with a clear buffish-grey; fresh feathers show narrow white tips. Long tertials reach almost to tip of folded primaries. Flight feathers dark brownish-grey, with some narrow whitish edging to secondaries. Back, rump and uppertail-coverts white; tail whitish or pale brown, lightly barred brown. Underparts white, with dark brown spotting and streaking on sides of lower neck and breast, extending lightly onto flanks as brown chevrons. Underwing and axillaries largely white. **Non-breeding:** Crown and upperparts become brownish-grey, fairly plain but with some darker streaking and white fringing. Wing-coverts are similar, but lesser coverts are rather darker grey. Forehead, lores and supercilium are whitish; underparts white, with grey suffusion and sometimes slight dark streaking on sides of neck and breast. **Juvenile:** As non-breeding, but upperparts are browner with buffish or whitish fringing; some feathers show dark submarginal lines.

AGE/SEX Juveniles are distinct at close range until Oct. Sexes are not known to differ in plumage, but females average slightly larger.

RACES No geographical variation is known.

MEASUREMENTS Length 220-250 mm (9¼"). Wing 128-148 mm; bill 36-45 mm; tarsus 47-57 mm; tail 49-62 mm.

REFERENCES Tolchin (1976), Kieser and Kieser (1982).

139 GREENSHANK *Tringa nebularia* Plate 55 (see also Plate 56)

Other names: Common or Greater Greenshank
The largest of the Palaearctic 'shanks', very similar to the American Greater Yellowlegs (141) in many aspects of its biology.

IDENTIFICATION A mainly pale brownish-grey and white wader with long greenish or yellowish legs and a longish, rather heavy, slightly-uptilted bill. In flight, its dark upperwings contrast with the mainly-white back, rump and uppertail. The most similar species is the rare Spotted Greenshank (140), but Spotted is clearly shorter-legged; in flight its toes fall about level with the tail-tip or project only slightly. Spotted can also be distinguished by its thickly-spotted breast in breeding plumage and all year by its more sharply two-toned bill. In the hand, Greenshank shows faint brown markings on axillaries and underwing-coverts (pure white on Spotted) and very little webbing between the toes (more obvious in Spotted). Confusion with Marsh Sandpiper (138) is also likely, but Greenshank's relatively shorter legs, heavier head and neck, and thicker, more uptilted bill, more extensively pale at the base, should enable identification. Calls are also useful to separate these three species. Other shanks should always be distinguishable by leg colour, but note that yellowish legs of some Greenshanks may suggest Greater Yellowlegs; latter effectively identical in call and bill shape, but is generally slightly darker in all plumages, especially on the breast, and shows just a square white rump-patch in flight. See also Willet (146). **Bare parts:** Bill thickish at base, tapering and uptilted towards tip; basal half tinged bluish- or greenish-grey, shading into blackish outer half. Iris dark brown. Legs pale greyish-green, sometimes greenish-yellow or dull yellowish; most of length of toes projects beyond tail-tip in flight. **VOICE** Usual flight call is a quick, ringing whistle of two, three or four syllables, most often 'teu-teu-teu'; also a sharp 'tchuk' or 'chip' in alarm. Voice is more varied when breeding; song is a melodious repetition of 'too-hoo-too-hoo...'.

HABITS Nests late Apr-Aug, chiefly in taiga and forest zones of Palaearctic; may nest in forest clearings, moorlands with scattered trees, or treeless upland bogs. Breeding range is generally more southerly than that of Spotted Redshank (136), more northerly than Redshank (137) and Marsh Sandpiper, but with considerable overlap. Male has a switchback display flight, sometimes at great height. Both sexes incubate, but usually only one parent leaves not long after hatching. Non-breeding habitat includes a wide variety of wetland types, both coastal and inland, but prefers estuaries to open coasts. Generally feeds singly, but may gather into large flocks at roost. Feeds most often in shallow water or at water's edge with steady walk, but often catches small fish by dashing rapidly through shallows. Usually fairly wary.

MOVEMENTS Departs from breeding grounds late June-Aug. Arrivals in winter quarters span July-Oct. Scottish breeders winter mainly in British Isles, but other populations are more strongly migratory. Return passage begins in Mar and continues to May. Some non-breeders remain south all year. Vagrant Newfoundland,

Iceland, Faeroes, Azores, Amsterdam I., Crozet Is., Kerguelen I., Macquarie I., Campbell I., Chatham Is., New Zealand, W Aleutians (regular), St Lawrence I. and Pribilofs.

DESCRIPTION Breeding: Crown and hindneck whitish, streaked brown. Indistinct, faintly-streaked whitish supercilium; lores are crossed by diffuse dark line which continues obscurely behind the eye; sides of head otherwise whitish, streaked brown. Mantle, scapulars and tertials show a mixture of brownish-grey feathers with white fringes and dark submarginal lines, and blackish feathers fringed or notched whitish. Wing-coverts grey-brown, fringed whitish. Primary coverts and flight feathers dark grey. Back, rump and uppertail largely white; longest uppertail-coverts and tail are irregularly barred dark brown. Underparts are whitish, with strong blackish-brown streaking on neck, breast and flanks; flanks show some dark chevrons. Underwing and axillaries are white, with faint markings of pale brown visible in the hand. **Non-breeding:** Head and neck whitish, suffused pale grey and slightly streaked darker grey. Upperparts pale

brownish-grey, with whitish fringing especially on larger feathers; tertials grey-brown with edges notched darker. Lesser coverts rather darker than medians. Underparts white, with light greyish streaking on sides of lower neck and of upper breast. **Juvenile:** Upperparts rather browner than non-breeding, with buffish-white fringes and dark submarginal lines or spotting; at a distance, not dissimilar to breeding plumage. Underparts as non-breeding, but with fine brown streaking on neck and breast, and some light brown barring on flanks.

AGE/SEX Evenly-fringed upperparts and brownish tinges of juvenile plumage are distinct at close range until Oct. Sexes are similar in plumage, but females average slightly larger.

RACES None described, but central Palaearctic breeders average slightly longer-winged.

MEASUREMENTS Length 300-340 mm (12½"). Wing 177-200 mm; bill 47-61 mm; tarsus 52-66; tail 70-83 mm.

REFERENCES Nethersole-Thompson and Nethersole-Thompson (1979), Tree (1979).

140 SPOTTED GREENSHANK *Tringa guttifer*   Plate 56

Other names: Armstrong's Sandpiper, Nordmann's Greenshank
A rarely-encountered, poorly-known and possibly decreasing sandpiper of E Asia. It nests in trees on Sakhalin Island.

IDENTIFICATION This species strongly resembles Greenshank (139) and requires careful observation to distinguish from that species. It is slightly smaller than Greenshank and has characteristically short, yellowish legs and a straighter bill with greenish-yellow at the base. In flight, it is like Greenshank in structure and has similar dark upperwings and long white wedge from back to uppertail. It differs in that the tips of toes only just reach the tail-tip, the white of underwing and axillaries is unmarked (lacking Greenshank's fine brownish barring) and secondaries are rather paler and greyer. In breeding plumage, shows large oval or heart-shaped black spots on lower neck, breast, belly and flanks; at the most, Greenshank shows small spots on upper breast and fore-flanks, never on belly. Thicker, two-toned bill and heavier build should always distinguish from Marsh Sandpiper (138) and from tattlers (150, 151); also, tattlers lack white on upperparts in flight. In breeding plumage beware confusion with Great Knot (188), which also has extensive black spotting underneath. **Bare parts:** Bill differs from Greenshank's in being almost straight, rather than upcurved, and slightly thicker; distinctly (but not sharply) two-toned, with outer half blackish and inner half greenish- or brownish-yellow. Iris dark brown. Legs from toes to feathering are nearly 40% shorter than on Greenshank, with diagnostic partial webbing between all toes unique in *Tringa*; leg colour varies from clear yellow to greenish- or brownish-yellow. Shortness of legs above the joint is particularly noticeable, and is the best field character out of breeding dress.

VOICE A piercing 'keyew', sometimes repeated, obviously sharper and less musical than calls of Greenshank. Male has a loud song in display flight on the breeding grounds.

HABITS Only known breeding grounds are on Sakhalin I., north of Japan, but may nest in adjacent continental USSR. Breeds June-Aug in sparse larch forests around marshy pools; all nests found to date have been in larch trees at heights of between 2.3 m and 4.5 m. The nests are built of larch twigs, moss and lichen (presumably not by the birds themselves). When not breeding, most often seen on muddy coasts or on saltpans. The stance is rather horizontal, and the feeding behaviour recalls a large Terek Sandpiper (147) with rapid runs after prey with bill held low. Food includes aquatic invertebrates and small fish. Often feeds up to belly in water. This is a wary bird which flies strongly.

MOVEMENTS Little known. Occurs as a rare winter visitor on mainland coasts from Bangladesh to Thailand, also on Hainan, and as a migrant in Japan, Korea, Taiwan, Hong Kong and China. Other records, presumably of vagrants, are from Assam, Borneo, Philippines, N Australia and Commander Is. (May 1883).

DESCRIPTION Breeding: Crown very dark brown, lores darkish; rest of head whitish, heavily streaked dark brown. Mantle, scapulars and tertials show a mixture of very dark brown feathers, fringed whitish, and dark grey-brown feathers, washed darker submarginally and fringed whitish. Lesser coverts darkish brown, rest of wing-coverts dull brown fringed whitish. Primary coverts and primaries blackish-brown; secondaries dark grey, with ill-defined paler tips. Lower back, rump and uppertail-coverts white; tail white, marked lightly and irregularly with pale grey. Underparts white, with bold blackish-brown oval, heart-shaped or almost semicircular spots on breast, upper belly and flanks. Underwing-coverts and axillaries pure white. **Non-breeding:** Forehead and supercilium whitish. Crown, nape, hindneck and ear-coverts are a pale but dull even brownish-grey, only slightly streaked. Upperparts are an even dull grey, edged paler; the dark lesser coverts are more contrasting in this plumage. Tail is washed pale grey. Underparts white, with light greyish suffusion and streaking on lower neck and breast. **Juvenile:** As non-breeding, but crown brownish, upperparts warm brown with long beaded buffish edgings to tertials and scapulars, wing-coverts brown fringed whitish-buff, and breast white obscurely washed and flecked brownish.

AGE/SEX Brownish colour and buff spotting of juvenile is discernible at close range to about Nov. Sexes are not known to differ.

RACES No geographical variation is known.

MEASUREMENTS Length 290-320 mm (11¾"). Wing 169-183 mm; bill 48-58 mm; tarsus 42-48 mm; tail 62-67 mm.

REFERENCES Nechaev (1978).

141 GREATER YELLOWLEGS *Tringa melanoleuca*   Plate 57

The larger of the American 'shanks', and the more southerly nester. It is similar in many respects to the Palaearctic Greenshank (139).

IDENTIFICATION Both this species and Lesser Yellowlegs (142) are tall, elegant waders with bright yellow, or sometimes orange, legs. They differ from other large *Tringa* in their square white rump-patches in flight and in their long wings which, when folded, project noticeably beyond the tail. Structurally and in call notes, Greater is very similar to Greenshank, but its longer wings, browner plumages and brighter legs are useful characters; Greenshank has at best pale yellow legs, and in flight shows a conspicuous white back. Bare-part colours of Greater also overlap with Redshank (137), but latter is a smaller, shorter-billed bird with white back and white secondaries conspicuous in flight. Greatest identification problem is separation from Lesser, particularly in the case of lone individuals where larger size of Greater is not apparent. Best feature is length and shape of bill: Greater's is roughly one-and-a-half times the distance from bill-base to nape, usually faintly uptilted, often with greenish, greyish or yellowish basal third; on Lesser, bill is shorter, only just over head length, thinner and straighter, all-dark or with some brownish or yellowish at the extreme base. In breeding plumage, breast and flanks of Greater are more heavily barred; in juvenile plumage, Greater's breast shows distinct streaks on a whitish background, while Lesser shows a brownish wash with faint darker streaking. In flight, Greater shows brownish notching on the secondaries extending onto the inner primaries; flight feathers are plain on Lesser. Lesser can also be distinguished by its lighter, daintier actions on the ground and in flight. **Bare parts:** Bill blackish, with greyish, greenish or yellow (sometimes orange) at base (see above). Iris dark brown. Legs usually bright yellow, sometimes orange or even orange-red.

VOICE Usual call is a loud clear 'teu-teu-teu' on a slightly descending scale, or a longer or shorter series of 'teu' syllables. This call is effectively identical to that of Greenshank, although sometimes slightly higher-pitched and faster, but is clearer and more ringing than Lesser's call and usually easily separable. A melodious 'too-whee' forms the basis of the rolling territorial song.

HABITS Nests May onwards, mainly in muskeg country (scattered trees, marshy ponds and open areas) and in northern margin of coniferous forest zone; range extends south to N Ontario and Nova Scotia. When not nesting, found on muddy coasts and at a variety of inland fresh or brackish wetland habitats, either singly or in small flocks. Like Greenshank, has

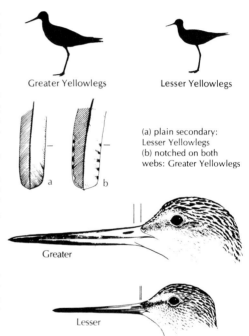

Greater Yellowlegs   Lesser Yellowlegs

(a) plain secondary: Lesser Yellowlegs
(b) notched on both webs: Greater Yellowlegs

Greater

Lesser

a variety of feeding techniques including dashing through the shallows after small fish. Often wades deeply. Fairly wary; often the first of a group of waders to flush and give the alarm.

MOVEMENTS Post-breeding departures begin mid-July, but some linger in N USA into early Nov. Arrivals in South America begin late Aug, and most depart again by Mar; some non-breeders remain all year. Return to breeding areas is very early, second only to Killdeer (91); most parts of range are re-occupied during Apr. Migrates both coastally and through the interior; in autumn and perhaps spring, some may overfly W Atlantic between NE USA and N South America. Vagrant Japan, Bermuda, Baffin I., Greenland, Iceland, Sweden, Britain and Ireland; much scarcer as a vagrant than Lesser Yellowlegs.

DESCRIPTION Breeding: Crown dark brown, streaked whitish; supercilium whitish, more streaked behind eye; lores dusky; sides of face whitish, streaked brown. Mantle, scapulars and tertials show a mixture of blackish and dull brown feathers, boldly spotted and notched whitish. Wing-coverts brownish, with whitish fringes. Primary coverts, primaries and secondaries are mainly dark brown; inner primaries and secondaries show paler notching. Back blackish-brown; rump and most of uppertail are white. Tail and longest uppertail-coverts are white, barred brown. Underparts white, but with heavy blackish-brown streaks on neck, becoming chevrons on lower breast and prominent bars on flanks and upper belly. Underwing-coverts and axillaries white, strongly barred brown. **Non-breeding:** As breeding, but upperparts brownish-grey, initially with many small dark spots and pale notches along feather edges, particularly on tertials. Underparts white, but with neck, breast and much of flanks lightly washed brownish-

grey and streaked or barred brown. **Juvenile:** As non-breeding, but with warmer brown upperparts liberally spotted and notched pale buff. Neck and breast show clear brown streaks on a whitish background, usually forming a fairly neat breast-band; flanks and undertail-coverts are lightly barred brown.
AGE/SEX Juvenile is distinct in the field until at least Nov. Sexes are similar in plumage and in size.
RACES No races described. Mean wing length is largest in centre of breeding range.
MEASUREMENTS Length 290-330 mm (12¼''). Wing 181-210 mm; bill 50-61 mm; tarsus 56-70 mm; tail 68-78 mm.
REFERENCES McNeil (1970), Burton and McNeil (1976), Wilds (1982).

142 LESSER YELLOWLEGS *Tringa flavipes*   Plate 57

A remarkably elegant American species, but often difficult to distinguish from its larger relative, Greater Yellowlegs (141).

IDENTIFICATION A slim, long-bodied wader with long, bright yellow (sometimes orange) legs and a relatively short bill. In flight, it shows dark upperwings and a squarish white patch on the rump. Care is needed to separate from Greater Yellowlegs (which see for a full discussion of characters); best features are size (Lesser averages 25-30% smaller), and length, shape and colour of bill, brownish notching on flight feathers (absent on Lesser), and call. The Eurasian Wood Sandpiper (145) is also very similar, especially to juvenile Lesser; both show brownish, heavily-spotted upperparts, squarish white rump and yellowish legs. Wood Sandpiper differs, however, in its relatively shorter legs, bill, neck and wings; it also has browner plumages, with longer, more contrasted supercilia. Beware confusion with Wilson's Phalarope (156) and Stilt Sandpiper (208), which are similar especially in flight. **Bare parts:** Bill straight, a little longer than the distance from bill-base to nape; black, usually tinged brownish or yellowish at the extreme base. Iris dark brown. Legs long, usually bright yellow, but sometimes more orange and suggesting Redshank (137).
VOICE Usual call is a whistled 'tew-tew' or 'tew', recalling Greater but less resonant, flatter and sometimes a little rougher; easily distinguishable from Greater with practice. On breeding grounds, gives a sharp 'kip' in alarm; song is a repeated musical 'pill-e-wee'.
HABITS Nests May-Aug in muskeg country, perhaps choosing drier and more sheltered sites than Greater in areas of range overlap, and also farther north, mainly in open woodlands. Tends to nest in loose colonies. Both sexes incubate and tend the brood. When not breeding, occurs widely on all types of inland and coastal wetlands; often feeds on flooded farmland or grassland. Flocks are typically larger than those of Greater, often concentrated in more sheltered sites. Feeds with delicate, high-stepping walk, picking from surface; rarely dashes after food. Often fairly tame and approachable.
MOVEMENTS In North America, peak of autumn migration is earlier, and spring migration later, than in Greater. Southward movement begins in early July

and continues to Oct; abundant on migration in E Canada, well east of breeding range, and probably many fly direct from there to N South America. Arrivals in South America begin late Aug. Relatively few winter in S USA. Return passage through USA spans late Mar-May. Many non-breeders remain south all year. Regular on Bermuda in autumn. Vagrant Japan, Australia, New Zealand, Falklands, Azores, Iceland, W Europe east to Sweden, Hungary and Italy, Nigeria and South Africa.
DESCRIPTION Breeding: Head and neck are whitish, streaked dark brown, with indistinct supercilium and whitish eye-ring. Mantle, scapulars and tertials are mainly brownish-black, with extensive whitish spots and notches; most wing-coverts are dull grey-brown, fringed whitish. Primary coverts and primaries are uniformly blackish-brown; secondaries indistinctly notched paler. Back is blackish-brown, contrasting with square white patch on rump and uppertail-coverts. Tail whitish, barred brown. Underparts mostly white, but with breast and anterior flanks fairly lightly streaked brown. Underwing-coverts and axillaries white, strongly barred brown. **Non-breeding:** As breeding, but upperparts are a much more even brownish-grey, lightly spotted whitish; tertials more prominently edged dark brown and notched whitish. Breast is suffused brownish-grey and very lightly streaked. **Juvenile:** As non-breeding, but mantle, scapulars, tertials and upperwing-coverts warmer brown, liberally spotted bright buff. The breast is washed grey and lightly streaked brown.
AGE/SEX Juveniles are distinct in the field until Oct, but can be identified later in the hand by retained juvenile coverts and worn primaries. Sexes are similar in plumage, but females average slightly longer-winged.
RACES None is described. There is very slight variation in average size: eastern birds are smallest, central birds largest.
MEASUREMENTS Length 230-250 mm (9½''). Wing 149-170 mm; bill 33-40 mm; tarsus 46-58 mm; tail 57-64 mm.
REFERENCES McNeil (1970), Burton and McNeil (1976), Wilds (1982), Tree and Kieser (1982).

143 GREEN SANDPIPER *Tringa ochropus* Plate 58

A distinctive blackish and white wader of inland fresh waters. Habitually nests in old tree-nests of other birds, particularly thrushes, sometimes in dense forest.

IDENTIFICATION A rather bulky, small *Tringa* with a rather hunched and horizontal·stance. At a distance, distinguished from Common Sandpiper (148) by larger size, darker legs, greater contrast between dark upperparts and white belly, and absence of a white 'peak' between the breast-patches and the folded wing. Compared with Wood Sandpiper (145), has darker, less strongly-patterned upperparts, a shorter supercilium, a bulkier outline, and shorter, darker legs. Flight pattern of dark back and wings and squarish white rump-patch is similar to that of Wood Sandpiper, but much more strongly-contrasted; the large white rump-patch is startlingly obvious in contrast to the almost blackish back, and extends onto the base of the tail. Toes do not project beyond the tail-tip. In addition, the wings are broad-based and blackish underneath, and the jerky, deep wingbeats and zigzag escape flight are almost like Common Snipe (175). Very similar to the Nearctic Solitary Sandpiper (144) in both plumage and habits, but about 10% larger in size: Green is easily distinguished in flight by conspicuous white rump and uppertail, and by broader wings which are slightly darker above and below. At rest, Solitary has a slimmer outline with neck, wings and tail paler than on Green Sandpiper.
Bare parts: Bill olive-green at base, shading through brown to a blackish tip; shortish and quite straight. Iris dark brown. Legs dull greyish-green, somewhat variable in shade, usually looking dark at a distance.
VOICE A noisy bird when flushed or when gathering on migration, with loud and highly distinctive sharp whistling calls. Commonest call is a high-pitched 'twit-wit-wit', sometimes preceded by a rising 'ko-wit'; often audible as birds migrate overhead at considerable heights. On breeding grounds, warning call is a rapid 'tit-ti-tit' and song a loud whistled 'loo-tit-ti-lhit' and variants.
HABITS Breeds late Apr-July in damp wooded regions, nesting usually in trees but occasionally on the ground among tree-roots. Does not build a nest, but uses the old nest of a thrush *Turdus* or Wood-pigeon *Columba palumbus*, a squirrel's drey or sometimes a natural platform. The young have to jump perhaps 10 m or more to the ground within hours of hatching. One parent, usually female, leaves territory as early as late May. Outside the breeding season, frequents inland fresh waters. Usually found singly, sometimes on quite small pools and narrow ditches, and normally the only wader found in such sites other than snipe species and Common Sandpiper. Favoured sites may attract small flocks, rarely of up to 30. Rare in intertidal habitats, even on migration. When feeding, moves rather slowly and deliberately around marginal vegetation and is easily overlooked. Usually a nervous bird, difficult to approach; flushes readily.
MOVEMENTS Leaves breeding grounds from early June onwards, and some remain on wintering grounds until early May. Does not migrate as far as its close relatives, and is rare beyond 10° S in Africa and beyond the equator elsewhere. Vagrant to outer Aleutians in spring, Jan Mayen I., Madeira, Cape Province in South Africa and N Australia.
DESCRIPTION Breeding: Distinct white supercilium in front of eye joins narrow white eye-ring; very dark line across lores, but eye-stripe indistinct behind eye. Crown and hindneck whitish, heavily streaked dark brown. Mantle and coverts very dark olive-brown, with very small whitish-buff spots; on the scapulars and tertials the spots are slightly larger. Rump and uppertail-coverts brilliant white. Tail white, with three or four broad dark brown bars. Chin, throat and breast whitish, with increasingly intense dark brown streaking; the streaks merge into irregular blotches on the breast and anterior flanks. Rest of underparts white, but underwing-coverts and axillaries blackish-brown with narrow white bars. **Non-breeding:** As breeding, but head and breast are a paler and more even greyish-brown, slightly streaked darker. Spots on scapulars and tertials are still smaller. **Juvenile:** As non-breeding in its smoothness of colour, but upperparts and breast are browner with small, deep buff spots on the scapulars and tertials which do not contrast so much as those of adults. Breast is more evenly coloured and lacks irregular spotting.
AGE/SEX Juvenile distinguishable on autumn passage, but as adult by Nov. Female averages larger, but is not known to differ in plumage.
RACES No geographical variation is known.
MEASUREMENTS Length 210-240 mm (8¾"). Wing 136-155 mm; bill 31-38 mm; tarsus 31-37 mm; tail 53-62 mm.
REFERENCES Oring (1968), Kirchner (1978), Kraatz and Beyer (1982, 1984).

144 SOLITARY SANDPIPER *Tringa solitaria* Plate 58

The Nearctic counterpart of the Old World Green Sandpiper (143). Not a gregarious bird, often living up to its name.

IDENTIFICATION A fairly slender, small, dark *Tringa* with dark wings and rump. At a distance may resemble Spotted Sandpiper (149) on the ground, but is slightly larger and more slender, has darker legs, and much greater contrast between the dark upperparts and white belly. Differs markedly from Green Sandpiper in flight in showing a dark rump and centre to the tail; also is narrower-winged and smaller, with wing-action more similar to Wood Sandpiper (145). Underwing and axillaries are dark, but white barring is broader than on Green Sandpiper. At rest, differs from latter in smaller size, slimmer outline with wings extending slightly beyond the tail, broader whitish eye-ring, and less hunched stance. The carpal and leading edge of the folded wing sometimes show as a dark line between the slightly paler outer median coverts and the white underparts. Three or four dark bars may be visible on the edge of the tail. **Bare parts:** Bill dull greenish at base, shading to blackish at tip; sometimes the bill-tip is faintly drooped. Iris brown. Legs dull greyish-green, sometimes tinged yellowish in juveniles.

VOICE Similar to that of Green Sandpiper, but calls are by comparison quieter, less complex and less frequent. Usual calls are a high 'tou-tou-twit' or 'peet-weet', and a single sharp 'tew' or 'pit'.

HABITS Nests in boreal forests of Canada and Alaska, rarely southwards into Minnesota. Like Green Sandpiper, frequently uses old tree-nests of other birds, particularly thrush species. Outside the breeding season, found on inland fresh waters; extremely rare in intertidal habitats. Often found on isolated ditches and tiny temporary ponds where waders would not otherwise be expected; sometimes found on muddy pools in woodland. Feeding action fairly slow and deliberate; pecks delicately. Bobs when alarmed; generally nervous, but vagrants often allow close approach. Aggressively territorial when feeding, but may gather in small flocks on migration.

MOVEMENTS Strong migrant. Southward movement begins in early July. Generally more numerous east of the Rockies. Some winter in SE USA, but main winter range extends from West Indies and Central America south to Argentina and Uruguay. Vagrant Bermuda, Greenland, Iceland, W Europe (in autumn), Galapagos, South Georgia (Nov 1975) and South Africa (Aug 1979).

DESCRIPTION Breeding: Prominent white eye-ring. Whitish supercilium, usually prominent, in front of eye, and dark line across the lores, but both eye-stripe and supercilium are poorly marked behind the eye. Rest of head and neck darkish olive-brown, finely speckled white. Breast greyish-white, heavily streaked with dark brown. Underwing-coverts and axillaries evenly barred blackish-brown and white; rest of underparts white. Upperparts are blackish-brown, with small whitish or buffy spots and notches. Wings, rump and central tail feathers dark brown; median and greater coverts are slightly darker than leading lesser coverts. Outer tail feathers and sides of uppertail white, boldly barred with blackish-brown. **Non-breeding:** As breeding, but a little paler and greyer particularly on head, neck and breast. Chin and throat almost white. Upperparts show less spotting. **Juvenile:** As breeding, but dark upperparts slightly browner, with pale spots on upperparts initially bright buff. Chin and upper throat whitish; the breast is washed brownish and finely streaked light brown.

AGE/SEX Juvenile is easily distinguished until Nov, but afterwards resembles adult. Females average slightly larger.

RACES Two races are recognised, but there is a wide zone of overlap and few individuals out of breeding range can be assigned to a particular race. Nominate race (eastern areas) averages smaller and has whitish-buff spots on the upperparts in breeding plumage; *cinnamomea* (western areas) is slightly larger and tends to have warmer brownish-buff spotting, sometimes almost cinnamon. Birds from all parts of the breeding area apparently intermingle in winter.

MEASUREMENTS Length 180-210 mm (7¾"). Wing 125-146 mm; bill 27-32 mm; tarsus 29-35 mm; tail 49-57 mm.

REFERENCES Oring (1968), Jehl (1976).

145 WOOD SANDPIPER *Tringa glareola*   Plate 58

One of the most abundant and widespread *Tringa* sandpipers, and one of the strongest migrants in the genus. Typically an inland wader.

IDENTIFICATION A slim, graceful, buffish-brown *Tringa* with a long pale supercilium and quite long legs. Most often confused with Green Sandpiper (143), but the distinctions between the two are obvious once learnt. Wood is paler, slimmer and longer-legged, and sports a supercilium which is obvious behind the eye and extends to the rear of the ear-coverts. In flight, the wings are conspicuously less broad at the base and the feet extend beyond the tail. The underwing is whitish, only slightly mottled with grey-brown, and the white rump-patch is smaller and less contrasted with the rest of the upperparts. The outer primary shows a white shaft. Lesser Yellowlegs (142) is actually the most similar species, especially in juvenile plumage; it is, however, larger and greyer, and has proportionately longer, clear yellow legs, and wings which extend well beyond the tail at rest. On Wood Sandpiper, the wings and tail are roughly equal in length. Beware confusion with three-quarter-grown Redshank chicks (137) and with Ruff (210). **Bare parts:** Bill shortish and straight, fairly deep at base, with a blackish distal half and an olive-green or yellow-green base; rather browner in juveniles. Iris dark brown. Legs dull yellowish, usually greenish- or brownish-yellow, always looking pale at a distance.

VOICE Flight call a whistled 'chiff-if' or 'chiff-if-iff'. Alarm call is a sharper 'chip', often repeated rapidly. The song, given in Redshank-like display flight (rarely when perched), is pleasant, repeated 'liltie', reminiscent of Redshank song but somewhat higher-pitched.

HABITS Breeds May-July in damp, open parts of boreal forests, or in marshes with dwarf deciduous scrub; more rarely nests away from trees in blanket bogs or in alpine zone. Nests usually in a lined scrape among dense ground cover, but occasionally, like Green and Solitary Sandpipers (144), uses the old tree-nest of another bird. Outside the breeding season, frequents inland fresh waters and marshes, sometimes small temporary pools; rarely seen in intertidal habitats. Often feeds in scattered groups and may gather in small flocks on migration or in winter. Typically towers high when flushed, uttering ringing calls.

MOVEMENTS Strongly migratory; winters mainly in the southern part of the Old World, although occasional individuals have been found as far north as Britain. Often abundant in sub-Saharan Africa and in India, but surprisingly scarce in Australia and only a vagrant to Tasmania. No records yet from New Zealand. As a migrant, scarce in westernmost Europe, particularly so in spring. Vagrant Iceland (has bred), Greenland, Faeroes, Azores, Madeira, New York State (Oct 1907), Bermuda, Barbados (Oct 1955), Hawaii and Alaska (occasionally breeds, regular in flocks on W Aleutians in spring).

DESCRIPTION Breeding: Long white supercilium from bill to rear of ear-coverts. Clear but thin dark line from bill to eye, but eye-stripe indistinct across ear-coverts. Narrow whitish eye-ring. Crown blackish-brown streaked whitish, hindneck paler; upperparts including mantle, scapulars, tertials, and larger coverts blackish-brown strongly barred and spotted pale grey-brown and white. Smaller coverts brown, fringed white. Rump and uppertail-coverts white; tail feathers pale brown, narrowly barred white. Chin and throat white, breast infused grey-buff and strongly streaked and spotted dark brown, fading into whitish underparts. Upper flanks strongly barred brown. Underwing white, slightly barred pale grey-brown.

Non-breeding: As above, but upperparts a more even grey-brown, spotted whitish. Breast suffused grey-brown, with indistinct brown streaks. Flank barring virtually absent. Juvenile: As breeding, but all upperparts dark warm brown extensively spotted and fringed bright buff-brown. Breast suffused grey-brown; pale feather tips give pale mottled appearance. Tail feathers infused buffish on pale bars. No flank bars.

AGE/SEX Juvenile very distinctly spotted with buff-brown; strong pale notchings on tertials can be seen until Feb on some individuals. Often, immatures renew their outer primaries in late winter or early spring; these are then contrastingly fresher and darker than worn inner primaries. Females average slightly larger.

RACES No geographical variation is known.

MEASUREMENTS Length 190-210 mm (7¾"). Wing 120-134 mm; bill 25-32 mm; tarsus 32-41 mm; tail 45-53 mm.

REFERENCES Kirchner (1978).

146 WILLET *Catoptrophorus semipalmatus* Plate 59

This rather odd American wader has a genus to itself, but seems to be closely related to the 'shanks' of genus *Tringa* (136-142) despite its unusual wing pattern.

IDENTIFICATION A rather heavy and inelegant wader on the ground, shank-like in proportions, perhaps closest to Redshank (137) in shape but larger than Greater Yellowlegs (141). In flight, appears more godwit-like; its black primary coverts and primaries crossed by a highly conspicuous broad white band, its white-based secondaries, white rump and pale grey tail-band form a unique pattern. The underwing-coverts are largely black, recalling the longer-billed Hudsonian Godwit (124), but the strongly-contrasted translucent white band across the bases of the primaries, the pale secondaries and leading lesser underwing-coverts, and the grey-tipped tail are distinctive. On the ground, the strong blue-grey legs and straight bill, shortish but fairly heavy, separate it from all similar species. All shanks have brighter legs, are slimmer and more elegant, and have patterned upperparts in all plumages. In winter, Willet is undistinguished dull grey with a broken white eye-ring and small white spot above the lores. Bare parts: Bill blackish-grey, usually with blue-grey base, brightest in winter; straight and fairly heavy. In some, the bill-base is a godwit-like pinkish-brown. Iris brown. Legs blue-grey, often quite bright, strongly built.

VOICE A noisy bird, quick to give its repeated 'kip' or 'wiek' alarm call; the calls increase in frequency and volume as the bird becomes more alarmed. In flight also a triple 'wee-wee-wee', but this is much harsher and less clear than in Greater Yellowlegs, for example. The Willet is named after its familiar call, a musical 'pill-will-willet'.

HABITS When breeding, eastern Willets are associated with short or patchy saltmarsh vegetation, and are essentially coastal; mid-western individuals occupy lakes and ponds of a wide range of salinity, but most are in the more alkaline habitats. In winter, both races are found on or near the ocean shore. They are versatile feeders and may be found on salt-

marshes, mudflats, sandy beaches or in rocky zones; sometimes feed on wet grassland. The steady walk is Redshank-like. In addition to pecking items from the surface, they frequently probe and may stalk larger prey in the water; small fiddler crabs are often taken. Strongly territorial throughout the year, but often forms loose breeding colonies or wintering groups. Has *Tringa*-like display flight on stiffly-held, downcurved wings; ground displays feature the underwing prominently. Some individuals are approachable, but generally they are of nervous disposition. Those feeding on the upper reaches of salt-marshes are often the first birds to utter alarm calls (as is Redshank in Eurasia).

MOVEMENTS Northern breeders are strongly migratory, but those breeding around the Gulf of Mexico and the Caribbean are probably fairly sedentary. The most northerly breeding areas are occupied by late Apr, but many adults depart again in June-July before the young have fledged. Eastern birds typically shift southwards along the Atlantic seaboard and into the Caribbean, some reaching N Brazil. Western birds migrate mostly to the Pacific coast from Oregon to N Peru, including Galapagos, but some enter the Caribbean and have reached Surinam. Vagrant to S British Columbia, Hudson Bay, Bermuda, once to Alaska (two, Aug 1961), and recently to the Azores (long dead, Mar 1979) and Finland (Sept 1983). There is also an old undated specimen from France, and other unconfirmed European records.

DESCRIPTION Breeding: Head pale grey, streaked brown; whitish area above lores together with narrow whitish eye-ring gives a spectacled appearance. Dark brownish line across the lores, but eye-stripe is indistinct behind eye. Chin is white. Neck, mantle, scapulars and tertials are grey-brown, barred whitish-buff and dark brown to a variable extent. Bases of tail feathers and uppertail-coverts form a squarish white rump-patch; central five pairs of tail feathers darkish but variably marked, outer pair whitish. Primary coverts black, bases of primaries white but tips black. Outer secondaries with little blackish-grey on tips, but essentially white. Greater, median and lesser coverts are mostly grey. Under-wing white, except for greyish lesser coverts, and black median and greater coverts, primary coverts, primary tips and axillaries. Underparts whitish, variably spotted on breast or irregularly barred brown on flanks. Rear belly whitish. **Non-breeding:** As breeding, but all upperparts almost plain pale grey, with mantle, coverts and scapulars narrowly fringed paler grey or white. Central tail feathers uniform grey. Underparts white, washed grey on throat, breast and flanks. **Juvenile:** As non-breeding, but feathers of mantle, coverts, scapulars and tertials all grey-brown with dark subterminal bar and quite broad buff fringes; larger feathers are also notched with buff. The inner 6 primaries are tipped white. Breast slightly browner than on adult.

AGE/SEX Most juvenile feathers are replaced by mid-winter, but the primaries are retained throughout the first year and become very worn. Females are larger on average, but otherwise the sexes are similar.

RACES Two: nominate *semipalmatus* ('Eastern Willet': coastal E North America south to N Mexico, also Bahamas, Greater Antilles and Los Roques Is. off Venezuela), and *inornatus* ('Western Willet': prairies of SW Canada and NW USA). Plumages distinct only when breeding: *inornatus* is larger and breeding plumage is paler; flank barring is indistinct, and central tail feathers are not barred as in nominate race but almost unmarked. There is, however, much individual variation.

MEASUREMENTS Length 330-410 mm (14½"). Wing 186-222 mm; bill 50-67 mm; tarsus 50-70 mm; tail 66-88 mm. Individuals smaller than wing 206 mm, bill 57 mm, tarsus 61 mm are almost certainly of the nominate race; those larger than wing 209 mm, bill 59 mm, tarsus 63 mm almost certainly *inornatus*. Many individuals fall in the overlap zone and are not racially identifiable on measurements.

REFERENCES Stenzel *et al*. (1976), Burger and Shisler (1978), Sordahl (1979), Howe (1982).

147 TEREK SANDPIPER *Xenus cinereus*   Plate 59

The only short-legged wader with a long upcurved bill. In many ways, a particularly charismatic wader.

IDENTIFICATION Attention is often first drawn by the amazingly active feeding habits of this bird; typically, it moves much faster than the calidrids and *Tringa* species among which it usually feeds, with abrupt changes of direction. In all plumages, the pale brownish-grey upperparts, head and breast-patches recall the smaller Common Sandpiper (148), but Terek is larger, deeper-chested and paler, with conspicuous orangey legs and a long, evenly-upcurved bill. At closer ranges, a blackish patch can be seen at the carpal joint of the folded wing and, for most of year, an irregular blackish line down the centre of each set of scapulars. In flight, pattern of black/grey/black/white across the inner half of the wing is diagnostic, as is the combination of a bold white trailing edge and a grey rump and tail. Only the tips of the toes protrude beyond the tail. Wing-beats are rather shallow and flicking. **Bare parts:** Bill blackish, usually with a small area of dull orange at base. Iris brown. Legs short (tarsus obviously shorter than bill), bright orange or orange-yellow, sometimes duller orange or greenish-yellow.

VOICE Typical flight note a sharp fluty 'twit-wit-wit-wit', recalling Common Sandpiper and Whimbrel (129); each syllable rises slightly in pitch. Also 'wit-e-wit', 'tuu-du' and a softer 'hu-hu-hu'. Alarm a sharper 'tu-li'. In display, a long melodious 'prerrr'.

HABITS Breeds May-July along larger rivers and shores of freshwater lakes of USSR and Finland. Winters mainly on tropical coasts, especially muddy bays and estuaries but also on reefs, brackish coastal lagoons and sandbars or mudflats at river mouths. Feeds mainly by chasing mobile food items on the surface; also probes deeply, sometimes with the bill-base pointing in towards the legs. Frequently runs with prey to nearby creek to wash item before it is swallowed. Occasionally feeds in shallow water, using

an avocet-like sideways sweeping action. Scattered when feeding, but forms communal roosts. Usually found in small numbers in large feeding flocks or roosts of other species such as Red-necked and Little Stints (192, 193), Curlew Sandpiper (205) and Redshank (137). Commonly perches at roost on mangrove branches, or partly-submerged posts or breakwaters, in Australia often with Grey-tailed Tattler (150).

MOVEMENTS Leaves breeding grounds from late July and returns during May. Numbers breeding in Finland have increased since 1950, and migrants are now more frequent in W Europe and W Africa. There are isolated winter records from S England (Nov 1973-May 1974) and Tunisia (Jan 1975). Many non-breeders remain on wintering grounds all year. In New Zealand first found in 1951, but now annual in small numbers. Common in New Guinea, E Indonesia and tropical Australia; only a vagrant to Tasmania. Vagrant to W and S Alaska in spring, sometimes in flocks.

DESCRIPTION Breeding: Whitish supercilium is obscure and does not extend much beyond the eye. Dark lores (variably conspicuous) and narrow dark line behind the eye. Upperparts grey-brown, all feathers with narrow blackish shaft-streaks; on the scapulars, the shaft-streaks are broad and conspicuous, forming long blackish lines (some of the small scapulars may be almost entirely black). Some individuals also show conspicuous blackish wedges in the centres of the mantle feathers. Rump, uppertail-coverts and tail often slightly paler grey than mantle and scapulars, with whitish tips when fresh. Longest uppertail-coverts show some blackish barring. Median coverts grey-brown, slightly mottled; lesser coverts blackish-brown, all but innermost primaries and their coverts blackish. Inner 4 primaries show narrow white tip. Secondaries blackish-brown,

broadly tipped white. Underparts white, but with a grey wash across the breast almost forming lateral breast-patches; the wash is very pale in the centre, but finely streaked with brown at the sides. Underwing white, but with grey-brown centres to the lesser coverts. **Non-breeding:** Upperparts a paler brownish- or sandy-grey, still finely streaked but lacking obvious scapular lines on most individuals. Breast markings are paler, with poorly-defined streaking. **Juvenile:** Like breeding plumage in pattern, but slightly darker grey-brown. Coverts and tertials are grey, with obscure subterminal bar and pale cinnamon-buff fringe.
AGE/SEX Some juvenile coverts and tertials are retained to Oct, and on most are still visible to Dec.

In late winter many juveniles moult the outer 4 or 5 primaries, and thus show a contrast between worn inner primaries and fresh outers; this contrast may be visible throughout the first summer. Females average slightly larger than males, but there are no consistent differences between the sexes.
RACES Geographical variation is slight, involving relative lengths of wing, bill and tarsus, and not yet understood.
MEASUREMENTS Length 220-250 mm (9¼"). Wing 126-142 mm; bill 39-52 mm; tarsus 26-32 mm; tail 47-57 mm.
REFERENCES Hosking and Ferguson-Lees (1959), Winkler (1980).

148 COMMON SANDPIPER *Actitis hypoleucos*   Plate 60

A familiar species of a variety of wetland habitats in the Old World. This species and Spotted Sandpiper (149), its Nearctic relative, share an extremely odd mode of flight.

IDENTIFICATION At rest, easily distinguished from all similar species except Spotted Sandpiper by its bobbing walk, short legs, and pattern of brown upperparts and patches on the sides of the upper breast. The lower breast is white, extending upwards as a white 'peak' between the breast-patch and the carpal area of the folded wing. Best distinguished from Green Sandpiper (143) at long range by smaller size, by paler upperparts contrasting less with the white belly, by shorter and paler legs, and by the white peak. Similar in size to some calidrids, but easily distinguished by almost constant bobbing of rear half of body (teetering), and by plumage pattern which resembles only the much smaller Temminck's Stint (194). In flight, easily distinguished from all other waders except Spotted Sandpiper by level flight, usually low over the water, in which wingbeats are spasmodic: each downbeat is suddenly curtailed just below the horizontal, and there are short glides on down-bowed wings between groups of flickering shallow wingbeats. Differs from Spotted Sandpiper in browner upperparts, contrasting more strongly with the white flanks and belly, duller greyish or straw-coloured legs (not usually yellowish), less conspicuous eye-ring, and longer tail extending well beyond folded wings; never shows spotted underparts or a bicoloured bill. In juvenile plumage, tertials of Spotted are normally plain except at the extreme tip, while in Common the tertial edges are strongly marked. In flight, white wingbar is conspicuous along the full length of the secondaries, while in Spotted the narrow white bases to the inner secondaries are obscured by the dark greater coverts. **Bare parts:** Bill short and straight, fairly deep at base; mainly dark brown, but with some ill-defined dull greenish or brownish at the base. Iris brown. Legs somewhat variable in colour, from greyish-olive to dull yellowish-brown like dead straw (rarely, a clearer yellow).
VOICE Noisy when breeding and on migration, but single birds are often rather silent. Flight call consists of penetrating thin piping notes 'tsee-wee-wee', typically given in a descending series; the typical call can be readily distinguished from that of Spotted, but there is some overlap between the two species. The

song, often heard in winter quarters or on migration, is a repeated, rising 'kittie-needie'.
HABITS Breeds Apr-July in vicinity of water, in a variety of habitat types including rivers (usually stony and fast-flowing), small pools, lakesides and sheltered sea-coasts. Nests on the ground, sometimes some distance from water among trees or shrubs. Has apparently bred in E Africa. On migration and in winter, found singly or in small parties in virtually all types of wetland habitat where waders occur, including ocean beaches, estuaries, and inland waters such as ponds and riverbanks, sometimes in urban or forested areas, but tends to avoid areas used by more gregarious species. Occasionally strays from water's edge to feed on grassland or along roadsides. Feeding action is slow and deliberate; teeters constantly, especially on landing. Perches freely on posts and waterside trees; often roosts on moored boats. Sometimes gathers in flocks, rarely of up to 200, before leaving on migration at dusk. When flying high or in flocks, may abandon its unusual mode of flight and resemble a small calidrid.
MOVEMENTS Southward migration begins in late June. Some birds winter well to the north in British Isles and Japan, but many reach the tips of the southern continents. There are relatively few New Zealand records (currently seven from North Island, two South Island). Vagrants regularly reach W Alaska in spring and autumn. One record from Hawaii, and also recorded on Amsterdam I. in the Southern Ocean.
DESCRIPTION Breeding: Crown, nape, hindneck and mantle greenish-brown, faintly glossy, with fine dark brown shaft-streaks. Indistinct whitish supercilium and eye-ring. Indistinct eye-stripe from bill to rear of ear-coverts. Scapulars, tertials, wing-coverts, rump and uppertail as mantle but, in addition to shaft-streaks, feathers show well-spaced irregular dark brown bars and a narrow buffish-brown tip when fresh. Greater coverts and outermost primary coverts broadly tipped white. Flight feathers dark brown, with white wingbar at bases of secondaries and on inner webs of all but outermost large primary, and white trailing edge formed by tips of secondaries and inner primaries. Wingbar and trailing edge may meet across

inner webs of inner secondaries. Central tail feathers as large scapulars in pattern, others progressively paler brown and with broader white tip; outer two pairs show extensive white along outer webs. Neck and breast white, lightly streaked with brown; sides of breast strongly infused greenish-brown to form breast-patches. Chin white, but throat lightly streaked. Belly, flanks and undertail white. Underwing strongly patterned brown and white. Coverts and axillaries are white, except for median coverts and greater primary coverts which are brown with narrow white tips. Flight feathers are brown underneath, except for wingbar and trailing edge which are clearly defined. **Non-breeding:** As breeding, except that shaft-streaks and barring are much less evident on upperparts, and neck and breast are virtually unstreaked. Coverts show narrow buffish tips when fresh. **Juvenile:** As non-breeding on head, breast, mantle and scapulars, except for initial faint buff fringes. Coverts (also

uppertail-coverts and central tail feathers) are strongly barred with buffish-brown at the tip. Tertials show a buffish fringe and dark brown submarginal notching along their entire outer edges.
AGE/SEX A difficult bird to age, since adults grow brown-barred wing-coverts during the autumn moult; juveniles are thus easily identified only early on. Further, the young mostly undergo a complete wing moult during Jan-Apr; only those retaining some juvenile inner primaries or secondaries can be identified as first-years when back on the breeding grounds. Female averages slightly larger, but no plumage differences are known.
RACES No geographical variation is known.
MEASUREMENTS Length 190-210 mm (8"). Wing 105-119 mm; bill 22-28 mm; tarsus 22-25 mm; tail 51-58 mm.
REFERENCES Pearson (1977), Holland *et al.* (1982).

149 SPOTTED SANDPIPER *Actitis macularia*   Plate 60

A common American wader, highly distinctive by virtue of its breeding plumage and its unusual way of flying. The curious jerky flight is shared by the Palaearctic Common Sandpiper (148), its close relative.

IDENTIFICATION Bold thrush-like blackish spotting on white underparts is diagnostic when present. Birds out of breeding plumage are easily separated from all species except Common Sandpiper (which see) by short legs, frequent bobbing of rear half of body (teetering), and pattern of greyish-brown upperparts and patches on the sides of the upper breast. The white 'peak' between the breast-patches and the carpal area of the folded wing, smaller size, paler legs and much paler upperparts are the best distinctions from Solitary and Green Sandpipers (144, 143). Not likely to be confused with calidrids owing to its almost constant teetering, but the plumage pattern resembles that of Temminck's Stint (194). In flight, note the white wingbar, almost plain rump and tail, and extremely odd wing-action. Differs from Common Sandpiper in its greyer upperparts, contrasting less strongly with the white flanks and belly, brighter legs (often yellow), faintly more obvious eye-ring, and shorter tail extending only a short distance beyond the folded wings. In breeding plumage, easily separated by blackish spotting (variable in extent) and by bicoloured bill. Juveniles show bolder barring on the coverts, but almost plain tertials, usually barred only at the tip; in Common, the tertials are notched along their entire length. In flight, far less white is visible on the inner secondaries and the outer edges of the tail; the wingbar is hardly evident on the innermost 3 secondaries, a clear distinction from Common in which the wingbar and white trailing edge converge across these feathers (on some the inner secondary is wholly white). **Bare parts:** Bill short and straight, fairly deep at base; mainly dark brown with some ill-defined dull greenish or brownish at base, but when breeding becomes quite bright pinkish or orange with a sharply-defined blackish tip. Iris brown. Legs variable in colour, from greyish-olive to fairly bright yellow-ochre, usually a dull yellow; on breeding birds, the legs become dull pinkish-brown.
VOICE Typical flight call is a series of similar but

faintly rising 'peet' notes; this call is readily distinguished from Common Sandpiper's descending series of more evenly-pitched notes. All calls have a thin, piping quality virtually identical to that of Common, and some calls are apparently common to both species. Lower-pitched than similar calls of Solitary Sandpiper.
HABITS Nesting habitats similar to Common Sandpiper's but differs in its mating system. Most breeding groups show polyandry: the females mate with several males, and lay several clutches of eggs over a short period (the eggs are smaller in proportion to the body size than those of Common Sandpiper). Habits on migration and in winter are similar to Common Sandpiper's.
MOVEMENTS Starts moving south in June. Some winter as far north as British Columbia, but the main range lies between S USA and N Chile and Argentina, including the West Indies and, in most years, Galapagos. Vagrant to Spitsbergen, W Europe, East Germany, Azores, Madeira and Tristan da Cunha, also E Siberia, and Marshall Is. in the W Pacific. Nested in Scotland in 1975.
DESCRIPTION Breeding: Crown, nape, hindneck, mantle, scapulars and tertials much as Common Sandpiper, but with shaft-streaking less evident and dark barring rather broader. Coverts as on Common Sandpiper, except that greater coverts lack white tips and the outer primary coverts show only narrow white tips. Secondaries differ in that white trailing edge is much narrower on inner feathers, and wingbar is visible beyond the greater coverts only on the outer secondaries; usually, wingbar and trailing edge are separated on the inner secondaries by at least 10 mm. Whitish is present on the outer edges of the outer one or two pairs of tail feathers. Underparts from chin and cheeks to undertail boldly spotted blackish on white background; breast-patches largely absent. Axillaries unspotted white; underwing pattern as on Common Sandpiper. **Non-breeding:**

Upperparts as breeding, except that shaft-streaks and barring are much less evident. Underparts white, with patches of grey-brown suffusion at sides of breast. Coverts show narrow buffish tips when fresh. **Juvenile:** As non-breeding, but coverts are strongly barred with buffish-brown at the tip. Other contour feathers of upperparts show narrow buff fringes when fresh, but these wear off rapidly to leave a rather isolated area of barring on the coverts of the folded wing. Tertials are plain grey-brown, except for a buffish tip and some subterminal brown barring.

AGE/SEX A difficult species to age (see Common Sandpiper). Females average slightly larger, and tend to show larger and blacker spots in breeding plumage. First-year females, however, may resemble males.

RACES Western individuals ('*rava*') tend to be greyer and less glossy above and with heavier and blacker spotting below, but most authorities regard the species as monotypic.

MEASUREMENTS Length 180-200 mm (7½"). Wing 99-113 mm; bill 21-27 mm; tarsus 21-25 mm; tail 44-53 mm.

REFERENCES Hays (1972), Wilson (1976), Oring *et al.* (1983).

150 GREY-TAILED TATTLER *Heteroscelus brevipes*   Plate 61

Other names: Polynesian or Siberian Tattler, Grey-rumped Sandpiper
This species and Wandering Tattler (151), once considered conspecific, are distinct from other waders in their plain slate-grey upperparts, long grey wings and tail, and short yellow legs.

IDENTIFICATION Resembles a 'shank' of the genus *Tringa* in build and proportions, except for short legs (tarsus shorter than bill) and long wings and tail; closest to Redshank (137) in size. Readily distinguished from all waders except Wandering Tattler by plain slate-grey upperparts, including entire wings and tail, well-defined white supercilium and dark lores, slate-grey underwing, and yellow legs. Differs from Wandering in breeding plumage in that dark grey barring on the underparts is finer and confined to the breast, flanks and the edge of the undertail-coverts; belly and vent are unbarred. Juvenile differs in being more spotted on upperparts and on tail. Grey-tailed is always a slightly paler bird and has a faintly broader supercilium. Uppertail-coverts show faint whitish barring. Also differs at all times in its typical flight call, the length of the nasal groove on the bill (visible only in close telescope views), and the pattern of scaling on the legs (useful only in the hand). Folded wings normally fall level with the tail-tip at rest. There is considerable overlap in non-breeding distributions, but Wandering is more typically a rocky-coast bird while Grey-tailed also frequents beaches and mudflats and sometimes even inland sites. **Bare parts:** Bill blackish, with yellowish basal third of lower mandible; nasal groove (the depression along upper mandible which includes the nostril opening) ends more than 17 mm from the bill-tip, at a point only just over half-way down the bill. Iris dark brown. Shortish, quite thick, bright yellow or yellow-ochre legs; the scales on the legs are scutellated, that is they form a laddered pattern, overlapping like tiles on a roof.

VOICE Usual call is a disyllabic, upslurred whistle 'tu-whip' recalling Ringed Plover (86) but with the second syllable rising to a higher pitch. Also a sharp monosyllable in alarm, and a strident 'klee-klee' or 'weet-eet'. Occasionally gives calls similar to those of Wandering, but normal calls are quite distinct.

HABITS Breeds along stony riverbeds in the mountains of NE Siberia, present late May-early Sept. It was not until 1959 that the first nest was found, and the breeding range is still poorly known. Perches freely in trees in the nesting area, and occasionally nests in old tree-nests of other birds. On migration, normally coastal on rocky, sandy or muddy areas but may occur inland on paddyfields. In winter, found on coasts and estuaries, usually where large expanses of mangrove-backed mud or sandflats are exposed at low tide, also on rocky coasts. Flight fast and apparently effortless, with flicking beats of long wings. Usually feeds singly or in loose groups; forms communal (often single-species) roosts at high tide, often perched on mangroves, breakwaters or causeways. Most allow close approach. Sometimes crouches rather than flies in response to danger. Walks with bobbing and teetering movements like those of Common and Spotted Sandpipers (148, 149).

MOVEMENTS Most leave breeding grounds during Aug. Wintering grounds are mainly on continental coasts and shores of larger islands where mudflats are available. There are, however, exceptional winter records from around hot springs in Kamchatka. First-year birds often stay well south during the southern winter, while the bulk of the population moves northward in Apr and May. Regular in small numbers in Tasmania and New Zealand. Vagrant to W Alaska north to Point Barrow, particularly in autumn, SE Alaska (once) and once to sewage-ponds 80 km inland from Los Angeles, California.

DESCRIPTION Breeding: Entire upperparts including crown, hindneck, wings and tail plain slate-grey (slightly tinged brownish), relieved only by faint whitish barring on uppertail-coverts and narrow white tips to the outer greater coverts and inner primary coverts. In very fresh plumage there are narrow pale tips to most feathers of the upperparts, but these wear off rapidly. The greater primary coverts and the outer 5 primaries are a darker grey, almost blackish. Head shows white supercilia which almost meet across forehead, dark grey lores and narrow post-ocular eye-stripe, and small clear white chin-patch. Ear-coverts, cheeks, the rear of supercilium, and sides and front of neck are white streaked with grey. Breast and upper flanks are white, with fairly narrow V-shaped grey bars; sometimes a few grey bars are visible on the sides of the undertail-coverts. Belly, lower flanks, vent and most of the undertail clear white. Axillaries and underwing-coverts dark grey with narrow whitish tips; underside of flight feathers is slightly paler and browner than the coverts. **Non-breeding:** As breeding, but underparts lack barring. Sides of neck and breast are suffused an even slate-grey, forming breast-patches which join only narrowly in the centre; chin, throat, front of neck, lower belly, vent and undertail-coverts are white. **Juvenile:** Underparts as non-breeding, except that breast and flanks are smudged and barred with grey rather than evenly washed. Wing-coverts, tertials and scapulars show whitish (initially buff-tinged) spotting and tipping. Tail shows whitish barring towards tip, particularly on central feathers.

AGE/SEX Spotted coverts of juveniles are usually replaced by about Dec. First-winter birds usually replace the outer 4 or 5 primaries (sometimes more) during Jan-Aug; thus during May-Sept worn primaries, or a contrast between worn inners and fresh outers, indicate a first-year bird. Those remaining south during their first summer do not attain full breeding plumage: the grey breast and flanks are often faintly vermiculated like those of the juvenile. Females average larger than males, but no plumage differences are known between the sexes.

RACES No geographical variation is known.

MEASUREMENTS Length 240-270 mm (10"). Wing 154-175 mm; bill 34-42 mm; tarsus 29-34 mm.

REFERENCES Neufeldt *et al.* (1961), Gibson (1978), Andreev (1980a).

151 WANDERING TATTLER *Heteroscelus incanus* Plate 61

An Alaskan breeder with a remarkable oceanic migration which takes it to some of the remotest islands in the Pacific. Forms a superspecies with the very similar Grey-tailed Tattler (150) of Siberia.

IDENTIFICATION A plain dark grey, 'shank'-like wader with short yellow legs and long wings and tail, barred below in breeding plumage. Distinguishing this bird in the field from Grey-tailed Tattler, out of breeding plumage, is possible only if diagnostic calls are heard or the longer nasal groove is seen. Additional pointers may be the pattern of the rump and uppertail-covert feathers (rarely visible except in the hand), whether the wings extend beyond the tail, and habitat. Wandering sometimes shows narrow whitish tips to the uppertail-coverts, but not faint barring as in most Grey-tailed. The folded wings normally extend a short distance beyond the tail-tip. Normally occurs only on rocky coasts and reefs or adjacent sandy or stony beaches, whereas Grey-tailed also occurs regularly on estuarine mudflats. Wandering averages about 5% larger. In the hand, the reticulated tarsus is diagnostic. In breeding plumage, grey bars on underparts are broader and cover almost the entire underside, leaving only a small clear white patch on the belly. Moulting birds may show a larger white belly, but wide bars and the presence of strong barring on the central feathers of the belly or undertail would confirm this species. Juveniles are plainer than those of Grey-tailed, less heavily spotted on upperparts and tail. **Bare parts:** Bill blackish, with yellowish wash to basal third or more of the lower mandible; nasal groove extends to within 15 mm of the tip, and ends almost three-quarters of the way down the bill. Iris dark brown. Shortish, quite thick, bright yellow or yellow-ochre legs; the scales on the tarsi are reticulated, that is they are non-overlapping and form a flush surface with a net-like pattern.

VOICE Characteristic flight call is a plaintive, whistled, rippling trill, usually of six to ten notes all on the same pitch, accelerating but with decreasing volume: a ringing, rather hollow-sounding 'pew-tu-tu-tu-tu-tu'. This is quite unlike Grey-tailed's usual plover-like upslurred whistle.

HABITS Similar to Grey-tailed, except for narrower range of winter habitats. Nests by mountain streams in parts of Alaska and, probably, extreme E Siberia where may overlap with Grey-tailed. The nest-site is a simple hollow in riverside gravel, or a more complex structure built of roots and twigs. Outside the breeding season, found almost exclusively on rocky coasts and reefs, sometimes adjacent beaches or freshwater pools; on migration, occasionally appears well inland in W USA and Canada. Occurs rarely at coastal estuaries. When feeding, bobs and teeters almost continuously like Spotted and Common Sandpipers (149, 148). Usually found singly or in small groups when feeding, but forms communal roosts. Often allows close approach. May crouch rather than fly in response to danger. Flight is fast and effortless, with flicking beats of long wings.

MOVEMENTS Present on breeding grounds late May-Aug. Southward migration is probably partly oceanic towards Hawaii, but many birds move along outer coast and islands of British Columbia. Winters on Pacific coast of America from central California south to Ecuador, and on Pacific islands west to the Great Barrier Reef in Australia, where it is found in small numbers among the Grey-tailed. Vagrant Manitoba, Ontario (probably) and Peru; regular in small numbers in Japan (on migration) and N New Zealand, vagrant Chatham Is. First-years often remain south during their first northern summer.

DESCRIPTION Breeding: Entire upperparts including crown and hindneck, wings and tail plain slate-grey, relieved only by very narrow white tips to uppertail-coverts, outer greater coverts and inner primary coverts. The greater primary coverts and the outer 5 primaries are rather darker grey than the rest of the wing. Head shows narrow white supercilia, dark lores, and narrow eye-stripe behind the eye. Ear-coverts, cheeks, the rear of the supercilium, chin and throat, and sides and front of neck are white streaked with grey. Rest of underparts, except for small area of clear white around central belly and vent, strongly marked with V-shaped dark grey bars. The feathers of the sides of the breast and upper flanks show more grey than white. Axillaries and underwing-coverts dark grey, with narrow whitish tips; underside of flight feathers is slightly paler than the underwing-coverts. **Non-breeding:** As breeding, except that the barring is lost from underparts, which become plain slate-grey except for whitish chin, throat, lower belly, vent and central undertail-coverts. **Juvenile:** Underparts as non-breeding, but grey of breast and flanks is faintly smudged and barred rather than an even wash. Wing-coverts, tertials and scapulars show small whitish tips and spotting, initially pale buffish. Central tail feathers also show some tiny whitish spotting along the edges.

AGE/SEX Spotted coverts and pale-edged tertials of juvenile are often completely replaced by Jan. Most juveniles moult the outer 4-5 primaries between Jan and Aug; birds with worn primaries, or a contrast between fresh outers and worn inners, can be identified as first-year. Those remaining south attain only

a partial breeding plumage: as in juveniles, the breast and flanks are often faintly vermiculated rather than evenly washed with grey. Females are larger than males on average, but no plumage differences are known.

RACES No geographical variation is known.

MEASUREMENTS Length 260-290 mm (10¾"). Wing 163-186 mm; bill 35-43 mm; tarsus 30-37 mm; tail 71-80 mm.

REFERENCES Weeden (1965), Sibson (1965).

152 TUAMOTU SANDPIPER *Prosobonia cancellata*   **Plate 56**

A most peculiar wading bird, perhaps related to the tattlers (150, 151). Former range spanned 3700 km of the central Pacific, but recently recorded from just five small atolls in a small area of the Tuamotu archipelago; it is in grave danger of extinction.

IDENTIFICATION A very small, dark brown bird with a short thin bill, unlikely to be mistaken for any other wader. The now-extinct White-winged Sandpiper (153) of Tahiti and Moorea was similar, but with a white chin, small white spot behind the eye, white fringes to the lesser coverts, and unbarred russet underparts. **Bare parts:** Bill black, short, slender and sharply pointed like that of an insectivorous passerine. Iris dark brown. Leg colour greyish or yellowish-brown; hind toe is unusually long for a wader.

VOICE A soft high-pitched whistle is the only call described.

HABITS Seen among vegetation as well as on the open ocean shore, lagoon beaches, and areas of bare gravel. Nest is constructed of bits of shell, coral debris and fragments of vegetation. Breeding was at a peak in mid-Aug on one island, but it is not clear whether the season is synchronised on different islands. One nest found in May on another atoll held two eggs. Food is chiefly insects, but plant matter is also taken. Populations have fared best on islands lacking permanent human population and free from introduced predators such as rats and feral cats.

MOVEMENTS Probably entirely sedentary, but recent records on Nakutavake and Rangiroa are the first from those atolls and may represent visitors from other islands. Apparently still present on Maturei-Vavao,

Pinaki, and Marutea du Sud.

DESCRIPTION All plumages: Crown and hindneck dark brown, flecked paler; lores brown; narrow creamy supercilia; ear-coverts dull brownish. Upperparts dark brown, with obscured whitish-brown bars; dull buffish spots and fringes on coverts. Greater coverts very narrowly tipped pale grey-brown, but not forming a noticeable wingbar. Tail dark brown, barred or notched with buffish-brown; feathers rather broad. Underparts pale creamy, usually unmarked on chin but rest of neck and throat spotted or streaked brown; irregular brown bars on breast become larger and broader along the flanks; belly is sometimes unbarred. Undertail-coverts strongly barred. Underwing and axillaries dull brownish-grey. The wing is strongly rounded (wingpoint 8=9, 10th -1 mm, 7th -2 mm).

AGE/SEX Considerable variations in coloration of the plumage occur within a single locality, but these are not known to be related to age, sex or time of year.

RACES No geographical variation is known.

MEASUREMENTS Length 155-165 mm (6¼"). Wing 103-112 mm; bill 15-16 mm; tarsus 22-26 mm; tail 47-50 mm.

REFERENCES Zusi and Jehl (1970), Lacan and Mougin (1974), Temple (1979).

153 WHITE-WINGED SANDPIPER   **No colour plate**
Prosobonia leucoptera

This is a Polynesian species known only from a handful of specimens, of which only one still exists. The species was discovered on Tahiti in 1773 during Captain Cook's voyages, but became extinct during the nineteenth century.

IDENTIFICATION A small sandpiper similar to Tuamotu Sandpiper (152) in structure, but with uniform dark brownish upperparts, reddish underparts, a tiny white spot above and behind the eye, a white chin, and a white band across the leading lesser coverts. Tuamotu Sandpiper has strongly-barred underparts and uniformly dark wings. **Bare parts:** Bill black. Iris blackish. Legs greenish.

VOICE Nothing is known.

HABITS Nothing is known of its behaviour, except that it was said to occur near small streams.

MOVEMENTS Unknown, but presumably sedentary.

DESCRIPTION Only specimen: Crown blackish, sides of face and hindneck browner, tinged russet around eye, on cheeks and above lores; small white mark above and behind the eye. Chin and throat buffish-white; rest of underparts russet. Axillaries sooty-brown, underwing-coverts brown with some white on leading lessers. Upperparts and wings uniformly sooty-brown except for russet rump and a narrow band of white across the leading lesser coverts.

AGE/SEX Nothing is known.

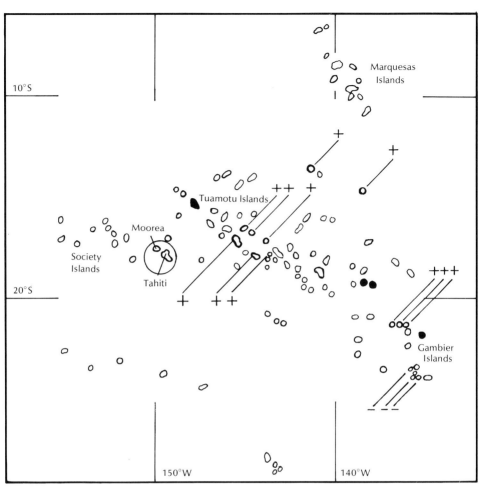

Recorded distribution of the extinct White-winged Sandpiper (153) and the endangered Tuamotu Sandpiper (152) in the south-central Pacific Ocean

Key: **Tuamotu Sandpiper** filled islands = recent records;

+=islands where recorded but status not known;

−=islands where it has disappeared

NB: There are also old records of Tuamotu Sandpiper from Christmas Island (Line Islands), 2°N 157°W

White-winged Sandpiper islands where recorded are circled.

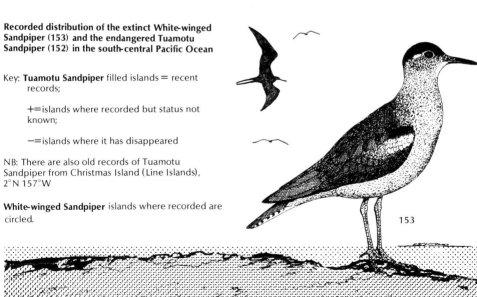

RACES Two: nominate (Tahiti) and *ellisi* (Moorea, 16 km northwest of Tahiti). The only specimen of *ellisi* is now lost. It did not differ sufficiently from *leucoptera* to be treated as a separate species.

MEASUREMENTS The single remaining specimen has wings measuring 111 mm and 113 mm, and a bill of 20 mm.
REFERENCES Zusi and Jehl (1970).

154 RUDDY TURNSTONE *Arenaria interpres* Plate 62

Other name: Turnstone
Breeds only in the Arctic, but may be found as a non-breeder on coasts almost throughout the world.

IDENTIFICATION A stocky, medium-sized wader with short orange-red legs and short, slightly-uptilted, wedge-shaped bill. Unmistakable in breeding plumage, with black markings on white head and bright chestnut on scapulars and coverts. In flight, shows a striking dark-and-white pattern on upperparts, shared only with Black Turnstone (155); has white back, blackish rump, white uppertail-coverts, and a broad black subterminal tail-band. Wings show a white triangle at base, plus a long white wingbar. Worn juveniles in particular may be confused with Black Turnstone, but note that chin is white (occasionally flecked dark), while that of Black Turnstone is always dark, and that legs are orange. **Bare parts:** Bill black, tinged pale on base of lower mandible. Iris dark brown. Legs orange-red, brighter when breeding; in juveniles initially yellow-brown, becoming increasingly orange.
VOICE Typical call a clear, rapid, rolled staccato 'trik-tuk-tuk-tuk' or shorter 'tuk-e-tuk'. When flushed, may give a short, sharp 'chick-ik' or a monosyllabic 'kuu'. Feeding birds have a low 'tuk' contact call, often rapidly repeated. On breeding grounds, also utters a long rolling rattle.
HABITS Breeds late May-early Aug on the coastal plain or lowlands around the Arctic Ocean, extending farther south on Baltic coasts than elsewhere. Outside the breeding season entirely coastal, except for a scattering inland especially on migration: found on most biologically-productive rocky or stony coasts which do not freeze, and also on sandy beaches with washed-up seaweed or where reefs are exposed at low tide. A relatively tame bird with fascinating feeding behaviour. The strong neck and bill are used to flick seaweed sideways or turn over small stones; food items underneath (such as small crustaceans) are pecked at or chased. In sandy areas, often digs substantial holes. Frequently scavenges, for example on items made available by oystercatchers, and may eat such items as coconuts and carrion. Walks with a rolling gait, but runs well. Flight is strong and direct, usually low, with rather stiff and shallow wingbeats. Flocks fly in tight groups when moving locally, but in loose lines when migrating.
MOVEMENTS Essentially moves south from breeding grounds, but birds from Greenland and NE Canada cross the Atlantic to W Europe and NW Africa. Palaearctic breeders mostly migrate farther south to tropical or subtropical coasts, including many Indian Ocean islands. Nearctic race *morinella* migrates to the Pacific islands and South America. Most one-year-olds remain south of the breeding grounds. Regular on Auckland and Chatham Is. Vagrants have reached Amsterdam I., St Paul I. and the Crozet Is. in the Southern Ocean.

DESCRIPTION Breeding: Head pattern individually variable, but is white with black line from forehead, through eye and then vertically downwards to neck. Crown variably streaked black and buff. Black breast-band covers front of neck and upper breast; rest of underparts white. Upperparts show strong contrast between chestnut-orange patches on coverts, scapulars and tertials, and blackish-brown tertials. Inner wing-coverts and bases of tertials form a triangular white patch at the base of each wing. Strong white wingbar is formed by bases of inner primaries, tips of inner primary coverts and all greater coverts, and by bases of secondaries; inner secondaries are wholly white. Tail black, outer five pairs of feathers narrowly tipped white. **Non-breeding:** As breeding, but lacks all chestnut on upperparts. Head smudged brown, darkest where black breeding pattern present; some palish patches above eye and on side of head. Rest of upperparts and breast-band dark slaty-grey with paler edges to feathers. **Juvenile:** As non-breeding, but with much more distinct pale patches on the head and all of the brown-washed dark feathers clearly fringed buffish-white.
AGE/SEX Buff-fringed juvenile wing-coverts and scapulars are much smaller than those of adults, and give a strikingly-scalloped appearance. Buff fringes rapidly fade and abrade, and are difficult to see after Dec. On adults the large, loose scapulars almost entirely overlap the wing-coverts. In the field, sexing of individuals in breeding plumage is sometimes possible but, because of individual variation, is reliable only with breeding pairs. Males tend to show more white and less streaking on the head, a cleaner black breast-band, and brighter chestnut on upperparts; females average fractionally larger.
RACES Two: nominate *interpres* (NE Canada, Palaearctic, Alaska) is slightly larger, and has more dark crown streaking and paler, more orangey colour on scapulars and coverts; *morinella* (SE of Canadian range, west to Alaska) shows a deep chestnut-red colour on coverts and scapulars, more extensively than in the nominate race. In juvenile plumage, *morinella* can show a pale chestnut-buff wash to covert fringes, so appearing warmer and paler than *interpres*. There is a cline in colour in the E Palaearctic.
MEASUREMENTS Length 210-255 mm (9¼"). Wing 145-165 mm (nominate), 141-163 mm (*morinella*); bill 19-25 mm; tarsus 24-28 mm; tail 54-65 mm.
REFERENCES Nettleship (1973), Thompson (1974), Branson *et al.* (1978), Ferns (1978), Groves (1978), Harris (1979).

155 BLACK TURNSTONE *Arenaria melanocephala* Plate 62

A close relative of the Ruddy Turnstone (154) but less migratory and much more restricted in range. It has a remarkable aerial display.

IDENTIFICATION Similar in size and flight pattern to Ruddy Turnstone, but is slightly more heavily built and broader-winged, always lacks chestnut in plumage, has dark legs, and always a dark chin not contrasting with the upper breast. Head is always dark, almost entirely so in non-breeding plumage except for tiny posterior supercilium, while Ruddy always has a white chin. Breeding plumage is stunningly black-and-white. Black or black-spotted breast-band extends farther down onto belly and upper flanks, an easily visible feature when in flight. White wing-bar is broader. Dark legs and bill, and white on back and coverts in flight, quickly distinguish it from Surfbird (186) and Rock Sandpiper (203), which often occur alongside, or vagrant Purple Sandpiper (202). **Bare parts:** Bill as Ruddy Turnstone in shape, but all-dark. Iris dark brown. Legs brownish-black, tinged pinkish or reddish but never as bright as on Ruddy. **VOICE** A trilling 'skirrr', similar to some calls of Ruddy Turnstone but higher-pitched and quite different from Ruddy's usual staccato notes.
HABITS Generally very similar to Ruddy Turnstone. Breeds on the coastal plain of W Alaska, May-July. Display includes dashing zigzag chases, and a display flight in which the male climbs high and dives down like a snipe, producing an audible note from the feather vibrations. At other seasons, found on rocky coasts and offshore islands; sometimes feeds on adjacent sandy beaches or mudflats. Feeding methods similar to Ruddy Turnstone's, although not so well studied. Blends superbly with its usual background of dark rocks. May roost in mixed flocks with Ruddy Turnstone, Surfbird, Rock Sandpiper and American Black Oystercatcher (14).
MOVEMENTS From breeding grounds migrates south along Nearctic Pacific coasts, occasionally as far as Sonora in Mexico. Vagrant inland in westernmost states and provinces, also Yukon Territory and Montana. Recorded west to Wrangel I. in USSR on spring migration. Some non-breeders remain south of breeding grounds all year.
DESCRIPTION Breeding: Slaty-black upperparts and breast contrast with white belly. Head black, with a little whitish streaking on crown and nape, a bold white spot at base of bill, and a small white crescent over eye. Ear-coverts, chin and throat black; sides of breast and lower neck black with feathers neatly tipped white, so appearing white-spotted. Upperparts all slaty-black, but with some scapulars and coverts narrowly edged white. Prominent white wingbar, formed by same feathers as in Ruddy Turnstone but with slightly more extensive white on each. As in Ruddy, white patches on inner wing, back, uppertail-coverts and tips to outer five pairs of tail feathers. Black of breast spreads onto upper belly, and black chevrons extend along flanks under anterior third of closed wing. **Non-breeding:** White spotting on head, nape and sides of breast is lost, so upperparts and breast are more evenly dark. Slightly paler posterior supercilium. White edges remain on some scapulars, tertials and coverts. Dark flank spotting reduced in extent, sometimes absent. **Juvenile:** As non-breeding, but all of blackish feathers tinged brown; most scapulars, tertials and coverts have buffish or buff-white edges and fringes. Breast-band brownish-grey. As in Ruddy Turnstone, the juvenile scapulars and tertials are smaller and neater than those of the adults.
AGE/SEX Following the post-juvenile body moult in Oct-Nov, juveniles cannot be distinguished except in the hand. In breeding plumage, the male tends to have a more distinct black-and-white head and breast pattern, with a larger white spot on the lores, but individual birds are very difficult to sex. Female averages slightly larger.
RACES No geographical variation is known.
MEASUREMENTS Length 220-250 mm (9¼"). Wing 147-162 mm; bill 21-25 mm; tarsus 24-27 mm; tail 59-65 mm.
REFERENCES Gill *et al.* (1983).

156 WILSON'S PHALAROPE *Phalaropus tricolor* Plate 63

The largest and most terrestrial of the phalaropes, wintering not at sea but on fresh and brackish waters in South America. Most unusually, shows seasonal changes in leg colour. Breeding range and extent of vagrancy are currently expanding eastwards.

IDENTIFICATION This is one of the most distinctive small waders, simply identified by unusual behaviour, odd shape, fairly long needle-shaped bill and mainly-whitish plumage. Breeding plumage of female is highly distinctive. Often swims, feeding by picking from the surface; also feeds on mud, when rapid walk and almost frenetic picking action instantly draw attention. Appears small-headed, long-necked and wide-bodied (pot-bellied) compared with other small waders. When swimming, most likely to be confused with Red-necked Phalarope (157), but larger and with a relatively longer and thinner bill. In flight, shows a squarish white rump and no wingbar. Lesser Yellowlegs (142) and Stilt Sandpiper (208) both resemble this species in flight, and to a lesser degree at rest, but have different proportions and behaviour and are not so white below. **Bare parts:** Long, needle-fine, black bill. Iris brown. Legs black during breeding, becoming straw-yellow or dull yellow (rarely bright yellow) June onwards and darkening again Dec-Jan; newly-fledged juveniles have pinkish- or greenish-yellow legs. Toes are not so distinctly lobed as on other phalaropes.
VOICE Rather silent, but a soft grunting 'aangh' is sometimes given in flight. Breeding birds also give repeated 'yna' calls, like tooting a tiny horn.

HABITS Breeds around shallow marshy wetlands on the North American prairies, often in loose groups. Females leave the nesting area usually before the eggs hatch, leaving the male to incubate the eggs and tend the brood. On migration, seen mostly on shallow ponds such as sewage-ponds, saltworks, and flooded fields, sometimes on mudflats. Rarely reported at sea (salt gland, well developed in the other two phalaropes, is rudimentary in this species). Spends Oct-Apr in South America, chiefly on ponds on Argentinian pampas but large flocks also seen on high-altitude lakes. Often very tame.

MOVEMENTS Spring passage in S USA spans late Mar-early June, while return begins in mid-June (mostly females) and continues to early Oct. Occasionally winters as far north as S California and Texas; one winter record from France. A frequent vagrant to W Europe: over 150 records since the first in 1954. There is evidence now for north-south migration of European vagrants, and individuals show remarkable tendency to reappear on migration in exactly the same spot in successive years. Also recorded in Bermuda, Martinique, Falklands, Morocco, Turkey, South Africa, New Zealand and Australia. In mid-Oct 1968, one was found dead on Alexander I., 71° S ; this is the most southerly record of any wader ever.

DESCRIPTION Breeding female: Crown, nape and hindneck pale pearly-grey; white patch above eye; black band from bill through eye and down sides of neck becomes chestnut-red on sides of mantle. Underparts white, with rich orange flush on sides of neck and onto breast. Mantle and coverts clean pale grey, with chestnut-red bands on edges of mantle and another across scapulars. In flight, wing almost uniform grey (no wingbar), tail grey, and rump and uppertail white, showing as a squarish patch. Legs black. **Breeding male:** Pale grey on crown, nape, mantle and scapulars of the female is replaced by blackish-brown, and chestnut-red bands are replaced by duller orange-brown. **Non-breeding:** Upperparts entirely pale ash-grey, underparts and face entirely white; grey band backwards from eye to join grey nape forms a less conspicuous 'phalarope-mark' than on the other species. Legs yellow, often quite bright. **Juvenile:** Upperparts all dark brown, with broad buffish feather edgings giving a scaly appearance. Sides of breast are washed with buff. Legs usually pinkish-yellow.

AGE/SEX Post-juvenile moult is very early in this species, and mantle and scapulars may be completely replaced by pale grey adult-type feathers by mid-Aug. Buff fringes on retained inner median coverts may be visible on birds in the hand until Apr-May. In the breeding season, one-year-olds show very worn primaries and may not attain full breeding plumage. Sexes are easily separable in breeding plumage. Size-dimorphism is marked: females average 9% longer in wing length and 35% heavier in breeding weight; wing length above 130 mm (adults) or 129 mm (juveniles) indicates female, and below these values indicates male.

RACES No geographical variation is known.

MEASUREMENTS Length 220-240 mm (9"). Wing 116-129 mm (males), 129-143 mm (females); bill 27-36 mm; tarsus 29-36 mm; tail 48-58 mm.

REFERENCES Höhn (1967), Johns (1969), Burger and Howe (1975), Howe (1975).

157 RED-NECKED PHALAROPE *Phalaropus lobatus*   Plate 63

Other name: Northern Phalarope

Like the Grey Phalarope (158) a largely marine species, but differs in having overland migration routes. One of the most confiding and approachable of all waders.

IDENTIFICATION Easily identified as a phalarope by small size combined with persistent swimming behaviour. In non-breeding plumages shows the 'phalarope-mark', a blackish mark through and behind the eye. Differs from Grey Phalarope in build by longer, finer bill (lacking lateral expansion), smaller size, and proportionately shorter wings. Differs from Grey and from Wilson's (156) in non-breeding plumage by conspicuous white lines along outer edges of mantle and scapulars (bright orange-buff on juvenile). Breeding plumage shows distinctive red on sides and base of neck, white chin and throat, and golden-buff lines above. Flight pattern of white wingbar and white sides to rump is similar to that of Grey Phalarope, but wingbeats are faster and the flight often more erratic with rapid twists and turns, more like a small calidrid. **Bare parts:** Bill about as long as distance from bill-base to nape, always all-black, needle-fine. Iris brown. Legs blue-grey or grey-black, very short for the size of the bird; toes are distinctly lobed.

VOICE Usual flight call is a single 'twick' or 'clip', lower-pitched than similar call of Grey Phalarope. On breeding grounds, gives a variety of buzzing alarm calls.

HABITS Breeds late May-Aug in freshwater marshes and bogs from sea-level up to at least 1300 m, often a considerable distance from the sea. Where range overlaps with that of Grey Phalarope, favours pools with emergent vegetation. Mating system is monogamous or serially polyandrous (simultaneous polyandry may occur). Female takes no part in incubation or caring for the young. On migration, found on inland lakes, reservoirs and sewage-ponds, and coastal marshes, as well as on the open sea. Winters chiefly at sea in the tropics. In some localities (e.g. W New Britain), makes extensive use of fresh water a short distance inland; also winters in small numbers on E African rift-valley lakes. Highly gregarious when not breeding. At all times remarkably tame and approachable. Feeds chiefly by picking from the water surface or from emergent stones or vegetation. When swimming, course is erratic; often spins repeatedly, rarely up-ends. Exceedingly tame.

MOVEMENTS Some females leave breeding grounds in late June, followed by successful males in late July and juveniles in Aug-early Sept. Migration routes are partly overland; large flocks use favoured lakes as staging-posts, e.g. 600,000 on Lake Tengiz (Kazakhstan) in late May 1959. European breeders move southeast towards the Caspian and Black Seas, then continue to wintering grounds in the Arabian Sea, where present late July to third week of May. Canadian population migrates chiefly southwest towards the Pacific coast; migration towards Peruvian coast is pelagic south of California. Destination of huge flocks which occur on passage in the Bay of Fundy (Nova Scotia/New Brunswick) is unknown; no major wintering areas have yet been discovered in the Atlantic. Alaskan birds probably join E Siberian ones to winter off the East Indies. Exceptionally, there are inland winter records as far north as Switzerland (two) and Morocco. A few winter annually at San Diego, California. Vagrants have occurred in inland South America, near Cape Town (regular in recent years), Sri Lanka, Australia and New Zealand.

DESCRIPTION Breeding female: Head and neck dark grey, except for white spot above and in front of eye, white chin and throat (often outlined in grey), and chestnut-red band from behind each eye down sides of neck to join across base of neck. Breast-band and flanks grey, rear flanks becoming white with dark smudges; belly and undertail white. Underwing white, with dark bar crossing the median underwing-coverts. Upperparts dark grey-brown, with golden-buff lines at edges of mantle and scapulars; larger scapulars, coverts and tertials edged rufous-buff. Clear white wingbar. Whitish sides to rump; rump and tail otherwise dark grey. **Breeding male:** Face, crown and breast lack clean

grey of female and are dull brown-grey. White above eye is more diffuse, and normally forms a short whitish supercilium. Upperparts are paler brown and have more feathers edged buff, particularly on the mantle. Neck-patch is pale rusty-brown. **Non-breeding:** Head mainly white, with conspicuous blackish mark through and behind eye ('phalarope-mark') and dark patch on rear crown. Underparts white, except for grey smudging on sides of breast and upper flanks. Upperparts and hindneck grey, with whitish edgings to larger feathers forming ill-defined lines at edges of mantle and scapulars. **Juvenile:** Crown, nape, hindneck, upperparts and sides of upper breast rich dark brown. Mantle lines and edges to tertials, larger coverts and scapulars are bright orange-buff. Front of neck and upper breast suffused pinkish-buff.

AGE/SEX Post-juvenile moult begins early but may continue until spring. The primaries are not replaced during the first winter and become very worn. First-winter individuals often show retained dark brown feathers in the cap, scapulars and tertials. Adults moult into non-breeding plumage mostly in July-early Aug, before the start of migration. Female averages about 5% longer in wing length than the male. Sexes are distinct in breeding plumage.

RACES No geographical variation is known.

MEASUREMENTS Length 180-190 mm (7¼"). Wing 102-114 mm (males), 109-118 mm (females); bill 19-23 mm; tarsus 19-22 mm; tail 45-53 mm.

REFERENCES Hildén and Vuolanto (1972).

158 GREY PHALAROPE *Phalaropus fulicarius* Plate 63

Other name: Red Phalarope
A truly marine wader, normally pelagic except while breeding or when storm-driven, rarely seen inland.

IDENTIFICATION Easily identified as a phalarope by habitual swimming, and, in non-breeding plumage, by blackish mark through and behind eye (the 'phalarope-mark'). White or whitish cheeks and red underparts in breeding plumage are highly distinctive. Differs from Red-necked Phalarope (157) in deeper and broader bill, usually with some yellowish at the base, distinctive breeding plumage, larger size, and paler and plainer non-breeding plumage. At sea, may be very difficult to distinguish from Red-necked: look for plain, paler grey mantle, proportionately larger wings, slower wingbeats, and short bill. In flight, pale plumage, strong wingbar and call may recall Sanderling (189), but note proportionately larger wings and the typical phalarope characters of small head, broad tail and 'phalarope-mark'. **Bare parts:** Bill about as long as distance from bill-base to nape, remarkably broad when viewed from above; black with extensive rich yellow base in breeding plumage, tinged yellow or yellowish-brown at the base in other plumages. Iris brown. Legs greyish or brownish, yellowish-brown when breeding; large, rounded, yellowish lobes along toes. The legs look very short for the size of the bird.

VOICE Contact and flight call is a shrill 'wit', recalling Sanderling and Little Stint (193). Disyllabic and twittering calls are made when breeding.

HABITS Breeds June-Aug on marshy tundra near

coasts of the Arctic Ocean. Where range overlaps with that of Red-necked, favours pools with muddy edges. Often has to wait at sea for two or three weeks for ground to thaw. Female normally deserts male as soon as eggs are laid, and may attempt to mate again. When not breeding, found at sea mainly in plankton-rich oceanic upwelling zones. Uses remarkably broad bill to seize prey, chiefly on or just below the surface. Mostly found singly or in small parties, occasionally gathers in flocks of over a thousand. Often gathers around cetaceans, and may pick parasites from their backs. Strong winds may drive these birds to coastal bays, inlets and marshes, occasionally inland to lakes and reservoirs. Juveniles in Sept-Oct are particularly likely to be storm-driven. When ashore, may feed by walking slowly along water's edge. When swimming, often spins rapidly, pecking outwards at food particles; sometimes up-ends. Has been seen eating carrion. Usually very tame.

MOVEMENTS In contrast to other phalaropes, and indeed to all other waders, the migration routes appear to be entirely oceanic. All populations apparently leave breeding grounds in an easterly direction and then move southeast across Atlantic or Pacific Oceans to reach major wintering grounds off Chile and W Africa. Occasionally blown onto European coasts in westerly autumn gales, sometimes in large numbers; singles may winter as far north as the North

Sea. In North America, much more numerous along Pacific coast than Atlantic, particularly Sept-Dec; in some years, also numerous in spring. Winters irregularly off both coasts, and may appear inshore during storms. Vagrant inland in most parts of northern continents, E African coast and lakes, India, Saudi Arabia, Australia, New Zealand, Argentina, Falklands, and Anvers I. off the Antarctic Peninsula where one was collected in full breeding plumage in Jan 1970.
DESCRIPTION Breeding: Dark brown area on chin extends around bill, over crown and down hindneck, contrasting strongly with bold oval white area on sides of head surrounding eye. Rest of head and underparts rich chestnut-red. Underwing and axillaries white. Mantle, scapulars and tertials blackish-brown, with rich rufous and buffish edgings. Upper surface of wing grey, with strong white wingbar. Tail grey, with central pair of feathers darker. Rump greyish with some rufous at sides. **Non-breeding:** Head and underparts white, except for blackish-grey cap (variable in extent: sometimes restricted to nape, sometimes extending onto hindneck), blackish crescent through and behind eye, and grey smudging on sides of breast and flanks. Hindneck, mantle, scapulars and coverts clean pale grey, initially with fine white fringing. White sides to grey rump. **Juvenile:**

Pattern as non-breeding, but crown, hindneck, mantle, scapulars, coverts and tertials blackish-brown with broad buffish-brown edgings or fringes. Underparts white, but face, sides of neck and upper breast initially show a strong pinkish-buff suffusion.
AGE/SEX Juvenile plumage is gradually lost during Aug-Nov, but buff-fringed coverts are retained and sometimes also a few dark feathers in the cap, back or rump. Adults are usually completely plain grey above by mid-Sept, and have all coverts grey with narrow white fringes. Female averages 6% longer than male in wing length. In breeding plumage, females can be distinguished by very dark brown, unstreaked cap, blackish-brown mantle with pale buff edgings, large pure white area on cheeks, and bright chestnut-red underparts. Males are duller and show streaked brown crown, smaller and more buffish-white cheek-patch, and often some white on belly even in full plumage.
RACES No geographical variation is known.
MEASUREMENTS Length 200-220 mm (8¼"). Wing 122-134 mm (males), 128-141 mm (females); bill 20-24 mm (males), 21-25 mm (females); tarsus 20-23 mm; tail 57-74 mm.
REFERENCES Kistchinski (1975), Schamel and Tracey (1977), Mayfield (1979), Ridley (1980).

159 EURASIAN WOODCOCK *Scolopax rusticola*

Plate 64
(see also Plate 65)

Other name: Woodcock

A woodland bird, widespread in the temperate forested zone of Eurasia and with a number of isolated southerly populations. Still hunted over much of its winter range. The breeding system is unusual and has attracted much attention.

IDENTIFICATION A fairly large, heavily-built wader with a longish bill and broad, rather blunt wings. Its plumage of mottled chestnuts, browns, buffs and grey provide superb camouflage in its typically woodland setting; as in all woodcock species, there are transverse blackish bars on the crown and nape. Most likely to be encountered in roding flight (see Habits) at dusk and dawn, or if flushed from the woodland floor, when rises almost vertically with a slight clatter of wings, then twists rapidly out of sight. Winter range includes Amami-Oshima, where Amami Woodcock (160) is resident; Eurasian is shorter-legged, but it is not known whether there are any reliable distinguishing field characters. Overlap with American Woodcock (164) has also been recorded, but Eurasian is very easily distinguished by greater size (almost twice as heavy), darker plumage, strongly-barred underparts, less obvious pale 'V' on mantle, and relatively longer primaries; outer primaries are not reduced. See also Dusky, Celebes and Obi Woodcocks (161-163), and Wood Snipe (169). **Bare parts:** Bill horn-brown, tinged yellowish or pinkish at base, darker on outer third. Iris dark brown. Legs usually greyish- or pinkish-brown, sometimes blue-grey or yellowish; very short for size of bird.
VOICE Almost always silent when flushed, but may give a harsh snipe-like 'schaap', sometimes repeated quickly. In roding display, male gives an accelerating series of barely audible guttural notes 'quorr-quorr-quo-ro' followed by a sharp, penetrating 'pietz',

sounding disyllabic; the sequence is repeated constantly, with brief intervals, throughout the flight. Males meeting during display may make loud excited chirrups.
HABITS Breeding habitat is woodland, coniferous or broad-leaved but requiring a large area, not too fragmented, which includes clearings or glades, dry areas with good ground cover for nesting, and damper, more open areas in which to feed. Nesting season begins in Mar and may last six months. Males perform roding flights at dawn and dusk, late Feb-Aug; fly with irregular flickering wingbeats just above treetop level, singing constantly, often for about 20 minutes at a stretch, searching for receptive females. Once mated, male may stay with female until laying, but takes no part in incubation or care of the brood. Several males often display over the same ground. Non-breeding habitat is similar, but may use smaller woods, scrub or even gardens; feeds mostly at night, sometimes on damp fields 3-4 km from daytime cover. In freezing weather, may feed on intertidal mud. When feeding, walks stealthily with steady rocking motion; probes deeply into moist soil, or picks from surface, even catching flying insects. Almost always solitary. Usually freezes when approached and flushes at a few metres. Female apparently can carry chicks in flight.
MOVEMENTS Sedentary on Atlantic islands, but otherwise migratory, although some W European and Himalayan birds may not move far. Winters close to limits of persistent frosts; autumn migration is late and

343

variable, with onward movements often provoked by severe mid-winter weather, and spring return early. Migrates almost entirely at night. Scarce in N Africa, and no confirmed records south of Sahara. Vagrant to North America from Quebec and Newfoundland to Ohio and Alabama, Greenland, Iceland, Spitsbergen, Kuwait, Sri Lanka, Andamans and Malaysia.

DESCRIPTION Breeding and non-breeding: Forehead and forecrown pale buff, streaked brown; rear crown and nape show broad blackish transverse bars. There is a narrow dark eye-stripe from bill to behind eye and a dark bar across the cheeks; sides of face are otherwise buff-brown, streaked brown. Upperparts show a complex pattern of blackish-brown and reddish-brown feather centres and whitish, greyish and reddish-buff fringes. Most coverts and tertials are strongly but irregularly barred with yellowish-buff and chestnut-brown; tail mainly blackish, but each feather is tipped silvery-white. Underparts, including underwing, are pale warm chestnut-buff, strongly barred dark brown, sometimes also whitish, with a strong infusion of chestnut on the sides of the breast. Longest undertail-coverts have bright white tips. **Juvenile:** Virtually identical, but tips of tail feathers are a duller silvery-grey,

and the pattern of the tips of the primary coverts differs: the terminal bar is quite broad and a similar shade of chestnut-brown to the rest of the bars on the feather (narrower and paler in adult).

AGE/SEX Ageing is possible only in the hand, with primary coverts the best feature. Note that juvenile tail feathers may be replaced by adult-type feathers during the first winter. Young birds show slightly greater degree of wear on primaries during the winter. No reliable sexing characters are known, but males average longer-tailed and shorter-billed than females.

RACES No races are generally recognised. Birds from the Azores are reported to be smaller. Those in Nepal and Assam are rather dark in plumage.

MEASUREMENTS Length 330-350 mm (13½"). Wing 182-218 mm (freshly-dead birds); bill 58-92 mm (but see below); tarsus 31-40 mm; tail 66-98 mm. Since 1948, an increasing number of abnormally short-billed woodcocks have been recorded in W Europe in winter; during 1981-84, there were almost a hundred reports in Britain and Ireland of individuals with bills down to half the normal length.

REFERENCES Shorten (1974), Hirons (1980).

160 AMAMI WOODCOCK *Scolopax mira*   Plate 65

This bird is a resident of Amami-Oshima, and perhaps also Tokunoshima, in the N Ryukyu chain, south of Japan. Eurasian Woodcock (159) is a winter visitor to these islands, and it is not clear whether it ever stays to nest there. The two forms are very similar and often treated as conspecific.

IDENTIFICATION This species is extremely difficult to identify owing to its apparent variability in plumage and its close similarity to Eurasian Woodcock. It is slightly larger and longer-legged than the visiting species and has much broader wings. An area of bare pinkish skin around and behind the eye is, when visible, a clear distinction from Eurasian Woodcock (159). The forehead is flatter and forms a shallower angle with the bill. The uppertail-coverts are paler sandy-rufous, contrasting more with back and tail. The middle secondaries are finely marbled with rufous-brown and whitish-buff, as well as being notched along the feather edges. The silvery spots underneath the tail-tip are smaller, duller and greyer than in Eurasian, and less sharply defined. At least some individuals, however, are paler than Eurasian, with rather uniform sandy or buffish wing-coverts. **Bare parts:** Bill dull horn-brown, tipped darker, rather thicker than in Eurasian. Iris dark brown. Legs dull

brown, perhaps tinged greyish or dull yellowish, longer than in Eurasian.

VOICE Little known. A continuous shrill 'reep-reep-reep' in distraction display.

HABITS Occurs in evergreen forests and surrounding areas, including sugar-cane fields. Habits appear to resemble Eurasian Woodcock's.

MOVEMENTS Entirely sedentary.

DESCRIPTION See Identification for differences from Eurasian Woodcock.

AGE/SEX Nothing is known.

RACES Monotypic.

MEASUREMENTS Length about 340-360 mm (14"). Wing 198-215 mm; bill 75-83 mm; tarsus 44-49 mm; tail 67-70 mm.

REFERENCES Hachisuka (1952).

161 DUSKY WOODCOCK *Scolopax saturata*   Plate 65

Other names: Javanese or East Indian Woodcock
This is an apparently rare woodcock known only from the primary montane forests of Sumatra, Java and New Guinea, where no other woodcock occurs.

IDENTIFICATION Shows the typical woodcock features of bulky body, long straight bill, and transverse bars on the nape, but it is smaller than Eurasian Woodcock (159) and differs markedly in dark plumage with whitish patch on the upper belly. It is very dark blackish and chestnut-brown above, and

strongly barred below with a brown-washed breast ending neatly against the whitish upper belly. Looks compact, dumpy and very dark in flight. **Bare parts:** Bill darkish horn-brown, tipped blackish or slaty-brown, heavy base tapers to relatively thin tip. Iris dark brown. Legs grey, usually tinged slaty or bluish.

VOICE In roding display, gives a nasal 'queet' and a rapid squealing 'quo-quo-quo-quo', which may also be given from the branch of a tree. Contact call is a repeated rattling 'krrr'.

HABITS Occurs in damp montane forests with moderate or dense understorey, at 1500-3000 m. Not recorded from secondary forest. Breeds in Java during wet season Feb-Apr; nest is on a bed of moss among ferns, slightly raised above the forest floor. There is a roding display flight at dawn and dusk, particularly around clearings. Roding has been observed during Aug-Sept in E New Guinea. If encountered on the ground, appears very tame and reluctant to fly; if flushed, may land again quickly.

MOVEMENTS Apparently entirely sedentary.

DESCRIPTION All plumages: Head basically rufous-brown, with black transverse bars on the rear crown and dark lores, ear-coverts and cheek lines; in New Guinea, also shows whitish or pale buffish chin, malar stripe and spot above the lores. Upperparts blackish, with irregular dark brownish-chestnut bars and notches. Primaries and secondaries dark brown, notched on the outer webs with a paler buffish- or chestnut-brown. Tail feathers blackish, with slight buff-brown notches and tipped silvery-grey. Underparts all strongly barred, especially the throat; neck and breast washed brown, forming a fairly neat junction with whitish-washed upper belly; middle and rear belly variably washed whitish, buffish or brownish. Underwing-coverts and axillaries dark brown, lightly barred paler buff-brown.

AGE/SEX Nothing is known.

RACES Two: nominate, 'Horsfield's Woodcock' (Sumatra and Java), and rosenbergii, 'Rosenberg's Woodcock' (New Guinea). These are sometimes treated as separate species. Nominate race has chin buffish, supercilium brownish-chestnut, barring on lower breast neat but lightish brown, and small whitish area on upper belly which contrasts with the brown-washed breast and with the central and rear belly, which are washed buffish-brown. The race rosenbergii is distinctly darker, with a whitish chin, a whitish malar streak, and usually a whitish spot above the lores; the whole of the belly is whitish, sometimes washed pale buffish towards the rear, so that the underpart barring contrasts strongly with the ground colour. It may average slightly shorter-billed.

MEASUREMENTS Length about 290-310 mm (12″). Wing 151-164 mm; bill 71-87 mm; tarsus 30-38 mm; tail 53-65 mm.

REFERENCES Rand and Gilliard (1968), Bishop and Andrew (in prep.).

162 CELEBES WOODCOCK *Scolopax celebensis*   Plate 65

Other name: Sulawesi Woodcock

This woodcock is a little-known species restricted to the island of Sulawesi (Celebes) in Indonesia, where two apparently distinct populations occur. Sometimes treated as conspecific with Obi Woodcock (163).

IDENTIFICATION This is a large, heavy-billed woodcock with a faintly-spotted pattern above and almost unbarred underparts. It differs from Obi Woodcock in smaller spots on upperparts; spots are mostly reddish-brown rather than yellowish-buff. Range alone should distinguish this from Eurasian Woodcock (159), but note that latter species is a winter visitor to the Philippines. Look for larger size, darker upperparts and strong contrast of dark upperparts and pale, almost plain ochre-buff underparts to distinguish from Eurasian. Bare parts: Bill slaty-grey. Iris dark brown. Legs slate-grey or blackish-grey.

VOICE Nothing is known.

HABITS Found in dense woodland at 1100-2500 m, especially where wet open ground is present under the canopy. Skulks away from danger. Very little is known about this species.

MOVEMENTS Apparently entirely sedentary.

DESCRIPTION All plumages: Forehead and sides of face dull olive-buff, contrasting with prominent blackish transverse bars on the rear crown and nape, and dark lines across lores, ear-coverts and rear cheeks. Upperparts blackish-brown, broken up by small rufous-brown spots and fringes and a few ochre-buff spots. Primaries and secondaries are darkish brown, with small dull ochre-buff notches. Tail blackish with hardly any pale notches, tipped silvery-grey. Underparts dull ochre-buff, virtually plain except for light and narrow brown barring at sides of breast. Underwing-coverts and axillaries barred darkish brown and dull ochre-buff.

AGE/SEX Nothing is known.

RACES Two have been described: nominate (central Sulawesi) and *heinrichi* (NE tip of Sulawesi). Although they are probably identical, *heinrichi* may be shorter-billed; it is known from only three specimens (all males).

MEASUREMENTS Length 300-335 mm (12¾″). Wing 191-200 mm; bill 86-90 mm (nominate), 76-80 mm (*heinrichi*); tarsus 44-49 mm.

REFERENCES Stresemann (1941).

163 OBI WOODCOCK *Scolopax rochussenii*   Plate 65

Other names: Maluku or Moluccan Woodcock

The woodcock is recorded only from the islands of Obi (major) and Batjan in the Moluccas, between Sulawesi and New Guinea.

IDENTIFICATION The largest woodcock and very distinct in plumage. It is about 25% more bulky than Eurasian Woodcock (159), with a much thicker bill. The upperparts are marked spectacularly with huge ochre-buff spots and are quite unlike those of other woodcocks; Celebes Woodcock (162) is also spotted above, but the spots are smaller and more rufous, contrasting much less. The underparts are bright ochre-buff and are barred only at the sides. No other woodcock has been recorded on these islands, but note that Eurasian occurs on the Philippines in winter and is a potential vagrant. **Bare parts:** Bill slaty-grey, slightly darker at tip. Iris dark brown. Legs grey; tibiae are largely unfeathered.

VOICE Nothing is known.

HABITS Virtually nothing is known about this species. Apparently a bird of dense moist montane forest.

MOVEMENTS Probably entirely sedentary.

DESCRIPTION Presumed adult: Forehead, forecrown and most of sides of face bright ochre-buff; lores are very contrastingly blackish, and there are also dark lines across the ear-coverts and rear cheeks. Crown and nape show striking transverse blackish bars. Upperparts blackish, with massive ochre-buff spots. Primaries and secondaries dark brown, boldly and contrastingly notched mid-buff. Tail feathers blackish-brown, notched palish-buff and tipped silvery-grey. Underparts all bright ochre-buff, lightly barred dark brown on the neck and more extensively barred pale brown on flanks. Axillaries and underwing-coverts blackish-brown, barred dull ochre-buff. **Juvenile:** Unknown.

AGE/SEX Nothing is known.

RACES Monotypic.

MEASUREMENTS Length 320-350 mm (13¼''). Wing 200-205 mm; bill 90-100 mm; tarsus 43-47 mm; tail 68-77 mm.

REFERENCES Hartert (1903).

164 AMERICAN WOODCOCK *Scolopax minor*

Plate 64
(see also Plate 65)

Other names: Woodcock, Timberdoodle, Mud-bat

The smallest woodcock, with uniquely attenuated outer primaries. Like Eurasian Woodcock (159) it is widely distributed, migratory, and still hunted.

IDENTIFICATION A typical woodcock with broad, rounded wings, a longish, straight and heavy bill, broad blackish transverse bars on crown and nape, unbarred underparts, and silvery spots at the tip of the tail. Uniquely, the outermost 3 primaries are greatly reduced in width. A woodland species which, when flushed, rises steeply, then twists away through the trees on whistling wings. Eurasian Woodcock has occurred rarely in North America, but it is clearly larger, heavier and darker than American, has whole underparts strongly barred, and less obvious grey lines on mantle and scapulars. **Bare parts:** Bill dull greenish- or yellowish-brown, darker towards tip. Iris dark brown. Legs short, greyish-, yellowish- or greenish-brown.

VOICE Virtually silent in winter. Male displaying on ground gives a muffled cooing 'chako' followed by a louder, buzzing 'peent'. He also has a musical twittering and bubbling song delivered in display flight, and a sharp 'cac-cac-cac' in aggressive encounters. Female has a wheezy call.

HABITS Mainly crepuscular and nocturnal. Typically found in rich moist, bushy, mixed or deciduous woodlands; chooses drier sites for breeding. Male has spectacular display at dusk and dawn which, unlike Eurasian's, occurs at special stations and serves to attract females to him. Display stations are on bare open ground, usually at a clearing or field edge; individual males may use more than one. The male begins by adopting an upright posture and 'peenting' repeatedly. At intervals, usually of only a few minutes, he rises vertically on twittering wings and delivers the song from a circular display flight about 100 m above the display ground, then returns in a rapid spiral. Display can continue for several hours. Aggression between displaying males is frequent. Display and nesting may begin in Jan in southern states, but not until Apr in north of range. Non-breeding habitats may include more open woodland and even gardens; often rests in woodland during day and flights out to feed nocturnally on damp fields and marshlands. When feeding, has a slow walk with a constant rocking motion of the body. Probes deeply

into moist ground, or picks from surface. Owing to superb camouflage, rarely seen until flushed, when rockets away from close range with clearly audible wing-noise, usually dropping quite quickly back into cover.

MOVEMENTS A summer visitor to north of range, present chiefly late Mar-Oct, sometimes later in mild weather, and a winter visitor in S Texas, S Louisiana and S Florida. Southern nesters are presumably mostly sedentary, but there is evidence that at least some early-hatched young may join the northward migration. Vagrant west to Montana and Colorado, and has occurred on Bermuda.

DESCRIPTION Breeding and non-breeding: Forehead, forecrown, supercilium and most of side of head fairly plain orange-buff; rear crown and nape show broad transverse blackish bars; narrow dark eye-stripe from bill to nape and another dark line across lower cheeks. Mantle, scapulars and tertials are blackish-brown with whitish, chestnut and grey fringes; there is a neat silver-grey 'V' on edges of mantle and less clear grey lines on scapulars. Wing-coverts are mottled with brown and dull chestnut and tipped greyish. Primaries dull brownish, outer 3 reduced to short, very narrow feathers; primaries 6 and 7 are

longest. Secondaries mostly mottled brown and chestnut; on the underside of the middle secondaries, tips do not contrast strongly with rest of feather. Rump and uppertail-coverts orange-buff, slightly mottled brownish and with a darker central area to rump; tail feathers blackish, each neatly tipped silvery-white. Underparts, including underwing-coverts and axillaries, virtually unbarred orange-buff. **Juvenile:** Almost identical, but on the underside of the middle secondaries the pale tip and dark subterminal bar usually contrast strongly with the rest of the feather. **AGE/SEX** Young birds can be distinguished only in the hand. Sexes alike in plumage, but female averages roughly 10% larger than male in wing and bill and has wider outer primaries: combined width of outer 3 primaries is at least 12.6 mm in females, 12.4 mm or less in males.
RACES No geographical variation is known.
MEASUREMENTS Length 265-295 mm (11"). Wing 128-146 mm (females mostly 140 mm or more, males mostly 134 mm or less); bill 62-73 mm; tarsus 29-35 mm; tail 53-61 mm.
REFERENCES Sheldon (1967), Smith and Barclay (1978), Dwyer *et al.* (1979), Marshall (1982).

165 NEW ZEALAND SNIPE *Coenocorypha aucklandica*   Plate 66

Other names: Subantarctic or Auckland Islands Snipe
This species and the Chatham Islands Snipe (166), often considered conspecific, constitute a group of apparently primitive snipes now restricted to remote vermin-free islands to the south and east of New Zealand. All populations are in severe danger of extinction; two subspecies have been lost in the last century. There are considerable similarities in plumage and structure, but not size, to the '*Chubbia*' group of South American snipes (179-181).

IDENTIFICATION A small snipe with longish, drooping bill and very short legs, restricted to certain remote oceanic islands. Normally the only snipe species found on these islands, but Japanese Snipe (168) may occur as a vagrant; there are probable records of latter species from Macquarie I. New Zealand Snipe is much smaller and shorter-legged, relatively poorly patterned, and in flight shows short, broad and rounded wings. The races differ quite markedly in shades of colour and precise patterning above and below; there is also a fair degree of individual variation. Chatham Islands Snipe has the palest underparts of any of the group, and can be distinguished from all races of New Zealand Snipe by its smaller size and proportionately smaller bill. **Bare parts:** Bill brown, paler at base. Iris brown. Legs and toes yellowish-brown, sometimes greyish or greenish; middle toe plus claw measures about 8-10 mm longer than tarsus.
VOICE A low 'chup-chup' is given by territorial males, often building up to a repeated whistle. Female's call is a softer 'chur'.
HABITS Found in tussock grass and lightly-wooded areas; usually in cover during the day, but more active at dusk and at night, emerging to feed in more open areas such as the fringes of penguin colonies. Probes soil and the bases of tussocks for amphipods, insect larvae and earthworms. Highly territorial when breeding, sometimes fighting vigorously with intruding birds. Two eggs are laid Nov-Apr in a grassy cup well concealed among vegetation. Both sexes incubate. Brood is divided between the parents, and no more than one chick is ever seen with an adult. This is a tame species and will often feed unconcerned within a few metres of an observer. If flushed, usually dashes off low with whirring flight and lands again quite quickly, but may move several hundred metres. Otherwise, rarely flies except at dusk and at night; some races are suspected of having a nocturnal drumming display flight.
MOVEMENTS Not suspected of moving even to adjacent islands within island groups.
DESCRIPTION All plumages: Crown brown with gingery feather edgings; buff crown-stripe from top of crown to nape, not reaching bill. Narrow brown eyestripe from bill; supercilium and cheeks buffish with brown spots. Chin unmarked buffish. Neck and breast suffused buffish, streaked and spotted brown. Flanks smudged brown; belly, vent and undertail variably buffish to yellowish-brown. Underwing-coverts pale brown, almost unpatterned. Hindneck brown with darker streaks. Mantle and scapulars centred blackish-brown, with irregular brown bars and buff fringes to outer webs of some feathers. Rump and uppertail brown with faint barring. Tail almost hidden by coverts, medium-brown with faintly-barred pattern; outer two pairs of feathers rather stiff and narrow. Wing-coverts and tertials brown, with poorly-defined barring and fringing. Greater primary coverts plain brown with whitish tips. Primaries and secondaries plain medium-brown.
AGE/SEX Ageing is very difficult; in *huegeli,* young are distinguished by greyer plumage with less contrast than adults and by grey legs and basal half of bill. Sexes are similar in plumage, but females are larger.
RACES Three, plus two recently exterminated by cats and rats: nominate *aucklandica* (Ewing, Disappointment, Enderby and Adams Islands of the Auckland Is. group), *meinertzhagenae* (Antipodes Is.), *huegeli* (Northeast and Broughton Is. in the Snares group), *barrierensis* (known only from a single specimen collected 1870 on Little Barrier I., near the coast of Auckland on North Island), and *iredalei* (South Cape Is., Jacky Lee I. and possibly other small islands off Stewart I.; last reported on Big South Cape I. in 1964, but now presumed extinct). The nominate race is largest and palest, with a large unbarred area of buffish on the belly. The race *meinertzhagenae* is the darkest, and has rather yellowish underparts. In *huegeli,* the underparts are barred all over. The race *iredalei* is, or was, the most rufous subspecies, with boldly-spotted throat and barred flanks and belly.
MEASUREMENTS Length 220-230 mm (9"). Wing 101-113 mm; bill 46-67 mm; tarsus 23-29 mm.
REFERENCES Oliver (1955), Anderson (1968), Tuck (1972).

166 CHATHAM ISLANDS SNIPE *Coenocorypha pusilla*   Plate 66

The smallest of the 'semi-snipes', restricted to four of the Chatham Is. and in considerable danger of extinction. Often considered conspecific with New Zealand Snipe (165).

IDENTIFICATION See New Zealand Snipe for general characters and distinctions from possible vagrant Japanese Snipe (168). Since all the forms of *Coenocorypha* are sedentary on well-separated island groups, range is entirely sufficient for identification. This species is smaller than all races of New Zealand Snipe, and proportionately shorter-billed. It also differs in having the palest underparts; there is a large area of unbarred buffish-white covering most of the belly. **Bare parts:** Bill brown, darker towards tip. Iris dark brown. Legs and toes dull greyish-yellow to pale orange-yellow.
VOICE Attention is often first drawn to the bird by its characteristic calls, given chiefly at dusk but also occasionally during the day. The call starts with a few soft low chirrups, followed by a series of eight to ten sharp, tuneful whistles pitched on high B. The female's call is similar, but lower-pitched. Feeding birds occasionally chirrup softly. The alarm call is a strident 'cheep'.
HABITS Formerly occurred throughout the Chathams group, but became confined to Southeast I. when the other populations were exterminated by introduced predators. Successfully re-introduced to Mangere I. in 1970, after feral cats had died out. On Southeast I., occurs mainly in bushed areas; feeds by probing leaf-mould on the forest floor and also among damp grasses and mosses in more open habitats. Often tame and approachable. Two (sometimes three) eggs are laid Oct-Jan, usually among sedges or grass under forest canopy. Both sexes incubate, and the brood is divided between the parents. Adults and young chicks are active all day and all night, but others are usually inactive in the afternoon. This species tends to fly more than New Zealand Snipe, and is suspected of having a nocturnal drumming display flight.
MOVEMENTS Has colonised Little Mangere I. from Mangere I. and (apparently) Star Keys from Southeast I. Otherwise sedentary.
DESCRIPTION See Identification section for differences from New Zealand Snipe.
AGE/SEX Juveniles have rather less well-defined markings, greyish legs and grey base to bill. Sexes are fairly easy to distinguish, since male is smaller in body size and bill length, and darker and more strikingly patterned above. Female's voice is lower-pitched.
RACES No geographical variation.
MEASUREMENTS Length about 200 mm (8"). Wing 99-106 mm; bill 40-45 mm (males), 45-48 mm (females); tarsus 22-25 mm.
REFERENCES Oliver (1955), Tuck (1972).

167 SOLITARY SNIPE *Gallinago solitaria*   Plate 68

A relatively large and distinctive snipe, found almost exclusively at high altitude.

IDENTIFICATION A typical snipe in basic pattern and structure, but larger than all other Palaearctic snipes except the broader-winged Wood Snipe (169), and with a unique combination of colours: plumage is generally gingery-brown and whitish, finely vermiculated whitish and chestnut. On the ground, whitish face and mantle lines and gingery-brown patch on sides of breast (contrasting strongly with white face) are best clues to identity. In flight, note also large size, relatively slow and heavy flight, pale wing-panel formed by white edges to median coverts, and contrastingly bright chestnut on tail. **Bare parts:** Bill brownish at base, blackish at tip; bill-base rather slender. Iris dark brown. Legs variably pale yellowish-green to yellowish-brown; toes do not project beyond tail-tip in flight.
VOICE When flushed, gives a harsh 'kensh', rather louder than Common Snipe (175). In display there is a vocal 'chok-a-chok-a', deeper than Common, and a mechanical bleating produced by the outer tail feathers, perhaps slightly shriller than Common.
HABITS Has discontinuous breeding range in mountains of E Asia. Nests May onwards in mountain bogs and river valleys well above the timber-line, around 2400 m, or as high as 5000 m in the Himalayas. Male has aerial drumming display typical of the genus. After breeding, occurs at lower altitude but in similar habitats; usually found singly along mountain streams or around unfrozen springs, often in areas shunned by other snipes. On migration or in winter, may occur in more usual snipe habitat such as paddyfields and marshes, even on the coast. Often approachable, but crouches when disturbed; if flushed, flies rather slowly and usually pitches down again quickly.
MOVEMENTS Many individuals are apparently sedentary at high altitude, but may be driven down by cold weather. Some, however, perform regular altitudinal movements or even longer migrations. Regular in winter in small numbers in NE Iran, Pakistan, N India and Japan, far from known breeding range. Vagrant Chilka Lake (coastal E India), Hong Kong.
DESCRIPTION All plumages: Head greyish-white, with contrasting dark gingery-brown crown, lores, upper ear-coverts, and line across lower cheeks; central crown-stripe is whitish, but narrow and often broken. Upperparts generally a medium-brown, with many narrow white and rufous fringes and bars which give a finely vermiculated appearance; tertials are often strongly barred pale brown and dark brown. At junction of mantle and scapulars are narrow but strongly contrasting whitish lines. Flight feathers are dark brown, with tips of secondaries and inner 7 primaries narrowly white, giving a thin pale trailing edge; narrow white tips also to greater coverts and greater primary coverts. Median coverts show broad brownish-white fringes. Tail is longish, wedge-shaped

or strongly rounded, and composed of between eight and 14 (usually ten) pairs of feathers, outer feathers are narrow, only 2-3 mm in width, and 20-30 mm shorter than central feathers. Tail shows narrow white tip and conspicuous bright rufous subterminal band on middle feathers. Breast is strongly infused with gingery-brown (especially on the sides), and mottled whitish; dark breast contrasts with white flanks, heavily barred brown, and unbarred white belly. Underwing and axillaries are barred with equal amounts of brown and white, usually looking dull brown.
AGE/SEX No reliable ageing characters are known. Sexes are similar in plumage, but female averages slightly larger.

RACES Two are described, but their validity is uncertain: nominate *solitaria* (most of range), and *japonica* (breeding range unknown, occurs in winter in Japan). The two are almost identical, but *japonica* may show richer red and less white above; it averages slightly shorter in wing length, marginally longer in bill and tarsus.
MEASUREMENTS Length 290-310 mm (12"). Wing 157-174 mm; bill 65-78 mm; tarsus 31-36 mm; tail 55-63 mm.
REFERENCES Zubarovskij (1976), Shcherbakov (1980).

168 JAPANESE SNIPE *Gallinago hardwickii*   Plate 68

Other names: Latham's Snipe, Australian Snipe
This snipe has rather small breeding and wintering ranges, but is one of the greatest migrants of the genus.

IDENTIFICATION A fairly large and heavy-looking snipe, proportionately long-winged and long-tailed. This species, together with Pintail and Swinhoe's Snipes (170, 171), shows the following differences from Common Snipe (175) and its allies: at base of bill, pale supercilium is conspicuously broader than dark head-stripes and eye-stripes (easily visible in a close view on the ground); trailing edge to the wing is only narrowly pale, and dull greyish rather than white; wing shows a fairly conspicuous pale panel across the median coverts, outlined by dark lesser and greater coverts. Within this group of three species, Japanese can be distinguished by its larger size, longer wings (measurement is diagnostic), longer tertials which overlap the long primaries almost completely, and longer tail (projecting well beyond folded wings) with slightly more white on outer feathers. Outer tail feathers are similar to Swinhoe's, but marginally broader. Pintail is the smallest of the three and is a rather short-tailed bird. See Table on page 394 for a summary of useful characters. **Bare parts:** Bill greenish-brown at base, becoming blackish at tip. Iris dark brown. Legs greenish, relatively long.
VOICE When flushed, a short rasping 'chak' or 'zak'. More vocal in display flight than Common; gives a regular 'zrack' or 'tchraak' between drumming dives.
HABITS Breeds late Apr to early Aug, at altitudes from sea-level to at least 1200 m. Locally still common on Hokkaido, but breeding range has contracted northwards during the last century. Preferred habitat is not marshland, but drier heathlands and moorlands, often among light woodlands of larch or birch. There is a typical drumming display, mainly around dusk, often by several males together. When not breeding, occurs around freshwater wetlands, often in parties of several dozen. In some localities, feeds mostly at night, taking refuge in denser, drier cover by day. If flushed, flies fairly heavily, with relatively few zigzags, and drops quickly back into cover.
MOVEMENTS Breeds only in Japan (mainly Hok-

kaido) and adjacent USSR (Kunashiri I. and perhaps others in the Kurils), and winters extensively in E Australia, but is rarely seen in intermediate areas. Recorded as a migrant in Taiwan, the Philippines and New Guinea. Migrants leave S Australia mainly late Feb or early Mar but do not arrive in Japan until early Apr. Some remain in winter quarters all year, and are joined by migrants from Aug onwards. Recorded also in NW Australia, New Guinea and New Zealand in winter. Vagrant Sakhalin (Sept 1958), Lord Howe I.; vagrant snipes on Macquarie I. are probably of this species.
DESCRIPTION Breeding and non-breeding: Main differences from Swinhoe's are as follows. Pale trailing edge to secondaries is slightly broader (2-3 mm), although still hardly visible in the field. Shaft of outer primary is much whiter distally. Primary tips on folded wing are more widely spaced, especially noticeable with primaries 7 and 8. Despite the long wing, the tertials overlie all except sometimes the longest primary. Outer tail feathers are slightly broader (outermost 4-6 mm, next pair 6-8 mm, at 20 mm from tip); all are white-tipped and have one or two whitish subterminal bars, separated by brown. **Juvenile:** As in most other snipes, the wing-coverts tend to have buffish-white fringes rather than brownish-buff paired spots at tip. Also, primaries show clearer and neater white fringes.
AGE/SEX Juvenile is separable at least until early Nov; later than this, ageing is very difficult. First-winter bird has a complete moult starting Dec-Jan. Sexes are similar in plumage, but male has longer outer tail feathers on average (at least in the breeding season), and female averages longer-billed.
RACES No geographical variation is known.
MEASUREMENTS Length 280-300 (11½"). Wing 157-168 mm; bill 66-77 mm; tarsus 34-39 mm; tail 58-68 mm.
REFERENCES Frith *et al.* (1977), Lane and Forest (1984), Fujimaki and Skira (1984).

Swinhoe's Snipe   Japanese Snipe

169 WOOD SNIPE *Gallinago nemoricola*   Plate 66

Other name: Himalayan Snipe
A large, little-known snipe of Himalayan woodlands.

IDENTIFICATION In size, rather rounded wings, entirely-barred belly, and habitat, this snipe is more woodcock-like than snipe-like. The typically snipe-like patterning, with pale parallel lines on the upperparts, should always distinguish it from Eurasian Woodcock (159). It is usually found only in woodland and dense tall herbage, particularly at relatively high altitude. It is much heavier and darker than Common (175) or Pintail (170) Snipes, but of similar bulk to Solitary (167) or Great (174). The blackish upperparts are normally fringed with dull buffish-grey, while the whitish underparts are entirely heavily barred with brown. Compared with Solitary, it is much darker above and below, and the bill-base is heavier. Great Snipe also has extensively-barred underparts, but its prominent white on the wing-coverts and tail-corners should preclude confusion. Wood Snipe is likely to be seen only when flushed; flight is slow and wavering, reminiscent of Eurasian Woodcock and Painted Snipe (9). The broad, rounded wings are distinctive for a snipe; note also a paler wing-panel formed by median and greater coverts, the narrow greyish trailing edge to the wing, and the virtual absence of white in the tail. **Bare parts:** Bill brownish at base, darkening to a blackish tip. Iris dark brown. Legs greyish-green.

VOICE When flushed, occasionally gives a low croaking 'chok-chok'.

HABITS Believed to breed only in wooded habitats at high altitude, from 1200 m to 4000 m, but breeding biology is virtually unknown; an egg is reported to have been found in June. There is reputed to be an aerial drumming display. Outside the breeding season, found at lower altitude in the Himalayas, usually in dense marshes and swamps in cover too thick for other snipes. Usually seen singly. When flushed, rarely flies far.

MOVEMENTS Some may be resident at comparatively low altitude in the Himalayas, but many move down to the foothills in winter. Part of the population, however, is migratory; there are records for hill ranges in most parts of India and Pakistan. Vagrant Sri Lanka, and Thailand (two records).

DESCRIPTION Breeding and non-breeding: Brownish-buff head shows typical snipe-like markings, but the pale crown-stripe is very narrow. Mantle and scapulars are blackish, fringed greyish- or brownish-buff; mantle lines are variable in strength, sometimes broken. Wing-coverts are dark brown, usually barred and spotted with pale buffish-grey. Flight feathers are dark brown, with narrow grey tips to secondaries and paler tips to all but outer primaries. Tail usually has nine pairs of feathers, outermost only 3-4 mm broad; all but central pair are tipped whitish-grey. Neck and upper breast are washed brown, with darker brown spots and streaks. Lower breast and belly are whitish, heavily barred with dark brown; flanks are washed brownish-buff. **Juvenile:** As adult, but with pale buff fringes to median coverts, neater white tips to primaries, and scaly, more vermiculated mantle and scapulars.

AGE/SEX Ageing is virtually impossible in the field, but juveniles and first-winter birds may be identifiable in the hand on primary wear and covert pattern. Sexes are not known to differ.

RACES No geographical variation is known.

MEASUREMENTS Length 280-320 mm (12"). Wing 142-156 mm; bill 61-72 mm; tarsus 34-39 mm; tail 63-74 mm.

170 PINTAIL SNIPE *Gallinago stenura*   Plate 67

Other name: Pin-tailed Snipe
The tail of this bird is composed of up to 28 feathers, whereas most waders have only the normal 12. In the field, it is difficult to separate from Swinhoe's (171) and Japanese (168).

IDENTIFICATION Similar in size to Common Snipe (175) but slightly shorter-billed and shorter-tailed. In flight, it lacks Common's broad white trailing edge to the wing and shows virtually no white on the tail-corners. Difference in wing pattern is obvious with the naked eye when bird is flushed. Shape of outer tail feathers is diagnostic, but visible in the field only in ideal conditions; the outer six to nine pairs (usually eight) are pin-shaped, less than 2 mm wide, and resemble a row of tiny paintbrushes. It shares several features with Japanese and Swinhoe's, including lack of white trailing edge, darker underwing than Common, pale median coverts forming a paler panel on upperwing, and face pattern with supercilium broader than eye-stripe at base of bill. Japanese is a larger bird, with proportionately longer wings, tertials and tail; on Pintail, tail projects only slightly beyond folded wings, and primary tips project slightly beyond tertials. Swinhoe's is extremely similar to Pintail in all but tail structure, and probably inseparable except in ideal conditions. The best features for field identification are probably as follows: tail is shorter on Pintail, and toes project farther beyond tail-tip; Pintail shows less white on tail-corners; Pintail is a slightly smaller and lighter bird on average. See Tables on pages 394 and 395, also Solitary and Wood Snipes (167, 169). **Bare parts:** Bill shortish for a snipe, greyish-green at base and dark brown at tip. Iris dark brown. Legs greyish-green or brownish-green; almost full length of toes projects beyond tail-tip in flight.

VOICE When flushed, may give a short rasping 'squik', 'etch' or 'chet', rather weaker and lower-pitched than Common Snipe, distinguishable with practice. Songs are a hoarse repetition of 'terre' or 'tcheka', and in display flight a remarkable crescendo of staccato and buzzing sounds.

HABITS Nests May-Aug in wide area of arctic and boreal USSR, typically in damp habitats but may use drier areas than Common Snipe. Males often display in a group (a 'tok'), which may be in some respects the aerial equivalent of a lek; the display includes the strange vocalisations, as well as fizzing and whistling noises from the outer tail feathers. Outside the breeding season, occurs in a wide variety of wetland habitats, often alongside Common, but may also resort to drier ground. When flushed, escape flight is typically shorter and less towering than in Common (although may accompany Common if both are flushed together). Feeds more by picking than does Common.

MOVEMENTS Normal winter range apparently extends from Pakistan to S China, Sulawesi and Timor. The commonest migrant snipe in S India and most of SE Asia, but less common than Common in Pakistan, and less common than Swinhoe's in the Philippines. Present in winter quarters late Aug-early May, but most arrive in Sept-Oct and depart in Mar-early Apr. Arrives later on breeding grounds than does Common. Occurs on passage west to Iran, and recorded as a vagrant in Oman, Socotra, Somalia, Kenya (possibly regular), Maldive Is., Christmas I., W and NW Australia, and Hawaii.

DESCRIPTION Breeding and non-breeding: Very similar to Common Snipe, but differs in the following features. Relatively narrow line across lores; super-cilium broad in front of eye. Fringes to mantle and scapulars are slightly narrower and less well defined. Larger lesser and median wing-coverts are paler brown than leading lessers and greater coverts, forming a pale patch in flight. Flight feathers mid-brown, with very narrow greyish-white trailing edge to secondaries and innermost primaries. Tail has 12-14 pairs of feathers, outer six to nine pairs extremely reduced to narrow dark vanes with whitish, slightly bulbous tip. Streaking on flanks is more extensive, giving smaller unbarred white belly-patch. Underwing-coverts and axillaries are uniformly darker, all with broad brown and narrower white bars; no white patch on underwing. **Juvenile:** Very like adult, but upperpart fringes even narrower, sometimes giving vermiculated appearance, and wing-coverts show a whitish-buff fringe rather than paired brownish-buff spots at tip.

AGE/SEX Juvenile coverts are very difficult to distinguish, even in autumn. By mid-winter, first-winter birds typically show rather more primary wear than adults. Sexes are similar in plumage, but female averages slightly longer-billed.

RACES No geographical variation is known.

MEASUREMENTS Length 250-270 mm (10¼"). Wing 125-143 mm; bill 55-70 mm; tarsus 29-36 mm; tail 42-55 mm.

REFERENCES Berman and Kuz'min (1965), Madge (1977a), Kitson (1978), Taylor (1984).

171 SWINHOE'S SNIPE *Gallinago megala*   Plate 68

Other names: Chinese or Forest Snipe
A rather poorly-known species, probably often overlooked among the very similar Japanese and Pintail Snipes (168, 170).

IDENTIFICATION Lack of a white trailing edge to the wing, relatively broad supercilia and narrow head-stripes and eye-stripes at base of bill, pale panel across the median and larger lesser coverts, and uniformly rather dark underwing are all clear distinctions from Common Snipe (175), but all are shared also by Japanese and Pintail; separation from last two species is much more difficult. Japanese differs in larger size (measurements are diagnostic), and relatively longer wings, tertials and tail. On Japanese the tertials normally completely overlap the primaries, while on Swinhoe's the primary tips project noticeably beyond the tertial tips; if the primary tips are visible, note the distance between the third and fourth outermost: wide on Japanese, relatively narrow on Swinhoe's. Also shaft of outer primary is mid-brown on Swinhoe's, white distally on Japanese. Compared with Pintail, Swinhoe's is slightly larger, and has a longer tail with more white visible on corners. Useful characters are summarised in the Table on page 394. See also Solitary and Wood Snipes (167, 169). **Bare parts:** Bill relatively long, brownish- or greyish-green at base and dark brown at tip. Iris dark brown. Legs relatively long, greenish or greenish-yellow.

VOICE Call when flushed is possibly slightly less hoarse than in Pintail and Japanese. Song in display is a repeated 'tchiki', given from the ground, a perch in a tree, or in flight. Other noises in display flight (see below) are presumed to be mechanical.

HABITS Nests May-Aug, mainly in open woodland along river valleys, choosing drier and more enclosed sites than Common Snipe. Male has crepuscular, usually solitary display flight in which he circles, singing, then dives steeply making a prolonged low-pitched bubbling whinny, alternating rapidly between two notes, presumably produced by the outer tail feathers; the dive often ends with a complex creaking sound. Habits outside the breeding season are not known to differ from those of Pintail Snipe; often chooses drier ground than Common, and flies more heavily with fewer zigzags.

MOVEMENTS Winter range is generally more easterly than in Pintail, extending from S and E India to S China, Taiwan, the Philippines, W Micronesia, New Guinea and N Australia. No recent records from Thailand. Much commoner than Pintail in area eastward from Philippines. Rarely arrives in Australia before Nov, and most depart before mid-Apr. Vagrant N Caucasus (Dec 1898) and Maldive Is. (Dec 1958).

DESCRIPTION Breeding and non-breeding: Hardly differs from Pintail Snipe, except for tail pattern. Tail has usually ten pairs of feathers (rarely nine or up to 13); outer pairs are 2-4 mm wide at 20 mm from the tip, with a small white tip, brown subterminal band, and grey-brown wash to the base of the feather. **Juvenile:** As adult, but wing-coverts and tertials show clear whitish-buff fringes (on adult, coverts have

paired dull buff spots at tip, and tertials are clearly barred buff and brown).
AGE/SEX Juvenile is very difficult to separate, except in ideal conditions. Primary wear is probably a more useful character after mid-winter. Sexes are similar in plumage, but female averages longer-billed.

RACES No geographical variation is known.
MEASUREMENTS Length 270-290 (11"). Wing 137-151 mm; bill 56-74 mm; tarsus 31-38 mm; tail 46-57 mm.
REFERENCES Naumov (1962), Poslavski and Sokolov (1980), Taylor (1984).

172 AFRICAN SNIPE *Gallinago nigripennis*   Plate 69

Other name: Ethiopian Snipe
This is the only snipe other than Painted Snipe (9) that breeds in Africa. It is closely related to the Common Snipe (175), and to the Magellan Snipe (176) of South America, and sometimes all are treated as conspecific.

IDENTIFICATION A typical snipe in all respects. Range and relatively short migrations preclude confusion with any except migrant Palaearctic snipes — Common, Pintail (170) and Great (174). Compared with Common, it is darker above and on wing-coverts (particularly lessers) and the bill is longer, but identification is almost impossible on the ground. The best characters are seen in flight: they are the rather slower flight, with fluttering wing-action on more rounded wings, the less zigzag line taken by flushed birds, and especially the large amount of white on the outer tail feathers, sometimes visible in level flight but usually obvious as the bird comes in to land. In the hand, the outer tail feather is almost all-white, with a few diffuse brownish spots but no barring, and the bill measurement is often diagnostic. Distinction from Pintail Snipe is much easier, since latter species lacks white on the trailing edge of the wing, has very little on the tail-corners, and is relatively short-billed. Neither Common nor Pintail has yet been recorded south of Zambia. Great Snipe is obviously larger and heavier, with a darker belly, conspicuous white spotting on the wing-coverts, and relatively short bill held almost horizontal in flight; white on tail-corners is even more conspicuous than on African, especially as the bird is landing. See Table on page 395 for a summary of characters, also Jack Snipe (182). **Bare parts:** Bill long, averaging 20% longer (more in southwest of range) than Common Snipe's; greenish-brown, becoming blackish towards tip. Iris dark brown. Legs brownish-green, sometimes tinged yellow.
VOICE Call on being flushed is similar to that of Common, but quieter and less rasping. On breeding grounds a repeated, far-carrying 'kip'.
HABITS Nests in wet moorlands and swamps only at very high altitudes, in E Africa from 1700 m to as high as 4000 m. Breeding season is irregular in tropics, depending on rains, chiefly Apr-Oct in S Africa. There is a drumming display like that of Common Snipe. Regular at lower altitudes, even to coastal lowlands, as a non-breeding visitor.
MOVEMENTS May disperse several hundred kilometres from known nesting grounds, but not known to have regular migrations. Not recorded as a vagrant.
DESCRIPTION Breeding and non-breeding: Very similar to Common Snipe. Mantle and scapulars are very slightly blacker in ground colour, but with rather more numerous rufous markings. Lesser and primary coverts are blacker, contrasting more with the small white tips. Tail has 16 feathers; outers are narrower than in Common (3.5-6 mm), and mostly white with a few diffuse pale brown marks. On underparts, white belly and whiter ground colour to breast contrast more with upperparts. Underwing and axillaries are variable: some individuals show underwing completely barred brown, others a whiter central bar along underwing. **Juvenile:** As adult, but wing-coverts are fringed whitish-buff rather than with distinct olive-buff spots at tip.
AGE/SEX Juvenile is doubtfully distinguishable in the field. Sexes are similar, but females average larger, particularly in bill length.
RACES Often regarded as monotypic, but up to three races have been described: *aequatorialis* (E Africa), *angolensis* (Angola, Zambia and Botswana) and nominate *nigripennis* (S Africa). The three are virtually identical, but *angolensis* averages longer in bill length.
MEASUREMENTS Length 255-285 mm (10½"). Wing 128-141 mm; bill 85-103 mm (*angolensis*), 67-96 mm (others); tarsus 34-41 mm; tail 51-60 mm.
REFERENCES Taylor (1980).

173 MADAGASCAR SNIPE *Gallinago macrodactyla*   Plate 69

This snipe, restricted to Madagascar, shows closest similarities to the Noble Snipe (177) of the northern Andes.

IDENTIFICATION This is a large, heavy, long-billed snipe, with a very dark underwing and extensive barring on the flanks. In flight, it shows only a very narrow pale greyish trailing edge to the secondaries; flight appears slower than in smaller snipe species. Range should be sufficient to identify it, since it is believed to be sedentary and no other snipes have yet been recorded on Madagascar; vagrant snipes in areas surrounding Madagascar are much more likely to be Palaearctic migrants, probably Common (175) or Pintail (170). Common differs in smaller size, paler underwing, and obvious white trailing edge to the wing. Pintail Snipe has a similar wing pattern to Madagascar, but is smaller, shorter-billed and shorter-tailed. African Snipe (172) is similar to Madagascar in proportions, but has a clear white trailing edge to the wing. See Table on page 395, and also Painted Snipe (9). **Bare parts:** Bill dark brown at base and blackish towards tip, proportionately long. Iris dark brown. Legs dark greenish-grey or slaty-grey.

VOICE Gives a hoarse cry when flushed, probably similar to those of Common and African Snipes.

HABITS Found mostly in E Madagascar, where it is fairly common in marshes and swamps with grass and sedges, also ricefields, from sea-level to 2500 m. In forested districts, it occurs in small bogs and on the banks of streams. Breeding season is poorly known, but includes July-Jan. There is an aerial drumming display as in Common Snipe.

MOVEMENTS Apparently entirely sedentary, although in 1840 described as a migrant on Île de Sainte-Marie.

DESCRIPTION Breeding and non-breeding: Chief differences from Common Snipe are as follows. The trailing edge of the secondaries is narrowly whitish-grey or greyish-buff. Underwing-coverts and axillaries show brown-and-white barring, the brown bars broader than the white ones. Barring on the flanks is slightly more extensive, reaching the sides of the belly. There are 16 tail feathers; the outermost is narrower than on Common Snipe, about 5-6 mm broad, with dark markings less prominent and more irregular. **Juvenile:** Very similar to adult, but the wing-coverts show neat, warm olive-buff fringes rather than colder spotting.

AGE/SEX Juveniles are very difficult to separate, even in the hand. Sexes are similar in plumage, but the female averages larger, especially in bill length.

RACES No geographical variation is known.

MEASUREMENTS Length 290-320 mm (12"). Wing 141-149 mm; bill 80-115 mm; tarsus 40-43 mm; tail 55-61 mm.

REFERENCES Benson et al. (1976).

174 GREAT SNIPE *Gallinago media*   **Plate 69**

Other name: Double Snipe
This snipe is unique among the genus in that it has no aerial display; instead there is complex lekking behaviour on the ground.

IDENTIFICATION A fairly bulky, large-headed snipe with a medium-length bill; it is the largest of the W Palaearctic and African species. Adult is easily distinguished from Common (175), African (172) and Pintail (170) by bold white spotting on wing-coverts, and bold unmarked white tail-corners, particularly evident on landing; juvenile has much less white on wing-coverts than adult, but white tail-corners (although lightly marked with brown) are obvious. In flight, Great is distinguished from all its smaller relatives by its bulky outline and relatively slow and level flight. There is a narrow white trailing edge to the wing; upperwing of adult shows a bold dark panel across the greater coverts, bordered narrowly by white fore and aft. In addition, the underparts, including the thighs and most of the belly, are heavily barred, the pale lines on mantle and scapulars are relatively indistinct, and the head pattern is usually obscured by brownish spotting. See Table on page 395 for a summary of useful characters. **Bare parts:** Bill dark brown, with yellowish or greenish-brown base; proportionately shorter than bill of Common Snipe, often with a faint downward angle half-way along upper mandible. Iris dark brown. Legs pale greyish-green or dull brownish-yellow.

VOICE When flushed, almost always gives a low single or double croak 'etch-etch'. A wide variety of unusual sounds is given in display at the lek, including bill-clattering, a vocal drumming and various tinkling, clicking and buzzing noises. Usually silent away from the lek arena.

HABITS Nests late May-early Sept, generally in moist areas of wooded boreal tundra, occasionally in drier woods bordering marshes or bogs. It has decreased enormously in W Europe this century. Males have complex display behaviour at traditional lekking sites; leks can be recognised in the absence of the birds by the pattern of trampled grass. Males gather towards dusk; in display, they adopt erect posture, with chest protruding and tail cocked and fanned, utter the song, and often leap into the air. Display postures are reminiscent of American Woodcock (164). The female alone builds the nest and incubates the eggs. When not breeding, found usually singly or in small numbers in marshy habitats along with Common and African Snipes, but also on drier ground. May resort to short grass on golf-courses or football pitches. If flushed, flies with comparatively straight and level flight and may drop again quickly. Take-off is much more shallow than in Common and African, bill is held more horizontally; flight is sometimes more like that of a large sandpiper or plover than a snipe.

MOVEMENTS Moves south from late Aug onwards. Generally well scattered in winter range; a scarce winterer in E Africa, but common in Zambia and Malawi. Vagrant New Jersey (Sept 1963), Spitsbergen, Madeira, Canary Is., Cape Town, Kuwait, India, Sri Lanka, Andaman Is. and Burma. Rarely seen on migration in Europe, and many may overfly. Has rarely wintered in Britain and S Scandinavia.

DESCRIPTION Breeding and non-breeding: Head pattern like Common, but line across lores is slightly narrower, ear-coverts are often more broadly dusky, supercilium appears narrower behind the eye, and pattern is somewhat obscured by heavy spotting on sides of face. Upperparts are dark brown, finely vermiculated with buff and pale brown; pale lines are rather narrow. Wing-coverts, except for leading lessers, are tipped white; white tips are very prominent on median, greater and greater primary coverts. Flight feathers are dark brown with a poorly-defined pale trailing edge to secondaries and inner primaries. Tail has normally eight pairs of feathers (sometimes seven or nine); outer three pairs are entirely white, except for dusky base. Neck and upper breast are suffused pale brown and heavily spotted and streaked dark brown; streaks form chevrons on lower breast. Flanks and belly obscured with heavy bars or chevrons, with only a small unbarred area on belly. Underwing-coverts and axillaries show broad brown and narrow white barring, and appear dark. **Juvenile:** As adult, but streaks on upperparts tend to be narrower, white covert tips are narrower and much less conspicuous, and outer tail feathers, although extensively white, show a small amount of brown barring.

AGE/SEX In autumn, adults are readily distinguishable in the field by their bold white spotting on the wing-coverts and clean white tail-corners. By midwinter, however, juveniles have gained many adult-

type feathers and are inseparable except in the hand. Sexes are similar in plumage, but (uniquely among lekking waders) females average larger than males, albeit fractionally.

RACES No geographical variation is known.

MEASUREMENTS Length 270-290 mm (11″). Wing 139-155 mm; bill 54-72 mm; tarsus 32-40 mm; tail 48-57 mm.

REFERENCES Lemnell (1978), Blankert (1980), Taylor (1980, 1981).

175 COMMON SNIPE *Gallinago gallinago* Plate 67
(see also Plate 69)

Other names: Snipe, Fantail Snipe

The most widespread and familiar of the Palaearctic snipes. Some authorities regard African Snipe (172) and some or all races of Magellan Snipe (176) as conspecific.

IDENTIFICATION The only small snipe likely to be seen in North America, and the only snipe of its size over most of the W Palaearctic; Jack Snipe (182) is conspicuously smaller and shorter-billed, and Great Snipe (174) slightly larger, obviously more bulky, and more heavily and extensively barred on the belly. Both these species fly more slowly than Common; Great shows bold white tail-corners and, except on juvenile, bold white spotting on the wing-coverts. Jack is further distinguished by its short, dark, wedge-shaped tail, and its lack of a crown-stripe. Identification problems arise mainly in N South America (with Magellan Snipe) and in Africa (with African Snipe); see those species and Tables on pages 396 and 395. In many cases, snipe species seen in the overlap zones during the northern winter may be best left unidentified. Among E Palaearctic *Gallinago*, Common has the largest white belly, the palest underwing (usually with a clearer white band along the inner median coverts), and the broadest white trailing edge to the wing. Pintail (170), Swinhoe's (171) and Japanese (168) all lack white on the trailing edge and look obviously dark-winged on take-off; they also differ in face pattern and number and shape of tail feathers (see Table on page 394). There is a rare melanistic form of Common, known as 'Sabine's Snipe'. **Bare parts:** Bill long and straight, dull reddish-brown at base, dark brown at tip. Iris dark brown. Legs yellowish-green or greenish-grey.

VOICE When flushed, gives a long harsh 'scaaap', typically with a slightly rising inflection. Display calls include a sharp 'chick' and a monotonously-repeated 'chip-per'.

HABITS Nests Apr-Aug, mainly in or near open fresh or brackish marshlands with rich or tussocky vegetation. Perches freely on posts or trees in the nesting area. As in most snipes, males have drumming display in which they circle high on rapid, clipped wing-beats then dive at a steep angle with outer tail feathers held out at almost a right angle to the body; air rushing over these feathers makes a characteristic loud bleating or drumming sound. Occupies similar habitats when not breeding, but also other wetlands including damp farmland and the upper reaches of estuaries. In some places, rests in cover during the day and feeds in more open sites chiefly at night. Feeding is by jerky, rhythmic, vertical probing, which is often compared with action of a sewing-

machine. Often gathers in flocks of several hundred, and may fly in flocks ('wisps'). When disturbed, freezes or runs quickly to cover, exploding away if approached closely; escape flight has steep rate of climb, with rapid zigzags, then high circling before a plunge to earth, usually some distance from where flushed.

MOVEMENTS Some populations are virtually sedentary, while others migrate to the northern tropics. Nearctic race normally penetrates South America only as far as Colombia and Venezuela; vagrant Surinam, and Bermuda and Britain on passage. Palaearctic races are unrecorded south of equator except in E Africa (small numbers reach Zambia) and marginally in Sumatra; they winter in large numbers in Atlantic and Mediterranean Europe, as well as in northern tropics. Many British birds are almost sedentary; some Icelandic ones even winter locally around warm springs, but most visit W Europe. Vagrant Bear I.

DESCRIPTION Breeding and non-breeding: Crown dark brown, with distinct buff central crown-stripe. Supercilium buff; ear-coverts show rather diffuse dark lines at upper and lower edges; brown bar across lower cheeks. Dark brown line across lores usually broadens noticeably towards bill; at base of bill supercilium is narrower than eye-stripe. Mantle, scapulars and tertials are blackish and dark brown, variably streaked and barred with dull reddish and buff, and fringed whitish-buff; there are broad, rich buff lines at edges of mantle and upper scapulars. Wing-coverts dark brown, patterned with brownish-buff and buffish-white spotting and fringing. Fine white tips to greater coverts and inner primary coverts form an obscure wingbar. Flight feathers dark brown, but with clear, relatively broad white tips to secondaries and inner primaries. Tail feathers basically dark brown, greyer towards outer ones; central feathers have variable reddish subterminal wash, and all feathers are narrowly tipped white. Chin and throat buffish-white, breast washed brownish-buff and streaked dark brown; rest of underparts are white, unbarred on belly but with flanks barred brown. **Juvenile:** Virtually identical, but wing-coverts more neatly fringed with buffish-white, giving a slightly scaly pattern. Pale lines on upperparts may be narrower.

AGE/SEX Juvenile coverts (with only a very thin dark shaft-streak at the tip) are distinguishable from adult coverts (fringe broken by broad shaft-streak) in the hand or at close range in the field. Most, however, are replaced early in the first winter. By spring, first-winter birds typically have more heavily-worn primaries than adults. Differences are clearest on Nearctic birds. Sexes do not differ in plumage, but females average slightly longer-billed. At least in breeding plumage, male has longer outer tail feathers (47 mm or more) than female (typically 43 mm or less).

RACES Three: nominate *gallinago* (most of Palaearctic), *faeroeensis* (Iceland, Faeroes, Orkney and Shetland) and *delicata* (N America). The race *faeroeensis* differs marginally from nominate in more rufous tones above and on breast; rufous markings are finer and form clearer bars. The race *delicata* ('Wilson's Snipe') is more distinct: typically it has eight pairs of tail feathers (typically seven in nominate race), of which the outers are usually 9 mm or less in width (9 mm or more in nominate); axillaries show wider brown bars, and are slightly more brown than white; white trailing edge to the wing is marginally narrower, usually 5 mm or less in width (6 mm or more in *gallinago*).

MEASUREMENTS Length 250-270 mm (10¼"). Wing 123-144 mm; bill 55-75 mm; tarsus 27-36 mm; tail 49-64 mm.

REFERENCES Tuck (1972), OAG Münster (1975).

176 MAGELLAN SNIPE *Gallinago paraguaiae*   Plate 70

Other name: Paraguayan Snipe
The three small snipes breeding in South America are treated here as races of a single species distinct from the Holarctic Common Snipe (175). Other authors have lumped them with Common Snipe, or recognised the yellow-legged 'Puna Snipe' *andina* as a separate South American species.

IDENTIFICATION This is a small snipe, with an obvious white trailing edge to the wing in flight, very similar to Common Snipe and African Snipe (172). The race *delicata* of Common Snipe is a non-breeding visitor only to N South America, but poses a considerable identification problem in the zone of overlap. See Table on page 396 for a summary of the characters of these races and species. The northern, nominate race of Magellan Snipe may just be distinguishable in the field by its shorter wings, slightly paler underwing, and more white on the sides of the tail. Farther south, Common Snipe is less likely to occur. The puna race *andina* of Magellan Snipe is quite distinct from all other snipes in having yellow legs; this race may also be separated by its call, very white outer tail feathers, whitish underwing and generally buffish coloration. Other snipe species in South America are either larger or much larger than Magellan Snipe; Noble Snipe (177) is the most similar, but is restricted in range, lacks a white trailing edge to the wing, and is much larger and broader-winged, almost woodcock-like in proportions. Beware confusion with South American Painted Snipe (10). **Bare parts:** Bill dull greenish or yellowish at base, otherwise dark. Iris dark brown. Legs greenish-grey, yellow in race *andina*.

VOICE Loud rasping alarm call, and drumming and repeated vocal 'chip-per' in display are very similar to those of Common Snipe. The puna race *andina* is said to be distinguishable from *magellanica* by its higher, shorter 'bzeep' when flushed.

HABITS Generally very much like Common Snipe in behaviour, feeding habits and display. The three races breed in slightly different habitats: the northern, nominate race in wet grassy savannas, the southern *magellanica* in peat-bogs, and *andina* along boggy rivers high in the Andes.

MOVEMENTS The nominate race is essentially sedentary, but performs short seasonal movements, withdrawing to the permanent marshlands during the dry winter months. Southern *magellanica* is more migratory, deserting Tierra del Fuego for the winter and spreading northwards to N Argentina and Uruguay in Apr-July; it is chiefly a summer visitor to the Falkland Is., but occasionally winters. The puna race *andina* winters at lower altitudes on the Argentinian pampas, often alongside *magellanica*.

DESCRIPTION Breeding and non-breeding: Very similar to Common Snipe; differences are summarised in Table on page 396. **Juvenile:** Very similar to the adults but, as in Common Snipe, the largest lesser and median coverts have neater pale buff fringes and a narrower dark shaft-streak.

AGE/SEX It is very difficult to age this snipe in the field, but with practice juveniles can be separated in the hand for several months after fledging. Females average very slightly larger, but no plumage differences are known between the sexes.

RACES Three: nominate *paraguaiae* (lowlands between the Atlantic coast and the Andes, Colombia, E Venezuela and E Peru south to N Argentina, also Trinidad and possibly Tobago), *magellanica* (central Chile and central Argentina south to Tierra del Fuego, also Falkland Is.) and *andina* (puna zone of high Andes, S Peru, W Bolivia, N Chile and NW Argentina). A few specimens of *andina* from the Loa River in Chile have almost pure white underwings, and have been separated as a fourth race 'innotata' by some authors. Nominate *paraguaiae* has short wings, prominent dark breast streaking, and rather cold brown infusion to the breast and fringes to the upperparts; *magellanica* is longer-winged, warmer buff on breast and upperparts (but variable), has less prominent breast streaking, and deep rufous tail spots; *andina* is small, short-winged and yellow-legged, has a pale or almost white underwing, whitish frosting to the outer webs of the alula and to at least the outermost primaries when fresh, and extensive rufous in the tail.

MEASUREMENTS Length 225-290 mm (10¼"). Wing 115-130 mm (nominate), 130-142 mm (*magellanica*), 115-127 mm (*andina*); bill 62-79 mm (nominate), 55-79 mm (*magellanica*), 47-60 mm (*andina*); tarsus 26-30 mm (*andina*), 30-37 mm (others); tail 44-55 mm (nominate), 52-58 mm (*magellanica*), 38-52 mm (*andina*).

REFERENCES Johnson (1965), Barlow (1967), Tuck (1972).

177 NOBLE SNIPE *Gallinago nobilis*

Plate 70
(see also Plate 71)

A medium-sized montane snipe of the northern Andes, perhaps with parallels to Madagascar Snipe (173) but considerably broader-winged.

IDENTIFICATION Very like the typical small snipes in plumage and build, but larger and restricted to wetlands above and just below the tree-line. Only the Andean Snipe (180) is known to occur alongside, while Giant Snipe (178), Magellan Snipe (176) and, in winter, migrant Common Snipe (175) are found in the nearby lowlands. Imperial Snipe (181) may occur in the region, but this is unconfirmed. Similar in size to Andean and Imperial, but differs in more typical snipe-like patterning, with unbarred white belly, conspicuous pale crown-stripe and lines on the upperparts, and more pointed wing. Easiest distinctions from Common and Magellan Snipes are the larger size, broader wings and the dark trailing edge to the secondaries. Giant Snipe is larger still, and has rounded wings with barred flight feathers. On the ground, Noble's proportionately very long, usually clearly two-toned bill should serve to identify it. See Table on page 396 for a summary of characters. **Bare parts:** Bill very long (just overlapping in measurement with Giant Snipe), with a blackish tip and usually pale horn at the base. Iris dark brown. Legs greenish-grey. **VOICE** The call is described as clear and melodious. **HABITS** Found in grassy wetlands, swamps and marshy edges of fresh water in mountainous areas, chiefly between 2000 m and 3300 m. Display flight involves a bleating noise from the outer tail feathers, like that of Common Snipe but much lower-pitched. Breeding season may start as early as Mar, while eggs have been found in late July. Usually encountered singly or in pairs; difficult to observe on the ground.

Probably similar to Common Snipe in most elements of behaviour.
MOVEMENTS Thought to be an entirely sedentary species.
DESCRIPTION All plumages: Generally very similar in colour and pattern to Common and Magellan Snipes, but darker on the breast and often with rather more chestnut on the back of the head, hindneck, breast, flanks and undertail-coverts. Breast contrasts strongly with large, clear white belly-patch. Axillaries and underwing show slightly wider brown bars than white ones. Well-marked crown-stripe and lines at edges of mantle and scapulars. No white on the trailing edge to the wing; inner primaries and secondaries are narrowly tipped with slightly paler grey-brown. Tail of normally 16 feathers shows similar pattern to Common and Magellan Snipes, but rump and uppertail are often more rufous.
AGE/SEX Some individuals may be identifiable as juveniles by their short, loosely-structured wing-coverts; these have dull colours, with a narrow whitish-buff fringe broken narrowly by a point of brown at the shaft. Sexes are similar in plumage and measurements, except that longer-billed birds are females.
RACES No geographical variation is known.
MEASUREMENTS Length 300-325 mm (12½"). Wing 145-156 mm; bill 83-104 mm; tarsus 37-45 mm; tail 50-66 mm.
REFERENCES Tuck (1972).

178 GIANT SNIPE *Gallinago undulata*

Plate 70

An aberrant South American snipe, well named since it is by far the largest of the group.

IDENTIFICATION Snipe-like shape and pattern but massive size should be sufficient for identification, although size-difference from Common and Magellan Snipes (175, 176) may be less obvious in the northern race. Further distinguished in flight by broad, rounded wings like Eurasian Woodcock (159); uniquely among snipes, the flight feathers are barred. The bill is long and very deep at the base; the culmen joins the skull high on the forehead, giving a curious flat-headed profile. The other large South American snipes, Cordilleran (179), Andean (180) and Imperial (181), are all upland species and unlikely to overlap in range; they are also smaller, less clearly patterned on head and upperparts, and lack unbarred white on the belly. Noble Snipe (177) is similarly broad-winged and may just overlap in bill length, but is a considerably smaller-bodied bird. **Bare parts:** Bill brownish-horn, at base becoming blackish towards tip; often looks all-dark. Iris dark brown. Legs greyish-horn or brownish. **VOICE** When flushed, utters a positive, usually disyllabic call 'kek-kek'. The display flight and calls appear to be given only at night; display call is a rasping, guttural trisyllabic note.

HABITS Virtually unknown, hardly ever watched on the ground. No nests of the northern race have ever been described. It is not known whether there is a drumming display. Found among tall vegetation in swamps and flooded grasslands, locally up to 1000 m; sometimes occurs in dry savannas with tall herbage. Very difficult to flush, normally flies only when almost trodden on, and almost always flushed singly. Possibly more active at night than during the day.
MOVEMENTS Seasonal in its occurrence at some sites, apparently arriving after rain, but almost nothing is known of this bird's movements. A record in Tierra del Fuego (Oct 1974) may represent vagrancy, since breeding is not suspected south of Paraguay.
DESCRIPTION All plumages: Pale creamy-white crown-stripe, supercilium, malar area and throat contrast strongly with dark brown head-stripes, eye-stripe from base of upper mandible to behind eye, and broad bar across the ear-coverts. Neck off-white, heavily streaked brown; breast and flanks barred more than streaked, and lightly suffused buffish-brown. Central belly unbarred white. Undertail suffused tawny. Axillaries and underwing-coverts evenly barred brown and white. Mantle and scapu-

lars blackish-brown, with broad tawny-chestnut edgings forming spots on the upper back and lines on the mantle edges and on the scapulars. Coverts mainly dark brown, barred pale brownish-buff particularly on the inner feathers. Primaries and secondaries brown, clearly but narrowly barred with pale buff. Rump mainly dark brown, but with tawny-chestnut tips; uppertail almost unmarked tawny-chestnut. Tail has 14 feathers, obscurely patterned with narrow brown bars on a mainly pale tawny-brown background. Outer feathers are relatively narrow (5-7 mm).

AGE/SEX No ageing or sexing characters are known for this species.

RACES Two, ranges incompletely known: *undulata*

(Colombia to N Brazil) and *gigantea* (SE Brazil, Paraguay, possibly also Uruguay and Argentina); species apparently absent over most of Brazil. The races hardly overlap in size: most *gigantea* have wing > 169 mm, bill > 120 mm and tarsus > 51 mm, and *undulata* wing < 171 mm, bill < 115 mm and tarsus < 52 mm; *gigantea* also tends to have bolder markings.

MEASUREMENTS Length 400-435 mm (16½"). Wing 160-170 mm (*undulata*), 170-183 mm (*gigantea*); bill 100-114 mm (*undulata*), 123-132 mm (*gigantea*); tarsus 49-51 mm (*undulata*), 52-56 mm (*gigantea*); tail 49-57 mm.

REFERENCES Haverschmidt (1974), Abramson (1977).

179 CORDILLERAN SNIPE *Gallinago stricklandii*　　　　Plate 71

Other name: Strickland's Snipe

This and the next two species are heavy woodcock-like snipes of the Andean range; they are sometimes separated into their own genus, *Chubbia*. Often considered conspecific with Andean Snipe (180).

IDENTIFICATION A dark, rather bulky snipe with longish, slightly drooping bill and strongly-rounded wings. Sympatric only with Magellan Snipe (176), which is easily distinguished by its obviously smaller size and bolder patterning with clear pale stripes on head and upperparts and rich chestnut and blackish in the tail. In flight, Cordilleran is obviously much heavier and more woodcock-like, and has broad wings which lack a white trailing edge. A recent report of Giant Snipe (178) in Tierra del Fuego suggests possible range overlap with this species, but the race *gigantea* of Giant is considerably larger than Cordilleran, more boldly patterned, and with barred flight feathers obvious when flushed. Range in Chile, Argentina and the Falkland Is. is the easiest distinction from its two close relatives Andean and Imperial Snipes (181). Differs from Andean chiefly in its darker and warmer coloration above and below, smaller unmarked throat-patch, and less clearly barred underparts; also, tends to have a longer bill and shorter tail. The very rare Imperial Snipe is darker still, and has a distinct, strongly-banded pattern across the belly and flanks. **Bare parts:** Bill deep-based, tapering and slightly drooping towards tip; darkish horn with a blackish tip. Iris dark brown. Legs greyish, tinged yellowish-green; tibiae are feathered almost to the joint.

VOICE Only the display calls have been described. These are 'chip-chip-chip' uttered frequently in flight, and a penetrating 'char-woo' which alternates with drumming sounds in the nocturnal aerial display.

HABITS Frequents marshy, peaty and rushy areas, sometimes with low scrub, from 3000 m or more in central Chile almost to sea-level, often on quite small islands in the Falklands and Tierra del Fuego. Very rare in the Falklands, common in Tierra del Fuego and decreasingly so northwards through the range. Apart from its calling and drumming in display flight, almost nothing is known of its habits. Food includes beetles.

MOVEMENTS Mainly sedentary, but appears to vacate Tierra del Fuego in winter. Sporadic nature of records on the Falkland Is. may be due either to

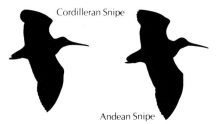

Cordilleran Snipe

Andean Snipe

the rarity of the species there or to occasional vagrancy from mainland South America.

DESCRIPTION Breeding and non-breeding: Generally rather rufous above and buffish below. Patterning is snipe-like, but rather indistinct. Dark, warm brown crown with narrow, indistinct pale crown-stripe. Face is warm buffish-brown, heavily flecked brown and crossed by broad, indistinct brown bars across lores and lower ear-coverts. Underparts are strongly suffused buff; breast is darkish buff, irregularly streaked dark brown; belly and flanks are paler, with fine, neat, brown barring and a small unbarred area in the centre of the belly. Axillaries and underwing-coverts are evenly barred with brown and pale buffish-brown. Upperparts are obscurely patterned with dark brown, blackish-brown and warm rufous-brown; edges to mantle and scapulars are paler, but do not form obvious lines. Wings are fairly evenly coloured, but with a narrow buffish trailing edge to the secondaries and inner primaries. Wing-tip is strongly rounded, with the outer three or four feathers almost equal in length. Tail has 14 feathers, blackish-brown barred with paler buffish-brown.

Juvenile: Probably shows pale buffish notches and tips on wing-coverts as described for Andean Snipe.

AGE/SEX Juveniles would be separable only in the hand. No differences are known between the sexes.

RACES No geographical variation is known.

MEASUREMENTS Length 290-300 mm (11½"). Wing 153-162 mm; bill 78-94 mm; tarsus 35-40 mm; tail 42-48 mm.

REFERENCES Johnson (1965), Humphrey *et al.* (1970), Tuck (1972), Woods (1975).

180 ANDEAN SNIPE *Gallinago jamesoni*   Plate 71

Other name: Jameson's Snipe
A large, high-altitude South American snipe. Often treated as conspecific with Cordilleran Snipe (179), but a distance of almost 2000 km separates their ranges.

IDENTIFICATION Like Cordilleran, a bulky, rather woodcock-like snipe with rather poorly-patterned plumage and a deep-based, tapering and slightly drooping bill. Sympatric with Magellan (176) and Noble (177) Snipes, but easily distinguished from both by larger size, indistinct patterning above, lacking clear pale lines on upperparts and reddish-chestnut on tail, and completely barred belly. In flight, further distinguished by broad, rounded wings, and from Magellan by lack of a white trailing edge to the wing. The race of Magellan Snipe normally found in the Andes (*andina*) has yellow legs. Also sympatric in SE Peru with Imperial Snipe (181). Latter species is very similar in plumage and build, but much darker and more rufous with a strongly-banded pattern on the belly and flanks; its underwing is blackish and the tail feathers unpatterned. Cordilleran Snipe is very similar indeed to Andean, but tends to be longer-billed and shorter-tailed. Andean differs in plumage by paler and colder brown-and-buff coloration, a larger unmarked throat-patch, and in having the whole belly and flanks fairly evenly barred with brown on an almost whitish background. **Bare parts:** As Cordilleran Snipe.
VOICE Only the display calls have been described. Displays are given at dusk and well into the night. The bird flies in wide, level circles giving double calls, written 'whee-tschwu' about twice per second, for a period of about 30 seconds to one minute, then slowly enters a dive to the ground. At the end of the dive there is a muffled bellowing sound, presumably made by vibration of wing or tail feathers.
HABITS Occurs in marshy areas where montane forest grades into grassland, chiefly around 3000-3500 m. Probably not rare, but difficult to flush and normally seen only when displaying. Habits are generally very poorly known.
MOVEMENTS Probably entirely sedentary.
DESCRIPTION Breeding and non-breeding: Generally very similar to Cordilleran Snipe, but with more cold buffish-brown and less rufous above, and less buffish below (particularly on belly, flanks and underwing). Belly is completely barred with brown. Axillaries and underwing-coverts are mainly brown, with narrow whitish-buff barring. **Juvenile:** As adult, but distinguished by pattern of larger coverts, rear scapulars and some tertials; these are notched with dark brown and tipped pale tawny-buff, in contrast to the adult pattern of dark brown feathers barred with cold buffish-brown.
AGE/SEX Juveniles are separable only in the hand. No differences are known between the sexes.
RACES No geographical variation is known.
MEASUREMENTS Length 290-300 mm (11½"). Wing 156-170 mm; bill 74-86 mm; tarsus 34-40 mm; tail 47-55 mm.
REFERENCES Vuilleumier (1969).

181 IMPERIAL SNIPE *Gallinago imperialis*   Plate 71

Other names: Banded Snipe, Bogota Snipe
For a century known only from two specimens (labelled Bogota), but recently rediscovered in Cordillera Vilcabamba near Cuzco, S Peru.

IDENTIFICATION This is a distinctively dark, blackish-brown snipe with a strongly-banded belly, known only from the timber-line of the Andes. Most likely to be detected and identified by its characteristic aerial display and loud calls, given at dawn and dusk; otherwise, very rarely encountered. Sympatric snipes in Peru are the Andean Snipe (180) and the puna race *andina* of the Magellan Snipe (176): both are much paler, and lack the strongly-banded belly. Andean Snipe shares with Imperial the heavy-bodied outline, slightly drooping bill, short, rather rounded wings, short tail and lack of distinct pale lines on the upperparts. It differs in having a larger white area on throat, pale barring on the underwing-coverts and a less contrasting whitish rear belly. The *andina* race of Magellan is much smaller, has obvious pale lines on the upperparts, an extensive area of unbarred white on the belly, and yellow legs. Imperial may be sympatric with Noble Snipe (177) in Colombia. See also Cordilleran Snipe (179), which however is a southern species. **Bare parts:** Bill rather heavy at base, but tapering and drooping slightly towards tip; dark brownish-grey. Iris dark brown. Legs medium-grey, feathered almost to the joint.
VOICE Shatteringly loud raucous song is given repeatedly in aerial display high over the forest at dawn and at dusk. The songs last about ten seconds, and are normally separated by about six seconds of silence; increasingly loud, sharp, single notes are followed by a series of loud double or triple notes, and then by single notes decreasing in volume. A separate call, possibly given on the ground, sounds like the final notes of the song, delivered more slowly and evenly.
HABITS The display flight follows a level, roughly circular path, but the bird enters a shallow dive to accompany the final notes of the song and then pulls out sharply with a clearly audible whirring noise, presumably caused by vibration of the wing feathers. The habitat is above 3000 m, around the tree-line, in damp, mountainous, forested country. Nothing is known of the feeding habits or nesting of this species. It occurs apparently at very low density. Displays were observed in July and Aug.
MOVEMENTS Completely unknown. The 'Bogota' specimens were probably local breeders rather than

migrants, but how close to Bogota they were collected is now unknown.

DESCRIPTION Adult: Crown blackish-brown, with narrow dark chestnut crown-stripe. Rest of head and upperparts generally barred dark chestnut and black. Tail of 12 feathers is brownish-grey, unpatterned, with the outer feather about 8 mm broad. Malar area is mid-brown. Rest of underparts shows two distinct patterns: throat to upper belly dark chestnut and black, as upperparts but more spotted and less clearly barred; lower belly to undertail strongly banded whitish and dark brown. Underwing-coverts are blackish, relieved only by tiny whitish tips. On the folded wing, the primary tips are completely covered by the tertials. The wing-point is primary 9, with primaries 8 and 10 both about 2 mm shorter. **Juvenile:** Unknown.

AGE/SEX It is presumed that the sexes are alike.

RACES No geographical variation is known. The Bogota specimens are closely similar to one from Peru.

MEASUREMENTS Length 290-310 mm (11¾"). Wing 161-162 mm; bill 87-94 mm; tarsus 32-38 mm; tail 58 mm.

REFERENCES Terborgh and Weske (1972).

182 JACK SNIPE *Lymnocryptes minimus*   **Plate 67**

The smallest of the snipes. It is sufficiently different from the other snipes to warrant being placed in its own genus.

IDENTIFICATION Considerably smaller and shorter-billed than other snipes occurring within its range. Only New Zealand (165) and Chatham Islands Snipes (166) are of comparable size, but both are restricted to oceanic islands off New Zealand. Most likely to be seen when flushed; it rises typically very close to the observer, and flies with relatively weak and fluttery wingbeats, dropping again after only a short distance. Take-off is far less abrupt and powerful than in Common Snipe (175), and small size is always evident; bill length is also a useful character. The tail is short and wedge-shaped, and never shows white on the sides. If seen on the ground, note small size and bill length, absence of a central crown-stripe, and the very dark mantle and scapulars which, uniquely for a snipe, are glossed with purple and green. Compare South American Painted Snipe (10) and Broad-billed Sandpiper (207), both of which are superficially similar. **Bare parts:** Basal two-thirds of bill dull pinkish-brown or greyish-yellow, terminal third blackish, straight and long, but typically at least 20 mm shorter than that of Common Snipe. Iris dark brown. Legs pale greenish, dull greenish-yellow or dull pinkish-brown.

VOICE Normally silent when flushed, but rarely gives a barely audible 'gah', much more subdued than Common's call. Contrastingly noisy when breeding; rhythmical song is likened to the sound of a galloping horse, a muffled gulping 'ogogoglK-ogoglK'; also makes knocking noises and a weak whistling, presumed to be vocal.

HABITS Nests May-early Sept in open boreal marshlands, often on floating bogs but sometimes on drier ground among bushes. Male holds a large territory, sometimes up to 20 ha, advertised by high aerial switchback display; song is given in display flight and from the ground. Display can occur at any time of day, but not usually in bright sunlight. Apparently, incubation is mostly or entirely by the female, but relatively little is known of breeding biology. Outside the breeding season, occurs mainly on inland freshwater marshes, usually with dense vegetation; prefers soft silty mud. Generally scarce, solitary and inconspicuous. Rarely flies by day unless flushed. When feeding, typically rocks body rhythmically up and down in the manner of a woodcock, as if on springs.

Capable of a crake-like run. Freezes when approached, and adopts remarkably effective camouflage postures in which the body may be tilted or angled to align the pale lines on the upperparts with the vegetation. Relies on camouflage on initial approach, and may flush at less than 1 m; there are records of birds actually being stepped on, or even captured by hand.

MOVEMENTS Adults and young remain in or near breeding range during moult in Aug-Sept, rarely appearing south until mid-Sept. Does not arrive in south of winter range until Nov, much later than other migratory snipes. Return passage is quite early; some are displaying on territory by mid-Apr. In Europe, winters as far north as Shetland and even Iceland on occasion. Vagrant Labrador (Dec 1927), Azores, Madeira, Africa south to Ghana, Nigeria, Zambia and Tanzania, Pribilof Is. (spring 1919), and California (Nov 1938).

DESCRIPTION All plumages: Crown glossy blackish-brown, flecked paler; broad yellowish-buff supercilia completely surround and isolate a dark line above the eye. Lores are crossed by a broad dark line; eye-stripe continues narrowly behind eye to join a dark spot on the lower ear-coverts and a diffuse dark line across the lower cheeks. Rest of sides of face, also chin and throat, are buffish-white. Hindneck is mottled brown and grey-brown, and flecked paler. Mantle, upper scapulars, rump and uppertail are brownish-black, glossed quite strongly with purple and green, contrasting markedly with four striking pale golden-buff parallel lines (at junctions of mantle and scapulars, and at lower border of upper scapulars). Lower scapulars are dark brown, marked with reddish-buff and pale buff. Upperwing-coverts are brown, fringed buffish. Flight feathers are dark brown, but secondaries and inner primaries are narrowly tipped white, as are greater coverts and greater primary coverts. Tail is dark brown, darkest in centre, markedly wedge-shaped, and composed of only six pairs of rather pointed feathers. Neck, breast and, to a lesser extent, anterior flanks are suffused and streaked brown; rest of underparts are whitish, although undertail is lightly streaked with brown. Underwing and axillaries are dull greyish-white, lightly streaked brown.

AGE/SEX Full juvenile differs marginally from adults in having smaller and fainter brown streaks on under-tail, and slightly more pointed tail feathers (most evident on pairs 2 and 3). These characters are typically lost during moult in Aug-Oct, but some first-winter individuals are separable. Sexes are similar in plumage, but males average longer in wing and tail.

RACES No geographical variation is known.
MEASUREMENTS Length 170-190 mm (7"). Wing 105-121 mm; bill 36-43 mm; tarsus 22-25 mm; tail 45-54 mm.
REFERENCES Nilsson and Nilsson (1978), Hollyer (1984).

183 SHORT-BILLED DOWITCHER *Limnodromus griseus* Plate 72

This and Long-billed Dowitcher (184) were generally regarded as a single species under the name *griseus* until 1950. This, compounded by various erroneous speculations in the literature, has led to much unwarranted confusion between the two species which is only now being resolved.

IDENTIFICATION The two North American dowitchers are easily separated from other waders by their rufous, brown or grey plumages and long snipe-like bills; unlike snipes, they do not have prominently-striped head and upperpart patterns, and there are seasonal changes in coloration. Godwits (123-126) and Asiatic Dowitcher (185) also have long bills, but are darker-legged and considerably larger. In flight, Short-billed and Long-billed show a rather plump outline, fairly narrow wings with a fine pale trailing edge to the secondaries, and a conspicuous white patch on the back, showing as a slit of white between the tertials as in Spotted Redshank (136); Asiatic has a brown-barred white rump, and a broad pale area on the wing covering the secondaries and bases of the inner primaries. The principal characters by which Short-billed and Long-billed can be separated are listed in the Table on page 397. Juveniles are easily separable by plumage characters; breeding adults require more care, particularly in view of racial variation in Short-billed; non-breeding birds are separable by plumage only in ideal views. Calls are diagnostic throughout the year and are easily learnt. Bill length is of little value in field conditions.
Bare parts: Bill blackish-brown, tinged greenish or yellowish-green over the basal half. Iris dark brown. Legs greyish- or brownish-green, more yellowish-green on juveniles.
VOICE Usual flight note is a rapid mellow 'tu-tu-tu', faster than similar call of Lesser Yellowlegs (142); in cadence (but not in tone) it recalls Ruddy Turnstone (154) to most observers. Other similar calls (see Table) are also distinct from calls of Long-billed. Song is a prolonged gurgling repetition of 'cha' syllables.
HABITS Nests late May-early Aug in muskegs and similar open marshes and bogs. Male has hovering song flight over the territory. Both sexes incubate, but female takes little part in raising the brood and may leave the breeding grounds in late June. Occurs on migration in a wide variety of wetland habitats, inland and coastal; essentially coastal in winter, feeding mostly on intertidal mudflats, often in large flocks. Feeds mainly by rapid, snipe-like vertical probing, like a sewing-machine. Usually feeds in water, often submerging head. When disturbed stands motionless, typically holding bill-tip just below water surface, or dashes away on strong, swift flight. Often roosts in large groups with other estuarine waders.
MOVEMENTS A relatively early autumn migrant; adults move south from late June, females first, and juveniles from late July. The three well-separated races

(see below) differ in normal migration routes: western race *caurinus* migrates mostly close to the Pacific coast, and winters from N California to Peru; central race *hendersoni* crosses the E Great Plains, straggling west at least to Utah and Arizona and east to the Atlantic coast (vagrant Quebec), and winters from Florida westwards and on both coasts of Central America south to Panama; eastern *griseus* moves chiefly along the Atlantic coast, straggling west to Texas, and winters North Carolina to Florida and south through the Caribbean to Brazil. Northward passage in USA spans early Mar-early June; routes used by each race in spring are broadly similar. Vagrant Galapagos and probably N Argentina. Reports of transatlantic vagrancy stem largely from misidentified Long-billed and old specimens of uncertain provenance; records are currently claimed from Norway, Sweden, Britain, Belgium, Spain and Ghana. All British records are under review.
DESCRIPTION Breeding: Crown dark brown, flecked pale; supercilium pale chestnut; lores are crossed by narrow, neat, dark brown line which extends for a short distance behind eye. Side of head pale chestnut, very lightly streaked brown. Hindneck variably pale chestnut or whitish, streaked brown. Mantle and scapular feathers are mainly black-centred and fringed rusty-buff or pale cinnamon; tertials are similar, but more barred. Wing-coverts are grey-brown, fringed paler or whitish. Secondaries dark, but with trailing edge partly washed whitish to give a palish bar which extends slightly onto inner primaries; primaries otherwise blackish-brown. Back and upper rump are white; lower rump and uppertail-coverts white, barred dark brown. Tail variably patterned with brown and white bars, about equal in width or with white bars broader. Neck and breast are washed pale chestnut-red; belly and vent may be chestnut-red or whitish; breast, flanks and undertail are variably spotted and barred dark brown. Underwing-coverts and axillaries white, lightly barred brown. Non-breeding: Crown, hindneck and upperparts grey-brown, fringed paler; lores are slightly darker grey-brown; supercilium whitish. Underparts mainly white, with throat and upper breast slightly washed greyish and usually finely spotted or streaked darker grey; rear flanks and undertail-coverts lightly spotted and barred. Juvenile: Mantle and scapulars darkish brown, broadly fringed warm chestnut-buff. Wing-coverts mid-brown, fringed buff, palest on lessers. Larger scapulars and tertials show extensive warm buff or pale chestnut internal markings; tertials may be strongly barred

brown and buff ('tiger-striped'). Underparts largely buffish-white, but washed with rich buff on sides of breast; breast, flanks and undertail are finely streaked and spotted.

AGE/SEX Juveniles are easily separable as long as characteristic scapulars and tertials are retained, usually to Dec-Jan. Sexes are not known to differ in plumage, but females average larger.

RACES Three: nominate *griseus* (E Canada), *hendersoni* (central Canada) and *caurinus* (S Alaska). Differences are mainly in size and breeding plumage; other plumages are virtually identical. Average size increases from east to west. In *griseus*, belly is largely white, even in full plumage, breast is densely spotted and flanks heavily barred. In *hendersoni*, entire underparts are usually reddish, almost unspotted in centre of breast but heavily spotted on breast-sides, upper flanks and undertail. The race *caurinus* is variable, and may show the whole range of underpart colour and pattern.

MEASUREMENTS Length 250-290 mm (10½"). Wing 135-156 mm; bill 51-68 mm; tarsus 31-41 mm; tail 50-57 mm.

REFERENCES Pitelka (1950), Nisbet (1961b), Wilds and Newlon (1983).

184 LONG-BILLED DOWITCHER *Limnodromus scolopaceus* Plate 72

A very similar bird to Short-billed Dowitcher (183) and separated only in 1950. In spite of its E Siberian and W Nearctic breeding grounds, this is the dowitcher which occurs regularly in Europe.

IDENTIFICATION Seé Short-billed Dowitcher, and Table on page 397. Separation from Short-billed is simple in juvenile plumage (in which most vagrants arrive), more difficult in breeding plumage (owing to the variability of Short-billed), and not safe in non-breeding plumage except in ideal views or in the hand. Calls, however, are diagnostic throughout the year, and are easily learnt. Asiatic Dowitcher (185) may overlap in range with Long-billed in E Asia, but is an obviously larger bird with proportionately longer dark grey legs and a flatter forehead; in flight, Asiatic has the white centred on the rump rather than on the back, and has a broad mottled area across the secondaries and inner primaries rather than a fairly sharp whitish trailing edge. **Bare parts:** As Short-billed, but bill and legs average longer.

VOICE Usual call is a high, thin 'keek', either a single note or up to five or six rapidly run together as an accelerating series. There is some similarity to calls of Wood Sandpiper (145), while distant single calls may suggest Sanderling (189) or even Little Stint (193). Experienced observers have little difficulty separating the two North American dowitchers on call. Song, given all year, is a very rapid repetition of 'pee-ter-wee-too' or part of this phrase.

HABITS Nests late May-Aug around grassy or sedgey swamps and marshes in the tundra. Male delivers song in hovering display flight. Both sexes incubate, but only male looks after the brood; females often leave breeding grounds early. When not breeding, differs noticeably from Short-billed in habitat choice, preferring fresh or brackish pools to intertidal habitats; migrant and coastal-wintering Long-billed do, however, use intertidal habitats regularly, often alongside Short-billed. Gregarious, but usually seen in smaller flocks than Short-billed. Behaviour generally is much as Short-billed.

MOVEMENTS A relatively late autumn migrant; adults move south from July onwards, but in greatest numbers in Aug-Sept, while juveniles do not appear on migration before mid-Aug and are rare before mid-Sept. There is a strong easterly element to the migration, which brings birds to the Atlantic coast regularly as far north as New England. A small number probably follow W Pacific coasts, since a few occur in Japan on passage; vagrants recently recorded

juvenile tertials

Long-billed Dowitcher

Short-billed Dowitcher

Bali, Brunei and Thailand. Winters in S USA and Central America, rarely south to Panama, but there are no certain records in S America. Spring migration in USA occurs late Mar-mid May, and follows a more westerly route; migrants are scarce east of the Mississippi and rare on Atlantic coast. Vagrant Quebec, Sable I. (Nova Scotia), and W Europe between Finland and Spain; juveniles are virtually annual in Britain and Ireland from Sept 20th onwards, and sometimes stay the winter.

DESCRIPTION Breeding: For minor differences from Short-billed, see that species and Table on page 397. Typically shows heavy spotting on foreneck, dense barring or spotting on breast, narrow barring on flanks, and unmarked chestnut-red belly. Whitish fringing to fresh upperparts and underparts wears off rapidly. **Non-breeding:** As Short-billed, but averaging slightly darker grey. Foreneck and breast are more solidly grey, lightly mottled but not speckled, ending fairly sharply against white belly. Tail pattern also differs (see Table). **Juvenile:** Mantle and scapulars dark brown, with fine, slightly-scalloped chestnut fringes and virtually no internal markings; tertials are solidly dark, except for narrow brownish-buff edges and, rarely, faint internal markings just inside the tip. On some individuals buff wash on sides of breast contrasts noticeably with grey sides of neck.

are retained at least to Nov and sometimes to Feb, enabling ageing at close range in the field. Sexes are not known to differ in plumage, but females average larger; size-dimorphism is greater than in Short-billed.

RACES No geographical variation is known.
MEASUREMENTS Length 270-300 mm (11¼''). Wing 140-159 mm; bill 54-78 mm; tarsus 34-46 mm; tail 51-62 mm.
REFERENCES Pitelka (1950), Nisbet (1961b), Wilds and Newlon (1983).

185 ASIATIC DOWITCHER *Limnodromus semipalmatus*   **Plate 49**

Other names: Asian Dowitcher, Snipe-billed Godwit, Semi-palmated Snipe
A rare species, for which the breeding and wintering ranges are as yet poorly known. Recently flocks of over a hundred have been found in NW Australia, 300 in Hong Kong, 500 in Thailand and 1,500 in Sumatra, and it is clearly more numerous than once supposed.

IDENTIFICATION This bird is clearly a dowitcher in its bill shape and feeding behaviour, but in size and shape and in plumages at all seasons it closely resembles Bar-tailed Godwit (125). It joins freely with flocks of that species, and is very easily overlooked. The best distinctions are as follows. Bill shape and colour are diagnostic (see below); bill is often held well below horizontal. Body size is clearly smaller. Eye-stripe is bolder, particularly across lores; long whitish supercilium extends well onto sides of forehead. In breeding and juvenile plumages, the flanks show narrow vertical dark bars, the undertail-coverts are barred, and the scapulars have dark brown centres and distinctive, narrow but conspicuous whitish-buff or pale chestnut fringes. In flight, the rump is barred brown and contrasts little with the back and tail, as in eastern Bartails, but the underwing is paler, almost completely white; as in Bartail, there is a paler band across the wing covering the secondaries and the bases of the inner primaries, but in Asiatic Dowitcher this area may be almost translucent, viewed against the light. Feeding behaviour differs in that the dowitcher feeds by almost continuous vertical probing (the 'sewing-machine' action), usually in knee-deep or belly-deep water, while the godwit hooks food forwards and upwards before swallowing, probes more slowly, covers more ground, and feeds more often on exposed mud. Black-tailed and Hudsonian Godwits (123, 124) differ further in bold wing and tail patterns. Short-billed and Long-billed Dowitchers (183, 184) share feeding behaviour, but are considerably smaller with shorter, green or yellowish-green legs and in flight a narrow white patch on the back and a sharper, whiter trailing edge to the wing. **Bare parts:** Bill of similar length to Bartail's, but straight rather than upcurved, solid blackish rather than two-toned, deep along its whole length and swollen laterally at tip; at close range, some pinkish may be visible at the base of the lower mandible. Iris dark brown. Legs longish, dark grey; whole length of toes projects beyond tail-tip in flight.
VOICE Contact calls are a yelping 'chep-chep' or 'chowp' and a soft moaning 'kiaow'. The latter call has a strange quality, like a distant human voice. On the breeding grounds, also gives a soft, repeated 'kewick' or 'kru-ru'.
HABITS Nests from late May onwards, in small colonies in sparsely-vegetated parts of grassy wetlands, both fresh and saline. Often allows close approach at the nest. Strictly coastal in winter, occurring on intertidal mudflats and fairly frequently on coastal

lagoons. Feeds and flies often in tight flocks. Mixes freely at roost with godwits and other waders. Flight is powerful, often aerobatic.
MOVEMENTS Normal winter range apparently extends from SE India through Thailand, Malaysia and Indonesia to NW Australia, but there are also records from Papua New Guinea and the Brisbane and Melbourne areas of SE Australia. Sumatra is apparently the stronghold. Occurs on passage in Japan, E China, Hong Kong, Vietnam and the Philippines. Some remain in non-breeding range all year. Vagrant Aden, and Kenya (Nov 1966).
DESCRIPTION Breeding: Crown and eye-stripe from bill brownish-chestnut. Rest of head, including supercilia and narrow eye-ring, also neck, clear chestnut-red; the chin may be paler. On the upperparts, the mantle, scapulars and tertials have dark brownish-black feather centres narrowly fringed whitish and chestnut. Wing-coverts are similar, but with slightly paler, grey-brown centres. Primary coverts, outer primaries and tips of inner primaries are darkish brown; bases of inner primaries and secondaries are paler brown. Back, rump and uppertail-coverts are buffish-white, heavily barred brown. Tail shows broad brown bars and narrower white ones. Breast is evenly chestnut-red, becoming blotched with white on upper belly; rest of belly and flanks mainly white, the latter with many narrow vertical brown bars. Undertail-coverts white, barred and spotted brown. Underwing-coverts and axillaries very white, with just a few brown tips. **Non-breeding:** All chestnut-red is lost. Supercilium, sides of head, neck and underparts become white, slightly mottled grey-brown especially on the breast; flanks are obscurely barred grey-brown. Upperparts generally dark grey-brown, with contrastingly whitish feather edgings. **Juvenile:** Upperparts paler than breeding adult, a uniform darkish brown with extensive neat buff fringes. Wing-coverts slightly paler than scapulars. Supercilium is clearer white and eye-stripe dark brown; underparts are whitish, but neck, breast and flanks are strongly washed warm buff and streaked slightly darker.
AGE/SEX Juvenile remains distinct in the field until about Nov. Female averages larger and is slightly duller, with less chestnut-red, in breeding plumage.
RACES No geographical variation is known.
MEASUREMENTS Length 340-360 mm (13¾''). Wing 174-188 mm; bill 75-88 mm; tarsus 46-54 mm; tail 60-67 mm.
REFERENCES Paige (1965), Smith (1974), Kitson (1978), Jaensch (1983).

186 SURFBIRD *Aphriza virgata*   Plate 62

An unusual calidrid-like wader, with a rather plover-like bill and turnstone-like feeding habits, which shows strong similarities in breeding plumage and breeding habitat to Great Knot (188).

IDENTIFICATION Easily distinguished from all similar species by short, rather thick and blunt-tipped bill, and in flight by white wingbar, uppertail and base of tail, and broad black tail-band. Grey plumage and rock-haunting habits are similar to those of Rock Sandpiper (203) and Black Turnstone (155), which share the northern part of its range. Best told from Rock Sandpiper by short, rather thick bill and by white rump in flight. Larger size, yellow legs and bill-base and paler plumage are ready distinctions from Black Turnstone. **Bare parts:** Bill rather short and plover-like, mainly dark brown, with a yellow or orangey patch covering cutting edge and base to lower mandible. Iris brown. Rather short, yellow legs.
VOICE A shrill, plaintive whistle 'kee-wee-ah'. Often silent.
HABITS Breeds late May-July on rocky ridges above the timber-line in mountains of central Alaska and adjacent Yukon Territory. Protects eggs from grazing sheep and caribou by sitting tight until the last moment and then flying in the face of the animal; humans may be treated similarly. Nest and eggs were unknown until 1926. Non-breeding habitat is rocky ocean shores and jetties. Feeds on seaweed-covered rocks close to the tideline, sometimes on adjacent sandy beaches. Occurs rarely on mudflats. Gregarious, often in large groups on migration. Often very tame.
MOVEMENTS Strongly migratory, some reaching Tierra del Fuego. Extremely rare away from Pacific coast. Southward movement of adults begins mid-July. Migration is mostly coastal, but a few may overfly W USA in spring from the head of the Gulf of California. Occurs rarely in spring on the Texas coast. One record from Pennsylvania. Non-breeders may remain in some parts of the wintering range all year.
DESCRIPTION Breeding: Cap, mantle and upper scapulars dark grey, with bold chestnut and whitish edgings. Rear scapulars have conspicuous paired golden-buff oval spots, which become more obvious as greyish or blackish tips wear off. Sides of head and neck are white, with blackish streaking; breast has heavier black spotting, and flanks show black V-shaped markings. Uppertail and base of tail are white; tail has broad black band, but extreme tail-tip is white. Long, narrow, white wingbar. Underwing mainly white. **Non-breeding:** Mantle, scapulars and wing-coverts become plain slate-grey. Breast slate-grey, with indistinct brownish spots. Belly white; flanks show brownish-grey spots and 'V's. **Juvenile:** Similar to non-breeding adult, but grey feathers of upperparts each show buff fringe and clear dark subterminal bar. Breast is mottled with brownish.
AGE/SEX Juvenile inner medians showing the clear subterminal bar may still be present until Apr. One-year-olds show very worn primaries, and attain only partial breeding plumage. Sexes are apparently similar.
RACES No geographical variation is known.
MEASUREMENTS Length 235-255 mm (9½"). Wing 169-185 mm; bill 22-27 mm; tarsus 29-32 mm; tail 63-69 mm.
REFERENCES Dixon (1927), Jehl (1968), Frisch (1978).

187 RED KNOT *Calidris canutus*   Plate 73

Other names: Knot, Lesser Knot
A classic high-arctic breeder and long-distance migrant. Winters in large concentrations in widely-scattered localities.

IDENTIFICATION A bulky calidrid with a pale greyish rump and tail and a whitish wingbar. Almost oval form emphasised by short greenish legs makes feeding birds look 'low-slung'. Pale rump and largish size distinguish it from all other calidrids except the noticeably larger and longer-billed Great Knot (188). Latter, however, has a whiter rump contrasting more strongly with mantle and tail, and in breeding plumage blackish-brown spotting on a white breast (underparts not red). Curlew Sandpiper (205) also has red underparts in breeding plumage and a pale rump, but is much smaller and slimmer, has a longer, more decurved bill, clearer white rump and longer black legs. **Bare parts:** Bill blackish, rather short for the size of the bird, faintly downcurved. Iris dark brown. Legs short, dull olive-green, more yellowish-green in juveniles.
VOICE Not particularly vocal; single individuals are almost always silent. A low, slightly harsh monosyllabic 'knutt', and variants, is heard from feeding birds and flocks in flight. On migration, a less harsh disyllabic 'knuup-knuup'. In display, the male has a fluty melodious song, a rather melancholy 'poor-me'.
HABITS Breeds June-Aug inland on moist tundra and upland glacial gravel. Display involves a high circling flight on still or quivering wings, ending in a rapid tumbling fall to land with wings upraised. Both sexes incubate, but the females disappear after hatching, leaving the males to tend the brood. Strictly coastal in winter, but occurs rarely inland on passage. Prefers large, essentially sandy estuaries, also beaches and rock shelves. A highly gregarious species which forms dense and spectacular feeding and roosting flocks, although occurring at relatively few sites. Feeds mainly by probing, but may also peck at surface foods. Flying flocks are typically ovoid, flat-bottomed when near the ground. Knot flocks at great distance appear 'grainier' than those of smaller species, and with slower, steadier changes in shade and direction resembling drifting smoke. On migration flies in lines or 'V's.
MOVEMENTS Populations from Greenland and NE

Canada cross the N Atlantic, often via Iceland, to winter in W Europe. Central Siberian birds use Great Circle route through W Europe to W Africa, and some penetrate to South Africa. E Siberian race winters chiefly in Australasia. W North American race winters on both coasts of North America and in South America, chiefly in Argentina, and may be a vagrant to Britain. Typically makes long flights between staging-posts. Normally strictly coastal but has overland migration routes, for example over W Africa and central Brazil, and stragglers may be seen well inland. Has bred Spitsbergen. Can occur almost anywhere on passage, but rare in E Africa and the Indian subcontinent. Vagrant to many oceanic islands, including Madeira and Cape Verde Is. in the Atlantic and Chatham Is. and Macquarie I. in the Southern Ocean. **DESCRIPTION Breeding:** Face and underparts chestnut-red, variable in shade, with variable amount of white and brown spotting on rear belly, and of flecks of white on rest of belly. Often slightly paler around base of bill. Underwing-coverts greyish and white. Feathers of mantle, scapulars and tertials are blackish-centred, initially edged rufous or yellowish and tipped pale grey; the tips and edges abrade to leave large blackish areas by Aug. Wing-coverts are grey, fringed whitish. Flight feathers are blackish, with distinct but narrow white wingbar formed mainly by tips of greater coverts and inner primary coverts. Lower rump and uppertail are whitish-grey, lightly flecked brown; tail is washed pale brownish-grey. **Non-breeding:** Upperparts, including crown and hindneck, rather plain grey; coverts are thinly fringed with white. Most grey feathers have a very fine blackish shaft-streak. Head pattern dull, with an indistinct

whitish supercilium. Underparts white, suffused and streaked grey on breast and upper belly. **Juvenile:** As non-breeding, but mantle, scapulars and coverts have a brownish wash; in addition, boldly-pencilled submarginal lines and white fringes on these feathers give a characteristic scaly pattern. Breast has a gentle pinkish-buff wash at first.
AGE/SEX The highly distinctive submarginal lines and brown coverts of the juvenile are detectable for most of the first year. One-year-old birds do not attain full summer plumage and mostly remain south of breeding grounds. Can be sexed in breeding plumage, although with difficulty, by males having red underparts more even in shade and more extensive on rear belly. Females average slightly larger.
RACES Four: *rufa* (W Nearctic, winters USA to South America) has pale chestnut underparts with large whitish rear belly, mantle fringes rufous; *rogersi* (E Siberia, winters Australasia) is shorter-billed, with medium-shade chestnut belly, moderate area of white on rear belly, mantle fringes rufous; nominate *canutus* (central Siberia, winters Africa) is long-billed, with deep chestnut underparts, little white on rear belly, mantle fringes dark chestnut; *islandica* (Greenland and NE Canada, winters in W Europe) is shorter-billed than nominate race, with medium-chestnut underparts, and mantle with many yellowish fringes.
MEASUREMENTS Length 230-250 mm (9½"). Wing 155-180 mm; bill 29-38 mm; tarsus 27-33 mm; tail 55-66 mm.
REFERENCES Hobson (1972), Prater (1972), Nettleship (1974), Dick *et al.* (1976), Dorogoy (1982), Harrington (1983).

188 GREAT KNOT *Calidris tenuirostris*   Plate 73

Other names: Greater Knot, Great Sandpiper
The largest calidrid; plumages and breeding haunts parallel those of the Surfbird (186) of Alaska, to which it may be closely related.

IDENTIFICATION Differs from other calidrids chiefly in its large size and in its highly distinctive black-spotted underparts in breeding plumage. Similar in shape to Red Knot (187), but longer-billed and longer-bodied, with a somewhat protruding breast; appears longer-winged and less compact in flight. Also differs in its poorer supercilium and wingbar and its clearer but narrower white rump, less obscured with black. The streaked appearance of the crown, nape and mantle is a clear distinction from Red Knot in all plumages. Never shows red on the underparts. **Bare parts:** Bill longer and deeper-based than Red Knot's, but tapers to a finer point; blackish-brown, becoming slightly greenish towards base. Iris dark brown. Legs dark slate or greenish-grey, paler and greener on juveniles, usually darker than on Red Knot.
VOICE Rather silent, although occasionally gives a disyllabic 'nyut-nyut' call like that of Red Knot. The first syllable is longer, with a rising inflexion, and the second is shorter and lower-pitched.
HABITS Breeds in the subarctic highlands of NE Siberia. As yet only two nests have been reported, and its breeding habits are very little known. Essentially coastal outside the breeding season, like Red

Knot occurring in large concentrations at favoured sites, but rare elsewhere except on passage. Prefers large sandy or muddy estuaries and coasts where a large tidal range leaves much mud uncovered at low tide; feeds mainly by probing. Flying flocks are often less dense than those of Red Knot, and have a looser, more linear form recalling Bar-tailed Godwit (125). Forms dense packs at roost, associating freely with Red Knot, godwits, sandplovers and Red-necked Stint (192).
MOVEMENTS From Siberian breeding grounds migrates to the Indian subcontinent, SE Asia and Australasia. Much larger numbers than previously suspected are now known to be regular in Australia, especially on NW and Gulf coasts. Only a scarce migrant in W Indonesia; most migrate via Philippines and New Guinea. Rare in New Zealand. Vagrant Arabia and Morocco (an adult in Aug 1980). First-years apparently do not return to the breeding area, spending the northern summer in, particularly, the tropical parts of the non-breeding range.
DESCRIPTION Breeding: Head and neck feathers have blackish-brown centres, giving a streaked pattern on a whitish background. Cap is darker; super-

cilium is poorly marked, although there is a diffuse whitish area above the lores; lores have a diffuse area of brown; chin and throat are clear white. Breast and flank feathers are white, with bold black subterminal spots or bars forming an almost solid black centre to the breast, especially in worn plumage; flanks and undertail show heart-shaped black spots. Belly and vent are clean white. Underwing mainly white; axillaries white, but slightly sullied with brown. Back is blackish-brown with narrow pale greyish tips, becoming almost solid black in worn plumage. Central two lines of scapulars have a pair of very large bright chestnut ovals on each feather, showing as a chestnut band above the folded wing. In worn plumage, the dark feather tips wear away revealing a blaze of almost unmarked chestnut. Coverts are grey with dark shaft-streaks and whitish fringes. The upperwing shows a narrow wingbar, formed by white tips to the greater and inner primary coverts; the shafts of the primaries are white, but there is only a very narrow edging of white on the webs of the inner primaries. Rump and uppertail-coverts are white, sparsely marked with blackish. Tail is plain dark grey. **Non-breeding:** Paler and greyer above and on breast; breast-band becomes finely streaked rather than spotted, although most birds retain some bold spotting.

Flanks are sparsely streaked; the undertail is white. Head and upperparts have clear streaks of blackish-grey, most evident on the crown and hindneck. **Juvenile:** Darker and browner than non-breeding adult; mantle and scapulars are darkish brown, with narrow whitish-buff fringes (slightly scalloped) giving a scaly pattern. Coverts and tertials are paler brown, with whitish-buff fringes and, on the larger feathers, dark brown subterminal bands. Crown is darker, forming a distinct cap, but as in the adult there is no clear supercilium. Breast is suffused with brownish-buff and streaked and spotted with dark brown.

AGE/SEX Juvenile plumage is rapidly lost after Oct, but some brownish coverts are retained until Mar-Apr. Only second-year birds and adults are in primary moult Sept-Dec. First-years often attain well-developed breeding plumage. Females are larger on average, and tend to have less chestnut in the scapulars in breeding plumage.

RACES No geographical variation is known.

MEASUREMENTS Length 260-280 mm (10½"). Wing 170-189 mm (males), 177-203 mm (females); bill 39-47 mm; tarsus 32-38 mm; tail 56-70 mm.

REFERENCES Andreev (1980b), Flint et al. (1980a), Gerasimov (1980), Prater and Grant (1982).

189 SANDERLING *Calidris alba*   Plate 74

This bird nests only in a few scattered areas of the high Arctic, to within 960 km of the North Pole, but is widespread and familiar in most parts of the world as a non-breeding visitor.

IDENTIFICATION One of the easiest calidrids to identify by virtue of its habits and habitat and by the extensive white in the plumages. It is a rather thickset small wader with black bill and legs, typically seen in small, highly active flocks on sandy beaches; the birds scamper along the tide edge, sometimes dashing after retreating waves. Sanderlings do, however, mix with other waders on estuaries and occur on migration at inland or freshwater sites, and it is these 'out-of-habitat' birds that may lead to confusion. In flight, it shows the broadest white wingbar of any calidrid, contrasting strongly with blackish trailing and leading edges to the wings. In breeding plumage, head, breast and upperparts become mainly rich dark chestnut, but lower breast and belly remain bright white; the general pattern is similar to Red-necked Stint (192), and to a lesser extent Little Stint (193), but Sanderling can be distinguished by its larger size (40% greater in total length) and by the more extensive greyish-white tipping to the upperparts. Compare also with Spoon-billed Sandpiper (206), which is superficially similar in all plumages. Non-breeding plumage is plain pale grey above, much paler than any other calidrid, but the black lesser and primary coverts form a contrasting patch at the bend of the folded wing; non-breeding Broad-billed (207) also shows this pattern, but is distinguished by its dark mask and whitish supercilium, and by its more contrasting dark feather centres above. On juvenile Sanderling, the upperparts are characteristically spangled with black and whitish. Flying birds may be confused with Grey Phalarope (158), but latter has a weaker wingbar, a broader tail with less contrasting pale

sides, and a bold blackish eye-patch. **Bare parts:** Bill black, rarely tinged paler; about head length, heavy-based but tapering and slightly drooped. Iris dark brown. Legs black or blackish.

VOICE Flight calls are a rather quiet 'twick' or 'kip', sometimes repeated, and occasionally a short trill. Song is a complex churring delivered in one- or two-second bursts during display flight.

HABITS Nests mainly in extreme arctic conditions on closest land to the North Pole, but some nest just south of the Arctic Circle. Season at such latitudes is extremely short. Eggs are laid from mid-June, later if snow has not melted. Female often lays two clutches, one to be incubated by the male. Occurs at inland waters on migration, and a few winter inland at some saline lakes. Prefers sandy ocean beaches and sandier outer reaches of estuaries, but also occurs on rocky or muddy shores. Often in large flocks, sometimes with other small waders; may join mixed roosts, or form a monospecific pack high on the beach. Often fairly tame; rarely flies far when disturbed. Feeds mostly by rapid probing or pecking, but at times has a more hesitant, plover-like action.

MOVEMENTS Migrations are largely offshore or coastal, but occurs regularly on many oceanic islands; vagrants have occurred in most inland continental regions. Adults depart breeding grounds mid-July to mid-Aug, and juveniles late Aug-early Sept. Both Greenland and Siberian breeders pass through British Isles in autumn, and some continue along Atlantic coast to South Africa. Siberian birds also cross USSR to coasts of Indian Ocean and SW Pacific. Canadian nesters migrate south as far as Tierra del

Fuego on Pacific and Atlantic coasts. Despite the very wide range, individuals are often faithful to wintering sites and migration stop-overs. Northward movement spans late Mar-late May; typically, large flocks fly long distances between favoured sites at which they can regain weight rapidly. Many non-breeders remain south all year.

DESCRIPTION Breeding: Feathers at base of bill are whitish, as is chin, but rest of head, neck and upper breast are strongly washed deep chestnut and streaked dark brown. Mostly-chestnut upper breast forms a sharp and neat division with white lower breast, belly and underwing. Mantle, scapulars and tertials are mainly blackish with rufous and grey fringes and whitish notches, at first broadly tipped whitish-grey. Median and greater coverts are grey, fringed paler grey or whitish, but lesser and primary coverts are contrastingly blackish. Flight feathers black, crossed by broad white wingbar; on several inner primaries (typically five), white fringe on outer web reaches the shaft. Rump and uppertail-coverts are white at sides, with broad blackish central line; central tail feathers are blackish-brown, outers pale grey. **Non-breeding:** Mostly plain pale whitish-grey on rear crown, nape, mantle, scapulars and tertials, with white forehead and lores. All of underparts white, except for greyish smudges on sides of breast. Blackish lesser coverts are prominent. **Juvenile:** Crown dark brown, fringed buff; supercilium whitish-buff; darkish patches on lores and ear-coverts. Mantle and scapulars blackish, with large paired buffish-white spots; tertials blackish, with wide buffish fringes. Wing-coverts brownish, with blackish subterminal patch and buffish-white fringe. Underparts are white, with upper breast initially washed buff and streaked brown at the sides.

AGE/SEX The spotted pattern of the juvenile is usually distinct in the field until Nov. One-year-old birds typically remain south, gain no breeding plumage and start wing moult early. Males tend to be slightly brighter in breeding plumage; females average slightly larger.

RACES None is described. Siberian breeders are more sexually dimorphic than those in Greenland; Greenland birds average slightly smaller than Canadian ones.

MEASUREMENTS Length 200-210 mm (8"). Wing 116-133 mm; bill 21-28 mm; tarsus 22-28 mm; tail 46-54 mm.

REFERENCES Parmelee (1970), Parmelee and Payne (1973), Summers (1976), Pienkowski and Green (1976).

190 SEMIPALMATED SANDPIPER *Calidris pusilla* Plate 75
(see also Plates 79, 80)

The four dark-legged stints often give rise to very difficult problems of identification. Semipalmated and Western Sandpipers (191) are the only calidrids with substantial webbing between the toes.

IDENTIFICATION Small size distinguishes stints from other calidrids, but remember that apparent size can be misleading in the absence of direct comparison. Only four true stints normally have dark legs, but see Spoon-billed Sandpiper (206) which is closely related; also, Temminck's (194) with black legs have been recorded. Separation from Western, Red-necked (192) and Little (193) demands a good view and careful observation; birds not seen well should be left unidentified. Features to look for depend on the plumage, which should normally be determined before identification to species. In breeding plumage, Semipalmated is the dullest of the four: mantle and scapular lines are faint or lacking and upperparts are dark brown with dull yellowish or orangey fringes, less rufous than Western; underparts are mostly white, with a band of streaking across the breast which may extend onto the fore-flanks. In juvenile plumage (also the dullest), upperparts generally of earthy and buffy-brown colours and with a rather uniform, faintly scaly pattern; may show a faint 'V' at mantle edges, but lacks clear 'braces' of Little and bright rufous colours of Western, Red-necked and Little. In non-breeding, plain grey plumage, is effectively indistinguishable from other dark-legged stints and field identification rests with structure of bill and legs, and call. Note that palmations are visible only in ideal conditions. See Table on page 398 for a summary of useful characters. Also see Temminck's, which is the dullest of the yellow-legged stints, and Baird's Sandpiper (198). **Bare parts:** Bill black, typically shorter than on Western (but measurements overlap) and not obviously drooped at tip; in profile, appears deep at base and rather blunt-tipped, many individuals also show some lateral expansion of the tip. Iris dark brown. Legs black, often tinged greenish or brownish; there is substantial webbing between the toes, particularly between middle and outer.

VOICE Typical calls are rather lower-pitched and hoarser than in other dark-legged stints, commonly a rather loud 'cherk' or 'chrup', sometimes 'chirrup' and variants; may give soft chittering call on take-off. Easily distinguished from Western by experienced observers. Song, given in display flight, is a monotonous repetition of 'ree-ree-ree' or 'di-jip-di-jip-di-jip'.

HABITS Nests late May-July on wet tundra, often near pools, rivers and lakes; mating is normally monogamous. In Alaska, often nests at high density alongside Western; aggression is frequent between these species when breeding and at other times. When not breeding, mainly coastal but also frequent at inland wetlands, particularly on migration. Highly gregarious, occurring in huge numbers at favoured estuaries. Feeding action may be slightly slower than in Little; in comparison with Western, probes less often and less deeply, and on mudflats shows less preference for tide edge.

MOVEMENTS A few winter in S Florida, but most migrate to West Indies and N South America. Three more-or-less separate breeding populations also differ in migration routes. Alaskan birds migrate chiefly across the Great Plains, but may occur farther east particularly in autumn. Central populations migrate south largely via James Bay, upper Bay of Fundy (where 100,000 are typically present in early Aug) and the W Atlantic, and northwards across Gulf of Mexico and the Great Plains. E Canadian birds join southward movement via W Atlantic, but return northwards largely along Atlantic coast. Many immatures remain in non-breeding range all year. Vagrant Greenland, Azores, Ireland, Britain, France, West Germany, Chile, Argentina, Paraguay, Falkland Is., and Pacific USA where regular in small numbers in spring and autumn.

DESCRIPTION Breeding: Crown is initially streaked dark brown and pale grey, but wear may reveal some reddish fringes; whitish supercilia, finely streaked brown; lores are dusky, ear-coverts paler and washed very pale chestnut. Hindneck pale grey, streaked brown. Mantle feathers and scapulars have broad blackish centres and are tipped pale grey; wear reveals narrow pale chestnut fringes. Tertials are darkish brown with paler fringes, wing-coverts mostly pale brown-grey. Narrow white wingbar is formed by tips of greater and inner primary coverts and bases of inner primaries. Central rump, uppertail and tail are dark brown; sides of rump are white, sides of tail grey. Underparts are white, except for fine brown streaking on breast and anterior flanks, becoming more obvious when worn. Underwing is white. **Non-breeding:** Upperparts pale, fairly uniform brownish-grey; underparts are mostly white, but with sides of breast washed grey and obscurely streaked (unlike most Westerns). **Juvenile:** Crown is streaked dark

brown and dull greyish-buff, sometimes with some pale chestnut; supercilia are white, lores and ear-coverts quite dark brownish, hindneck paler greyish. Mantle and scapulars are blackish-brown, fringed whitish-buff and with only a little pale chestnut; lower rows of scapulars have greyer bases. Whitish fringes may form indistinct lines at edges of mantle. Tertials and wing-coverts are dull grey-brown, fringed very pale buff and whitish. Underparts white except for a brownish-buff wash on breast, overlain with diffuse streaking particularly at sides.

AGE/SEX Juvenile may remain distinct until Oct-Nov, but in winter is identifiable only in the hand by retained juvenile coverts or very worn primaries. Some first-winter birds replace the outer primaries and show contrasting fresh outers and worn inners during spring and summer. Females average larger, but do not differ in plumage.

RACES Monotypic, but the three more-or-less separate breeding populations (see Movements) show slight trends of increasing wing and bill measurements from west to east.

MEASUREMENTS Length 130-150 mm (5½"). Wing 93-104 mm; bill 15-23 mm; tarsus 19-24 mm; tail 35-45 mm.

REFERENCES Phillips (1975), Ashkenazie and Safriel (1979), Harrington and Morrison (1979), Jonsson and Grant (1984).

191 WESTERN SANDPIPER *Calidris mauri*

Plate 75
(see also Plates 79, 80)

Closely related to Semipalmated Sandpiper (190), which see, and often difficult to distinguish from this and the other dark-legged stints, Red-necked (192) and Little (193). Nests only in E USSR and Alaska.

IDENTIFICATION See Table on page 398 for a summary of useful characters. This is marginally the largest of the stints, and differs in longer, slightly droop-tipped bill recalling shorter-billed races of Dunlin (204); small size, however, is always a clear distinction from Dunlin. Differs from other dark-legged stints as follows. In breeding plumage, has highly distinctive blackish streaking on breast and 'V's or arrowheads on flanks and sometimes sides of undertail, and much chestnut above, particularly on scapulars, crown-sides, nape and ear-coverts. In juvenile plumage, also much more rufous than Semipalmated, and less scaly and less uniform; centre of mantle and the upper two rows of scapulars are edged bright chestnut, while lower scapulars are contrastingly greyish with dark anchor shapes towards tips. Most show faint pale lines at edges of mantle and upper scapulars. In non-breeding plumage, virtually indistinguishable in the field from other dark-legged stints except by bill, palmations and call. Paler and greyer than Dunlin in non-breeding plumage. **Bare parts:** Bill black or brownish-black, typically longer than on other stints, roughly 2½-3 times distance from bill-base to front edge of eye; tip is finer than in Semipalmated and faintly decurved. Iris dark brown. Legs black, sometimes tinged greenish or brownish; toes partially webbed as in Semipalmated.

VOICE Typically a thin, rather sharp and high-pitched 'jeet' or 'cheet', longer and less distinctive than similar call of White-rumped Sandpiper (197), but distinguishable with practice from typical calls of Semi-

palmated. Also gives shorter, hoarser calls which may be indistinguishable from Semipalmated. Short song consists of a few notes rising in pitch, followed by a purring or trilling 'tweer-tweer-tweer'.

HABITS Nests late May-July, chiefly on drier tundra than Semipalmated but in parts of Alaska both species nest together at high density. Interspecific aggression is frequent. Mating is normally monogamous. Appears at inland wetlands on migration, but is mostly coastal when not breeding. Feeds more in water and probes more than Semipalmated. Like other stints, highly gregarious and often in large flocks. Often tame and approachable.

MOVEMENTS Birds from E USSR join Alaskan ones in southeasterly autumn migration, early July-late Nov. Regular in E USA north to Massachusetts, but very rare in E Canada. Much more abundant on Pacific coasts than Semipalmated. Northward movement through USA occurs early Apr-early June. Many immatures remain in non-breeding range all year. Vagrant Lake Baikal in USSR (Sept), Japan, Australia, S Peru, Azores, Ireland, Britain, France and Denmark.

DESCRIPTION Breeding: Crown feathers are dark brown, fringed chestnut, often with clear chestnut on nape; supercilia white, finely streaked brown; lores are dusky-brown, but ear-coverts contrastingly chestnut or reddish-brown. Hindneck greyish, heavily streaked dark brown. Mantle feathers blackish, narrowly fringed greyish and chestnut; scapulars have extensive deep chestnut-red fringes and black subterminal crescents, and are tipped pale grey in fresh plumage. Upperwing-coverts and tertials grey-brown, fringed paler. Narrow white wingbar is formed by tips of greater and inner primary coverts, and bases of inner primaries. Central rump, uppertail and tail are dark brown; sides to rump are white, sides of tail grey. Underparts are basically white; chin is unstreaked, but neck and especially breast are heavily streaked dark brown, with streaks or chevrons extending along flanks to lateral undertail-coverts. Underwing white. **Non-breeding:** Essentially pale, cold greyish above with fine brown streaking on the crown, and fairly clear white supercilium; underparts are white, with sides of breast washed grey, overlain by clear-cut, fine blackish streaks which often join across breast (unlike Semipalmated). **Juvenile:** Crown buff-grey, streaked pale brown; fairly clear white supercilium; fairly dusky lores and ear-coverts; hindneck pale greyish, finely streaked brown. Mantle blackish, fringed rufous; lateral feathers have more whitish at edges, giving faint mantle lines on some individuals. Upper

rows of scapulars are centred black and fringed rich rufous; lower scapulars are centred mainly grey, with a blackish shaft-streak which expands into an irregular spot or anchor shape towards the tip. Tertials are grey-brown with some rufous edging. Upperwing-coverts brown-grey with pale buff fringes. Underparts are white, with pale orange-buff wash on breast overlain by clear but narrow dark streaking.

AGE/SEX Rufous-fringed upper scapulars of juvenile may be evident to mid-winter, but many first-winter birds are indistinguishable except in the hand. Female averages larger, especially in bill length; bill-tip tends to be more obviously drooped in females.

RACES No geographical variation is known.

MEASUREMENTS Length 140-170 mm (6"). Wing 94-103 mm; bill 21-30 mm; tarsus 20-25 mm; tail 38-45 mm.

REFERENCES Page and Fearis (1971), Holmes (1973), Senner and Martinez (1982), Jonsson and Grant (1984).

192 RED-NECKED STINT *Calidris ruficollis*

Plate 76
(see also Plates 79, 80)

Other names: Rufous-necked Stint/Sandpiper

This stint is largely an eastern replacement for Little Stint (193), but there is overlap in both breeding and non-breeding ranges. The two species are very similar and were long considered conspecific.

IDENTIFICATION Considerable care is needed to separate from Little and from the other dark-legged stints —Semipalmated (190), which see, and Western (191). Little and Red-necked differ from the two mainly-American species in unwebbed toes, proportionately longer wings, bright juvenile plumage with pale lines at edges of mantle and upper scapulars, and in breeding plumage at least some rufous on the breast and sides of neck. Red-necked is on average the longest-winged and shortest-legged of the four, and the brightest in breeding plumage. See Table on page 398 for a summary of useful features. Also see Spoon-billed Sandpiper (206), which is particularly similar in breeding plumage. Chief differences from Little are as follows. In profile, bill-tip looks slightly thicker, wings longer and legs shorter; measurements are usually diagnostic. In breeding plumage, typically shows unmarked rich chestnut-red face, neck and upper breast, with sometimes complete necklace of brownish spotting on lower breast below the chestnut-red; throat is usually chestnut-red. Mantle lines are weaker than on Little. Wing-coverts and tertials, sometimes some lower scapulars, often remain grey as in non-breeding plumage. Note that the much larger Sanderling (189) is similar in breeding plumage and can cause confusion. In juvenile plumage, very similar to Little but pale lines at edges of mantle are less distinct, pale lines at edges of upper scapulars are faint or absent, and crown has a less distinct dark ridge along the centre. Wing-coverts and lower scapulars are mainly grey, fringed buffish, contrasting with the dark-centred chestnut-fringed feathers of mantle and upper scapulars. Tertials are mainly grey, with a fine dark shaft-streak, whitish edging, and some pale rufous fringing at tip. In non-breeding plumage, effectively identical to Little and separable with certainty only by measurements (not all individuals). Call may be helpful. **Bare parts:** Bill black, slightly

deeper at tip than in Little, but less deep than in Semipalmated and less laterally expanded at the tip. Iris dark brown. Legs blackish, averaging slightly shorter than in related species; toes unwebbed.

VOICE Calls are very similar to those of Little Stint and generally of little value in separating these two species. Typically calls 'chit' or 'prip', slightly coarser than Little's call and perhaps lower-pitched, also recalling Semipalmated. Also a sharp squeak 'week', less high-pitched than Western's call. Often gives a short trill when flushed. Song is a prolonged steady repetition of 'yek' or a deep 'ooah'.

HABITS Nests late May-July on tundra, usually drier areas at low altitude; breeds alongside Little in E Taimyr and Lena delta. Mainly coastal when not breeding, but also occurs at inland wetlands, particularly on migration. Highly gregarious. Feeds mostly with constant pecking action, as Little Stint; sometimes probes.

MOVEMENTS Alaskan birds join those from USSR to winter chiefly in SE Asia from Burma to S China and in Australasia. Occurs on passage in Micronesia, suggesting that some make a direct crossing of the W Pacific, and in Japan. First adults reach Australia by late Aug and arrivals continue until Nov; departure is chiefly Mar-Apr. Many immatures remain in non-breeding range all year. Westward limit of normal winter range is unknown, but Red-necked has occurred with Little as far west as Cape Province; also recorded India (scarce but regular), Seychelles, Somalia, Kenya, Mozambique and Natal. Relatively scarce but increasing in New Zealand. Vagrant West Germany (Aug 1968), East Germany (July 1979), Volga River (W USSR), Auckland Is., SE Alaska, British Columbia, Oregon, California, Atlantic USA and Bermuda.

DESCRIPTION Breeding: Head, neck and upper breast are usually rich chestnut, with crown streaked dark brown, lores dusky, a whitish area on chin and around base of bill, and supercilium pale behind eye; in fresh plumage the chestnut is obscured by pale fringes. Even in full plumage, the chestnut can be paler and may be reduced to a wash on ear-coverts and neck, surrounding a whitish chin and throat. Underparts are otherwise white, except for some clear dark brown breast spotting especially on sides of breast below the chestnut. Mantle and scapulars are dark brown with chestnut and a few greyish edges, tipped whitish-grey when fresh; wing-coverts are mainly plain brownish-grey. Tertials grey-brown, edged whitish or pale rufous. White wingbar is formed by tips of greater coverts, inner primary coverts and bases of inner primaries. Central rump, uppertail and tail are dark brown; sides of uppertail are white and of tail pale grey. **Non-breeding:** Essentially grey-brown above and white below, with slight greyish streaking on sides of breast. Supercilium white, quite prominent. **Juvenile:** Crown pale grey-buff, lightly streaked brown; supercilium whitish; lores and narrow eye-stripe behind eye are dusky.

Hindneck pale greyish. Mantle dark brown fringed deep rufous, with whitish on outer edges of lateral feathers forming slight mantle lines. Upper rows of scapulars centred dark with rufous and white fringes, but lower rows much greyer with dusky subterminal patch and whitish fringes. Wing-coverts including inner medians are pale brown-grey with pale buff fringes; tertials grey-brown, fringed pale buff. Underparts mainly white, with breast washed greyish-buff and faintly streaked at sides.

AGE/SEX Juvenile is often distinct in the field to Nov. In the hand, retained juvenile inner medians are more difficult to distinguish than on Little Stint owing to mainly-grey colour and paler fringing. Females average slightly larger in wing and bill.

RACES No geographical variation is known.

MEASUREMENTS Length 130-160 mm (5¾"). Wing 94-112 mm; bill 16-21 mm; tarsus 18-21 mm; tail 38-48 mm. Wing:tarsus ratio is 5.0 or greater (5.1 or less in Little).

REFERENCES Flint *et al.* (1980b), Jonsson and Grant (1984).

193 LITTLE STINT *Calidris minuta*

Plate 76
(see also Plates 79, 80)

An abundant small wader of the W and central Palaearctic, Africa and India, closely similar to Red-necked Stint (192) but generally more westerly in distribution.

IDENTIFICATION One of the four dark-legged stints, requiring considerable care to separate from Red-necked, Semipalmated (190), which see, and Western (191). See Table on page 398 for a summary of useful characters. In breeding plumage, shows some rufous on neck and upper breast, but differs from Red-necked in paler, more orangey colour (not brick-red), brown spotting overlain on orangey wash at sides of breast, and in white throat. Creamy lines at edges of mantle and upper scapulars are normally obvious. Wing-coverts, lower scapulars and tertials are mostly blackish-brown fringed with chestnut (except for a few retained non-breeding feathers), and do not form an obvious contrast with the mantle and upper scapulars. In juvenile plumage, Little is the brightest of the four dark-legged stints, differing from Red-necked as follows. Crown normally shows a darker 'ridge' along the centre, and a fine whitish line each side which joins the supercilia in front of the eye (supercilium appears 'split'). Pale lines at edges of mantle and upper scapulars are conspicuous in fresh plumage. Wing-coverts, lower scapulars and tertials are mainly dark in the centre and fringed rich chestnut, thus not contrasting in colour and pattern with the mantle and upper scapulars. In non-breeding plumage, note thinner bill-tip than Red-necked and Semipalmated, and lack of palmations. Call may be helpful. Even in the hand, some may not be separable from Red-necked, although measurements are usually diagnostic. **Bare parts:** Bill black, rather fine at tip, sometimes faintly decurved. Iris dark brown. Legs normally black or greyish-black, but sometimes tinged brownish; toes unwebbed.

VOICE Typical call is a short, incisive 'stit', probably distinct from other stints, but also makes calls very similar to those of Red-necked, including 'chit', 'see-

seet' and a short trill. Song is a repeated weak 'svee-svee-svee'.

HABITS Nests June-Aug on high-arctic tundra, mainly on drier ground at low altitude, but also on marshy ground and in Sweden at up to 1100 m. Mating systems include serial polygamy in which males and females incubate separate clutches. Mainly coastal when not breeding, but frequently uses inland wetlands on migration and is common at many inland sites in Africa. Highly gregarious, often in large flocks, but at some sites individuals defend feeding territories aggressively against conspecifics and other small waders. Feeds mostly with rapid pecking action, but sometimes probes. Often tame and approachable.

MOVEMENTS Adults begin moving south in July and juveniles in late Aug; passage continues until late Oct. A few winter as far north as Britain in most years. Return passage is chiefly Apr-early June. Much commoner in Britain in autumn (mostly juveniles) than in spring. Many immatures remain in non-breeding range all year. Vagrant to Alaska and W Aleutians, California (Sept 1983), James Bay (Canada), Atlantic Canada and USA, Antigua, Bermuda, South Georgia (breeding plumage, Dec 1977), Cape Verde Is., Iceland, Faeroes, Spitsbergen, Bear I., Burma, Japan, Brunei, Papua New Guinea and Australia.

DESCRIPTION Breeding: Crown streaked pale chestnut and dark brown; supercilium whitish, sometimes slightly infused pale chestnut; lores dusky; ear-coverts washed pale chestnut; chin and throat always white. Sides of head, also hindneck, variably pale chestnut streaked brown. Upper breast and sides of neck are washed variably with pale chestnut and streaked or spotted mid-brown. Mantle feathers blackish, fringed chestnut; there are distinct creamy-white lines at sides of mantle. Scapulars have blackish centres and bright mid-chestnut fringes, tipped whitish-grey when fresh. Tertials brownish, edged pale chestnut. Wing-coverts mostly pale brown, fringed fairly deep chestnut-buff. Patterns of wing and tail are as Red-necked. **Non-breeding:** Grey-brown above and on breast, white below. Upperpart feathers are variably dark-centred, sometimes with a prominent dark wedge but often just a thin dark shaft-streak. **Juvenile:** Crown warm chestnut streaked with brown, darker along the centre forming a dark 'ridge' and with an indistinct whitish lateral crown-stripe (giving the impression of a split supercilium). Supercilium is whitish and lores dusky; ear-coverts have a pale chestnut wash. Hindneck is contrastingly pale and greyish. Mantle feathers are centred blackish and fringed deep rufous; whitish fringes to lateral feathers form a prominent 'V' at edges of mantle. Scapulars are all dark-centred and fringed chestnut and whitish; whitish fringes at edges of upper scapulars form whitish lines parallel to the mantle 'V'. Tertials dark brown, fringed chestnut. Wing-coverts brown, clearly fringed deep buff or chestnut: inner medians are fringed rich chestnut.

Dark rump feathers are tipped pale chestnut; central tail feathers have a broad pale chestnut fringe and a sharp point to the dark central area of the feathers. Underparts are white, but sides of breast are washed orange-buff and clearly streaked with darkish brown. **AGE/SEX** Juvenile is often distinct in the field until Dec, but after post-juvenile moult some are separable only in the hand by retained chestnut-fringed inner medians. Many first-winter birds undergo a complete primary moult, after which they resemble adults, but others moult outer primaries only and may be recognised later by the pattern of worn inners and fresh outers. Females average larger in wing, bill and tail. **RACES** No geographical variation is known. **MEASUREMENTS** Length 120-140 mm (5"). Wing 91-104 mm; bill 16-20 mm; tarsus 19-23 mm; tail 37-44 mm. Wing:tarsus ratio is 5.1 or less (5.0 or greater in Red-necked). **REFERENCES** Middlemiss (1961), Tree (1974), Pearson (1984), Jonsson and Grant (1984).

194 TEMMINCK'S STINT *Calidris temminckii* Plate 77
(see also Plates 60, 79, 80)

This is the most distinctive of the seven small calidrids, both in appearance and in calls.

IDENTIFICATION Like Long-toed and Least Sandpipers (195, 196), this is a tiny calidrid with pale, usually yellowish legs. Its plumages, however, are distinctively plain throughout the year, lacking bright colours and patterns in breeding and juvenile plumages and never showing whitish lines on mantle and scapulars. General pattern of plain head and upperparts and clouded breast suggests a diminutive Common (148) or non-breeding Spotted Sandpiper (149). In flight it shows white tail-sides; obvious on take-off and landing and when the bird jinks in flight; this feature is unique for a sandpiper and recalls small plovers, particularly Kentish (98) and allies. It is the longest-tailed of the stints, the tail usually projecting noticeably beyond folded wing-tips; head is rather small and rounded. In breeding plumage, darker rufous than Little Stint (193), with a less obvious paler throat, and without lines on mantle. In non-breeding plumage, breast and upperparts are an even grey, less brownish than in Long-toed and Least and with less obvious dark feather centres. In juvenile plumage, scaly brown upperparts with dark submarginal lines and buff fringes are diagnostic for a bird of this size. **Bare parts:** Bill blackish or blackish-brown, but often with the base of the lower mandible tinged paler brown, greyish-green or dull yellow; rather slender, tapering to a fine point. Iris dark brown. Legs variable in colour from greenish or greenish-grey to yellow or yellowish-brown, usually obviously pale but on some may be dark grey or even blackish. **VOICE** Usual flight call is a distinctive, rapid, cricket-like 'tiririririr', often repeated, or a trilled 'tirr'. Song, delivered from ground or in display flight, is a sustained reeling 'kilililililililili' interspersed with more musical variations. **HABITS** Breeds late May-Aug, avoiding severest arctic conditions and often choosing more sheltered sites on woodland fringes, even around human habitation; range includes S Scandinavia and sometimes Britain. Breeding is by a rapid double-clutch system involving bigamy by both sexes; each clutch and brood is normally cared for by only one adult. Male has spectacular hovering or circling display flight during which he may sing continuously for several minutes. When not breeding, uses a wide variety of wetland types but generally avoids open coasts, and shows a preference for inland and freshwater sites. Unlike Little and Red-necked (192), usually seen singly or in small parties (although up to 200 may gather on migration); Temminck's is more ready than these species to enter vegetation at wetland fringes, and feeds by slower systematic searching, covering far less ground. Often crouches when approached; if flushed, typically gains height rapidly with fast jinking flight. **MOVEMENTS** Adults may leave breeding grounds in July, before young have fledged; passage of juveniles begins in Aug. Most winter in northern tropics, but extending just south of equator in E Africa; smaller numbers winter in Europe, occasionally as far north as England. Northward passage peaks in Apr-May. Vagrant Azores, Canaries, E Africa south to Zambia, Seychelles, Maldive Is., Philippines, Borneo, Aleutians, W Alaska and Vancouver B.C. (Sept 1982). **DESCRIPTION Breeding:** Crown and hindneck are streaked dark brown and pale grey-brown, with some dull chestnut on crown; faint white supercilium is obscured by fine brown streaking and is often visible only behind the eye; lores are dusky, and ear-coverts washed grey-brown and finely streaked. Most feathers of mantle, scapulars and tertials are centred dark brown, edged pale chestnut, and are tipped pale grey when fresh; a variable number of plain non-breeding-type feathers are admixed. Upperwing-coverts brown, mainly fringed brownish-buff. Flight feathers are blackish, with a narrow white wingbar formed by tips of greater coverts and slight wash on bases of inner primaries. Rump, uppertail-coverts and base of central tail feathers dull grey-brown; central tail tipped darker; sides of uppertail and tail are white. Outer three pairs of tail feathers are all-white, or sometimes slightly sullied with grey. Neck and breast are mottled with buff and grey-brown, very slightly streaked darker; chin and throat are paler, but not contrastingly so. Rest of underparts including underwing and axillaries are white. **Non-breeding:** As breeding in general appearance, but all feathers of upperparts are an even, fairly dark grey-brown. Breast is also grey-brown, sometimes forming large and diffuse lateral patches. **Juvenile:** Similar to non-breeding, but basic colour a slightly warmer dull brown; mantle feathers, scapulars, tertials and upperwing-coverts each show a clear dark submarginal line and a narrow buff or rufous-buff fringe. Chin and throat are whitish and breast dull brown, initially with buffish wash.

AGE/SEX The faintly scaly pattern of the juvenile may be discernible in close views as late as Oct-Nov, but later can be aged only in the hand. Young birds often moult only outer primaries during Dec-May, and subsequently show a characteristic pattern of worn inners and fresh outers. Sexes are not known to differ in plumage, but females average fractionally larger.

RACES No geographical variation is known.

MEASUREMENTS Length 130-150 mm (5½"). Wing 94-105 mm; bill 15-19 mm; tarsus 17-19 mm; tail 42-51 mm.

REFERENCES Hildén (1975, 1978), Tomkovich and Fokin (1983), Jonsson and Grant (1984).

195 LONG-TOED STINT *Calidris subminuta* Plate 78
(see also Plates 79, 80)

This E Palaearctic stint shares many features with the American Least Sandpiper (196), and careful observation is needed for satisfactory identification. The extra length of the toes on this bird perhaps helps it to walk on floating vegetation.

IDENTIFICATION Tiny size and pale legs characterise the three pale-legged stints, Long-toed, Least and Temminck's (194). The last species is easily distinguished by its generally plain plumages, strongly-clouded but largely unstreaked breast, and longer tail with white sides in flight. The four dark-legged stints should also be considered, particularly if there is uncertainty about leg colour. See Tables on pages 398 and 399 for a summary of useful characters. Long-toed differs from Least more in shape than in plumage. It is markedly longer-necked, as well as longer-legged, with proportions recalling Pectoral and Sharp-tailed Sandpipers (199, 200), or even Wood Sandpiper (145), rather than a stint. Juvenile and non-breeding plumages of Sharp-tailed are so similar that confusion may arise, even though Sharp-tailed averages more than 60% larger in total length. Toe length is diagnostic in the hand, but of little value in field conditions. Weaker wingbar is a constant difference from Least: shafts of all primaries except outermost (10) are brownish. In breeding plumage, head pattern is slightly more contrasted, showing paler nape, heightening the capped appearance, and often a 'split' supercilium; the supercilia, however, do not meet across the forehead. Upperparts tend to show broader, brighter rufous edgings. Sides of breast are strongly streaked, but centre may be unstreaked. In non-breeding plumage, Long-toed tends to have larger, more sharply-defined dark feather centres on upperparts and wing-coverts, and a similar but more muted difference in head pattern to that shown in summer plumage. Both Long-toed and Least are browner above than dark-legged stints. In juvenile plumage, head-pattern and breast-pattern differences from Least are as in breeding plumage. Upperparts of both are rather darker than on other stints; Long-toed tends to have richer rufous fringes to mantle and scapulars, and paler, more whitish-buff fringes to wing-coverts. **Bare parts:** Bill blackish, usually with base of lower mandible tinged brownish or greenish-yellow; short, faintly drooped, fairly fine at tip. Iris dark brown. Legs and toes variably yellowish-brown, greenish-yellow, or greenish, sometimes pale orange-yellow; toes, including hind toe, are longer than on other stints, with central toe always obviously longer than the bill.

VOICE Usual call is a fairly short, soft, rippling 'prrt', 'chrrup' or 'chulip', sometimes recalling Curlew Sandpiper (205). Other calls include a sharp 'tik-tik-tik'. Song is a slow, repeated 'kroer'.

HABITS Nests early June onwards, apparently in a wide variety of arctic and boreal habitats, regularly south to 50° N. Range is incompletely known and nesting little studied: there is no evidence yet that females ever incubate or attend the brood. Male has a high circling display flight during which he sings. Outside breeding season found mainly around fresh waters, often with Little or Red-necked and Temminck's; like Temminck's, may also venture on to tidal mudflats. Generally feeds singly or in small flocks, occasionally up to 50, often among vegetation at water's edge or on floating weed or algae. When alarmed, stands upright with neck extended, recalling a miniature Sharp-tailed or Ruff (210); may crouch low if disturbed. If flushed, towers high like Temminck's; wingbeats sometimes appear rather weak and fluttery.

MOVEMENTS Like breeding areas, migration routes are also poorly known. Southward passage of adults begins by mid-July, but peak of passage is in Aug-Sept; present in winter quarters Aug-early Apr; spring passage through China occurs Apr-May. Most winter in SE Asia and Philippines, but a few hundred reach Australia (chiefly W.A.); small numbers in Iran, Oman, Saudi Arabia and Aden on passage suggest that a few may winter regularly in E Africa. Vagrant Sweden (Oct-Nov 1977), England (Aug-Sept 1982), Ethiopia (Jan 1964), Kenya, Seychelles, Christmas I., W Aleutians (regular), W Alaska and Oregon.

DESCRIPTION Breeding: Crown streaked dark brown and rufous, contrasting with relatively indistinct pale supercilia; ill-defined dusky line across the lores and dusky ear-coverts form a mask from eye; hindneck pale brown, streaked darker. Mantle and scapulars are blackish-centred, with deep rufous, orange-chestnut and whitish fringes, initially with broad greyish-white tips; some show indistinct whitish lines at edges of mantle. Tertials broadly edged rufous; they normally overlap tips of all primaries. Coverts brown, fringed warm buff and pale chestnut. Narrow white wingbar is formed chiefly by tips of greater coverts: narrow white tips to inner primary coverts form a very indistinct outer bar. Primary shafts brown, except outermost which is whitish. Central rump and tail are dark brown; sides of rump and uppertail are narrowly whitish, sides of tail grey. Underparts white, but breast shows a grey-buff wash, and dark streaking which is often indistinct in centre but can be prominent on sides. **Non-breeding:** Rather dull grey-brown above, with white underparts except for breast quite heavily washed and streaked grey-brown. Supercilium relatively indistinct. Scapulars show prominent dark brown centres and pale grey-brown fringes; coverts are also rather dark-centred. **Juvenile:** Crown dark brown, streaked bright rufous. Super-

cilia rather broad and contrastingly pale, not meeting on forehead but extending to rather pale hindneck; lores show small areas of brown near bill and near eye, and ear-coverts a diffuse brown area. Hindneck pale greyish, heightening capped appearance. Mantle, scapulars and tertials are black-centred, edged mainly rich chestnut; whitish edges to mantle may form clear lines. Wing-coverts are brown, fringed pale buff. Underparts white, except for breast which is washed buffish and streaked brown, especially at sides.

AGE/SEX Juveniles are distinct in the field to late Nov, but later may be identifiable only in the hand. Most one-year-olds gain breeding plumage, but retain worn juvenile primaries. Sexes are not known to differ in plumage; females average fractionally larger.

RACES No geographical variation is known.

MEASUREMENTS Length 130-150 mm (5½"). Wing 88-100 mm; bill 16-20 mm; tarsus 19-24 mm; central toe 20-23 mm (to base of claw), 21-26 mm (including claw); tail 35-41 mm.

REFERENCES Tomkovich (1980), Jonsson and Grant (1984).

196 LEAST SANDPIPER *Calidris minutilla*

Plate 78
(see also Plates 79, 80)

Marginally the smallest wader in the world. It is very similar to the Siberian Long-toed Stint (195) and has in the past been considered conspecific with it. Its breeding range extends farther south than that of any other calidrid, except perhaps Dunlin (204).

IDENTIFICATION Requires care and a good view to separate from Long-toed (which see for a detailed comparison of plumage characters). In breeding and juvenile plumages, head pattern differs subtly in that supercilia meet narrowly across forehead but are less sharply defined, lores are darker, and a dark area on the ear-coverts is separated from the eye by a diffuse pale area. The breast of Least tends to be more uniformly streaked than in Long-toed, lacking a clearer area in the centre. Least is a smaller and more compact bird, and more stint-like in postures than Long-toed, less frequently adopting a long-necked, upright posture. Least has a stronger wingbar, with white on shafts of inner primaries, and may appear slightly narrower-winged. Toe length is diagnostic in the hand, but of little value in normal field conditions; all three pale-legged stints, Least, Long-toed and Temminck's (194), often have central toe longer than tarsus, but only Long-toed has central toe obviously longer than bill. Temminck's shares small size and pale legs with Least and Long-toed, but is plainer in all plumages and has unique white tail-sides. Dark-legged stints should also be considered, especially if there is uncertainty about leg colour. In non-breeding plumage, Least is browner above than Semipalmated (190) and Western (191) and has more extensive dark feather centres; it is also a smaller and finer-billed bird. See Tables on pages 398 and 399 for a summary of useful characters. **Bare parts:** Bill blackish, sometimes tinged brownish or yellowish at the base of lower mandible; fairly fine-tipped, slightly drooping. Iris dark brown. Legs variably yellowish, greenish or brownish, rarely orange-yellow; usually yellowish in juveniles.

VOICE Rather variable, but usual calls are distinguish-

able from those of other stints with practice: a high-pitched, shrill, rising 'trreee', often delivered in a slow irregular series, and a lower 'prrrt'. A monotonous song is delivered in display flight or from the ground, with single notes repeated at about two per second.

HABITS Nests mid-May (south of range) to Aug, in a wide variety of subarctic and boreal habitats including coastal and upland tundra, marshy areas in spruce forests, and flat sandy islands; breeds regularly at Sable I. and Cape Sable I., Nova Scotia, and has bred (1979) near Cape Cod, Massachusetts, at 42° N. Males advertise territory by singing continuously in display flight, often for several minutes. Males take major part in incubation and care of the brood; double-clutching has not been found in populations studied. Outside breeding season, differs marginally from Long-toed in being more gregarious and in feeding more often on open coasts and mudflats; like that species, however, is attracted to inland wetlands and feeds readily among vegetation. When disturbed may stretch neck upwards, but this is not a constant feature of behaviour. If flushed, may rise steeply, but 'towering' is less frequent than in Temminck's and Long-toed. Often very tame.

MOVEMENTS Southward movement begins in early-mid July and continues to Oct; first adults reach S America by mid-July, first juveniles mid-Aug. Despite small size, many migrate direct from SE Canada to South America over W Atlantic. Return passage spans Apr-early June, peaking in USA during late Apr and early May. A few non-breeders remain in winter quarters all year. Regular in autumn in Bermuda. Vagrant Japan, St Lawrence I. (Alaska), Baffin I., Iceland, Azores, Ireland, Britain, France, West Germany, Finland and Austria. Some records published as *C. minutilla* in fact refer to Long-toed.

DESCRIPTION Breeding: Crown streaked dark brown and whitish, with a little pale chestnut; supercilia whitish and finely streaked, rather indistinct, often meeting on forecrown. Lores dark; rear ear-coverts show a diffuse brown patch separated from the eye (compare Long-toed). Rest of sides of head and neck whitish, streaked brown. Mantle and scapulars blackish-centred and fringed yellowish-chestnut, whitish and grey; whitish fringes may form lines at edges of mantle. Tertials blackish-brown fringed rufous, almost completely overlapping all primary tips. Wing-coverts brown, fringed buff. White wing-bar is formed chiefly by tips of greater and primary coverts, and by primary shafts. Rump and central uppertail and tail dark brown; sides of rump are whitish, sides of tail grey. Underparts white, with breast washed buff and heavily streaked dark brown. **Non-breeding:** Dull grey-brown upperparts, and white underparts with strong grey-brown wash to breast. All upperpart feathers are narrowly centred darker, becoming paler towards edges; rear scapulars have broadest dark centres. **Juvenile:** Very much brighter than adult. Crown is streaked dark brown and chest-

nut. Distinct white supercilia often meeting above bill. Head pattern otherwise as described for breeding adult. Hindneck washed buff-brown and streaked brown. Mantle and scapulars blackish, mostly fringed deep rufous; whitish fringes at edges of mantle form distinct lines. Tertials and wing-coverts brown, fringed deep buff or pale chestnut. Underparts white, with breast washed bright buff and distinctly streaked brown; on a minority of individuals there is little streaking on the centre of the breast.

AGE/SEX Juvenile is distinct to late Oct or later in the field. In S America, post-juvenile moult may include all primaries, leaving moulted juvenile indistinguishable from adult, or just outers, giving characteristically worn inners and fresh outers. Sexes are similar in plumage, but females average slightly larger, especially in bill length.

RACES No geographical variation is known.

MEASUREMENTS Length 130-150 mm (5½"). Wing 86-96 mm; bill 16-19 mm (males), 18-21 mm (females); tarsus 17-21 mm; central toe 16-19 mm (to base of claw), 18-21 mm (including claw); tail 33-40 mm.

REFERENCES Miller (1983a, b), Jonsson and Grant (1984).

197 WHITE-RUMPED SANDPIPER *Calidris fuscicollis*   Plate 81

This long-winged Nearctic calidrid is not well-named, since it is the uppertail which is white, not the rump.

IDENTIFICATION A smallish calidrid, intermediate in body size between stints and larger species such as Dunlin (204) and Curlew Sandpiper (205). Along with Baird's Sandpiper (198), it shows remarkably long wings which extend well beyond the tail-tip and give the feeding bird an elongated appearance; the wing-tips describe characteristically large ovals as the bird walks and dips forward. Wing length averages longer than in Dunlin. In flight it shows a relatively weak wingbar, but there is a conspicuous white band across the uppertail which recalls Curlew Sandpiper; in the latter species, however, the white band is broader and slightly farther from the tail-tip, and the wingbar is more prominent. In breeding plumage, the flanks and lower breast are heavily marked with blackish streaks and 'V's, recalling Western Sandpiper (191) but lacking the latter's rufous cap and ear-coverts. Western is also smaller, shorter-winged, and has a dark-centred uppertail. In non-breeding plumage, White-rumped is a stint-like plain brownish-grey above, much greyer and with a bolder supercilium than Baird's. Juveniles are rather scaly above, with bright rufous and buff fringes and whitish lines at edges of mantle, and a contrastingly pale hindneck.

Bare parts: Bill blackish, with base of lower mandible often tinged greenish or yellowish-brown; tip is slightly drooped. Iris dark brown. Legs are rather short in comparison with body length; black or blackish-grey, often faintly tinged greenish.

VOICE Flight call is a distinctive, high, thin squeak; 'jeeet' or 'eeet', often compared to a mouse or a bat; other calls include a clear short 'tit' or 'teep'. Songs include a series of 'poing-zee' notes and various rattling and bubbling sounds.

HABITS Nests June-Aug on arctic tundra, mainly near the coast. Males are polygynous; they display often

for only a week or so at the start of the breeding season, and leave the breeding grounds once egg-laying is completed. There are hovering display flights, in which the female sometimes participates. On migration and in winter it uses a variety of wetland habitats both inland and coastal, including mudflats, coastal lagoons, freshwater marshes and lakes, and wet grassland and fields. Occurs in large flocks on mudflats in S South America. Feeding action is generally quite brisk, but at times moves more inconspicuously. Flight is powerful on long wings; the bird seems larger in flight than on the ground. Gregarious, often forming single-species flocks or joining with other waders.

MOVEMENTS Southward passage spans July-early Dec; juveniles are late migrants, with first arrivals in New York not until late Sept. Route apparently follows Great Circle from breeding grounds to N South America, via E Canada or NE USA and W Atlantic. Return passage is very late, beginning in South America in Mar, and passing through USA during late Apr to mid-June; route is through central North America but small numbers are found regularly on the Atlantic coast in spring. In some years large flocks reach Falkland Is. Frequent vagrant to Iceland and W Europe (far more common in Britain than in California), with records east to Austria; vagrant also Spitsbergen, Franz Josef Land, S Africa, Tristan da Cunha, South Georgia, New Zealand, SE Australia, Galapagos and W North America (particularly in late spring).

DESCRIPTION Breeding: Crown and ear-coverts buffish-brown or dull chestnut, streaked dark brown; hindneck whitish, streaked brown; supercilium long and whitish, curving up over eye, down behind eye and kinking upwards again at rear of ear-coverts; lores dusky; chin and throat white. Mantle, scapulars and tertials blackish-brown edged chestnut, grey and buff; coverts grey-brown fringed whitish. Flight feathers dark brown; a narrow white wingbar is formed by white tips to greater coverts and inner primary coverts. Uppertail-coverts white, contrasting strongly with grey tail. Underparts white, with neck, breast and flanks spotted and streaked brown; flanks show some blackish 'V's. Underwing and axillaries white. **Non-breeding:** As breeding, but crown, nape and upperparts are dull brownish-grey, with clear dark shaft-streaks. Supercilium is often shorter. Underparts are white, but with breast and upper flanks variably suffused greyish and lightly streaked grey-brown. **Juvenile:** Crown streaked brown and chestnut, contrasting with pale greyish hindneck. Mantle, scapu-

lars and tertials are blackish, brightly fringed whitish, chestnut and buff; whitish fringes form narrow but clear lines at edges of mantle and upper scapulars. Upperwing-coverts are greyish-brown, with dark sub-marginal marks and pale buff fringes. Underparts white, but neck, upper breast and upper flanks are suffused buffish-grey and finely streaked brown. **AGE/SEX** Neatly scaly plumage of juvenile is clear until at least Nov, sometimes until Feb. Sexes are similar in plumage, but females average slightly larger. **RACES** No geographical variation is known. **MEASUREMENTS** Length 150-180 mm (6½"). Wing 118-131 mm; bill 21-26 mm; tarsus 23-26 mm; tail 46-53 mm. **REFERENCES** Parmelee *et al.* (1968).

198 BAIRD'S SANDPIPER *Calidris bairdii*   Plate 81

This calidrid is more distinctive in its long-winged shape than in its plumages, which are rather plain.

IDENTIFICATION A smallish calidrid, intermediate in body size between stints and Dunlin (204), short-legged and short-billed but with proportionately very long wings; wing length averages longer than in Dunlin. As in White-rumped (197), the wing-tips project well beyond the tail-tip when folded, and describe characteristically large ovals as the bird walks and dips forward. All plumages are rather buffy-brown with breast finely streaked and upperparts with bold dark feather centres; a weak eye-stripe gives a rather bland expression to the face. Although White-rumped is very similar in size and shape, it differs markedly from Baird's in its brighter breeding and juvenile plumages, plainer and greyer non-breeding plumage, and in its white uppertail-coverts. Baird's in flight shows a very weak wingbar and a poor contrast between the dark centre and greyish-buff sides to the rump and uppertail. There is a rare grey 'morph' in which all plumage tones are greyer. **Bare parts:** Bill blackish, sometimes tinged greenish at the base; remarkably fine-tipped, and very slightly drooped. Iris dark brown. Legs are short in comparison to body length; black or blackish-grey, often faintly tinged greenish. **VOICE** Usual call is a low trilling 'preeet, or a rough grating 'krrt'; also a sharp 'tsick'. Song is a prolonged guttural trilling given in display flight. **HABITS** Nests June-July in chiefly upland, high-arctic tundra; range extends from extreme E Siberia to NW Greenland. Males are territorial and have circling song flights; both parents incubate and tend the brood. Essentially an inland species on migration and in winter, preferring margins of inland wetlands or grassland (often some distance from water) to coastal habitats. Tends to feed on higher parts of shore or dry fringes of wetland sites, often among vegetation; wades relatively infrequently. Less gregarious than most calidrids, and usually seen singly or in small groups; some individuals defend feeding territories. Feeding action is usually brisk, but slower than in stints. Generally a fairly tame species; may crouch when approached or stand upright in alarm. **MOVEMENTS** Adults and juveniles begin southward movement from early July (males slightly later than females, and juveniles later still); most migrate via North American prairies and N Andes, overflying

Central America. First juveniles reach Argentina by late Aug. Return begins early Mar, with main spring passage in USA in Apr and early May. Vagrant Japan, Hawaii, Galapagos, N and SE Australia, Tasmania, New Zealand, Falkland Is., South Africa, Senegal, Azores, and NW Europe east to Sweden and Poland. Vagrants have exceptionally wintered in Europe, although there are no documented records for North America after Dec. **DESCRIPTION Breeding:** Crown brown, streaked buffish, sometimes dull chestnut; supercilium long and pale buff, rather strongly downcurved; lores and ear-coverts warm brown, forming a diffuse dusky eye-stripe; narrow buff eye-ring; head otherwise fairly plain buffish. Mantle, scapulars and tertials have dark brown centres and clear warm buff fringes; wing-coverts are mostly grey-brown, fringed paler. Flight feathers blackish-brown; wingbar consists of narrow white tips to greater coverts and paler bases of primaries, and may be virtually absent in worn plumage. Rump, uppertail-coverts and central tail feathers are blackish-brown; rump and uppertail are narrowly edged buffish or grey-buff, and tail-sides are greyish. Chin and throat are very pale buffish; upper neck and breast are buffish, finely streaked brown; belly white, but flanks are occasionally suffused

buffish. Underwing-coverts and axillaries are white.
Non-breeding: Very similar to breeding, but slightly
duller; upperparts are grey-brown, fringed grey-buff.
Juvenile: Supercilium is slightly less distinct than in
breeding plumage, and chin is whiter. Most feathers
of upperparts show a grey-brown centre, shading to
a blackish-brown submarginal area which contrasts
with a buffish-white fringe; the pattern of the upperparts is strongly scaly. Wing-coverts are grey-brown,
fringed rich brown and chestnut-buff. Breast and neck
are washed buff and distinctly streaked brown; streaks

sometimes may form lateral breast-patches.
AGE/SEX The scaly upperparts of juveniles are distinct in the field until Nov; retained coverts may enable birds to be aged later than this in the hand. Sexes
are similar in plumage, but females average slightly
larger.
RACES No geographical variation is known.
MEASUREMENTS Length 140-170 mm (6"). Wing 118-
135 mm; bill 20-26 mm; tarsus 21-26 mm; tail 45-53
mm.
REFERENCES Jehl (1979).

199 PECTORAL SANDPIPER *Calidris melanotos*   Plate 82

The breeding range of this bird is almost as extensive in N Siberia as in North America, yet the vast bulk
of the population winters in S South America. On the breeding grounds, males have an astonishing hooting
display call.

IDENTIFICATION A rather large calidrid with a fairly
short, faintly-decurved bill and shortish, usually yellowish legs. It can be recognised in all plumages by
the feature for which it is named: the streaking on
the breast is sharply demarcated from the unmarked
white belly, with the line of division running across
the lower breast. Breeding and juvenile plumages are
similar in rufous edges to crown feathers and to
upperparts; in juvenile plumage, whitish fringes at
edges of mantle and upper scapulars form fairly clear
pale lines. Non-breeding plumage is brownish-grey
above with darker brown feather centres. Flight pattern in all plumages shows a weak wingbar, a narrow whitish trailing edge to the secondaries and a
broad black centre to the rump and uppertail. Sharp-
tailed (200) is very similar in size, structure and
appearance, but always lacks Pectoral's sharply-
demarcated streaked breast. In breeding plumage,
Sharp-tailed shows heavy blackish chevrons on breast
and flanks, extending to undertail, while in juvenile
plumage it is exceptionally bright rufous on cap and
buff on breast, with a bold whitish supercilium. Ruff
(210) is always larger and longer-necked; in flight, Ruff
shows large white ovals on uppertail and a stronger
wingbar. See also Cox's Sandpiper (201). **Bare parts:**
Bill brownish-black, with paler yellowish-brown or
greenish-brown basal third, sometimes contrasting
strongly. Iris dark brown. Legs variably dull greenish, brownish or yellowish; toes do not project
beyond tail-tip in flight.
VOICE Typical flight call is a loud, harsh, reedy
'churk' or 'trrit', often irregularly repeated. In song
flight, male makes a sonorous foghorn-like hooting
'oo-ah' about two to three times per second.
HABITS Nests June-July on arctic tundra, usually on
dry fringes of well-vegetated wetlands. Mating system is promiscuous: males display vigorously for a
short period during June and often mate several
times, while females may visit territories of other
males. Male in display sports a pendulous, fat-filled
sac beneath the feathering of the breast, which dis-
tends the breast and emphasises the contrast between
breast and belly; in song flight, the sac is pumped
up and down in time with the hooting calls. Most
males then leave the breeding grounds before the
eggs hatch. When not nesting, typically a species of
wet grassland and freshwater margins, but also occurs

in coastal habitats. Feeds usually on drier areas away
from water's edge, often among vegetation;
feeding action is a fast and steady walk with pecks
and shallow probes. Often gathers in large flocks at
suitable sites, but some individuals defend feeding
territories. Generally tame and approachable.
MOVEMENTS Siberian breeders are believed mostly
to join those of North America in migration to South
America, largely by a Great Circle route over W Atlantic. Uncommon in W USA in autumn. A smaller number winter regularly in Australia and New Zealand.
Adults begin southward movement in late June, and
juveniles appear from early Aug; most still in North
America in Sept-Oct are juveniles. Northward movement spans Mar-early June and is mainly more
westerly, via interior North America, but avoiding W
USA. Westerly storms in Sept-Oct bring juveniles
regularly to W Europe, where it is the commonest
transatlantic wader; such migrants apparently continue south towards Africa, and some may return
through Europe in subsequent seasons. Regular on
passage on Phoenix and Line Is. Vagrant Hawaii, Falkland Is., South Georgia, S and E Africa, Morocco,
Azores, Madeira, Europe east to Austria and Poland,
Malta, Iceland, Spitsbergen and Bear I.
DESCRIPTION Breeding: Crown brown, streaked
dull chestnut and pale olive-brown; supercilium is
whitish, but dull and often virtually absent; lores and
ear-coverts brownish. Mantle, scapulars and tertials
are blackish-brown, with variable chestnut, pale
brown or brownish-buff fringes sometimes forming
ill-defined lines at edges of mantle. Wing-coverts are
grey-brown, fringed paler. Flight feathers are blackish except for narrow whitish tips to secondaries;
greater coverts show very narrow white tips. Centre
of rump, uppertail and tail is blackish-brown. Sides
of rump are narrowly white, and lateral tail feathers
dull grey-brown; outer three pairs of tail feathers are
roughly equal in length and rounded at tip. Underparts white, but neck and breast are heavily suffused
brown-buff and streaked or blotched brown, with a
sharp border against the unstreaked belly; flanks
show slight streaking. Underwing-coverts and axillaries are white, slightly smudged greyish. **Non-
breeding:** As breeding, but plainer and duller; all
chestnut tones are lost on upperparts, which become
brownish, with irregular paler buff-brown feather

edges. Supercilium may be slightly more distinct. **Juvenile:** As breeding, but crown and upperparts more brightly fringed chestnut, white and buff. On the mantle and scapulars the whitish fringes form distinct white 'V's. Supercilium is prominent, although finely streaked behind the eye; sometimes there is a faint 'split-supercilium' effect. Breast is heavily streaked brown on a buffish wash, ending sharply against the whitish belly. Wing-coverts are neatly fringed buffish.
AGE/SEX Neatly-fringed upperparts of juvenile may remain distinct in the field until Nov. Sexes are separa-

ble with difficulty in breeding plumage: breast feathers of male are blackish-brown with paired white spots at tip, giving a dark and strongly-mottled pattern; female tends to have finer brown streaking on breast. At all times males are larger than females, with almost no overlap in wing length; the size difference may even be of value for sexing birds in the field.
RACES No geographical variation is known.
MEASUREMENTS Length 190-230 mm (8¼"). Wing 136-150 mm (males), 124-138 mm (females); bill 24-32 mm; tarsus 24-31 mm; tail 46-62 mm.

REFERENCES Kieser and Smith (1982), Myers (1982).

200 SHARP-TAILED SANDPIPER *Calidris acuminata* Plate 82

Other name: Siberian Pectoral Sandpiper
The breeding range of this Siberian species is, remarkably, entirely enclosed within that of its closest relative, Pectoral Sandpiper (199).

IDENTIFICATION This is a rather large and angular calidrid, with brownish plumages, pale legs and a short, faintly-decurved bill. It is almost identical to Pectoral in size and shape, but averages shorter-billed and shorter-necked, and has a slightly flatter crown. Sharp-tailed always differs in its cleaner, brighter supercilium, often broader behind the eye than in front, more contrasting dark cap, broader pale eye-ring, and lack of heavy breast streaking and sharp pectoral division. In breeding plumage it shows diagnostic blackish chevrons on breast, flanks and central undertail. The juvenile is one of the most striking calidrids, with chestnut-red crown and brownish eye-stripe contrasting strongly with whitish eye-ring and broad whitish supercilium; the foreneck and breast are strongly suffused buff (sometimes ending sharply against whiter belly), and there is a narrow gorget of fine streaking across the upper neck. In flight, patterns of wing and tail are effectively as Pectoral, although the wingbar averages slightly more prominent; the diagnostic pointed tail feathers and evenly-graduated tail shape are rarely evident in field conditions. Confusion with Ruff (210) is possible, although even a female Ruff is obviously larger than Sharp-tailed, and Ruff is a proportionately longer-necked and longer-legged bird which never shows a prominent eye-stripe or whitish supercilium. Compare also the much smaller Long-toed Stint (195). **Bare parts:** Bill blackish-brown, with paler greyish or yellowish-brown tinge at the base, particularly of the lower mandible. Iris dark brown. Legs variably greenish, brownish or yellowish, usually dull greenish-grey. Tips of toes project very slightly beyond tail-tip in flight.
VOICE Calls are softer and less reedy than Pectoral's calls: in flight typically 'wheep', 'pleep' or 'trrt', often in a short twittering sequence such as 'teet-teet-trrt-trrt' or 'prtt-wheet-wheet' recalling Barn Swallow *Hirundo rustica*. Song includes an extraordinary low-pitched, aspirated 'hoop', and a long muffled reeling trill.
HABITS Nests late May-July in Siberian tundra, mainly in areas which include wet peaty hollows and drier hummocks or raised polygons; generally less numerous and apparently more specialised in habitat than Pectoral. Breeding habits are still inadequately known. Male has a song flight with short

ascents followed by planing down on upraised wings. When not breeding, feeds extensively on grassland and on drier margins of wetlands as does Pectoral; like Pectoral often feeds among vegetation and may crouch, snipe-like, to avoid detection. Often very tame. In some localities, feeds habitually on intertidal mudflats as well as on coastal lagoons. Gregarious, often in large flocks, sometimes with Curlew Sandpiper (205) and Red-necked Stint (192).
MOVEMENTS Main migration is to Australia, where it is one of the commonest and most widespread visiting waders, and to New Zealand. Most depart breeding grounds July-Sept; arrivals in Australia begin in late Aug and continue to Nov. Northward passage spans Mar-early June. Very few non-breeders remain south during southern summer. Major route in both directions crosses E USSR (mainly east of Lake Baikal), coastal China, Philippines and Indonesia; also occurs regularly on passage east to W Alaska, Japan and Phoenix and Line Is. Vagrant N India, Sri Lanka, SE Asia and Pacific coast of Canada and USA. In some years, a few birds apparently join eastward movement of Pectorals from Siberia across North America and even reach W Europe (Britain, Ireland, France, Norway, Sweden and Finland); some possibly reach Europe from the east. Vagrant also Tristan da Cunha (June 1950).
DESCRIPTION Breeding: Crown streaked dark brown and dull chestnut; supercilium in front of eye is relatively poorly marked and sometimes streaked brown, but whitish and clearer behind eye; lores and ear-coverts pale brownish, slightly streaked darker. Hindneck streaked brown and whitish. Mantle, scapulars and tertials are blackish-brown, mostly fringed dull chestnut and whitish-buff; wing-coverts grey-brown, fringed paler. Flight feathers dark brown, crossed by a very narrow white wingbar which is formed by narrow white tips to greater coverts and even narrower primary-covert tips; some birds show paler bases to inner primaries. Centre of rump and uppertail-coverts is blackish; sides of rump are narrowly white. Tail is brownish, darkest in the centre; all feathers are rather pointed, and the tail itself is evenly wedge-shaped. Chin, throat, face, neck and upper breast are suffused buffish and heavily streaked brown; streaks become bold chevrons on the white background of the lower breast and flanks. Undertail-

coverts white, streaked brown. Underwing-coverts and axillaries are white, slightly smudged grey. **Non-breeding:** As breeding, but cap duller and supercilium more distinct; darker patch on ear-coverts. Mantle feathers show big brown centres and buff-brown fringes; scapulars are brown-centred and fringed whitish-buff. Underparts are mostly whitish, with neck and breast suffused greyish and finely streaked brown; some show darkish breast-band, especially during moult. **Juvenile:** Cap is bright rufous, contrasting very markedly with long creamy-white supercilium and dark reddish lores and ear-coverts. Supercilium is typically more conspicuous behind the eye. Hindneck is washed buff and finely streaked brown. Mantle, scapulars and tertials are blackish-brown, fringed boldly with chestnut, white

and bright buff; wing-coverts are brown, fringed chestnut-buff. Underparts mostly whitish, but breast and foreneck are strongly washed with orange-buff, and there is a narrow gorget of fine brown streaks (sometimes broken in centre) across the upper neck, and some streaking at sides of upper breast.

AGE/SEX The beautifully-marked juvenile remains distinct in the field at least until late Nov. Sexes are similar in plumage, but males average about 8% longer-winged than females and measurements hardly overlap.

RACES No geographical variation is known.

MEASUREMENTS Length 170-210 mm (7½"). Wing 133-145 mm (males), 124-137 mm (females); bill 22-28 mm; tarsus 26-32 mm; tail 47-59 mm.

REFERENCES Webb and Conry (1979), Britton (1980).

201 COX'S SANDPIPER *Calidris paramelanotos*   **Plate 82**

This new species was described by S.A. Parker in 1982 on the basis of two S Australian specimens collected by J.B. Cox. More than 20 calidrids of unusual type observed by F.T.H. Smith and others in Australia since 1955 and thought to be either a stereotyped hybrid or a previously-undescribed race of Dunlin (204) are now generally believed to have been this species, despite a possible discrepancy in the description of the uppertail-covert pattern. A live bird was caught and photographed in 1981. All records are so far from Australia. Since breeding is completely unknown, it is yet possible that this 'species' may be a stereotyped hybrid.

IDENTIFICATION This is a large calidrid with a longish, downcurved bill, a fairly weak white wing-bar, darkish centre and whitish sides to uppertail, and shortish, yellowish-green or dark olive legs. On present knowledge, it is a very difficult species to identify. In life it resembles a cross between Sharp-tailed (200) and Curlew Sandpipers (205), also recalling Pectoral Sandpiper (199) and Dunlin. Differs from Pectoral and Sharp-tailed in longer, darker bill, slightly stronger wingbar, and in extensive whitish at sides of rump and uppertail-coverts. Lacks clear white on uppertail shown by Curlew Sandpiper; in close views, central uppertail shows blackish chevrons on a white or grey-brown background. Breeding plumage (as described from moulting birds in Mar) perhaps most resembles Pectoral, but breast may be tinged rufous and lacks the clear pectoral division from the white belly. In non-breeding plumage, upperparts are less variegated than on Pectoral and Sharp-tailed, but more so than on Dunlin and Curlew Sandpiper. Best distinctions from Dunlin are probably the slightly larger size, yellowish or greenish (rather than black) legs, and the more brownish upperparts with contrasting dark centres to the scapulars. Further characters will undoubtedly emerge as a full picture of plumage changes is built up. Juvenile is at present completely unknown. **Bare parts:** Bill longish, slightly downcurved, very Dunlin-like in shape and length; mainly black, but at least sometimes with a patch of yellowish at base of lower mandible. Iris colour not different from relatives. Legs strongly built as on Pectoral and Sharp-tailed; yellowish-green, brownish-green or dark olive, always noticeably paler than on Dunlin and Curlew Sandpiper in good light.

VOICE Usual calls are a shrill 'trilt' and an undistinguished 'prrrp', quite similar to Pectoral but shorter, quieter and less ringing; also has other Pectoral-like calls.

HABITS Breeding grounds and nesting habits are

unknown. Australian observations suggest that species is close to Sharp-tailed and Curlew Sandpipers in general behaviour, and it sometimes roosts with those species. Has been seen on intertidal mud and in brackish coastal pools and sewage-farms. Tends to feed in water like Curlew Sandpiper. Evidently it is a rare bird, occurring singly among large flocks of other species.

MOVEMENTS Present records are all on south and east Australian coasts between Sept and Mar. Since all other calidrids breed at between 42° and 83° N, it must be presumed that this species nests somewhere in this zone, probably in the USSR. If so, it should be looked for on migration in intermediate areas and as a potential vagrant in other continents. Some records of Dunlin and Pectoral Sandpiper well outside usual range may need to be re-examined.

DESCRIPTION See also Identification section. **Breeding:** Rufous tinges to ear-coverts. Upperparts show variable buffy or pale chestnut fringes. Narrow wingbar, intermediate between Sharp-tailed and Curlew Sandpiper. Rump blackish-brown with broad pale fringes. Central uppertail-coverts whitish, washed pale grey-buff and marked with heavy blackish-brown bars and chevrons. Tail feathers rounded at tip (not pointed as on Sharp-tailed), but with central pair longer and more pointed. Underparts mainly white, but with extensive, quite heavy dark streaking on throat and breast and a few dark bars along flanks to sides of undertail. Breast lacks a sharp line of demarcation from white of belly, and may show some rufous tinges. **Non-breeding:** Greyer above than Pectoral and Sharp-tailed, with less contrasting dark feather centres; dark centres to scapulars, however, give a more contrasting pattern than Dunlin and Curlew Sandpiper. Supercilium less obvious than on Curlew Sandpiper. Underparts as breeding, but lacking rufous on breast and dark bars on flanks. **Juvenile:** Unknown as yet.

AGE/SEX Nothing is known. It may be significant that the male specimen measures 10 mm longer in the wing than the female one, since male is larger than female in both Pectoral and Sharp-tailed.
RACES No geographical variation is known.

MEASUREMENTS Length 190 mm (7½″) (one live bird, not stretched). Wing 134-144 mm; bill 33-37 mm; tarsus 30-32 mm; tail 54-57 mm.
REFERENCES Cox (1976), Lane *et al*. (1981, and correction in next issue), Parker (1982), Smith (1982).

202 PURPLE SANDPIPER *Calidris maritima*   Plate 83

This is a rock-haunting sandpiper of exposed coasts of the N Atlantic. It is very similar to its N Pacific equivalent, Rock Sandpiper (203), and many are effectively indistinguishable except on range; the two species are often considered conspecific.

IDENTIFICATION A rather large, dumpy calidrid with a longish, slightly-drooped, yellowish-based bill, very short yellowish legs, and wings typically falling short of the tail-tip. Purple and Rock are the only calidrids likely to be seen on wave-washed seaweedy rocks. Non-breeding plumage is mainly dark slate-grey on head, breast, flanks and upperparts, relieved by a whitish throat and small white spots above the lores and behind the eyes; a faint purple gloss to the mantle and scapulars is rarely visible in field conditions. Breeding and juvenile plumages are also rather dark, with chestnut fringes to upperparts, and breast and flanks heavily streaked. In flight it shows white sides to the uppertail, a strong white wingbar and a narrow white trailing edge to the secondaries; often one or two inner secondaries are almost completely white. Separation from Rock Sandpiper is confounded by wide variation within the latter species; most races of Rock are more similar to Purple than they are to nominate Rock. All races of Rock have slightly more white on outer webs of inner primaries than in Purple (sometimes reaching shaft), and more extensive white on inner secondaries. Nominate Rock (Pribilof Is.) differs from Purple in breeding plumage in its extensive pale yellowish fringing on upperparts, mainly-whitish sides of head and foreneck, contrasting with a dark spot on the ear-coverts, and mainly-white underparts with a large blackish patch on the lower breast; in non-breeding plumage it is paler than Purple, more ash-grey. Other races of Rock differ from Purple in breeding plumage in darker chestnut fringes to upperparts and rather broader black centres to feathers of lower breast, often forming a solid blackish patch; in non-breeding and juvenile plumages they are virtually identical, but tend to have more sharply-defined spotting on lower breast and flanks. Juvenile Rock often has buffy-brown background colour to foreneck and upper breast, much brighter than on juvenile Purple. **Bare parts:** Bill longish and slightly downcurved, not unlike Dunlin (204) in shape; blackish towards tip, but virtually always with basal third or more dull yellow. Iris dark brown. Legs shorter than bill, rather strongly built, dull yellow often tinged brownish or greenish. Bill-base and legs are often tinged with orange in spring.
VOICE Rather quiet away from breeding grounds; gives short, conversational 'tit', 'whit' or 'tweet', sometimes disyllabic, becoming a low twitter from feeding or roosting flocks. When breeding, has a wide vocabulary of wheezing and trilling calls, and a variable song which may include several changes of rhythm.
HABITS Nests mid-May to Aug in Iceland and

Faeroes, but from mid-June in more northerly areas; nesting habitats include arctic coasts and upland fringes of permanent snow, in Scandinavia sometimes at altitudes above 1300 m. Has recently nested in upland Scotland. Male takes major share in incubation and normally only he tends the chicks. There is a well-developed rodent-run display to distract potential predators from the nest. When not breeding, shows strong attachment to rocky sea-coasts, particularly fairly exposed shores where wave action is strong and tidal range wide. Often makes use of concrete sea-defences, groynes and breakwaters. Sometimes feeds on sandy or muddy beaches; occasional on coastal pools and, on migration, fringes of inland waters. In typical habitat feeds largely on small gastropod molluscs, often at fringes of surf; in stormy weather spends much time avoiding waves. Swims well if necessary. Fairly gregarious, usually seen in small single-species flocks or mixed with Ruddy Turnstones (154). Tame throughout the year; if flushed, typically flies low over water.
MOVEMENTS In winter, appears to shift south just far enough to accommodate whole population on ice-free coasts. In July-Aug, adults moult on coasts mostly close to nesting grounds, before onward passage to wintering grounds mainly late Sept-Nov. Juveniles follow a similar schedule, but a few unmoulted juveniles appear in winter range from mid-Sept. E Greenland nesters winter mostly in Iceland. Normal southern limits in winter are N Carolina and N Portugal; has straggled south to Texas and Morocco, also Azores and Madeira. Return passage is mainly Apr-May; south of winter range is deserted, but many non-breeders summer just south of breeding grounds. Vagrant inland in North America to Lake Winnipeg, Great Lakes (rare but regular), W Tennessee and Oklahoma, and in Europe east to Hungary and Greece and south to Italy and Malta.
DESCRIPTION Breeding: Crown, mantle, scapulars and tertials are mainly blackish-brown, fringed mid-chestnut and whitish. Supercilium is whitish, contrasting with dark lores and large reddish-dusky patch on ear-coverts; rest of face whitish, obscured by brown streaking. Flight feathers are mainly blackish, with clear white wingbar formed by narrow (about 1 mm wide) white outer webs of inner primaries, neat white greater-covert tips and whitish on outer webs of secondaries; one or two inner secondaries may be almost completely white. Rump, uppertail-coverts and central tail feathers are slaty-black; sides of rump and uppertail show a little white, and sides of tail dull brownish. Underparts whitish, but with throat, neck and breast distinctly spotted and streaked mid-brown,

most intensely on lower breast (sometimes forming a darker patch), and some spotting on flanks. **Non-breeding:** Head and neck dark slate-grey, with slightly paler chin and tiny obscure patches above the lores and behind the eyes. Upperparts dark slate-grey, with faint purple gloss on mantle and scapulars. Wing-coverts are fringed grey (outers) or whitish (inners). Breast is slate-grey with distinct dark grey streaks on flanks, sometimes forming long lines. Undertail-coverts white with grey spotting. **Juvenile:** Cap is brownish, edged pale chestnut. Mantle and scapular feathers are smaller and neater than those of adults, and are fringed pale chestnut, white and buff. Wing-coverts are brown, with neat fringes of pale buff (outers) or chestnut-buff (inners). Foreneck and breast are washed brownish-grey and finely but distinctly

streaked brown. Belly is white; flanks show some brown streaking.

AGE/SEX The small buff-fringed coverts of the juvenile are distinct until at least Oct; some first-winter birds may retain juvenile coverts visible in the field until Feb. Sexes are similar in plumage, but females average slightly larger, particularly in bill length.

RACES None is widely accepted, but there is marked variation in size between populations; Icelandic birds are largest and those from Greenland, Spitsbergen and Norway marginally the smallest.

MEASUREMENTS Length 200-220 mm (8¼"). Wing 123-142 mm; bill 26-37 mm; tarsus 21-26 mm; tail 52-67 mm.

REFERENCES Feare (1966), Atkinson *et al.* (1975), Bengtson (1975), Morrison (1976).

203 ROCK SANDPIPER *Calidris ptilocnemis* Plate 83

The Pacific counterpart of the N Atlantic Purple Sandpiper (202), and widely regarded as conspecific. The nominate race of Rock is, however, consistently different from all other forms of the two species.

IDENTIFICATION A rather large, dumpy calidrid of the N Pacific, typically seen on rocky coasts. Purple Sandpiper (which see) is virtually identical to most Rock Sandpipers (all except nominate race of the Pribilof Is.) in size, structure and in plumages. The only known constant differences of non-nominate Rocks from Purple are as follows: a slightly greater amount of white on the inner primaries and inner secondaries of Rock; rather more sharply-defined spotting on lower breast and flanks in non-breeding and juvenile plumages; brighter, more buffy-brown foreneck and upper breast in juvenile plumage; and, in breeding plumage, darker chestnut fringes above, and rather broader black centres to feathers of lower breast, often forming a blackish patch. On present knowledge it is unlikely that a vagrant Purple in the Pacific could be detected as such. Rock Sandpipers breeding on the Pribilofs, however, differ strikingly in all plumages from other races and from Purple Sandpiper, and average larger. In breeding plumage, upperpart fringing is pale yellowish and pale chestnut, and face and underparts are largely white, contrasting with a dark spot on the ear-coverts and a large black patch on the lower breast. Pattern recalls Dunlin (204), which, however, has no obvious ear-patch, a streaked breast, and a larger black patch which is on the belly rather than the breast. In juvenile and non-breeding plumages, upperparts and breast are paler — ash-grey rather than slate-grey. In E Pacific, often associates with Black Turnstone (155) and Surfbird (186), but differs in slightly drooping yellow-based bill, and in flight by the lack of white on the base of the tail. Black Turnstone differs additionally in blacker plumage, dark legs, and white on back and inner wing-coverts in flight. Surfbird is similar to Rock in non-breeding colour and pattern, but differs obviously in larger size and plumper shape and in its stubby plover-like bill and pied tail pattern. Compare also Wandering Tattler (151). **Bare parts:** See Purple Sandpiper.

VOICE Not known to differ from Purple Sandpiper. Contact calls may be fractionally higher-pitched. On breeding grounds, has rolling calls and rough trills.

HABITS Habits on breeding grounds and in winter are not known to differ from Purple Sandpiper. Breeding range is mainly coastal; probably nests less extensively at high altitude than does Purple. Reported to have a fluttering display flight.

MOVEMENTS Like Purple, a late migrant in autumn but returns to vicinity of nesting grounds relatively early. Occurs in California only from mid-Nov to early Apr (once lingering to mid-May). Occurs regularly in winter as far south as Tokyo area, Japan, and N California; vagrant south to Los Angeles, California. Extremely rare inland, but recorded Atlin, NW British Columbia (Oct 1932). The race *tschuktschorum* is probably responsible for all N American records south of Alaska. More southerly races are presumed to be resident.

DESCRIPTION Breeding: Crown is brownish-black, edged chestnut; supercilia are whitish, sometimes just meeting on forehead, contrasting with dark triangle in front of eye and prominent dark patch on rear ear-coverts; sides of head otherwise whitish, slightly streaked darker. Mantle, scapulars and tertials are blackish-brown, fringed deep rich chestnut and pale buff; wing-coverts brownish-grey or grey, fringed white. Flight feathers blackish, with strong wingbar formed by broad (2 mm or more wide) white fringes to outer webs of inner primaries (often reaching the shaft), white tips to greater coverts and white outer webs of secondaries, most prominent on inner feathers. Rump and uppertail are mainly blackish, with narrow whitish sides; tail is mostly dark. Chin is whitish; upper breast is washed buffish and variably streaked brown, while lower breast has larger brownish-black spots often fusing to form blackish patch (but see Races); belly and flanks are white, with variable amounts of brown streaking. **Non-breeding:** Many individuals are indistinguishable from Purple Sandpiper, except for pattern of white in wings and rather sharper spotting on lower breast and flanks. Nominate race, however, is paler: crown is pale brownish-grey, fringed white; forehead is pale and often joins a short supercilium; chin is whitish. Breast is off-white with obscure pale brown mottling and streaking; flanks show a little streaking. Wing-coverts are grey, fringed white; mantle and scapulars are a slightly darker brownish-grey. **Juvenile:** Upperparts show dark brown feather centres, fringed pale chestnut and buff; wing-coverts are grey-brown, mostly broadly fringed buff. Underparts white, but with neck and breast suffused buffish, and breast finely streaked brown; flanks show very few streaks.

AGE/SEX Juveniles are distinct in the field until at least Sept. Sexes differ slightly in breeding plumage, and females average larger, particularly in bill length.

RACES Four: nominate *ptilocnemis*, (Pribilof Is.), *tschuktschorum* (E Siberia and W Alaska), *couesi*

(Aleutians and S Alaska) and *quarta* (Commander and Kuril Is.). All except the nominate race have dark chestnut fringes to scapulars and tertials in breeding plumage. In *ptilocnemis*, the fringes are pale yellowish-chestnut, the neck and breast are distinctively pale, and the lower breast shows a prominent black patch. There are marked differences in size: the nominate race is largest and *couesi* smallest.

MEASUREMENTS Length 200-230 mm (8½"). Wing 112-145 mm; bill 23-38 mm; tarsus 21-25 mm; tail 50-55 mm (*couesi*).

REFERENCES Tomkovich (1982).

204 DUNLIN *Calidris alpina*

Plate 84 (see also Plate 74)

Other name: Red-backed Sandpiper

This circumpolar breeder is the common small winter wader on many northern hemisphere coasts. Only in Africa, however, does it penetrate regularly south of 20° N. Vagrants south of the equator must be identified with caution.

IDENTIFICATION A very well-known bird in North America and Europe. The classic Dunlin features are black bill, longish and noticeably drooped at the tip, black legs, rather hunched 'neckless' stance, and black on belly: breeding birds show a solid black belly-patch, while juveniles show blackish spotting on lower breast and sides of belly. In flight it shows a clear white wingbar, white sides to uppertail, and grey tail-sides. It is a rather variable species, however, particularly in bill length, body size and colour of upperparts when breeding. All races are larger than stints but slightly smaller than Curlew Sandpiper (205). No other small wader shows a black belly-patch, but compare breeding Rock Sandpiper (203), which has a smaller blackish patch on the lower breast. Most likely to be misidentified in non-breeding plumage, when plain grey-brown plumage and black legs invite confusion with dark-legged stints (190-193), Curlew Sandpiper and Broad-billed (207). Upperparts and coverts are darker and browner than in the stints and Broad-billed, and lack the latter's blackish-centred scapulars and blackish lesser coverts. Curlew Sandpiper is longer-legged than Dunlin, has a longer and more evenly-downcurved bill, a white rump-patch and a clearer white supercilium. See also Cox's Sandpiper (201). **Bare parts:** Bill black, rather longer than distance from bill-base to nape (but with much variation in length), and noticeably downcurved at the tip. Iris dark brown. Legs black or blackish-grey.

VOICE Flight call is a distinctive, slurred, reedy 'kree' or 'treeep'. Flocks feeding or at roost make a soft twittering sound. On the breeding grounds, may give a sharp 'quoi' in alarm. Most frequent song is a prolonged reedy trill on a descending scale.

HABITS Nests late Apr-Aug in a wide variety of habitats, from upland moorland, wet coastal grassland and saltmarshes in south of range to high-arctic tundra. Has nested at 36° N in S Spain and in E China. Both sexes incubate and tend the brood. Non-breeding habitats include muddy inland freshwater sites, but most gather in muddy estuaries; scarce on sandy coasts. Flocks are often huge and perform co-ordinated aerial manoeuvres with rapid changes of direction. Feeds by pecking or probing vigorously and

in rapid series, often interspersed with short runs; feeds mostly near the water's edge, often wading shallowly, or on wet mud.

MOVEMENTS Less migratory than most congeners. Populations are rather variable in timing of southward passage: in Europe and W Africa, adults move south mainly in July-Aug and moult in large concentrations on or near wintering grounds, dispersing Oct-Nov, while N American birds rarely appear on either coast before mid-Sept. Juveniles appear on passage in Europe from mid-July. Return movement spans Mar-early June. Some immatures spend all year in non-breeding range, but most return to breeding grounds. Has nested Spitsbergen and Bear I. Vagrant Costa Rica, Panama, Peru, French Guiana, Argentina, South Africa, E Africa, Maldive Is., Australia (mainly N Queensland) and New Zealand.

DESCRIPTION Breeding: Crown streaked chestnut and brown; supercilium whitish; lores dusky; ear-coverts rather pale, slightly streaked. Hindneck variably greyish or brownish, streaked brown. Mantle, scapulars and tertials are blackish, fringed chestnut of varying shade, grey or whitish; wing-coverts grey-brown, fringed pale grey or whitish. Flight feathers blackish, with clear white wingbar formed by tips of greater and primary coverts and bases of secondaries and inner primaries. Centre of rump, uppertail-coverts and tail is blackish-brown; sides of rump and uppertail are white, and sides of tail grey. Chin is white; foreneck whitish, with slight dark brown streaking which becomes more prominent on breast; belly is bordered white, but has a large black patch centrally. Vent and undertail, also axillaries and underwing, are white. **Non-breeding:** Crown, ear-coverts, hindneck, mantle, scapulars and wing-coverts are rather plain dull grey-brown. Supercilium is whitish and fairly clear. Underparts are white, but with sides of breast suffused and lightly streaked grey-brown. **Juvenile:** Lores and ear-coverts warm brown; hindneck buffish-brown. Mantle and scapulars blackish-brown with chestnut and whitish-buff fringes. Wing-coverts are brownish, clearly fringed buff or chestnut. Underparts white, with buff suffusion and brown streaks on foreneck and breast; belly mostly white, but with clear blackish-brown spots on sides of upper belly and on flanks.

AGE/SEX The juvenile is distinct at least to late Oct in the field; later, ageing is usually possible in the hand by retained juvenile inner medians. Virtually all one-year-old birds gain full breeding plumage; a variable proportion show some fresh buff-fringed coverts, difficult to distinguish from true juvenile feathers. In breeding plumage, male has whitish or pale grey hindneck, lightly streaked with brown, and the female a brownish hindneck contrasting less with the cap and mantle. Females average larger and longer-billed in all populations, but sexing is difficult unless race is known.

RACES Six: nominate *alpina* (N Scandinavia and NW USSR, winters W Europe and Mediterranean to W India), *schinzii* (SE Greenland, Iceland, Britain and S Scandinavia, winters mainly W Africa), *arctica* (NE Greenland, winters mainly W Africa), *sakhalina* (NE USSR and N Alaska, winters China and Japan), *pacifica* (W Alaska, winters Pacific USA and Mexico) and

hudsonia (central Canada, winters SE USA). There is considerable variation in size: *schinzii* and *arctica* are smallest, *alpina* and *sakhalina* intermediate, and the two American races largest and longest-billed. Races vary also in colour of upperparts in breeding plumage: *alpina* has rusty-red fringes, *schinzii* more yellowish-red, while in *arctica* the fringes are pale reddish-yellow and less extensive. In *sakhalina*, fringes are a brighter, deeper red than in *alpina*, and the two American races are the brightest and richest red of all; *hudsonia* differs further in that breast streaking butts onto the belly-patch, without an intervening white band.

MEASUREMENTS Length 160-220 mm (7½"). Wing 105-131 mm; bill 23-44 mm; tarsus 22-30 mm; tail 40-59 mm.

REFERENCES Holmes (1966), Soikkeli (1966), Page (1974), Pienkowski and Dick (1975), Mascher and Marcström (1976), Pienkowski *et al.* (1979), Greenwood (1979, 1984), Ferns (1981), Clark (1983).

205 CURLEW SANDPIPER *Calidris ferruginea* Plate 85

This elegant wader nests regularly only in a small area of N USSR, but is a common non-breeding visitor from W Africa east to New Zealand.

IDENTIFICATION The relatively long, clearly-decurved bill is the feature for which this calidrid was named; the bill shape, slim neck, and longish legs give it a characteristic outline. In breeding plumage its mainly chestnut-red head and underparts are like those of Red Knot (187), but the latter species can easily be distinguished by its greater bulk, shorter bill, and shorter, paler legs. Non-breeding plumage is rather plain grey-brown, recalling the shorter-legged Dunlin (204), but supercilium of Curlew Sandpiper is always more distinct, and bill averages longer and is more evenly decurved. Juvenile also has a clear supercilium, clean underparts with a buff suffusion on the breast, and neatly scaly upperparts. In flight, shows a clear white wingbar and a white band across the uppertail-coverts and lower rump; in breeding plumage, the white area is often partly obscured by rufous or brown spotting. Flight pattern suggests the smaller-bodied White-rumped Sandpiper (197), but in Curlew Sandpiper the wingbar and the white band above the tail are broader. Stilt Sandpiper (208) is superficially very similar in outline, except for its obviously longer legs; Stilt also differs, however, in its straighter-based, blunter-tipped bill, and flatter forehead. In flight, Stilt has a similar white patch above the tail, but it lacks a clear wingbar and its legs project well beyond the tail-tip, giving a characteristic cross-shaped outline. **Bare parts:** Bill black, sometimes tinged brownish or greenish at base. Iris dark brown. Legs black or blackish-grey, rarely tinged brownish or greenish; tips of toes project beyond tail-tip in flight.

VOICE A gentle rippling 'chirrup' recalling a very soft Ruddy Turnstone (154) or even Greater Sandplover (108). The song is a complex series of chatters, trills and whinnies.

HABITS Nests June-July on high-arctic coastal tundra, mainly in central Siberia (has nested N Alaska).

Male has a song flight around the territory with slow wingbeats and glides. Apparently only females incubate, and males may leave the nesting grounds by late June. Outside breeding season prefers muddy, poorly-vegetated wetland fringes both inland and coastal, including intertidal mudflats. Feeds on wet mud by Dunlin-like pecking and probing, or in water, where wades more deeply than its congeners; this habit may segregate Curlew Sandpipers from mixed feeding flocks of calidrids. Gregarious, often in large flocks, mixing freely with other small waders when feeding or roosting.

MOVEMENTS Has major migration routes to Africa, via W Europe (common in autumn, relatively rare in spring) and Black and Caspian Seas, to Indian subcontinent, and to Australasia. A few winter annually in Europe. Adults gather south of the breeding grounds to moult July-Aug, males preceding females; main migration of juveniles is in Aug-Sept. Return passage is mainly Apr-May. Many non-breeders remain in winter range all year. Vagrant Spitsbergen, Bear I., Iceland, Madeira, Cape Verde Is., Barbados (Sept 1969, having been ringed 14 days earlier in Belgium), both coasts and many inland areas of USA and Canada, Peru, Argentina, also Amsterdam I. in the Southern Ocean.

DESCRIPTION Breeding: Supercilium, sides of head and all of underparts are rich dark chestnut-red, relieved only by whitish undertail-coverts, some blackish bars on belly and flanks, and pale areas around base of bill and sometimes around eye. Chestnut feathers are mostly broadly tipped whitish when fresh. Crown and mantle feathers are dark brown, fringed dark chestnut, and scapulars dark brown, fringed chestnut and whitish. Wing-coverts are grey-brown, fringed whitish. Flight feathers blackish; a clear wingbar is formed by broad white tips to greater coverts, white tips to inner primary coverts, and white bases of inner primaries. Back and upper rump are mainly dark brown. Lower rump and uppertail-coverts are white, often slightly obscured by dark brown bars. Tail grey-brown, darkest in centre. Underwing-coverts and axillaries white. **Non-breeding:** Crown and upperparts grey-brown with darker shaft-streaks; wing-coverts grey, fringed whitish. Supercilium long and distinctly white, emphasised by a narrow darkish line across the lores and dusky ear-coverts. Underparts white, but sides of breast are suffused and sparsely streaked pale grey-brown. Rump and uppertail are clearer white. **Juvenile:** As non-breeding, but feathers of crown, mantle, scapulars and tertials are darkish brown, neatly fringed pale buff. Wing-coverts are slightly paler brown, with dark submarginal lines and pale buff fringes. Supercilium buffish-white. Neck and breast are suffused pale buff, and there is faint brown streak-

ing on upper breast; rest of underparts white.
AGE/SEX The scaly appearance of the juvenile is evident in the field until Nov; some juvenile coverts are normally retained throughout the first winter. One-year-old birds do not gain a full breeding plumage. Females average larger than males, particularly in bill length where there is very little overlap in measurements. In breeding plumage, females tend to have paler chestnut underparts with more white feathers admixed and more brown barring.
RACES No races are described. Females of eastern populations show less brown barring on underparts in breeding plumage than those in the west.
MEASUREMENTS Length 180-230 mm (8"). Wing 125-139 mm; bill 32-39 mm (males), 38-44 mm (females); tarsus 27-33 mm; tail 41-50 mm.
REFERENCES Holmes and Pitelka (1964), Elliott *et al.* (1976), Wilson *et al.* (1980).

206 SPOON-BILLED SANDPIPER
Eurynorhynchus pygmaeus

Plate 74
(see also Plates 79, 80)

Other name: Spoonbill Sandpiper
This is a highly charismatic wader, owing to its extraordinary bill shape, obvious even in young chicks, and to its rarity. The population has been estimated (optimistically?) at between 2,000 and 2,800 pairs.

IDENTIFICATION In size, shape, bare-part colours and plumage patterns, this bird shows a strong resemblance to Red-necked Stint (192); in juvenile and non-breeding plumages it also resembles the other dark-legged stints— Semipalmated (190), Western (191) and Little (193). The easiest and safest distinction from these species is the characteristic spatulate bill-tip, which is quite unlike that of any other wader. The 'spoon' is less evident in side views, however, and must be looked for carefully; a glint of light reflected from the bill-tip is often a good clue, but when lit from the side the bill looks darker-tipped. Spoon-billed always looks heavier-headed than stints, often stands more upright, and has a highly distinctive feeding action. In breeding plumage, face, neck and upper breast are mainly chestnut-red, giving a strong resemblance to Red-necked, but lower scapulars are not contrastingly grey. In non-breeding plumage, Spoon-billed is rather whiter on face and breast than the stints, even suggesting a diminutive Sanderling (189). In juvenile plumage, shows more buffish-white and fewer chestnut fringes above than Red-necked, and more white on the face which often contrasts with a broad dark mask through the eye. In flight, shows white sides to uppertail and grey tail-sides like stints, but white wingbar is slightly more prominent.
Bare parts: Bill rather broad and deep at base, tapering towards tip, but with tip flattened and expanded, spatulate in shape; whole bill black, but faint greyish cast may be visible over the basal two-thirds. Iris dark brown. Legs black.
VOICE Contact call is a quiet rolled 'preep' or a shrill 'wheet'. Song, given in display flight, is an intermittent cicada-like buzzing trill 'preer-prr-prr' on a descending scale.
HABITS Nests June-July in coastal tundra, preferring grassy areas near freshwater pools. The male has a display flight, including brief hovers during which he

sings, circling, and rapid dives. Apparently, he takes the major part in incubation and care of the brood. On the breeding grounds, feeds largely on insects around freshwater pools. Winters on muddy coasts or coastal lagoons, often occurring in tiny numbers among large flocks of Red-necked or Little Stints. Feeds mostly in shallow water or soft wet mud, typically using a side-to-side motion of the bill: the bird walks forward with head down and sweeping from side to side, and may even turn back on its course without raising the bill — a 'vacuum cleaner' to the 'sewing-machine' of snipes and dowitchers.
MOVEMENTS Winters coastally from SE India to Singapore and SE China, but is nowhere common. Only two records for Thailand by 1984. Occurs on passage in Korea, Japan, Hong Kong and E China, chiefly in late Apr-May and Sept. Vagrant Assam, W Aleutians, W Alaska and Vancouver B.C. (July-Aug 1978).
DESCRIPTION Breeding: Forehead, crown and hindneck are suffused chestnut-red and streaked dark brown. Supercilium chestnut-red and dark brown, paler behind the eye. Feathering around bill, including chin, is whitish; lores show a dusky area, and the eye-stripe continues narrowly behind the eye. Rest of face, neck and upper breast are chestnut-red, faintly streaked brown. Lower breast is paler chestnut, with distinct streaking at the sides sometimes forming a complete band of brownish spots. Rest of underparts white, including underwing and axillaries. Mantle, scapulars and tertials are blackish-centred with mainly-chestnut fringes; whitish fringes on the mantle may form faint whitish lines. Flight feathers are blackish, with a broad white wingbar formed by large white tips to greater coverts, and white bases of secondaries and inner 7 primaries; inner secondaries show more extensive white at base. Central uppertail and tail are blackish; sides of uppertail are white and of tail pale grey. **Non-breeding:** Crown and

upperparts are brownish-grey, with slightly darker shaft-streaks; hindneck is paler. Wing-coverts grey, with narrow white fringes. Forehead, supercilium and underparts are bright white; sides of neck and upper breast are lightly streaked grey-brown. **Juvenile:** Crown dark brown, fringed buffish-chestnut. Forehead and supercilium are creamy-white, contrasting with a dusky spot on the lores and a well-marked dusky patch across the ear-coverts. Mantle, scapulars and tertials are blackish-brown, with mainly buffish and whitish fringes; the latter may form faint 'V's at edges of mantle and upper scapulars. Coverts are brown, with pale buff and reddish-buff fringes.

Underparts are white, but with sides of breast washed buff and showing small areas of brown streaking; the buff wash may join across the centre of the breast. **AGE/SEX** Juveniles are distinct in the field to at least Oct. Sexes are not known to differ in plumage, but females average slightly larger.
RACES No geographical variation is known.
MEASUREMENTS Length 140-160 mm (6"). Wing 98-106 mm; bill 19-24 mm, breadth of bill-tip 10-12 mm; tarsus 19-22 mm; tail 37-39 mm.
REFERENCES Dixon (1918), Portenko (1957), Burton (1971), Sauppe et al. (1978).

207 BROAD-BILLED SANDPIPER *Limicola falcinellus*　　　Plate 77

A rather scarce and elusive calidrid-like wader whose breeding and wintering ranges are not yet fully elucidated.

IDENTIFICATION Calidrid-like, except for its unusually broad bill. It is intermediate in size between Dunlin (204) and the stints (190-196), almost overlapping with smallest Dunlins. The bill is Dunlin-like in relative length, and shows a similar kink towards the tip; the breadth of the bill is not a usable field character. Breeding and juvenile plumages are snipe-like: very dark brown above and on breast, with a contrasting double supercilium and thin whitish lines at edges of mantle and scapulars. The pale face is crossed by a long dark eye-stripe, while belly and undertail are white. In non-breeding plumage, it becomes a pale grey-brown stint-like bird, greyer than Dunlin and with more conspicuous dark feather centres, particularly to the scapulars; the dark eye-stripe and pale double supercilium are still present, but contrast little with the rest of the face. In flight, it shows a black leading edge to the wing, like Sanderling (189), conspicuous in non-breeding plumage, a fairly narrow white wingbar, and a dark central rump and tail. See also Western (191), Curlew (205) and Cox's (201) Sandpipers, and Jack Snipe (182).
Bare parts: Bill black, sometimes tinged greenish or brownish, or with a tinge of yellow at the base; longish, decurved at tip, tapering in profile, but from above remarkably broad and parallel-sided, tapering sharply to a pointed tip. Iris dark brown. Legs rather short, appearing blackish-grey at a distance, but often tinged greenish, yellowish or brownish.
VOICE An unmusical buzzing trill 'chrrreet' is the usual call in flight, but also has shorter calls 'tzit' and 'trr'; may recall Temminck's Stint (194). Songs are a rhythmic buzzing 'sprrr-sprrr-sprrr' and a faster, wheezier, more whirring trill.
HABITS Nests June-Aug in wettest parts of montane or lowland bogs. The nest itself is often in the top of a tussock. Male has song flight at alternating fast and slow speeds. Breeding birds often skulk, rail-like, to avoid detection. Occurs at inland wetlands on migration, but chiefly coastal outside the breeding season; prefers areas of soft intertidal mud, also occurring in similar habitats a short distance inland. In winter usually found in small numbers among stint flocks, and many are probably overlooked; some sites may hold up to a few dozen. Parties of up to a few hundred can occur on migration. Feeding actions are

usually like Dunlin, but typically it holds its head farther in front of the body and the bill a little more vertical. Slower feeding action and persistent vertical probing are unlike stints. Often fairly tame; may crouch, snipe-like, when approached.
MOVEMENTS Adults move south from early July and juveniles from Aug. Some reach winter range by late July (adults) or late Aug (juveniles), but passage may continue to end Oct. Route of Scandinavian breeders is largely southeasterly, mostly via Black or Caspian Seas or E Mediterranean, probably towards India and E Africa. Breeding range and movements of Siberian birds are poorly known; most winter in SE Asia and Australia. Return passage is rather late, mainly late Apr-May. A few non-breeders remain south all year. Vagrant W Aleutians, New Zealand, Iceland, Bear I., most European countries, Morocco, Chad, Nigeria, Namibia, SE Africa and E African lakes; further regular sites probably remain to be discovered in W and S Africa.
DESCRIPTION Breeding: Crown is blackish-brown, except for a fine whitish line each side which joins the supercilium in front of the eye—a 'split supercilium'. Main supercilium is broad and brownish-white, extending from bill to nape. A dark line across the lores and broadly dark ear-coverts form a mask through the eye; cheeks and throat are contrastingly brownish-white, lightly streaked brown. Mantle, scapulars and tertials are blackish-brown, fringed whitish and pale chestnut and initially broadly tipped greyish-white; whitish edges to mantle and scapulars form contrasting lines along upperparts. Wing-coverts are brown, except for blackish lesser and primary coverts; medians are fringed whitish. Flight feathers are mostly blackish; white wingbar is formed mainly by narrow white tips to primary and greater coverts. Rump and uppertail-coverts white at sides and blackish-brown in the centre. Central pair of tail feathers are dark brown, other pairs pale greyish. Underparts white, but with neck and breast infused grey-brown and heavily but neatly streaked mid-brown, sharply defined against the white belly; anterior flanks also show some streaking. **Non-breeding:** Supercilia are white; main supercilium is well marked, upper supercilium variably distinct. Dark lines across the lores and dusky ear-coverts form

a strong eye-stripe. Feathers of crown and upperparts pale grey-brown, with prominent blackish centres or shaft-streaks and fine white fringes. Underparts mainly white, but with breast lightly streaked grey-brown. **Juvenile:** As breeding, but mantle, scapulars and tertials are fringed paler buff-chestnut and whitish, and wing-coverts broadly fringed buff. Breast is washed brownish-buff and only faintly streaked; hardly any streaks extend onto flanks.

AGE/SEX Juvenile is distinct at close range to Nov, and some as late as Jan; adults are normally in full non-breeding plumage by Oct. Sexes are similar in plumage, but females average larger.

RACES Two: nominate *falcinellus* (Scandinavia and W USSR) and *sibirica* (central and E USSR), but their geographical separation is as yet uncertain. The race *sibirica* differs in brighter, more rufous fringes to the upperparts and a cinnamon wash to the breast in breeding plumage; the upper supercilium is less well defined. In juvenile plumage, buff fringes are broader than on nominate race.

MEASUREMENTS Length 160-180 mm (6¾"). Wing 100-115 mm; bill 27-36 mm; tarsus 20-24 mm; tail 33-40 mm.

REFERENCES Nisbet (1961a), Flint (1973).

208 STILT SANDPIPER *Micropalama himantopus*   Plate 85

This calidrid-like American wader is similar in many ways to the Palaearctic Curlew Sandpiper (205), but differs markedly in leg length and in feeding behaviour.

IDENTIFICATION A largish sandpiper with a long, decurved bill and comparatively long greenish legs. It is usually seen feeding in belly-deep water, often with the much larger dowitchers (183, 184), using a dowitcher-like 'sewing-machine' feeding action with rapid, irregular vertical probes. Curved bill, long legs and slim neck are similar to Curlew Sandpiper, but Stilt always differs in longer, paler legs, straighter-based, slightly thicker bill, and in less rounded head shape; forehead of Stilt always appears long and sloping. Folded wings project slightly beyond tail-tip. In flight it shows a white patch on the lower rump and uppertail, as in Curlew Sandpiper, but virtually no wingbar; it also differs obviously from Curlew Sandpiper in that its pale greenish toes and part of the tarsus project beyond the tail-tip. Breeding plumage is unmistakable, with reddish nape and mask, and underparts strongly barred blackish-brown and white. Flight pattern may suggest Lesser Yellowlegs (142) or Wilson's Phalarope (156); the former species is obviously larger, however, and in the latter the toes project less beyond the tail-tip. **Bare parts:** Bill laterally compressed and straight at base, but downcurved and slightly laterally expanded at tip; black, sometimes tinged greyish or brownish at base. Iris dark brown. Legs long and slender, dull greenish or yellowish-green; toes are partially webbed.

VOICE Usual flight call is a soft rattling trill 'kirrr' or 'grrrt'; also a clearer 'whu'. Song is a complex series of guttural trills, braying and whining sounds.

HABITS Nests June-Aug in relatively open, dry tundra, north of the tree-line. Males advertise territories by prolonged song flights. Both sexes incubate, males mostly by day and females at night. Initially both parents tend the brood, but both typically leave before the young fledge, females preceding males. Outside the breeding season, found principally on inland waters and coastal pools, rarely on open shores. Typical feeding behaviour is dowitcher-like (see above); also feeds on wet mud by calidrid-like pecking and probing. Flight is strong and powerful on relatively large wings. Usually occurs singly with dowitchers or in small single-species groups; large flocks may gather on migration.

MOVEMENTS Adults move south from mid-July, juveniles from mid-Aug. Main route is through interior

Canada and USA, but a proportion migrates via E USA and W Atlantic to N South America. Return movement occurs Mar-May. Some non-breeders remain in winter quarters all year. Scarce on passage in Pacific USA, but a few winter regularly in S California. Regular in Bermuda on autumn passage. Vagrant Japan, Darwin, N Australia (Aug-Sept 1980), Britain, Ireland, Sweden, Finland, Austria, and Majorca (May 1983).

DESCRIPTION Breeding: Crown heavily streaked brown, fringed chestnut and whitish. Supercilium white, long and distinct; lores washed chestnut and streaked brown; ear-coverts fairly bright chestnut; rest of sides of face, also neck, whitish heavily streaked brown. Mantle and most scapulars are centred blackish and edged whitish; tertials are dark brown, fringed narrowly paler. Upperwing-coverts are grey-brown, fringed whitish. Flight feathers are brownish, darkest on outer primaries; there is a very indistinct whitish wingbar formed by narrow white tips to greater coverts. Lower rump and uppertail-coverts are white, variably obscured by brown bars; tail is washed rather pale grey. Underparts have a whitish ground colour, with upper breast streaked brown and flanks, belly and undertail-coverts strongly barred dark brown. Underwing-coverts and axillaries are white, with some indistinct grey smudges. **Non-breeding:** Head pattern is much as breeding but lacks chestnut; distinct pale supercilium and dark eye-stripe. Upperparts are fairly plain brownish-grey, with darker shaft-streaks and some paler fringes; wing-coverts are fringed whitish. Underparts white, with fine grey streaking on throat and foreneck which becomes more prominent on breast, and indistinct streaks on flanks and undertail-coverts. Lower rump and upper-tail are clearer white. **Juvenile:** Crown is darkish brown, streaked buffish-white; mantle, scapulars and tertials are centred blackish-brown and fringed whitish-buff; wing-coverts are grey-brown, fringed pale buff. Underparts are whitish, with throat, fore-neck and upper breast washed buff and showing some brownish streaks.

AGE/SEX The neat scaly pattern of the juvenile may be distinct into Oct. Sexes are difficult to separate even in full breeding plumage; underpart barring of males is blackish, of females more brownish. Female averages slightly larger in wing and bill.
RACES No geographical variation is known.
MEASUREMENTS Length 180-230 mm (8"). Wing 124-140 mm; bill 37-44 mm; tarsus 35-46 mm; tail 45-52 mm.
REFERENCES Jehl (1970, 1973).

209 BUFF-BREASTED SANDPIPER *Tryngites subruficollis*   Plate 86

A wader of inland habitats, in some ways a Nearctic equivalent of the Old World Ruff (210). Formerly much more numerous, but severely reduced by shooting pressure in the late nineteenth century.

IDENTIFICATION Easily identified by buff face and underparts, scaly brown-and-buff upperparts, bright yellow legs, unusually steep forehead, and rather small-looking head. Closest resemblance is to a juven-ile Ruff, but is much smaller even than a female Ruff, has much brighter legs, and has distinctive bland expression. Differs in flight in lack of white wingbar and sides to rump: upperwing shows an indistinct buffish bar, and sides of the rump are also buff, poorly contrasted with the rest of the upperparts. Note gleaming white axillaries, contrasting with buff flanks and belly, and narrow dark bar at the tips of the under primary coverts. Flight is easier and more graceful than any calidrid, but less so than Ruff. **Bare parts:** Bill short and straight like small *Calidris*, dark brown with a tinge of yellow at base of lower mandible. Iris brown. Legs are bright yellow-ochre.
VOICE Usually silent, but a low growling flight call 'pr-r-r-reet' is sometimes heard and rapid clicking noises are given in display.
HABITS Nests June-Aug on arctic tundra. Males indulge in a form of lekking behaviour, with much display of the silvery-white undersides of the wings. The territories defended by males at the lek are larger than in other lekking birds, ranging from less than 1 ha to over 4 ha. Successful males may mate with several females, but they take no further part in the nesting cycle. Display may occur well south of the breeding grounds during northward migration. When not breeding, typically a wader of short-grass plains. On migration usually seen on golf-courses or airfields or on baked mud around rivers, inland lakes and reservoirs, rarely beside water. Many individuals defend small feeding territories on South American grasslands, yet they roost in large monospecific flocks. Gait is typically high-stepping. Usually a very tame species.
MOVEMENTS Migrates across central North America, east of the Rockies, towards winter quarters on S South American grasslands. There appears to be a second southward migration route via Hudson Bay, New England, the W Atlantic and NE South America. Rare autumn migrant on both North American coasts, south from Labrador and S Alaska, but far more regu-lar on the Atlantic side. In Argentina, most arrive in mid-Sept; many depart in late Jan, but a few are still present in Mar. Spring movement is again across cen-tral North America; coastal records at this season are exceptional. In spite of its comparative rarity on the North Atlantic coast, this is one of the most numer-ous of the Nearctic waders seen in Europe in autumn: more than 60 in Britain and Ireland during late Aug-early Oct 1975. Vagrant also to most parts of con-tinental Europe, Spitsbergen, Azores, Tunisia (Dec 1963), Egypt (Feb 1928), Sierra Leone (Nov 1973), Kenya (Dec 1973), South Africa (Dec 1977), Sri Lanka (Mar 1960), Amurland, Kurils, Japan, Hawaii and other central Pacific islands, Papua New Guinea, and Australia (Dec-May). One wintered Poland 1982/83.
DESCRIPTION Breeding: Head and underparts rich buff, paler on belly, vent and undertail, with brown spotting or streaking on crown, hindneck and sides of breast. Buff feathers are all slightly paler-fringed, giving a faintly-mottled appearance, particularly on the breast. Lesser underwing-coverts are rich deep buff; primary underwing-coverts strongly mottled dark brown and with a bold brown subterminal bar; axillaries and other underwing-coverts silky-white. Undersides of all flight feathers of wing and tail strongly mottled distally with dark brown spots on a whitish background. Mantle, scapulars, rump, uppertail and wing-coverts all show buffish-brown feather edgings and mainly narrow and lanceolate dark brown feather centres. Flight feathers, outer greater coverts, bastard wing and primary coverts show a buffish-white fringe, a dark subterminal spot or bar, and dark brown mottling on the proximal part of each feather; outer 2 primaries, however, effec-tively lack a pale fringe, and the central pair of rec-trices is almost all-dark. **Non-breeding:** Almost identical, except that buffish-brown edgings to upper-part feathers tend to be broader and browner, less buff. **Juvenile:** Head and underparts as adult, except that paler fringes to buff feathers are broader, show-ing paler particularly on belly, flanks and undertail. Mantle and scapulars as adult's in coloration, but fringes are a paler, whiter buff; pattern differs in that dark feather centres are rounded, giving a more scaly appearance. Wing-coverts show a central subtermi-nal spot, sometimes broadened into a bar, inside a pale buff fringe. Flight feathers are less strongly pat-terned than on adult. The outer primaries show pale tips approaching 1 mm broad when fresh.
AGE/SEX The scaly upperparts and subterminal cov-ert markings of the fresh juvenile are clear distinc-tions from the adult. Some juvenile coverts are retained until the spring. The undersides of the primaries are finely speckled dark brown in juven-

ile, while adults show bolder blackish spotting. Males are larger than females and are always separable on measurements. In the field, parties may be sexed on size-differences (with practice).

RACES No geographical variation is known.

MEASUREMENTS Length 180-200 mm (7½"). Wing 133-140 mm (males), 124-132 mm (females); bill 19-21 mm (males), 18-20 mm (females); tarsus 31-34 mm (males), 27-31 mm (females); tail 51-60 mm (males), 46-56 mm (females).

REFERENCES Prevett and Barr (1976), Myers (1979, 1980).

210 RUFF *Philomachus pugnax*   **Plate 86**

Other name: Reeve (females only)

A relatively large and powerfully-built calidrid-like wader which is remarkable in its sexual dimorphism in size and in breeding plumage; breeding males are highly spectacular in their variably-coloured ruffs and ear-tufts.

IDENTIFICATION In spite of wide variability in size, plumage and leg colours, Ruff is a distinctive and easily recognised species. Much of its special 'jizz' is accounted for by odd shape: head is rather small, bill is shortish and slightly drooped, neck is longish, and body rather deep-bellied and hump-backed. Breeding plumage males are unmistakable; moulting males may be mostly grey-brown on head and neck, but still show black or chestnut patches on sides of breast and flanks. Breeding females are variable, but usually show extensive blackish feather centres above and on breast and flanks. Non-breeding plumage is mainly mottled grey-brown above and on foreneck and breast; scapulars and tertials are rather long and loose and are often raised by the wind. Some birds show a fairly sharp contrast between whitish sides of neck and darker ground colour to hindneck; all have pale lores. A minority of males (exceptionally females) show a variable amount of unmarked white on head, neck and breast. Many non-breeding Ruffs recall Redshank (137) in bare-part colours and superficially in plumage and shape; Redshank, however, is longer-billed, slightly greyer, lacks dark feather centres on upperparts, and has white secondaries and back which are conspicuous in flight. Juveniles are washed buff on underparts (variable in shade) and have a neatly scaly upperpart pattern with small, buff-fringed scapulars, tertials and wing-coverts; as in adults, lores are pale. Compare juvenile with Sharp-tailed (200) and Buff-breasted (209) Sandpipers. In flight, Ruff looks large-winged and powerful and may fly with measured, rather slow wingbeats. There is a narrow white wingbar; sides to uppertail-coverts are broadly white, forming a unique pattern of large white ovals (usually joined at tip) overlying the base of the tail. **Bare parts:** Bill mostly blackish-brown, sometimes tinged brownish or reddish at base, but in breeding males may be variably yellowish, orange or pinkish-red, with or without a blackish tip; rather short and slightly downcurved. Facial warts of breeding males may be greenish, yellowish, orange or red. Iris dark brown. Legs of juvenile are dull yellowish-brown or greenish, but from first winter onwards become mottled with some orange or orange-pink; adult colours of pinkish-red or orange-red are attained after about two years (rate of colour change appears to be variable). Some adult males show seasonal change in leg colour and are yellow-legged when breeding.

VOICE Rarely makes any sound. A variety of low hoarse grunts such as 'kurr', 'kuk-uk' and 'kook' are sometimes given by feeding birds, winter flocks, females disturbed at the nest, and at the lek; a shrill rising 'hoo-ee' may be heard from migrating flocks.

HABITS Nests May-Aug in extensive lowland freshwater marshlands and damp grasslands. Males have a complex lek display at which some defend particular 'residences' about 1 m apart, using posturing and sometimes kicking and pecking; others, 'satellite males', move more freely around the arena and behave opportunistically. Females visit the lek and are mated by one or several males; they then nest and raise the brood, inconspicuously and often 400 m or more from the lek. Rudimentary lek behaviour may begin on spring migration. When not breeding, occurs on grassland, plough, rice-paddies and similar habitats, and around inland freshwaters and coastal pools; rarely uses intertidal habitats. Feeds mainly using a steady Redshank-like walk and pecking action. May wade deeply and submerge head when feeding; on saline lakes in E Africa often swims, phalarope-like, pecking at surface items. Occurs in vast concentrations, particularly in W Africa; nearly one million were estimated at one roost in Senegal. Flies to and from roost very rapidly and purposefully, usually low and in dense flocks.

MOVEMENTS Non-breeding range is wide, but the vast bulk of the population winters in Africa, including E Siberian breeders. Many migrate south via W Europe, but spring migration is generally more easterly. Males begin leaving breeding grounds in late June, followed by females and juveniles from mid-July; some males arrive in W Africa by mid-July, but main arrival in winter range occurs Aug-Sept. Males outnumber females in Britain in winter, but females predominate in E Africa and South Africa. Return passage spans Feb-May. Many non-breeders spend all year in winter quarters. Regular also east to Burma, S China, Philippines, New Guinea and S Australia. Vagrant Bear I., Iceland, Bermuda, Cape Verde Is., Madagascar, New Zealand, Alaska (regular, nested 1976), both coasts and many inland areas of USA and Canada (perhaps nests), Guatemala, Panama, Barbados, Trinidad, Peru and Venezuela.

DESCRIPTION Breeding male: Most of face is bare, with small warts and wattles. Ear-tufts, covering sides of nape, and ruff, covering neck and breast, are variable and largely independent in colour; either may be chestnut, buff, white, or black glossed with purple, barred blackish or unbarred. Mantle, scapulars and tertials may also show admixed chestnut and/or black; coverts mostly grey-brown, fringed paler. Flight feathers dark brown, with narrow white wingbar formed by greater-covert tips and white at bases of the inner primaries. Rump is mostly dark brown; uppertail-coverts are rather long, brown in centre but white at sides, forming two large white ovals; tail feathers themselves are mainly dull grey. Underparts white, but with some black or chestnut, sometimes extensive, on lower breast and flanks. **Breeding female:** Lacks bare face, head-tufts and ruff. Upperparts are mainly greyish-brown, fringed whitish, but a variable number of mantle feathers and scapulars are centred blackish. Underparts show fairly prominent blackish blotching on breast and flanks. **Non-breeding:** Like breeding female, but plainer above and below. Face off-white; upperparts all dull grey-brown with darker feather centres; underparts whitish, with foreneck, breast and flanks slightly mottled grey. A small proportion (almost always males) show a conspicuous patch of white or creamy-white on the breast and around base of neck; some have head, neck and breast (even upper mantle) almost unmarked white. **Juvenile:** As typical non-breeding,

but with head, neck, breast and upper belly strongly washed buff. Mantle, scapulars and tertials are blackish, neatly fringed pale chestnut-buff and whitish; wing-coverts darkish brown, fringed buffish.

AGE/SEX The scaly upperparts and buff-washed breast of the juvenile enable identification in the field up to Nov; brownish or greenish legs are subsequently a good indicator of a first-winter bird. One of the easiest waders to sex since breeding plumages are completely different and sexes hardly overlap in size: with experience it is usually possible to sex even a lone Ruff in the field.

RACES No geographical variation is known.

MEASUREMENTS Length: males 260-320 mm (11½"), females 200-250 mm (8¾"). Wing 170-210 mm (males), 132-170 mm (females); bill 30-42 mm (males), 26-34 mm (females); tarsus 45-55 mm (males), 37-46 mm (females); tail 62-70 mm (males), 49-60 mm (females).

REFERENCES Hogan-Warburg (1966), van Rhijn (1973), Shepard (1976), Pearson (1981), Prater (1982).

211 RUFOUS-BELLIED SEEDSNIPE *Attagis gayi* Plate 87

The largest and hardiest seedsnipe, resident at high altitude.

IDENTIFICATION Rufous belly and underwing are diagnostic. This species and White-bellied Seedsnipe (212) are easily distinguished from the *Thinocorus* seedsnipes (213, 214) by their obviously larger size, bulky, quail-like rather than passerine-like outline, and plain-coloured rather than contrastingly-patterned underwing and axillaries. Overlaps in range with White-bellied in S Chile and Argentina, but is slightly larger and heavier-billed and differs obviously in rufous rather than white underparts and underwing. In addition, the upperparts are paler owing to more extensive and finer vermiculations, and the flight feathers have broader, neatly-defined tawny fringes. Beware confusion with tinamous of genus *Nothoprocta*. **Bare parts:** Bill quite heavy, dull grey-brown. Iris brown. Legs dull yellow or yellowish-brown, short, with thickly-feathered tibiae.

VOICE A rasping 'tchaa' when flushed, snipe-like but noticeably louder.

HABITS A bird of the high Andes throughout the year. Often around the snow-line at over 4000 m; in the south, may be found as low as 2000 m. Found in sparse grasslands and rocky areas. Nest may be on barren slopes or among sparse vegetation. Gregarious, may gather in sizeable flocks in winter. Feeds as other seedsnipes by grazing plants and pecking seeds. Quite approachable; when flushed, flies in rapid, low zigzag, but ordinary flight is more direct. Wings are broad-based and pointed and wingbeats are rapid, recalling the Old World sandgrouse (Pteroclididae).

MOVEMENTS Sedentary, hardly ever moving to lower altitudes even in severe weather.

DESCRIPTION Breeding and non-breeding: Whole upperparts mid-brown, extensively fringed and vermiculated with very fine whitish or rufous bars; these are rather broader and more rufous on wing-coverts. Primaries and secondaries brown, with neat, pale

rufous fringes to secondaries, inner primaries, and greater primary coverts. Tail, mostly hidden by long coverts above and below, mid-brown with buff-olive barring; 14 feathers. Entire underparts washed cinnamon-brown to chestnut; darker breast-band has usually fairly narrow and irregular dark brown crescents; belly feathers often have broad paler fringes, forming a mottled pattern. Underwing-coverts and axillaries unmarked cinnamon. **Juvenile:** As adult, but vermiculations even finer; the primary fringes are slightly more buffish and extend onto outer 3 primaries, which are all-dark in adults.

AGE/SEX Juveniles are distinguishable only in the hand. No differences are known between the sexes.

RACES Three: *latreillii* (Ecuador), *simonsi* (Peru, Bolivia, NW Argentina) and *gayi* (Chile, Patagonia). Very similar in size, with very slight trends towards longest tarsus in *latreillii* and longest bill in *gayi*. In *latreillii*, upperparts are darker and have fewer and finer vermiculations (almost approaching White-bellied); underparts are rich chestnut with neat, dark breast markings and strong flank bars. The race *gayi* is palest above and below; *simonsi* is intermediate, but much closer to *gayi*.

MEASUREMENTS Length 290-310 mm (11¾"). Wing 187-207 mm; bill 15-19 mm; tarsus 23-27 mm; tail 71-93 mm.

REFERENCES Johnson (1965).

212 WHITE-BELLIED SEEDSNIPE *Attagis malouinus*   **Plate 87**

A beautifully-marked seedsnipe of wild habitats at the southern tip of South America.

IDENTIFICATION The mainly-white underparts and pure white axillaries and underwing distinguish this from Rufous-bellied Seedsnipe (211), which is otherwise very similar. Also differs in slightly smaller size, proportionately smaller bill, more rufous upperpart fringes, pale rufous tips to crown and nape, and more striking scalloped pattern on the breast. Larger size should distinguish it easily from female Grey-breasted Seedsnipe (213), but note also the streaked breast and black axillaries of latter species. **Bare parts:** Bill dusky-brown, with greyish at base of lower mandible. Iris brown. Legs yellowish-grey or brownish.

VOICE In flight, a melancholy 'too-ee' recalling Grey Plover (84). When flushed, a sharper repeated 'tu-whit', very different from Rufous-bellied's snipe-like call.

HABITS Inhabits barren mountains and exposed moorland of the southernmost Andes and Tierra del Fuego. Usually seen in pairs in summer, but gathers in flocks in winter and may visit lowland flats in severe conditions. Lays four eggs in a simple depression among short vegetation, lined with mosses and lichens. Food is chiefly crowberry and other plant material. When flushed, dashes away with wild, twisting flight; usually disappears over the nearest ridge, but may land on a high vantage point.

MOVEMENTS Sedentary, but driven to lower altitudes by heavy snowfalls. Recorded on the Falkland Is. in 1783 and 1859.

DESCRIPTION Breeding and non-breeding: Face, hindneck, chin and throat pale buff, spotted brown. Buffish and chestnut tips on crown. Upperparts, including coverts, richly coloured, essentially brownish-black scaled with rufous and whitish; each feather has a dark centre, then alternating bands of rufous or whitish, and dark brown towards the edge. Patterning is finest on mantle and scapulars. Flight feathers uniform medium-brown. Tail darkish brown, obscurely barred with paler brown and narrowly tipped whitish. Breast off-white, neatly and boldly scalloped with dark brown. Rest of underparts white, but with some large irregular brown chevrons on flanks and undertail-coverts. Underwing-coverts and axillaries pure white. **Juvenile:** As adult, but with many more neat whitish crescents over upperpart feathers, appearing paler and more scaly. Ground colour of chin, neck and breast is whiter.

AGE/SEX Juveniles are very difficult to distinguish. No differences are known between the sexes.

RACES Northern birds have been separated as *'cheeputi'*, but the species is probably best considered monotypic.

MEASUREMENTS Length 265-290 mm (11"). Wing 167-180 mm; bill 14-15 mm; tarsus 21-24 mm; tail 75-91 mm.

REFERENCES Johnson (1965), Humphrey *et al.* (1970).

213 GREY-BREASTED SEEDSNIPE *Thinocorus orbignyianus*   **Plate 88**

This is the larger of the two small, sexually-dimorphic seedsnipes. Like the two large species of the genus *Attagis* (211, 212), it is essentially an upland species.

IDENTIFICATION A turnstone-sized bird, clearly larger than Least Seedsnipe (214) but considerably smaller and less bulky than Rufous-bellied (211) or White-bellied (212). Shows obvious strong affinities with Least: both male and female plumages are similar, and the unusual black-and-white underwing pattern is virtually identical in the two species. Always distinguishable from Least by larger size, slightly darker and warmer brown upperparts, extensive brown chevrons on flanks, and more uniform wing with less obvious pale trailing edge. The male has more extensive grey, of a richer, bluer shade, on the forecrown, hindneck and breast, and never shows a black central line joining the throat- and breast-bands as in Least. The female has heavier breast streaking and a less obvious brown outline to the throat-patch. **Bare parts:** Bill yellowish, with black tip. Eye prominent, iris dark brown. Legs yellowish, rather short and often strongly flexed.

VOICE When flushed, a snipe-like rasping 'bzeep' as Least Seedsnipe, but the normal flight call is a deeper disyllabic 'wuk-wuk'. When very agitated, may give a sharp 'pik-pik'. The song, given in flight or from a perch on a rock, is a cooing 'puku-puku' repeated at the rate of two to three per second for up to five minutes.

HABITS A bird of the high puna zone of the Andes in the north of its range, sometimes above 4000 m, occurring at decreasing altitudes southwards to Tierra del Fuego and Staten I., where it may be found near the coast. The display flight is low, rarely above 10 m, ending with a shallow glide on downcurved wings; unlike Least, it does not raise its tail just before landing. When disturbed, usually crouches motionless, relying on camouflage. If flushed, dashes off with zig-zag flight and rapid shallow wingbeats; sometimes lands again quickly. Bobs head vigorously when alarmed. Despite short legs, can run quickly and easily.

MOVEMENTS Mainly sedentary, but descends from highest altitudes (and apparently vacates Tierra del Fuego) during severe winter weather.

DESCRIPTION Breeding and non-breeding plumages are similar. **Male:** Head, neck and breast entirely clean deep blue-grey, except for small white throat-patch outlined in black, brownish lores and ear-coverts, and rich buffish-brown rear crown with dark brown streaking. On some individuals, the breast is bordered below by a black line against the buffish upper belly. Flanks show a strong brown wash and dark brown crescent-shaped barring; belly and undertail are buffish-white or off-white, with a faint pinkish-buff wash. Axillaries and lesser and median underwing-coverts are black, contrasting with white on greater underwing-coverts and lesser primary coverts, and mostly-white undersides to the secondaries. Upperparts show mostly dark brown feather centres, with crescent-shaped tawny-brown bars and whitish-buff fringes. Back and rump, overlain by scapulars, are plainer and darker brown. Primaries and secondaries are brown, with paler edgings to secondaries and tips to inner primaries; the outer 2 primaries have white shafts. Tail is rounded, mostly dark brown, with some buffish notching on middle feathers and a pale buffish or whitish outer edge and tip to outer feathers. **Female:** As male, but lacking all blue-grey on foreparts. Throat-patch is buffish-white, indistinctly outlined in brown. Crown, neck and breast are infused cold buffish-brown, irregularly streaked dark brown or marked with brownish crescents. **Juvenile:** Very like adult female, but breast-

band is slightly more buff and upperparts are slightly paler. Feathers with a broad tawny-brown submarginal band, a narrow dark subterminal line and a broad whitish-buff fringe may be typical of this plumage.
AGE/SEX Sexual dimorphism is obvious in adults, but juveniles are not safely separable from adult females in the field. Only adult males show blue-grey on the breast, forehead or hindneck.
RACES Two: nominate *orbignyianus* (Tierra del Fuego to N Chile) and *ingae* (N Chile to Peru). They are effectively identical in plumage, but *ingae* averages smaller in wing and tarsus measurements.
MEASUREMENTS Length 215-240 mm (8¾"). Wing 142-159 mm (nominate), 137-150 mm (*ingae*); bill 11-13 mm; tarsus 22-25 mm (nominate), 21-23 mm (*ingae*); tail 55-73 mm.
REFERENCES Johnson (1965), Maclean (1969).

214 LEAST SEEDSNIPE *Thinocorus rumicivorus*   **Plate 88**

Other name: Patagonian Seedsnipe
The smallest seedsnipe, this species (unlike the others, which are mountain species) occurs widely in the coastal plains and Andean foothills. Like its congener, Grey-breasted Seedsnipe (213), it is sexually dimorphic in plumage.

IDENTIFICATION A very small ground-living bird, hardly bigger than a lark or a longspur *Calcarius*, but identifiable as a seedsnipe by its rather scaly upperpart patterning and dumpy, small-headed shape. In flight, shows quite narrow, pointed wings, obviously wader-like, and may give a snipe-like call. Generally very similar to Grey-breasted Seedsnipe in both male and female plumages, and shows an almost identical pattern of black and white on the underwing. The best distinction is the noticeably smaller size of Least, and its bolder whitish trailing edge to the wing in flight. Males have less extensive grey, of a paler, less blue shade, and a black vertical line in the centre of the breast (lacking in Grey-breasted). Females have the breast more finely spotted and streaked, the white throat more clearly outlined in brown, and less extensive brown markings on the flanks than female Grey-breasted. The two *Attagis* seedsnipes (211, 212) are very much larger, and lack black on the axillaries and underwing. **Bare parts:** Bill short and stubby, yellowish-brown with a dark tip. Iris dark brown. Legs short and yellow.
VOICE Quite vocal. When flushed, gives a snipe-like rasping 'bzeep'; also in flight, a disyllabic 'kirik'. On the ground, may give repeated 'kru'; with young a sharp 'kikik', a soft nasal 'krim-krim' or a mournful 'piiiii'. The song is a repeated 'wikiti-wikiti-wikiti', followed by a hooting dove-like 'puku-puku-puku' or a deep 'whoop-whoop-whoop', and may be given either in flight or from a high perch on a rock or bush.
HABITS Found in arid or sparsely-vegetated plains, including cultivated land, near the Pacific coast, also in the puna zone of the central Andes (*bolivianus*). In Chile, breeding begins in Aug in the north, Sept or Oct farther south, and Nov in the extreme south. The display flight features a rapid, steep descent on stiffly-downcurved wings; the tail is cocked upwards just before landing. Usually seen in loose groups and

may nest semi-colonially. In keeping with its dry habitat, the metabolic rate is unusually low for a bird of its size. Walks with gently nodding head, feeding on seeds and succulent vegetation. Runs rapidly, crouches or freezes when alarmed, but flies rapidly with zigzag flight when flushed.
MOVEMENTS The nominate race in the south of the range is partly migratory, spreading northwards in winter as far as Uruguay along the Atlantic coastal plain. Vagrants have occurred on the Falkland Is.; last recorded there in 1955.
DESCRIPTION Breeding and non-breeding plumages are similar. **Male:** Forecrown grey; rear crown, nape and hindneck dark brown, with rich buff-brown feather edgings. Lores indistinctly whitish, and ear-coverts brownish; sides of face, neck and upper breast are otherwise ash-grey. White chin and throat are outlined broadly in black; black continues as a vertical central line on the breast to join a black breast-band, which divides the grey sides of the upper breast from the whitish lower breast, belly and undertail. Flanks are mostly white, but show a small patch of brown suffusion and barring bordering the upper breast. Axillaries and most of leading underwing-coverts are black, contrasting with white tips to the greater underwing-coverts and the mostly-white undersides to the secondaries. Upperparts have dark brown feather centres and brownish to buffish-white fringes, often also crescent-shaped submarginal barring of tawny- or olive-brown. Back and rump, overlain by scapulars, are plainer and darker. Sides to the rump are narrowly white bordering the rear flanks. Flight feathers are brown, with faint wingbar formed by whitish tips to greater coverts and greater primary coverts, and fairly clear but narrow whitish trailing edge to secondaries and inner 5 primaries. Shafts of outer primaries are white. Tail is wedge-shaped, mainly blackish with bold white tips to all but cen-

tral pair of feathers, and a narrow white outer edge to the outer feathers. **Female:** As male, but lacking all grey and black. Grey of head and breast is replaced by buffish-brown, streaked dark brown. Most females show a strong dark brown outline to the throat-patch, and some also show a dark brown line down the centre of the breast and a narrow breast-band (black on male). Upperparts tend to be slightly paler, with broader fringes. **Juvenile:** Very like adult female, but dark brown lines on breast and outlining throat are absent or very poorly defined. Upperparts tend to have broader tawny-brown submarginal barring and whiter fringes. Primaries are slightly more pointed than those of adults, and show clear pale tips to the inner eight, sometimes nine feathers.

AGE/SEX Adults are clearly sexually dimorphic, but juveniles after a few weeks become indistinguishable in the field from adult females. In the hand, whitish tipping on primaries 8 and 9 is diagnostic of juvenile; juvenile primaries are also more pointed and often more worn than those of adults.

RACES Three: nominate *rumicivorus* (Tierra del Fuego to N Chile), *bolivianus* (puna zone of N Chile, NW Argentina and SW Bolivia), and *cuneicauda* (mainly coastal, N Chile to Ecuador). All are very similar and difficult to separate in the field. The nominate race is darkest in plumage, but intermediate in size; *bolivianus* is the largest, with rather pale and pinkish plumage; *cuneicauda* is the smallest and palest, with rather buffish plumage.

MEASUREMENTS Length 160-190 mm (7"). Wing 110-132 mm (nominate), 125-132 mm (*bolivianus*), 101-120 mm (*cuneicauda*); bill 9-11 mm; tarsus 15-19 mm; tail 50-66 mm.

REFERENCES Wetmore (1926), Johnson (1965), Maclean (1969).

RACIAL CHARACTERS OF BLACK-WINGED STILTS (24)

	Eurasian & African (*himantopus*)	Australasian (*leucocephalus*)	N & Central American (*mexicanus*)	Hawaiian (*knudseni*)	South American (*melanurus*)
Adult					
Centre and rear of crown	white or blackish	white	black	black	white
Lower ear-coverts	white	white	black	black	black
Upper hindneck	white or mostly white	black	black	black	black
Base of hindneck	white	white	black	black	white
Mantle colour of female	brown	blackish-brown	brown	blackish-brown	brown
Juvenile					
Centre and rear of crown	dark grey	dark grey	dark grey-brown	dark grey-brown	mid-grey
Upper hindneck	pale grey	pale grey	dark brown	blackish-brown	blackish
Base of hindneck	pale grey	pale grey	blackish-brown	blackish-brown	mid-grey
Mantle colour	brown	dark brown	dark brown	brown	brown
Average size (mm)					
Wing	236	228	220	233	237
Bill	63	61	64	76	63
Legs from feathers (exposed tibia+tarsus)	176 (S Africa), 202 (Palaearctic)	157 (NZ), 180 (Australia)	180	204	181

PRINCIPAL CHARACTERS SEPARATING THE THREE SPECIES OF GOLDEN PLOVERS

	Eurasian (81)	Pacific (82)	American (83)
At all times			
Underwing and axillaries	mostly white	dull grey	dull grey
Wing-tip v. tail-tip	wings slightly longer than or equal to tail	wings clearly longer	wings clearly longer
Size and shape	large, bulky, small-billed	noticeably small and slim	fairly bulky
Leg length	relatively short, little tibia exposed	relatively long, particularly above 'knee'	relatively long, particularly above 'knee'
Breeding plumage			
White flank line	broad but irregular	narrow, often inconspicuous	flanks mostly black with very little white
White 'shoulder-patch' (sides of breast)	absent or relatively small	relatively small	large, conspicuous
Undertail-coverts	white or whitish, sometimes barred	blotched black and white	black or mainly black
Non-breeding			
Supercilium	buffish, indistinct	yellowish-buff, distinct	whitish, striking
Upperparts	pale brown, spotted yellowish	brown, spotted bright yellow	brown-grey, spotted whitish and pale yellow
Breast	streaked dark grey-brown, mottled yellowish	buffish, mottled bright yellow	dull greyish, mottled off-white
Juvenile			
Supercilium	buffish, inconspicuous	whitish-yellow, conspicuous	whitish, conspicuous
Upperparts	brown, spotted yellow	brown, spotted bright yellow	dark brown, spotted pale yellow and whitish
Breast	pale brown, mottled yellow	buff, mottled bright yellow	greyish, mottled white
Underpart barring	belly and flanks	flanks only	upper belly and flanks
Central tail feathers	broadly notched/barred yellow	narrowly spotted/edged pale yellow	narrowly spotted/edged pale yellow

PRINCIPAL FEATURES SEPARATING LESSER AND GREATER SANDPLOVERS

	Lesser Sandplover (107)	Greater Sandplover (108)
At all times		
Bill	noticeably more delicate, never with prominent gonys, length roughly equal to distance from base of bill to rear of eye	heavier, many eastern birds with pronounced gonys; length greater than distance from base of bill to rear of eye
Head shape	nearly always rounded	variable, sometimes rounded, often more angular with sloping forehead
Leg length	long, but shorter than Greater, especially above the 'knee'; toes fall roughly level with tail-tip in flight	very leggy; toes project beyond tip of tail in flight
Leg colour	generally darkish grey	variable, generally much paler; grey with greenish or even yellow tinge
White wingbar	inner bar relatively prominent; primary bar usually with parallel edges	inner bar slightly less prominent; primary bar bulges on primaries 2-5
Tail pattern	little white at sides or tip; tends to appear evenly dark	tends to show more white, especially on lateral uppertail-coverts; strongly contrasting dark subterminal bar
Call	sharp, hard 'chitik'	quiet, long, rolling or trilling 'tritrictrick', or shorter 'trrri'
Breeding plumage		
Breast-band	typically broad chestnut band which extends onto flanks and even upper belly; in some, neatly bordered by black above	typically narrower chestnut band, sometimes irregularly bordered dusky above

MAIN IDENTIFICATION FEATURES OF THE FOUR TYPICAL SNIPES OF THE E PALAEARCTIC

See also Solitary (167), Wood (169) and Great (174) Snipes

	Common Snipe (175) Eurasia : N America	Pintail Snipe (170)	Swinhoe's Snipe (171)	Japanese Snipe (168)
In the field, in flight				
General size	moderate	moderate	moderate	largish
Bill length	moderate	shortish	moderate	moderate
Median coverts and larger lessers	as rest of upperparts	paler, forming a contrasting pale wing-panel	as Pintail	as Pintail
Trailing edge of wing	broad, white: medium, white	very narrow, pale greyish-white	as Pintail	as Pintail but slightly more prominent
Tail length	longish	shortest	shortish	longest
White on outer tail feathers	variable, often fairly clear	virtually none	relatively little	as Swinhoe's or slightly more prominent
Escape flight	long, zigzag, towering	intermediate	shortish, some zigzag	as Swinhoe's
Wing-action	relatively agile	intermediate	relatively heavy	as Swinhoe's but even heavier
Call	harsh, long rasp	weaker and less harsh	as Pintail but even less harsh	as Pintail
Underpart colour	large white belly, pale underwing	small white belly, dark underwing	as Pintail	as Pintail
In the field, on the ground				
Supercilium width at base of bill	narrower than eye-stripe	broader than eye-stripe	as Pintail	as Pintail
Primary extension beyond tertials	intermediate	short	long	short or none
Tail extension beyond primaries	longish	short	longish	long
In the hand				
Number of tail feathers (range)	14 (12-18): 16	26 (24-28)	20 (18-26)	18
Width of outer tail feather	7-12 mm	1-2 mm	2-4 mm	4-6 mm
Length of central tail feather	52-63 mm	42-55 mm	46-57 mm	58-68 mm
Wing length	126-144 mm	125-143 mm	137-151 mm	157-168 mm
Wing point to 7th primary	11-17.5 mm	9-14 mm	10-15 mm	15-20 mm

PRINCIPAL FIELD CHARACTERS OF LARGER SNIPES IN AFRICA

	Common Snipe (175)	African Snipe (172)	Great Snipe (174)	Pintail Snipe (170)	Madagascar Snipe (173)
Trailing edge of secondaries	white	white	narrow, white	very narrow, greyish	very narrow, greyish
Covert pattern	mainly brown/buff	as Common but white spotting sometimes more obvious	prominent white spots, very striking on adults	much as Common	much as Common
Bill length (average)	65 mm	94 mm (SW Africa), 82 mm elsewhere	63 mm	63 mm	98 mm
Underwing colour	whitish	variable	mainly brown	mainly brown	mainly brown
White in tail	some	more obvious than in Common	extensive, very striking on adults	very little	some
Call	harsh, long rasp	less rasping than Common	low croak	shorter and weaker than in Common	?
Escape flight	fast, long, zigzag, towering	slightly weaker than Common; wings rather more rounded	relatively slow, short and straight	weaker than Common, fewer zigzags, towers less	?

COMPARATIVE FEATURES OF THE SMALLER TYPICAL SOUTH AMERICAN SNIPES

	Common Snipe (175)	Magellan Snipe (176)			Noble Snipe (177)
	G.g.delicata	*G.p.paraguaiae*	*G.p.magellanica*	*G.p.andina*	*G.nobilis*
Range	north S America (mainly Sept-Mar)	lowland east S America	south S America	central Andes	north Andes
Trailing edge of wing	white	white	white	white	brownish
White v. brown on underwing	more brown	as much brown as white	more brown	more white	more brown
Outer tail feather					
colour	fairly dark	fairly dark	some white	much white	fairly dark
barring	broad, irregular	medium, regular	medium, regular	narrow, regular	medium, irregular
width (mm)	6-9	4-6	3-5	3.3-5.5	6-7
length (mm)	40-55	35-47	41-53	37-44	mean 52.8
Wing length (average)	131 mm	122 mm	136 mm	121 mm	151 mm
Bill length (average)	64 mm	70 mm	67 mm	54 mm	94 mm
Tarsus length (average)	30 mm	34 mm	34 mm	28 mm	41 mm

KEY DIFFERENCES BETWEEN THE AMERICAN DOWITCHERS

Note: Wilds and Newlon (1983), from which paper this Table is adapted, is strongly-recommended reading for anyone interested in this group

	Short-billed Dowitcher (183)	Long-billed Dowitcher (184)
At all times Voice	Alarm and flight: mellow 'tu-tu-tu' (often extended or curtailed). Feeding: usually silent; rarely an abrupt 'tu' or 't'tu'	A high 'keek': shrill and strident in alarm, thinner in flight or when feeding. May be multiple. Flocks talkative
Shape		One bird in six has an obviously longer bill or longer legs than any Short-billed Dowitcher
Plumage	Tail pattern variable. Light bars on tail usually (not always) wider than black bars	Light bars on tail never wider than black bars; usually much narrower
Breeding plumage (Apr-Aug)	Belly or vent partly or entirely white or whitish; foreneck, centre of breast, belly, and vent very lightly to moderately spotted. Red normally paler, more orange, or brownish	All-red underparts plus densely-spotted foreneck and barred upper breast, clear red belly (may be barred white); vent may be barred black-and-white. Red normally darker, less orange
	(Note: Both species may have chevron-like bars on sides of breast, bars on flanks, spots or bars on undertail-coverts, all-red underparts, or cinnamon or white bars on tail)	
Non-breeding plumage (Aug-Apr; some all year)	Throat and upper breast light grey, finely speckled; lower edge of breast often spotted	Throat and entire breast grey, unspeckled, ending abruptly at white belly. Breast and upperparts darker than on Short-billed
	(Note: Few dowitchers in non-breeding plumage can be identified visually in the field except at close range and under ideal conditions)	
Juvenile plumage (July-Nov/Dec)	Scapulars and inner wing-coverts broadly edged with bright reddish-buff, with conspicuous internal markings. Tertials broadly edged, striped, and/or barred with reddish-buff. West Coast race has narrower, redder edges. Underparts as non-breeding plumage, but with bright reddish-buff wash; fine streaks and spots on breast	Scapulars, inner wing-coverts, and tertials narrowly edged with dark reddish-buff; internal markings inconspicuous or lacking. Scapulars and tertials normally retained to end of year. Underparts as non-breeding plumage, but with reddish-buff wash on breast and belly. Head and neck sometimes noticeably greyer than breast
	(Note: In both species, feather edgings and markings may fade to buff by late Sept)	

PRINCIPAL IDENTIFICATION FEATURES OF THE FOUR DARK-LEGGED STINTS

Adapted from Jonsson and Grant (1984)

	Semipalmated Sandpiper (190)	Western Sandpiper (191)	Red-necked Stint (192)	Little Stint (193)
At all times				
Bill shape	straight, tip usually thickened	drooping, longish, tip fairly fine	straight, tip slightly thickened	almost straight, tip fine
Toes	partly webbed	partly webbed	unwebbed	unwebbed
Call	low, harsh 'chrup' or 'kreet'	thin, sharp 'jeet'	longish, rough 'chit'	short 'stit-tit'
Primary projection	short	very short	medium	long
Breeding plumage				
Throat, supercilium	whitish	whitish	reddish	whitish
Scapulars, upperparts	black, fringed dull grey, a little pale rufous	rich chestnut, spotted black	black, fringed rufous and white	black, fringed rufous and white
Mantle/scapular lines	virtually absent	virtually absent	slight	prominent
Breast	white, fairly clearly streaked	white, strongly streaked dark brown	pale, clear ring of streaks	slight orange wash, streaked lightly
Flank streaking	very slight	prominent	none	none
Non-breeding				
Upperpart colour	brownish-grey	typically rather uniform pale grey	mid-grey	brownish-grey
Breast pattern	diffuse streaking at sides, not joining across centre of breast	majority have complete breast-band of very fine streaks	diffuse streaking at sides	some have grey, finely-streaked band right across breast
Juvenile				
'Split supercilium' effect	shown rarely	not shown	shown rarely	pale lateral crown-stripe ('split supercilium') accentuates dark ridge along central crown
Mantle/scapular lines	virtually absent	very slight	slight	prominent
Mantle fringes	pale buff/rufous	mainly rufous	mainly rufous	mainly rufous
Scapulars	darkish; lowers have pale base, dark anchor-shaped distal area with whitish tips and pale rufous edges; scaly appearance	uppers deep rufous, spotted blackish; lowers greyer, pattern as Semipalmated but bolder dark areas and less scaly appearance	uppers as Little Stint, lowers dull greyish, fringed buff, with dark anchor-shaped distal area; lowers look pale, washed out	all dark-centred, rufous and white fringes
Tertials	grey centre, buff or pale rufous edges	grey-brown centre, whitish and rufous edges	grey centre, off-white edges	blackish centre, usually edged rufous
Wing-coverts	grey-brown, whitish or pale buff fringes	grey-brown, pale rufous fringes	pale greyish, pale rufous fringes	brown, clear deep buff or rufous fringes
Breast pattern	buff wash, extensive diffuse streaks	orange-rufous wash, clearly but narrowly streaked at sides	greyish-orange wash, extensive faint/diffuse streaks	orange-rufous wash, sides clearly streaked

PRINCIPAL DIFFERENCES BETWEEN LONG-TOED STINT AND LEAST SANDPIPER

	Long-toed Stint (195)	Least Sandpiper (196)
At all times		
Shape	often looks long-legged and long-necked	generally hunched
Length of middle toe	very long (obviously longer than bill and tarsus)	shorter (about same as bill length)
Length of hind toe	rather long (5.5-7.0 mm)	normal length (4.0-4.5 mm)
Bill colour	black, but majority show pale base to at least lower mandible	all-black, or black tinged brown at base
Flight silhouette	about half toe length projects beyond tail	tips of toes only just project beyond tail
Primary shaft colours	only outermost whitish	most are whitish
Call	a short, soft rippled 'chu-ilp' or 'chrrup'	a shrill 'kreeep' or purring 'prrrt'
Breeding plumage		
Head pattern	supercilium whitish, quite prominent; lores fairly pale; ear-covert patch contiguous with eye	supercilium off-white, less clear; lores show prominent dark line; isolated patch on rear of ear-coverts forming diffuse spot
Fringes of scapulars/tertials	usually broader and bright rufous	usually narrower and paler
Non-breeding plumage		
Scapular pattern	all with rather uniform dark brown centres and neat pale grey-brown fringes	at a distance as Long-toed, but at closer range sharper dark shaft-streak visible; colour becomes steadily paler towards fringe
Juvenile		
Head pattern	supercilium whitish, usually clearly 'split'; crown distinctly rufous-fringed; lores and ear-coverts as breeding	supercilium whitish, occasionally 'split'; crown normally less rufous; lores and ear-coverts as breeding
Scapular/tertial fringes	deep rufous, some white tips	often slightly paler rufous
Wing-covert fringes	pale buff to whitish	deep buff to pale chestnut
Breast	washed grey-buff; streaking less extensive, often absent in centre of breast	washed brighter buff; streaking more extensive, often forming distinct band

Appendix

20. Pied Oystercatcher. New Zealand race *finschi* (SIPO) has occurred northwards to Lord Howe I. and Vanuatu, and record of Pied Oystercatcher from Norfolk I. also probably concerned this race.

24. Black-winged Stilt. Nominate race has also been recorded as a vagrant in W Aleutians.

31. Stone-curlew. Sexes are now known to be separable on plumage. In the adult male, the dark covert bars are sharply defined and the covert panel is clean grey with sharp dark streaks. The female has more diffuse dark bars and at least the upper half of the grey covert panel partly obscured by buff feather edgings. The juvenile head pattern also differs from adults: in juvenile, pale supercilium is restricted to a narrow band immediately above the eye, not extending in front of or behind the eye, and the ear-coverts are virtually uniformly white whereas in adult they are strongly streaked brown (RE Green and CGR Bowden, *Brit. Birds* 79: 419-22). The species is listed as a vagrant in Seychelles.

51. Oriental Pratincole. A vagrant was recorded in W Aleutians in spring 1985.

73. Pied Plover. In most individuals, the outer tail feather is black-tipped, not all-white as stated in the text. Photographs examined show the iris to be dark brown; references in earlier literature to pinkish or grey iris colour may be erroneous.

91. Killdeer. Has occurred as vagrant also on St Lawrence I.

92. Piping Plover. Vagrants have occurred north to Lake Athabasca in spring.

107. Lesser Sandplover. Species is probably regular as a vagrant in W Alaska, where it has even bred.

126. Marbled Godwit. Species is a scarce passage migrant in S Alaska, where it has recently been found nesting in the southwest.

133. Far Eastern Curlew. The present world population of this species may be only 10,000-15,000 individuals.

142. Lesser Yellowlegs. Vagrants have also been recorded in Sumatra, Gambia, Zambia, Uganda and Zimbabwe.

143. Green Sandpiper. Has been recorded as a vagrant also on St Lawrence I.

146. Willet. In eastern North America, inland migrants and late coastal records in autumn are probably all referable to the western race *inornatus*. The species has been recorded as a vagrant also in Finland (Sept 1983).

147. Terek Sandpiper. Has been recorded in winter in Mauritania (Dec 1984).

159. Eurasian Woodcock. This species is apparently regular in winter in Brunei.

162. Celebes Woodcock. Although range should distinguish this species from Eurasian Woodcock (159), note that latter occurs in winter as far south as Brunei as well as in Philippines.

163. Obi Woodcock. Re-examination of study skins shows that there is, as in Amami Woodcock (160), an area of bare skin around and behind the eye.

188. Great Knot. Has been recorded as a vagrant in W Alaska (ten records by 1984), Sri Lanka (1981), Laccadives, Seychelles (1981 and 1984), and Israel (Oct 1985), as well as in the Arabian peninsula (Oman, Sept 1982) and Morocco, and one was reported also in Spain in Apr 1979. The Australian population has recently been estimated at 253,500 in Nov-Dec.

190. Semipalmated Sandpiper. Note that this species has a *hovering* display flight (cf. 191 below).

191. Western Sandpiper. This species has a *diving* display flight (cf. 190 above), during which song is given. Has been recorded as a vagrant also in New Zealand and in Poland.

200. Sharp-tailed Sandpiper. Following the removal of this species from the Dutch list in 1985, it should be noted that there are now no records of Sharp-tailed Sandpipers with flesh-coloured legs.

202. Purple Sandpiper. In addition to the vagrants noted in the text, a single individual wintered in 1984/85 at Key West, Florida. This is the most southerly record of the species to date.

204. Dunlin. Has been recorded as a vagrant also in Venezuela and in Brunei.

The authors would be very pleased to hear of errors, omissions, or new material which could be used to improve any future editions of this book. Please write to JH Marchant, British Trust for Ornithology, Beech Grove, Station Road, Tring, Hertfordshire HP23 5NR, England, or to AJ Prater, Royal Society for the Protection of Birds, Aldwych House, Bethel Street, Norwich, Norfolk NR2 1NR, England.

General Bibliography

Bent, AC (1927, 1929) Life Histories of North American Shorebirds. *US. Natl. Mus. Bull.* 142 and 146. Washington.

Blake, ER (1977) *Manual of Neotropical Birds. Vol. 1.* Chicago.

Britton, PL (ed) (1980) *Birds of East Africa.* Nairobi.

Clements, JF (1982) *Birds of the World: a Checklist.* London.

Cramp, S, and Simmons, KEL (eds) (1983) *The Birds of the Western Palearctic. Vol. 3.* Oxford.

Dementiev, GP, and Gladkov, NA (1951) *Birds of the Soviet Union. Vol. 3.* Jerusalem.

Glutz von Blotzheim, UN, *et al.* (1975) *Handbuch der Vögel Mitteleuropas. Vols. 6 and 7.* Wiesbaden.

Godfrey, WE (1966) *The Birds of Canada.* Ottawa.

Johnsgard, PA (1981) *The Plovers, Sandpipers and Snipes of the World.* Lincoln.

Kozlova, EV (1961, 1962) *The Fauna of the USSR.* Nos. 80 and 81. Moscow.

McLachlan, GR, and Liversidge, R (1978) *Birds of South Africa.* Cape Town.

Prater, AJ, *et al.* (1977) *Guide to the identification and ageing of Holarctic waders.* BTO Guide 17: Tring.

Roberson, D (1980) *Rare Birds of the West Coast.* Pacific Grove.

Sálim Ali and Ripley, SD (1969) *Handbook of the Birds of India and Pakistan. Vols. 2 and 3.* Oxford.

Stout, GD (ed) (1967) *The Shorebirds of North America.* New York.

Specific Bibliography

Abramson, IJ (1977) Photographic confirmation of Giant Snipe in Argentina. *Auk* 94: 357.

Ade, B (1979) Some observations on the breeding of Crowned Plovers. *Bokmakierie* 31: 9-16.

Allan, D (1983) Black-winged Plover (R243) in the Transvaal. *Witwatersrand Bird Club News* 120: 8.

Allen, AA, and Kyllingstad, H (1949) The eggs and young of the Bristle-thighed Curlew. *Auk* 66: 343-50.

Allen, JN (1980) The ecology and behavior of the Long-billed Curlew in southeastern Washington. *Wildl. Monogr.* No. 73.

Anderson, RA (1968) Notes on the Snares Island Snipe. *Notornis* 15: 223-7.

Andreev, AV (1980a) (Biology of the Grey-rumped Sandpiper (*Tringa brevipes*).) In Flint, V, (ed) *New Studies on the Biology and Distribution of Waders.* Moscow; (1980b) (A nesting biology study of Great Knot (*Calidris tenuirostris*) in the river Kolyma basin.) *Ornitologiya* 15: 207-8.

Appert, O (1971) Die Limikolen des Mangokygebietes in Südwest-Madagaskar. *Orn. Beob.* 68: 53-77.

Ashkenazie, S, and Safriel, UN (1979) Breeding cycle and behaviour of the Semipalmated Sandpiper at Barrow, Alaska. *Auk* 96: 56-67.

Atkinson, NK, *et al.* (1978) The winter distribution of Purple Sandpipers in Britain. *Bird Study* 25: 223-8.

Bagg, AM (1967) Factors affecting the occurrence of the Eurasian Lapwing in eastern North America. *Living Bird* 6: 87-122.

Bainbridge, IP, and Minton, CDT (1978) The migration and mortality of the Curlew in Britain and Ireland. *Bird Study* 25: 39-50.

Baker, AJ (1973) Distribution and numbers of New Zealand Oystercatchers. *Notornis* 20: 128-44; (1974a) Criteria for ageing and sexing New Zealand Oystercatchers (*H.o.finschi*). *N.Z.J. Mar. Freshwater Res.* 8: 211-21; (1974b) Prey-specific feeding methods of New Zealand Oystercatchers. *Notornis* 21: 219-33; (1975) Morphological variation, hybridization and systematics of New Zealand oystercatchers. *J. Zool., Lond.* 175: 357-90; (1977) Multivariate assessment of phyletic affinities of Australasian oystercatchers (Aves: Charadriiformes). *Bijdr. Dierk.* 47: 156-64.

Banks, RC (1977) The decline and fall of the Eskimo Curlew. *Am. Birds* 31: 127-34.

Bannerman, DA (1969) A probable sight record of a Canarian Black Oystercatcher. *Ibis* 111: 257.

Barlow, JC (1967) Autumnal breeding of the Paraguay Snipe in Uruguay. *Auk* 84: 421-2.

Barlow, M (1972) The establishment, dispersal and distribution of the Spur-winged Plover in New Zealand. *Notornis* 19: 201-11.

—, *et al.* (1972) Breeding data on the Spur-winged Plover in Southland, New Zealand. *Notornis* 19: 212-49.

Bates, RSP, and Lowther, EHN (1952) *Breeding Birds of Kashmir.* London.

Beddgood, GW (1977) Field notes on the southern stone curlew in Victoria. *Aust. Bird Watcher* 7: 35-40.

Begg, GW, and Maclean, GL (1976) Belly-soaking in the Whitecrowned Plover. *Ostrich* 47: 65.

Bengtson, S-A (1975) (Observations on the breeding biology of the Purple Sandpiper *Calidris maritima* on Svalbard.) *Fauna* 28: 81-6.

Benson, CW, *et al.* (1976) Contribution de l'ornithologie de Madagascar. *L'Oiseau et RFO* 46: 103-34, 209-42.

Bergstrom, PW (1982) Ecology of incubation in Wilson's Plover (*Charadrius wilsonia*). PhD, Univ. Chicago.

Berman, DI, and Kuz'min, IF (1965) (The Pintail Snipe in the Tuva, USSR.) *Ornitologiya* 7: 209-16.

Betts, BJ (1973) A possible hybrid Wattled Jacana x Northern Jacana in Costa Rica. *Auk* 90: 687-9.

Beven, JO (1913) Notes and observations on the Painted Snipe (*Rostratula capensis*) in Ceylon. *Ibis* 10: 527-34.

Bishop, KD, and Andrew, P (in prep.) Notes on little-known birds of the Greater Sundas.

Blankert, JJ (1980) (Identification of Great Snipe and occurrence in the Netherlands.) *Dutch Birding* 2: 106-15.

Bock, WJ (1964) The systematic position of the Australian Dotterel *Peltohyas australis*. *Emu* 63: 383-404.

Bomford, M (1978) The behaviour of the Banded Dotterel *Charadrius bicinctus*. MSc, Univ. Otago, Dunedin.

Bowen, DE, Jr (1977) Coloniality, reproductive success and habitat interactions in Upland Sandpipers, *Bartramia longicauda*. PhD, Kansas State Univ.

Branson, NJBA, and Minton, CDT (1976) Moult, measurements and migrations of the Grey Plover. *Bird Study* 23: 257-66.

—, *et al.* (1978) Turnstone migrations in Britain and Europe. *Bird Study* 25: 181-7.

Britton, D (1980) Identification of Sharp-tailed Sandpipers. *Br. Birds* 73: 333-45.

—, *et al.* (1972) Breeding data on the Spur-winged Plover in Southland, New Zealand. *Notornis* 19: 212-49.

Britton, PL (1977) The Madagascar Pratincole in Africa. *Scopus* 1: 94-7.

Broekhuysen, GJ (1963) (A description and discussion of threat- and anxiety-behaviour of *Burhinus capensis* (Lichtenstein) during incubation.) *Zoöl. Meded., Leiden* 39: 240-8.

Brosselin, M (1968) Observation d'un Courlis à bec grêle *Numenius tenuirostris* en Vendée. *Nos Oiseaux* 29: 274.

Brosset, A (1979) (The breeding cycle of *Glareola nuchalis*: its ecological and behavioural determinants.) *La Terre et la Vie* 33: 95-108.

Brown, LH (1948) Notes on birds of the Kabba, Ilorin and N. Benin Provinces of Nigeria. *Ibis* 90: 525-37.

Bryant, CE (1947) Notes on avocets breeding near Melbourne. *Emu* 46: 241-5; (1948) More observations on nesting avocets. *Emu* 48: 89-92.

Burbidge, AA, and Fuller, PJ (1982) Banded Stilt breeding at Lake Barlee, Western Australia. *Emu* 82: 212-16.

Burger, J, and Howe, M (1975) Notes on winter feeding behavior and moult in Wilson's Phalaropes. *Auk* 92: 442-51.

—, and Shisler, J (1978) Nest site selection of Willets in a New Jersey salt marsh. *Wilson Bull.* 90: 599-607.

Burnier, E (1977) Sur l'hivernage du pluvier guignard en Algérie. *Nos Oiseaux* 34: 74.

Burton, J, and McNeil, R (1976) Age determination of six species of North American shorebirds. *Bird-Banding* 47: 201-9.

Burton, PJK (1971) Comparative anatomy of head and neck in the Spoon-billed Sandpiper, *Eurynorhynchus pygmeus* and its allies. *J. Zool., Lond.* 163: 145-63.

Byrkjedal, I (1978) Variation and secondary intergradation in S.W. Norwegian Golden Plover (*Pluvialis apricaria*) populations. *Ornis Scand.* 9: 101-10.

Cadbury, CJ, and Olney, PJS (1978) Avocet population dynamics in England. *Br. Birds* 70: 102-21.

Cadman, M (1979) Territorial behaviour in American Oystercatchers *Haematopus palliatus*. *Wader Study Group Bull.* 27: 40-1.

Cairns, WE (1982) Biology and behaviour of breeding

Piping Plovers. *Wilson Bull.* 94: 531-45.

—, and McLaren, IA (1980) Status of the Piping Plover on the east coast of North America. *Am. Birds* 34: 206-8.

Cheke, RA (1980) A small breeding colony of the Rock Pratincole *Glareola nuchalis liberiae* in Togo. *Bull. Br. Orn. Club* 100: 175-8; (1982) Additional information on the Rock Pratincole *Glareola nuchalis* in Togo. *Bull. Br. Orn. Club* 102: 116-17.

Chekmenev, DI (1961) (On the biology of the Sociable Plover.) *Trudy ISAN Kas. SSR Alma Ata* 15: 143-6.

Cheltsov-Bebutov, AM (1976) (Geographical variability of the Greater Sand Plover (*Charadrius leschenaultii*) and its possible causes.) *Ornitologiya* 12: 200-6.

Christen, W (1980) (Status and ecology of the Stone Curlew *Burhinus oedicnemus* population in the Alsace.) *Orn. Beob.* 77: 201-8.

Clark, A (1982a) Some observations on the breeding behaviour of Kittlitz's Sandplover. *Ostrich* 53: 120-2; (1982b) Some observations on the behaviour of the Three-banded Plover. *Ostrich* 53: 222-7.

Clark, NA (1983) The ecology of Dunlin (*Calidris alpina* L.) wintering on the Severn Estuary. PhD, Univ. of Edinburgh.

Close, DH (1982) Recent records of the Oriental Plover. *S. Aust. Ornithol.* 28: 205-6.

—, and Newman, OMG (1984) The decline of the Eastern Curlew in south-eastern Australia. *Emu* 84: 38-40.

Collar, NJ, and Stuart, SN (1985) *Threatened Birds of Africa and related Islands.* Cambridge.

Connors, PG (1983) Taxonomy, distribution and evolution of Golden Plovers (*Pluvialis dominica* and *Pluvialis fulva*). *Auk* 100: 607-20.

Cox, JB (1976) The Pectoral Sandpiper: an unusual specimen. *S. Aust. Ornithol.* 27: 110-11.

Crawford, DN (1978) Notes on Little Curlew on the subcoastal plains, Northern Territory. *Aust. Bird Watcher* 7: 270-2.

Cunningham, JM (1973) The Banded Dotterel (*Charadrius bicinctus*): Pohowera or tuturiwhatu? Call notes and behaviour. *Notornis* 20: 21-7.

Cunningham-van Someren, GR, and Robinson, C (1962) Notes on the African Lily-trotter *Actophilornis africana* (Gmelin). *Bull. Br. Orn. Club* 82: 67-72.

Cyrus, DP (1982) Blackwinged Plovers nesting on the coastal plain of Zululand. *Ostrich* 53: 248.

Dabelsteen, T (1978) An analysis of the song flight of the Lapwing (*Vanellus vanellus*). *Behaviour* 66: 136-78.

Dann, P (1981) Breeding of the Banded and Masked Lapwings in Southern Victoria. *Emu* 81: 121-7.

Dare, PJ, and Mercer, AJ (1973) Foods of the Oystercatcher in Morecambe Bay, Lancashire. *Bird Study* 20: 173-84; (1974) The white collar of the Oystercatcher. *Bird Study* 21: 180-4.

Davis, MM (1980) Red-capped Dotterel in North Canterbury. *Notornis* 27: 367-8.

Dean, AR, et al. (1977) White-tailed Plover: new to Britain and Ireland. *Br. Birds* 70: 465-71.

Demaree, SR (1975) Observations on roof-nesting Killdeers. *Condor* 77: 487-8.

Dhondt, AA (1975) Note sur les échassiers (Charadrii) de Madagascar. *L'Oiseau et RFO* 45: 73-82.

Dick, WJA, et al. (1976) Distribution and geographical origins of Knot *Calidris canutus* wintering in Europe and Africa. *Ardea* 64: 22-47.

Dixon, J (1918) The nesting grounds and nesting habits of the Spoon-billed Sandpiper. *Auk* 35: 387-404; (1927) The surfbird's secret. *Condor* 29: 3-16.

Dorogoy, IV (1982) (Materials on Knot biology on Vrangel Island.) *Vest. Zool.* 5: 65-9.

Dowsett, RJ, et al. (1977) The voice of the courser *Rhinoptilus cinctus*. *Bull. Br. Orn. Club* 97: 73-5.

Dukes, PA (1980) Semipalmated Plover: new to Britain and Ireland. *Br. Birds* 73: 458-64.

Dwyer, TJ, et al. (1979) The technical literature on the American Woodcock, 1927-1978. *U.S. Fish Wildl. Serv. Spec. Sci. Rep. — Wildl.* 213.

Edgar, AT (1969) Estimated population of the Red-breasted Dotterel. *Notornis* 16: 85-100.

Edwards, PJ (1982) Plumage variation, territoriality and breeding displays of the Golden Plover *Pluvialis apricaria* in southwest Scotland. *Ibis* 124: 88-96.

Eley, TJ (1976) Extension of the breeding range of the Black Oystercatcher in Alaska. *Condor* 78: 115.

Elliott, CCH, et al. (1976) The migration system of the Curlew Sandpiper *Calidris*

ferruginea in Africa. *Ostrich* 47: 191-213.

Espin, PMJ, et al. (1983) Age and foraging success in Black-winged Stilts, *Himantopus himantopus*. *Ardea* 71: 225-8.

Evans, PR, and Dugan, PJ (1984) Coastal birds: numbers in relation to food resources. In Evans, PR, et al. (eds) *Coastal Waders and Wildfowl in Winter.* Cambridge.

Farrand, J, Jr (1977) What to look for: Eskimo and Little Curlews compared. *Am. Birds* 31: 137.

Feare, CJ (1966) The winter feeding of the Purple Sandpiper. *Br. Birds* 59: 165-79.

Ferguson-Lees, IJ (1959) Photographic studies of some less familiar birds 95. Terek Sandpiper. *Br. Birds* 52: 85-90; (1965) Studies of less familiar birds 132. Spur-winged Plover. *Br. Birds* 58: 47-51.

Ferns, PN (1978) Individual differences in the head and neck plumage of Ruddy Turnstones (*Arenaria interpres*) during the breeding season. *Auk* 95: 753-5; (1981) Identification, subspecific variation, ageing and sexing in European Dunlins. *Dutch Birding* 3: 85-98.

Fitzner, JN (1978) The ecology and behaviour of the Long-billed Curlew (*Numenius americanus*) in Southeastern Washington. PhD, Washington State Univ.

Flint, VE (1973) (On the biology of the Broad-billed Sandpiper, *Limicola falcinellus sibiricus*.) In Flint, V, (ed) *Fauna and Ecology of Waders.* Moscow.

—, (ed) (1980a) (Breeding biology of the Great Knot (*Calidris tenuirostris*).) In Flint, V, (ed) *New Studies on the Biology and Distribution of Waders.* Moscow; (1980b) (New information on spreading and breeding biology of the Rufous-necked Stint (*Calidris ruficollis*).) In Flint, V, (ed) *New Studies on the Biology and Distribution of Waders.* Moscow.

Freese, CH (1975) Notes on nesting in the Double-striped Thick-knee (*Burhinus bistriatus*) in Costa Rica. *Condor* 77: 353-4.

Friedmann, H, and Smith, FD (1955) A further contribution to the ornithology of northeastern Venezuela. *Proc. U.S. Nat. Mus.* 104: 349-465.

Frisch, R (1978) Surfbirds in Ogilvie and Richardson Mountains, Yukon Territory. *Can. Field Nat.* 92: 401-3.

Frith, HJ, et al. (1977) Aspects of

the biology of the Japanese Snipe *Gallinago hardwickii*. *Aust. J. Ecol.* 2: 341-68.

Fry, CH (1983a) Incubation, brooding and a structural character of the African Jacana. *Ostrich* 54: 175-6; (1983b) The jacanid radius and *Microparra*, a neotenic genus. *Gerfaut* 73: 173-84.

Fujimaki, Y, and Skira, IJ (1984) Notes on Latham's Snipe *Gallinago hardwickii* in Japan. *Emu* 84: 49-51.

Fuller, RJ, and Lloyd, D (1981) The distribution and habitats of wintering Golden Plovers in Britain 1977-78. *Bird Study* 28: 169-85.

Gerasimov, NN (1980) (Spring migration of the Great Knot (*Calidris tenuirostris*) and Knot (*C. canutus*) along the western coast of Kamchatka.) In Flint, V, (ed) *New Studies on the Biology and Distribution of Waders.* Moscow.

Gibson, DD (1978) Separation of tattlers and snipe. *'Elepaio* 39: 8.

Gibson, F (1971) The breeding biology of the American Avocet (*Recurvirostra americana*) in central Oregon. *Condor* 73: 444-54.

Gill, RE, Jr, et al. (1983) Memorial to a Black Turnstone: an exemplar of breeding and wintering site fidelity. *N. Am. Bird Bander* 8: 98-101.

Glue, DE, and Morgan, RA (1974) Breeding statistics and movements of the Stone Curlew. *Bird Study* 21: 21-8.

Goriup, PD (1982) Behaviour of Black-winged Stilts. *Br. Birds* 75: 12-29.

Goss-Custard, JD (1969) The winter feeding ecology of the Redshank *Tringa totanus*. *Ibis* 111: 338-56.

Grant, PJ (1980) Judging the size of birds. *Br. Birds* 73: 227-8; (1983a) Spotted Redshanks flying with legs retracted. *Br. Birds* 76: 136-7; (1983b) Size-illusion. *Br. Birds* 76: 327-34.

Graul, WD (1975) Breeding biology of the Mountain Plover. *Wilson Bull.* 87: 6-31.

—, and Webster, LE (1976) Breeding status of the Mountain Plover. *Condor* 78: 265-7.

Graves, GR (1981) New Charadriiform records from coastal Peru. *Gerfaut* 71: 75-9.

Greenwood, JG (1979) Geographical variation in the Dunlin *Calidris alpina* (L.) PhD, Liverpool Polytechnic; (1984) Migrations of Dunlin *Calidris alpina*: a worldwide overview. *Ringing & Migration* 5: 35-9.

Groves, S (1978) Age-related differences in Ruddy Turnstone foraging and aggressive behavior. *Auk* 95: 95-103.

Hachisuka, MU (1952) What is the Amami Woodcock? *Bull. Br. Orn. Club* 72: 77-81.

Hagar, JA (1966) Nesting of the Hudsonian Godwit at Churchill, Manitoba. *Living Bird* 5: 5-43.

Hale, WG (1971) A revision of the taxonomy of the Redshank *Tringa totanus*. *Z. Jour. Linn. Soc.* 50: 199-268; (1973) The distribution of the Redshank *Tringa totanus* in the winter range. *Z. Jour. Linn. Soc.* 53: 177-236.

—, and Ashcroft, RP (1982) Pair formation and pair maintenance in the Redshank (*Tringa totanus*). *Ibis* 124: 471-90.

Hall, KRL (1958) Observations on the nesting sites and nesting behaviour of the Kittlitz's Sandplover *Charadrius pecuarius*. *Ostrich* 29: 113-25; (1959) A study of the Blacksmith Plover *Hoplopterus armatus* in the Cape Town area. I. Distribution and breeding data. *Ostrich* 30: 117-26; (1964) A study of the Blacksmith Plover *Hoplopterus armatus* in the Cape Town area. II. Behaviour. *Ostrich* 35: 3-16.

Hamilton, RB (1975) Comparative behaviour of the American Avocet and Black-necked Stilt. *Ornithol. Monogr.* 17.

Harrington, BA (1983) The migration of the Red Knot. *Oceanus* 26: 44-8.

—, and Morrison, RIG (1979) Semipalmated Sandpiper migration in North America. *Studies in Avian Biology* 2: 83-100.

Harris, MP (1967) The biology of Oystercatchers *Haematopus ostralegus* on Skokholm Island, S. Wales. *Ibis* 109: 180-93.

Harris, PR (1979) The winter feeding of the Turnstone in North Wales. *Bird Study* 26: 259-66.

Harrison, P (1983) *Seabirds: an identification guide.* London.

Hartert, E (1903) The birds of the Obi group, Central Moluccas. Notes on *Neoscolopax rochussenii*. *Nov. Zool.* 1903 (10): 17.

Harting, JE (1873) On rare or little-known Limicolae. *Ibis* 15: 260-9.

Hartwick, EB (1974) Breeding ecology of the Black Oystercatcher *Haematopus bachmani*. *Syesis* 7: 83-92; (1976) Foraging strategy of the Black Oystercatcher *Haematopus bachmani*.

Can. J. Zool. 54: 142-55; (1978a) The use of feeding areas outside the territory of breeding Black Oystercatchers. *Wilson Bull.* 90: 650-2; (1978b) Some observations on foraging by Black Oystercatchers *Haematopus bachmani*. *Syesis* 11: 55-60.

Haverschmidt, F (1963) *The Black-tailed Godwit.* Leiden; (1974) The occurrence of the Giant Snipe *Gallinago undulata* in Surinam. *Bull. Br. Orn. Club* 94: 132-4.

Hayman, PJ (1956) A note on field-identification of pratincoles. *Br. Birds* 49: 312-13.

Hays, H (1972) Polyandry in the Spotted Sandpiper. *Living Bird* 11: 43-57.

Heather, BD (1973) The Black-fronted Dotterel (*Charadrius melanops*) in the Wairarapa. *Notornis* 20: 251-61; (1977) Foot-trembling by the Black-fronted Dotterel. *Notornis* 24: 1-8.

Heppleston, PB (1971) The feeding ecology of Oystercatchers *Haematopus ostralegus* L. in winter in northern Scotland. *J. Anim. Ecol.* 40: 651-72; (1972) The comparative breeding ecology of Oystercatchers *Haematopus ostralegus* L. in inland and coastal habitats. *J. Anim. Ecol.* 41: 23-51.

Higgins, KF, and Kirsch, LM (1975) Some aspects of the breeding biology of the Upland Sandpiper in N. Dakota. *Wilson Bull.* 87: 96-102.

Hildén, O (1975) (Breeding system of Temminck's Stint *Calidris temminckii.*) *Ornis Fenn.* 52: 117-46; (1978) (Population dynamics in Temminck's Stint *Calidris temminckii.*) *Oikos* 30: 17-28; (1979) (The timing of arrival and departure of the Spotted Redshank *Tringa erythropus* in Finland.) *Ornis Fenn.* 56: 18-23.

—, and Vuolanto, S (1972) Breeding biology of the Red-necked Phalarope *Phalaropus lobatus* in Finland. *Ornis Fenn.* 49: 57-85.

Hindwood, HA (1940) Notes on the distribution and habits of the Jacana or lotusbird. *Emu* 39: 261-7.

Hingston, RWG (1932) Habits of the Indian Spur-winged Plover (*Hoplopterus ventralis*). *J. Bombay Nat. Hist. Soc.* 32: 219-20.

Hirons, G (1980) The significance of roding by Woodcock, *Scolopax rusticola*: an alternative explanation based on observations of marked birds. *Ibis* 122: 350-4.

Hobbs, JN (1972) Breeding of Red-capped Dotterel at Fletcher's Lake, Dareton, N.S.W. *Emu* 72: 121-5.

Hobson, W (1972) The breeding biology of the Knot. *Proc. Western Found. Vert. Zool.* 2: 5-26.

Hockey, PAR (1981) Morphometrics and sexing of the African Black Oystercatcher. *Ostrich* 52: 244-7; (1982) The taxonomic status of the Canary Island Oystercatcher *Haematopus (niger) meadewaldoi. Bull. Br. Orn. Club* 102: 77-83; (1983a) Aspects of the breeding biology of the African Black Oystercatcher. *Ostrich* 54: 26-35; (1983b) The distribution, population size, movements and conservation of the African Black Oystercatcher *Haematopus moquini. Biol. Conserv.* 25: 233-62.

—, and Cooper, J (1982) Occurrence of the European Oystercatcher *Haematopus ostralegus* in southern Africa. *Ardea* 70: 55-8.

Hoffman, A (1950) Zur Brutbiologie des Wasserfasans. *Ornithol. Beri.* 2: 119-26.

Hogan-Warburg, AJ (1966) Social behaviour of the Ruff *Philomachus pugnax* (L.). *Ardea* 54: 109-229.

Höhn, EO (1967) Observations on the breeding biology of Wilson's Phalarope *Steganopus tricolor* in central Alberta. *Auk* 84: 220-44; (1975) Notes on Black-headed Ducks, Painted Snipe and Spotted Tinamous. *Auk* 92: 566-75.

Holland, PK, et al. (1982) The breeding biology of the Common Sandpiper *Actitis hypoleucos* in the Peak District. *Bird Study* 29: 99-110.

Hollyer, JN (1984) Camouflage postures of Jack Snipe at day roost. *Br. Birds* 77: 319-20.

Holmes, RT (1966) Breeding ecology and annual cycle adaptations of the Red-backed Sandpiper (*Calidris alpina*) in Northern Alaska. *Condor* 68: 3-46; (1973) Social behaviour of breeding Western Sandpipers *Calidris mauri*. *Ibis* 115: 107-23.

—, and Pitelka, FA (1964) Breeding behavior and taxonomic relationships of the Curlew Sandpiper. *Auk* 81: 362-79.

Hoogerwerf, A (1966) On the validity of *Charadrius alexandrinus javanicus* Chasen, and the occurrence of *Ch.a.ruficapillus* Temm. and of *Ch. peronii* Schl. on Java and New Guinea. *Philipp. J. Sci.* 95: 209-14.

Hopkins, N (1976) Further notes on the Australian Pratincole. *North Qd Nat.* 168.

Howe, MA (1975) Behavioral aspects of the pair bond in Wilson's Phalaropes. *Wilson Bull.* 87: 248-70; (1982) Social organisation in a nesting population of Eastern Willets (*Catoptrophorus semipalmatus*). *Auk* 99: 88-102.

Howell, TR (1980) Breeding biology of the Egyptian Plover, *Pluvianus aegyptius*. *Univ. Calif. Publs. Zool.* 113.

Hoy, G (1967) The eggs and nesting ground of the Puna Plover. *Auk* 84: 130-1.

Hudson, WH (1920) *Birds of La Plata.* London.

Humphrey, PS, et al. (1970) *Birds of Isla Grande (Tierra del Fuego).* Washington D.C.

Hussell, DJT, and Page, GW (1976) Observations on the breeding biology of Black-bellied Plover on Devon Island, N.W.T., Canada. *Wilson Bull.* 88: 632-53.

Imboden, C (1974) (Migration, dispersal and breeding period of the Lapwing *Vanellus vanellus* in Europe.) *Orn. Beob.* 71: 5-134.

Jaensch, RP (1982) Little Ringed Plover at Little Bool Lagoon. *S. Aust. Ornithol.* 28: 201-4; (1983) The Asian Dowitcher in north-western Australia. *The Stilt* 4: 2-5.

Jayakar, SD, and Spurway, H (1965a) The Yellow-wattled Lapwing, a tropical dry-season nester (*Vanellus malabaricus* (Boddaert) Charadriidae). I. The locality and the incubatory adaptations. *Zool. Jb. (Syst.)* 92: 53-72; (1965b) The Yellow-wattled Lapwing *Vanellus malabaricus* (Boddaert), a tropical dry-season nester. II. Additional data on breeding biology. *J. Bombay Nat. Hist. Soc.* 62: 1-14; (1968) The Yellow-wattled Lapwing, *Vanellus malabaricus*, a tropical dry-season nester. III. Two further seasons' breeding. *J. Bombay Nat. Hist. Soc.* 65: 369-83.

Jeffery, RG, and Liversidge, R (1951) Notes on the Chestnut-banded Sandplover, *Charadrius pallidus pallidus*. *Ostrich* 22: 68-76.

Jehl, JR, Jr (1968) The systematic position of the Surfbird *Aphriza virgata*. *Condor* 70: 206-10; (1970) Sexual selection for size differences in two species of Sandpipers. *Evolution* 24: 311-19; (1973)

Breeding biology and systematic relationships of the Stilt Sandpiper. *Wilson Bull.* 85: 115-47; (1975) *Pluvianellus socialis:* biology, ecology and relationships of an enigmatic Patagonian shorebird. *Trans. San Diego Soc. Nat. Hist.* 18: 29-73; (1976) Shorebird in a tree. *Beaver* (winter): 54-7; (1978) A new hybrid oystercatcher from South America, *H. leucopodus* x *H. ater. Condor* 80: 344-6; (1979) The autumn migration of Baird's Sandpiper. *Studies in Avian Biol.* 2: 55-68.

Jenni, DA, and Betts, BJ (1978) Sex differences in nest construction, incubation and parental behaviour in the polyandrous American Jacana (*Jacana spinosa*). *Anim. Behav.* 26: 207-18.

—, and Collier, G (1972) Polyandry in the American Jacana (*Jacana spinosa*). *Auk* 89: 743-65.

—, *et al.* (1974) Acoustic behavior of the Northern Jacana. *Living Bird* 13: 193-210.

Johns, AD, and Thorpe, RI (1981) On the occurrence of long-distance movement in the Yellow-wattled Lapwing, *Vanellus* (= *Lobipluvia*) *malabaricus.* J. *Bombay Nat. Hist. Soc.* 78: 597-8.

Johns, JE (1969) Field studies of Wilson's Phalarope. *Auk* 86: 660-70.

Johnson, AW (1965) *The Birds of Chile and Adjacent Regions of Argentina, Bolivia and Peru.* Vol. 1. Buenos Aires; (1972) *Supplement to the Birds of Chile.* Buenos Aires.

Johnson, OW, and Macfarlane, RW (1967) Migration and bioenergetics of flight in the Pacific Golden Plover. *Condor* 69: 156-68.

Jones, A (1979) Notes on the behaviour of Variable Oystercatchers. *Notornis* 26: 47-52.

Jones, E (1983) The current reporting of wader sizes. *Aust. Bird Watcher* 10: 28-32.

Jones, J (1945) The Banded Stilt. *Emu* 45: 1-36, 110-18.

Jonsson, L, and Grant, PJ (1984) Identification of stints and peeps. *Br. Birds* 77: 293-315.

Jonsson, PE (1983) (The Kentish Plover in Sweden, its status and breeding ecology). *Anser* 22: 209-30.

Kålås, JA, and Byrkjedal, I (1984) Breeding chronology and mating system of the Eurasian Dotterel (*Charadrius morinellus*). *Auk* 101: 838-47.

Kenyon, KW (1949) Observations on behavior and populations of Oystercatchers in Lower California. *Condor* 51: 193-9.

Khrokov, VV (1978) (The Sociable Plover, *Chettusia gregaria*). *Priroda, Mosk.* 1978 (12): 92-6.

Kieser, JA, and Kieser, GA (1982) Field identification of common waders: Marsh Sandpiper and Greenshank. *Bokmakierie* 34: 63-6.

—, and Liversidge, R (1981) Identification of White-fronted Sandplover. *Dutch Birding* 3: 81-4.

—, and Smith, FTH (1982) Field identification of the Pectoral Sandpiper *Calidris melanotos. Aust. Bird Watcher* 9: 137-46.

King, WB (1981) *Endangered Birds of the World.* Washington.

Kirchner, K (1978) *Bruchwasserläufer und Waldwasserläufer.* Wittenberg.

Kistchinski, AA (1975) Breeding biology and behaviour of the Grey Phalarope *Phalaropus fulicarius* in east Siberia. *Ibis* 117: 285-301.

Kistyakovski, AB (1980) (Does the Slender-billed Curlew (*Numenius tenuirostris*) still exist?) In Flint, V, (ed) *New Studies on the Biology and Distribution of Waders.* Moscow.

Kitson, AR (1978) Identification of Long-toed Stint, Pintail Snipe and Asiatic Dowitcher. *Br. Birds* 71: 558-62.

—, *et al.* (1980) Greater Sand Plover: new to Britain and Ireland. *Br. Birds* 73: 568-73.

Klomp, H (1954) (Habitat selection in the Lapwing.) *Ardea* 42: 1-139.

Komeda, S (1983) Nest attendance of parent birds in the Painted Snipe (*Rostratula benghalensis*). *Auk* 100: 48-55.

Kraatz, S, and Beyer, K-H (1982) Zur Brutbiologie des Waldwasserläufers (*Tringa ochropus*). *Beitr. Vogelk.* 28: 231-56; (1984) (Further observations on the breeding biology of the Green Sandpiper *Tringa ochropus* L.) *Beitr. Vogelk.* 30: 33-47.

Kuroda, N (1936) *The Birds of the Island of Java.* Vol. 2. Tokyo.

Labutin, YV, *et al.* (1982) The Little Curlew *Numenius minutus* in Siberia. *Ibis* 124: 302-19.

Lacan, F, and Mougin, J-L (1974) Les oiseaux des Iles Gambier et de quelques atolls orientaux de l'archipel des Tuamotu (Océan Pacifique). *L'Oiseau et RFO* 44: 192-280.

Lane, BA (1982) Hooded Plover survey, October 1981. *The Stilt* 2: 46.

—, and Forest, BS (1984) Preliminary results from banding Latham's Snipe *Gallinago hardwickii* in Southern Victoria. *Victorian Wader Study Group Bull.* 8: 2-11.

Lane, SG, *et al.* (1981, 1982) A hybrid wader? *Corella* 5: 114-15; 6: 18.

Larkins, D, and McGill, A (1978) Oriental Dotterels at Bankstown Airport, N.S.W. *Aust. Birds* 12: 59-60.

Lemnell, PA (1978) Social behaviour of the Great Snipe *Capella media*, at the arena display. *Ornis Scand.* 9: 146-63.

Lenington, S (1980) Bi-parental care in Killdeer: an adaptive hypothesis. *Wilson Bull.* 92: 8-20.

Lessells, CM (1984) The mating system of Kentish Plovers *Charadrius alexandrinus. Ibis* 126: 474-83.

Little, J de V (1967) Some aspects of the behaviour of the Wattled Plover *Afribyx senegallus* (L.). *Ostrich* 38: 259-80.

Lowe, VT (1963) Observations on the Painted Snipe. *Emu* 62: 221-37.

McCrie, N (1984) Further records of the Oriental Plover and a reassessment of some problems in field identification. *S. Aust. Ornithol.* 29: 106-7.

McGill, AR (1944) The Red-kneed Dotterel in coastal south-eastern Australia. *Emu* 43: 225-8.

McGilp, J, and Morgan, AM (1931) The nesting of the Banded Stilt. *S. Aust. Ornithol.* 11: 37-53.

McKenzie, HR (1980) Some Red-capped Dotterel records. *Notornis* 27: 291-2.

Maclean, GL (1967) The breeding biology and behaviour of the Double-banded Courser *Rhinoptilus africanus* (Temm.). *Ibis* 109: 556-69; (1969) A study of Seedsnipe in southern South America. *Living Bird* 8: 33-80; (1973) A review of the biology of the Australian desert waders, *Stiltia* and *Peltohyas. Emu* 73: 61-70; (1976a) A field study of the Australian Pratincole. *Emu* 76: 171-82; (1976b) A field study of the Australian Dotterel. *Emu* 76: 207-15; (1977) Comparative notes on Black-fronted and Red-kneed Dotterels. *Emu* 77: 199-207.

—, and Moran, VC (1965) The choice of nest site in the White-fronted Sandplover *Charadrius marginatus* Vieillot. *Ostrich* 36: 63-72.

McNamara, JA (1980) Nocturnal feeding of the Inland Dotterel (*Peltohyas australis*). *Emu* 80: 39-40.

McNeil, R (1970) Hivernage et estivage d'oiseaux aquatiques nord-américains dans le Nord-Est du Venezuela (mue, accumulation de graisse, capacité de vol et routes de migration). *L'Oiseau et RFO* 40: 185-302.

Mace, TR (1978) Killdeer breeding densities. *Wilson Bull.* 90: 442-3.

Madge, SC (1977) Field identification of Pintail Snipe. *Br. Birds* 70: 146-52.

Makkink, GF (1936) An attempt at an ethogram of the European Avocet. *Ardea* 25: 1-74.

Marchant, JH (1984) Identification of Slender-billed Curlew. *Br. Birds* 77: 135-40.

Marshall, WH (1982) Minnesota Woodcock. *Loon* 54: 203-11.

Mascher, JW, and Marcström, V (1976) Measures, weights and lipid levels in migrating Dunlins *Calidris a. alpina* at Ottenby Bird Observatory, South Sweden. *Ornis Scand.* 7: 49-59.

Mathew, DN (1964) Observations on the breeding habits of the Bronze-winged Jacana (*Metopidius indicus* (Latham). *J. Bombay Nat. Hist. Soc.* 61: 295-302.

Mayfield, HF (1979) Red Phalaropes breeding on Bathurst Island. *Living Bird* 17: 7-40.

Medway, Lord, and Wells, DR (1976) *The Birds of the Malay Peninsula.* Vol. 5. London.

Middlemiss, E (1961) Biological aspects of *Calidris minuta* while wintering in south-west Cape. *Ostrich* 32: 107-21.

Miller, EH (1983a) Structure of display flights in the Least Sandpiper. *Condor* 85: 220-42; (1983b) Habitat and breeding cycle of the Least Sandpiper (*Calidris minutilla*) on Sable Island, Nova Scotia. *Can. J. Zool.* 61: 2880-98.

—, and Baker, AJ (1980) Displays of the Magellanic Oystercatcher (*Haematopus leucopodus*). *Wilson Bull.* 92: 149-68.

Moon, SJ (1983) Little Whimbrel: new to Britain and Ireland. *Br. Birds* 76: 438-45.

Morrison, RIG (1976) Moult of the Purple Sandpiper *Calidris maritima* in Iceland. *Ibis* 118: 237-46.

Mülder, T (1972) De Grutto in Nederland. *Wetensch Meded. Kon. Nederl. Natuurhist. Veren.* 90.

Muller, K (1975) Threat display of the Australian Painted Snipe. *Emu* 75: 28-30.

Mundahl, JT (1982) Role specialization in the parental care and territorial behaviour of the Killdeer. Wilson Bull. 94: 515-30.

Myers, JP (1978) One deleterious effect of mobbing in the Southern Lapwing (Vanellus chilensis). Auk 95: 419-20; (1979) Leks, sex, and Buff-breasted Sandpipers. Am. Birds 33: 823-5; (1980) Territoriality and flocking by Buff-breasted Sandpiper: variations in non-breeding dispersal. Condor 82: 241-50; (1982) The promiscuous Pectoral Sandpiper. Am. Birds 36: 119-22.

—, and Myers, LP (1979) Shorebirds of coastal Buenos Aires Province, Argentina. Ibis 121: 186-200.

Naik, RM, et al. (1961) Some observations on the behaviour of the incubating Red-wattled Lapwing Vanellus indicus indicus (Bodd.). J. Bombay Nat. Hist. Soc. 58: 223-30.

Naumov, RI (1962) (The biology of Capella megala in central Siberia.) Ornitologiya 4: 160-9.

Nechaev, VA (1978) (A contribution to the biology and behaviour of Tringa guttifer on Sakhalin Island.) Zool. Zh. 57: 727-37.

Neelakantan, KK, et al. (1980) The Crab Plover (Dromas ardeola) in Kerala. J. Bombay Nat. Hist. Soc. 77: 508.

Nethersole-Thompson, D (1973) The Dotterel. London.

—, and Nethersole-Thompson, M (1979) Greenshanks. Berkhamsted.

Nettleship, DN (1973) Breeding ecology of Turnstones Arenaria interpres at Hazen Camp, Ellesmere Island, N.W.T. Ibis 115: 202-17; (1974) The breeding of the Knot Calidris canutus at Hazen Camp, Ellesmere Island, N.W.T. Polarforschung 44: 8-26.

Neufeldt, I, et al. (1961) Studies of less familiar birds. 110. Grey-rumped Sandpiper. Br. Birds 54: 30-3.

Newman, M (1982) Hooded Plover: is Tasmania the real stronghold? The Stilt 3: 8-9.

Nielsen, BP (1975) Affinities of Eudromias morinellus (L.) to the genus Charadrius (L.). Ornis Scand. 6: 65-82.

—, and Colston, PR (1984) Breeding plumage of female Caspian Plover. Br. Birds 77: 356-7.

Nilsson, SG, and Nilsson, IN (1978) Population, habitat and display activity of the Jack Snipe Lymnocryptes minimus in southern Sweden. Vår Fågelvärld 37: 1-8.

Nisbet, ICT (1961a) Studies of less familiar birds. 113. Broad-billed Sandpiper. Br. Birds 54: 320-3; (1961b) Dowitchers in Great Britain and Ireland. Br. Birds 54: 343-56.

North, MEW (1937) Breeding habits of the Crested Wattled Plover. Jl. E. Africa Nat. Hist. Soc. 13: 132-45.

Nowicki, T (1973) A behavioral study of the Marbled Godwit in North Dakota. MSc, Central Michigan Univ.

OAG Münster (1975) (Migration, moult and biometrics of the Snipe G. gallinago in the sewage farms of Münster.) J. Orn. 116: 455-88.

Okugawa, KT, et al. (1973) (An ecological study of Macrosarcops cinereus (Blyth), Grey-headed Lapwing (Charadriidae), at the Ogura Farm area, Kyoto.) Bull. Kyoto Univ. Ed. ser. B 37: 3-87.

Oliver, WRB (1955) New Zealand Birds (2nd Edition). Wellington.

Oring, LW (1968) Vocalizations of the Green and Solitary Sandpipers. Wilson Bull. 80: 395-420.

—, et al. (1983) Population studies of the polyandrous Spotted Sandpiper. Auk 100: 272-85.

Osborne, DR (1982) Replacement nesting and polyandry in the Wattled Jacana. Wilson Bull. 94: 206-8.

—, and Bourne, GR (1977) Breeding behavior and food habits of the Wattled Jacana. Condor 79: 98-105.

Page, G (1974) Age, sex, moult and migration of Dunlins at Bolinas Lagoon. Western Birds 5: 1-12.

—, and Fearis, B (1971) Sexing Western Sandpipers by bill-length. Bird-Banding 42: 297-8.

Paige, JP (1965) Field identification and winter range of the Asiatic Dowitcher. Ibis 107: 95-7.

Panov, E (1963) (Taxonomic position of the Ussuri plover, Charadrius hiaticula placidus on the basis of ethological data.) Zool. Zh. 42: 1546-53.

Parker, SA (1982) A new sandpiper of the genus Calidris. S. Aust. Nat. 56: 63.

Parmelee, DF (1970) Breeding behavior of the Sanderling in the Canadian high arctic. Living Bird 9: 97-146.

—, et al. (1968) Summer schedule and breeding biology of the White-rumped Sandpiper in the central Canadian Arctic. Wilson Bull. 80: 1-29.

—, and Payne, RB (1973) On multiple broods and the breeding strategy of Arctic Sanderlings. Ibis 115: 218-26.

Parr, R (1980) Population study of Golden Plover Pluvialis apricaria, using marked birds. Ornis Scand. 11: 179-89.

Pearson, DJ (1977) The first year moult of the Common Sandpiper Tringa hypoleucos in Kenya. Scopus 1: 89-94; (1981) The wintering and moult of Ruffs Philomachus pugnax in the Kenyan rift valley. Ibis 123: 158-82; (1984) The moult of the Little Stint Calidris minuta in the Kenyan Rift Valley. Ibis 126: 1-15.

Pedler, L (1982) An Oriental Plover in the mid-north of South Australia. S. Aust. Ornithol. 28: 207.

Penny, MJ (1971) Migrant waders at Aldabra, September 1967-March 1968. Phil. Trans. R. Soc. Lond., ser. B, 260: 549-59.

Penry, EH (1979) The Rock Pratincole (Glareola nuchalis) at Greystone, Kitwe, and a review of its migratory movements. Bull. Zambian Orn. Soc. 11: 20-32.

Pettet, A (1982) Feeding behaviour of White-tailed Plover. Br. Birds 75: 182.

Phillips, AR (1975) Semipalmated Sandpiper: identification, migrations, summer and winter ranges. Am. Birds 29: 799-806.

Phillips, BT (1945) Photographing the Ibis-bill (Ibidorhyncha struthersii Gould). J. Bombay Nat. Hist. Soc. 45: 347-52.

Phillips, RE (1977) Notes on the behaviour of the New Zealand Shore Plover. Emu 77: 23-7; (1980) Behaviour and systematics of New Zealand plovers. Emu 80: 177-97.

Phillips, WWA (1942) Some observations on the nesting habits of the Indian Courser Cursorius coromandelicus (Gmelin). J. Bombay Nat. Hist. Soc. 43: 200-5.

Pienkowski, MW (1984) Breeding biology and population dynamics of Ringed Plovers Charadrius hiaticula in Britain and Greenland: nest predation as a possible factor limiting distribution and timing of breeding. J. Zool., Lond. 202: 83-114.

—, and Dick, WJA (1975) The migration and wintering of Dunlin Calidris alpina in north-west Africa. Ornis Scand. 6: 151-67.

—, and Green, GH (1976) Breeding biology of Sanderlings in north-east Greenland. Br. Birds 69: 165-77.

—, et al. (1979) Seasonal and migrational weight changes in Dunlins. Bird Study 26: 134-48.

Pierce, RJ (1979) Foods and feeding of the Wrybill (Anarhynchus frontalis) on its riverbed breeding grounds. Notornis 26: 1-21; (1980a) The Black Stilt — endangered bird of the high country. Forest Bird 13: 15-18. (1980b) Habitats and feeding of the Auckland Island Banded Dotterel (Charadrius bicinctus exilis Falla 1978) in autumn. Notornis 27: 309-24; (1982) A comparative ecological study of Pied and Black Stilts in South Canterbury. PhD, Univ. Otago; (1983) Charadriiformes of a high-country river valley. Notornis 30: 169-85; (1984a) The changed distribution of stilts in New Zealand. Notornis 31: 7-18; (1984b) Plumage, morphology and hybridisation of New Zealand stilts Himantopus spp. Notornis 31: 106-30; (in prep.) Observations of behaviour and foraging of the Ibisbill Ibidorhyncha struthersii in Nepal.

Pitelka, FA (1950) Geographic variation and the species problem in the genus Limnodromus. Univ. Calif. Publs. Zool. 50: 1-108.

Pitman, CRS (1965) The eggs and nesting habits of the St Helena Sand-Plover or Wirebird Charadrius pecuarius sanctae-helenae (Harting). Bull. Br. Orn. Club 85: 121-9.

Portenko, LA (1957) Studien an einigen seltenen Limicolen aus dem nördlichen und östlichen Sibirien. I — Die Löffelschnepfe — Eurynorhynchus pygmaeus (L.). J. Orn. 98: 454-66.

Poslavski, AN (1978) (On the biology of Charadrius asiaticus (Pallas).) Vest. Zool. 1978: 85-7.

—, and Sokolov, AI (1980) (Number and biology of the Swinhoe's Snipe (Gallinago megala) in the South Kuzbass.) In Flint, V, (ed) New Studies on the Biology and Distribution of Waders. Moscow.

Postage, A (1984) The behaviour of breeding African Jacanas. Bokmakierie 36: 12-14.

Potter, J (1934) Lotus-birds found breeding on Hawkesbury River, N.S.W. Emu 33: 298-305.

Prater, AJ (1972) The ecology of Morecambe Bay III. The food and feeding habits of the Knot (Calidris canutus L.) in Morecambe Bay. J. Appl. Ecol. 9: 179-94; (1981) Estuary Birds of Britain and Ireland. Calton; (1982) Identification of Ruff. Dutch Birding 4: 8-14.

—, and Grant, PJ (1982) Waders in Siberia. Br. Birds 75: 272-81.

Prevett, JP, and Barr, JF (1976) Lek behavior of the Buff-breasted Sandpiper. Wilson Bull. 88: 500-3.

Purdue, JR (1976) Adaptations of the Snowy Plover on the Great Salt Plains, Oklahoma. Southwest. Nat. 21: 347-57.

Pym, A (1982) Identification of Lesser Golden Plover and status in Britain and Ireland. Br. Birds 75: 112-24.

Rand, AL (1936) The distribution and habits of Madagascar birds. Bull. Am. Mus. Nat. Hist. 72: 143-499.
—, and Gilliard, ET (1968) Handbook of New Guinea Birds. Garden City.
Ratcliffe, DA (1976) Observations on the breeding of the Golden Plover in Great Britain. Bird Study 23: 63-116.
Reed, SM (1981) New Zealand Dotterel (Charadrius obscurus) — an endangered species? Notornis 28: 129-32.
Reynolds, JF (1968) Observations on the White-headed Plover. E. Afr. Wildl. J. 6: 142-4.
Richards, DK (1980) Distribution of the Chestnut-banded Sandplover Charadrius pallidus in Tanzania. Scopus 4: 24.
Ridley, MW (1980) The breeding behaviour and feeding ecology of Grey Phalarope Phalaropus fulicarius in Svalbard. Ibis 122: 210-26.
Riley, JW, and Rooke, KB (1962) Sociable Plover in Dorset. Br. Birds 55: 233-5.
Rittinghaus, H (1961) Der Seeregenpfeifer. Wittenberg.
Russell, RP, Jr (1983) The Piping Plover in the Great Lakes Region. Am. Birds 37: 951-5.
Ryan, MR (1982) Marbled Godwit habitat selection in the northern prairies. PhD, Iowa State Univ.

Sakane, M (1957, 1958) Notes on the Grey-headed Lapwing in Kinki, W. Honshu. Tori 14: 25-37, 15: 13-17.
Saunders, CR (1970) Observations on breeding of the Long-toed or White-winged Plover Hemiparra crassirostris leucoptera (Reichenow). Honeyguide 62: 27-9.
Sauppe, B, et al. (1978) First Canadian and third North American record of the Spoon-billed Sandpiper (Eurynorhynchus pygmaeus). Am. Birds 32: 1062-4.
Schamel, D, and Tracy, D (1977) Polyandry, replacement clutches and site tenacity in the Red Phalarope (Phalaropus fulicarius) at Barrow, Alaska. Bird-Banding 48: 314-24.
Schwartz, CW, and Schwartz, ER (1951) The Hawaiian stilt. Auk 68: 505-6.
Senner, SE, and Martinez, EF (1982) A review of Western Sandpiper migration in interior North America. Southwest. Nat. 27: 149-59.
Serle, W (1956) Notes on Anomalophrys superciliosus (Reichenow) in West Africa with special reference to its nidification. Bull. Br. Orn. Club 76: 101-4.
Shcherbakov, VV (1980) (Biology of the Eastern Solitary Snipe (Gallinago solitaria) in the Western Altai Mountains.) In Flint, V, (ed) New Studies on the Biology and Distribution of Waders. Moscow.

Sheldon, WG (1967) The Book of the American Woodcock. Amherst.
Shepard, JM (1976) Factors influencing female choice in the lek mating system of the Ruff. Living Bird 14: 87-111.
Shorten, M (1974) The European Woodcock (Scolopax rusticola). Report on a search of the literature since 1940. Game Conservancy Rep. 21.
Sibson, RB (1963) A population study of the Wry-billed Plover (Anarhynchus frontalis). Notornis 10: 146-53; (1965) A note on Wandering Tattlers in Fiji. Notornis 12: 248-50; (1966) Increasing numbers of South Island Pied Oystercatchers visiting northern New Zealand. Notornis 13: 94-7.
Simmons, KEL (1956) Territory in the Little Ringed Plover Charadrius dubius. Ibis 98: 390-7.
Sinclair, JC, and Nicholls, GH (1980) Winter identification of Greater and Lesser Sandplovers. Br. Birds 73: 206-13.
Skead, CJ (1955) A study of the Crowned Plover Stephanibyx coronatus coronatus (Boddaert). Ostrich 26: 88-98.
Skeel, MA (1983) Nesting success, density, philopatry and nest-site selection of the Whimbrel (Numenius phaeopus) in different habitats. Can. J. Zool. 61: 218-55.
Smith, FTH (1974) A Victorian record of the Asiatic Dowitcher. Aust. Bird Watcher 5: 111-18; (1982) Dunlins undone. The Stilt 2: 10-11.
Smith, NG (1969) Polymorphism in Ringed Plovers. Ibis 111: 177-88.
Smith, PC, and Evans, PR (1973) Studies of shorebirds at Lindisfarne, Northumberland. I. Feeding ecology and behaviour of the Bar-tailed Godwit. Wildfowl 24: 135-9.
Smith, RW, and Barclay, JS (1978) Evidence of westward changes in the range of the American Woodcock. Am. Birds 32: 1122-7.
Smythies, BE (1968) The Birds of Borneo. Edinburgh.
Soikkeli, M (1966) On the variation in bill- and wing-length of the Dunlin (Calidris alpina) in Europe. Bird Study 13: 256-69.
Sordahl, TA (1979) Vocalizations and behavior of the Willet. Wilson Bull. 91: 551-74.
Stenzel, LE, et al. (1976) Feeding behavior and diet of the Long-billed Curlew and Willet. Wilson Bull. 88: 314-31.
Stepanjan, LS (1979) (Possible relations of Ibidorhyncha struthersii and notes on the history of the family Haematopodidae.) Zool. Zh. 58: 1671-9.
Stephens, ML (1984a) Intraspecific distraction displays of the polyandrous Northern Jacana Jacana spinosa. Ibis 126: 71-3; (1984b) Interspecific aggressive behaviour of the polyandrous Northern Jacana Jacana spinosa. Auk 101: 508-18.

Sterbetz, I (1974) Die Brachschwalbe. Wittenberg.
Stidolph, RHD (1973) Plumages of Variable Oystercatchers. Notornis 20: 311-13.
Stinson, CH (1977) The spatial distribution of wintering Black-bellied Plovers. Wilson Bull. 89: 470-2.
Stresemann, E (1941) Die Vögel von Celebes, Part 3. J. Orn. 89: 1-112.
Summers, RW (1976) The origins of South African Sanderlings, Siberia or Greenland? Safring News 5: 17-18.
—, and Hockey, PAR (1980) Breeding biology of the White-fronted Plover (Charadrius marginatus) in the southwestern Cape, South Africa. J. Nat. Hist. 14: 433-45.
Sutton, GM, and Parmelee, DF (1955) Breeding of the Semipalmated Plover on Baffin Island. Bird-Banding 26: 137-47.
Symmes, TCL (1952) Some observations on the breeding of the Crowned Plover. Ostrich 23: 85-7.

Tarboton, WR, and Nel, F (1980) On the occurrence of the White-crowned Plover in the Kruger National Park. Bokmakierie 32: 19-21.
Taylor, PB (1980) The field separation of Common, Ethiopian and Great Snipe Gallinago gallinago, G. nigripennis and G. media. Scopus 4: 1-5; (1981) Field characters and habitat preferences of Great Snipe and Snipe. Dutch Birding 3: 52-4; (1982) Field identification of sand plovers in East Africa. Dutch Birding 4: 113-30; (1983) Field identification of sand plovers in East Africa. Dutch Birding 5. 37-66, (1984) Field identification of Pintail Snipe and recent records in Kenya. Dutch Birding 6: 77-90.
Taylor, RC (1974) A method for sexing adult Ringed Plovers Charadrius hiaticula L. in summer plumage. Wader Study Group Bull. 11: 15-17; (1978) Geographical variation in the Ringed Plover Charadrius hiaticula. PhD, Liverpool Polytechnic; (1979) Moult of the Long-billed Ringed Plover, Charadrius placidus. Bull. Br. Orn. Club 99: 98-102; (1980) Migration of the Ringed Plover Charadrius hiaticula. Ornis Scand. 11: 30-42.
Temple, S (ed) (1979) Red Data Book. Vol. 2. Aves. Morges.
Terborgh, J, and Weske, JS (1972) Rediscovery of the Imperial Snipe in Peru. Auk 89: 497-505.
Thomas, DG (1969) Breeding biology of the Australian Spur-winged Plover. Emu 69: 81-102.

Thomas, DH (1983) Aposematic behaviour in the Blacksmith Plover. Ostrich 54: 51-2.
Thompson, MC (1974) Migratory patterns of Ruddy Turnstones in the central Pacific region. Living Bird 12: 5-23.
Tolchin, VA (1976) (Distribution and ecology of the Marsh Sandpiper in central Siberia.) Nauch. Dokl. vyssh. Shk., biol. nauki 5: 42-8; (1980) (Spreading of the Far Eastern Curlew (Numenius madagascariensis) in East Siberia.) In Flint, V, (ed) New Studies on the Biology and Distribution of Waders. Moscow.
Tomkins, IR (1944) Wilson's Plover in its summer home. Auk 61: 259-69; (1947) The Oystercatcher of the Atlantic coast of northern America and its relation to oysters. Wilson Bull. 59: 204-8.
Tomkovich, PS (1980) (The biology of the Long-toed Stint (Calidris subminuta).) Ornitologiya 15: 104-10; (1982) (Sexual dimorphism of the Rock Sandpiper Calidris ptilocnemis.) Zool. Zh. 61: 1110-13.
—, and Fokin, S Yu (1983) (On the ecology of Temminck's Stint in Northeast Russia.) Ornitologiya 18: 40-56.
Townshend, DJ, et al. (1984) The unsociable plover — use of intertidal areas by Grey Plovers. In Evans, PR, et al. (eds) Coastal Waders and Wildfowl in Winter. Cambridge.
Tree, AJ (1974) Ageing and sexing the Little Stint. Safring News 3: 31-3; (1982) Greenshank studies. Safring News 11: 18-20.
—, and Kieser, JA (1982) Field separation of Lesser Yellowlegs and Wood Sandpiper. Honeyguide 110: 40-1.
Tuck, L (1972) The Snipes. Ottawa.
Tyler, S (1978) Observations on the nesting of the Three-banded Plover. Charadrius tricollaris. Scopus 2: 39-41.

Urban, EK, et al. (1972) Four descriptions of nesting, previously undescribed, for Ethiopia. Bull. Br. Orn. Club 92: 162-4.
Uys, CJ, and Underhill, GD (1977) Nesting of Double-banded Courser in the Worcester district. Bokmakierie 29: 43-5.

Väisänen, RA (1969) Evolution of the Ringed Plover (Charadrius hiaticula L.) during the last hundred years in Europe. A new computer method based on egg dimensions. Ann. Acad. Sci. Fenn. (A) IV 149: 1-90.

van den Berg, AB (1984) Occurrence of Sociable Plover in Western Europe. *Dutch Birding* 6: 1-8.

van Rhijn, JG (1973) Behavioural dimorphism in male Ruffs, *Philomachus pugnax* (L.). *Behaviour* 47: 153-229.

van Tets, GF, *et al.* (1967) Nesting distribution and nomenclature of Australasian vanelline plovers. *Emu* 67: 85-93.

Vaurie C (1963) Systematic Notes on Palearctic Birds. No. 51. A review of *Burhinus oedicnemus*. *Am. Mus. Novit.* 2131: 1-13.

Vernon, CJ (1973) Polyandrous *Actophilornis africanus*. *Ostrich* 44: 85.

Verschuren, J (1977) Note sur la fauna ornithologique du Burundi, principalement près de Bujumbura. *Gerfaut* 67: 3-20.

Vinter, SV (1980) (The Far Eastern Curlew (*Numenius madagascariensis*) on the lower Bureya river.) In Flint, V, (ed) *New Studies on the Biology and Distribution of Waders.* Moscow.

von Helversen, O (1963) Beobachtungen zum Verhalten und zur Brutbiologie des Spornkiebitzes (*Hoplopterus spinosus*). *J. Orn.* 104: 89-96.

Vuilleumier, F (1969) Field notes on some birds from the Bolivian Andes. *Ibis* 111: 599-608.

Wallis, CA, and Wershler, CR (1981) Status and breeding of Mountain Plover (*Charadrius montanus*) in Canada. *Can. Field Nat.* 95: 133-6.

Walmsley, JG (1970) Une Glaréole de Nordmann *Glareola nordmanni* en Camargue, première observation et premier cas de nidification pour la France. *Alauda* 38: 295-305; (1976) Une Glaréole à ailes noires *Glareola nordmanni* en Camargue. *Alauda* 44: 334-5.

Walters, J (1979) Interspecific aggressive behaviour by Long-toed Lapwings (*Vanellus crassirostris*). *Anim. Behav.* 27: 969-81.

—, and Walters, BF (1980) Co-operative breeding by Southern Lapwings (*Vanellus chilensis*). *Ibis* 22: 505-9.

Webb, BE, and Conry, JA (1979) A Sharp-tailed Sandpiper in Colorado with notes on plumage and behaviour. *Western Birds* 10: 86-91.

Webster, JD (1941) The breeding of the Black Oystercatcher. *Wilson Bull.* 53: 141-56; (1942) Notes on the growth and plumages of the Black Oystercatcher. *Condor* 44: 205-11.

Weeden, RB (1965) Further notes on Wandering Tattlers in central Alaska. *Condor* 67: 87-9.

Weston, FM, and Williams, EA (1965) Recent records of the Eskimo Curlew. *Auk* 82: 493-6.

Weston, IL (1978) Banding jacanas — lotus birds in Papua New Guinea. *Bull. Fish. Res. Dev. Agency Busan* 553-4: 103.

Westwood, NJ (1983) Breeding of Stone Curlews at Weeting Heath, Norfolk. *Br. Birds* 76: 291-304.

Wetmore, A (1926) Birds of Argentina, Paraguay, Uruguay and Chile. *Bull. 133. Smithsonian Inst.*

Widrig, RS (1983) December nesting of the Collared Plover in western Mexico. *Am. Birds* 37: 273-4.

Wilcox, L (1959) A twenty year banding study of the Piping Plover. *Auk* 76: 129-52.

Wilds, C (1982) Separating the Yellowlegs. *Birding* 14: 172-8.

—, and Newlon, M (1983) The identification of Dowitchers. *Birding* 15: 151-66.

Williams, MD (1981) Description of the nest and eggs of the Peruvian Thick-knee (*Burhinus superciliaris*). *Condor* 83: 183-4.

Wilson, G (1974) Incubating behaviour of the African Jacana. *Ostrich* 45: 185-8.

Wilson, GE (1976) Spotted Sandpipers nesting in Scotland. *Br. Birds* 69: 288-92.

Wilson, JH (1977) Camouflage posture of Bronze-wing Courser. *Honeyguide* 92: 48.

Wilson, JR, *et al.* (1980) The migration through Europe and wintering in West Africa of Curlew Sandpipers. *Wildfowl* 31: 107-22.

Winkler, H (1980) (On the feeding of Terek Sandpipers in winter quarters.) *Egretta* 23: 56-60.

Woods, RW (1975) *The Birds of the Falkland Islands.* Oswestry.

Zubarovskij, VM (1976) (On the biology of the eastern Solitary Snipe (*Gallinago solitaria*) in the Altai.) *Ornitologiya* 12: 114-17.

Zusi, RL, and Jehl, JR, Jr (1970) The systematic relationships of *Aechmorhynchus*, *Prosobonia* and *Phegornis* (Charadriiformes, Charadrii). *Auk* 87: 760-80.

Index of Vernacular and Scientific Names

Figures in bold refer to plate numbers. In cases of alternative vernacular names, only main text page reference is given.